CENTURY 21 ACCOUNTING

ROBERT M. SWANSON

Professor of Business Education and Office Administration
College of Business
Ball State University
Muncie, Indiana

LEWIS D. BOYNTON

Professor Emeritus
Formerly Chairman, Department of Business Education
Central Connecticut State College
New Britain, Connecticut

KENTON E. ROSS

Chairman, Department of Accounting
College of Business Administration
University of North Florida
Jacksonville, Florida

ROBERT D. HANSON

Chairman, Department of Business Education
Central Michigan University
Mount Pleasant, Michigan

Published by

B20 **SOUTH-WESTERN PUBLISHING CO.**

CINCINNATI   WEST CHICAGO, ILL.   DALLAS   PELHAM MANOR, N.Y.
PALO ALTO, CALIF.   BRIGHTON, ENGLAND

CENTURY 21®
ACCOUNTING

 First-Year Course

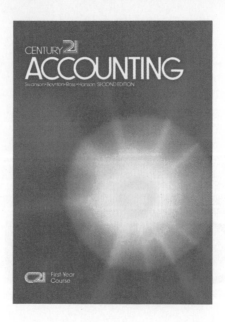

ON THE COVER

The cover of this book portrays the brilliance of a laser beam and symbolizes the future of accounting at the dawning of a new and exciting century. This spirit is captured in CENTURY 21 ACCOUNTING. The design element represents a cross section view of a laser beam now being used in increasingly prominent ways in business, industry, and medicine. Continuing experiments with a laser beam promise even broader applications, perhaps in accounting, in this micro/electronic era.

The design element gives the impression of a beginning, of emergence, of development that is appropriate for a student exploring careers and starting a foundation for an occupation. The colors dramatically represent a wide spectrum of career opportunities for the student of accounting in Century 21.

Copyright © 1977
Philippine Copyright 1977
by South-Western Publishing Co.
Cincinnati, Ohio

ISBN: 0-538-02200-0

Library of Congress Catalog Card Number: 75-1821

15 16 17 18 19 20 K 4 3 2

Printed in the United States of America

Preface

The future holds an opportunity for young people to develop careers. The future also offers young people a chance to assume the rights and responsibilities which go with earning a living. The future requires that young people manage their economic lives so that they are able to do productive and satisfying work as well as have enjoyable leisure-time experiences. Education leads young people to their future.

Building a career in accounting

The study of high school accounting offers a starting point for building a career. Such study teaches basic skills and develops values and attitudes useful in gaining entry into the field of accounting. Many opportunities are available for young people who seek to become accountants, accounting clerks, or bookkeepers. Also, a knowledge of accounting is important for young people seeking to enter computer related jobs or various other office positions.

The study of accounting also helps young people develop an overall picture of the total process of business systems. Such understanding is a good base for further study and career advancement in the business world.

There will be some young people whose careers lead them to ownership of small businesses. They will become the future farmers, service station operators, beauty shop owners, and managers. Success in owning and managing a business is directly related to success in having important financial information available. For these people, an understanding of accounting principles and procedures may be the difference between success and failure.

There are many career opportunities in accounting and related fields. Along with increases in employment possibilities in automated data processing

v

areas, there is a continuing demand for bookkeepers and accountants. This demand is described in the *1974–1975 Occupational Outlook Handbook*.

> *Bookkeeping Workers.* High school graduates who have taken business arithmetic, bookkeeping, and accounting meet the minimum requirements for most bookkeeping jobs.
>
> Although the number of bookkeepers will increase slowly through the mid-1980's, thousands of workers will be needed each year.
>
> . . . the need for bookkeeping workers probably will outpace the impact of labor-saving office machines over the next decade.
>
> *Accountants.* Employment of accountants is expected to increase rapidly through the mid-1980's as business and government agencies continue to expand in size and complexity.
>
> Greater use of accounting information in business management, changing tax systems, and growth of large corporations that must provide financial reports to stockholders, all point to excellent opportunities for accountants.

These facts and opinions from the United States Department of Labor give support to the value of the study of high school accounting.

In this cybernetic age no organization can operate successfully without financial records. This is true of profit-seeking businesses. It is also true of social and governmental organizations. The family and the individual also need accounting records to manage successfully.

Accounting as personal economic education

The process of daily living includes a constant need to make personal economic decisions. How much of my pay check should be saved? How much spent on food? On housing? On entertainment? Personal decisions are wiser if financial facts are organized, summarized, and easily available to the citizens. The study of high school accounting includes learning how to organize and summarize personal financial facts and how to interpret the economic message the facts convey.

Accounting, therefore, is not just for the accountant. Accounting is not just for the person who will work in business. Accounting is also for the individual, for the family, for the stockholders, the business owners, the business managers, and the secretaries. Accounting is for all persons who need to understand financial records so that improved economic decisions can be made.

THIS REVISION MOVES INTO THE FUTURE

This second edition of *Century 21 Accounting* continues the traditions of the 23 editions of its predecessor, *20th Century Bookkeeping and Accounting*. The study of accounting is kept up to date and out front as it has been in the 70 years of the existence of this series. *Century 21 Accounting* moves into the future with a presentation of basic accounting principles applied to manual *as well as* automated data processing systems. This is a first for high school accounting texts and expands the whole scope of occupational information for those young people who study accounting.

Basic accounting principles have not changed. However, technology has provided business with tools to increase the efficiency of its operation. A rapidly increasing number of businesses are using computers to process business data. To have maximum career opportunities, young people must be capable of applying accounting principles to either manual or automated data processing systems. This second edition of *Century 21 Accounting* meets this new challenge for career preparation.

Integration of manual and automated accounting systems. The role of the accountant in automated accounting systems is presented in three new chapters — Chapters 18, 19, and 20. For this second edition, these three chapters have been completely rewritten and updated. The student studies automated accounting systems after studying manual procedures for both a service business and a merchandising business. In these three new chapters the student learns about: the basic concepts of automated data processing systems as applied to the manual accounting systems; how a business converts from a manual to an automated accounting system; how to prepare the necessary accounting forms to send needed accounting data to a computer center for processing; how a computer center prepares accounting data for computer processing; how accounting data flow through a computer system and back to the business.

After the student has gained an understanding of automated accounting for a merchandising business, automated accounting principles are included as an integral part of the discussion in eight of the remaining chapters in the text.

Up-to-date terms. In addition to the big step into the automated future, steps have also been taken to modernize the vocabulary and forms illustrated. For example, accountants now prefer the term *revenue* in place of *income* and *plant assets* instead of *fixed assets*.

The individual student as the center of learning. *Century 21 Accounting* recognizes that each accounting student is an individual with special needs and aptitudes. Few accounting textbooks provide as many helpful facilities to encourage individualized teaching and competency-based learning as does *Century 21 Accounting*. Some of the aids in the textbook are:

1. *An easier reading level.* The reading level (as determined by *A Formula for Predicting Readability*, by Edgar Dale and Jeanne S. Chall, Bureau of Educational Research, Ohio State University) is appropriate for the average student and is an encouraging aid to the reader.
2. *Varying levels of assignments.* End-of-chapter problems provide a choice for different levels of difficulty. Teachers have a variety of choices of assignment levels that can be used with students with various learning levels.
3. *Flexible organization.* There are flexible time schedules for schools using either the quarter or the semester plan. Versions of the text are available for (a) short, adult evening classes, (b) quarter-year courses, (c) half-year or semester courses, and (d) one-year or two semester courses. A second-year (advanced) text is available for those schools offering three or four semesters of high school accounting.
4. *Improved visual aids.* Colorful, appropriate, and realistic illustrations are frequent aids to motivation and learning. A CENTURY 21 Trans-Vision® insert provides help in learning the preparation of an eight-column work sheet.

A wealth of teaching and learning materials provides the accounting teacher with a wide choice in the kind and the extent of individual learning activities. Teachers have available the materials needed to establish performance objectives appropriate for the students in their own particular situation.

Among the many materials available for use with the textbook is *Computer Oriented Accounting*. This is a supplemental learning package devoted exclusively to the accountant's work in an automated accounting system. A student with no prior knowledge of a computer can do the work in this supplemental material. The content of the learning package easily correlates with the student's study of *Century 21 Accounting*. Of most interest, a student does not have to be a computer operator in order to study these materials.

ACKNOWLEDGMENTS

This second edition of *Century 21 Accounting*, like its predecessors, reflects the combined efforts of many people. Innumerable teachers who have used previous editions have been most helpful with their criticisms and useful suggestions. Students, too, have contributed many worthwhile suggestions. Professional accountants and specialists in automated data processing have been consulted and have given freely of their professional knowledge.

To all of these people, as well as those who have worked behind the scenes at the publishing and printing companies, we wish to express our sincere appreciation for their suggestions and help.

Robert M. Swanson
Lewis D. Boynton
Kenton E. Ross
Robert D. Hanson

Contents

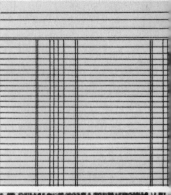

1

THE ACCOUNTING CYCLE IN ITS SIMPLEST FORM

EVERY BUSINESS NEEDS AN INFORMATION SYSTEM.
A system of records which shows (a) how well the business is succeeding, and (b) how much it is worth is an accounting information system. An accounting system supplies the kind of information needed for managing a business properly and for preparing financial reports.

Information in an accounting system may be recorded by hand, on bookkeeping and accounting machines, or on automated equipment. The kind and size of a business determines how its accounting records are best kept. Regardless of the data processing methods used for keeping accounting records, the principles of accounting are the same.

An easy way to learn accounting principles is to apply them to problems using manual procedures — doing accounting work by hand. Therefore, the early part of this textbook centers on the application of basic accounting principles and procedures by hand. The use of machines and automated equipment for processing data is introduced later.

SOME BUSINESSES SELL ONLY SERVICE. Many kinds of businesses and professional people render services and must keep accounting records. Among these are: hotels, motels, laundromats, car washes, physicians, dentists, lawyers, accountants, etc.

In the first part of this textbook we shall learn how a small service business, *Rainbow Car Wash*, uses the principles of accounting in keeping its financial records. We shall also see how the financial reports prepared from these records provide valuable information about the operation of the business.

RAINBOW CAR WASH
CHART OF ACCOUNTS

---

(1) ASSETS	Account Number
Cash..........................	11
Operating Supplies	12
Car Wash Equipment........	13
Office Equipment	14

(2) LIABILITIES	
Auto Wash Equipment Co ..	21
Marco Plumbing Company .	22

(3) CAPITAL	
Harry Shaw, Capital.........	31
Income Summary	32

(4) REVENUE	Account Number
Sales	41

(5) EXPENSES	
Advertising Expense.........	51
Fuel Expense	52
Miscellaneous Expense	53
Rent Expense	54
Utilities Expense	55

The chart of accounts for Rainbow Car Wash is illustrated above for ready reference as you study Part 1 of this textbook.

Starting an Accounting System

A business must keep good records in order to operate successfully. This is true for the smallest as well as the largest business. Every profit-making organization — the smallest farm, the corner grocery store, the largest corporation — must have exact records. This is also true of non-profit organizations — a family, a church, the American Red Cross, the United States Government.

Reasons for business information systems

There are two reasons why every business must have a system for collecting and reporting information about itself.

First, information is required for sound decisions, for sensible planning, and for proper control of the business. No matter how rich a business may be today, survival in the future depends upon making wise decisions about the use and control of its resources. Accurate information about all activities of a business helps in making right decisions.

Second, both profit-making and nonprofit organizations must report to persons outside the organization. Income tax reports must be filed with the government. Businesses wishing to borrow money from banks must report their financial condition. Profit-making businesses must send financial reports to their owners. Nonprofit organizations give financial reports to those who provide their funds. The reported information gives assurance to the banker that the loan can be repaid; to the owners that their investment is being managed properly; to the members of non-profit organizations that their contributions are being spent wisely.

WHAT IS ACCOUNTING?

Much of the information a business collects about itself is written in dollars and cents values. Orderly records of the financial activities of an individual or of a business are called accounting records. Planning how to keep these records, summarizing them for convenient interpretation, and analyzing them to advise what should be done is called accounting. A person who plans, summarizes, and analyzes financial records is called an accountant. A person who earns a living by recording financial activities of a business is called an accounting clerk. Accounting clerks are sometimes referred to as bookkeepers.

The work of the accountant

The accountant's work, training, and experience go beyond that of an accounting clerk. The accountant is trained to interpret and to audit (check for accuracy and fairness) the accounting records of a business. He or she may be asked to advise about the kinds of business forms and records best suited for a particular business. Accountants usually have completed some study beyond high school.

An accountant may be licensed by a state as a certified public accountant (CPA). To earn the license, the candidate must meet the state requirements and pass a challenging examination.

WHY STUDY ACCOUNTING?

Courses in accounting are offered in various kinds of schools and colleges: secondary schools — public and private, technical and vocational; colleges — public and private, two-year and four-year, liberal arts and business; and graduate colleges. There are different reasons why so many people study accounting on so many different levels.

Accounting as a career

The most important reason for studying accounting is to prepare for making it one's life work. Thousands of people each year study accounting to become accountants, accounting clerks, payroll clerks, or to work in some other accounting-type position. There are, however, other reasons why so many people study accounting.

Accounting used in business management

Accounting is necessary for the best management of any organization. The management of a profit-making business uses information from its accounting system to make such decisions as: What are its resources? What debts does it owe? How large are its profits? Its losses? Should selling prices be increased? Should more workers be employed? Should a new product be introduced? Should the plant be enlarged?

A knowledge of accounting is also essential for the person planning to operate a service station, farm, beauty parlor, restaurant, or store. Lack of proper financial records and lack of understanding of such records are frequent causes of business failure.

Accounting used by all business workers

Accounting has been called the language of business. Everyone engaged in business activity uses this language. A typist may type financial statements and other accounting reports. A secretary may take dictation and transcribe information dealing with accounting terms and records. A sales clerk may have to count items in stock and assist with inventory work.

Accounting also helps the automated data processing worker appreciate the accounting work done by computers and other modern business equipment. Business workers who have studied accounting are able to perform their tasks with greater confidence and understanding. As a result, their chances for promotion are improved.

Accounting used in everyday life

Every adult engages in business activities in some way. Every responsible adult is concerned with the financial aspects of individual as well as family life.

Everyone who has taxable income must keep records that may be checked by federal, state, and local income tax authorities. Everyone is faced with the problem of balancing expenses with income and of providing for the future. Nearly everyone who is employed contributes to social security and in many cases to pension plans. Many persons put their savings to work by purchasing savings bonds, by opening savings accounts with banks, by buying a home, and by investing in American business. Almost everyone has business dealings with banks, merchants, utility companies, and employers. In each case, the person who knows the basic principles of accounting is better able to handle these personal business affairs.

DATA PROCESSING IN ACCOUNTING

An accounting clerk records financial information consisting of many items. Detailed or factual items are called data. When data are used to supply helpful information, they are said to be processed. For example, in football, keeping a record of yards gained, passes completed, and touchdowns made is the processing of data. This is data processing at its simplest. The recording, sorting, classifying, calculating, summarizing, and reporting of facts is called data processing.

The size of a business and the kind and extent of its activities help determine the best way to process its business data. Over 95 percent of the businesses in the United States have less than 100 employees. The accounting clerks in many of these smaller businesses process data manually — by hand, using pen and paper. Other businesses use bookkeeping and accounting machines to record financial data. Still others use computers and machines that process the data automatically with a minimum amount of human effort. Keeping accounting records by means of machines and equipment that operate automatically is called automated data processing (ADP). ADP equipment is expensive and is normally used by companies that have large quantities of data to process. However, if a small business wishes to have some of its data processed automatically, it may buy the services of a data processing company.

All data processing procedures — manual and automated — use the same principles of accounting that are included in this textbook. The easiest way to learn the principles of accounting is by use of manual procedures. Therefore, the early part of this book describes a manual method of processing accounting data.

STARTING AN ACCOUNTING SYSTEM

Harry Shaw operates a self-service car wash called Rainbow Car Wash. He pays a monthly rent for the use of a corner lot containing two carwash units called bays. Mr. Shaw furnishes such car-wash equipment as an electric water pump, a gas hot water heater and boiler, and the hoses with attachments used for spraying the cars with detergent and rinse water. He also provides operating supplies such as a low-sudsing detergent, buckets, and cloths.

Mr. Shaw has decided to start a new accounting system for the car wash to obtain more complete information about the operation of his business. To start his new accounting system, he first needs to know:

1. What the business owns.
2. What the business owes.
3. What the business is worth.

Mr. Shaw lists and totals in one column what his business owns. He lists and totals in another column what his business owes. These facts are shown below.

WHAT IS OWNED		WHAT IS OWED	
Cash on hand and in the bank	$ 650.00	Auto Wash Equipment Co.	$ 850.00
Operating supplies	250.00	Marco Plumbing Company	150.00
Car wash equipment	3,600.00	Total owed	$1,000.00
Office equipment	500.00		
Total owned	$5,000.00		

Mr. Shaw next finds out what his business is worth. He does this by subtracting the total that his business owes, $1,000.00, from the total of what it owns, $5,000.00. His business is worth $4,000.00.

Total owned...........	$5,000.00
Less total owed	1,000.00
Equals what the business is worth	$4,000.00

THE BALANCE SHEET

In accounting, a business form that lists (1) what is owned, (2) what is owed, and (3) what a business is worth on a specific date is called a balance sheet. Because the purpose of a balance sheet is to show the financial position of a business on a particular date, it is sometimes known as a position statement. After a business knows what it owns, what it owes, and what it is worth, a balance sheet is prepared.

The beginning balance sheet of Rainbow Car Wash on August 1, prepared by Mr. Shaw, is shown below.

Rainbow Car Wash				
Balance Sheet				
August 1, 1977				
Assets			*Liabilities*	
Cash	65000		Auto Wash Equip. Co.	85000
Operating Supplies	25000		Marco Plumbing Co.	15000
Car Wash Equipment	360000		Total Liabilities	100000
Office Equipment	50000			
			Capital	
			Harry Shaw, Capital	400000
Total Assets	500000		Total Liab. and Capital	500000

Beginning balance sheet of Rainbow Car Wash

Heading of a balance sheet

The heading of a balance sheet contains three items: (1) the name of the business for which the balance sheet is prepared; (2) the name of the form; and (3) the date of the form. On the balance sheet of Rainbow Car Wash, these items are listed on separate lines in the heading as follows:

Line 1.	WHO?	Name of business	*Rainbow Car Wash*
Line 2.	WHAT?	Name of the form	*Balance Sheet*
Line 3.	WHEN?	Date of the form	*August 1, 1977*

Body of a balance sheet

The body of a balance sheet has three sections that show: (1) what is owned, (2) what is owed, and (3) what the business is worth. A special business term is used to describe each of these three sections as follows:

1. Assets. Anything of value that is owned is called an asset. Assets are listed on the left-hand side of the balance sheet, as shown in the diagram at the right.

BALANCE SHEET

1. ASSETS (What is owned)	2. LIABILITIES (What is owed) and 3. CAPITAL (What the business is worth)
(Left-hand side)	(Right-hand side)

2. Liabilities. An amount that is owed is called a liability. Liabilities are listed on the right-hand side of the balance sheet.

> The liabilities of a business are the debts of a business. The one to whom an amount is owed is called a creditor

3. Capital. The amount that remains after the total liabilities are subtracted from the total assets is what the business is worth. What the business is worth is called capital. For example:

Total assets on the balance sheet of Rainbow Car Wash	$5,000.00
Less total liabilities on the balance sheet of Rainbow Car Wash..........	1,000.00
Equals the amount of the capital of Rainbow Car Wash....................	$4,000.00

The amount of the capital is shown beneath the liabilities on the right-hand side of the balance sheet.

> An owner of a business is called a proprietor. The capital section of a balance sheet is therefore sometimes known as proprietorship or owner's equity.

Assets equal equities — why a balance sheet has two sides

The assets of a business are listed on the left-hand side of the balance sheet. The claims against these assets are listed on the right-hand side of the balance sheet. The claims against the assets of a business are called equities

There are two types of equities: (1) the liabilities are the equities of the creditors and (2) the capital is the equity of the owner. Since equities represent the total claims against the assets, the assets must equal the equities. Creditors have first claim against the assets of the business. Therefore, creditors' claims are listed first on the right-hand side of the balance sheet.

On a complete and accurate balance sheet, the total of the left-hand side is always equal to the total of the right-hand side. The two sides of a balance sheet must be "in balance." The total of the left-hand side of the balance sheet of Rainbow Car Wash, $5,000.00, is equal to the total of the right-hand side, $5,000.00. This is shown in the diagram below.

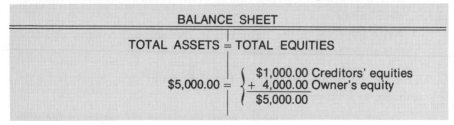

BALANCE SHEET

TOTAL ASSETS = TOTAL EQUITIES

$$\$5,000.00 = \left\{ \begin{array}{l} \$1,000.00 \text{ Creditors' equities} \\ + \ \ 4,000.00 \text{ Owner's equity} \\ \overline{\$5,000.00} \end{array} \right.$$

STEPS IN PREPARING A BALANCE SHEET

The following five steps are used in preparing a balance sheet. As you study these steps, check each one in the illustration of the balance sheet of Rainbow Car Wash shown below.

☐ 1 Write the heading on three lines; center each item in the heading.

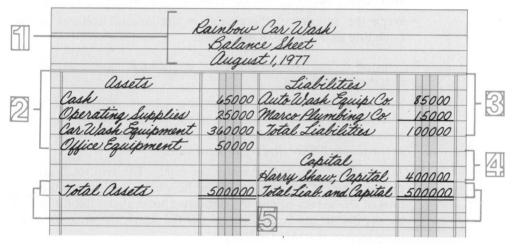

A balance sheet showing the five steps in its preparation

☐ 2 Prepare the assets section on the left-hand side, as follows:

- Write the word *Assets* in the center of the first line of the wide column on the left.

- List the name and amount of each asset, using a brief title to describe it. Begin on the next line.

☐ 3 Prepare the liabilities section on the right-hand side, as follows:

- Write the word *Liabilities* in the center of the first line of the wide column on the right.

- List the name and amount of each liability, using a brief title to describe it. Begin on the next line.
- Rule a single line across the amount column directly under the last amount.
- Write the total of the liabilities in the amount column and label this amount *Total Liabilities*.

☐ 4 Prepare the capital section on the right-hand side, beneath the liabilities, as follows:

- Skip one line and write the word *Capital* in the center of the wide column.
- Write the name of the owner and the word *Capital* on the next line.

    In some accounting systems the word written after the owner's name on the balance sheet may be *Investment*, or *Net Worth*, or *Proprietor*, or *Capital*. In this textbook the word *Capital* is used.

- On a separate sheet of paper, find the amount of the capital by subtracting the total liabilities from the total assets.
- Write the amount of the capital in the amount column on the same line as the name of the owner.

☐ 5 Determine if the balance sheet is "in balance" and complete its preparation as follows:

- Rule a single line across the amount column on the right-hand side directly under the amount of the capital. Rule a single line across the amount column on the left-hand side on the same line as the single line on the right-hand side.
- Add each column and compare the totals. The two totals should be the same. If the two totals are the same, this proves that the total of the assets equals the combined total of the liabilities and the capital. (If the final totals are not the same, the error or errors must be found and corrected.)
- Record the totals directly under the addition line on each side. Do not skip a space.
- Write the words *Total Assets* on the same line as the left-hand total.
- Write the words *Total Liabilities and Capital* on the same line as the right-hand total.

    If necessary, the words on this line may be abbreviated to *Total Liab. and Cap.*

- Rule double lines across both amount columns directly under each total. The double lines show that the work is completed and that the balance sheet is "in balance."

KEEPING BUSINESS RECORDS AND PERSONAL RECORDS SEPARATE

The owner of a business has personal assets as well as business assets. The owner also has personal liabilities as well as business liabilities. In order to provide helpful data for managing the business, the accounting records of the business must be kept separate from the owner's personal records. When a balance sheet for the business is prepared, only the assets and the liabilities of the business are reported.

COMMON ACCOUNTING PRACTICES

The following illustrations of the right-hand section of a balance sheet are used to point out six common accounting practices.

1. Words are written in full when space is adequate. Words may be abbreviated when space is inadequate, as shown below in the labeling of the *Total Liab. and Cap.*

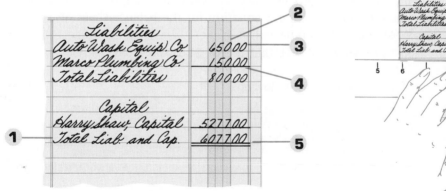 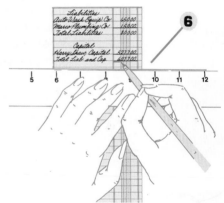

Some common accounting practices

2. Dollar signs, cent signs, and decimal points are not used when amounts are written in ruled columns of accounting paper. A color tint in the amount columns separates dollars from cents. A heavy vertical ruling may also be used in an amount column to separate dollars from cents and to serve as the decimal point.

3. Two zeros are written in the cents column when an amount is in even dollars. This is the way an accounting machine or an adding machine prints "no cents." If the cents column were left blank, there

might be some doubt later as to whether the recording of the cents was overlooked.

Some accountants use a dash (—) instead of two zeros for indicating "no cents."

4. When the accountant rules a single line beneath an amount, this single line indicates that either a total or a remainder will follow.
5. A double ruling across an amount column indicates that the work above the double lines is complete and accurate.
6. For neat accounting work a ruler or other straight edge is needed for drawing single and double rulings.

THE ACCOUNTING EQUATION

On any balance sheet, *Assets = Equities*. Since there are two types of equities — (1) the *equity* of the creditors (liabilities) and (2) the *equity* of the owner (capital) — the equation is expanded as follows:

ASSETS = LIABILITIES + CAPITAL

The statement that assets equal liabilities plus capital is called the accounting equation. This equation is true of all complete balance sheets. For example, the accounting equation for the balance sheet of Rainbow Car Wash illustrated on page 9 is:

ASSETS OF $5,000.00 = LIABILITIES OF $1,000.00 + CAPITAL OF $4,000.00

Using Business Terms

✦ What is the meaning of each of the following?

- accounting records
- accounting
- accountant
- accounting clerk
- data
- data processing
- automated data processing (ADP)
- balance sheet
- asset
- liability
- creditor
- capital
- proprietor
- equities
- accounting equation

Questions for Individual Study

1. What are two reasons why every business has a system for collecting and reporting information about itself?
2. State the four basic reasons why people study accounting.
3. What are the three general ways by which business data are processed?
4. How can the owner of a business find out how much the business is worth?
5. Name the three items in the heading of a balance sheet.
6. What are the three sections of the body of a balance sheet?
7. Why does a balance sheet have two sides?

8. What is meant when it is said that a balance sheet is "in balance"?
9. What are the five steps in preparing a balance sheet?
10. Why are dollar signs, cent signs, and decimal points omitted when recording amounts in ruled columns of accounting paper?
11. Why should the cents column of ruled accounting paper be filled in when an amount in even dollars is recorded?
12. What does a double ruling across an amount column indicate?

CASE 1 Mary Hess is the proprietor of a beauty parlor. Her balance sheet for the year just ended shows that her capital is less than it was when she made her balance sheet a year ago. What are some of the reasons for this decrease in capital?

CASE 2 The balance sheet of Rainbow Car Wash, page 7, shows that the business owes $1,000.00 to creditors. However, there is only $650.00 in cash to pay these bills. From what sources might the car wash obtain additional cash to pay its creditors?

CASE 3 The South Street Car Wash and Ezy-Do Car Wash each have assets totaling $10,000.00. The owner's equity in South Street Car Wash is $1,000.00. The owner's equity in Ezy-Do Car Wash is $9,000.00. Each business submits its balance sheet to a bank and each asks to borrow $3,000.00. Based on this information, which of these two businesses would find it easier to get the loan? Why?

DRILL 1-D 1 Using business terms

The first step in learning accounting is to learn business terms. A list of common, everyday words and phrases is given at the right. This drill is planned to help you learn the language of business and to give you practice in using business terms. If you do not have a workbook, prepare a form similar to the one shown here.

Instructions: Write in the right-hand column the business term for each of the everyday words and phrases listed in the left-hand column. For example, in business the first item, a thing of value, is called an asset.

Words and Phrases	Terms
1. A thing of value...............	*Asset*
2. A debt...........................	
3. One to whom money is owed..............................	
4. The amount a business is worth.............................	
5. An owner of a business......	
6. Claims against the assets of a business........................	
7. Detailed items of information..................................	
8. Handling detailed items of information......................	
9. Handling detailed items of information by automated means	
10. The owner's claim against the assets of a business	

DRILL 1-D 2 Classifying assets, liabilities, and capital

In preparing a balance sheet, it is necessary to classify each item as an asset, a liability, or capital. This drill is planned to give you practice in classifying and locating items on balance sheets. If you do not have a workbook, prepare a form similar to the one shown at the top of the next page.

Instructions: Classify each of the following balance sheet items by writing the word *asset*, *liability*, or *capital* in the proper column. For example, the first item, Cash, is an asset. Because assets appear on the left-hand side of the balance sheet, the word *Asset* is written in the left-hand column.

Items	Balance Sheet	
	Left-hand side	Right-hand side
1. Cash	Asset	
2. Amount owed to creditor		
3. Office machines		
4. Delivery equipment......................................		
5. Amount a business is worth		
6. Machinery		
7. Factory building		
8. Unpaid electric bill.....................................		
9. Office furniture..		
10. Any amount owned......................................		
11. Any amount owed..		
12. Difference between total assets and total liabilities		

DRILL 1-D 3 ● Using the accounting equation

The accounting equation is true of all complete balance sheets. This drill gives you practice in using the accounting equation. If you do not have a workbook, prepare a form similar to the one below.

Instructions: Find the missing amount in the accounting equation for each of the businesses listed below. Enter this amount in the Answers column. The answer to Business No. 1 is given as an example.

Business No.	Assets	=	Liabilities	+	Capital	Answers
1.	$ 4,000.00	= $	1,000.00	+	?	$ 3,000.00
2.	20,000.00	=	4,000.00	+	?	
3.	9,500.00	=	?	+ $	5,500.00	
4.	5,495.95	=	1,345.30	+	?	
5.	?	=	6,780.00	+	6,220.00	
6.	364,777.50	=	110,107.50	+	?	
7.	?	=	978.10	+	2,009.60	

Problems for Applying Concepts

PROBLEM 1-1 ● Balance sheet for a self-service laundry

The following are the assets and the liabilities of Harvey's Coin Laundry, owned and operated by Robert Harvey:

Assets		Liabilities	
Cash...................................	$ 620.20	Jay's Repair Shop................	$ 45.70
Furniture and Fixtures.........	173.50	Marvel Appliances..............	1,000.00
Drying Equipment..............	1,080.00	OK Laundry Supply Co.	28.00
Washing Equipment	2,240.00		

Instructions: Prepare a balance sheet for Harvey's Coin Laundry. Use the date September 1 of the current year. Follow the five steps for preparing a balance sheet given on pages 9 and 10. Use as your model the balance sheet illustrated on page 9.

Self-checking: Check the accuracy and the completeness of your work with the following questions:

1. Is each of the three items in the heading centered and on a separate line?
2. Is each of the sectional headings in the body of the balance sheet centered?
3. Are the assets, liabilities, and capital listed immediately below the appropriate heading without skipping a line?
4. Are the liabilities section and the capital section separated by a blank line?
5. Is the amount of the total assets at the bottom of the left-hand side of the balance sheet on the same line as the amount of the total liabilities and capital at the bottom of the right-hand side?
6. Are the two totals at the bottom of the balance sheet the same amount?
7. Are the single and double lines drawn across the amount columns only?
8. Is your work neat? Is your writing legible? Can it be read with ease?

PROBLEM 1-2 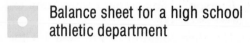 Balance sheet for an attorney

Irving Zeller, an attorney, has the following business assets and liabilities:

Assets		Liabilities	
Cash	$ 450.00	Atlantic Furniture Co.	$1,500.00
Office Supplies	280.00	Scott Supply Company	40.00
Automobile	3,200.00	South End Garage	120.00
Legal Library	600.00		
Furniture and Fixtures	2,100.00		
Office Machines	970.00		

Instructions: Prepare a balance sheet for Attorney Irving Zeller dated June 1 of the current year. Use as your model the balance sheet on page 9.

Self-checking: Check your work with the questions under Problem 1-1.

PROBLEM 1-3 Balance sheet for a high school
athletic department

The Athletic Department of the Canton High School has the following assets and liabilities on May 1 of the current year:

Assets		Liabilities	
Cash	$1,660.00	General Printing Company	$ 65.00
Baseball Equipment	1,400.00	K D Sporting Goods Co.	535.00
Basketball Equipment	820.00	Rick's Sport Shop	850.00
Football Equipment	3,650.00		
Golf Equipment	275.00		
Tennis Equipment	275.00		
Swimming Equipment	180.00		

Instructions: Prepare a balance sheet for the Canton High School Athletic Department. Use the date May 1 of the current year. The amount of the capital should be labeled, *Canton H. S. Athletic Dept., Cap.* Use as your model the balance sheet illustrated on page 9.

Self-checking: Check your work with the questions under Problem 1-1.

**MASTERY
PROBLEM 1-M** Balance sheet for a small garage

The following are the assets and the liabilities of the A1A Garage, owned by Robert Ott:

Assets		Liabilities	
Cash	$ 840.00	Eddy Supply Company	$ 40.00
Supplies	660.00	Edison Equipment Company	450.00
Tools	320.00	Samson Motor Company	1,150.00
Garage Equipment	5,550.00		
Office Equipment	660.00		

Instructions: Prepare a balance sheet for the A1A Garage dated July 1 of the current year. Use the balance sheet on page 9 as your model.

Self-checking: Check your work with the questions under Problem 1-1.

**BONUS
PROBLEM 1-B** Balance sheet for an individual

In Problem 1-1, the amount of the capital in Harvey's Coin Laundry was found for September 1 of the current year. This was the amount of the investment in the business by the owner, Robert Harvey.

Mr. Harvey wishes to know the total amount that he is worth on this same date. He supplies the following information:

Has cash on hand and in his personal bank account amounting to $340.00.
Owns U.S. Savings Bonds worth $117.00.
Owns Harvey's Coin Laundry. (See solution to Problem 1-1 for amount of his owner's equity in Harvey's Coin Laundry.)
Owes his father, John Harvey, $40.00.
Owes Central Community College, where he is taking night courses, $60.00.
Owns an automobile worth $2,100.00. Still owes Auto Finance Company $800.00.
Recently bought a color TV set for $430.00. Still owes the seller, Collier Sales Company, $225.00.
Owes pledge made earlier in the year to the United Fund, $15.00.
Owns transistor radio worth $30.00.
Owns clothing valued at $410.00.

Instructions: Prepare a balance sheet for Robert Harvey dated September 1 of the current year. Use as your model the balance sheet on page 9.

Self-checking: Check your work with the questions under Problem 1-1.

Recording the Opening Entry

2

The beginning balance sheet shows the beginning financial position of the business. The balance sheet is, therefore, the starting place for a new accounting system.

Periodically, every business needs to know its up-to-date financial position. For example, from month to month Mr. Shaw, the proprietor of Rainbow Car Wash, will want to know how well his business is doing. Is the business making a profit? Operating at a loss? Is the business worth more or less this month than last? How much more? How much less?

To provide the necessary data for future balance sheets and for other financial statements, an orderly accounting system must be used. A new accounting system is started by making the data on the beginning balance sheet a part of the permanent records. This is done by recording the data on the beginning balance sheet in one of the books of the business.

THE JOURNAL — A BOOK OF ORIGINAL ENTRY

The first book in which the records of a business are written is called a journal. Each record in a journal is called an entry. The entry that records the data shown on a beginning balance sheet is called an opening entry. Because a journal is the first book in which entries are recorded, a journal is also known as a book of original entry.

The general journal

There are different kinds of journals. The nature of a business and the extent of its activities determine the types of journals that are needed. A journal may have one or more amount columns. A journal with two amount columns in which all kinds of entries may be recorded is called a general journal

The standard form of two-column general journal used by Rainbow Car Wash is shown at the top of the next page.

GENERAL JOURNAL					PAGE	
DATE	ACCOUNT TITLE	POST. REF.	DEBIT	CREDIT		
1						1
2						2

Standard form of two-column general journal

The source document

When an accounting clerk makes an entry in a journal, there should be some written evidence to support the entry. This evidence is usually some business paper. The business paper from which a journal entry is made is called a source document.

The source document for an opening entry

The beginning balance sheet of Rainbow Car Wash, shown below, is the source document for the opening entry made in the general journal.

Beginning balance sheet of Rainbow Car Wash

Rainbow Car Wash Balance Sheet August 1, 1977				
Assets		**Liabilities**	
Cash	65000	Auto Wash Equip. Co.	85000
Operating Supplies	25000	Marco Plumbing Co.	15000
Car Wash Equipment	360000	Total Liabilities	100000
Office Equipment	50000		
		Capital	
		Harry Shaw, Capital	400000
Total Assets	500000	Total Liab. and Capital	500000

The amounts on the left-hand side of the balance sheet are recorded in the left-hand amount column of the two-column general journal. The left-hand amount column of a two-column general journal is called the *debit column*. The amounts on the right-hand side of the balance sheet are recorded in the right-hand amount column of the journal. The right-hand amount column of a two-column general journal is called the *credit column*.

The meaning of *debit* and *credit* is explained in Chapter 3.

BEGINNING BALANCE SHEET

Assets	Liabilities and Capital

GENERAL JOURNAL

Debit column	Credit column

Relationship of items on beginning balance sheet to general journal columns

The parts of a journal entry

Every journal entry has four parts: (1) a date, (2) a debit part, (3) a credit part, and (4) a brief explanation or an indication of the source document.

STEPS IN RECORDING THE OPENING ENTRY

The steps in recording the opening entry on page 1 of the general journal of Rainbow Car Wash are:

☐ 1 **Date of the entry.** Write the date of the opening entry in the Date column as shown below.

DATE	ACCOUNT TITLE	POST. REF.	DEBIT	CREDIT
1977 Aug. 1				

■ Write the *year* in small figures at the top of the column. The year is written only once on a journal page.

■ Write the *month* below the year on the first line in the first column. A month is generally written only once on a page.

> Because the Date column is narrow, the name of the month may be abbreviated.

■ Write the *day* of the month on the first line in the second column immediately after the name of the month.

The date is written once and only once for each entry, regardless of how many lines are used for the entry.

☐ 2 **Debit part of the entry.** Write the debit part of the entry as shown below.

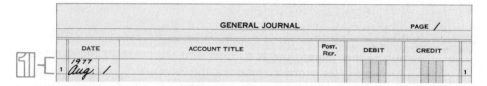

DATE	ACCOUNT TITLE	POST. REF.	DEBIT	CREDIT
1977 Aug. 1	Cash		65000	
	Operating Supplies		25000	
	Car Wash Equipment		360000	
	Office Equipment		50000	

■ Write the name of each asset at the extreme left edge of the Account Title column.

■ Write the amount of each asset in the Debit column.

☐ 3 **Credit part of the entry.** Write the credit part of the entry as shown below.

	GENERAL JOURNAL			PAGE /	
DATE	ACCOUNT TITLE	POST. REF.	DEBIT	CREDIT	
1977 Aug. 1	Cash		65000		1
	Operating Supplies		25000		2
	Car Wash Equipment		360000		3
	Office Equipment		50000		4
	Auto Wash Equipment Co.			85000	5
	Marco Plumbing Company			15000	6
	Harry Shaw, Capital			400000	7
					8
					9

- Write the name of each liability and the name of the owner, followed by the word Capital, in the Account Title column. Indent each name about one-half inch (about 1.3 centimeters) from the left edge of the Account Title column. Indenting these items helps to separate the credit part of the entry from the debit part.

- Write the amount of each credit item in the Credit column.

☐ 4 **Reason for or source of the entry.** Write a brief explanation or indicate the source document used for making the entry.

	GENERAL JOURNAL			PAGE /	
DATE	ACCOUNT TITLE	POST. REF.	DEBIT	CREDIT	
1977 Aug. 1	Cash		65000		1
	Operating Supplies		25000		2
	Car Wash Equipment		360000		3
	Office Equipment		50000		4
	Auto Wash Equipment Co.			85000	5
	Marco Plumbing Company			15000	6
	Harry Shaw, Capital			400000	7
	August 1 balance sheet.				8
					9
					10

- Write the explanation or indicate the source document in the Account Title column immediately below the last credit item. Indent about one inch from the left edge of the Account Title column.

- If the explanation takes more than one line, each line should be indented about one inch (about 2.5 centimeters).

The purpose of an explanation or an indication of the source document is to supply the reason for the journal entry or to identify its source in case further information is needed.

The complete opening entry

The complete opening entry in the general journal of Rainbow Car Wash is shown below.

	DATE	ACCOUNT TITLE	POST. REF.	DEBIT	CREDIT	
		GENERAL JOURNAL			PAGE *1*	
1	*1977* *Aug.* 1	*Cash*		65000		1
2		*Operating Supplies*		25000		2
3		*Car Wash Equipment*		360000		3
4		*Office Equipment*		50000		4
5		*Auto Wash Equipment Co.*			85000	5
6		*Marco Plumbing Company*			15000	6
7		*Harry Shaw, Capital*			400000	7
8		*August 1 balance sheet.*				8
9						9

Opening entry of Rainbow Car Wash

The use of the Post. Ref. column will be explained in Chapter 3.

CHECKING FOR ACCURACY

Accuracy is extremely important in keeping books. An accounting clerk has frequent opportunities to check the accuracy of the work.

Every journal entry must be "in balance"

An accounting clerk checks the accuracy of the balance sheet by seeing that it is in balance. When the total of the left-hand side of the balance sheet is equal to the total of the right-hand side, the balance sheet is in balance. Similarly, every journal entry must be in balance. The sum of the amounts in the debit part of a journal entry must equal the sum of the amounts in the credit part.

Making corrections

When the sum of the debit amounts in a journal entry does not equal the sum of the credit amounts in the entry, the error or errors must be found and corrected. If an error is made in writing an amount, the incorrect amount is canceled by drawing a line through it. The correct amount is then written immediately above the canceled amount. Similarly, if an error is made in any other part of the entry, the entry is corrected. This is done by drawing a line through the incorrect part. The correction is written immediately above the canceled part. A correction is shown below.

	DATE	ACCOUNT TITLE	POST. REF.	DEBIT	CREDIT	
1	1977 Sept. 1	Cash		50000		1
2		Office Supplies		5000		2
3		Office Equipment		205000		3
4		Regal Supplies Company			20000	4
5		Paul Dayton, Capital			~~240000~~ ~~250000~~	5
6		September 1				6
7		balance sheet.				7

GENERAL JOURNAL — PAGE 1

Correcting an error in an amount

✦ What is the meaning of each of the following?

- journal
- entry
- opening entry
- general journal
- source document

Questions for Individual Study

1. Why is a beginning balance sheet the starting place for a new accounting system?
2. How is a new accounting system started?
3. What is the source document for making an opening entry?
4. What are the four parts of every entry in a general journal?
5. Where are the month, the day, and the year of the opening entry written?
6. When an opening entry is recorded, what kinds of balance sheet items have their amounts recorded in the Debit column of the general journal?
7. When an opening entry is recorded, what kinds of balance sheet items

have their amounts recorded in the Credit column of the general journal?
8. How far should the name of each credit item be indented in a general journal entry?
9. Why is the credit part of the opening entry indented?
10. What is the purpose of writing a brief explanation or indicating the source document in the opening entry?
11. If the sum of the debit amounts in a journal entry does not equal the sum of the credit amounts in the entry, what should the accounting clerk do?
12. How is an error in writing an amount corrected?

Cases for Management Decision

CASE 1 Dan Morgan started a grass cutting business that he called Morgan's Lawn Service. During his first month in business, he failed to establish an accounting system. He calls upon you to start such a system.

What steps would you take and to what sources might you go for securing the information needed for an opening entry in the general journal?

CASE 2 Jack Kern learned the real estate business by working for a large real estate agency. He decided to start a new agency

for himself. On October 1, 1977, before he had rented or furnished an office, Mr. Kern deposited $4,000.00 in a local bank in the name of his new business, Kern Realty Agency. At that time, the agency had no other assets and no liabilities.

Mr. Kern did not make an opening entry in his accounting records. He believed that until he had assets other than cash, he could not prepare a balance sheet. He believed that he needed a beginning balance sheet before he could make an opening entry. Mrs. Kern indicated that she believed he should make an opening entry. Do you agree with Mr. Kern or Mrs. Kern? Why?

DRILL 2-D 1 **Classifying balance sheet items and indicating their debit and credit parts when recorded in an opening entry**

Drill for Mastering Principles

This drill is planned to give you practice (a) in classifying balance sheet items, and (b) in determining which kinds of balance sheet items are recorded in the Debit column and which kinds are recorded in the Credit column in an opening entry. A form listing the balance sheet items is provided in your workbook.

Instructions: □ **1.** Classify each item by writing the word *asset, liability*, or *capital* in one of the Balance Sheet columns to indicate on which side of the balance sheet it should be listed.

□ **2.** If the amount of the item is written in the Debit column of the general journal when making an opening entry, make a check mark in the Debit column of the form. If the amount of the item is written in the Credit column of the journal when making an opening entry, make a check mark in the Credit column of the form. The first item, Delivery equipment, is given as an example on the form below.

	Balance Sheet		General Journal	
Balance Sheet Items	Left-hand side	Right-hand side	Column in which amount in opening entry is recorded	
			Debit column	Credit column
1. *Delivery equipment*	*Asset*		√	

If you do not have a workbook, copy the form above on a sheet of paper and use the following list of balance sheet items:

(1) Delivery equipment
(2) Land
(3) Jeff Owen (creditor)
(4) Cash
(5) Sue Ann Page, Capital
(6) Crosby Equipment Company (creditor)
(7) Dry cleaning equipment
(8) Dry cleaning supplies
(9) Building
(10) Any amount owed
(11) Any amount owned
(12) Any owner's equity

Instructions: □ **3.** Now cover your answers and see how rapidly you can do this drill mentally without looking at your answers. Repeat this drill several times for increased speed and accuracy.

PROBLEM 2-1 Opening entry for a farm

Instructions: □ **1.** Prepare page 1 of a general journal by writing the proper heading at the top of each column. Use the same headings as shown in the general journal on page 18.

□ **2.** Record the opening entry in this journal from the following balance sheet. Use July 1 of the current year as the date of the entry.

Sunnybrook Farm
Balance Sheet
July 1, 19—

Assets			Liabilities		
Cash...................................	210	00	Grange Credit Union.................	5 000	00
Livestock..............................	1 750	00	Red River Feed Company..........	140	00
Machinery and Equipment.........	3 850	00	River City Feed and Grain Store..	110	00
Buildings	10 500	00	Total Liabilities........................	5 250	00
Land...................................	12 000	00			
			Capital		
			Dale Hiller, Capital...................	23 060	00
Total Assets...........................	28 310	00	Total Liabilities and Capital	28 310	00

Self-checking: Compare your opening entry with the illustration on page 21 and check the accuracy of your work by asking yourself the following questions:

1. Are the year, the month, and the day written at the top of the Date column?
2. Is each debit item written at the extreme left edge of the Account Title column?
3. Is each credit item in the Account Title column indented about one-half inch (about 1.3 centimeters)?
4. Is either a brief explanation of the entry or an indication of the source document given? Is this indented about one inch (about 2.5 centimeters)?
5. Does the sum of the amounts of the debit part of the entry equal the sum of the amounts in the credit part?

PROBLEM 2-2 Opening entry for a real estate agency

Instructions: Record an opening entry on page 1 of a general journal from the balance sheet below. Use October 1 of the current year as the date of the entry.

Rhodes Realty Agency
Balance Sheet
October 1, 19—

Assets			Liabilities		
Cash...................................	371	00	Adams Company......................	91	00
Automobile	3 170	00	Daniels Company	300	00
Office Furniture......................	745	60	Star Garage...........................	1 250	00
Office Machines......................	254	40	Total Liabilities........................	1 641	00
			Capital		
			Ralph Rhodes, Capital..............	2 900	00
Total Assets	4 541	00	Total Liabilities and Capital	4 541	00

Self-checking: Check the accuracy of your opening entry by asking yourself the questions given at the end of Problem 2-1.

**MASTERY
PROBLEM 2-M** Balance sheet and opening entry for a
secretarial service

Rose Pierce, a public stenographer, owns and operates Pierce Secretarial Service. The following are the assets and the liabilities of her business.

Assets		Liabilities	
Cash	$ 670.50	Crown Equipment Company	$450.00
Office Supplies	140.50	Knoll Products, Inc.	45.50
Office Furniture	840.00	Scheve Stationery Company	28.20
Office Machines	1,680.00		

Instructions: □ **1.** Prepare a balance sheet for the Pierce Secretarial Service dated October 1 of the current year.

□ **2.** Record the opening entry on page 1 in a general journal.

Self-checking: Check your balance sheet with the questions listed under Problem 1-1, page 15. Check your opening entry with the questions listed under Problem 2-1, page 24.

**BONUS
PROBLEM 2-B** Balance sheet and opening entry for a dry
cleaning business; separating business
records from personal records

Jerald Rooney has been the owner and operator of Jerry's Cleaners, a dry cleaning business, for the past month. During this time he failed to keep any records of either his dry cleaning business or his personal affairs. The following information, however, which is a mixture of Mr. Rooney's business and personal assets as well as his business and personal liabilities, is available.

Assets. Cash in Mr. Rooney's personal checking account, $312.50; cash in the checking account of Jerry's Cleaners, $624.00; delivery truck, $2,776.00; furniture in Mr. Rooney's home, $2,770.00; dry cleaning equipment, $2,110.00; store equipment, $1,340.00; family automobile, $3,200.00; house in which he lives, $19,500.00; store building in which his business is located, $8,000.00; land on which his corner store is located, $6,000.00; land on which his home is located, $6,000.00.

Liabilities. To Auto Finance Company, $1,600.00, for payments yet to be made on the delivery truck; to Collier County National Bank for payments yet to be made on family automobile, $800.00; to Haskins Supply Company, $1,000.00, for amount still due on dry cleaning equipment; to Merchants National Bank, $8,500.00, of which $4,000.00 is for the mortgage on his home and the remaining $4,500.00 for the mortgage on his corner store building and lot.

Instructions: □ **1.** Prepare a balance sheet for Jerry's Cleaners. Use August 1 of the current year as the date.

□ **2.** Record the opening entry on page 1 of a general journal.

Self-checking: Check your balance sheet with the questions under Problem 1-1, page 15. Check your opening entry with the questions under Problem 2-1, page 24.

3

Posting the Opening Entry

The beginning balance sheet shows the beginning financial position of the business. The opening entry in the journal is made from the beginning balance sheet. The opening entry, therefore, is a complete record of the assets, the liabilities, and the capital *at the time an accounting system is started*.

The business transaction

As a business conducts day-to-day operations, changes occur in the value of its assets, liabilities, and capital. Goods and services are bought and sold. Cash is received and paid out. Debts are incurred and paid.

An exchange of property or services is called a business transaction. Each wash that Rainbow Car Wash sells to a customer is a business transaction. For example, the five-minute use of its equipment is exchanged for the fifty cents a customer deposits in a coin box. Each business transaction causes a change in the amount of some balance sheet items. An accounting system must show not only what a business has, but also the changes in its assets, its liabilities, and its capital.

THE LEDGER — A BOOK OF SECONDARY ENTRY

Accounting records for showing the increases and the decreases in assets, liabilities, and capital include a separate page, sheet, or card for each balance sheet item.

An accounting form that is used to sort and summarize the changes caused by business transactions is called an account. A group of accounts is called a ledger. In manual accounting, the ledger is usually a loose-leaf book. Because the information recorded in the ledger is secured from the journal, the ledger is also known as a book of secondary entry. In machine accounting, the ledger may consist of ledger sheets or ledger cards kept in a tray or a file.

Two-column account form

Accounts are ruled in various ways. One form of ruling is with two amount columns — one Debit column and one Credit column. This two-column account form is shown below. It is often used in systems where accounting is done manually.

Two-column account form

Debit and credit

The two-column account form is divided into two halves, each with the same ruling. The left-hand side of a two-column account form is called the debit side. The right-hand side of a two-column account form is called the credit side. Except for the headings of the debit and the credit columns, the headings are the same on each side of the account.

An entry on the left-hand side of a two-column account form is called a debit entry, or merely a debit. An entry on the right-hand side of a two-column account form is called a credit entry, or merely a credit.

The words *debit* and *credit* are also used as verbs. You *debit* an account when you make an entry on the left-hand side. You *credit* an account when you make an entry on the right-hand side.

The abbreviations *Dr.* for debit and *Cr.* for credit (derived from the words debitor and creditor) are frequently used in accounting.

Chart of accounts

Each account has a name and a number. The name given to an account is called the account title. The number given to an account to show its location in the ledger is called the account number. There is an account in the ledger for each item on the beginning balance sheet.

A list of account titles along with their numbers showing the arrangement of the accounts in the ledger is called a chart of accounts. The accounts are arranged in the ledger in numerical order. As a result, they can be located quickly. A part of the chart of accounts of Rainbow Car Wash is shown below. The complete chart of accounts is on page 2.

<table>
<tr><td colspan="4" align="center">**Rainbow Car Wash**
Chart of Accounts</td></tr>
<tr><td align="center">**(1) Assets**</td><td align="center">**Account Number**</td><td align="center">**(2) Liabilities**</td><td align="center">**Account Number**</td></tr>
<tr><td>Cash...............................</td><td align="center">11</td><td>Auto Wash Equipment Co. ..</td><td align="center">21</td></tr>
<tr><td>Operating Supplies.............</td><td align="center">12</td><td>Marco Plumbing Co. ....</td><td align="center">22</td></tr>
<tr><td>Car Wash Equipment..........</td><td align="center">13</td><td></td><td></td></tr>
<tr><td>Office Equipment ....</td><td align="center">14</td><td align="center">**(3) Capital**</td><td></td></tr>
<tr><td></td><td></td><td>Harry Shaw, Capital............</td><td align="center">31</td></tr>
</table>

Partial chart of accounts for Rainbow Car Wash

The first digit of each account number tells in which *division* of the ledger the account is located. In the partial chart of accounts given above, there are three divisions: division 1, assets; division 2, liabilities; division 3, capital. Therefore, all asset account numbers begin with 1, all liability account numbers begin with 2, and the capital account number begins with 3.

The second digit of each account number tells the *position* of the account within its *division* of the ledger. For example, the account number for Car Wash Equipment is 13. This number shows that the car wash equipment account is in the *first* division of the ledger, the assets division, and that it is the *third* account in the division.

> For reasons that will be explained in other chapters, some businesses use a three-digit numbering system for their chart of accounts and some use a four-digit system. For example, a business larger than Rainbow Car Wash might assign the number 111 to the cash account.

Opening accounts in the ledger

Writing the account title and the account number on the first line of a ledger account form is called opening an account. An account needs to be opened in the ledger for each account listed on the chart of accounts. As additional accounts are needed, they are listed on the chart of accounts and are opened in the ledger.

Cash is the first account to be opened in the ledger of Rainbow Car Wash because it is the first account in the chart of accounts. The cash account is opened by □ 1 writing the name of the account *Cash* at the left on the first line of the first page of the ledger, and □ 2 writing the number of the cash account, *11*, in the upper right-hand corner of the ledger page.

The cash account, after it is opened, appears in the ledger as follows:

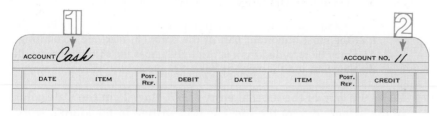

The cash account
after it is opened

The procedure in opening each of the remaining accounts is the same as that followed in opening the cash account.

POSTING THE OPENING ENTRY TO THE LEDGER

Each amount in the opening entry of Rainbow Car Wash shown below is transferred to the proper ledger account. Transferring the entries in a journal to the accounts in a ledger is called posting . Posting sorts the data in the journal bringing all data of one kind together. For example, all data about changes in cash are sorted from the other data in the journal and brought together in the cash account.

The first three steps in posting debit items of the opening entry

The first three steps in posting Line 1 of the journal are shown below and explained on the next page.

The first three steps in
posting a debit item

	DATE	ACCOUNT TITLE	POST. REF.	DEBIT	CREDIT	
	GENERAL JOURNAL				PAGE 1	
1	1977 Aug. 1	Cash		65000		1
2		Operating Supplies		25000		2
3		Car Wash Equipment		360000		3
4		Office Equipment		50000		4
5		Auto Wash Equipment Co.			85000	5
6		Marco Plumbing Company			15000	6
7		Harry Shaw, Capital			400000	7
8		August 1 balance sheet.				8
9						9
10						10

ACCOUNT Cash   ACCOUNT NO. 11

DATE	ITEM	POST. REF.	DEBIT	DATE	ITEM	POST. REF.	CREDIT
1977 Aug. 1	Balance		65000				

☐ **1** Write the *amount* of the cash debit, *$650.00*, in the Debit column of the cash account in the ledger as shown on page 29.

> In manual accounting, the amount is usually written first because it is the most important part of the entry. In machine accounting, data may be recorded from left to right across the account form with the date first and the amount last.

☐ **2** Write the *date* of the journal entry, *1977, Aug. 1*, in the Date column of the ledger account the same as it is written in the journal entry as shown on page 29.

> The year and the name of the month are written only once during the month on the side of the account that is used.

☐ **3** Write the word *Balance* in the Item column of the account.

> Accounting clerks distinguish between the beginning amount in an account and the amounts recorded later as a result of normal business operations. The beginning amount or balance in the cash account is therefore labeled with the single word *Balance* in the Item column.

The final two steps in posting — cross-referencing

The posting of an entry is not complete until a cross-reference is made between the journal and the ledger. This cross-referencing is shown below and explained in Steps 4 and 5 on page 31.

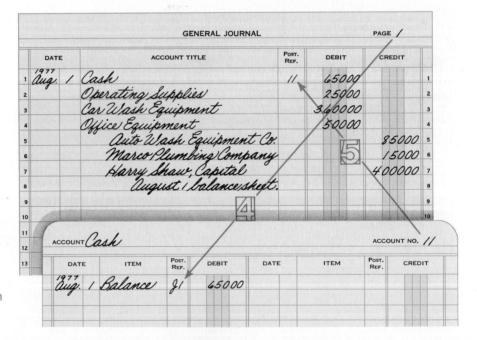

The final two steps in posting — cross-referencing

□ **4** Write *J1* in the Post. Ref. column of the cash account. *J1* is written in the Post. Ref. column of the account to show that this debit to Cash came from page 1 of the general journal.

> *J* is the abbreviation for *general journal*. *Post. Ref.* is the abbreviation for *Posting Reference*.

□ **5** Return to the journal and write in the Post. Ref. column of the journal the number of the account, *11*, to which the item was posted.

Writing the number 11 in the Post. Ref. column of the general journal shows that this item was posted to account number 11. The number also indicates that all the details of the posting of this line have been completed. For each entry the Post. Ref. figure in the journal is written as the *last* step in posting. When the accounting clerk is interrupted in posting, the proper use of Post. Ref. numbers makes it easier to resume the posting quickly at the right place. For this reason, recording the posting reference numbers in the journal *must* be the last step in the posting procedure.

Posting the remaining debit items of the opening entry

The same steps used in posting the first debit item of the opening entry are followed in posting the remaining debit items. The accounts to which all debit items have been posted are shown below. Each account is a separate page of the ledger.

Asset accounts with all debit items in opening entry posted

ACCOUNT *Cash* — ACCOUNT NO. *11*

DATE	ITEM	POST. REF.	DEBIT	DATE	ITEM	POST. REF.	CREDIT
1977 Aug. 1	Balance	J1	65000				

ACCOUNT *Operating Supplies* — ACCOUNT NO. *12*

DATE	ITEM	POST. REF.	DEBIT	DATE	ITEM	POST. REF.	CREDIT
1977 Aug. 1	Balance	J1	25000				

ACCOUNT *Car Wash Equipment* — ACCOUNT NO. *13*

DATE	ITEM	POST. REF.	DEBIT	DATE	ITEM	POST. REF.	CREDIT
1977 Aug. 1	Balance	J1	360000				

ACCOUNT *Office Equipment* — ACCOUNT NO. *14*

DATE	ITEM	POST. REF.	DEBIT	DATE	ITEM	POST. REF.	CREDIT
1977 Aug. 1	Balance	J1	50000				

Posting the credit items of the opening entry

The credit items in the general journal are posted in the same manner as the debit items. The exception is that the credit items are posted to the *credit side* of the accounts. The five steps in posting the first credit item are illustrated below.

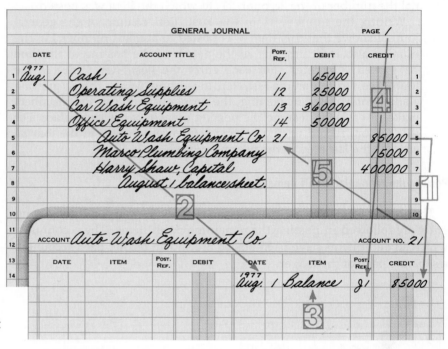

The posting of a credit item

The accounts to which all the credit items have been posted are shown at the top of the next page.

Post. Ref. column of the general journal after posting

After the posting of the opening entry has been completed, the Post. Ref. column in the general journal appears as shown at the bottom of the next page.

Use of Post. Ref. numbers

The numbers in the posting reference columns in the journal and in the ledger are useful for cross-reference. An accounting clerk looking at an entry in the journal can find the number of the account to which the journal entry was posted. With this information, the account can be quickly located in the ledger. Also, the accounting clerk looking at a ledger account can find the number of the journal page from which the posting was made. With this information, the entry in the journal can be quickly located. This cross-reference information is useful when the accuracy of the posting is being checked. Accuracy is extremely important in all accounting work.

ACCOUNT Auto Wash Equipment Co.							ACCOUNT NO. 21
DATE	ITEM	POST. REF.	DEBIT	DATE	ITEM	POST. REF.	CREDIT
				1977 Aug. 1	Balance	J1	85000

ACCOUNT Marco Plumbing Company							ACCOUNT NO. 22
DATE	ITEM	POST. REF.	DEBIT	DATE	ITEM	POST. REF.	CREDIT
				1977 Aug. 1	Balance	J1	15000

ACCOUNT Harry Shaw, Capital							ACCOUNT NO. 31
DATE	ITEM	POST. REF.	DEBIT	DATE	ITEM	POST. REF.	CREDIT
				1977 Aug. 1	Balance	J1	400000

Liability and capital accounts with all credit items in the opening entry posted

GENERAL JOURNAL				PAGE 1	
DATE	ACCOUNT TITLE	POST. REF.	DEBIT	CREDIT	
1977 Aug. 1	Cash	11	65000		1
	Operating Supplies	12	25000		2
	Car Wash Equipment	13	360000		3
	Office Equipment	14	50000		4
	Auto Wash Equipment Co.	21		85000	5
	Marco Plumbing Company	22		15000	6
	Harry Shaw, Capital	31		400000	7
	August 1 balance sheet.				8
					9
					10
					11
					12
					13

Opening entry of Rainbow Car Wash after posting

SUMMARY OF STARTING AN ACCOUNTING SYSTEM

A diagram that shows the sequence of all the steps involved in a particular activity or procedure is called a flowchart. The flowchart below summarizes the activities involved in starting an accounting system:

1. A beginning balance sheet is prepared listing the assets, the liabilities, and the capital of the business as of the day the new accounting system is started.

2. The data on the beginning balance sheet are recorded as an opening entry in the journal — a book of original entry. The assets are recorded as debits; the liabilities and the capital are recorded as credits.

3. The items recorded in the opening entry in the journal are posted to individual accounts in the ledger — a book of secondary entry.

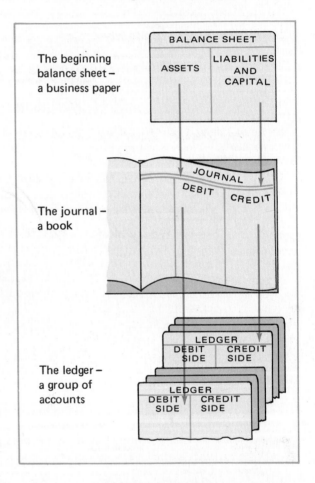

Flowchart showing the start of an accounting system

✦ What is the meaning of each of the following?

- business transaction
- account
- ledger
- debit side
- credit side

- debit or debit entry
- credit or credit entry
- account title
- account number

- chart of accounts
- opening an account
- posting
- flowchart

1. In addition to showing the assets, liabilities, and capital of a business, what else must an accounting system show?
2. What columnar headings on the two sides of a two-column form of account are the same?
3. In the partial chart of accounts of Rainbow Car Wash on page 28, what is the first digit of (a) all asset account numbers, (b) all liability account numbers, (c) the capital account number?
4. What does an accounting clerk write as the heading of an account to open an account?
5. What are the five steps in the procedure for posting each amount of the opening entry?
6. Why is the word *Balance* written in the Item column of the ledger account when posting each item of the opening entry?
7. What is the purpose of writing a journal page number in the Post. Ref. column of the ledger account?
8. What are the two purposes of writing a ledger account number in the Post. Ref. column of the general journal?
9. After an opening entry has been posted, what kind of balance has (a) each asset account, (b) each liability account, (c) the capital account?
10. How does the posting of a debit amount differ from the posting of a credit amount to a ledger account?
11. What are the three steps necessary to start an accounting system?

CASE 1 When Barry Heath started a new accounting system for his lumber business, he numbered each account consecutively — the same as he numbered the pages in his ledger. Thus his seven asset accounts were numbered 1 through 7, his four liability accounts were numbered 8 through 11, and his capital account was numbered 12. Why is Mr. Heath's system for numbering accounts in his ledger not as satisfactory as the system described in this chapter?

CASE 2 The owner of Lacy's Cafeteria notices that an accounting clerk has neglected to record in the Post. Ref. column of the general journal the ledger account numbers to which the various items in the opening entry were posted. How can this omission of cross-references cause trouble for the accounting clerk?

CASE 3 Alva Hicks is interrupted by a telephone call while in the midst of posting her general journal. If she has been following correct accounting procedure in her posting, how can she tell quickly where she left off in the journal at the time her work was interrupted by the telephone conversation?

DRILL 3-D 1 Numbering accounts

Eric Snyder, grocer, uses the same two-digit numbering system for the chart of accounts of his grocery business as that of Rainbow Car Wash described on page 28. Mr. Snyder's ledger, however, has eight asset accounts, five liability accounts, and one capital account.

Instructions: □ **1.** The location of different accounts in the ledger is given in the form on page 36. On this form in your workbook, write the account number that would be assigned each of these accounts. Use the Account Number column for your answers. For example, the account number for the first item would be 23.

If you do not have a workbook, prepare your own form on a sheet of paper. Use a form similar to the one shown at the right.

Location of the account in the ledger	Account Number
1. The third liability account	23
2. The second liability account......	
3. The first asset account	
4. The eighth asset account	
5. The capital account..................	
6. The fifth asset account.............	
7. The fifth liability account.........	
8. The first liability account	
9. The seventh asset account........	
10. The second asset account.........	

☐ **2.** Now cover the Account Number column and see how accurately you can recall the correct account numbers.

DRILL 3-D 2   Indicating the balance side of balance sheet accounts

Instructions: The names of ten balance sheet accounts are listed below on the form. To the right of the list of account titles is a diagram indicating the two sides of an account. On this form in your workbook, write the word *Balance* opposite each account title on the side where the amount of the opening entry will always appear in that account. The solution for the first account in the list, Cash, is given as an example.

ACCOUNT TITLE	Sides of an Account	
	Left-hand side DEBIT SIDE	Right-hand side CREDIT SIDE
1. Cash............................	*Balance*	_____
2. Delivery Equipment.......	_____	_____
3. Pine Street Garage (creditor).............................	_____	_____
4. Office Furniture.............	_____	_____
5. John Norman (creditor)...	_____	_____
6. Daniel Strong, Capital....	_____	_____
7. Office Machines.............	_____	_____
8. Office Supplies..............	_____	_____
9. Frank Harper (creditor)...	_____	_____
10. Building......................	_____	_____

If you do not have a workbook, prepare your own form on a sheet of paper. Use a form similar to the one shown above.

PROBLEM 3-1   Recording and posting the opening entry for a veterinarian

Luther York, a veterinarian, owns and operates York Animal Hospital. The balance sheet of York Animal Hospital on August 1 of the current year is on page 37.

Instructions: ☐ **1.** Record the opening entry on page 1 of a general journal. Use August 1 of the current year as the date.

☐ **2.** Open accounts in a ledger for all the account titles listed on the balance sheet. Allow one fourth of a page in your ledger for each account. Number the accounts as follows: asset accounts, 11 to 16; liability accounts, 21 and 22; and the veterinarian's capital account, 31.

☐ **3.** Post the opening entry.

York Animal Hospital
Balance Sheet
August 1, 19—

Assets			Liabilities		
Cash....................................	850	00	Avery Drug Company	50	00
Medical Supplies	750	00	Veterinary Supply Company	1 700	00
Office Supplies.......................	450	00	Total Liabilities.....................	1 750	00
Automobile	2 700	00			
Medical & Surgical Equipment..	2 000	00	**Capital**		
Building and Kennels..............	15 000	00	Luther York, Capital	20 000	00
Total Assets	21 750	00	Total Liabilities and Capital	21 750	00

Self-checking: Compare your accounts with the model accounts on pages 31 and 33. Check the accuracy of your posting by asking yourself the following:

1. Are the year, month, and day written at the top of the Date column on the side of each account that is used?
2. Are all the debits in the journal posted to the debit side of the six asset accounts?
3. Are all the credits in the journal posted to the credit side of the liability and the capital accounts?
4. Is the journal page number written in the Post. Ref. column of each account?
5. Is an account number written in the Post. Ref. column of the journal for each line of the journal that was posted? Was this your last step in posting the general journal?

**MASTERY
PROBLEM 3-M** Preparing a chart of accounts; recording and posting an opening entry

The balance sheet of World-Wide Travel Agency is shown below. The owner, Isabelle Lyle, has employed you to set up a new accounting system for her.

World-Wide Travel Agency
Balance Sheet
July 1, 19—

Assets			Liabilities		
Cash....................................	1 455	00	Auto Finance Company...........	1 250	00
Automobile	2 800	00	Bert's Garage	51	00
Office Furniture.....................	780	00	Office Supply Company..........	89	00
Office Machines.....................	895	00	Regal Equipment Company......	560	00
			Total Liabilities	1 950	00
			Capital		
			Isabelle Lyle, Capital..............	3 980	00
Total Assets	5 930	00	Total Liabilities and Capital	5 930	00

Instructions: ☐ **1.** Prepare a partial chart of accounts similar to the one illustrated on page 28.

□ **2.** Open accounts in a ledger for all the accounts listed on the partial chart of accounts. Allow one fourth of a page in your ledger for each account.

□ **3.** Record the opening entry on page 1 of a general journal. Use July 1 of the current year as the date.

□ **4.** Post the opening entry.

Self-checking: Check the completeness of your posting by using the questions listed under Problem 3-1.

BONUS		Preparing a chart of accounts and a beginning
PROBLEM 3-B		balance sheet; recording and posting an opening entry

Harry Guest, a photographer, owns and operates Guest Portrait Studio. He has never kept a formal set of accounting records. On October 1 of the current year he decides to start an accounting system for his photography business. He has gathered the following financial information about his studio:

Cash. Currency and coins in the cash drawer, $43.50; checks on hand received from customers, $133.50; and a bank balance according to the checkbook of $980.80.

Office Supplies. Assorted office supplies valued at $54.00.

Photographic Supplies. Assorted film, plates, developing chemicals, paper, and other supplies which cost $860.00. Mr. Guest owes Photo Supply Company $110.00 for the last order of supplies that was received.

Studio Equipment. Assorted cameras, attachments, lenses, stands, and other equipment which cost $2,450.00. Except for the $340.00 owed to Rollex Camera Company for one of the cameras, the other items of studio equipment have been fully paid for.

Office Equipment. Typewriter, $180.00; adding machine, $140.00; two filing cabinets, $160.00; desk, $140.00; desk chair, $28.00.

Mr. Guest owes Mid-Town Realty Company $150.00 for the rent of his studio. He also owes Mountain County Power Company $34.40 for heat and light.

Instructions: □ **1.** Prepare a partial chart of accounts for Guest Portrait Studio.

□ **2.** Open a ledger account for each account title listed in the chart of accounts. Allow one fourth of a page in your ledger for each account. Number the accounts as shown on your chart.

□ **3.** Prepare a balance sheet dated October 1 of the current year.

□ **4.** Record the opening entry on page 1 of a general journal.

□ **5.** Post the opening entry.

Self-checking: Check the completeness of your work by using the questions listed under Problem 3-1.

Debit and Credit of
Business Transactions Affecting
Balance Sheet Accounts

4

The opening entry in Chapter 3 was posted to accounts in the ledger of Rainbow Car Wash. After the opening entry is posted, all balance sheet accounts in the ledger have beginning amounts. Each of these beginning amounts is on one side of the account or the other. Each asset account has a beginning amount on its debit side. Each liability account and the capital account have a beginning amount on the credit side. You will learn in this chapter how amounts in these accounts are changed.

ACCOUNT BALANCES

The difference between the totals of the amounts posted to the two sides of an account is called the account balance. When an account has only one posting, this single amount is the account balance. This was true of accounts with only beginning balances in the previous chapter. As business transactions are recorded and posted, amounts will be found on both sides of some accounts.

ANY BALANCE SHEET	
ANY ASSET ACCOUNT	**ANY LIABILITY ACCOUNT**
Balance is always a debit	Balance is always a credit
	THE CAPITAL ACCOUNT
	Balance is always a credit

Diagram showing normal balances of balance sheet accounts

When the total of the debit amounts in an account exceeds the total of its credit amounts, the account has a debit balance . When the total of the credit amounts in an account exceeds the total of its debit amounts, the account has a credit balance .

Each asset account normally has a left-hand or debit balance. Assets, therefore, are found listed on the left-hand side of the balance sheet. Each liability account and the capital account normally have right-hand or credit balances. Liability accounts and the capital account, therefore, are found listed on the right-hand side of the balance sheet.

Business transactions change account balances

Every business transaction increases or decreases the balances of two or more accounts. These increases or decreases are shown in the records when the transaction is recorded in a journal and then posted to a ledger. For example, if Rainbow Car Wash sells its old adding machine for $10.00, the balances of both the cash account and the office equipment account are changed.

The balance of the cash account is *increased* $10.00. The balance of the office equipment account is *decreased* $10.00. Cash is increased because Rainbow Car Wash now has $10.00 more cash. Office Equipment is decreased because the Car Wash now owns less office equipment.

Why a ledger account has two sides

The first illustration below shows how increases and decreases in a cash account would be recorded if only one amount column were used.

The cash account as it would appear if it had only one amount column

Cash

Beginning balance	4,000.00
Increase (Receipt of cash)	+ 500.00
Decrease (Payment of cash)	− 300.00
Decrease (Payment of cash)	− 200.00
Increase (Receipt of cash)	+ 800.00
Decrease (Payment of cash)	− 500.00
Increase (Receipt of cash)	+ 400.00

The sides of a two-column ledger account, however, are used to show the increases and decreases in account balances. *All increases are recorded on the balance side of the account. All decreases are recorded on the side opposite the balance side of the account.* This makes it easy to find the total of each column, to subtract the smaller total from the larger total, and to find the new balance of the account.

The second illustration at the left shows how increases and decreases in cash are recorded when the cash account has two sides.

The cash account with two amount columns

Cash

(Receipts)		(Payments)	
Balance	4,000.00	Decrease	300.00
Increase	500.00	Decrease	200.00
Increase	800.00	Decrease	500.00
Increase	400.00		1,000.00
	5,700.00		

The new account balance for this cash account is figured as shown at the top of the next page.

Total of debit side (balance and increase side) of cash account $5,700.00
Total of credit side (decrease side) of cash account 1,000.00
Difference between the two sides of cash account .... New balance= $4,700.00

ANALYZING BUSINESS TRANSACTIONS

Every business transaction is recorded first in a journal — a book of original entry. Before a transaction can be recorded in a journal, it must be analyzed to determine in what ways the assets, the liabilities, or the capital have been increased or decreased by the transaction. This analysis determines the accounts to be debited and credited. When analyzing the effect of a transaction on accounts, the following three questions are answered:

☐ 1 What are the names of the accounts affected?

☐ 2 What is the classification of each account affected? (Is it an asset, a liability, or a capital account?)

☐ 3 How is the balance of each of these accounts changed? (Is the balance increased or decreased?)

The remainder of this chapter shows how several transactions that affect balance sheet accounts are analyzed into their debit and credit parts. To simplify the illustrations of the accounts that are affected, some of the rulings of the two-column account are eliminated. The result is the mere outline of an account that looks like a capital T. A skeleton form of ledger account that shows only the account title and the debit and credit sides is called a T account.

Cash

T account

TRANSACTION NO. 1 — THE SALE OF AN ASSET FOR CASH

August 1, 1977. Received cash from the sale of an old adding machine, $10.00.

In this transaction one asset is increased and another is decreased.

Analysis of Transaction No. 1

☐ 1 What are the names of the accounts affected?

Cash and *Office Equipment.*

☐ 2 What is the classification of each account affected?

Cash is an *asset account. Office Equipment* is also an *asset account.*

□ 3 How is the balance of each of these accounts changed?

Cash. The Rainbow Car Wash now has $10.00 more cash after receiving $10.00 for the old adding machine. The balance of the cash account, an asset account, is *increased* $10.00. The *balance side* of every asset account is the *debit side*. An increase in any account balance is always recorded on the balance side of the account. The cash account is therefore *debited* for the amount of the increase.

Cash	
(debit)	*(credit)*
Balance 650.00	
Increase 10.00	

The cash account above shows that a debit balance of $650.00 was in the account before the transaction took place. The $10.00 increase in the cash balance is recorded as a debit so that it can be added to this balance.

Office Equipment. The Rainbow Car Wash owns less office equipment as a result of selling an old adding machine. The balance of the office equipment account, an asset account, is *decreased* $10.00. The *balance side* of every asset account is the *debit side*. A decrease in any account balance is always recorded on the side opposite the balance side. The office equipment account is therefore *credited* for the amount of the decrease.

Office Equipment	
(debit)	*(credit)*
Balance 500.00 Decrease	10.00

The office equipment account had a debit balance of $500.00 before this transaction took place. The decrease of $10.00 is recorded as a credit to show a decrease in this balance.

The basic meaning of *debit* and *credit* is related to the two sides of a two-column account. This is why a T-account analysis of business transactions is used to determine the debit and the credit of journal entries. The business transactions analyzed in Chapters 4 and 5 are shown recorded in a journal in Chapter 6.

The debit amount equals the credit amount in each transaction

Each business transaction has two parts — a debit part and a credit part. The debit part must always equal the credit part. When Transaction No. 1 is recorded in a journal and the journal entry is posted, the debit of $10.00 to the cash account is equal to the credit of $10.00 to the office equipment account. The debit part of the transaction equals the credit part as shown below.

Debit part (Cash $10.00)   *EQUALS*   Credit part (Office Equipment $10.00)

Cash		Office Equipment	
(debit) 10.00	=		*(credit)* 10.00

Summary of increases and decreases in asset accounts

Increases and decreases in asset accounts are recorded as follows:

An increase in an asset is recorded as a debit. The balance of any asset account is always recorded on the *left-hand side* of the account as a *debit. An increase in any account balance is always recorded on the balance side of the account.* An increase in any asset account is therefore recorded on the *debit side.* As a result, the amount can be added easily to the balance of the asset account.

ANY ASSET ACCOUNT	
+	−
Debit side	Credit side
is	is
balance side	decrease side
and	
increase side	

A decrease in an asset is recorded as a credit. *A decrease in any account balance is always recorded on the side opposite the balance side of the account.* A decrease in any asset account is therefore recorded on the *credit side* of the account.

TRANSACTION NO. 2 — PART PAYMENT OF A LIABILITY

> *August 1, 1977. Paid cash to the Auto Wash Equipment Co. in part payment of the amount owed, $200.00.*

In this transaction an asset is decreased and a liability is decreased.

Analysis of Transaction No. 2

☐ **1** What are the names of the accounts affected?

> *Auto Wash Equipment Co.* and *Cash*.

☐ **2** What is the classification of each account affected?

> *Auto Wash Equipment Co.* is a *liability account. Cash* is an *asset account*.

☐ **3** How is the balance of each of these accounts changed?

Auto Wash Equipment Co. The Rainbow Car Wash decreases its liability to Auto Wash Equipment Co. by $200.00 as a result of this part payment of an amount owed. The balance of the Auto Wash Equipment Co. account, a liability account, is *decreased* $200.00. The *balance side* of every liability account is the *credit side. A decrease in any account balance is always recorded on the side opposite the balance side of the account.* The Auto Wash Equipment Co. account is therefore *debited* for the amount of the decrease.

Auto Wash Equipment Co.		
(debit)		*(credit)*
Decrease 200.00	Balance	850.00

The Auto Wash Equipment Co. account shows that a credit balance of $850.00 was in the account before this transaction took place. The $200.00 decrease is recorded as a debit to show a decrease in this balance.

Cash. The Rainbow Car Wash has less cash as a result of having paid $200.00 to Auto Wash Equipment Co. The balance of the cash account, an asset account, is *decreased* $200.00. *A decrease in any account balance is recorded on the side* opposite *the balance side.* The cash account is therefore *credited* for the amount of the decrease. The cash account shows this $200.00 decrease on the credit side of the account.

	Cash		
	(debit)		(credit)
Balance	650.00	Decrease	200.00
Increase	10.00		

When Transaction No. 2 is recorded in a journal and the journal entry is posted, the debit of $200.00 to the Auto Wash Equipment Co. account is equal to the credit of $200.00 to the cash account. A liability account balance is decreased and an asset account balance is decreased.

Summary of increases and decreases in liability accounts

Increases and decreases in liability accounts are recorded as follows:

An increase in a liability is recorded as a credit. The balance of any liability account is always recorded on the *right-hand side* of the account as a *credit. An increase in any liability account is therefore recorded on the* balance side *of the account.* An increase in any liability account is therefore recorded on the *credit side*. As a result, the amount can be added easily to the balance of the liability account.

ANY LIABILITY ACCOUNT	
−	+
Debit side is decrease side	Credit side is balance side and increase side

A decrease in a liability is recorded as a debit. *A decrease in any account balance is recorded on the side* opposite *the balance side of the account.* A decrease in any liability account is therefore recorded on the *debit side* of the account.

TRANSACTION NO. 3 — ADDITIONAL INVESTMENT OF CAPITAL BY PROPRIETOR

August 1, 1977. Received cash from the proprietor, Harry Shaw, as an additional investment in the business, $500.00.

In this transaction an asset is increased and the capital is increased.

Analysis of Transaction No. 3

☐ 1 What are the names of the accounts affected?

Cash and *Harry Shaw, Capital.*

☐ **2** What is the classification of each account affected?

> *Cash* is an *asset account. Harry Shaw, Capital* is the proprietor's *capital account.*

☐ **3** How is the balance of each of these accounts changed?

Cash. The Rainbow Car Wash has $500.00 more cash as a result of receiving this additional investment. The balance of the cash account, an asset account, is *increased* $500.00. The *balance side* of every asset account is the *debit side. An increase in any account balance is recorded on the* balance side *of the account.* The cash account is therefore *debited* for the amount of the increase. The cash account at the right shows this $500.00 increase.

Cash			
(debit)		*(credit)*	
Balance	650.00	Decrease	200.00
Increase	10.00		
Increase	500.00		

Harry Shaw, Capital. Mr. Shaw has increased his investment in Rainbow Car Wash as a result of this transaction. The balance of Harry Shaw, Capital is *increased* $500.00. The balance side of any proprietor's capital account is the *credit side. An increase in any account balance is recorded on the* balance side *of the account.* The proprietor's capital account, Harry Shaw, Capital, is therefore *credited* for the amount of the increase in investment.

The capital account, Harry Shaw, Capital, shows that a balance of $4,000.00 was in the account before this transaction took place. The additional investment of $500.00 is recorded as a credit to show an increase in this balance.

Harry Shaw, Capital		
(debit)	*(credit)*	
	Balance	4,000.00
	Increase	500.00

When Transaction No. 3 is recorded in a journal and the journal entry is posted, the debit of $500.00 to the cash account is equal to the credit of $500.00 to the capital account.

Summary of increases and decreases in the proprietor's capital account.

Increases and decreases in the proprietor's capital account are recorded as follows:

An increase in capital is recorded as a credit. The balance of any proprietor's capital account is always recorded on the *right-hand side* of the account as a *credit. An increase in any account balance is recorded on the* balance side *of the account.* An increase in the proprietor's capital account is therefore recorded on the *credit side.*

ANY PROPRIETOR'S CAPITAL ACCOUNT	
−	+
Debit side is decrease side	Credit side is balance side and increase side

A decrease in capital is recorded as a debit. *A decrease in any account balance is recorded on the side* opposite *the balance side of the account.* A decrease in the proprietor's capital account is therefore recorded on the *debit side* of the account.

SUMMARY OF THE PRINCIPLES OF DEBIT AND CREDIT FOR BALANCE SHEET ACCOUNTS

ANY BALANCE SHEET			
ANY ASSET ACCOUNT		**ANY LIABILITY ACCOUNT**	
+	−	−	+
Debit side is balance side and increase side	Credit side is decrease side	Debit side is decrease side	Credit side is balance side and increase side
		ANY PROPRIETOR'S CAPITAL ACCOUNT	
		−	+
		Debit side is decrease side	Credit side is balance side and increase side

Diagram showing the principles of debit and credit for balance sheet accounts

Using Business Terms

✦ What is the meaning of each of the following?

- account balance
- debit balance
- credit balance
- T account

Questions for Individual Study

1. After an opening entry has been posted, the beginning amounts are on which side of (a) the asset accounts? (b) the liability accounts? (c) the capital account?
2. How does the side on which an account is listed on the balance sheet compare with the kind of balance that account has?
3. How many ledger accounts are affected by each business transaction?
4. Why does a ledger account have two sides?
5. What three questions are answered when analyzing the effect of a business transaction on accounts?
6. On which side of an account is an increase always recorded?
7. Why is an increase in an asset account recorded as a debit?
8. On which side of an account is a decrease always recorded?
9. Why is a decrease in an asset account recorded as a credit?
10. Why is an increase in a liability account recorded as a credit?
11. Why is a decrease in a liability account recorded as a debit?
12. Why is an increase in the proprietor's capital account recorded as a credit?
13. Why is a decrease in the proprietor's capital account recorded as a debit?

CASE 1 The Fair Winds Insurance Agency bought an electric typewriter for $410.00. The agency's secretary, who keeps their accounting records, analyzes this cash transaction as shown in the two T accounts at the right.

What two principles of accounting has the secretary failed to follow in analyzing this transaction?

Cash	
410.00	

Office Equipment	
410.00	

CASE 2 When Ms. Eva Winn applied for an office position, she was shown the four T accounts presented below.

Ms. Winn was then told that these accounts contained the debits and the credits for each of three business transactions, and she was asked to show her knowledge of accounting by describing each transaction. Describe each of these three transactions. The debits and credits of the transactions are labeled (a), (b), and (c) respectively.

Cash			
Balance 6,500.00	(a)	200.00	
(b) 1,000.00	(c)	400.00	

Nemo Supply Company			
(a)	200.00	Balance	200.00

Office Equipment		
Balance	600.00	
(c)	400.00	

Harold Hart, Capital			
		Balance	10,400.00
		(b)	1,000.00

DRILL 4-D 1   The effect of business transactions on balance sheet accounts

This drill is planned to give you practice in recognizing when assets, liabilities, and capital are increased or decreased as a result of business transactions.

Instructions: □ **1.** Prepare a form with the headings shown below.

Trans. No.	ASSETS		LIABILITIES		CAPITAL	
	+	−	−	+	−	+
1.	35.00	35.00				

□ **2.** Indicate the amount of the increase or the decrease in assets, liabilities, and capital resulting from each of the seven transactions at the top of the next page. Do this by writing the amount of the increase or the decrease in each of the proper two columns for each transaction. Copy the answer to Transaction No. 1 which is given as an example.

Transaction
Number   *Transactions*

1. Received cash from sale of typewriter, $35.00.
2. Paid cash in part payment of amount owed, $150.00.
3. Received cash from the proprietor as an additional investment in the business, $800.00.
4. Paid cash for an electric typewriter, $400.00.
5. Received cash from sale of old check writing machine, $10.00.
6. Paid cash in full payment of amount owed, $50.00.
7. Received cash from sale of old desk, $30.00.

DRILL 4-D 2 The sides of balance sheet accounts —
debit, credit, balance, increase,
and decrease

Instructions: □ **1.** Make a T account for each of the account titles listed below

Automobile
_____|_____
                   |

and write the proper account title on each T account. The automobile account is shown at the left as an example.

Account Titles

Automobile	Land	Office Equipment
Building	Merchants National	Company (creditor)
C. R. Miller, Capital	Bank (creditor)	Office Supplies
Cash	Office Furniture	Office Machines

Instructions: □ **2.** Write the words *Debit side* on the debit side of each T account and write the words *Credit side* on the credit side of each T account. The asset account, Automobile, is shown as an example.

Automobile
_____|_____
Debit side | Credit side

□ **3.** Write the words *Balance side* on the debit side of each account that usually has a debit balance. Write the words *Balance side* on the credit side of each account that usually has a credit balance. The asset account, Automobile, is shown as an example.

Automobile
_____|_____
Debit side | Credit side
Balance side |

□ **4.** In each T account make a plus sign (+) on the side of the account that is the increase side. Make a minus sign (−) on the side that is the decrease side. The asset account, Automobile, is shown as an example.

Automobile
_____|_____
Debit side | Credit side
Balance side | −
+ |

DRILL 4-D 3 Self-checking oral drill on debit and credit

Instructions: Without looking at your written answers to Drill 4-D 2, check your understanding of debit and credit by seeing how fast and accurately you can answer the questions given at the top of page 49.

1. What classification of account has its balance side on the debit side?   ·

2. What classifications of accounts have their balance side on the credit side? ·

3. What classification of account has all increases written on the debit side? ·

4. What classifications of accounts have all increases written on the credit side? ·

5. What classifications of accounts have all decreases written on the debit side? ·

6. What classification of account has all decreases written on the credit side? .

DRILL 4-D 4 Analyzing the effect of transactions on accounts

The balance sheet accounts along with a list of transactions of the Daniel J. Egan Insurance Agency are given in Problem 4-1 below and on the next page.

Instructions: □ **1.** Prepare a form with the headings shown below for use in checking your understanding of how business transactions affect account balances. Allow two lines for each transaction.

Trans. No.	(a) Account Titles Affected	(b) Classification of Account	(c) Effect of Transaction on Balance of Account		(d) Recorded on Which Side of the Account?	
			Increase	Decrease	Debit	Credit
1.	Cash	Asset	✓		✓	
	Office Machines	Asset		✓		✓
2.						

Instructions: □ **2.** For each of the thirteen transactions in Problem 4-1: (a) Write the account titles affected. (b) Identify the classification of each account affected. (c) Indicate whether the balance of each of these accounts is increased or decreased. (d) Indicate on which side of the account the amount is to be recorded. Copy the analysis of Transaction No. 1, which is given as an example on the form above.

PROBLEM 4-1 Analyzing transactions into their debit and credit parts

Mr. Daniel J. Egan operates an insurance agency. His ledger contains the following balance sheet accounts:

Cash
Office Supplies
Automobile
Office Furniture

Office Machines
Anthony's Garage (creditor)
Hart Stationery Store (creditor)

Roper Equipment Company
   (creditor)
Daniel J. Egan, Capital

Problems
for
Applying
Concepts

Instructions: Use a pair of T accounts to analyze each of the transactions listed below. Analyze each transaction into its debit and credit parts as follows:

Cash	
25.00	

Office Machines	
	25.00

(a) Write the account title and the debit amount in the first T account.

(b) Write the account title and the credit amount in the second T account.

The analysis of Transaction No. 1 is given at the left.

Transaction
Number   *Transactions*

1. Received cash from sale of old typewriter, $25.00.
2. Paid cash for an electric typewriter, $320.00.
3. Paid cash to Roper Equipment Company in payment of amount owed, $120.00.
4. Paid cash for office supplies, $15.00.
5. Received cash from sale of old office desk and chair, $35.00.
6. Paid cash to Anthony's Garage in part payment of amount owed, $50.00.
7. Paid cash for a new office desk, $220.00.
8. Received cash from sale of old adding machine, $10.00.
9. Paid cash to Hart Stationery Store in payment of amount owed, $20.00.
10. Paid cash for office supplies, $18.00.
11. Received cash from sale of old automobile, $850.00.
12. Paid cash for new automobile, $3,200.00.
13. Received cash from Daniel J. Egan, the proprietor, as an additional investment in the business, $1,500.00.

PROBLEM 4-2   Analyzing transactions into their debit and
                       credit parts

Mr. John Sirko, the owner of the Rosebud Restaurant, is selling some of his old equipment and replacing it with new. On June 1, his ledger contained the following balance sheet accounts with balances as shown in the T accounts below.

Cash		B & W Wholesale Company	
Balance 1,640.00			Balance 70.00

Restaurant Supplies		Food Service Equipment Company	
Balance 420.00			Balance 1,400.00

Kitchen Equipment		R & W Supply Company	
Balance 2,100.00			Balance 250.00

Restaurant Equipment		John Sirko, Capital	
Balance 1,460.00			Balance 3,900.00

Instructions: □ **1.** On a sheet of paper, copy the T accounts as shown on page 50 with their balances. Allow seven lines for the cash account and three lines for each of the other accounts.

□ **2.** Analyze each of the following transactions into its debit and credit parts. Write the debit amount and transaction number on the proper side of the account. Write the credit amount and transaction number on the proper side of the account.

The analysis of the first two transactions and their effect on the accounts is shown at the right.

Cash		
Balance 1,640.00	(2)	400.00
(1) 83.00		

Restaurant Equipment		
Balance 1,460.00	(1)	83.00

Food Service Equipment Company		
(2) 400.00	Balance 1,400.00	

Transaction
Number   *Transactions*

1. Received cash from sale of old dining room chairs, $83.00.
2. Paid cash to Food Service Equipment Company in part payment of amount owed, $400.00.
3. Received cash from sale of old kitchen table, $40.00.
4. Received cash from sale of old dining room tables, $178.00.
5. Paid cash for new dishes and other restaurant supplies, $163.00.
6. Paid cash for new piece of kitchen equipment, $70.00.
7. Received cash from sale of old restaurant equipment, $75.00.
8. Paid cash to R & W Supply Company in part payment of amount owed, $200.00.
9. Received cash from sale of old restaurant counter, $60.00.
10. Paid cash for new stove, $460.00.
11. Paid cash for new restaurant chairs, $120.00.
12. Paid cash to B & W Wholesale Company in full payment of amount owed, $70.00.

MASTERY PROBLEM 4-M   Analyzing transactions into their debit and credit parts

Mr. James Pond owns and operates a private detective agency. On September 1, his ledger contains the following balance sheet accounts with balances as shown in the T accounts below and on page 52.

Cash	
Balance 1,240.00	

Furniture and Fixtures	
Balance 1,140.00	

Automobile	
Balance 3,200.00	

Office Machines	
Balance 330.00	

Chestnut Street Garage	
	Balance 64.00

Family Finance Company	
	Balance 1,450.00

Crown Supply Company	
	Balance 36.00

James Pond, Capital	
	Balance 4,360.00

Instructions: ◻ **1.** On a sheet of paper, copy the T accounts as shown with their balances. Allow seven lines for the cash account and four lines for each of the other accounts.

◻ **2.** Analyze each of the following transactions into its debit and credit parts. Write the debit amount and the transaction number on the proper side of the account. Write the credit amount and the transaction number on the proper side of the account.

Transaction
Number   *Transactions*

1. Paid cash to Chestnut Street Garage in payment of amount owed, $64.00.
2. Received cash from sale of old rug, $10.00.
3. Paid cash for new rug, $115.00.
4. Paid cash to Family Finance Company for payment due on car, $100.00.
5. Paid cash for a check-writing machine, $48.00.
6. Paid cash for two new chairs, $140.00.
7. Received cash from sale of old desk, $20.00.
8. Received cash from Mr. Pond, the owner, as an additional investment in the business, $1,000.00.
9. Received cash from sale of old desk chair, $5.00.
10. Paid cash for new desk, $265.00.
11. Paid cash to Crown Supply Company in payment of amount owed, $36.00.

BONUS
PROBLEM 4-B   ● Analyzing transactions in T accounts

Walter Powell, a registered architect, started a business of his own with an investment of cash, $6,500.00, and some used drafting equipment worth $500.00. The opening entry for his investment and the first ten transactions completed by the business are recorded in the T accounts listed below and on the next page.

Cash			
Balance 6,500.00	(1)	140.00	
(3)	2,500.00	(2)	60.00
(9)	40.00	(4)	3,000.00
		(5)	450.00
		(8)	100.00
		(10)	180.00

Automobile		
(4)	3,000.00	

Drafting Equipment		
Balance	500.00	(9) 40.00
(2)	60.00	
(7)	180.00	

Palmer County Bank	
	(3) 2,500.00

Office Furniture	
(1)	140.00
(5)	450.00
(6)	240.00

Zemo Copying Equipment Company	
(8) 100.00	(6) 240.00

Arnold Supply Company	
(10) 180.00	(7) 180.00

Walter Powell, Capital
Balance 7,000.00

Instructions: ◻ **1.** Indicate for each debit and for each credit in each of the ten transactions (a) the name and the classification of the account affected, and (b) whether the account was increased (+) or decreased (−).

◻ **2.** Write a brief description of each transaction.

Answers should be presented in the following form, with Transaction No. 1 given as an example.

Trans. No.	ACCOUNT DEBITED			ACCOUNT CREDITED			DESCRIPTION OF TRANSACTION
	Name	Classification	Effect	Name	Classification	Effect	
1.	*Office Furniture*	*Asset*	+	*Cash*	*Asset*	−	*Bought office furniture for $140.00*

5

Debit and Credit of Revenue and Expense Transactions

All of the business transactions described in Chapter 4 were debited and credited to balance sheet accounts. Some transactions are recorded in other than balance sheet accounts. In this chapter transactions are explained that cause changes in capital but which are debited and credited to accounts other than the capital account.

REVENUE TRANSACTIONS

An increase in capital that results from the operation of a business is called revenue. Revenue is also known as income. The Rainbow Car Wash receives its revenue from the service provided to customers for washing their cars.

The purpose of Rainbow Car Wash, like that of most businesses, is to make money. When the total revenue exceeds the total cost of operating a business, the difference is called a profit. When the total costs exceed the total revenue, the difference is called a loss.

Need for revenue accounts

All revenue transactions cause an increase in capital. Crediting all revenue transactions to the capital account would make that account large and hard to analyze. Therefore, revenue is recorded in revenue accounts instead of the capital account.

The management of a business needs to be able to determine the total amount of each kind of revenue. Detailed information about each kind of revenue enables the manager or owner to see what sources of revenue are increasing or decreasing and how much. This information helps in making such decisions as the amount of money to be spent on advertising or the number of employees needed by the business.

Different kinds of businesses have various names for revenue: a store has revenue from *sales;* a bank has revenue from *interest;* a doctor or lawyer has revenue from *fees;* real estate and insurance agencies have revenue from *commissions;* the owner of an apartment building has revenue from *rent.*

Every kind of business needs detailed revenue records. As a result, a business with different kinds of revenue keeps not only a capital account but also a separate account for each kind of revenue. For example, a large, fully equipped car wash could have the following revenue accounts: (1) Car Wash Sales; (2) Car Wax Sales; (3) Vacuum Sales; (4) Vending Machine Sales; (5) Telephone Commissions (from pay telephones).

The only source of revenue for the small Rainbow Car Wash is from the use of its car wash equipment. The Rainbow Car Wash, therefore, records all of its revenue in a single revenue account titled Sales. The sales account is placed in the fourth division of the ledger, as shown in the chart of accounts on page 2. If the business had other sources of revenue, a separate account would be opened for each kind of revenue.

TRANSACTION NO. 4 — A REVENUE TRANSACTION

August 1, 1977. Received cash from sales for one day, $82.00.

In this transaction an asset is increased and revenue is also increased.

Analysis of Transaction No. 4

The same questions that must be answered when analyzing transactions affecting assets, liabilities, and capital are used in analyzing revenue transactions. These questions are:

☐ 1 What are the names of the accounts affected?

>   *Cash* and *Sales*.

☐ 2 What is the classification of each account affected?

>   *Cash* is an *asset account*. *Sales* is a *revenue account.*

☐ 3 How is the balance of each of these accounts changed?

> **Cash.** The Rainbow Car Wash has more cash as a result of receiving $82.00 from its sales for one day. The balance of the cash account, an asset account, is *increased* $82.00. The *balance side* of every asset account is the *debit side. All increases in any account balance are always recorded on the* balance side *of the account.* The cash account is therefore *debited* for the amount of the increase, $82.00.

Cash		
(debit)		*(credit)*
Balance	650.00	Decrease 200.00
Increase	10.00	
Increase	500.00	
Increase	**82.00**	

Sales. The revenue of Rainbow Car Wash has been increased $82.00 as a result of receiving cash for the use of its car wash equipment. The *balance side* of every revenue account is the *credit side*. All increases in any account are recorded on the *balance side* of the account. Therefore, the revenue account, Sales, is *credited* for the amount of the increase, $82.00.

Sales	
(debit)	*(credit)*
	Increase 82.00

Summary of increases and decreases in revenue accounts

Every revenue transaction has a debit part and a credit part. The debit part always equals the credit part.

An increase in revenue is recorded as a credit. Revenue accounts always have *credit* balances. *Increases in the balance of any account are recorded on the* balance side *of the account.* Therefore, an increase in the balance of any revenue account is always recorded on the *credit* side of the revenue account.

ANY REVENUE ACCOUNT	
−	+
Debit side is decrease side	Credit side is balance side and increase side

A decrease in revenue is recorded as a debit. *Decreases in the balance of any account are always recorded on the side* opposite *the balance.* Therefore, decreases in the balance of any revenue account are always recorded on the *debit side* of the revenue account.

Debits to revenue accounts are not very common. An example of a transaction calling for a debit (decrease) to a revenue account would be if Rainbow Car Wash gave a cash refund to a customer. In this case, **Sales** would be debited for the amount of the refund and **Cash** would be credited for the same amount.

EXPENSE TRANSACTIONS

A decrease in capital that results from the operation of a business is called an expense. Business expenses are the costs of items and services used to produce revenue. For example, Rainbow Car Wash pays for advertising to attract customers. It also pays for fuel (natural gas) to heat the water used for washing the cars.

All businesses have some expenses. To operate at a profit, the total revenue of a business must exceed the total expenses.

Need for expense accounts

All expense transactions cause a decrease in capital. Debiting all expense transactions to the capital account would make that account large and hard to analyze. Therefore, expenses are recorded in expense accounts instead of the capital account.

Separate expense accounts show the management of a business how much is being spent for each kind of expense. The separate expense accounts also show which expenses are increasing and how much each is increasing. With these facts, the manager can plan ways to cut down expenses that are too high.

The Rainbow Car Wash uses five expense accounts. All are placed in alphabetical order in the fifth division of the ledger. These expense account titles and numbers are shown in the chart of accounts on page 2. Whenever Rainbow Car Wash has other kinds of frequent expenses, a separate account will be opened for each.

> Car washes similar to Rainbow Car Wash commonly use an expense account for repairs and another to record the cost of water. These expense accounts are not needed by Rainbow Car Wash. Mr. Shaw, the owner, is a skilled repairman and performs his own repairs. Furthermore, no water has to be purchased because of the deep well on the property.

TRANSACTION NO. 5 — AN EXPENSE TRANSACTION

August 2, 1977. Paid cash for rent of the car wash for August, $350.00.

In this transaction an expense is increased and an asset is decreased.

Analysis of Transaction No. 5

The same questions that are answered when analyzing transactions affecting assets, liabilities, capital, and revenue are answered when analyzing expense transactions. These questions are:

☐ 1 What are the names of the accounts affected?

> *Rent Expense* and *Cash*.

☐ 2 What is the classification of each account affected?

> *Rent Expense* is an *expense account*. *Cash* is an *asset account.*

☐ 3 How is the balance of each of these accounts changed?

> **Rent Expense.** The operating expenses of Rainbow Car Wash have been *increased* $350.00 as a result of paying the monthly rent for the car wash. The *balance side* of any expense account is the *debit side*. *All increases in any account balance are always recorded on the* balance side *of the account*. Therefore, the expense account, Rent Expense, is *debited* for the amount of the increase, $350.00, as shown in the T account at the right.

Rent Expense	
(debit)	*(credit)*
Increase 350.00	

Cash. The Rainbow Car Wash has $350.00 less cash as a result of having paid the monthly rent. The balance of the cash account, an asset account, is *decreased* $350.00. *All decreases in any account balance are always recorded on the side* opposite *the balance side*. The cash account is therefore *credited* for the amount of the decrease, $350.00, as shown in the T account at the left.

Cash		
(debit)	(credit)	
Balance 650.00	Decrease 200.00	
Increase 10.00	Decrease 350.00	
Increase 500.00		
Increase 82.00		

Summary of increases and decreases in expense accounts

Every expense transaction has a debit part and a credit part. The debit part must always equal the credit part.

An increase in an expense is recorded as a debit. Expense accounts always have *debit* balances. *Increases in the balance of any account are recorded on the* balance side *of the account.* Therefore, an increase in the balance of any expense account is always recorded on the *debit side* of the expense account.

ANY EXPENSE ACCOUNT	
+	−
Debit side is balance side and increase side	Credit side is decrease side

A decrease in an expense is recorded as a credit. *Decreases in the balance of any account are always recorded on the side* opposite *the balance side*. Therefore, decreases in the balance of any expense account are always recorded on the *credit side* of the expense account.

Credits to expense accounts are not very common. An example of a transaction calling for a credit (decrease) to an expense account would be if Rainbow Car Wash overpaid its monthly rent and was given a cash refund. In this case, **Cash** would be debited for the amount of the refund and **Rent Expense** would be credited for the same amount.

SUMMARY OF THE PRINCIPLES OF DEBIT AND CREDIT FOR REVENUE AND EXPENSE ACCOUNTS

All revenue transactions cause an increase in capital. All expense transactions cause a decrease in capital. Instead of crediting the capital account directly for revenue, a separate revenue account is credited for each different kind of revenue transaction. Similarly, instead of debiting the capital account directly for expenses, a separate expense account is debited for each different kind of expense.

The use of separate revenue accounts and separate expense accounts provides the kind of detailed information needed for the best management of a business. The use of separate accounts keeps the capital account from becoming cluttered with numerous debit and credit entries. Revenue and expense accounts used to store detailed information until it is summarized and transferred to the capital account are called temporary capital accounts.

The procedure for summarizing revenue and expenses and recording the profit or the loss in the capital account is discussed in Chapter 11.

Revenue and expense accounts never appear on the balance sheet. However, their relationship to the capital account is diagrammed below.

ANY PROPRIETOR'S CAPITAL ACCOUNT	
−	+
Debit side is decrease side*	Credit side is balance side and increase side

ANY EXPENSE ACCOUNT		ANY REVENUE ACCOUNT	
+	−	−	+
Debit side is balance side and increase side*	Credit side is decrease side	Debit side is decrease side	Credit side is balance side and increase side

*Although debits to expense accounts signify *increases in expense,* they may also be referred to as *decreases in capital.*

Diagram showing the principles of debit and credit for revenue and expense accounts and their relationship to the capital account

Using Business Terms

✦ What is the meaning of each of the following?

- revenue
- profit
- loss
- expense
- temporary capital accounts

Questions for Individual Study

1. What effect does a revenue transaction have on capital?
2. What is the advantage of recording revenue transactions in separate revenue accounts instead of crediting all revenue transactions to the capital account?
3. What are some different names that businesses have for revenue?
4. From what sources other than car wash sales do some large car washes secure revenue?
5. Which side of a revenue account is the balance side?
6. On which side of a revenue account is an increase in its balance recorded?
7. What effect does an expense transaction have on capital?
8. Why is a separate ledger account kept for each kind of expense?
9. Which side of an expense account is the balance side?
10. On which side of an expense account is an increase recorded?
11. What are two advantages of using revenue and expense accounts instead of recording revenue and expense transactions in the capital account?

Cases for Management Decision

CASE 1 The Rainbow Car Wash has three utility expenses — telephone, electricity, and gas for heating the water used for washing the cars. The telephone costs and electricity costs are charged to one expense account, Utilities Expense. The third utility expense, the cost of the gas, is charged to a separate account, Fuel Expense. Why do you believe a separate expense account is used for this third utility?

CASE 2 Ollie Santos owns and operates a beauty shop. She receives revenue from services rendered to customers and from the sale of cosmetics. In the past she has recorded all revenue in one account with the title Revenue. She has decided that she would like to know how much revenue she receives from services rendered customers and how much revenue she receives from the sale of cosmetics. What changes would you suggest she make in her accounting procedures?

CASE 3 Vincent Lester is the new owner of a sports shop. He has never studied accounting and does not understand why the receipt of cash from the sale of an old cash register should not be recorded as revenue. How would you explain to him that all cash received is not necessarily revenue?

DRILL 5-D 1 The sides of accounts: debit, credit, balance, increase, and decrease

Twelve accounts of Carter's Painting and Paperhanging Service are listed below.

Cash	Utilities Expense	Tom's Garage (creditor)
Equipment	Painting Revenue	Paperhanging Revenue
Advertising Expense	Scott Carter, Capital	Miscellaneous Expense
Daniels Hardware (creditor)	Pickup Truck	Truck Expense

Instructions: □ **1.** Make a T account for each of the account titles listed above and write the proper account title on each T account.

□ **2.** Write the words *Debit side* on the debit side of each T account and write the words *Credit side* on the credit side of each T account.

□ **3.** Write the words *Balance side* on the proper side of each account to show where the balance normally appears in that account.

□ **4.** Make a plus sign (+) on the side of each T account that is the increase side. Make a minus sign (−) on the side of each T account that is the decrease side.

The cash account is shown at the right as an example.

Cash	
Debit side	Credit side
Balance side	
+	−

DRILL 5-D 2 Self-checking oral drill on debit and credit

Instructions: Without looking at your written answers to the drill above, check your understanding of debit and credit by seeing how fast and accurately you can answer the following questions:

1. What two classifications of accounts have their balances on the debit side?
2. What three classifications of accounts have their balances on the credit side?
3. What two classifications of accounts have each increase recorded on the debit side?
4. What three classifications of accounts have each increase recorded on the credit side?

DRILL 5-D 3   Analyzing the effect of transactions on accounts

The chart of accounts along with a list of transactions of a skating rink, Reed's Rollarena, are given in Problem 5-1 below.

Instructions: □ **1.** Prepare a form with the headings shown below for use in checking your understanding of how business transactions affect account balances. Allow two lines for each transaction.

Trans. No.	(a) Account Titles Affected	(b) Classifica-tion of Account	(c) Effect of Transaction on Balance of Account		(d) Recorded on Which Side of the Account?	
			Increase	Decrease	Debit	Credit
1.	Utilities Expense	Expense	✓		✓	
	Cash	Asset		✓		✓

Instructions: □ **2.** For each of the transactions in Problem 5-1 on page 62: (a) Write the account titles affected. (b) Identify the classification of each account affected. (c) Indicate whether the balance of each of these accounts is increased or decreased. (d) Indicate on which side of the account the amount is to be recorded. Copy the analysis of Transaction No. 1, which is given as an example on the form above.

PROBLEM 5-1   Analyzing transactions into their debit and credit parts

Problems for Applying Concepts

Bert Reed is the owner and operator of a skating rink called Reed's Rollarena. His chart of accounts is shown below.

**Reed's Rollarena
Chart of Accounts**

(1) Assets	Account Number	(4) Revenue	Account Number
Cash....................................	11	Admissions Revenue.............	41
Furniture and Fixtures...........	12	Vending Machine Revenue	42
Office Equipment	13		
Skating Equipment	14	**(5) Expenses**	
		Advertising Expense.............	51
(2) Liabilities		Miscellaneous Expense..........	52
Noonan Repair Shop.............	21	Rent Expense........................	53
		Utilities Expense	54
(3) Capital			
Bert Reed, Capital.................	31		

Instructions: Use a pair of T accounts to analyze each of the transactions listed on page 62.

Analyze each transaction into its debit and credit parts as follows:

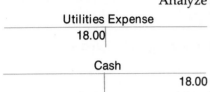

(a) Write the account title and the debit amount in the first T account.

(b) Write the account title and the credit amount in the second T account.

The analysis of Transaction No. 1 is given at the left.

Transaction
Number   *Transactions*

1. Paid cash for telephone expense, $18.00.
2. Received cash from admissions revenue, $150.00.
3. Paid cash for rent of skating rink, $200.00.
4. Paid cash to Noonan Repair Shop in payment of amount owed, $60.00.
5. Received cash from admissions revenue, $130.00.
6. Paid cash for repair of floor, $10.50. (Miscellaneous Expense)
7. Received cash from vending machine revenue, $18.00.
8. Paid cash for electricity expense, $26.50.
9. Paid cash for newspaper advertising, $40.00.
10. Paid cash for new skating equipment, $175.00.
11. Received cash from Bert Reed, the owner, as an additional investment in the business, $500.00.
12. Paid cash for purchase of new office desk, $160.00.
13. Received cash from sale of old office desk, $20.00.

PROBLEM 5-2 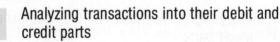 Analyzing transactions into their debit and credit parts

Marie Nunn is the proprietor of the Drive-In Laundromat and pays a monthly rent for the use of the building. Her revenue is obtained from two sources: (1) coins collected from washing machines, and (2) coins collected from drying machines.

On November 1, her ledger accounts had the following balances: Cash, $750.00; Furniture and Fixtures, $250.00; Washing Machines, $3,800.00; Drying Machines, $1,200.00; Fourth Street National Bank (creditor), $2,500.00; and Marie Nunn, Capital, $3,500.00.

Instructions: □ **1.** On a sheet of paper prepare a T account for each account above and record the account balance. Prepare a T account for each of the following revenue and expense accounts: Drying Machines Revenue, Washing Machines Revenue, Advertising Expense, Electricity Expense, Machine Repairs Expense, Miscellaneous Expense, Rent Expense, and Water Expense. There are no account balances on November 1 in the two revenue accounts and six expense accounts. Allow ten lines for the cash account and three lines for each of the other accounts.

□ **2.** Analyze each of the transactions at the top of the next page into its debit and credit parts. Write the debit amount and the transaction number on the proper side of the account. Write the credit amount and the transaction number on the proper side of the account.

*Transaction
Number*   *Transactions*

1. Paid cash for November rent, $300.00.
2. Received cash from sale of old washing machine, $20.00.
3. Received cash from washing machines revenue, $34.00.
4. Received cash from drying machines revenue, $12.00.
5. Paid cash to Fourth Street National Bank in part payment of amount owed, $200.00.
6. Paid cash for electric bill, $42.00.
7. Received cash from washing machines revenue, $68.00.
8. Received cash from drying machines revenue, $19.00.
9. Paid cash for a newspaper ad advertising the laundromat, $18.00.
10. Received cash from Marie Nunn, the owner, as an additional investment in the business, $400.00.
11. Paid cash for water bill, $32.00.
12. Received cash from washing machines revenue, $51.00.
13. Received cash from drying machines revenue, $14.00.
14. Paid cash to cleaning woman, $20.00. (Miscellaneous Expense)
15. Paid cash for repairs to one of the washing machines, $28.00.
16. Paid cash for new chairs for customers to use while waiting, $60.00.

**MASTERY
PROBLEM 5-M** Analyzing transactions into their debit and credit parts

Chester Kirkwood owns and operates the City-Wide Delivery Service. On February 1 his ledger accounts have the following balances: Cash, $750.00; Delivery Equipment, $4,800.00; Office Equipment, $850.00; Carlson Motors (creditor), $2,100.00; and Chester Kirkwood, Capital, $4,300.00.

Instructions: □ **1.** On a sheet of paper prepare a T account for each of the accounts above and record the account balance. Also prepare a T account for each of the following accounts: Delivery Revenue, Advertising Expense, Delivery Truck Expense, Miscellaneous Expense, and Telephone Expense. There are no account balances on February 1 in the revenue account and the four expense accounts. Allow eight lines for the cash account and three lines for each of the other accounts.

□ **2.** Analyze each of the transactions below and on page 64 into its debit and credit parts. Write the debit amount and the transaction number on the proper side of the account. Write the credit amount and the transaction number on the proper side of the account.

*Transaction
Number*   *Transactions*

1. Paid cash for telephone expense, $25.50.
2. Received cash from delivery revenue, $240.00.
3. Paid cash for gas and oil for delivery truck, $12.50.
4. Paid cash for office desk and chair, $165.00.
5. Received cash from sale of old office desk and chair, $12.00.

6. Paid cash for washing the delivery truck, $2.00. (Delivery Truck Expense)
7. Paid cash for gas and oil for delivery truck, $14.40.
8. Paid cash for advertising expense, $18.00.
9. Received cash from delivery revenue, $425.00.
10. Paid cash for leather work gloves, $4.00. (Miscellaneous Expense)
11. Paid cash to Carlson Motors in part payment of amount owed, $500.00.
12. Received cash from delivery revenue, $180.00.

BONUS PROBLEM 5-B ● Analyzing T accounts

The nine accounts of Dan's Tree Service, owned and operated by Daniel Lawrence, are shown below. In addition to the beginning balance in each account, the debit and credit amounts of twelve transactions are shown in the accounts.

Cash

Balance	450.00	(1)	24.00
(3)	500.00	(4)	20.00
(6)	3,700.00	(5)	18.00
(8)	500.00	(7)	4,500.00
(11)	150.00	(9)	45.00
		(10)	8.00
		(12)	200.00

Daniel Lawrence, Capital

| | Balance | 4,600.00 |
| | (3) | 500.00 |

Service Revenue

| | (8) | 500.00 |
| | (11) | 150.00 |

Truck

| Balance | 3,700.00 | (6) | 3,700.00 |
| (7) | 4,500.00 | | |

Advertising Expense

| (1) | 24.00 |
| (5) | 18.00 |

Equipment

| Balance | 850.00 |
| (2) | 350.00 |

Miscellaneous Expense

| (4) | 20.00 |
| (10) | 8.00 |

Tree-Cutting Equipment Co.

| (12) | 200.00 | Balance | 400.00 |
| | | (2) | 350.00 |

Truck Expense

| (9) | 45.00 |

Instructions: ☐ **1.** Indicate for each debit and for each credit in each of the twelve transactions (a) the name and the classification of the account affected, and (b) whether the account was increased (+) or decreased (−).

☐ **2.** Write a brief description of each transaction.

Answers should be presented in the following form, with Transaction No. 1 given as an example.

| Trans. No. | ACCOUNT DEBITED | | | ACCOUNT CREDITED | | | DESCRIPTION OF TRANSACTION |
	Name	Classification	Effect	Name	Classification	Effect	
1.	Advertising Expense	Expense	+	Cash	Asset	−	Paid cash for advertising expense, $24.00

Journalizing Business Transactions

6

Different kinds of business transactions were *analyzed* into their debit and credit parts in Chapters 4 and 5. As each transaction is analyzed into its debit and credit parts it is *recorded* in a journal. Recording each part of a business transaction in a journal is called journalizing.

Reasons for journalizing transactions

A journal provides an orderly record from which postings are made to accounts in the ledger. The reasons why business transactions are recorded first in a journal and not recorded directly in ledger accounts are:

1. Journalizing increases accuracy. When the debit and credit parts of a transaction are recorded together in a journal entry, the equality of the two amounts is readily seen. Thus, if only a part of the transaction is journalized, the omission is seen easily and the error can be corrected immediately.

If transactions were recorded directly in ledger accounts, the accounting clerk could forget to record both parts of the transaction. An interruption in the work might cause the accounting clerk to record only part of the transaction and forget to record the other part. An error of this kind would be very difficult to locate.

2. Journalizing provides a record of transactions in their chronological order. A journal contains the day-to-day transactions in the life of a business. Therefore, when facts about a transaction are needed some months or days after it occurred, the journal is an easy source to consult.

If transactions were recorded directly into ledger accounts, the debit would be on one page and the credit on another page. Thus, it would be more difficult to find both the debit part and the credit part of a single transaction.

Double-entry accounting is complete accounting

The recording of the debit part and the credit part of each transaction is called double-entry accounting. Double-entry accounting is used in practically all well-organized businesses. It is the only method that provides a complete record of the effect of each business transaction on the ledger accounts. Complete accounting, then, is double-entry accounting.

Source documents used for journalizing transactions

At the time a business transaction occurs, a business paper is prepared to describe the transaction in detail. For example, a check stub is filled out and a check is written for each cash payment. The check stub is the source document used by the accounting clerk for making the journal entry for the cash payment. Similarly, when a business issues receipts for all cash received, the stub of the receipt can be the source document used by the accounting clerk in journalizing the cash receipt.

JOURNALIZING CASH TRANSACTIONS IN A GENERAL JOURNAL

A two-column general journal was used by Rainbow Car Wash for recording its opening entry. This kind of journal can be used for recording all the transactions of a business. If Rainbow Car Wash continued to use its general journal for journalizing the first five transactions analyzed in Chapters 4 and 5, these entries would appear as shown below.

		GENERAL JOURNAL			PAGE *1*
DATE		ACCOUNT TITLE	POST. REF.	DEBIT	CREDIT
	1	Cash		1000	
		Office Equipment			1000
		Receipt No. 1.			
	1	Auto Wash Equipment Co.		20000	
		Cash			20000
		Check No. 1.			
	1	Cash		50000	
		Harry Shaw, Capital			50000
		Receipt No. 2.			
	1	Cash		8200	
		Sales			8200
		Receipt No. 3.			
	2	Rent Expense		35000	
		Cash			35000
		Check No. 2.			

Cash transactions recorded in a two-column general journal

JOURNALIZING CASH TRANSACTIONS IN A CASH JOURNAL

Mr. Shaw, the proprietor of Rainbow Car Wash, finds that he can journalize and post his transactions more easily if he uses a journal for cash transactions only. A journal that is used to record only one type of entry is called a special journal. A special journal in which all cash transactions and only cash transactions are recorded is called a cash journal.

Cash journal used by Rainbow Car Wash

The cash journal used by Rainbow Car Wash is shown below. The five transactions journalized in it are the same five as those journalized in the two-column general journal on the opposite page.

> The entry on Line 1 of the cash journal is not for a business transaction and is explained on page 68.

The form of the cash journal is different from that of the general journal. However, the entry for each transaction is still divided into a debit part and a credit part. For example, on Line 2 of the cash journal, the $10.00 debit to Cash is equal to the $10.00 credit to Office Equipment.

The cash journal below has a special amount column for each account that is debited or credited frequently during the month. For Rainbow Car Wash, these accounts are Cash and Sales. The cash account requires two special amount columns — a Cash Debit column for cash receipts and a Cash Credit column for cash payments. The car wash sales account requires only one amount column headed Sales Credit. A General Debit column and a General Credit column are used for accounts that are not debited or credited very often.

> Note that in this cash journal all debit columns are at the left of the Account Title column. All credit columns are at the right of the Account Title column.

CASH JOURNAL									PAGE /
1	2						3	4	5
CASH DEBIT	GENERAL DEBIT	DATE	ACCOUNT TITLE	NO.	POST. REF.	GENERAL CREDIT	SALES CREDIT	CASH CREDIT
		1977 Aug. 1	Balance on hand, $650.00		✓				1
1000		1	Office Equipment	R1		1000			2
	20000	1	Auto Wash Equipment Co	Ck1				20000	3
50000		1	Harry Shaw, Capital	R2		50000			4
8200		1		R3	✓		8200		5
	35000	2	Rent Expense	Ck2				35000	6

Cash transactions recorded in a cash journal

Advantages of using a cash journal

A cash journal with special amount columns has several advantages:

1. *Less space is required for recording* journal entries in a cash journal than in a two-column general journal. For example, compare the entry in each journal for the first transaction, which records the sale of an old adding machine for $10.00. Each entry records the same information. But the entry in the general journal requires three lines, while the entry in the cash journal requires only one line. Thus, if a two-column general journal were used to record all transactions, the general journal would be much bulkier than the cash journal.

2. *Less time is required for recording* cash transactions in a cash journal than in a two-column general journal. A general journal entry requires that the title of each account in the transaction be written in the Account Title column. A cash journal entry, however, requires that the title of no more than one account be written. This is true because the "cash" part of a transaction is always recorded in one of the special Cash columns. If both the debit amount and the credit amount of a transaction are recorded in special columns, it is not necessary to write any account title in the Account Title column. For example, in Transaction No. 4 on Line 5 of the cash journal, page 67, both the debit amount and the credit amount are recorded in special columns. A check mark ($\sqrt{}$) is placed in the Account Title column to show that no account title needs to be written in this wide column. The check mark also indicates that the writing of an account title in the Account Title column has not been overlooked.

When a two-column general journal is used, additional time and labor are required to write an account title for both parts of every transaction.

3. *Less time is required for posting* from the cash journal than from the general journal. Every amount that is recorded in a two-column general journal is posted separately. The amounts entered in special columns of the cash journal are not posted separately. Only the total of a special column is posted. Therefore, special columns in a cash journal save both time and labor in the later posting of the cash journal. Posting from a cash journal is explained in Chapter 7.

> Each business plans the special columns in its cash journal to fit its needs. For example, a larger car wash than Rainbow Car Wash might provide special columns in its cash journal for those revenue or expense items that occur frequently. Such a car wash might have special columns for Car Wash Sales, Wax Sales, and Vacuum Sales. Examples of journals with various special columns are given in Chapters 12, 23, and 24.

Recording the cash on hand in a cash journal

It is sometimes necessary to know the amount of cash that was on hand at the beginning of the month. To avoid referring frequently to the cash account in the general ledger, the first line of the cash journal is used each month to record this information. This entry is not posted since this amount is already in the cash account. An entry to record information that is not to be posted is called a memorandum entry.

On August 1, 1977, Rainbow Car Wash has $650.00 cash on hand. As shown on Line 1 of the cash journal, page 67, the memorandum entry, including the amount, is written in the Account Title column. The year, month, and day are written in the Date column. A check mark is placed in the Post. Ref. column to show that nothing is to be posted from this line. Nothing is written in the amount columns.

TRANSACTION NO. 1 — JOURNALIZING THE SALE OF AN ASSET FOR CASH

August 1, 1977. Received cash from the sale of an old adding machine, $10.00. Issued Receipt No. 1.

Source document for the sale of an asset

A written acknowledgment given when something is acquired is called a receipt. Each time Mr. Shaw, the proprietor of Rainbow Car Wash, receives cash, he records the transaction in a receipt book. Before writing the receipt, he first fills out the stub of the receipt. The receipt stub is the source document for each cash received transaction. Journal entries for all cash receipts are then made from the information on the receipt stubs. The receipt is given to the person from whom the cash or other asset is received.

The illustration below shows the receipt stub and receipt issued by Mr. Shaw for the $10.00 received for the old adding machine.

Receipt stub and receipt

Journalizing Transaction No. 1

The transaction to be recorded is first analyzed into its debit and credit parts. A quick review of the analysis of the sale of the old adding machine for $10.00 (explained in detail on pages 41 and 42) follows:

Cash

	(debit)	(credit)
Balance	650.00	
Increase	10.00	

Office Equipment

	(debit)	(credit)
Balance	500.00	Decrease 10.00

This transaction causes (1) the balance of an asset account, Cash, to increase $10.00, and (2) the balance of another asset account, Office Equipment, to decrease the same amount. Therefore, both of these accounts must be updated to show the changes caused by this transaction. Cash is debited for $10.00 and Office Equipment is credited for $10.00.

The record of a business transaction and its effect on accounts in the ledger is first recorded in a journal — a book of original entry. Line 2 of the illustration below shows Transaction No. 1 recorded in the cash journal of Rainbow Car Wash.

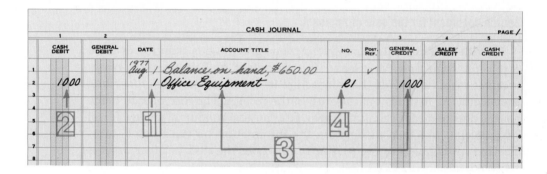

The same four steps taken in journalizing the opening entry in the general journal are followed in journalizing business transactions in the cash journal. For Transaction No. 1 these four steps are:

☐ **1** **Date of entry.** Write the date in the Date column. Since the year and the month have already been written on this page of the cash journal, only the day, *1*, needs to be written.

☐ **2** **Debit part of entry.** Debit the cash account by writing *$10.00* in the Cash Debit column on Line 2. It is not necessary to write *Cash* in the Account Title column. The column heading, *Cash Debit*, identifies this column as the one in which to record all amounts debited to the cash account. The cash account is debited because the balance of the asset account Cash is increased.

☐ **3** **Credit part of entry.** Credit the office equipment account (a) by writing *$10.00* in the General Credit column and (b) by writing the account title *Office Equipment* in the Account Title column. Office

Equipment is credited because the sale of an old adding machine decreases the balance of this asset account.

The General Debit and General Credit columns are used for accounts for which there are no special columns. When an amount is recorded in one of the General columns, the name of the account debited or credited is written in the Account Title column.

☐ 4 **Indication of source document.** Write *R1* in the No. column to show that Receipt No. 1 is issued in this transaction. The letter *R* in the No. column stands for *receipt* and is followed by the number of the receipt. The number is obtained from the stub of the receipt.

The journal entry does not show what item of office equipment was sold nor to whom it was sold. At a later date, such data may be needed. *R1* in the No. column of the cash journal shows where detailed data about this transaction may be obtained — from the stub of Receipt No. 1 in the file. Therefore, it is not necessary to repeat such details in the journal entry.

TRANSACTION NO. 2 — JOURNALIZING THE PART PAYMENT OF A LIABILITY

August 1, 1977. Paid cash to Auto Wash Equipment Co. in part payment of the amount owed, $200.00. Issued Check No. 1.

Source document for the payment of a liability

An order in writing, signed by the depositor, ordering the bank to pay cash from the depositor's account is called a check. Most businesses use checks to make all major cash payments. Checks are safer than money to send through the mail. After a check has been cashed, the bank returns it to the business that wrote it. The returned check is evidence that payment has been made and serves as a receipt for the payment.

The source document for recording a cash payment is the check stub that is prepared at the time each check is written. Each check stub should

Check stub and check

be filled out completely and retained in the checkbook. The check stub should contain all the information needed for making the journal entry to record a cash payment transaction.

The illustration on page 71 shows the first check stub and check prepared by Mr. Shaw, proprietor of Rainbow Car Wash, for the part payment of the liability owed to Auto Wash Equipment Co.

Journalizing Transaction No. 2

The analysis of this transaction into its debit and credit parts is explained on pages 43 and 44. Line 3 of the illustration below shows how Transaction No. 2 is recorded in the cash journal of Rainbow Car Wash.

The four steps in journalizing this transaction are:

☐ 1 **Date of entry.** Write the day of the month, *1*, in the Date column.

☐ 2 **Debit part of entry.** Debit the Auto Wash Equipment Co. account (a) by writing $200.00 in the General Debit column and (b) by writing the account title *Auto Wash Equipment Co.* in the Account Title column. The Auto Wash Equipment Co. account is debited because the balance of this liability account is decreased.

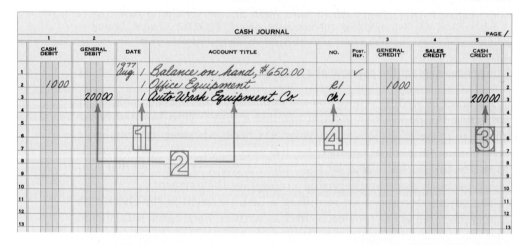

☐ 3 **Credit part of entry.** Credit Cash by writing $200.00 in the Cash Credit column. The column heading, *Cash Credit*, identifies this column as the one in which to record all amounts credited to the cash account. The cash account is credited because this cash payment transaction decreases the balance of the asset account Cash.

☐ 4 **Indication of source document.** Write *Ck1* in the No. column to show that Check No. 1 is issued in this transaction. The letters *Ck* in the No. column stand for *check*. The check number is obtained from the check stub.

The check number in the No. column shows which check stub contains additional details about the transaction. Since these data can be located quickly when needed, it is not necessary to record any of these details in the cash journal.

TRANSACTION NO. 3 — JOURNALIZING AN ADDITIONAL INVESTMENT OF CAPITAL BY THE PROPRIETOR

August 1, 1977. Received cash from Harry Shaw, the proprietor, as an additional investment in the business, $500.00. Issued Receipt No. 2.

Source document for an additional investment

All receipts of cash by Rainbow Car Wash are recorded in the receipt book. Therefore, when Mr. Shaw took $500.00 out of his personal funds and invested it in his business, he issued Receipt No. 2 to himself. The stub of Receipt No. 2 furnishes all the information needed to record Transaction No. 3.

Journalizing Transaction No. 3

After this transaction is analyzed into its debit and credit parts, as explained on pages 44 and 45, the following entry is made on Line 4 of the cash journal:

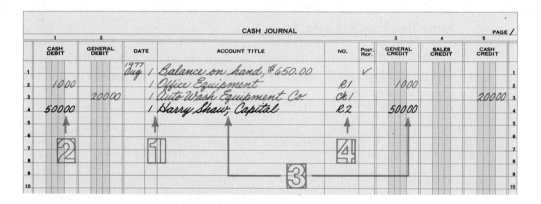

The four steps in journalizing this transaction are:

☐ 1 **Date of entry.** Write the day of the month, *1*, in the Date column.

☐ 2 **Debit part of entry.** Debit the cash account by writing *$500.00* in the Cash Debit column. The cash account is debited because the balance of the asset account Cash is increased.

□ 3   **Credit part of entry.** Credit the proprietor's capital account (a) by writing *$500.00* in the General Credit column and (b) by writing the account title *Harry Shaw, Capital* in the Account Title column. The proprietor's capital account is credited because the additional investment increases the balance of the capital account.

□ 4   **Indication of source document.** Write *R2* in the No. column to show that the stub for Receipt No. 2 is the source document.

TRANSACTION NO. 4 — JOURNALIZING A REVENUE TRANSACTION

> *August 1, 1977. Received cash from car wash sales for one day, $82.00. Issued Receipt No. 3.*

Source document for a revenue transaction

Each customer of Rainbow Car Wash inserts two quarters (50¢) in a coin box as the price for a car wash. This activates the equipment for five minutes. The customer is then able to spray the car with a detergent, followed by a rinse of clear water.

Mr. Shaw, the proprietor, removes the cash from the coin boxes each day that the car wash has been used. He then prepares a receipt showing the total cash taken from the coin boxes. The total on the stub of the receipt is the amount used for making an entry for revenue received from the car wash sales for the day.

Journalizing Transaction No. 4

After this transaction is analyzed into its debit and credit parts, as explained on pages 55 and 56, the following entry is made on Line 5 of the cash journal:

The first four steps in journalizing a revenue transaction in the cash journal are the same as those in journalizing other kinds of transactions.

☐ 1 **Date of entry.** Write the day of the month, *1*, in the Date column.

☐ 2 **Debit part of entry.** Debit the cash account by writing *$82.00* in the Cash Debit column. The cash account is debited because the balance of the asset account Cash is increased.

☐ 3 **Credit part of entry.** Credit the sales account by writing *$82.00* in the Sales Credit column. It is not necessary to write the word *Sales* in the Account Title column. The heading of the special column, Sales Credit, shows clearly that the sales account is credited for $82.00. Place a check mark (√) in the Account Title column to indicate that no account title needs to be written for this entry. The sales account is credited because this revenue transaction increases the balance of the revenue account Sales.

> Revenue from sales occurs almost daily at Rainbow Car Wash. Thus, a special column labeled *Sales Credit* is provided in the cash journal for recording this frequent source of revenue. This special column saves time in journalizing as well as in the later posting to the ledger.

☐ 4 **Indication of source document.** Write *R3* in the No. column to show that the stub for Receipt No. 3 is the source document for this entry.

☐ 5 **For cash sales only.** Place a check mark (√) in the Post. Ref. column. This check mark indicates that no individual amounts are to be posted from the entry on this line. Posting from special columns is further explained in Chapter 7.

TRANSACTION NO. 5 — JOURNALIZING AN EXPENSE TRANSACTION

> *August 2, 1977. Paid cash for rent of car wash for August, $350.00. Issued Check No. 2.*

Source document for an expense transaction

The source document for this payment of rent is the check stub that was prepared when the check was written.

Journalizing Transaction No. 5

After this transaction is analyzed into its debit and credit parts, as explained on pages 57 and 58, the entry shown on page 76 is made.

CASH JOURNAL   PAGE 1

CASH DEBIT	GENERAL DEBIT	DATE	ACCOUNT TITLE	NO.	POST. REF.	GENERAL CREDIT	SALES CREDIT	CASH CREDIT
		1977 Aug. 1	Balance on hand, $650.00		✓			
1000		1	Office Equipment	R1		1000		
	2000	1	Auto Wash Equipment Co.	Ck1				2000
50000		1	Harry Shaw, Capital	R2		50000		
8200		1		R3	✓		8200	
	35000	2	Rent Expense	Ck2				35000

The four steps in journalizing an expense transaction in the cash journal are the same as those in journalizing other transactions.

☐ **1** **Date of entry.** Write the day of the month, 2, in the Date column.

☐ **2** **Debit part of entry.** Debit the rent expense account (a) by writing $350.00 in the General Debit column and (b) by writing the account title *Rent Expense* in the Account Title column. The rent expense account is debited because this expense transaction increases the balance of the expense account Rent Expense. The balance of every expense account is always a debit balance.

☐ **3** **Credit part of entry.** Credit the cash account by writing $350.00 in the Cash Credit column. The cash account is credited because the balance of the asset account Cash is decreased.

☐ **4** **Indication of source document.** Write *Ck2* in the No. column to show that Check No. 2 is issued in this transaction.

JOURNALIZING OTHER BUSINESS TRANSACTIONS

The transactions for the remainder of August are similar to those that have been discussed. The complete cash journal of Rainbow Car Wash for August is shown on page 77.

The Rainbow Car Wash maintains five expense accounts: Advertising Expense, Fuel Expense, Miscellaneous Expense, Rent Expense, and Utilities Expense. The miscellaneous expense account is debited for all expenses that cannot be charged to any of the other expense accounts. The utilities expense account is debited for all telephone and electricity bills.

PROVING THE ACCURACY OF THE CASH JOURNAL ENTRIES

The accuracy of journalizing must be checked. The process of verifying the accuracy of work is known as proving.

Footing the cash journal

The first step in proving the accuracy of the entries in the cash journal is to add all the amount columns. The total of each amount column is

CASH JOURNAL   PAGE 1

CASH DEBIT	GENERAL DEBIT	DATE	ACCOUNT TITLE	NO.	POST. REF.	GENERAL CREDIT	SALES CREDIT	CASH CREDIT
		1977 Aug. 1	Balance on hand, $650.00		✓			
1000		1	Office Equipment	R1		1000		
	20000	2	Auto Wash Equipment Co.	Ck1				20000
50000		3	Harry Shaw, Capital	R2		50000		
8200		4	✓	R3	✓		8200	
	35000	5 2	Rent Expense	Ck2				35000
7050		6 2	✓	R4	✓		7050	
1800		7 3	✓	R5	✓		1800	
	4200	8 4	Fuel Expense	Ck3				4200
5450		9 4	✓	R6	✓		5450	
	1800	10 5	Advertising Expense	Ck4				1800
10200		5	✓	R7	✓		10200	
	300	6	Miscellaneous Expense	Ck5				300
11100		8	✓	R8	✓		11100	
7600		9	✓	R9	✓		7600	
3300		10	✓	R10	✓		3300	
4550		11	✓	R11	✓		4550	
	2650	12	Utilities Expense	Ck6				2650
5200		12	✓	R12	✓		5200	
1800		13	Office Equipment	R13		1800		
117250	6450 70400	15	Operating Supplies	Ck7		52800	64450	6450 70400
1250		16	✓	R14	✓		1250	
1800		17	✓	R15	✓		1800	
	4200	18	Utilities Expense	Ck8				4200
10800		18	✓	R16	✓		10800	
	1400	20	Miscellaneous Expense	Ck9				1400
7250		22	✓	R17	✓		7250	
6800		23	✓	R18	✓		6800	
8000		24	✓	R19	✓		8000	
	3150	25	Fuel Expense	Ck10				3150
9600		26	✓	R20	✓		9600	
	250	27	Miscellaneous Expense	Ck11				250
10200		29	✓	R21	✓		10200	
7900		30	✓	R22	✓		7900	
	1200	30	Miscellaneous Expense	Ck12				1200
3800		31	✓	R23	✓		3800	
184650	80600	31	Totals			52800	131850	80600

Cash journal of Rainbow Car Wash for August

written in small pencil figures immediately below the line of the last entry. Pencil totals written in small figures are commonly called footings. Footings are always made at the end of the month. They may also be made at any time during the month when the equality of debits and credits in the journal is being proved. The cash journal, page 77, shows that footings were made on August 15 as well as at the end of the month.

Proving the equality of debits and credits in the cash journal

The footings of the debit columns are listed on a separate sheet of paper and added. The footings of the credit columns are also listed and added. The end-of-month figures for proving the cash journal on page 77 are shown below.

Cash Debit footing..........	$1,846.50	General Credit footing.....	$ 528.00
General Debit footing......	806.00	Sales Credit footing.........	1,318.50
		Cash Credit footing.........	806.00
Total debits	$2,652.50	Total credits..................	$2,652.50

The sum of the totals of all *debit* columns should equal the sum of the totals of all *credit* columns.

> If the sum of all debit totals does not equal the sum of all credit totals, one or more errors have been made. The error or errors should be located and corrected.

Proving cash on hand

Determining that the amount of cash on hand agrees with the accounting records is called proving cash. Cash on hand is the bank balance plus all cash not deposited. Cash is proved daily in many businesses. Cash should always be proved when the cash journal is footed at the end of a month.

The following calculations are made to prove cash after the cash journal of Rainbow Car Wash is footed and proved on August 31.

Cash balance at the beginning of the month as shown by the memorandum entry (Line 1 of the cash journal)	$ 650.00
Plus cash received during the month (footing of Cash Debit column of the cash journal)..	1,846.50
Total of beginning balance plus cash received	$2,496.50
Less cash paid during the month (footing of Cash Credit column of cash journal)	806.00
Amount of cash that should be on hand	$1,690.50

The Rainbow Car Wash deposits all cash as it is received. The last check stub used in the checkbook shows a bank balance of $1,690.50. This proves that cash on hand agrees with the cash journal record.

RULING THE CASH JOURNAL

After proving the equality of debits and credits and the cash on hand, the cash journal is ruled. A single line is drawn across all amount columns of the cash journal under the last entry. The totals of the columns are written in ink. The last day of the month is written in the Date column on the line with the totals. The word *Totals* is written in the Account Title column. A double line is drawn across all amount columns under the totals. This common method of ruling the cash journal used by Rainbow Car Wash is shown in the illustration, page 77. A ruler or other straight edge should always be used in drawing lines.

Another method of ruling the cash journal is shown below. If a page that is almost full is totaled, the printed rulings at the bottom of the page may be used. The spaces between the last entry and the printed rulings are canceled by drawing a diagonal line across the Account Title column. The diagonal line is drawn from the Date column to the No. column.

A cash journal with totals at the bottom of the page

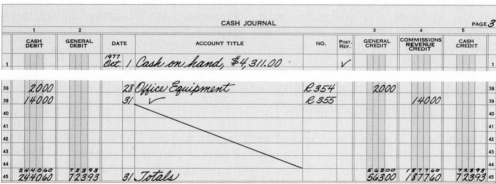

+ What is the meaning of each of the following?

- journalizing
- double-entry accounting
- special journal

- cash journal
- memorandum entry
- receipt

- check
- footings
- proving cash

1. What is the purpose of a journal?
2. What are the two reasons why business transactions are not recorded directly in ledger accounts?
3. From where is the information obtained that is needed to journalize a business transaction?
4. What are several advantages of using a cash journal instead of a general journal?
5. What business paper does the Rainbow Car Wash use for the source document for each of its cash received transactions?
6. What is the meaning of R1 in the No. column on Line 2 in the cash journal on page 77?
7. What business paper does Rainbow Car Wash use for the source document for each cash payment?

8. What is the meaning of Ck1 in the No. column on Line 3 in the cash journal on page 77?

9. Why is a check mark (√) placed in the Account Title column when journalizing a transaction showing revenue from car wash sales?

10. Why does the cash journal of Rainbow Car Wash have a special column labeled Sales Credit?

11. How is the equality of debits and credits in the cash journal proved?

12. How is cash proved?

Cases for Management Decision

CASE 1 Nancy Waldo, the owner and operator of a dance studio, refers to all of her cash payments as "my expenses." What examples of cash payments can you give to Ms. Waldo to prove that all cash payments are not expenses?

CASE 2 When Mr. Fernandez, proprietor of the Villa Motor Inn, makes a cash payment, he first fills in the check stub before writing the check. When Mr. Carlton, proprietor of the Edgewater Beach Motel, makes a cash payment, he first writes the check and signs it before filling in the check stub. Is one system better than the other? Why?

CASE 3 Mr. Schmidt of Atomic Sales Company records all of his transactions in a two-column general journal. He claims that it is easier to use and it makes checking the equality of debits and credits for each transaction easier. Mr. Roth of Up-Town Cleaning Service uses a special multicolumn cash journal similar to the one illustrated on page 77. He claims that it is easier to use and that he can check easily the equality of debits and credits for each transaction. Which journal do you think provides the most advantages for recording cash transactions?

Drills for Mastering Principles

DRILL 6-D 1 Analyzing transactions that have been journalized

Instructions: Turn to the completed cash journal on page 77. On a form similar to the one shown below, prepare an analysis of each of the entries recorded on Lines 2 through 11 of the cash journal. Allow two lines for each analysis. Copy the first analysis, which is given as an example.

	(a)	(b)	(c)		(d)	
			Is Account		Effect of Transaction on Balance of Account	
Trans. No.	Account Titles Affected	Classification of Account	Debited?	Credited?	Increase	Decrease
1.	Cash	Asset	√		√	
	Office Equipment	Asset		√		√
2.						

DRILL 6-D 2 Analyzing transactions

The first 12 transactions in March for Ronald Swift, a land surveyor, are listed at the top of the next page.

Transaction
Number   *Transactions*

1. Received cash from fees revenue.
2. Paid cash for advertisement in local paper.
3. Paid cash for March rent.
4. Paid cash for telephone bill. This is a utilities expense.
5. Received cash from sale of old office chair.
6. Received cash from fees revenue.
7. Paid cash for gas and oil for automobile.
8. Paid cash for postage stamps. This is a miscellaneous expense.
9. Paid cash to Plimpton Company in partial payment of amount owed.
10. Paid cash for electric bill. This is a utilities expense.
11. Paid cash for a new calculating machine.
12. Received cash from fees revenue.

Some of the account titles in the ledger of Ronald Swift, surveyor, are listed below. These are not all the accounts, but they are all you will need in this drill.

Cash   Plimpton Company (creditor)   Miscellaneous Expense
Office Equipment   Advertising Expense   Rent Expense
Surveying Equipment   Automobile Expense   Utilities Expense
Fees Revenue

Instructions: □ **1.** On a form similar to the one shown below, copy the analysis of Transaction No. 1, which is given as an example.

	(a)	(b)	(c)		(d)	
		Classifica-	Is Account		Effect of Transaction on Balance of Account	
Trans. No.	Account Titles Affected	tion of Account	Debited?	Credited?	Increase	Decrease
1.	*Cash*	*Asset*	✓		✓	
	Fees Revenue	*Revenue*		✓	✓	
2.						

Instructions: □ **2.** Write a similar analysis of Transactions No. 2 through 12, using the proper account titles in Column (a) of your form.

PROBLEM 6-1 Journalizing cash transactions for an architect

Problems for Applying Concepts

Ernest Lema, a registered architect, obtains his revenue from fees for designing buildings and for other architectural services.

Instructions: □ **1.** Prepare a cash journal similar to the one on page 77 by writing the proper headings at the top of each column. Number the page 5.

□ **2.** Record as a memorandum entry the cash balance for May of the current year. The cash balance on May 1 was $400.00.

☐ **3.** Record the May transactions, using the account titles shown in the following chart of accounts. Source documents are abbreviated as: check, Ck; receipt, R. Begin numbering checks with Ck501. Begin numbering receipts with R220.

Ernest Lema, A.I.A.
Chart of Accounts

(1) Assets	Account Number	(4) Revenue	Account Number
Cash......................................	11	Fees Revenue.......................	41
Automobile	12		
Drafting Equipment..............	13	**(5) Expenses**	
Office Equipment	14	Automobile Expense.............	51
		Miscellaneous Expense..........	52
(2) Liabilities		Rent Expense	53
Amaro Copying Equipment ...	21	Utilities Expense	54
(3) Capital			
Ernest Lema, Capital.............	31		

May 1. Paid cash for rent of office for May, $200.00.
   1. Paid cash for parking space for May, $20.00. (Automobile Expense)
   2. Received cash from sale of old office desk, $25.00.
   2. Received cash for planning a 20-unit motel, $650.00.
   2. Paid cash for gas and oil for automobile, $6.20.
   3. Paid cash for new desk and chair, $240.00.
   4. Received cash for planning a municipal garage, $1,200.00.
   5. Received cash for plans to remodel a men's shoe store, $450.00.
  12. Paid cash for drafting equipment, $85.00.
  14. Received cash for plans to add two rooms to a ranch-style house, $200.00.
  17. Paid cash to Amaro Copying Equipment for amount owed, $48.00.
  21. Paid cash for electric bill, $21.50.
  25. Received cash for planning a tri-level house, $450.00.
  29. Paid cash for telephone bill, $18.75.
  31. Received cash for plans to remodel a toy store, $150.00.
  31. Paid cash for postage stamps, $16.00. (Miscellaneous Expense)

Instructions: ☐ **4.** Foot each of the amount columns of your cash journal, using small pencil figures. Place these tiny pencil figures close to the line above so that they seem to hang from it. Study the model cash journal on page 77.

☐ **5.** Prove the equality of debits and credits in your cash journal by finding the sum of all the debit totals and the sum of all the credit totals. The sum of the two debit totals should equal the sum of the three credit totals.

☐ **6.** Prove cash. The cash balance on hand was recorded on May 1 as a memorandum entry. The last check stub shows a bank balance of $2,869.55 at the end of the month. All cash received has been deposited.

☐ **7.** If the sum of the totals of the debits in your cash journal is equal to the sum of the totals of the credits, rule a single line across all amount columns of your cash journal. Compare your work with the cash journal on page 77.

◻ **8.** Write the totals of each column in ink. Write the date on the line with the totals. Label the totals by writing the word *Totals* in the Account Title column. All of the totals should be on the same line.

◻ **9.** Rule double lines across all amount columns immediately below the totals. Use as your model the cash journal on page 77.

PROBLEM 6-2   Journalizing cash transactions of a real estate business

Hiram Sims is a real estate agent and obtains his revenue from commissions that he earns on property sold and property rented. The title that he uses for his revenue account is Commissions Revenue.

Instructions: ◻ **1.** Record the cash balance of Sims Realty as a memorandum entry on page 11 of a five-column cash journal. Use the current year in recording the date. The cash balance on October 1 was $860.50.

◻ **2.** Record the October transactions given below and on page 84. Use the account titles shown in the chart of accounts. Begin numbering checks with Ck101. Begin numbering receipts with R81.

<table>
<tr><td colspan="4" align="center">Sims Realty
Chart of Accounts</td></tr>
<tr><td align="center">**(1) Assets**</td><td align="center">**Account Number**</td><td align="center">**(4) Revenue**</td><td align="center">**Account Number**</td></tr>
<tr><td>Cash......................................</td><td align="center">11</td><td>Commissions Revenue ....</td><td align="center">41</td></tr>
<tr><td>Automobile ....</td><td align="center">12</td><td></td><td></td></tr>
<tr><td>Office Furniture...................</td><td align="center">13</td><td align="center">**(5) Expenses**</td><td></td></tr>
<tr><td>Office Machines...................</td><td align="center">14</td><td>Advertising Expense ....</td><td align="center">51</td></tr>
<tr><td></td><td></td><td>Automobile Expense ....</td><td align="center">52</td></tr>
<tr><td align="center">**(2) Liabilities**</td><td></td><td>Miscellaneous Expense..........</td><td align="center">53</td></tr>
<tr><td>Hadley Company..................</td><td align="center">21</td><td>Rent Expense ....</td><td align="center">54</td></tr>
<tr><td>Rick's Garage......................</td><td align="center">22</td><td></td><td></td></tr>
<tr><td align="center">**(3) Capital**</td><td></td><td></td><td></td></tr>
<tr><td>Hiram Sims, Capital..............</td><td align="center">31</td><td></td><td></td></tr>
</table>

Instructions: ◻ **3.** Debit the account Miscellaneous Expense for all expenses that cannot be charged to any other expense account.

Oct. 1. Paid cash for rent of office for October, $200.00.
     2. Received cash as commission from sale of a house, $700.00.
     3. Received cash from sale of old office furniture, $18.00.
     4. Paid cash for gas and oil for automobile, $5.75.
     5. Received cash as commission from renting a house, $80.00.
     7. Paid cash to Hadley Company in part payment of account, $85.00.
    10. Paid cash for new office furniture, $144.00.
    12. Paid cash to Rick's Garage in payment of amount owed, $92.50.
    15. Paid cash for a new office machine, $225.00.

Oct. 17. Received cash as commission from sale of a house, $420.00.
     19. Paid cash for repair to automobile, $12.00.
     23. Paid cash for advertisement in newspaper, $6.50.
     25. Received cash as commission from renting a warehouse, $265.00.
     27. Paid cash for telephone bill, $12.00.
     30. Paid cash for electric bill, $6.50.
     31. Received cash as commission from sale of two house lots, $260.00.

Instructions: □ **4.** Foot each of the amount columns of your cash journal. Use small pencil figures.

□ **5.** Prove the equality of debits and credits in your cash journal.

□ **6.** Prove cash. The last check stub shows a bank balance at the end of the month of $1,814.25. All cash received has been deposited.

□ **7.** Write the column totals and the date. Write the word *Totals* in the Account Title column.

□ **8.** Rule the cash journal.

This problem will be continued in the next chapter. If it is collected by your teacher at this time, it will be returned to you before it is needed in Problem 7-1.

**MASTERY
PROBLEM 6-M**   Journalizing cash transactions for a
                      taxi business

Norman Tower owns and operates the Tower Taxi Service. The title that he uses for his revenue account is Fares Earned.

Instructions: □ **1.** Record the cash balance of the Tower Taxi Service as a memorandum entry on page 9 of a five-column cash journal. Use the current year in recording the date. The cash balance on February 1 was $343.50.

□ **2.** Record the February transactions given on page 85. Use the account titles in the chart of accounts. Begin numbering checks with Ck91. Begin numbering receipts with R31.

Tower Taxi Service Chart of Accounts			
(1) Assets	Account Number	**(4) Revenue**	Account Number
Cash..................................	11	Fares Earned......................	41
Supplies.............................	12		
Equipment	13	**(5) Expenses**	
		Advertising Expense.............	51
(2) Liabilities		Gas & Oil Expense...............	52
Duke Street Garage..............	21	Rent Expense......................	53
First National Bank..............	22	Repairs & Maintenance Exp....	54
		Utilities Expense	55
(3) Capital			
Norman Tower, Capital.........	31		

Feb. 1. Received cash from fares earned, $63.00.
    2. Paid cash for rent of garage for February, $25.00.
    3. Paid cash for gas and oil, $7.50.
    3. Received cash from fares earned, $81.50.
    5. Paid cash for telephone bill, $14.00.
    6. Received cash from fares earned, $106.00.
    6. Paid cash to Duke Street Garage in settlement of account, $43.50.
    7. Received cash from fares earned, $64.50.
    8. Paid cash for repairs to front bumper, $8.00.
    9. Paid cash for gas and oil, $8.80.
   10. Received cash from fares earned, $120.00.
   12. Paid cash to First National Bank in partial settlement of account, $100.00.
   13. Paid cash for electric bill, $16.00.
   15. Received cash from fares earned, $44.00.
   16. Paid cash for gas and oil, $9.40.
   18. Received cash from fares earned, $83.00.
   19. Paid cash for purchase of two spare tires, $48.00. (Debit Supplies Account)
   21. Received cash from fares earned, $21.50.
   23. Paid cash for gas and oil, $6.60.
   24. Received cash from fares earned, $111.00.
   25. Paid for newspaper advertisement, $7.50.
   27. Received cash from fares earned, $36.50.
   28. Paid cash to First National Bank in final settlement of account, $200.00.

Instructions: ☐ **3.** Foot each of the amount columns of your cash journal. Use small pencil figures.

☐ **4.** Prove the equality of debits and credits in your cash journal.

☐ **5.** Prove cash. The last check stub shows a bank balance at the end of the month of $580.20. All cash received has been deposited.

☐ **6.** Write the column totals and the date. Write the word *Totals* in the Account Title column.

☐ **7.** Rule the cash journal.

BONUS PROBLEM 6-B ● Journalizing cash transactions of a travel agency

The International Travel Agency is owned and operated by Jane Rose. Ms. Rose uses a cash journal that has the same columnar headings as the cash journal used in Problem 6-2, but the arrangement of the columns is not the same. The amount columns in Ms. Rose's cash journal are those illustrated below.

CASH JOURNAL								Page 15
Cash		Date	Account Title	No.	P. R.	General		Commissions Revenue Credit
Debit	Credit					Debit	Credit	

Some of the account titles in the ledger of International Travel Agency are listed below. These are not all the accounts in its ledger, but they are all that you will need in this problem.

Cash	Advertising Expense
Office Furniture	Automobile Expense
Office Equipment	Miscellaneous Expense
Commissions Revenue	Rent Expense

Instructions: □ **1.** Record the cash balance as a memorandum entry in a cash journal ruled like the form on page 85. Use the current year in recording the date. The cash balance on February 1 was $1,650.00.

□ **2.** Record the following selected transactions, using the account titles shown above. Begin numbering the checks with Ck28. Begin numbering the receipts with R24.

Transactions

Feb. 1. Received commission on sale of European tour for two, $225.00.
    1. Paid for repairs to the automobile, $60.50.
    2. Paid rent for February, $200.00.
    4. Received commission from TransAtlantic Air Lines for sale of tickets in January, $350.00.
    5. Received refund from Lamont Equipment Company for an overcharge on office equipment bought from them last month, $10.00. This refund decreases the cost of the equipment.
    5. Paid refund to a customer of a part of the commission received from him last month, $15.00.
    7. Paid for advertising in local newspaper, $12.00.
    9. Paid to have the office cleaned, $15.00.
    11. Paid for gas and oil for the automobile, $18.30.
    15. Received commission on the sale of world tour for two, $575.00.
    18. Received commission from Pan Pacific Air Lines for sale of tickets in January, $480.00.
    19. Received cash from sale of old furniture, $42.00.
    22. Paid cash for entertaining a customer, $9.50.
    25. Paid cash for advertising in local newspaper, $16.50.
    28. Received commission for sale of group tour, $800.00.

Instructions: □ **3.** Foot each of the amount columns of your cash journal. Use small pencil figures.

□ **4.** Prove the equality of debits and credits in your cash journal.

□ **5.** Prove cash. The last check stub shows a bank balance at the end of the month of $3,785.20. All cash received has been deposited.

□ **6.** Write the column totals and the date. Write the word *Totals* in the Account Title column.

□ **7.** Rule the cash journal.

The balance sheet of Rainbow Car Wash in Chapter 1 shows the financial position of the business on a specific date — August 1, 1977. Between August 1 and August 31 the car wash was in operation, and many changes occurred in its financial position. Each business transaction caused a change. Revenue was earned and expenses were paid.

Each business transaction for Rainbow Car Wash is recorded in the cash journal as shown on page 77. The cash journal, however, does not sort the entries into accounts. Neither does it summarize the effect of transactions on accounts. For example, the cash journal does not show in one place the total amount spent for fuel expense. Furthermore, a journal does not supply account balances for preparing an up-to-date balance sheet.

Need for posting

In order to know how transactions have changed the account balances, posting from the cash journal to the accounts is necessary. Posting is a sorting process that transfers amounts in journals to appropriate accounts in the ledger. The debits and the credits in each account can then be added and new balances determined easily and quickly.

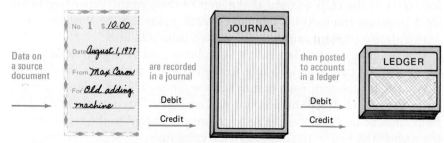

The order for arranging accounts in the ledger

Accounts in the ledger are arranged in the same order as they appear on financial reports. This arrangement makes them easy to locate.

The first group of accounts to be listed on a balance sheet is assets. The asset accounts are followed by the liabilities, and then the capital. In the ledger, therefore, the asset accounts appear first, followed by the liability accounts, and then the capital account. Each of these groups of accounts is a division of the ledger. In addition to these three groups of balance sheet accounts, the ledger of Rainbow Car Wash has a division for revenue accounts and a division for expense accounts. These five divisions are arranged in the ledger in the order shown at the left.

(1) Assets
(2) Liabilities
(3) Capital
(4) Revenue
(5) Expenses

The chart of accounts of a business outlines the order of the accounts in its ledger. The chart of accounts also serves as a guide in journalizing by showing the account titles that are to be used when recording business transactions.

Chart of accounts of Rainbow Car Wash

The chart of accounts of Rainbow Car Wash is shown on page 2. This chart of accounts has five divisions and uses a two-digit numbering system. For example, the rent expense account is numbered 54. The first digit, 5, is the number of the ledger division in which all expense accounts are located. The second digit, 4, shows that Rent Expense is the fourth account in the expenses division of the ledger.

> The ledgers of some businesses contain more than five divisions. Furthermore, businesses with numerous accounts usually use a numbering system with more than two digits.

POSTING THE GENERAL COLUMNS OF THE CASH JOURNAL

A portion of the cash journal of Rainbow Car Wash for August before being posted is shown on the next page. (The complete cash journal before posting and showing all the transactions in August is illustrated on page 77.)

The memorandum entry on the first line of the cash journal shows that $650.00 is in the cash account at the start of the month. This entry is not for a business transaction. The check mark placed in the Post. Ref. column indicates that nothing is to be posted from this line.

The amounts in the General Debit column and in the General Credit column of the cash journal apply to the different accounts named in the Account Title column. Each amount in the General Debit column is posted to the *debit* side of the account named in the Account Title column. Each amount in the General Credit column is posted to the *credit* side of the account named in the Account Title column.

		CASH JOURNAL							PAGE /
CASH DEBIT	GENERAL DEBIT	DATE	ACCOUNT TITLE	NO.	POST. REF.	GENERAL CREDIT	SALES CREDIT	CASH CREDIT	
		1977 Aug. 1	Balance on hand, $650.00		✓				1
1000		1	Office Equipment	R1		1000			2
	20000	1	Auto Wash Equipment Co.	Ck1				20000	3
50000		1	Harry Shaw, Capital	R2		50000			4
8200		1	✓	R3	✓		8200		5
	35000	2	Rent Expense	Ck2				35000	6
7050		2	✓	R4	✓		7050		7
1800		3	✓	R5	✓		1800		8
	4200	4	Fuel Expense	Ck3				4200	9
5450		4	✓	R6	✓		5450		10
	1800	5	Advertising Expense	Ck4				1800	11
10200		5	✓	R7	✓		10200		12
	300	6	Miscellaneous Expense	Ck5				300	13

Each amount is posted during the month to the debit side of the ledger account named in the Account Title column

Each amount is posted during the month to the credit side of the ledger account named in the Account Title column

Steps in posting from the General Credit column

The entry on Line 2 of the cash journal shows a debit to Cash and a credit to Office Equipment. The debit to Cash in the Cash Debit column is not posted separately. At the end of the month this special column is added, and the total is posted as one amount.

The steps in posting the credit to Office Equipment are shown and explained below and on the next page.

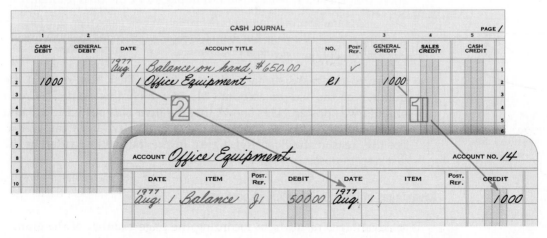

The first two steps in posting from the General Credit column of the cash journal

□ **1** Write the *amount* of the credit, *$10.00*, in the Credit column of the office equipment account as shown in the illustration on the preceding page.

□ **2** Write the *date* of this journal entry in the Date column on the credit side of the office equipment account.

> Since this is the first entry on the credit side of the office equipment account, the complete date, *1977, Aug. 1*, is written.

The posting of an entry is not complete until a cross-reference is made between the journal and the ledger. This cross-referencing is explained in Steps 3 and 4 and is shown below.

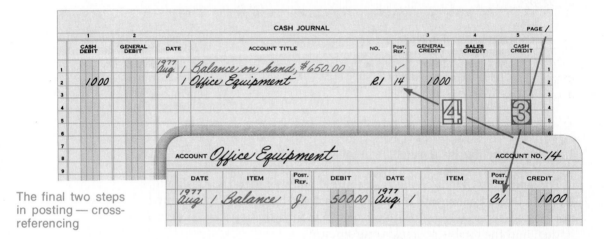

The final two steps in posting — cross-referencing

□ **3** Write *C1* in the Post. Ref. column of the account in the ledger to show that this entry was posted from page 1 of the cash journal.

> *C* is the abbreviation for *cash journal*. When more than one journal is used, the page number of the journal is coded to show from which journal the amount was posted.

□ **4** Return to the cash journal and write in the Post. Ref. column the number of the ledger account, *14*, to which this General Credit amount was posted. This shows that the item was posted to account number *14* and that all details of the posting have been completed. For this reason the Post. Ref. figure in the journal is written as the last step in posting.

Advantages of cross-referencing in posting

Two advantages result from recording the page number of the journal entry in the ledger account and the account number in the journal. First, the numbers in the Post. Ref. columns serve as a cross-reference between the journal and the ledger. For example, when examining a particular account, an accounting clerk may want to see the journal entry or trace back to the source document of a transaction. The page number of the journal in the Post. Ref. column of the account directs the search. Second, cross-referencing in posting shows how much of the posting has been completed. For example, the posting may be interrupted and then resumed. When this happens, it is clear that the remaining amounts to be posted are those for which there are no account numbers in the Post. Ref. column of the journal.

Steps in posting from the General Debit column

The entry on Line 3 of the cash journal shows a debit to Auto Wash Equipment Co. and a credit to Cash. The credit to Cash is not posted individually. This entry will be included when the total of the Cash Credit column is posted to the cash account at the end of the month. The steps in posting the debit to Auto Wash Equipment Co. are shown and explained below and on the next page.

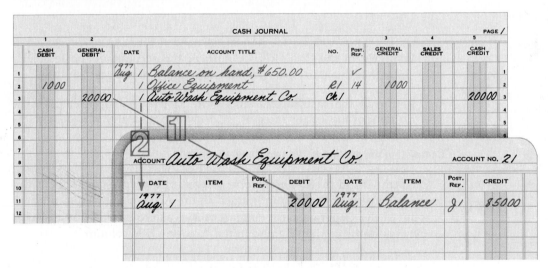

The first two steps in posting from the General Debit column of the cash journal

☐ 1 Write the *amount* of the debit, $200.00, in the Debit column of the Auto Wash Equipment Co. account as shown above.

☐ 2 Write the *date* of this journal entry in the Date column on the debit side of the Auto Wash Equipment Co. account.

Since this is the first entry on the debit side of the Auto Wash Equipment Co. account, the complete date, *1977, Aug. 1*, is written.

The final two steps in posting, indicating the cross-referencing between the journal and the ledger, are shown and explained below.

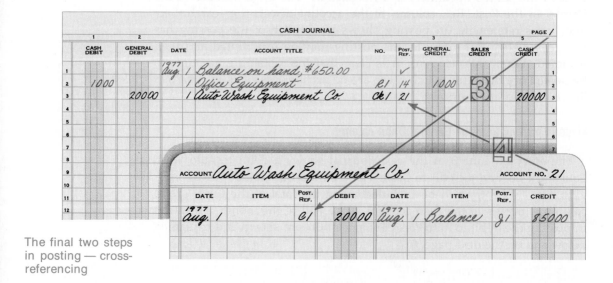

The final two steps
in posting — cross-
referencing

□ **3** Write *C1* in the Post. Ref. column of the account in the ledger to show that this entry was posted from page 1 of the cash journal.

□ **4** Return to the cash journal and write in the Post. Ref. column the number of the ledger account, *21*, to which the entry was posted.

Completing the posting of the two General columns

Each amount in the General Debit column of the cash journal is posted to the debit side of the account named in the Account Title column. Each amount in the General Credit column of the cash journal is posted to the credit side of the account named in the Account Title column.

> The amounts recorded in the General Debit and the General Credit columns of the cash journal are usually posted at frequent intervals during the month. Frequent posting (1) keeps accounts in the ledger up to date and (2) prevents the accumulation of work at the end of the month.

Because the individual amounts that make up the total of a General column are posted separately, the total of each General column is not posted. The total of a column is posted only when the heading of the column is the name of an account.

A check mark in parentheses (√) is placed under the total of each of the two General columns to show that these totals are not to be posted. (The illustration on page 93 shows a check mark under the total of each of the two General columns of the cash journal.)

POSTING THE SPECIAL COLUMNS OF THE CASH JOURNAL

The bottom portion of the cash journal of Rainbow Car Wash indicating the necessary posting of column totals is shown below.

Posting of column totals

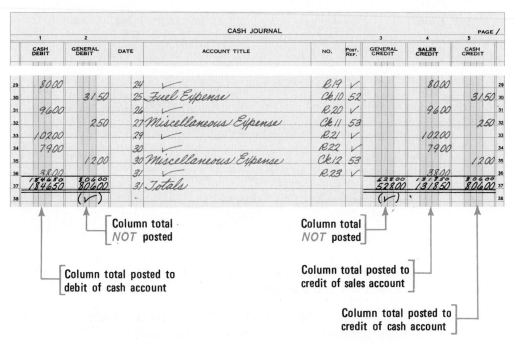

In the cash journal of Rainbow Car Wash, the Cash Debit column, the Cash Credit column, and the Sales Credit column are special columns. The heading of each of these special columns contains the name of an account in the ledger that is debited or credited frequently during the month. The individual amounts entered in special columns are not posted separately. Only the total of a special column is posted. This saves labor and time in posting.

The total of each special column is posted to the account named in the column heading. For example, the total of the Cash Debit column is posted to the debit side of the cash account. The total of the Cash Credit column is posted to the credit side of the cash account. The total of the Sales Credit column is posted to the credit side of the sales account.

When both the debit and credit amounts of an entry are recorded in special columns, a check mark (√) is placed in the Post. Ref. column of the journal. The check mark indicates that the amount in the special column is not to be posted separately. For example, a check mark was placed in the Post. Ref. column of the cash journal above for the entry on Line 29 in the Sales Credit column to show that no separate posting is required for this line.

Posting the total of the Cash Debit column

The steps in posting the total of the Cash Debit column are shown and explained below.

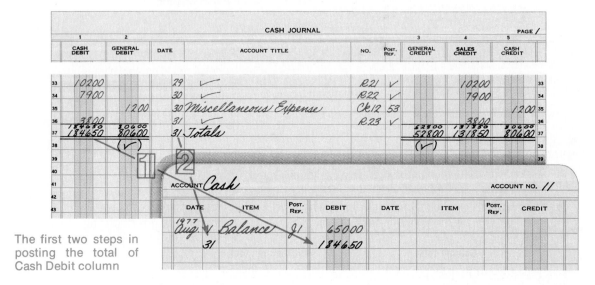

The first two steps in posting the total of Cash Debit column

□ **1** Write the *amount* of the debit, *$1,846.50*, in the Debit column of the cash account in the ledger.

□ **2** Write the *day* found on the Totals line of the cash journal, *31*, in the Date column on the debit side of the cash account.

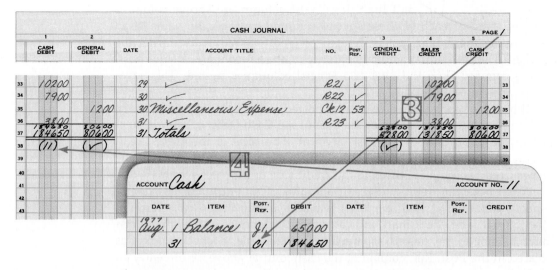

The final two steps in posting the total of the Cash Debit column — cross-referencing

This is the second entry on the debit side of the cash account. The date of the first entry in the cash account is 1977, Aug. 1. The date of the second entry is also the same year and the same month; therefore, it is not necessary to repeat 1977 and Aug. on the debit side of the cash account.

☐ 3 Write *C1* in the Post. Ref. column of the cash account in the ledger to show that this entry was posted from page 1 of the cash journal.

☐ 4 Return to the cash journal and write the account number of the cash account in parentheses, *(11)*, immediately under the total of the Cash Debit column.

Posting the total of the Cash Credit column

The steps in posting the total of the Cash Credit column of the cash journal are:

☐ 1 Write the *amount* of the total, *$806.00*, in the Credit column of the cash account in the ledger.

☐ 2 Write the *day* found on the Totals line of the cash journal in the Date column on the credit side of the cash account. Since this is the first entry on the credit side of the cash account, the complete date, *1977, Aug. 31*, is written.

☐ 3 Write *C1* in the Post. Ref. column of the cash account in the ledger to show that this entry was posted from page 1 of the cash journal.

ACCOUNT *Cash*							ACCOUNT NO. *11*
DATE	ITEM	Post. Ref.	DEBIT	DATE	ITEM	Post. Ref.	CREDIT
1977 Aug. 1	Balance	J1	65000	1977 Aug. 31		C1	80600
31		C1	184650				

☐ 4 Return to the cash journal and write the account number of the cash account in parentheses, *(11)*, immediately under the total of the Cash Credit column. (See the completed cash journal on page 99 showing this final step in the posting of the Cash Credit column.)

Posting the total of the Sales Credit column

The steps in posting the total of the Sales Credit column of the cash journal are on page 96.

☐ **1** Write the *amount* of the total, $1,318.50, in the Credit column of the sales account in the ledger.

☐ **2** Write the *day* found on the Totals line of the cash journal in the Date column on the credit side of the sales account. Since this is the first entry on the credit side of the sales account, it is necessary to write the complete date: *1977, Aug. 31*.

☐ **3** Write *C1* in the Post. Ref. column of the sales account in the ledger to show that this entry was posted from page 1 of the cash journal.

ACCOUNT	*Sales*							ACCOUNT NO. *41*
DATE	ITEM	POST. REF.	DEBIT	DATE	ITEM	POST. REF.	CREDIT	
				1977 *Aug. 31*		*C1*	*1318 50*	

☐ **4** Return to the cash journal and write the account number of the sales account in parentheses, *(41)*, immediately under the total of the Sales Credit column. (See the complete cash journal on page 99 showing this final step in the posting of the Sales Credit column.)

Summary of the principles for posting from the cash journal to the ledger

The cash journal of Rainbow Car Wash after posting has been completed is shown on page 99. The principles for posting from the cash journal are much the same as for posting from any journal.

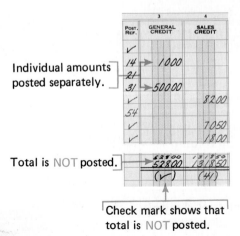

Individual amounts posted separately.

Total is NOT posted.

Check mark shows that total is NOT posted.

Posting from General columns. The principles for posting from the General columns of the cash journal are shown in the illustration at the left. *Individual amounts in General Debit and General Credit columns ARE posted separately to accounts named in the Account Title column. Each time an individual amount in a General column is posted, the number of the account to which it is posted is recorded in the Post. Ref. column of the journal.*

The total of a General column is NOT posted to the ledger. A check mark (√) is placed in parentheses under the total of a General column to show that the total of the column is not posted.

Posting from special columns. The principles for posting from special columns of the cash journal are shown in the illustration at the right. *Individual amounts in special columns of a journal are NOT posted separately.* A check mark (√) is placed in the Post. Ref. column of the journal at the time of the entry to show that each individual amount in a special column is *not* to be posted.

The total of a special column in a journal IS posted to the account named in the heading of the column. The total is posted to the sales account as a credit. The account number is placed in parentheses, (41), under the total of the special column to show to which account in the general ledger the total is posted.

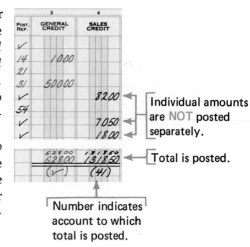

The ledger after posting

The ledger of Rainbow Car Wash after all posting for the month of August has been completed is shown below and on page 98.

Ledger of Rainbow Car Wash after posting all transactions for August

ACCOUNT *Cash* — ACCOUNT NO. *11*

DATE	ITEM	POST. REF.	DEBIT	DATE	ITEM	POST. REF.	CREDIT
1977 Aug. 1	Balance	J1	65000	1977 Aug. 31		C1	80600
31		C1	184650				

ACCOUNT *Operating Supplies* — ACCOUNT NO. *12*

DATE	ITEM	POST. REF.	DEBIT	DATE	ITEM	POST. REF.	CREDIT
1977 Aug. 1	Balance	J1	25000				
15		C1	6450				

ACCOUNT *Car Wash Equipment* — ACCOUNT NO. *13*

DATE	ITEM	POST. REF.	DEBIT	DATE	ITEM	POST. REF.	CREDIT
1977 Aug. 1	Balance	J1	360000				

ACCOUNT *Office Equipment* — ACCOUNT NO. *14*

DATE	ITEM	POST. REF.	DEBIT	DATE	ITEM	POST. REF.	CREDIT
1977 Aug. 1	Balance	J1	50000	1977 Aug. 1		C1	1000
				13		C1	1800

ACCOUNT *Auto Wash Equipment Co.* — ACCOUNT NO. *21*

DATE	ITEM	POST. REF.	DEBIT	DATE	ITEM	POST. REF.	CREDIT
1977 Aug. 1		C1	20000	1977 Aug. 1	Balance	J1	85000

ACCOUNT *Marco Plumbing Company*   ACCOUNT NO. 22

DATE	ITEM	POST. REF.	DEBIT	DATE	ITEM	POST. REF.	CREDIT
				1977 Aug. 1	Balance	J1	15000

ACCOUNT *Harry Shaw, Capital*   ACCOUNT NO. 31

DATE	ITEM	POST. REF.	DEBIT	DATE	ITEM	POST. REF.	CREDIT
				1977 Aug. 1	Balance	J1	400000
				1		C1	50000

ACCOUNT *Sales*   ACCOUNT NO. 41

DATE	ITEM	POST. REF.	DEBIT	DATE	ITEM	POST. REF.	CREDIT
				1977 Aug. 31		C1	131850

ACCOUNT *Advertising Expense*   ACCOUNT NO. 51

DATE	ITEM	POST. REF.	DEBIT	DATE	ITEM	POST. REF.	CREDIT
1977 Aug. 5		C1	1800				

ACCOUNT *Fuel Expense*   ACCOUNT NO. 52

DATE	ITEM	POST. REF.	DEBIT	DATE	ITEM	POST. REF.	CREDIT
1977 Aug. 4		C1	4200				
25		C1	3150				

ACCOUNT *Miscellaneous Expense*   ACCOUNT NO. 53

DATE	ITEM	POST. REF.	DEBIT	DATE	ITEM	POST. REF.	CREDIT
1977 Aug. 6		C1	300				
20		C1	1400				
27		C1	250				
30		C1	1200				

ACCOUNT *Rent Expense*   ACCOUNT NO. 54

DATE	ITEM	POST. REF.	DEBIT	DATE	ITEM	POST. REF.	CREDIT
1977 Aug. 2		C1	35000				

ACCOUNT *Utilities Expense*   ACCOUNT NO. 55

DATE	ITEM	POST. REF.	DEBIT	DATE	ITEM	POST. REF.	CREDIT
1977 Aug. 12		C1	2650				
18		C1	4200				

Ledger of Rainbow Car Wash after posting all transactions for August (concluded)

CASH JOURNAL   PAGE 1

	CASH DEBIT	GENERAL DEBIT	DATE	ACCOUNT TITLE	NO.	POST. REF.	GENERAL CREDIT	SALES CREDIT	CASH CREDIT	
1			1977 Aug. 1	Balance on hand, $650.00		✓				1
2	10 00		1	Office Equipment	R1	14	10 00			2
3		200 00	1	Auto Wash Equipment Co.	Ck1	21			200 00	3
4	500 00		1	Harry Shaw, Capital	R2	31	500 00			4
5	82 00		1	✓	R3	✓		82 00		5
6		350 00	2	Rent Expense	Ck2	54			350 00	6
7	70 50		2	✓	R4	✓		70 50		7
8	18 00		3	✓	R5	✓		18 00		8
9		42 00	4	Fuel Expense	Ck3	52			42 00	9
10	54 50		4	✓	R6	✓		54 50		10
11		18 00	5	Advertising Expense	Ck4	51			18 00	11
12	102 00		5	✓	R7	✓		102 00		12
13		3 00	6	Miscellaneous Expense	Ck5	53			3 00	13
14	111 00		8	✓	R8	✓		111 00		14
15	76 00		9	✓	R9	✓		76 00		15
16	33 00		10	✓	R10	✓		33 00		16
17	45 50		11	✓	R11	✓		45 50		17
18		26 50	12	Utilities Expense	Ck6	55			26 50	18
19	52 00		12	✓	R12	✓		52 00		19
20	18 00		13	Office Equipment	R13	14	18 00			20
21	1172 50	64 50 704 00	15	Operating Supplies	Ck7	12	528 00	644 50	64 50 704 00	21
22	12 50		16	✓	R14	✓		12 50		22
23	18 00		17	✓	R15	✓		18 00		23
24		42 00	18	Utilities Expense	Ck8	55			42 00	24
25	108 00		18	✓	R16	✓		108 00		25
26		14 00	20	Miscellaneous Expense	Ck9	53			14 00	26
27	72 50		22	✓	R17	✓		72 50		27
28	68 00		23	✓	R18	✓		68 00		28
29	80 00		24	✓	R19	✓		80 00		29
30		31 50	25	Fuel Expense	Ck10	52			31 50	30
31	96 00		26	✓	R20	✓		96 00		31
32		2 50	27	Miscellaneous Expense	Ck11	53			2 50	32
33	102 00		29	✓	R21	✓		102 00		33
34	79 00		30	✓	R22	✓		79 00		34
35		12 00	30	Miscellaneous Expense	Ck12	53			12 00	35
36	38 00		31	✓	R23	✓		38 00		36
37	1846 50	806 00	31	Totals			528 00	1318 50	806 00	37
38	(11)	(✓)					(✓)	(41)	(11)	38

Cash journal of Rainbow Car Wash
for August after posting is completed

Questions for Individual Study

1. What caused changes in the financial position of Rainbow Car Wash during the month of August?
2. In spite of the useful purposes that a journal serves, what does it not do?
3. Why is it necessary to post from the cash journal of Rainbow Car Wash to the accounts?
4. How are accounts arranged in the ledger?
5. What are the five divisions in the ledger of Rainbow Car Wash?
6. What meaning does each of the two digits have in account number 54, which is assigned to Rent Expense in the chart of accounts on page 2?
7. Why is the amount in the Cash Debit column on Line 2 of the cash journal not posted as a separate amount to the cash account?

8. What are the four steps in posting an amount in the General Credit column of the cash journal?

9. What are the two advantages of cross-referencing in posting?

10. What are the four steps in posting an amount in the General Debit column of the cash journal?

11. How do you show in the cash journal that the total of each of the two General columns is not posted?

12. When, in addition to a memorandum entry, is a check mark placed in the Post. Ref. column of the cash journal? Why?

13. What are the four steps in posting the total of the Cash Debit column of the cash journal?

14. What are the four steps in posting the total of the Cash Credit column of the cash journal?

15. What are the four steps in posting the total of the Sales Credit column of the cash journal?

Cases for Management Decision

CASE 1 Mr. Packer arranges all of his ledger accounts in alphabetical order. Mr. Gale arranges his ledger accounts as shown in the chart of accounts on page 2. What are the disadvantages of the plan used by Mr. Packer?

CASE 2 When Agnes Ernst, owner of Oceanside Candy Shop, started a new accounting system, she thought it a waste of time to record entries in a journal and then to transfer this same information to another book of record — the ledger. She decided, therefore, to use only a ledger in her accounting system. What useful purposes of a journal is Ms. Ernst ignoring?

CASE 3 Barry Tate has dozens of accounts in his ledger and numerous pages in his journal. While examining one of his ledger accounts, he becomes interested in getting some additional information about one of the transactions. He wants to trace this ledger entry back to the source document from which the journal entry was made and then posted. How can he quickly secure this desired information?

Drills for Mastering Principles

DRILL 7-D 1 Reviewing account numbers

William Gill, a landscape contractor, uses the same two-digit numbering system for the chart of accounts of his business as that used by Rainbow Car Wash illustrated on page 2. Mr. Gill's ledger has seven asset accounts, six liability accounts, one capital account, two revenue accounts, and eight expense accounts.

Location of the account in the ledger	Account Number
1. The second liability account...	22
2. The second revenue account ..	
3. The third liability account	
4. The third asset account	
5. The first expense account.......	
6. The first revenue account.......	
7. The capital account..............	
8. The seventh asset account......	
9. The seventh expense account .	
10. The sixth expense account	
11. The sixth liability account......	
12. The fourth expense account ...	

Instructions: □ **1.** The location of different accounts in the ledger of Mr. Gill is given in the form at the left. If you do not have a workbook, on a sheet of paper prepare a form similar to the one at the left. Write the account number that would be assigned to each of these accounts. Use the Account Number column for your answers. "The second liability account" is given as an example.

□ **2.** Now cover the Account Number column and see how accurately you can recall the correct account numbers.

DRILL 7-D 2 Analyzing the cash journal after posting

Instructions: Turn to page 99 in your textbook showing the cash journal of Rainbow Car Wash for August after posting. Answer the following questions:

1. How many entries for business transactions were recorded in the journal of Rainbow Car Wash during August?
2. How many checks were written in August? How many receipts?
3. Why was a check mark (√) placed in the Post. Ref. column for each entry in the Sales Credit column?
4. How could you find out the exact kind of office equipment that was sold on August 13?
5. How could you find out for what kind of utilities expense the $42.00 was spent on August 18?
6. How many postings were made to Account No. 53? to Account No. 11? to Account No. 41?
7. On what dates were fuel bills paid?
8. Was more cash received than paid out in the month of August? If so, how much more?
9. How many times in August did Rainbow Car Wash make a cash payment?

DRILL 7-D 3 Analyzing the ledger

Instructions: Turn to pages 97 and 98 in your textbook showing the ledger of Rainbow Car Wash after all transactions for August have been posted. Answer the following questions:

1. How much fuel expense did Rainbow Car Wash have in August?
2. From what journal page was the $150.00 credit to Marco Plumbing Company posted on August 1?
3. How much is owed to Auto Wash Equipment Co. on August 31?
4. From what journal page was the $18.00 debit to Advertising Expense posted?
5. Mr. Shaw has asked you, the accounting clerk, why the miscellaneous expense account was debited for $14.00 on August 20. What orderly steps should you take to find the answer to his question?
6. What expense account had the largest total in August?

PROBLEM 7-1 Posting the cash journal of a real estate business

Problem for Applying Concepts

The cash journal completed in Problem 6-2 of Chapter 6 is required for this problem. If Problem 6-2 has not been returned to you or if you are not using the workbook correlating with this textbook, complete Review Problem 7-R 1.

The ledger accounts of Sims Realty as they appeared on October 1 are in your workbook.

Instructions: □ **1.** Turn to the cash journal you completed for Problem 6-2. Post each amount recorded in the General Debit and the General Credit columns. Place a check mark under the General Debit and General Credit columns to indicate that these totals are not to be posted.

□ **2.** Post the totals of the three special columns of your cash journal to the proper accounts in your ledger.

**MASTERY
PROBLEM 7-M** Journalizing and posting the transactions of a motion picture theater

George Rice is the owner and operator of the Majestic Theater. You will need to prepare the ledger before you can do the work in this problem.

Instructions: □ **1.** Open the twelve accounts in the ledger that will be needed for this problem. Place six accounts on each page of your ledger. The Majestic Theater's chart of accounts is given below.

Majestic Theater Chart of Accounts			
(1) Assets	Account Number	**(4) Revenue**	Account Number
Cash.................................	11	Admissions Revenue...........	41
Equipment	12		
		(5) Expenses	
(2) Liabilities		Advertising Expense...........	51
Motion Picture Rental Co.....	21	Film Rental Expense...........	52
Carter's Electrical Service.....	22	Miscellaneous Expense........	53
		Rent Expense....................	54
(3) Capital		Salary Expense..................	55
George Rice, Capital...........	31	Utilities Expense	56

Instructions: □ **2.** Copy the following balances in the proper accounts in your ledger, using July 1 of the current year as the date. Whenever a balance is copied in a ledger account, write the word *Balance* in the Item column and place a check mark in the posting reference column.

	Debit Balance	Credit Balance
Cash..	$ 2,280.00	
Equipment	10,250.00	
Motion Picture Rental Co..		$ 350.00
Carter's Electrical Service		180.00
George Rice, Capital		12,000.00

Instructions: □ **3.** Record the cash balance as a memorandum entry on page 7 of a cash journal similar to the model journal on page 99.

□ **4.** Record the July transactions given on the next page. Number all checks, beginning with Ck111. Number all receipts, beginning with R40.

July 2. Paid cash for rent for July, $400.00.
    3. Paid cash for advertising, $54.85.
    5. Paid cash for projection equipment, $255.00.
    7. Received cash from admissions revenue for the week, $501.50.
   11. Paid cash to Motion Picture Rental Co. on account, $165.00.
   12. Received cash from sale of old equipment, $25.00.
   13. Received cash from admissions revenue for the week, $481.50.
   14. Paid cash for printing admission tickets, $18.50. (Miscellaneous Expense)
   16. Paid cash to Carter's Electrical Service on account, $100.00.
   18. Paid cash for telephone bill, $8.75. (Miscellaneous Expense)
   20. Received cash from admissions revenue for the week, $603.20.
   24. Paid cash for advertising, $47.50.
   27. Received cash from admissions revenue for the week, $588.00.
   30. Paid cash for film rentals, $1,000.00.
   31. Paid cash for salaries, $522.50.
   31. Paid cash for electricity expense, $101.85. (Utilities Expense)
   31. Received cash from admissions revenue, $281.50.

Instructions: ☐ **5.** Foot each amount column with small pencil figures.

☐ **6.** Prove the equality of debits and credits in your cash journal.

☐ **7.** Prove cash. The last check stub showed a bank balance at the end of the month of $2,086.75. All cash receipts have been deposited.

☐ **8.** Total and rule the cash journal.

☐ **9.** Post the individual amounts in the General Debit and General Credit columns to the accounts in the ledger. Place a check mark under the General Debit and General Credit columns to indicate that these totals are not to be posted.

☐ **10.** Post the totals of the three special columns.

**BONUS
PROBLEM 7-B** Journalizing and posting the transactions of a psychiatrist's office

You will need to prepare the ledger of Ann K. Frost, a psychiatrist, before you can do the work in this problem.

Instructions: ☐ **1.** Open the twelve accounts in the ledger that will be needed for this problem. Place four accounts on each page of your ledger. A chart of accounts showing account titles and numbers is given at the top of page 104.

☐ **2.** Copy the following account balances on the appropriate sides of the proper accounts in the ledger. Use August 1 of the current year as the date. Whenever a balance is copied in a ledger account, write the word *Balance* in the Item column and place a check mark in the Post. Ref. column.

Cash, $4,210.00; Automobile, $4,200.00; Office Furniture, $3,360.00; Medical Equipment, $4,500.00; Hanser Furniture, $1,870.00; Medex Supplies, Inc., $3,420.00; Ann K. Frost, Capital, $10,980.00.

Ann K. Frost, M.D.
Chart of Accounts

(1) Assets	Account Number	(4) Revenue	Account Number
Cash.................................	11	Professional Fees................	41
Automobile	12		
Office Furniture..................	13		
Medical Equipment.............	14	**(5) Expenses**	
		Automobile Expense...........	51
(2) Liabilities		Miscellaneous Expense........	52
Hanser Furniture................	21	Rent Expense.....................	53
Medex Supplies, Inc.............	22	Salary Expense..................	54
(3) Capital			
Ann K. Frost, Capital	31		

Instructions: □ **3.** Record the cash balance as a memorandum entry. Use page 10 of a cash journal similar to the one in Bonus Problem 6-B, page 85.

□ **4.** Journalize the transactions for August given below. The revenue column should be entitled *Professional Fees Credit*. Number all checks, beginning with Ck263. The receipt numbers are given after each cash receipt transaction.

Aug. 1. Paid cash for August rent, $450.00.
2. Received cash from professional fees, $135.00. Receipt No. 374.
3. Paid cash for office furniture, $180.00.
4. Paid cash for stationery, $30.50.
9. Received cash from professional fees, $680.00. Receipts No. 375–379.
10. Paid cash to Hanser Furniture in part payment of amount owed, $460.00.
15. Paid cash for salary expense, $200.00.
16. Paid cash for automobile expense, $80.00.
19. Received cash from professional fees, $620.00. Receipts No. 380–386.
20. Received cash from sale of old office furniture, $80.50. Receipt No. 387.
21. Paid cash to Medex Supplies, Inc., in part payment of amount owed, $710.00.
23. Paid cash for postage, $14.60.
24. Received cash from professional fees, $710.00. Receipts No. 388–395.
31. Received cash from professional fees, $616.00. Receipts No. 396–404.
31. Paid cash for salary expense, $230.00.
31. Paid cash for telephone bill, $24.60.
31. Paid cash for automobile expense, $49.80.

Instructions: □ **5.** Foot each amount column with small pencil figures.

□ **6.** Prove the equality of debits and credits in your cash journal.

☐ **7.** Prove cash. The cash balance is $4,622.00. All cash receipts for the month have been deposited.

☐ **8.** Total and rule the cash journal.

☐ **9.** Post the individual amounts in the General Debit and General Credit columns to the accounts in the ledger. Place a check mark under the General Debit and General Credit columns to indicate that these totals are not to be posted.

☐ **10.** Post the totals of the three special columns.

8

Proving the Accuracy of Posting

Accounting records must be accurate. One accounting error can cause other errors. For example, an error in journalizing will result in an error in an account. An error in an account can cause a balance sheet to be out of balance. The same error can cause the profit of a business to be misstated. Such an error might also cause a business to overpay or underpay its federal taxes.

All good accounting clerks are careful to avoid errors. Furthermore, they must know how to check the accuracy of their work to make sure errors have not been made. Two methods of checking the accuracy of accounting records are:

1. Proving the accuracy of the cash account.
2. Proving the accuracy of the ledger.

Finally, the accounting clerk must know how to correct errors when they are found.

PROVING THE ACCURACY OF THE CASH ACCOUNT

Cash, more than any other asset, is subject to loss, theft, or misuse. As a result, control over cash is important to both the owner and the employees of a business. Close control over cash protects this asset of the owner and helps the employee avoid suspicion of being dishonest or careless. One means of controlling cash is to prove frequently that the amount of cash on hand agrees with the balance of the cash account.

Steps in figuring and recording the balance of the cash account

The cash account of Rainbow Car Wash with the balance recorded in small pencil figures is shown at the top of the next page.

ACCOUNT *Cash*					ACCOUNT NO. *11*		
DATE	ITEM	POST. REF.	DEBIT	DATE	ITEM	POST. REF.	CREDIT
1977 Aug. 1	Balance	J1	650 00	1977 Aug. 31		C1	806 00
31		C1	1 846 50				
	1,690.50		2 496 50				

The three steps in figuring and recording the cash balance follow:

☐ **1** Foot the columns. Add the amounts in the Debit column; write the total in small pencil figures immediately under the last amount in that column. The footing is written very small so that the next line can be used for another entry.

Add the amounts in the Credit column and record the footing. Since there is only one entry on the credit side of Rainbow Car Wash's cash account, a pencil footing on the credit side of this account is not necessary.

☐ **2** Figure the account balance. Find the difference between the totals of the Debit and the Credit columns.

Total of debit side of cash account... $2,496.50
Less total of credit side of cash account 806.00
Equals difference between the two sides of the account.............. $1,690.50

The difference between the totals of the amounts posted to the two sides of an account is the account balance. The cash account has a debit balance of $1,690.50.

☐ **3** Record the account balance. Write the account balance in small pencil figures in the Item column of the account on the side with the larger total. Write this amount in line with the small pencil footing of the Debit column.

In the cash account above, the account balance, $1,690.50, is written on the debit side of the account.

Comparing the amount of cash on hand with the balance of the cash account

On August 31, the last check stub of Rainbow Car Wash shows a balance of $1,690.50. Because all cash receipts have been deposited, the check-stub balance shows the actual amount of cash on hand. The balance of the cash account in the ledger is also $1,690.50. When the cash on hand is found to agree with the balance of the cash account, the cash account is said to be proved.

A disagreement between the cash account balance and the amount of cash on hand indicates that one or more errors have been made. Errors may have been made (a) on the check stubs, (b) in posting to the cash account, or (c) in calculating the balance of the cash account. Any errors found should be corrected immediately.

PROVING THE ACCURACY OF THE LEDGER

In double-entry accounting the debit amount must equal the credit amount for each business transaction recorded in a journal. This double-entry system provides various opportunities for checking the accuracy of accounting work.

For example, proving the accuracy of the cash journal of Rainbow Car Wash is described in Chapter 6. The sum of the totals of all debit columns was found to equal the sum of the totals of all credit columns. If no errors are made when posting, the total of the debit amounts in the ledger should equal the total of the credit amounts in the ledger. Furthermore, the total of the debit balances of the accounts in the ledger should equal the total of the credit balances.

The trial balance

The proof of the equality of the debits and the credits in the ledger is called a trial balance. (See the illustration of a trial balance on page 111.)

The trial balance consists of: (1) a heading, (2) a list of ledger account titles, (3) the balance of each account in either a debit or a credit amount column, and (4) the total of each amount column.

When the two totals of a trial balance are equal, it proves that the ledger is in balance. As will be seen in subsequent chapters, the trial balance is a helpful step toward finding the profit or loss of a business.

Footing the accounts and finding their balances

The accounts in the ledger are footed and the account balances are calculated before the trial balance is prepared.

When an account has several entries on each side, both the Debit column and the Credit column are footed. The footing of the smaller side is subtracted from that of the larger side. The difference between the two footings is written in the Item column on the side of the account that has the larger total. This amount is the account balance. Account No. 11, Cash, in the ledger on page 109 shows this method of footing and calculating the account balance.

If the sides of an account are equal, a small –0– is written in the Item column on the balance side of the account. The account title is included on the trial balance and a short dash (–) is inserted in the proper amount column.

When an account has two or more entries on one side only, that side is footed. The balance is not written in the Item column because the footing is the balance. Account No. 12, Operating Supplies, in the ledger below shows this method of recording the balance.

When an account has only one debit entry and one credit entry, footings are not needed in the Debit and the Credit columns. The account balance is written in the Item column on the side that has the larger amount. Account No. 21, Auto Wash Equipment Co., in the ledger on page 110 shows this method.

When an account has only one entry, writing a footing or a balance is not necessary. The one amount in the account serves as the footing and the balance. Such an account is Account No. 22, Marco Plumbing Company, shown in the ledger on page 110.

A complete ledger showing account balances

The complete ledger of Rainbow Car Wash containing the necessary footings and balances for all accounts is below and on pages 110 and 111.

A ledger with the accounts footed

ACCOUNT Cash   ACCOUNT NO. 11

DATE	ITEM	POST. REF.	DEBIT	DATE	ITEM	POST. REF.	CREDIT
1977 Aug. 1	Balance	J1	65000	1977 Aug. 31		C1	80600
31		C1	184650				
	1,690.50		249650				

ACCOUNT Operating Supplies   ACCOUNT NO. 12

DATE	ITEM	POST. REF.	DEBIT	DATE	ITEM	POST. REF.	CREDIT
1977 Aug. 1	Balance	J1	25000				
15		C1	6450				
			31450				

ACCOUNT Car Wash Equipment   ACCOUNT NO. 13

DATE	ITEM	POST. REF.	DEBIT	DATE	ITEM	POST. REF.	CREDIT
1977 Aug. 1	Balance	J1	360000				

ACCOUNT Office Equipment   ACCOUNT NO. 14

DATE	ITEM	POST. REF.	DEBIT	DATE	ITEM	POST. REF.	CREDIT
1977 Aug. 1	Balance 472.00	J1	50000	1977 Aug. 1		C1	1000
				13		C1	1800
							2800

ACCOUNT *Auto Wash Equipment Co.*   ACCOUNT NO. *21*

DATE	ITEM	POST. REF.	DEBIT	DATE	ITEM	POST. REF.	CREDIT
1977 Aug. 1		C1	20000	1977 Aug. 1	Balance 650.00	J1	85000

ACCOUNT *Marco Plumbing Company*   ACCOUNT NO. *22*

DATE	ITEM	POST. REF.	DEBIT	DATE	ITEM	POST. REF.	CREDIT
				1977 Aug. 1	Balance	J1	15000

ACCOUNT *Harry Shaw, Capital*   ACCOUNT NO. *31*

DATE	ITEM	POST. REF.	DEBIT	DATE	ITEM	POST. REF.	CREDIT
				1977 Aug. 1	Balance	J1	400000
				1		C1	50000 450000

ACCOUNT *Sales*   ACCOUNT NO. *41*

DATE	ITEM	POST. REF.	DEBIT	DATE	ITEM	POST. REF.	CREDIT
				1977 Aug. 31		C1	131850

ACCOUNT *Advertising Expense*   ACCOUNT NO. *51*

DATE	ITEM	POST. REF.	DEBIT	DATE	ITEM	POST. REF.	CREDIT
1977 Aug. 5		C1	1800				

ACCOUNT *Fuel Expense*   ACCOUNT NO. *52*

DATE	ITEM	POST. REF.	DEBIT	DATE	ITEM	POST. REF.	CREDIT
1977 Aug. 4		C1	4200				
25		C1	3150 7350				

ACCOUNT *Miscellaneous Expense*   ACCOUNT NO. *53*

DATE	ITEM	POST. REF.	DEBIT	DATE	ITEM	POST. REF.	CREDIT
1977 Aug. 6		C1	300				
20		C1	1400				
27		C1	250				
30		C1	1200 3150				

A ledger with the accounts footed (continued)

A ledger with the accounts footed (concluded)

ACCOUNT	Rent Expense							ACCOUNT NO. 54	
DATE	ITEM	POST. REF.	DEBIT	DATE	ITEM	POST. REF.	CREDIT	
1977 Aug. 2		C1	35000					

ACCOUNT	Utilities Expense							ACCOUNT NO. 55	
DATE	ITEM	POST. REF.	DEBIT	DATE	ITEM	POST. REF.	CREDIT	
1977 Aug. 12		C1	2650					
18		C1	4200 6850					

Steps in preparing a trial balance

The five steps in preparing a trial balance are explained and illustrated below and on page 112. As you study these steps, check each one with the illustration of the trial balance of Rainbow Cash Wash.

Trial balance

1

2

Rainbow Car Wash
Trial Balance
August 31, 1977

ACCOUNT TITLE	ACCT. NO.	DEBIT	CREDIT
Cash	11	169050	
Operating Supplies	12	31450	
Car Wash Equipment	13	360000	
Office Equipment	14	47200	
Auto Wash Equipment Co.	21		65000
Marco Plumbing Company	22		15000
Harry Shaw, Capital	31		450000
Sales	41		131850
Advertising Expense	51	1800	
Fuel Expense	52	7350	
Miscellaneous Expense	53	3150	
Rent Expense	54	35000	
Utilities Expense	55	6850	
		661850	661850

3
4
5

☐ 1 Write the trial balance heading at the top of a sheet of paper that has two amount columns. The heading consists of three lines: (1) the name of the business, (2) the words *Trial Balance*, and (3) the date. The date is the month, the day, and the year for which the trial balance is prepared. Center each line of the heading.

☐ 2 Enter on the trial balance each account in the ledger and its balance. In each case record the account title, the account number, and the balance. Enter debit balances in the left-hand or debit column. Enter credit balances in the right-hand or credit column.

☐ 3 Rule a single line across both amount columns of the trial balance under the last amount listed.

☐ 4 Add each amount column and compare the totals. If the two totals are the same, write the totals on the first line below the single ruling. (If the totals are not the same, the error or errors must be found and corrected.)

☐ 5 Rule a double line under the totals across the amount columns. Note how the totals have been entered and the trial balance has been ruled in the illustration.

> A double ruling indicates that the work has been completed. The double line is not drawn until the trial balance is in balance.

FINDING AND CORRECTING ERRORS

A trial balance that is in balance does not *always* prove the complete accuracy of the accounting records.

Errors not disclosed by a trial balance

The following are two common kinds of errors in journalizing and posting which are not detected by a trial balance:

1. If the journalizing of a transaction is omitted, the ledger will still be in balance, but the error will not be indicated by the trial balance. If, however, the omitted transaction affects cash, the error will be found when cash is proved. Until the error is corrected, the balance of the cash account will not agree with the cash on hand.

2. If an amount is posted to the correct side, but to the wrong account, the trial balance will still be in balance. For example, if the $42.00 debited to the fuel expense account on August 4 had been posted by mistake to the debit side of the advertising expense account, the trial balance would still be in balance. If an error of this kind is not found at the time the trial balance is prepared, the error should be discovered when the financial reports are prepared.

Common errors that cause a trial balance not to balance

Some typical errors that cause a trial balance to be out of balance include the following:

1. Errors in the addition of the trial balance columns.
2. Listing an account balance in the wrong column of the trial balance.
3. Mistakes in arithmetic when figuring account balances.
4. Copying an amount incorrectly when journalizing, posting, or preparing the trial balance.
5. Posting only one amount of a journal entry.

Steps for locating errors when a trial balance does not balance

When a trial balance fails to balance, a systematic procedure for locating the error or errors should be followed. The recommended steps are:

☐ **1** Re-add the trial balance columns to prove the accuracy of the addition of these columns.

☐ **2** Find the difference between the totals of the trial balance columns. Look in the ledger to see if the amount of the difference is an account balance that was omitted from the trial balance.

☐ **3** Divide the amount of the difference between the two totals of the trial balance by 2. Look through the accounts to see if this amount has been recorded on the wrong side of an account. Also, check to see if this amount has been written in the wrong column of the trial balance. For example, if the difference between the two columns of the trial balance is $80.00, look for $40.00 on the wrong side of an account or in the wrong column of the trial balance.

☐ **4** Divide the amount of the difference between the two totals of the trial balance by 9. If this difference is evenly divisible by 9, look for an amount in the trial balance in which the digits have been transposed in copying the balance from the ledger. Also, look through the accounts for an amount in which the digits have been transposed in posting from the journal. For example, if the trial balance is out of balance $27.00, this amount is evenly divisible by 9, with a quotient of 3.00. The amount of the quotient indicates that there is a difference of 3 between the two digits that have been transposed. Look, therefore, for amounts containing at least four digits with the transposition between the third and the fourth digits from the right, such as $14.55 written as $41.55, or $25.40 written as $52.40, or $136.84 written as $163.84.

The amount of a difference that is evenly divisible by 9 may indicate that the decimal point has been incorrectly moved one or more spaces to the right or the left. An example of such an error, known as a slide, would be writing $12.00 as $1.20 or $120.00.

□ **5** Compare the balances on the trial balance with the balances in the ledger accounts. An error may have been made in copying an account balance on the trial balance.

□ **6** Verify the pencil footings and the account balances in the ledger. An error may have been made in footing an account or in calculating the balance.

□ **7** Verify the posting of each item in the journal. As each posting is verified, place a small check mark ($\checkmark$) on the double vertical line at the left of the corresponding amount in both the journal and the ledger. An item may have been posted twice, not posted at all, entered on the wrong side of an account, or copied incorrectly. Examine first the journal and then the ledger to find items not checked or items that have been checked twice.

When the preceding seven steps are followed, all of the work has been retraced and the error or errors should have been found. In most instances, errors are usually located before reaching Step 5.

Preferred ways of correcting errors

Errors in accounting records should be avoided by careful and attentive work. When an error is made, it should be corrected so that both the error and the correction are obvious. For example, if an error is made in an amount, the amount is canceled by drawing a line through the incorrect figure. The correct amount is then written immediately above the canceled amount. When an error is corrected in this manner, the accounting clerk is indicating that a mistake was found and corrected. Concealed errors, on the other hand, suggest possible dishonesty and can create suspicion.

Correcting errors in the trial balance

If an account balance has been omitted from the trial balance, the amount should be inserted in its proper position. If an account balance has been placed in the wrong column of the trial balance, the amount should be canceled with a line and written in the correct column. A similar correction should be made for a balance copied incorrectly. The trial balance totals should also be corrected.

Correcting errors in the ledger

If an item has been posted to the wrong side of an account, a line should be drawn through the incorrect posting. The item should then be posted correctly, as shown on the next page.

ACCOUNT *Office Machines*							ACCOUNT NO. *15*
DATE	ITEM	POST. REF.	DEBIT	DATE	ITEM	POST. REF.	CREDIT
1977 *Jan.* 1	*Balance*	*J1*	2254 40	*1977* *Jan.* 11		*C1*	215 00
13		*C1*	476 00	~~13~~		~~C1~~	~~476 00~~

Correction of the
posting to the wrong
side of an account

If an incorrect amount has been posted to the right account, a line should be drawn through the incorrect amount. The correct amount should then be written above it, as shown below.

ACCOUNT *Plaza Market*							ACCOUNT NO. *24*
DATE	ITEM	POST. REF.	DEBIT	DATE	ITEM	POST. REF.	CREDIT
1977 *Jan.* 4		*C1*	*125 00* ~~125 0~~	*1977* *Jan.* 1	*Balance*	*J1*	391 00

Correction of the
posting of an incor-
rect amount

If an item has been posted to the wrong account, a line should be drawn through the incorrect posting and the item should be posted correctly. If the posting of an item has been omitted, the amount should be posted at once. If an item has been posted twice, a line should be drawn through the second posting in the account.

An error in a pencil footing in the ledger should be erased and replaced by the correct pencil footing.

✦ What is the meaning of the following?

- trial balance

**Using
Business
Terms**

**Questions
for
Individual
Study**

1. What two methods of checking the accuracy of accounting records were presented in this chapter?
2. What are the steps used in figuring and recording the balance of the cash account?
3. Where is the pencil footing of each side of an account written?
4. Why should the pencil footings of an account in the ledger be written very small?
5. When can it be said that the cash account is proved?
6. What is the purpose of a trial balance?
7. Name two uses of a trial balance.

8. What are the three parts of the heading of a trial balance?
9. What are the steps in preparing a trial balance?
10. What kind of errors in journalizing and posting are not detected by a trial balance even though it is in balance?
11. What are some common errors that cause a trial balance not to balance?

12. What, in general, is the preferred way of correcting an accounting error?
13. How is the posting of an amount to the wrong side of a ledger account corrected?
14. How is the posting of an incorrect amount to the right ledger account corrected?

Cases for Management Decision

CASE 1 After all posting to the cash account has been completed, the balance of D. R. Emery's cash account does not agree with the amount of cash on hand. What steps should he take to find the error?

CASE 2 Which of the following errors would not be indicated by the trial balance? Explain your answers.

(a) In posting the August cash journal of Rainbow Car Wash, the debit of $200.00 to Auto Wash Equipment Co. was posted to the debit side of the Marco Plumbing account.

(b) On August 6 the debit of $3.00 to Miscellaneous Expense was posted to the credit side of that account.
(c) The office equipment account balance of $472.00 was not listed on the trial balance.
(d) The debit balance of $18.00 in the advertising expense account was written in the credit column of the trial balance.

CASE 3 Explain the method of correcting each of the errors listed in Case 2.

Drills for Mastering Principles

DRILL 8-D 1 Analyzing the ledger

Instructions: Turn to pages 109, 110, and 111 in your textbook. The illustrations show the ledger of Rainbow Car Wash after all of the transactions for August have been posted and the accounts have been footed. Refer to these ledger accounts as you answer the following questions:

1. Which asset accounts have a larger balance at the end of the month than at the beginning of the month?

2. Did Rainbow Car Wash owe more money or less money on August 31 than on August 1? How much more or how much less?

3. Why does the sales account show only one entry for the month when it is true that Rainbow Car Wash received revenue from many customers during August?

DRILL 8-D 2 Classifying accounts and entering their balances on a trial balance

The ledger accounts of Nelson Corey, commercial photographer, are listed at the top of the next page. These accounts are arranged alphabetically, and the end-of-month balance is shown for each account.

1. Advertising Expense, $60.00
2. Automobile, $3,400.00
3. Automobile Expense, $23.00
4. Brighton Garage (creditor), $80.00
5. Cash, $4,502.00
6. Nelson Corey, Capital, $10,602.00
7. Drake Company (creditor), $63.00
8. Fees Revenue, $970.00
9. Miscellaneous Expense, $17.25
10. Photography Equipment, $4,410.00
11. Photography Supplies, $98.25
12. Parker Company (creditor), $1,140.00
13. Rent Expense, $320.00
14. Utilities Expense, $24.50

Instructions: □ **1.** Rule a form like the one shown below:

1	2	3	4
		Trial Balance	
Account Title	Classifi-cation	Debit	Credit
1. *Advertising Expense*	E	60.00	

Instructions: □ **2.** Copy in the Account Title column (column No. 1) the ledger account titles in the order given above.

□ **3.** Classify each account on your list as an asset, a liability, a capital, a revenue, or an expense account. Indicate the classification by writing in the Classification column (column No. 2) A for asset; L for liability; C for capital; R for revenue; and E for expense.

□ **4.** Record the balance for each account in the appropriate Debit or Credit column (columns No. 3 or No. 4). All accounts have normal balances. The first account is given as an example.

□ **5.** Prove the accuracy of your work by adding columns No. 3 and No. 4. Compare the totals. If the totals are the same, double rule the amount columns.

□ **6.** Now cover your answers and see how rapidly you can classify each account and tell whether it has a debit or a credit balance. Repeat this oral drill several times for increased speed and accuracy.

PROBLEM 8-1 Taking a trial balance

If you are not using the workbook correlating with this textbook, complete Review Problem 8-R 1 instead of this problem.

The ledger accounts of Garrison Travel Bureau are in your workbook.

Instructions: □ **1.** Foot the ledger accounts. Write the footings in very small figures with a sharp pencil and place each footing close to the last item. If an account has entries on both sides, write the balance in small pencil figures in the Item column of the larger side.

Problems
for
Applying
Concepts

□ **2.** Prove the cash account. The bank balance according to the checkbook on October 31 is $2,199.37. All cash receipts have been deposited. The bank balance should agree with the balance of the cash account in the ledger.

□ **3.** Prepare a trial balance dated October 31 of the current year. If the two totals of the trial balance are equal, rule double lines as shown on page 111.

Self-checking: Compare your ledger with the illustrations on pages 109, 110, and 111 and ask yourself the following questions:

1. Are the pencil footings written in small figures with a sharp, firm pencil?
2. Is each amount column of an account footed when, and only when, it contains two or more entries?
3. For each account having one or more entries on both the debit and the credit sides, is the balance of the account written in small pencil figures in the Item column of the larger side?

PROBLEM 8-2 Finding and correcting errors indicated by a trial balance

If you are not using the workbook correlating with this textbook, complete Review Problem 8-R 2 instead of this problem.

The journal and the ledger of Harry Gordon, owner of a tax service, for November of the current year, are given in the workbook.

Instructions: □ **1.** Foot the ledger accounts. Write the footings in very small figures with a sharp pencil and place each footing close to the last item. If an account has entries on both sides, write the balance in small pencil figures in the Item column of the larger side.

□ **2.** Prove the cash account. The bank balance according to the checkbook on November 30 is $1,092.37. All cash receipts have been deposited.

□ **3.** Prepare a trial balance dated November 30 of the current year. In the heading, use the business name, Gordon's Tax Service. If the totals of the trial balance are not equal, proceed as you were directed in Steps 1–7, pages 113 and 114, to find the error or errors. Correct any errors in the journal or the ledger, using the methods explained and illustrated on pages 114 and 115. Then complete the trial balance.

Journalizing, Posting, and Taking a Trial Balance

This project makes use of all the steps in the accounting process that have been developed in the preceding eight chapters. These steps are:

1. Opening accounts in the ledger.
2. Recording the opening entry.
3. Posting the opening entry.
4. Journalizing business transactions.
5. Footing, proving, and ruling the cash journal.
6. Posting to ledger accounts.
7. Preparing a trial balance.

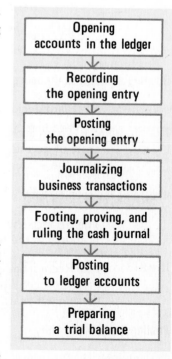

| Opening accounts in the ledger |
| Recording the opening entry |
| Posting the opening entry |
| Journalizing business transactions |
| Footing, proving, and ruling the cash journal |
| Posting to ledger accounts |
| Preparing a trial balance |

MOUNTAIN VIEW MOTEL

Philip Plant operates a small motel called Mountain View Motel. He pays a monthly rent for its use and receives revenue from the rental of its rooms to customers. The chart of accounts is shown on page 120.

Use made of revenue account

All cash received from room rentals is credited to the revenue account, Room Sales.

119

Use made of expense accounts

The expense accounts that are to be debited for the expense transactions of Mountain View Motel are:

Advertising Expense ..... for all advertising.

Laundry Expense.......... for the cost of having bed linens and towels laundered.

Miscellaneous Expense .. for expenses such as postage, stationery, and any expense item not covered by other expense accounts.

Rent Expense .... for rent of the motel.

Utilities Expense .... for water, electricity, and telephone service.

MOUNTAIN VIEW MOTEL
Chart of Accounts

(1) Assets	Account Number	(4) Revenue	Account Number
Cash...	11	Room Sales..............................	41
Housekeeping Supplies..............	12		
Furniture and Fixtures.................	13	**(5) Expenses**	
Office Equipment	14		
		Advertising Expense...................	51
(2) Liabilities		Laundry Expense.......................	52
		Miscellaneous Expense	53
Ryan Plumbing Company	21	Rent Expense...........................	54
Motel Equipment Company	22	Utilities Expense	55
(3) Capital			
Philip Plant, Capital...................	31		

Opening accounts in the ledger

Mr. Plant decides to open a new set of books for Mountain View Motel.

Instructions: 1. Open accounts in the new ledger in the order in which they are listed in the chart of accounts above. Allow four lines for each account. Number the accounts with the account numbers given in the chart of accounts.

Recording the opening entry

The balance sheet of Mountain View Motel as of the close of business on January 31 is shown at the top of the next page.

Instructions: 2. Record the opening entry on page 1 of a two-column general journal. Use the balance sheet illustrated on the opposite page. Date the opening entry February 1 of the current year.

Posting the opening entry

Instructions: 3. Post the opening entry. Remember to indicate in the Item column of the ledger accounts that each of these amounts is a "Balance."

```
                        MOUNTAIN VIEW MOTEL
                           Balance Sheet
                          January 31, 19—
```

Assets			Liabilities		
Cash......................................	865	00	Ryan Plumbing Company..........	350	00
Housekeeping Supplies.............	650	00	Motel Equipment Company	1 300	00
Furniture and Fixtures...............	5 950	00	Total Liabilities........................	1 650	00
Office Equipment	685	00	**Capital**		
			Philip Plant, Capital.................	6 500	00
Total Assets............................	8 150	00	Total Liab. and Capital.............	8 150	00

Instructions: 4. Record the cash balance as of February 1 of the current year as a memorandum entry on page 1 of a cash journal. Use a cash journal similar to the one illustrated on page 99. In this cash journal, use the column heading *Room Sales Credit* instead of *Sales Credit*.

Journalizing business transactions

Instructions: 5. Record the following transactions in the cash journal. All cash payments are made by check. Begin numbering checks with Ck21. Mr. Plant each day totals his copies of cash receipts for room sales. The one total amount is used to record the revenue from room sales for the day. Receipt numbers are given for all revenue transactions.

February
1. Paid February rent, $400.00.
1. Received cash from room sales, $137.00. Issued Receipts No. 1–8.
2. Sold old TV set, $20.00. Issued Receipt No. 9.
2. Paid cash in part payment of amount owed to Motel Equipment Company, $300.00.
3. Received cash from room sales, $78.00. Issued Receipts No. 10–15.
3. Paid for newspaper advertising, $30.00.
4. Received cash from room sales, $155.00. Issued Receipts No. 16–24.
5. Bought additional furniture for motel rooms, $125.00.
7. Bought postage stamps, $10.00.
8. Received cash from room sales, $73.00. Issued Receipts No. 25–29.
8. Paid laundry bill, $44.50.
9. Received cash from room sales, $47.00. Issued Receipts No. 30–32.
10. Bought motel registration cards and receipts, $9.50.
11. Paid for advertising signs, $73.00.
12. Received cash from room sales, $170.00. Issued Receipts No. 33–42.
14. Bought housekeeping supplies, $21.00.
15. Received cash from Mr. Plant, the proprietor, as an additional investment in the business, $800.00. Issued Receipt No. 43.
16. Received cash from room sales, $134.00. Issued Receipts No. 44–51.
17. Paid telephone bill, $48.50.
18. Received cash from room sales, $78.00. Issued Receipts No. 52–56.

February	**19.**	Received cash from room sales, $34.00. Issued Receipts No. 57–58.
	21.	Paid electric bill, $38.40.
	22.	Received cash from room sales, $121.00. Issued Receipts No. 59–65.
	23.	Bought stationery, $16.00.
	24.	Paid Ryan Plumbing Company in full for amount owed, $350.00.
	25.	Received cash from room sales, $30.00. Issued Receipts No. 66–67.
	26.	Bought postage stamps, $15.00.
	28.	Received cash from room sales, $62.00. Issued Receipts No. 68–71.
	28.	Paid laundry bill, $42.50.

Footing, proving, and ruling the cash journal

Instructions: **6.** Foot all columns of the cash journal.

7. Prove the equality of debits and credits in the cash journal. Find the sum of all the debit totals and the sum of all the credit totals. The sum of the totals of the two debit columns must equal the sum of the totals of the three credit columns.

8. Prove cash. The bank balance according to the checkbook is $1,280.60. All cash receipts have been deposited.

9. Total and rule the cash journal. Refer to the illustration on page 77.

Posting to ledger accounts

Instructions: **10.** Post each amount in the General Debit column and in the General Credit column. Place a check mark in parentheses under the total of the General Debit column and the General Credit column. These check marks show that the totals of these columns are not to be posted. Refer to the illustration on page 99.

11. Post the total of each of the three special columns of the cash journal: Cash Debit, Cash Credit, and Room Sales Credit. Write the proper account number in parentheses under each total after the posting is completed. Refer to the illustration on page 99.

Preparing the trial balance

Instructions: **12.** Foot the accounts in the ledger that have more than one entry on either side of the account. If an account has entries on both sides of the account, write the balance in small pencil figures in the Item column on the side that has the larger total. Use as your guide the illustrations on pages 109, 110, and 111.

13. Prepare a trial balance. Refer to the illustration on page 111.

The Six-Column Work Sheet

9

The owner of a business needs to know whether the business transactions have resulted in a profit or a loss. Knowing how well the business is doing helps the owner make good decisions about future operations.

The information needed to find the profit or the loss of a business is contained in the ledger accounts. This information, however, needs to be summarized and analyzed. Although a trial balance summarizes the information in the ledger accounts, the summary does not show the amount of profit or loss.

ANALYZING THE ACCOUNTS IN THE TRIAL BALANCE

Certain accounts in the trial balance must be analyzed before the profit or the loss of a business can be determined. The use of the six-column work sheet is presented in this chapter as a step toward (a) finding the profit or the loss of a business and (b) preparing up-to-date financial statements.

Analysis paper and the work sheet

Accounting paper with a number of amount columns that can be used to sort and analyze information is called analysis paper. The amount columns are used to classify and summarize amounts in the trial balance. The number of amount columns used depends on the kind and size of business.

Analysis paper on which the financial condition of a business is summarized is called a work sheet. The work sheet is used (a) to summarize the financial condition of a business and (b) to assist in the preparation of financial reports. The preparation of financial reports is described in Chapter 10. The work sheet is not a part of the permanent records of the business and may be prepared in pencil.

The fiscal period

A business analyzes its financial condition and prepares financial statements at regular intervals. The length of time for which an analysis of business operations is made is called a fiscal period. A fiscal period is also known as an accounting period. Fiscal periods may consist of a month, a quarter of a year, a half year, or a year. An accounting period of twelve consecutive months is called a fiscal year. The fiscal year does not always begin in the same month as the calendar year. However, many businesses do use the calendar year as their fiscal period.

THE WORK SHEET

The Rainbow Car Wash uses a six-column work sheet on which to analyze and summarize its financial position at the end of each month. The work sheet of Rainbow Car Wash for the month ended August 31, 1977, is shown on page 125.

Analyzing the six-column work sheet

The three-line heading on the work sheet shows the name of the business, the name of the form, and the fiscal period for which the analysis is made.

The Account Title column contains a list of the ledger accounts. The Acct. No. column lists the account numbers. The six amount columns on this work sheet are composed of pairs of Debit and Credit columns under the major headings of *Trial Balance, Income Statement,* and *Balance Sheet.*

The Trial Balance columns are used to sort the general ledger account balances in the proper Trial Balance Debit or Credit column. The trial balance of Rainbow Car Wash in the illustration is the same trial balance that was developed in Chapter 8, page 111.

The trial balance is generally recorded directly on the work sheet. A trial balance may be taken at other times, however, to prove the accuracy of the ledger. At such times the trial balance may be recorded on two-column accounting paper instead of on a six-column work sheet. At other times the debits and then the credits may be totaled on an adding machine and the totals compared for accuracy.

The Income Statement columns of a work sheet are used to list all the expenses and all revenue. The balance of each expense account is listed in the Income Statement Debit column. The balance of each revenue

Rainbow Car Wash
Work Sheet
For Month Ended August 31, 1977

ACCOUNT TITLE	ACCT. NO.	TRIAL BALANCE DEBIT	TRIAL BALANCE CREDIT	INCOME STATEMENT DEBIT	INCOME STATEMENT CREDIT	BALANCE SHEET DEBIT	BALANCE SHEET CREDIT	
Cash	11	169050				169050		1
Operating Supplies	12	31450				31450		2
Car Wash Equipment	13	360000				360000		3
Office Equipment	14	47200				47200		4
Auto Wash Equipment Co.	21		65000				65000	5
Marco Plumbing Company	22		15000				15000	6
Harry Shaw, Capital	31		450000				450000	7
Sales	41		131850		131850			8
Advertising Expense	51	1800		1800				9
Fuel Expense	52	7350		7350				10
Miscellaneous Expense	53	3150		3150				11
Rent Expense	54	35000		35000				12
Utilities Expense	55	6850		6850				13
		661850	661850	54150	131850	607700	530000	14
Net Income				77700			77700	15
				131850	131850	607700	607700	16

Six-column work sheet

account is listed in the Income Statement Credit column. The difference between the totals of these two columns shows whether the business is operating at a profit or a loss. When the total revenue is larger than the total expenses, the difference is called net income. When the total expenses are larger than the total revenue, the difference is called net loss. Thus the Income Statement columns of the work sheet are used for finding the amount of net income or net loss for the fiscal period.

The Balance Sheet columns are used to list the up-to-date balances of accounts that will be reported on the balance sheet. The balance of each asset account is listed in the Balance Sheet Debit column. The balance of each liability account and the balance of the capital account are listed in the Balance Sheet Credit column.

Steps in preparing the six-column work sheet

The nine steps that are followed in preparing the six-column work sheet are discussed on the following pages. As you study these nine steps, check each one with the illustration of the work sheet of Rainbow Car Wash shown above.

☐ 1   Write the heading on three lines; center each item in the heading. The date indicates the length and the closing date of the fiscal period for which the analysis is made, *For Month Ended August 31, 1977.*

☐ 2   Write the column headings (if they are not preprinted on the work sheet). Reading from left to right these column headings are: Account Title, Acct. No., Trial Balance Debit and Credit, Income Statement Debit and Credit, and Balance Sheet Debit and Credit.

☐ 3   Record the trial balance. For each account in the general ledger list the account title in the Account Title column, the account number in the Acct. No. column, and the account balance in the appropriate Trial Balance Debit or Credit column. Rule a single line across both Trial Balance columns under the last amount listed. Add the Trial Balance columns. If the totals of the debit and the credit columns are equal, draw double lines below the totals in Columns 1 and 2. If the totals are not equal, find the errors and correct them before completing the work sheet.

☐ 4   Extend the balance sheet items into the Balance Sheet columns as follows:

    ■ Extend the balance of each asset account from the Trial Balance Debit column (Column 1) into the Balance Sheet Debit column (Column 5).

    ■ Extend the balance of each liability account and the balance of the capital account from the Trial Balance Credit column (Column 2) into the Balance Sheet Credit column (Column 6).

		1	2	3	4	5	6
ACCOUNT TITLE	ACCT. NO.	TRIAL BALANCE		INCOME STATEMENT		BALANCE SHEET	
		DEBIT	CREDIT	DEBIT	CREDIT	DEBIT	CREDIT
ASSETS		XXXX				XXXX	
		XXXX				XXXX	
		XXXX				XXXX	
LIABILITIES			XXXX				XXXX
			XXXX				XXXX
			XXXX				XXXX
CAPITAL			XXXX				XXXX

☐ 5   Extend the revenue and expense items into the Income Statement columns, as follows:

    ■ Extend the balance of each revenue account from the Trial Balance Credit column (Column 2) into the Income Statement Credit column (Column 4).

ACCOUNT TITLE	ACCT NO.	TRIAL BALANCE		INCOME STATEMENT		BALANCE SHEET	
		1	2	3	4	5	6
		DEBIT	CREDIT	DEBIT	CREDIT	DEBIT	CREDIT
REVENUE					XXXX ──────→XXXX		
EXPENSES		XXXX ────→XXXX					
		XXXX ────→XXXX					
		XXXX ────→XXXX					
		XXXX ────→XXXX					
		XXXX ────→XXXX					

- Extend the balance of each expense account from the Trial Balance Debit column (Column 1) into the Income Statement Debit column (Column 3).

☐ 6 Total the Income Statement columns and the Balance Sheet columns as follows:

- Rule a single line across the Income Statement columns and the Balance Sheet columns to indicate addition.

- Add each column and write the totals on the same line as the Trial Balance totals.

☐ 7 Figure and record the net income (or the net loss) as follows:

- Subtract the smaller total in the Income Statement columns from the larger total as follows:

Total of Income Statement Credit column (revenue)............... $1,318.50
Total of Income Statement Debit column (expenses) 541.50
Net Income (revenue minus expenses) .... $ 777.00

   When the total of the Income Statement Debit column is larger, subtract the total of the credit column from the total of the debit column to find the net loss.

- Write the amount of the net income, *$777.00*, immediately below the smaller of the two totals in the Income Statement columns.

- Write the words *Net Income* in the Account Title column on the same line as the amount of the net income.

- Rule a single line across the Income Statement columns and add these columns. Write the proving totals on the next line.

   When these two proving totals of the Income Statement columns are equal, the amount of the net income (or the net loss) is assumed to be correct.

☐ **8** Extend the net income into the Balance Sheet Credit column (Column 6) as follows:

■ Extend the amount of the net income, *$777.00*, into the Balance Sheet Credit column. This amount shows the increase in capital as a result of the net income earned by the business during the month of August.

> If there is a net loss for the month, the capital is decreased. The amount of a net loss is therefore extended into the Balance Sheet Debit column.

■ Rule a single line across the Balance Sheet columns and add these columns.

> When these two proving totals of the Balance Sheet columns are equal, the amount of the net income (or the net loss) is assumed to be correct. If the two proving totals of the Balance Sheet columns are not equal, the error must be found and corrected.

☐ **9** Rule double lines below the final totals of the Income Statement columns and the Balance Sheet columns. The double lines show that all work has been completed and is assumed to be correct.

Using Business Terms

✦ What is the meaning of each of the following?

- analysis paper
- work sheet
- fiscal period
- fiscal year
- net income
- net loss

Questions for Individual Study

1. Where is the information needed to find the profit or the loss of a business located?
2. What two uses are made of a trial balance in this chapter?
3. Why may a work sheet be prepared in pencil?
4. What are some intervals of time generally chosen by businesses as fiscal periods?
5. What are the three items in the heading of the work sheet?
6. Aside from the heading, what are the three major sections of the six-column work sheet?
7. To what columns in the six-column work sheet are the debit amounts in the trial balance extended?
8. To what columns in the six-column work sheet are the credit amounts in the trial balance extended?

9. When the total of the Income Statement Credit column is larger than the total of the Income Statement Debit column, what is the amount of the difference called?
10. When the total of the Income Statement Debit column is larger than the total of the Income Statement Credit column, what is the amount of the difference called?
11. Why is the amount of the net income that is obtained from the Income Statement columns of the work sheet extended to the Balance Sheet Credit column?
12. Why is the amount of the net loss that is obtained from the Income Statement columns of the work sheet extended to the Balance Sheet Debit column?

CASE 1 When extending the amounts in the Trial Balance columns of a work sheet, the accounting clerk made the error of extending the amount of Advertising Expense to the Balance Sheet Debit column.

(a) What effect will this error have in calculating the net income on the work sheet? (b) When would such an error most likely be discovered?

CASE 2 The beginning balance sheet of Rainbow Car Wash for August 1, 1977, shown on page 7, lists the balance of Operating Supplies as $250.00 and the balance of Office Equipment as $500.00. However, the Balance Sheet Debit column of the work sheet at the end of August, illustrated on page 125, shows that these account balances are different from those on the beginning balance sheet. What kinds of transactions could have caused the differences in these account balances?

CASE 3 After comparing some of the amounts on the August 31 work sheet, shown on page 125, with some of the amounts on the August 1 balance sheet, on page 18, one student was puzzled over the amounts shown at the right.

The student did not understand why. the cash account during a fiscal period did not increase by the same amount as the net income for the period.

August 31 balance in Cash	$1,690.50
Less August 1 balance in Cash	650.00
Resulted in a net increase in the	
cash account	$1,040.50
Yet net income for the month was .	$ 777.00

Give some illustrations of transactions during August which increased or decreased the cash account but did not affect the net income for the period.

DRILL 9-D 1 Sorting account balances on the work sheet

The following is an alphabetically arranged list of accounts of the Central Travel Agency.

Advertising Expense
Bradley Shipping Company (creditor)
Cash
Commissions Revenue
Entertainment Expense
Miscellaneous Expense

Office Furniture
Office Machines
Rent Expense
Roy Travis, Capital
Wages Expense
Western Air Lines (creditor)

Instructions: □ **1.** If you do not have a workbook, prepare a form similar to the one shown below. In the Account Title column, copy the account titles given above.

□ **2.** Determine whether the balance of each of these accounts would be extended to the Income Statement columns or to the Balance Sheet columns. Then, after each

	3	4	5	6
	Income Statement		Balance Sheet	
Account Title	Debit	Credit	Debit	Credit
1. *Advertising Expense*	✓			

account title, place a check mark in the appropriate debit or credit column of either the Income Statement columns or the Balance Sheet columns of the work sheet. The first item is given as an example.

Problem
for
Applying
Concepts

PROBLEM 9-1 Work sheet for a real estate agency

The account balances in the ledger of the Tanner Real Estate Agency on May 31 of the current year, the end of a fiscal period of one month, are as follows:

Cash 11	Hall & Taylor 21	Automobile Expense 51
3,328.00	75.00	192.50

Office Supplies 12	Hughs Company 22	Entertainment Expense 52
136.00	63.00	43.00

Automobile 13	Valley Printers 23	Miscellaneous Expense 53
4,200.00	215.50	29.50

Office Furniture 14	Alice Tanner, Capital 31	Rent Expense 54
960.00	7,499.00	300.00

Office Machines 15	Commissions Revenue 41	Utilities Expense 55
726.00	2,140.50	78.00

Instructions: Prepare a six-column work sheet for the Tanner Real Estate Agency for the month ended May 31 of the current year. Write the proper heading at the top of each column of the analysis paper. Use the account titles, numbers, and balances given in the T accounts. Use as your model the work sheet on page 125.

Self-checking: Compare your completed work sheet with the work sheet on page 125. Check the accuracy of your work by asking yourself these questions.

1. Did you rule a single line across all six amount columns on the line immediately above the trial balance totals?
2. Do the two totals of your trial balance agree?
3. Did you rule a double line under both trial balance totals across two amount columns only?
4. Did you write a total for each of the two Income Statement columns and for each of the two Balance Sheet columns? Did you place all four of these totals on the same line?
5. Did you write the words *Net Income* in the account title column? Did you write the amount of the net income in the Income Statement Debit column and also in the Balance Sheet Credit column?
6. Did you rule a single line across the last four amount columns immediately under the amount of the net income?
7. Do the two proving totals of the Income Statement columns agree?
8. Do the two proving totals of the Balance Sheet columns agree?
9. Are the proving totals of the last four amount columns on the same line?
10. Did you rule a double line across the last four amount columns immediately under the proving totals to show that your work sheet has been completed?

This problem will be continued in the next chapter. If it is collected by your teacher at this time, it will be returned to you before it is needed in Problem 10-1.

MASTERY
PROBLEM 9-M Work sheet for a travel agency

The account balances in the ledger of the Tyler Travel Agency on November 30 of the current year, the end of a fiscal period of one month, are shown below.

Cash	$1,750.70	Commissions Revenue	$1,230.60
Office Supplies	146.00	Advertising Expense	88.00
Office Furniture	1,120.50	Entertainment Expense	46.60
Office Machines	788.00	Insurance Expense	61.00
Southern Air Lines (creditor)	682.30	Miscellaneous Expense	11.20
United Shipping Co. (creditor)	450.10	Rent Expense	300.00
Western Express Co. (creditor)	95.00	Utilities Expense	96.00
Janet Tyler, Capital	1,950.00		

Instructions: Prepare a six-column work sheet for the Tyler Travel Agency owned by Miss Janet Tyler. Use the account titles and the account balances given above.

Self-checking: Except for the omission of account numbers, is your work sheet similar in all respects to the model on page 125?

BONUS
PROBLEM 9-B Work sheet for a theater

The account balances in the ledger of the Grand Theater on September 30 of the current year, the end of a fiscal period of one month, are:

Cash	$ 346.00	Admissions Revenue	$1,389.00
Air Conditioning Equipment	2,950.00	Vending Machine Revenue	163.00
Projection Equipment	9,000.00	Advertising Expense	193.10
Sound Equipment	1,442.00	Electricity Expense	146.40
Film Producers, Inc. (creditor)	389.40	Film Rental Expense	810.20
Global Sound Service (creditor)	83.60	Maintenance Expense	27.00
Majestic Films (creditor)	129.30	Projection Expense	22.20
Midwest Studios (creditor)	238.60	Rent Expense	350.00
Tri-State Supply Co. (creditor)	36.10	Water Expense	42.10
Wayne Tilman, Capital	12,900.00		

Instructions: Prepare a six-column work sheet for the Grand Theater, Wayne Tilman, proprietor, using the account titles and account balances given above.

Self-checking: 1. Did you write the amount of the net loss in the Income Statement Credit column and in the Balance Sheet Debit column?

2. Did you write the words *Net Loss* in the Account Title column on the same line with the amount of the net loss?

10

The Income Statement and the Balance Sheet

The six-column work sheet is used to summarize the account balances from the ledger as described in Chapter 9. Two important financial statements are prepared from the data summarized on the work sheet.

FINANCIAL STATEMENTS

Financial statements show the financial condition of a business. They become a part of the business' permanent records. The report that shows the revenue, the expenses, and the net income or the net loss for a fiscal period is called an income statement. The balance sheet shows what is owned, what is owed, and what a business is worth on a specific date.

Need for financial statements

The owner of a business needs the information provided on financial statements to make management decisions. Financial statements are helpful in answering questions such as: What does the business own? What debts are owed? Is net income increasing or decreasing? Should selling prices be increased or decreased? Should additional money be invested in the business?

Financial statements also provide information needed by people considering the investment of some of their money in a business. In addition, a business that needs to borrow money for future operations must often provide its financial statements to a bank or other lending agency.

Time period covered by financial statements

The income statement shows the revenue, the expenses, and the net income (or the net loss) of a business over a *specific period of time* — usually a fiscal period. The balance sheet lists all the assets, the liabilities, and the capital *on a specific date*. The financial *progress* of a business for a fiscal period is shown by the income statement for that period. The financial *condition* of a business on a particular date is shown by the balance sheet of that date.

				77 JST			
	S	M	T	W	T	F	S
		1	2	3	4	5	6
	7	8	9	10	11	12	13
	14	15	16	17	18	19	20
	21	22	23	24	25	26	27
	28	29	30	31			

Income Statement

Reports financial *progress* August 1 through August 31, 1977

Balance Sheet

Reports financial *condition* on August 31, 1977

PREPARING THE INCOME STATEMENT

The income statement of Rainbow Car Wash shows the financial progress of the business for the entire month of August.

Source of data for the income statement

The income statement of Rainbow Car Wash is prepared from information found in two parts of the work sheet. *First,* the Account Title column of the work sheet includes the names of all accounts to be listed on the income statement. *Second,* the Income Statement columns of the work sheet include the amounts needed in preparing the income statement.

The parts of the work sheet for Rainbow Car Wash shown on page 134 are needed to prepare the income statement shown on page 135.

Steps in preparing the income statement

Five steps are followed in preparing the income statement. As you study these, check each with the income statement on page 135.

☐ **1** Prepare the heading.

Write the heading on three lines; center each item in the heading. Like the heading on the work sheet, the date is for a period of time.

☐ **2** Prepare the revenue section.

The amounts for preparing the revenue section of the income statement are obtained directly from the Income Statement Credit column of the work sheet (Column 4).

The heading of the revenue section of an income statement is the word *Revenue.* The heading is written on the first line, beginning at the vertical line at the left. The title of the revenue account, **Sales,** is written on the second line, indented about one-half inch (about 1.3

ACCOUNT TITLE	ACCT. NO.	INCOME STATEMENT	
		3 DEBIT	**4** CREDIT
8 *Sales*	41		1318 50
9 *Advertising Expense*	51	18 00	
10 *Fuel Expense*	52	73 50	
11 *Miscellaneous Expense*	53	3 50	
12 *Rent Expense*	54	350 00	
13 *Utilities Expense*	55	68 50	
14		541 50	1318 50
15 *Net Income*		777 00	
16		1318 50	1318 50
17			

Rainbow Car Wash / *Work Sheet* / *For Month Ended August 31, 1977*

Parts of work sheet used in preparing the income statement

centimeters). Since Rainbow Car Wash receives revenue from sales only, the amount of the sales is also the total revenue. The amount of sales, *$1,318.50*, is therefore written in the second amount column, which is used for totals.

> When an income statement is handwritten, blank lines are not usually left between the major sections of the report. However, when an income statement is typewritten, a blank line (double spacing) is usually left between the major sections of the statement.

☐ **3** Prepare the expenses section.

The amounts for preparing the expenses section of the income statement are obtained directly from the Income Statement Debit column of the work sheet (Column 3).

The heading of the second section of the income statement is the word *Expenses*. This heading is written at the left margin. The titles of the individual expense accounts are listed in the same order in which they are given on the work sheet. Each account title is indented one-half inch (about 1.3 centimeters) from the vertical line. The amount of each expense account is written in the first amount column of the income statement. A single line is drawn across the first amount column to indicate the addition of all expense amounts. The words *Total Expenses* are written on the line beneath the last expense account title and the amount of the total expenses, *$541.50*, is written in the second amount column.

☐ **4** Figure the net income (or net loss).

A single line is ruled across the second amount column to indicate subtraction of the total expenses, *$541.50*, from the total revenue,

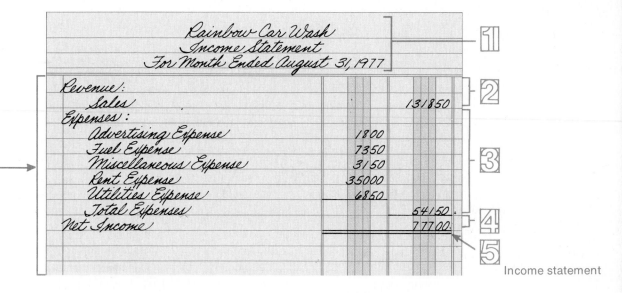

Rainbow Car Wash
Income Statement
For Month Ended August 31, 1977

Revenue:		
Sales		131850
Expenses:		
Advertising Expense	1800	
Fuel Expense	7350	
Miscellaneous Expense	3150	
Rent Expense	35000	
Utilities Expense	6850	
Total Expenses		54150
Net Income		77700

Income statement

$1,318.50. The result, $777.00, is written beneath the single ruled line in the second amount column. The words *Net Income* are written at the left margin. The amount of the net income shown on the income statement should, of course, agree with the amount of the net income previously calculated and recorded on the work sheet.

A net loss result is recorded in the same manner except that it is labeled *Net Loss*.

☐ **5** Rule the income statement.

Double lines are ruled across the amount columns to show that all work has been completed and is assumed to be correct.

PREPARING THE BALANCE SHEET

The balance sheet of Rainbow Car Wash shows the financial position of the business on one day, August 31, 1977.

Source of data for the balance sheet

The parts of the work sheet of Rainbow Car Wash shown on page 136 are needed to prepare the balance sheet on page 137.

Steps in preparing the balance sheet

The steps followed in preparing the August 31 balance sheet from the work sheet are described on the following pages. (Compare these steps with those on pages 9 and 10 for the August 1 balance sheet.)

	ACCOUNT TITLE	ACCT. NO.	BALANCE SHEET	
			DEBIT (5)	**CREDIT** (6)

Rainbow Car Wash
Work Sheet
For Month Ended August 31, 1977

#	ACCOUNT TITLE	ACCT. NO.	DEBIT	CREDIT	#
1	Cash	11	169050		1
2	Operating Supplies	12	31450		2
3	Car Wash Equipment	13	360000		3
4	Office Equipment	14	47200		4
5	Auto Wash Equipment Co.	21		65000	5
6	Marco Plumbing Company	22		15000	6
7	Harry Shaw, Capital	31		450000	7
14			607700	530000	14
15	Net Income			77700	15
16			607700	607700	16
17					17

Parts of work sheet used for preparing a balance sheet

☐ 1 Prepare the heading.

Write the heading on three lines; center each item in the heading. Since this balance sheet is being prepared for the specific date of August 31, 1977, that is the date written in the heading.

☐ 2 Prepare the assets section.

The amounts for the assets section of a balance sheet are obtained from the Balance Sheet Debit column of the work sheet (Column 5). The titles of the asset accounts are written on the left-hand side of the balance sheet in the same order as shown on the work sheet. The total of the left-hand side of the balance sheet is written on the same line as the final total on the right-hand side. Therefore, the *Total Assets* line and the amount of the total cannot be written until after the *Total Liabilities and Capital* line has been determined.

☐ 3 Prepare the liabilities section.

The amounts for the liabilities section of the balance sheet are obtained from the Balance Sheet Credit column of the work sheet (Column 6). The liability accounts are written on the right-hand side of the balance sheet in the same order as shown on the work sheet. A single line is ruled across the amount column under the amount of the last liability. The amount of the total and the words *Total Liabilities* are written as shown in the illustration.

☐ 4 Prepare the capital section.

The amounts for the capital section of the balance sheet of Rainbow Car Wash are obtained from the Balance Sheet Credit column

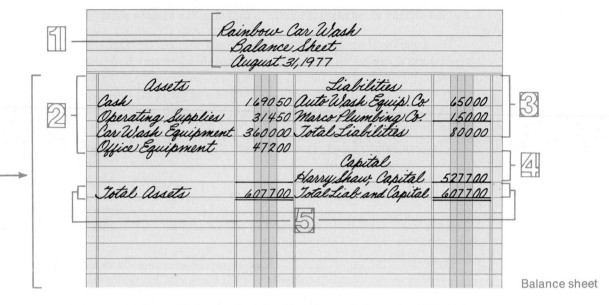

⊓	*Rainbow Car Wash*	
①	*Balance Sheet*	
	August 31, 1977	

Assets		*Liabilities*	
Cash	169050	*Auto Wash Equip. Co.*	65000
Operating Supplies	31450	*Marco Plumbing Co.*	15000
Car Wash Equipment	360000	*Total Liabilities*	80000
Office Equipment	47200		
		Capital	
		Harry Shaw, Capital	527700
Total Assets	607700	*Total Liab. and Capital*	607700

Balance sheet

of the work sheet (Column 6). Mr. Shaw's capital at the close of business on August 31, 1977, as shown on the work sheet consists of two items: (1) the balance in his capital account and (2) the net income his business has earned. These amounts are totaled as follows:

The balance in the owner's capital account (as shown on
 Line 7 of the work sheet)... $4,500.00
Plus the net income for August (as shown on Line 15 of the
 work sheet)... 777.00
Amount of present capital to be shown on balance sheet..... $5,277.00

The amount of the present capital, $5,277.00, is written in the right-hand amount column of the balance sheet.

□ **5** Prove and rule the balance sheet.

A single line is ruled across the amount column under the amount of the capital and on the same line across the amount column of the asset section. The present capital, $5,277.00, is added to the total liabilities, $800.00, to obtain the *Total Liabilities and Capital*, $6,077.00. The assets are added to obtain the *Total Assets, $6,077.00*, which is written in the assets section on the same line as the total liabilities and capital. The amount of the total liabilities and capital is compared with the amount of the total assets. If these two amounts agree, all calculations on the balance sheet are assumed to be correct.

In the balance sheet of Rainbow Car Wash, the two proving totals are *$6,077.00*. Double lines are then ruled under the two proving totals to indicate that the balance sheet has been completed and found to be in balance.

Another method of reporting the owner's capital on the balance sheet

The balance sheet of Rainbow Car Wash shown on page 137 reports the owner's capital in one amount. How this amount is figured is not shown.

In some businesses the calculation of the present capital is shown on the balance sheet. When this is done, the capital section of a balance sheet would appear as follows:

Ruth Adkins, Capital, October 1, 1977		$ 8,000.00
Additional Investment................................	$ 800.00	
Net Income...	1,300.00	2,100.00
Ruth Adkins, Capital, October 31, 1977........................		$10,100.00

The amounts needed to prepare the above section of the balance sheet are obtained from the following sources:

$8,000.00 — October 1 Capital — from the capital account in the ledger
  800.00 — Additional Investment — from the capital account in the ledger
1,300.00 — Net Income — from the Income Statement section of the work sheet

After showing the calculations on the balance sheet, the present capital, $10,100.00, is then added to the total liabilities to obtain *Total Liabilities and Capital*.

✦What is the meaning of the following?

• income statement

1. What are some of the major uses of financial statements?
2. What is the purpose of the income statement?
3. What is the purpose of a balance sheet?
4. What is the source of data for preparing an income statement?
5. What two parts of a work sheet supply all the information needed for preparing an income statement?
6. What are the three parts of the heading of an income statement?
7. What are the two main sections of the body of the income statement?
8. How is the net income calculated from the information on the income statement?
9. How do you prove the accuracy of the amount of the net income shown on the income statement?
10. What two parts of a work sheet supply all the information needed for preparing a balance sheet?
11. How does the heading of the balance sheet differ from the heading of the income statement?
12. What are the three main sections of the body of the balance sheet?

CASE 1 Mr. Shaw, who operates Rainbow Car Wash, is considering the installation of two additional car wash bays. The additional bays would require that a larger water pump, hot water heater, and boiler be installed. What factors should Mr. Shaw consider before making a decision?

CASE 2 Mr. Shaw, who operates Rainbow Car Wash, finds that his net income for the month of August is $777.00, as shown on the income statement on page 135. Mr. Shaw has been offered $800.00 a month to manage a large automatic car wash. What decisions must he make in order to determine whether to continue to rent property and operate Rainbow Car Wash or to manage a large automatic car wash?

DRILL 10-D 1 Classifying accounts

Drills for Mastering Principles

This drill is planned to give you additional skill in classifying accounts and in indicating on which financial statement each kind of account is reported.

Instructions: □ **1.** On a sheet of paper, rule a form similar to the one below. Fill in the headings and number the columns as shown in the illustration.

1	2	3	4	5	6	7	8
Account Title	KIND OF ACCOUNT					FINANCIAL STATEMENT	
	Asset	Liability	Capital	Revenue	Expense	Income Statement	Balance Sheet
1. Cash	✓						✓

Instructions: □ **2.** In the Account Title column (Column 1), copy the list of account titles given below.

1. Cash
2. Office Supplies
3. Utilities Expense
4. Sales
5. Office Equipment
6. Advertising Expense
7. Alice Osborn, Capital
8. Page Company (creditor)
9. Miscellaneous Expense
10. Commissions Revenue
11. Central Supply Company (creditor)
12. Office Machines
13. Rent Expense
14. Thomas Turner, Capital

Instructions: □ **3.** For each account title listed, (a) place a check mark in either Column 2, 3, 4, 5, or 6 to show what kind of account it is, and also (b) place a check mark in either Column 7 or 8 to show on which financial statement the account is reported.

The first item, Cash, is given as an example. Since this is an *asset* amount appearing on the *balance sheet*, check marks are placed in Columns 2 and 8.

DRILL 10-D 2 Using the accounting equation for figuring (a) net income and net loss and (b) the total capital at the end of a fiscal period

At the time a work sheet is completed, the total capital consists of two amounts: (1) the balance in the proprietor's capital account and (2) either the net income or the net loss for the period.

The data below show the total assets, the total liabilities, and the balance in the capital account *as shown on the work sheets* of seven businesses.

Instructions: □ **1.** Use the information shown below to figure the net income or the net loss of each business for the period. If there is a net income, record the amount in Column 5 in your workbook. If there is a net loss, record the amount in Column 6. The answers for Businesses A and B are given as examples.

1	2	3	4	5	6	7
	TOTAL ASSETS	= TOTAL LIABILITIES +	TOTAL CAPITAL			Total Capital at End of Fiscal Period
Busi-ness			Capital + Acct. Bal.	Net or − Income	Net Loss	
A	$ 8,000.00	$ 2,000.00	$ 5,000.00	$1,000.00		$ 6,000.00
B	18,000.00	6,000.00	13,000.00		$1,000.00	12,000.00
C	12,500.00	4,450.00	6,200.00			
D	9,750.00	2,325.00	5,875.00			
E	22,800.00	9,875.00	11,650.00			
F	63,275.00	23,550.00	45,100.00			
G	31,450.00	7,850.00	24,750.00			

Instructions: □ **2.** In Column 7 list the total amount of capital that will be reported on the balance sheet of each business at the close of this fiscal period. Business A, for example, will report a total of $6,000.00 — the balance in the capital account, $5,000.00, plus the net income for the period, $1,000.00. Business B will report a total of $12,000.00 — the balance in the capital account, $13,000.00, less the net loss for the period, $1,000.00.

Problems for Applying Concepts

PROBLEM 10-1 Financial reports for a real estate agency

The work sheet prepared in Problem 9-1 of Chapter 9 is required for this problem. If it has not been returned to you, complete Review Problem 10-R 1.

Instructions: □ **1.** Prepare an income statement from the Income Statement columns of the work sheet that you completed in Problem 9-1. Use as your model the income statement on page 135.

Self-checking: Ask yourself the following about your income statement:

1. Did you center each line of the heading?
2. Did you place the headings of the two sections, Revenue and Expenses, close to the vertical line at the left of the wide column?
3. Did you keep an even indention for all the account titles listed?
4. Did you rule a double line across both amount columns under the amount of the net income to show completion of all work?

Instructions: ▢ **2.** Prepare a balance sheet from the Balance Sheet columns of the work sheet that you completed in Problem 9-1. Use as your model the balance sheet illustrated on page 137.

Self-checking: Ask yourself these questions about your balance sheet:

1. Did you center each of the three lines of the heading?
2. Did you center the heading of each of the three main sections: Assets, Liabilities, and Capital?
3. Is the amount of the total assets at the bottom of the left-hand side on the same line as the amount of the total liabilities and capital at the bottom of the right-hand side?
4. Did you neatly rule the double lines across the amount columns only, under the two proving totals?

PROBLEM 10-2 Work sheet and financial reports for a bowling center

The account balances of the Metro Bowling Lanes on May 31 of the current year, at the end of a fiscal period of one month, are as shown below.

Instructions: ▢ **1.** Prepare a six-column work sheet using the account balances given. Use as your model the work sheet on page 125.

Cash...............................	$ 1,625.00	Ward Cleaners (creditor).....	$ 93.20
Bowling Supplies...............	1,360.50	Sally Denton, Capital	25,201.30
Office Supplies..................	410.30	Bowling Revenue...............	3,560.10
Bowling Equipment...........	27,000.00	Advertising Expense..........	83.20
Office Equipment	1,340.20	Maintenance Expense.........	134.30
Baxter Shoe Company		Miscellaneous Expense.......	32.60
(creditor)......................	1,200.00	Rent Expense....................	450.00
Garcia Company (creditor)..	2,719.40	Utilities Expense	134.60
United Repair Company		Wages Expense	400.00
(creditor)......................	196.70		

Instructions: ▢ **2.** Prepare an income statement from the Income Statement columns of the work sheet. Use as your model the income statement that is illustrated on page 135.

▢ **3.** Prepare a balance sheet from the Balance Sheet columns of the work sheet. Use as your model the balance sheet on page 137.

Self-checking: 1. Except for the omission of account numbers, is your work sheet similar in all respects to the model on page 125?

2. Check the accuracy of your financial reports by asking yourself the questions listed in Problem 10-1.

MASTERY Financial reports for an automobile
PROBLEM 10-M driving school

The work sheet for Riley's Driving School for the month of November of the current year is given below.

Instructions: □ **1.** Prepare an income statement.

□ **2.** Prepare a balance sheet.

Riley's Driving School
Work Sheet
For Month Ended November 30, 19—

Account Title	Acct. No.	Trial Balance		Income Statement		Balance Sheet	
		Debit	Credit	Debit	Credit	Debit	Credit
Cash	11	1 714 50				1 714 50	
Office Supplies	12	63 20				63 20	
Automobiles	13	10 400 00				10 400 00	
Classroom Equipment....	14	930 70				930 70	
Office Equipment	15	835 50				835 50	
Auto Finance Company..	21		3 800 00				3 800 00
Downtown Garage	22		93 60				93 60
Nelson Tire Company....	23		160 20				160 20
Western Supply Co.	24		66 40				66 40
Jack Riley, Capital	31		9 165 80				9 165 80
Fees Revenue	41		1 600 00		1 600 00		
Advertising Expense......	51	42 00		42 00			
Auto Repairs Expense....	52	93 60		93 60			
Gas and Oil Expense......	53	146 40		146 40			
Miscellaneous Expense...	54	27 10		27 10			
Rent Expense................	55	175 00		175 00			
Salary Expense..............	56	425 00		425 00			
Utilities Expense...........	57	33 00		33 00			
		14 886 00	14 886 00	942 10	1 600 00	13 943 90	13 286 00
Net Income				657 90			657 90
				1 600 00	1 600 00	13 943 90	13 943 90

BONUS
PROBLEM 10-B Financial reports for a laundry

The work sheet for the Eastside Laundry for the month of May of the current year is given at the top of the next page.

Instructions: □ **1.** Prepare an income statement.

□ **2.** Prepare a balance sheet.

Eastside Laundry
Work Sheet
For Month Ended May 31, 19—

Account Title	Acct. No.	Trial Balance		Income Statement		Balance Sheet	
		Debit	Credit	Debit	Credit	Debit	Credit
Cash	11	420 75				420 75	
Laundry Supplies..........	12	260 35				260 35	
Delivery Truck..............	13	3 800 00				3 800 00	
Machinery	14	11 000 00				11 000 00	
Office Equipment..........	15	765 65				765 65	
Anderson Equip. Co......	21		3 300 00				3 300 00
Martinez Repair Co.	22		130 60				130 60
Weaver's Garage...........	23		28 00				28 00
Martha Stevens, Capital .	31		12 979 30				12 979 30
Sales	41		1 360 00		1 360 00		
Advertising Expense......	51	48 25		48 25			
Delivery Expense	52	162 40		162 40			
Electricity Expense	53	68 30		68 30			
Miscellaneous Expense...	54	26 20		26 20			
Rent Expense................	55	420 00		420 00			
Wages Expense.............	56	790 00		790 00			
Water Expense..............	57	36 00		36 00			
		17 797 90	17 797 90	1 551 15	1 360 00	16 246 75	16 437 90
Net Loss					191 15	191 15	
				1 551 15	1 551 15	16 437 90	16 437 90

Self-checking: 1. Compare your income statement with the model on page 135. Did you use the words "Net Loss" instead of "Net Income" in your solution to this problem?

2. Compare your balance sheet with the model on page 137. In calculating the present capital, did you subtract the net loss for the period from the balance of the owner's capital account?

11

Closing the Ledger

The revenue and expense transactions occurring during a fiscal period change the capital of a business. A revenue transaction increases capital. An expense transaction decreases capital. The capital account, however, is not used to record changes caused by individual revenue and expense transactions. Rather, revenue and expense accounts are used to classify and summarize changes in capital that occur during the fiscal period. This procedure avoids having the capital account become cluttered with many debit and credit entries. This procedure also permits easy identification of the amount and kind of revenue and expense transactions that change capital.

Separate revenue accounts are credited for the different kinds of revenue. Similarly, separate expense accounts are debited for the different kinds of expenses. At the close of the fiscal period, the account balances for these temporary capital accounts are recorded on the work sheet. The account balances of these temporary capital accounts on the work sheet provide the information needed to prepare the income statement.

After the income statement is completed, the temporary revenue and expense accounts have served their purpose. The difference between the account balances of the revenue and expense accounts represents the net increase or net decrease in capital. This amount is then transferred to the capital account so that the balance of the capital account agrees with the amount of capital shown on the balance sheet.

CLOSING ENTRIES

The balance of each revenue account and the balance of each expense account are transferred to one ledger account to summarize the increases and decreases in capital.

The income summary account

The account to which the balance of each revenue and each expense account is transferred at the end of the fiscal period is titled *Income Summary*. The income summary account is sometimes known as the income and expense summary account. The income summary account is placed in the capital division of the ledger because the account is used to summarize the net increase or the net decrease in capital.

The balances of the revenue accounts and the expense accounts are transferred to Income Summary by journal entries. An entry that transfers the balance from one account to another is called a closing entry. An account that has its balance transferred to another account is called a closed account.

After the balances are transferred, the income summary account shows the total expenses on the debit side and the total revenue on the credit side. The difference between the two sides of the account shows the net increase or the net decrease in capital. The balance of the income summary account is transferred to the proprietor's capital account. The process of transferring the balances of the revenue and the expense accounts through a summary account to the proprietor's capital account is called closing the ledger.

Steps in closing the ledger

Three steps are taken in closing the ledger of Rainbow Car Wash. The chart below diagrams these three steps.

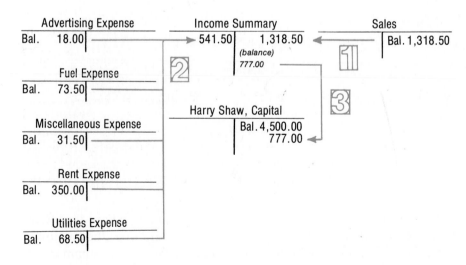

Diagram showing three closing entries

☐ 1 Transfer the credit balance of the revenue account to the credit side of the income summary account.

□ **2** Transfer the sum of the debit balances of the expense accounts *as a single amount* to the debit side of the income summary account.

□ **3** Transfer the credit balance of the income summary account to the credit side of the proprietor's capital account.

After these transfers of account balances have been completed, Mr. Shaw's capital account shows the net increase in capital for the fiscal period. As a result, his capital account in the ledger now agrees with the amount shown in the capital section of the balance sheet.

Closing Entry No. 1 — closing the revenue accounts

The end-of-period balances for all accounts are summarized on the work sheet. Therefore, the information needed for closing all revenue and expense accounts is readily found in the Income Statement columns of the work sheet. The balance of the sales account, $1,318.50, is shown in the Income Statement Credit column below.

			1	2	3	4
ACCOUNT TITLE		ACCT. NO.	TRIAL BALANCE		INCOME STATEMENT	
			DEBIT	CREDIT	DEBIT	CREDIT
8	Sales	41		1318 50		1318 50

Before any closing entry is made, the sales account and the income summary account appear as shown below.

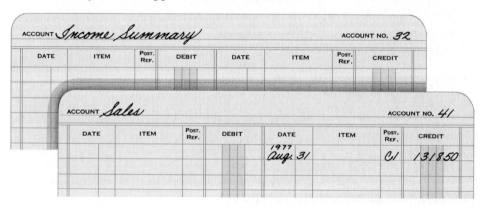

The balance of the sales account is a *credit* balance before it is transferred to the income summary account. After the transfer, the amount of the balance, $1,318.50, will be a *credit* item in the income summary account. To show that the balance of the sales account has been transferred, Sales will be debited for $1,318.50. This debit closes the revenue account, Sales.

The general journal entry to transfer the credit balance of the sales account to the credit side of the income summary account is shown below.

	GENERAL JOURNAL			PAGE /
DATE	ACCOUNT TITLE	POST. REF.	DEBIT	CREDIT
	Closing Entries			
31	*Sales*	41	1 31850	
	Income Summary	32		1 31850

Closing Entry No. 1 — closing the revenue account

The words *Closing Entries* are written in the Account Title column before the first closing entry is made. Since this heading explains the nature of the three closing entries, a separate explanation or indication of a source document for each closing entry is unnecessary.

> If the closing entries are started on a new page of the journal the heading is written on Line 1. The complete date including the year, month, and day would be written on Line 2.

After Closing Entry No. 1 has been posted, the two accounts affected appear as follows:

ACCOUNT *Income Summary*							ACCOUNT NO. 32	
DATE	ITEM	POST. REF.	DEBIT	DATE	ITEM	POST. REF.	CREDIT	
				1977 Aug. 31		J1	1 31850	

ACCOUNT *Sales*							ACCOUNT NO. 41	
DATE	ITEM	POST. REF.	DEBIT	DATE	ITEM	POST. REF.	CREDIT	
1977 Aug. 31		J1	1 31850	1977 Aug. 31		C1	1 31850	

The original *credit* balance of the sales account, $1,318.50, has now been transferred to the *credit* side of the income summary account. Therefore, the sales account is now closed.

> If there were other revenue accounts, their balances would also be transferred to the credit side of Income Summary.

Closing Entry No. 2 — closing the expense accounts

The balances of the expense accounts are shown in the Income Statement Debit column of the work sheet shown on page 148. The balances of the expense accounts are transferred to the income summary account as a single amount.

	ACCOUNT TITLE	ACCT. NO.	TRIAL BALANCE		INCOME STATEMENT	
			DEBIT	CREDIT	DEBIT	CREDIT
9	Advertising Expense	51	1800		1800	
10	Fuel Expense	52	7350		7350	
11	Miscellaneous Expense	53	3150		3150	
12	Rent Expense	54	35000		35000	
13	Utilities Expense	55	6850		6850	

The expense accounts are closed in the order in which they appear on the work sheet. All the expense account balances are transferred to the income summary account in one entry. An entry that contains two or more debits or two or more credits is called a combined entry.

All the expense account balances are *debits* before the transfer is made. After the transfer, the total of all the expense account balances will be shown as a single *debit* item in the income summary account. The sum of the expense account balances is $541.50. The amount to be *debited* to the income summary account is therefore $541.50. Each of the expense accounts is credited for the amount of its balance in order to close these accounts.

The general journal combined entry to transfer the debit balances of the expense accounts to the debit side of the income summary account is shown below.

		GENERAL JOURNAL			PAGE 1	
	DATE	ACCOUNT TITLE	POST. REF.	DEBIT	CREDIT	
13	31	Income Summary	32	54150		13
14		Advertising Expense	51		1800	14
15		Fuel Expense	52		7350	15
16		Miscellaneous Expense	53		3150	16
17		Rent Expense	54		35000	17
18		Utilities Expense	55		6850	18
19						19
20						20
21						21
22						22

Closing Entry No. 2 — closing the expense accounts

After Closing Entry No. 2 has been posted, the income summary account and the first of the expense accounts appear as illustrated at the top of the next page.

ACCOUNT *Income Summary*							ACCOUNT NO. *32*
DATE	ITEM	POST. REF.	DEBIT	DATE	ITEM	POST. REF.	CREDIT
1977 Aug. 31		J1	541 50	*1977* Aug. 31		J1	1318 50

ACCOUNT *Advertising Expense*							ACCOUNT NO. *51*
DATE	ITEM	POST. REF.	DEBIT	DATE	ITEM	POST. REF.	CREDIT
1977 Aug. 5		C1	18 00	*1977* Aug. 31		J1	18 00

The credits to the other expense accounts are posted in the same manner as the credit to Advertising Expense. All expense accounts are shown in the complete ledger on page 155.

Closing Entry No. 3 — closing the income summary account

The net income shown on the work sheet, page 125, of Rainbow Car Wash is $777.00. This amount is the same as the balance in the income summary account. (A credit of $1,318.50 minus a debit of $541.50 equals a credit balance of $777.00.) The next step in closing the ledger is to transfer this credit balance of the income summary account to the credit side of the proprietor's capital account.

The general journal entry to transfer the credit balance of the income summary account to the credit side of the proprietor's capital account is shown below.

GENERAL JOURNAL			PAGE *1*	
DATE	ACCOUNT TITLE	POST. REF.	DEBIT	CREDIT
31	*Income Summary*	32	777 00	
	Harry Shaw, Capital	31		777 00

Closing Entry No. 3 — closing the income summary account

After Closing Entry No. 3 has been posted, the income summary account and the proprietor's capital account appear as shown on page 150.

The income summary account now has a zero balance. As a result, it is said to be in balance and therefore closed. Mr. Shaw's capital account now shows: (1) the amount of capital at the start of this fiscal period, $4,000.00, (2) the additional investment by Mr. Shaw, $500.00, and (3) the net increase in capital that came from operating the car wash during this fiscal period, $777.00. The sum of these three amounts now equals

ACCOUNT *Income Summary*							ACCOUNT NO. *32*	
DATE	ITEM	POST. REF.	DEBIT	DATE	ITEM	POST. REF.	CREDIT	
1977 *Aug.* 31		*J1*	541 50	*1977* *Aug.* 31		*J1*	1318 50	
31		*J1*	777 00					

ACCOUNT *Harry Shaw, Capital*							ACCOUNT NO. *31*	
DATE	ITEM	POST. REF.	DEBIT	DATE	ITEM	POST. REF.	CREDIT	
				1977 *Aug.* 1	*Balance*	*J1*	4000 00	
				1		*C1*	500 00	
				31		*J1*	4500 00 777 00	

his present capital, $5,277.00. Since the present capital shown on the balance sheet is also $5,277.00, Mr. Shaw's capital account now agrees with the capital section of the balance sheet.

Summary of closing entries

The three closing entries as they appear in the general journal of Rainbow Car Wash after being posted are:

	GENERAL JOURNAL			PAGE *1*	
DATE	ACCOUNT TITLE	POST. REF.	DEBIT	CREDIT	
	Closing Entries				10
31	*Sales*	41	1318 50		11
	Income Summary	32		1318 50	12
31	*Income Summary*	32	541 50		13
	Advertising Expense	51		18 00	14
	Fuel Expense	52		73 50	15
	Miscellaneous Expense	53		31 50	16
	Rent Expense	54		350 00	17
	Utilities Expense	55		68 50	18
31	*Income Summary*	32	777 00		19
	Harry Shaw, Capital	31		777 00	20

Closing Entry No. 1 (lines 11–12)
Closing Entry No. 2 (lines 13–18)
Closing Entry No. 3 (lines 19–20)

Closing entries for Rainbow Car Wash after posting

The three closing entries are made from the work sheet illustrated on page 125 in the following order:

☐ 1 **Closing Entry No. 1.** Close the revenue accounts by (a) debiting each revenue account for its end-of-period balance and (b) crediting Income Summary for the total of all revenue account balances.

☐ **2** **Closing Entry No. 2.** Close the expense accounts by (a) debiting Income Summary for the total of all expense account balances and (b) crediting each expense account for its end-of-period balance. Note that the debit part of a general journal combined entry is always written first. The amount of the debit in this entry is found by adding the credit amounts.

☐ **3** **Closing Entry No. 3.** Close the income summary account by (a) debiting Income Summary for the amount of the net income and (b) crediting the capital account for the same amount, increasing capital by the amount of the net income.

> When a business has a net loss instead of a net income, the income summary account is closed by (a) crediting Income Summary for the amount of the net loss and (b) debiting the capital account for the same amount.

The following diagram summarizes the use of Income Summary as a "clearing" account for closing revenue and expense accounts and for transferring the net income (or net loss) to the capital account.

INCOME SUMMARY	
CLOSING ENTRY NO. 2	CLOSING ENTRY NO. 1
Debited	*Credited*
For the total of all expense account balances	For the total of all revenue account balances

CLOSING ENTRY NO. 3	
Debited → → → →	*or Credited*
When there is a *net income* to be transferred to the capital account	When there is a *net loss* to be transferred to the capital account

Income Summary, therefore, is an account that is used only at the end of a fiscal period when the ledger is being closed.

After the three closing entries in the journal are posted, the accounts in the revenue, expense, and capital divisions of the ledger are as follows:

1. Each revenue account is now in balance and closed because its credit balance has been transferred to the credit side of Income Summary.
2. Each expense account is now in balance and closed because its debit balance has been transferred to the debit side of Income Summary.
3. The account Income Summary is in balance and closed because its balance has been transferred to the proprietor's capital account.
4. The proprietor's capital account now shows the increase or decrease in capital due to the net income or the net loss.

> In case of a net loss, the proprietor's capital account will show the decrease in capital on its debit side.

RULING AND BALANCING ACCOUNTS

As a result of posting the closing entries, each revenue account, each expense account, and the income summary account are in balance and are said to be closed. In order to show that these accounts are closed, the accounts are ruled.

Ruling accounts that are closed

Ruling closed accounts prevents the amounts now recorded in these accounts from being confused with the amounts for the following fiscal period. The fuel expense account after ruling is shown below.

The following three steps are usually taken in ruling a revenue or an expense account:

☐ **1** Rule a single line under the last amount in the column with the most entries and on the same line in the opposite amount column. This single line indicates addition.

☐ **2** Write the totals of the debit side and the credit side of the account on the same line under the single line.

☐ **3** Rule double lines on the line under the totals across all columns except the Item columns to show that the account is closed.

When an account that is closed has only one debit and one credit, totaling the amount columns is unnecessary. The debit equals the credit. The account is ruled with double lines across all columns except the Item columns as shown below.

Balancing and ruling accounts that are open

After the closing entries are posted, an account with a balance remaining is called an open account. The only accounts that are open are the balance sheet accounts. When a balance sheet account contains one or more entries on each side, the balance of the account should be determined. The amount of the balance should be recorded on the proper side of the account. After the account is totaled and ruled, the entries of a new fiscal period are clearly separated from those of the previous period. The process of determining the balance of an account and bringing the balance into the new section of the account is called balancing an account.

The following three steps are usually taken when balancing an asset, a liability, or a capital account with one or more entries on each side. (These three steps are illustrated in the cash account at the top of page 154.)

☐ **1** Write the balance of the account on the side having the smaller total. Write the last day of the fiscal period in the Date column and the word *Balance* in the Item column. Place a check mark (√) in the Post. Ref. column to show that this item was not posted from a journal.

☐ **2** Total and rule the account in the same manner in which a revenue or an expense account is totaled and ruled when it is closed.

☐ **3** Write the balance again, this time below the double ruling on the side originally having the larger footing. Write the complete date (year, month, and day) of the new balance, using the first day of the new fiscal period. Write the word *Balance* in the Item column, and place a check mark (√) in the Post. Ref. column to show that this item was not posted from a journal.

In the ledger illustrated on pages 154 and 155, the asset and liability accounts that are balanced are Cash, Office Equipment, and Auto Wash Equipment Co.

The asset account Operating Supplies and the capital account of Harry Shaw are neither balanced nor ruled because they have entries on one side of the account only. However, these accounts are pencil footed so that the balance of the account is readily apparent.

Ledger that has been closed, balanced, and ruled

The ledger of Rainbow Car Wash, after the closing entries have been posted and the accounts have been balanced and ruled, is illustrated on pages 154 and 155.

ACCOUNT *Cash*   ACCOUNT NO. *11*

DATE	ITEM	POST. REF.	DEBIT	DATE	ITEM	POST. REF.	CREDIT
1977 Aug. 1	Balance	J1	65000	1977 Aug. 31		C1	80600
31		C1	184650	31	Balance	✓	169050
	1,690.50		249650				
			249650				249650
1977 Sept. 1	Balance	✓	169050				

ACCOUNT *Operating Supplies*   ACCOUNT NO. *12*

DATE	ITEM	POST. REF.	DEBIT	DATE	ITEM	POST. REF.	CREDIT
1977 Aug. 1	Balance	J1	25000				
15		C1	6450				
			31 450				

ACCOUNT *Car Wash Equipment*   ACCOUNT NO. *13*

DATE	ITEM	POST. REF.	DEBIT	DATE	ITEM	POST. REF.	CREDIT
1977 Aug. 1	Balance	J1	360000				

ACCOUNT *Office Equipment*   ACCOUNT NO. *14*

DATE	ITEM	POST. REF.	DEBIT	DATE	ITEM	POST. REF.	CREDIT
1977 Aug. 1	Balance	J1	50000	1977 Aug. 1		C1	1000
	472.00			13		C1	1800
				31	Balance	✓	*2 800* 47200
			50000				50000
1977 Sept. 1	Balance	✓	47200				

ACCOUNT *Auto Wash Equipment Co.*   ACCOUNT NO. *21*

DATE	ITEM	POST. REF.	DEBIT	DATE	ITEM	POST. REF.	CREDIT
1977 Aug. 1		C1	20000	1977 Aug. 1	Balance	J1	85000
31	Balance	✓	65000		*650.00*		
			85000				85000
				1977 Sept. 1	Balance	✓	65000

ACCOUNT *Marco Plumbing Company*   ACCOUNT NO. *22*

DATE	ITEM	POST. REF.	DEBIT	DATE	ITEM	POST. REF.	CREDIT
				1977 Aug. 1	Balance	J1	15000

ACCOUNT *Harry Shaw, Capital*   ACCOUNT NO. *31*

DATE	ITEM	POST. REF.	DEBIT	DATE	ITEM	POST. REF.	CREDIT
				1977 Aug. 1	Balance	J1	400000
				1		C1	50000
							450000
				31		J1	77700
							527700

Ledger of Rainbow
Car Wash closed,
balanced, and ruled

ACCOUNT *Income Summary* ACCOUNT NO. *32*

DATE	ITEM	POST. REF.	DEBIT	DATE	ITEM	POST. REF.	CREDIT
1977 Aug. 31		J1	541 50	1977 Aug. 31		J1	1 318 50
31		J1	777 00				
			1 318 50				1 318 50

ACCOUNT *Sales* ACCOUNT NO. *41*

DATE	ITEM	POST. REF.	DEBIT	DATE	ITEM	POST. REF.	CREDIT
1977 Aug. 31		J1	1 318 50	1977 Aug. 31		C1	1 318 50

ACCOUNT *Advertising Expense* ACCOUNT NO. *51*

DATE	ITEM	POST. REF.	DEBIT	DATE	ITEM	POST. REF.	CREDIT
1977 Aug. 5		C1	18 00	1977 Aug. 31		J1	18 00

ACCOUNT *Fuel Expense* ACCOUNT NO. *52*

DATE	ITEM	POST. REF.	DEBIT	DATE	ITEM	POST. REF.	CREDIT
1977 Aug. 4		C1	42 00	1977 Aug. 31		J1	73 50
25		C1	31 50				
			73 50				73 50

ACCOUNT *Miscellaneous Expense* ACCOUNT NO. *53*

DATE	ITEM	POST. REF.	DEBIT	DATE	ITEM	POST. REF.	CREDIT
1977 Aug. 6		C1	3 00	1977 Aug. 31		J1	31 50
20		C1	14 00				
27		C1	2 50				
30		C1	12 00				
			31 50				31 50

ACCOUNT *Rent Expense* ACCOUNT NO. *54*

DATE	ITEM	POST. REF.	DEBIT	DATE	ITEM	POST. REF.	CREDIT
1977 Aug. 2		C1	350 00	1977 Aug. 31		J1	350 00

ACCOUNT *Utilities Expense* ACCOUNT NO. *55*

DATE	ITEM	POST. REF.	DEBIT	DATE	ITEM	POST. REF.	CREDIT
1977 Aug. 12		C1	26 50	1977 Aug. 31		J1	68 50
18		C1	42 00				
			68 50				68 50

Ledger of Rainbow Car Wash closed, balanced, and ruled

POST-CLOSING TRIAL BALANCE

After the closing entries have been posted and the accounts have been balanced and ruled, debits must still equal credits. It is customary to take a trial balance to test the equality of debits and credits in the ledger. The trial balance taken after the closing entries have been posted is called a post-closing trial balance. The post-closing trial balance of Rainbow Car Wash is shown below.

ACCOUNT TITLE	ACCT. NO.	DEBIT	CREDIT
Rainbow Car Wash			
Post-Closing Trial Balance			
August 31, 1977			
Cash	11	169050	
Operating Supplies	12	31450	
Car Wash Equipment	13	360000	
Office Equipment	14	47200	
Auto Wash Equipment Co.	21		65000
Marco Plumbing Company	22		15000
Harry Shaw, Capital	31		527700
		607700	607700

Post-closing trial balance of Rainbow Car Wash

Only accounts that are open at the end of the fiscal period are listed on the post-closing trial balance. The accounts that are open are the asset, liability, and capital accounts with balances. The accounts are listed in the same order as they appear in the ledger. No revenue or expense account is included on the post-closing trial balance because each of these accounts has been closed.

The post-closing trial balance illustrated above shows the total of the debit balances, $6,077.00, to be the same as the total of the credit balances. Thus, the equality of debits and credits after posting the closing entries is proved for the general ledger. The amounts shown on the post-closing trial balance agree with the account balances shown on the balance sheet on page 137. The post-closing trial balance is used as a final means of checking to see that the ledger is in balance and ready for use in the new fiscal period.

SUMMARY OF THE ACCOUNTING CYCLE

In this and the preceding chapters a complete series of business activities for the Rainbow Car Wash has been presented for a fiscal period — the month of August, 1977. The complete series of activities involved in double-entry accounting during a fiscal period is called the accounting cycle. This accounting cycle begins with the analysis and the recording of transactions in a journal and ends with the post-closing trial balance. The flowchart below shows all the steps in the cycle.

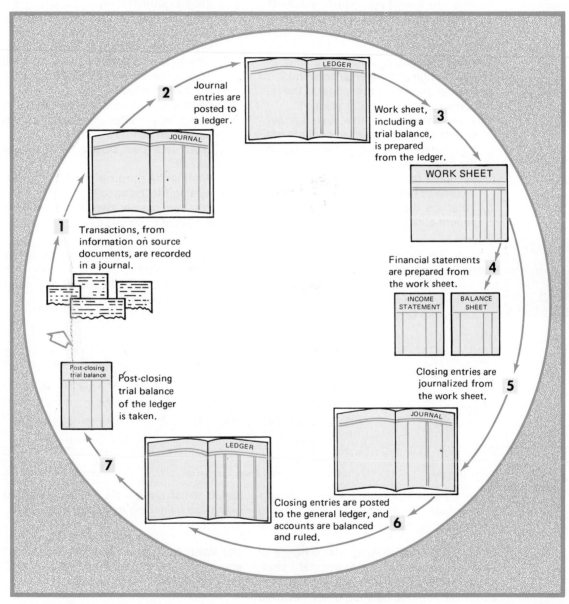

1 Transactions, from information on source documents, are recorded in a journal.

2 Journal entries are posted to a ledger.

3 Work sheet, including a trial balance, is prepared from the ledger.

4 Financial statements are prepared from the work sheet.

5 Closing entries are journalized from the work sheet.

6 Closing entries are posted to the general ledger, and accounts are balanced and ruled.

7 Post-closing trial balance of the ledger is taken.

Flowchart of the steps in the accounting cycle

✦ What is the meaning of each of the following?

- closing entry
- closed account
- closing the ledger

- combined entry
- open account
- balancing an account

- post-closing trial balance
- accounting cycle

Using Business Terms

Questions
for
Individual
Study

1. How do revenue and expense transactions that occur during a fiscal period change the capital of a business?
2. Why are temporary capital accounts used instead of the capital account for recording revenue and expense transactions?
3. What account is used to summarize the revenue and expense accounts?
4. In what division of the ledger is the income summary account placed?
5. After balances of the revenue accounts and the expense accounts are transferred, what item is shown (a) on the debit side of the income summary account? (b) on the credit side of the income summary account?
6. What are the three steps in the procedure of closing the ledger?

7. What two columns of the six-column work sheet are used as a guide for preparing the closing entries in the general journal?
8. After the first two closing entries have been posted, what kinds of accounts in the ledger have been closed?
9. Why is the income summary account in balance after Closing Entry No. 3 has been posted?
10. What kinds of accounts remain open in the ledger after the closing entries have been posted?
11. When is a post-closing trial balance taken?
12. What is the purpose of taking a post-closing trial balance?
13. What are the six steps for completing the accounting cycle?

Cases for
Management
Decision

CASE 1 The income summary account of Valley Recreation Center after the ledger was closed, December 31, 1977, is below.
(a) What does the $6,250.00 on the credit side of the account represent?
(b) What does the $5,100.00 on the debit side represent?
(c) What does the $1,150.00 on the debit side represent?

Date		Item	Post. Ref.	Debit		Date		Item	Post. Ref.	Credit	
1977 Dec.	31		J1	5 100	00	1977 Dec.	31		J1	6 250	00
	31		J1	1 150	00						
				6 250	00					6 250	00

CASE 2 Helen Morrison, owner of Helen's Beauty Salon, does not rule and balance her accounts at the end of each fiscal period. What are the disadvantages of not ruling and balancing the ledger accounts?

CASE 3 The post-closing trial balance of Rainbow Car Wash for August 31, 1977, page 156, shows Mr. Shaw's capital to be $5,277.00. The trial balance of the Rainbow Car Wash for the same date on page 111 shows Mr. Shaw's capital to be $4,500.00. How do you account for the difference?

Drills for
Mastering
Principles

DRILL 11-D 1 Identifying accounts as open or closed after closing entries are posted

The complete list of accounts used by Garver Delivery Service is given at the top of the next page.

1. Delivery Revenue
2. Foley Garage (creditor)
3. Sam Garver, Capital
4. Advertising Expense
5. Delivery Truck Expense
6. Baxter Company (creditor)
7. Cash
8. Delivery Truck

9. Warehouse Equipment
10. Utilities Expense
11. Wilson Trucking (creditor)
12. Miscellaneous Expense
13. Income Summary
14. Insurance Expense
15. Rent Expense
16. Office Equipment

Instructions: □ **1.** On a sheet of paper rule a form similar to the one illustrated at the right. Fill in the headings as shown in the illustration. In the Account Title column, copy the list of account titles given above.

Account Title	Answers
1. *Delivery Revenue*	C

□ **2.** If the account is closed after the closing entries are posted, write a capital C (for *Closed*) in the Answers column. If the account remains open after all closing entries are posted, write a capital O (for *Open*). The first item is an example.

□ **3.** Now cover your answers and see how rapidly you can do this drill mentally. Repeat this drill several times for increased speed and accuracy.

DRILL 11-D 2 Analyzing amounts that affect total capital during a fiscal period

The following information is available for twelve businesses:

Business	Balance in Capital Account at Start of Period	Additional Investment by Owner During Period	Net Income (+) or Net Loss (−) During Period	Balance Capital Account after Ledger is Closed
1.	$13,500.00	$1,500.00	+$4,640.00	$19,640.00
2.	28,000.00	None	− 1,860.00	26,140.00
3.	42,600.00	3,000.00	+ 6,450.00	?
4.	18,300.00	2,500.00	+ 3,380.00	?
5.	32,400.00	None	− 1,480.00	?
6.	23,800.00	1,800.00	− 1,250.00	?
7.	52,000.00	4,500.00	?	53,460.00
8.	38,850.00	None	?	43,200.00
9.	74,000.00	5,500.00	?	83,330.00
10.	36,880.00	?	+ 2,640.00	42,520.00
11.	92,500.00	?	− 1,380.00	92,620.00
12.	?	None	+ 2,370.00	26,830.00

Instructions: On a separate sheet of paper, fill in the missing amount for the last 10 businesses. Data for Businesses 1 and 2 are given as examples.

Problems for Applying Concepts

PROBLEM 11-1   Recording closing entries in a general journal

Those parts of the work sheet for Quick-Clean Car Wash needed to record the closing entries for the month ended June 30 of the current year are shown below.

Quick-Clean Car Wash
Work Sheet
For Month Ended June 30, 19—

Account Title	Acct. No.	Income Statement Debit	Income Statement Credit
Malcolm Holmes, Capital	31		
Income Summary	32		
Sales	41		1 360 00
Advertising Expense	51	43 40	
Electricity Expense	52	38 00	
Miscellaneous Expense	53	18 40	
Rent Expense	54	250 00	
Repairs Expense	55	18 50	
Wages Expense	56	425 00	
Water Expense	57	35 20	
		828 50	1 360 00
Net Income		531 50	
		1 360 00	1 360 00

Instructions: Record in a two-column general journal the three closing entries required at the end of the fiscal period.

Self-checking: Compare your work with the closing entries on page 150. (Note: No entries are made in the Post. Ref. column in this problem.)

PROBLEM 11-2   Recording closing entries in a general journal

Those parts of the work sheet of Skyline Motel needed to record the closing entries for the month ended March 31 of the current year are shown at the top of the next page.

Instructions: Record in a two-column general journal the three closing entries required at the end of the fiscal period.

Self-checking: Compare your work with the closing entries on page 150. (Note: No entries are made in the Post. Ref. column in this problem.)

Skyline Motel
Work Sheet
For Month Ended March 31, 19—

Account Title	Acct. No.	Income Statement	
		Debit	Credit
Carol Jenkins, Capital.........................	31		
Income Summary........................	32		
Room Sales..............................	41		1 130 00
Vending Machine Sales	42		42 75
Advertising Expense	51	74 50	
Laundry Expense........................	52	108 00	
Miscellaneous Expense	53	35 60	
Rent Expense..........................	54	450 00	
Utilities Expense	55	153 40	
Wages Expense	56	450 00	
		1 271 50	1 172 75
Net Loss...............................			98 75
		1 271 50	1 271 50

PROBLEM 11-3 Closing the ledger

If you are not using the workbook correlating with this textbook, complete Review Problem 11-R 1 instead of this problem.

Instructions: ◻ **1.** Foot the ledger accounts of the David Kiley Company provided for this problem in the workbook. If an account has entries on both sides, write the balance in small pencil figures in the proper Item column.

◻ **2.** Prove cash. The checkbook balance on September 30, 19—, is $1,823.70. This amount should agree with the balance in the cash account in the ledger. All cash receipts have been deposited.

◻ **3.** Prepare a work sheet on six-column analysis paper for the monthly fiscal period ended September 30. List *all* ledger accounts on the work sheet.

◻ **4.** Prepare an income statement.

◻ **5.** Prepare a balance sheet.

◻ **6.** Record the closing entries on page 2 of a general journal.

◻ **7.** Post the closing entries.

◻ **8.** Rule the income summary, revenue, and expense accounts.

◻ **9.** Balance all asset, liability, and capital accounts that need to be balanced.

◻ **10.** Prepare a post-closing trial balance.

Self-checking: 1. Were the footings written in your ledger in small figures with a sharp, firm pencil?

2. Was each amount column of an account footed when, and only when, it contained two or more entries?

3. Is your work sheet similar to the model on page 125?

4. Is your income statement similar to the model on page 135?

5. Is your balance sheet similar to the model on page 137?

6. Are your closing entries similar to the model on page 150?

7. After you have closed, ruled, and balanced your ledger, is it similar to the model ledger on pages 154 and 155?

8. Is your post-closing trial balance similar to the model on page 156?

The Complete Accounting Cycle

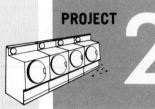

The preceding eleven chapters developed the steps in the complete accounting cycle. This project is designed to give you the opportunity to review and complete all of these steps:

1. Journalizing business transactions.
2. Posting to ledger accounts.
3. Preparing a trial balance and completing a work sheet.
4. Preparing financial statements.
5. Closing the ledger.
6. Preparing a post-closing trial balance.

| Journalizing business transactions |
| Posting to ledger accounts |
| Preparing a trial balance and completing a work sheet |
| Preparing financial statements |
| Closing the ledger |
| Preparing a post-closing trial balance |

CLEAN-RITE CENTER

The Clean-Rite Center, owned and operated by Dale Baker, is a self-service, coin-operated dry cleaning and laundry center. Mr. Baker rents the building in which the center is located. The center is equipped with automatic washers, automatic dryers, and automatic dry cleaners. Furniture and fixtures such as chairs, sorting tables, and carts are also provided for the customers. Clean-Rite Center uses the chart of accounts shown on page 164.

Opening accounts in the ledger

The Clean-Rite Center will use the same ledger for March of the current year as it used in February and previous months. Therefore, an opening entry is not required because a new set of books is not started in March.

Instructions: **1.** Open accounts in the ledger in the order listed in the chart of accounts, page 164. Number the accounts with the numbers given in the chart of accounts. Allow six lines for each account.

CLEAN-RITE CENTER
Chart of Accounts

(1) Assets	Account Number	(4) Revenue	Account Number
Cash..	11	Dry Cleaning Sales.....................	41
Furniture and Fixtures.................	12	Laundry Sales	42
Dry Cleaning Equipment.............	13		
Laundry Equipment....................	14	**(5) Expenses**	
		Advertising Expense..................	51
(2) Liabilities		Dry Cleaning Fluid Expense.........	52
Bay Appliance Co.	21	Maintenance Expense.................	53
Central Repair Service	22	Miscellaneous Expense...............	54
Superior Supplies Co.	23	Rent Expense	55
		Utilities Expense	56
(3) Capital			
Dale Baker, Capital	31		
Income Summary........................	32		

Instructions: 2. Copy the following balances in the ledger, using the date March 1 of the current year. As you copy these balances, write the word *Balance* in the Item column of each account and place a check mark (√) in the Post. Ref. column.

	Debit Balance		Credit Balance
Cash....................................	$ 920.00	Bay Appliance Co.	$ 1,730.00
Furniture and Fixtures.............	260.00	Central Repair Service	78.00
Dry Cleaning Equipment.........	7,100.00	Superior Supplies Co.	86.00
Laundry Equipment...............	4,620.00	Dale Baker, Capital	11,006.00

Journalizing business transactions

A business may have as many amount columns in its cash journal as it desires. Amount columns should be added in the journal when they will (a) save time and effort in posting or (b) supply additional data helpful in the management of the business. The six-column cash journal used by Clean-Rite Center is shown below.

CASH JOURNAL   PAGE 8

	CASH DEBIT	GENERAL DEBIT	DATE	ACCOUNT TITLE	NO.	POST. REF.	GENERAL CREDIT	DRY CLEANING SALES CREDIT	LAUNDRY SALES CREDIT	CASH CREDIT	
1			Feb. 1	Balance on hand $435.00		√					1
2		275.00	1	Rent Expense	Ck42	55				275.00	2
3		34.50	1	Advertising Expense	Ck43	51				34.50	3
4	187.00		2	√	R11	√		71.00	116.00		4
5		21.00	5	Maintenance Expense	Ck44	53				21.00	5
19	13.50		28	Furniture + Fixtures	R16	12	13.50				19
20		38.00	28	Utilities Expense	Ck45	56				38.00	20
21	1380.00 / 1380.00	812.00 / 812.00	28	Totals			46.00 / 46.00	320.50 / 320.50	930.50 / 930.50	895.00 / 895.00	21
22	(11)	(√)					(√)	(41)	(42)	(11)	22

Mr. Baker keeps two revenue accounts in his ledger — Dry Cleaning Sales and Laundry Sales. The two revenue accounts enable him to compare the revenue from both operations. He collects the coins from the automatic machines daily and deposits the total accumulated revenue in the bank twice a week. He journalizes both types of revenue transactions at the time of deposit. He therefore provides special columns for Dry Cleaning Sales Credit and Laundry Sales Credit in his six-column cash journal.

Instructions: **3.** Record the cash balance as of March 1 of the current year as a memorandum entry on page 8 of a six-column cash journal similar to the one on page 164.

4. Record in the cash journal the following transactions completed by the Clean-Rite Center during the month of March. Begin numbering checks with Ck46 and cash receipts with R17.

Transactions

March

1. Paid Superior Supplies Co. in full for amount owed, $86.00.
1. Paid for advertising in suburban newspaper, $46.00.
1. Paid March rent, $275.00.
3. Received revenue collected from machines for dry cleaning, $70.00, and laundry, $155.00; total, $225.00.

> Mr. Baker, the owner of the Clean-Rite Center, prepares receipts as his record of the revenue from the automatic machines when he removes the cash from the coin boxes. On the receipt form Mr. Baker writes in the total amount collected from each type of machine. The receipt serves as a source document to record receipt of cash from the automatic machines.
>
> Each revenue transaction for the Clean-Rite Center is journalized by a combined entry on one line of the cash journal. Line 4 of the cash journal, page 164, is an example.

4. Bought metal sorting table, $18.50.
6. Received revenue collected from machines for dry cleaning, $78.00, and laundry, $169.00; total, $247.00.
9. Bought postage stamps, $9.00.
10. Received revenue collected from machines for dry cleaning, $72.00, and laundry, $162.00; total, $234.00.
12. Bought filters for the dry cleaning machines, $38.00.
13. Received revenue collected from machines for dry cleaning, $81.00, and laundry, $152.00; total, $233.00.
14. Paid cash in part payment of amount owed to Bay Appliance Co., $250.00.
15. Sold old chair, $17.50.
15. Paid for washer repairs, $36.00.
16. Paid yearly magazine subscription, $15.00.
16. Bought new chair for reception area, $65.00.
17. Received revenue collected from machines for dry cleaning, $52.00, and laundry, $161.00; total, $213.00.
19. Bought clothes rack, $39.50.

March
20. Received revenue collected from machines for dry cleaning, $73.50, and laundry, $164.00; total, $237.50.
22. Bought dry cleaning fluid, $73.30.
23. Sold old washer, $20.00.
23. Paid teenager for washing the Center's windows, $6.00.
24. Bought new washer, $350.00.
24. Received revenue collected from machines for dry cleaning, $56.00, and laundry, $157.00; total, $213.00.
26. Paid Central Repair Service for amount owed, $78.00.
27. Received revenue collected from machines for dry cleaning, $74.00, and laundry, $166.00; total, $240.00.
27. Paid for special janitorial service, $18.00.
29. Bought dry cleaning steamer, $215.00.
30. Paid *Daily Gazette* for March advertising, $68.00.
31. Paid March gas bill, $115.00.
31. Paid March water bill, $98.00.
31. Paid March electrical bill, $106.00.
31. Paid March bill for newspaper subscription, $5.20.
31. Received revenue collected from machines for dry cleaning, $78.00, and laundry, $173.00; total, $251.00.

Footing, proving, and ruling the cash journal

Instructions: **5.** Foot all columns of the cash journal.

6. Prove the equality of debits and credits in the cash journal.

7. Prove cash. The bank balance according to the checkbook is $1,040.50. All cash receipts have been deposited.

8. Total and rule the cash journal. Refer to the illustration on page 164.

Posting to ledger accounts

Instructions: **9.** Post each amount in the General Debit column and in the General Credit column. Verify that a check mark was placed in the Post. Ref. column where both amounts of a transaction were entered in special columns. Place a check mark in parentheses under the total of each General column to show that the total is not to be posted.

10. Post the total of each of the four special columns in the cash journal. Write the proper account number in parentheses under each total.

Preparing a trial balance and completing a work sheet

Instructions: **11.** Foot the accounts in the ledger that have more than one entry on either side. If an account has entries on both sides, write the balance in small pencil figures in the Item column.

12. Prepare a trial balance on a six-column work sheet, using the first two amount columns for the trial balance.

13. Complete the work sheet. Refer to the illustration on page 125.

Preparing financial statements

Instructions: **14.** Prepare the income statement. Refer to the illustration on page 135.

15. Prepare the balance sheet. Refer to the illustration on page 137.

Closing the ledger

Instructions: **16.** Record the closing entries on page 7 of a two-column general journal. Use as your guide the illustration of closing entries on page 150.

17. Post the closing entries.

18. Rule the income summary account, the revenue accounts, and the expense accounts. Use as your guide the model accounts on pages 154 and 155.

19. Balance and rule all asset, liability, and capital accounts that need to be balanced. Use as your guide the model accounts on pages 154 and 155.

Preparing a post-closing trial balance

Instructions: **20.** Prepare a post-closing trial balance. Refer to the illustration on page 156.

THE ACCOUNTING CYCLE WITH THE COMBINATION JOURNAL AND SUBSIDIARY LEDGERS

MANY BUSINESSES HAVE DIFFERENT NEEDS FOR ACCOUNTING INFORMATION SYSTEMS. Large businesses may need an accounting information system that will handle thousands of transactions each month and provide many highly detailed reports. Smaller businesses may have less than a hundred transactions each month and need only a few accounting reports.

One manual accounting information system adopted by many small and medium size businesses uses a multi-column journal called a combination journal. The combination journal is used with a general ledger as well as additional ledgers called subsidiary ledgers.

SOME BUSINESSES SELL GOODS. A merchandising business is a business that buys and sells goods. Department stores, grocery stores, and automotive supply stores are examples.

In Part 2 of this textbook, we shall learn how a small merchandising business, *Gift World*, prepares financial reports. The financial reports are prepared by using a combination journal; the ledger accounts Purchases, Sales, Merchandise Inventory, Accounts Receivable, and Accounts Payable to account for goods it buys and sells; and the three ledgers, General Ledger, Accounts Receivable Ledger, and Accounts Payable Ledger.

GIFT WORLD
CHART OF ACCOUNTS

(1) ASSETS	Account Number	(4) REVENUE	Account Number
Cash...........................	11	Sales	41
Accounts Receivable	12		
Merchandise Inventory	13		
Supplies	14	**(5) COST OF MERCHANDISE**	
Prepaid Insurance	15	Purchases	51

(2) LIABILITIES		(6) EXPENSES	
Accounts Payable...........	21	Delivery Expense	61
		Insurance Expense	62
		Miscellaneous Expense	63
(3) CAPITAL		Rent Expense	64
Debra Horn, Capital	31	Salary Expense..............	65
Debra Horn, Drawing	32	Supplies Expense...........	66
Income Summary	33		

The chart of accounts for Gift World is illustrated above for ready reference as you study Part 2 of this textbook.

Journalizing Transactions of a Merchandising Business

12

Rainbow Car Wash, described in Part 1, sells a service. The service is washing cars. In Part 2, a business is described that sells small gifts, stationery, greeting cards, paper products, party supplies, and specialty items used for home decorating. The business, Gift World, is a gift shop owned by Miss Debra Horn. A business that buys and resells goods is called a merchandising business. A person or firm to whom a business sells merchandise is called a customer. The goods that a merchandising business purchases for resale to customers are called merchandise.

COMBINATION JOURNAL

The Rainbow Car Wash uses a multicolumn cash journal to record all cash transactions. All other transactions are recorded in a two-column general journal. Gift World has many noncash transactions that would take much time to enter in a general journal. Therefore, Gift World uses a journal in which all transactions can be entered yet has many of the time-saving features of the cash journal. A multicolumn journal that combines all journals into one book of original entry is called a combination journal. Gift World's combination journal is shown on pages 174 and 175.

Column headings in the combination journal

The cash journal used by Rainbow Car Wash has five amount columns: Cash Debit, General Debit, General Credit, Sales Credit, and Cash Credit. Gift World's combination journal has five more columns: Accounts Receivable Debit, Accounts Receivable Credit, Accounts Payable Debit, Accounts Payable Credit, and Purchases Debit. These additional amount columns are used to record the frequent transactions related to the purchase and sale of merchandise.

Arrangement of column headings in the combination journal

In the cash journal of Rainbow Car Wash, page 99, all debit columns are at the left of the Account Title column and all credit columns are at the right. Gift World's combination journal has twice the number of columns. Therefore, the columns are arranged to make accurate recording and posting easier. The debit and credit columns for Cash, Accounts Receivable, and Accounts Payable are arranged in pairs. This arrangement helps to avoid errors in recording amounts in the wrong columns. Since the Cash Debit and Credit columns are used in almost every transaction, they are placed at the left of the Account Title column. The remaining columns are placed at the right of the Account Title column. The General Debit and Credit columns are placed first. In this position, amounts for which special columns are not provided will be close to the account titles written in the Account Title column.

Recording the beginning cash balance in the combination journal

A memorandum entry for the beginning cash balance is recorded in the combination journal at the beginning of each month. A similar entry was made by Rainbow Car Wash in its cash journal. The entry is recorded in the journal so that the beginning cash balance is readily available for proving cash. Since this entry is not posted, a check mark is placed in the Post. Ref. column. The memorandum entry for Gift World on November 1, 1977, is on Line 1 of the combination journal, pages 174 and 175.

JOURNALIZING PURCHASES OF MERCHANDISE AND CASH PAYMENTS FOR PURCHASES

The value of the goods a business purchases to resell to customers is called the cost of merchandise. All costs of merchandise are deductions from the revenue of the business. Therefore, the costs of merchandise are recorded as debits. Costs of merchandise are kept in a separate division of the general ledger. This is shown in the chart of accounts, page 170.

A merchandising business frequently purchases merchandise for resale to customers and buys supplies and equipment for use in conducting the business. The account that shows the cost of merchandise purchased for resale to customers is titled Purchases. A more exact title for this account would be Merchandise Purchases. Common usage has shortened the title to Purchases. This account is used only for merchandise bought for resale. Therefore, only purchases of merchandise are recorded in the Purchases Debit column of the combination journal. All other items bought are recorded in the General Debit column.

The purchases account has a debit balance just as an expense account has a debit balance. Therefore, the purchases account is increased on its balance side which is its debit side. The purchases account is decreased on its credit side.

Purchase of merchandise for cash

Gift World pays cash for some purchases. However, payment is usually made several days after the merchandise has been received. Regardless of when payment is made, Gift World makes all payments by check.

Source document for a cash purchase of merchandise. The source document for a cash purchase transaction is the check stub of the check issued in payment. The source document for the transaction below is the check stub for Check No. 124.

Analyzing a cash purchase of merchandise. Gift World purchased for cash the following merchandise:

> November 2, 1977. Purchased merchandise for cash, $248.00. Check No. 124.

This cash purchase of merchandise transaction increases the balance of the purchases account. The cost account Purchases has a debit balance and is increased on its debit side. Thus Purchases is debited for $248.00.

Purchases	51
248.00	

Cash	11
	248.00

This transaction also decreases the balance of the cash account. The asset account Cash has a debit balance and is decreased on its credit side. Therefore, Cash is credited for $248.00.

Recording a cash purchase of merchandise. The entry to record this cash purchase of merchandise is on Line 3 of the combination journal on pages 174 and 175.

The date of the transaction, 2, is written in the Date column. The debit amount, $248.00, is written in the Purchases Debit column. The credit amount, $248.00, is written in the Cash Credit column. A check mark is placed in the Account Title column to show that no account title needs to be recorded. The check number, Ck124, is written in the Doc. No. column. A check mark is placed in the Post. Ref. column to show that amounts on this line are not to be posted individually.

> Gift World has many transactions recorded as debits to Purchases. For this reason, a special amount column headed Purchases Debit is included in the combination journal.

Purchase of merchandise on account

A transaction in which merchandise is purchased with an agreement to pay at a later date is called a purchase of merchandise on account. The business from which merchandise is purchased on account is known as a creditor.

PAGE 1 — COMBINATION JOURNAL

	1 CASH DEBIT	2 CASH CREDIT	DATE	ACCOUNT TITLE	DOC. NO.	POST. REF.	3 GENERAL DEBIT	4 GENERAL CREDIT	
1			1977 Nov. 1	Balance on hand, $3,400.00		✓			1
2		500 00	1	Rent Expense	Ck123		500 00		2
3		248 00	2	✓	Ck124	✓			3
4			3	Lotus Crafts	P21				4
5		360 00	4	Mac Nary Company	Ck125				5
6									6

Combination journal with purchases of merchandise transactions (left page)

Purchase order

Purchase order. A form prepared by a buyer describing what he desires to buy is called a purchase order. Gift World prepares purchase orders in duplicate as shown at the left. The original copy is sent to the firm from which the merchandise is to be purchased. The carbon copy is filed at Gift World. The purchase order is only an offer to buy. It does not represent a completed transaction. Therefore, the purchase order is not used as a source document for a journal entry.

PURCHASE ORDER

Gift World
814 Melrose Avenue
Medford, OR 97501
503-221-6475

No. 1048
DATE 10/8/77
SHIP BY Truck

TO
Lotus Crafts
1810 Woodstock Blvd.
Portland, OR 97200

DATE REQUIRED Dec. 1, 1977

PLEASE SHIP THE FOLLOWING

Quantity	Description	Price	Per	Amount
60 boxes	Assorted greeting cards #GC143	.50	box	30 00
30	Walnut ash trays #TA408	1.50	ea.	45 00
40	Desk sets #SD016	4.00	ea.	160 00
25	Novelty clocks #CN662	5.00	ea.	125 00
50 boxes	Playing cards #CP132	4.00	box	200 00
40 boxes	Game tally sheets #TG914	2.50	box	100 00
20	Music boxes #BK281	5.50	ea.	110 00
			TOTAL	770 00

ORIGINAL — ORDERED BY Debra Horn

DUPLICATE

Source document for a purchase of merchandise on account. When a seller sends merchandise to a buyer, the seller prepares a form showing what has been sent. A form describing the goods shipped, the method of shipment, the quantity, and the price of the goods is called an invoice. A copy of an invoice that the seller uses as the source document for recording a sale of merchandise is called a sales invoice. A copy of an invoice that the buyer uses as the source document for recording the purchase of merchandise is called a purchase invoice.

A purchase invoice received by Gift World is illustrated at the left. This purchase invoice lists the quantity, a brief description, the price of each item shipped, the total amount of the invoice as well as Gift World's purchase order number.

Lotus Crafts

RECD NOV 3 21

To
Gift World
814 Melrose Avenue
Medford, OR 97501

Date 11/3/77 — Salesperson Madden
Inv. No. 9057 — Shipped Via Truck
Terms 30 days — Your Order No. 1048

Lotus Crafts
1810 Woodstock Boulevard Portland, Oregon 97200

Quantity	Cat. No.	Description	Unit Price	Total
60✓ boxes	GC143	Assorted greeting cards	.50	30.00✓
30✓	TA408	Walnut ash trays	1.50	45.00✓
40✓	SD016	Desk sets	4.00	160.00✓
25✓	CN662	Novelty clocks	5.00	125.00✓
50✓ boxes	CP132	Playing cards	4.00	200.00✓
40✓ boxes	TG914	Game tally sheets	2.50	100.00✓
20✓	BK281	Music boxes	5.50	110.00✓
		Total		770.00 DH

Purchase invoice

FOR MONTH OF *November* 19 77						PAGE *1*	
	5	6	7	8	9	10	
	ACCOUNTS RECEIVABLE		SALES CREDIT	ACCOUNTS PAYABLE		PURCHASES DEBIT	
	DEBIT	CREDIT		DEBIT	CREDIT		
1							1
2							2
3						248.00	3
4					770.00	770.00	4
5				360.00			5
6							6

Combination journal with purchases
of merchandise transactions (right page)

When Gift World receives a purchase invoice, the date and a number are stamped in the upper right-hand corner. These numbers are assigned in sequence to identify all purchase invoices. The *21* stamped on the invoice shown on page 174 is the number assigned by Gift World to that purchase invoice. This number should not be confused with the seller's invoice number which is printed as *9057.*

The buyer needs to know that all of the items ordered have been received at the correct prices. The check marks on the invoice indicate that the items and amounts have been checked and are correct. The initials near the total are those of the person who checked the invoice.

The purchase invoice can be paid after the total has been verified. The agreement between the buyer and the seller as to payment for merchandise is called the terms of sale. The terms of sale on the invoice, page 174, are 30 days. This means payment is expected within 30 days from the date of the invoice. The invoice is dated November 3. Therefore, payment must be made by December 3.

Single general ledger account for all creditors. Some businesses buy on account from only a few companies. Therefore, they keep a separate account in the general ledger for each creditor. Rainbow Car Wash included separate accounts in its ledger, pages 97 and 98, for Auto Wash Equipment Co. and Marco Plumbing Company. However, a business that purchases on account from many firms will have numerous accounts with creditors. To avoid a bulky general ledger, the total amount owed to all creditors can be summarized in a single general ledger account. The general ledger account that summarizes the amount owed to all creditors is titled Accounts Payable which is a liability account.

Analyzing a purchase of merchandise on account. Gift World made the following purchase of merchandise on account:

November 3, 1977. Purchased merchandise on account from Lotus Crafts, $770.00. Purchase Invoice No. 21.

This transaction increases the balance of the purchases account. The cost account Purchases has a debit balance and is increased on its debit side. Purchases, therefore, is debited for $770.00.

Purchases	51
770.00	

Accounts Payable	21
	770.00

This transaction also increases the amount owed to creditors. The liability account Accounts Payable has a credit balance and is increased on its credit side. Accounts Payable, therefore, is credited for $770.00.

The way Gift World keeps records of the amount owed to each creditor is described in Chapter 13.

Recording a purchase of merchandise on account. The entry to record this purchase of merchandise on account is shown on Line 4 of the combination journal, pages 174 and 175.

The date, *3*, is written in the Date column. The amount of the debit to Purchases, *$770.00*, is written in the Purchases Debit column. The amount of the credit to Accounts Payable, *$770.00*, is written in the Accounts Payable Credit column. The name of the creditor, *Lotus Crafts*, is written in the Account Title column. The number of the purchase invoice, *P21*, is written in the Doc. No. column.

> Both debit and credit amounts are recorded in special amount columns, Purchases Debit and Accounts Payable Credit. It is not necessary to write the name of either account in the Account Title column. However, the name of the creditor is recorded in the Account Title column to show to whom the amount is owed.

Cash payment on account

Gift World pays for all merchandise purchased on account within the terms of sale stated on the seller's invoice.

Source document for a cash payment on account. The check stub for the check written to pay a creditor is the source document for a cash payment on account.

Analyzing a cash payment on account. Gift World made the following cash payment:

November 4, 1977. Paid on account to MacNary Company, $360.00. Check No. 125.

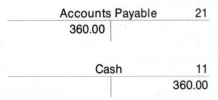

Accounts Payable	21
360.00	

Cash	11
	360.00

This cash payment on account decreases the amount owed to a creditor. The liability account Accounts Payable has a credit balance and is decreased on its debit side. Accounts Payable, therefore, is debited for $360.00.

This transaction also decreases the balance of the asset account Cash. Therefore, Cash is credited for $360.00.

Recording a cash payment on account. The entry to record this cash payment on account is on Line 5 of the combination journal, pages 174 and 175.

The date, *4*, is written in the Date column. The amount debited to Accounts Payable, *$360.00*, is written in the Accounts Payable Debit column. The amount credited to Cash, *$360.00*, is written in the Cash Credit column. The name of the creditor, *MacNary Company*, is written in the Account Title column. The number of the check, *Ck125*, is written in the Doc. No. column.

Summary of purchase of merchandise transactions

A summary of purchase of merchandise transactions and the combination journal columns in which they are recorded is shown below.

	CASH		GENERAL		ACCOUNTS RECEIVABLE		SALES CREDIT	ACCOUNTS PAYABLE		PURCHASES DEBIT
	1	2	3	4	5	6	7	8	9	10
	DEBIT	CREDIT	DEBIT	CREDIT	DEBIT	CREDIT		DEBIT	CREDIT	
Purchase of merchandise for cash		X								X
Purchase of merchandise on account									X	X
Cash payment on account		X						X		

Summary of purchase of merchandise transactions

JOURNALIZING SALES AND CASH RECEIPTS FOR SALES

A sale in which cash is received for the full amount at the time of the transaction is called a cash sale. Gift World sells most of its merchandise for cash.

Cash sales

Gift World uses a cash register to record all cash sales. The cash register prints a tape showing the amount of each cash sale. The amounts on the cash register tape may be totaled daily or weekly. This total amount of cash sales then may be recorded in the combination journal. Gift World records the total cash sales for each week.

Source document for cash sales. Gift World uses the cash register tape as the source document for the week's cash sales transactions. The tape is marked with the symbol *T* and the day of the month it is removed from the cash register. The total cash sales for the week are then recorded as a single transaction.

Analyzing a week's cash sales. The cash register tape at the close of business on November 5, 1977, shows the following:

> *November 5, 1977. Cash sales for the week, $1,432.00. Cash Register Tape No. T5.*

The tape for this transaction is marked *T5*. This cash sales transaction increases the balance of the asset account Cash. Cash, therefore, is debited for $1,432.00.

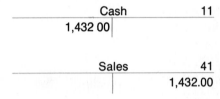

Gift World has one revenue account Sales in the revenue division of the general ledger. All sales of merchandise are recorded in this account. This transaction increases the balance of the revenue account Sales. Because Sales has a credit balance, the account is increased on its credit side. Sales, therefore, is credited for $1,432.00.

Recording cash sales. The entry for this cash sale is on Line 6 of the combination journal, below and on page 179.

The date, *5*, is written in the Date column. The amount debited to Cash, *$1,432.00*, is written in the Cash Debit column. The amount credited to Sales, *$1,432.00*, is written in the Sales Credit column. A check mark is placed in the Account Title column to show that no account title needs to be written for this transaction. The cash register tape number, *T5*, is written in the Doc. No. column. A check mark is placed in the Post. Ref. column to show that amounts on this line do not need to be posted individually.

> The entry for sales in the cash journal, Line 5, page 77, and the entry in the combination journal below, Line 6, are similar. The only difference is that Rainbow Car Wash records cash sales daily and Gift World records cash sales weekly.

| CASH | | DATE | ACCOUNT TITLE | Doc. No. | Post. Ref. | GENERAL | |
DEBIT	CREDIT					DEBIT	CREDIT
6	1432 00		5	✓	T5	✓			6
7			7	*Medford Interiors*	842				7
8	110 00		7	*Lavon Starks*	R101				8
9									9

PAGE 1 — COMBINATION JOURNAL

Combination journal with sales of merchandise transactions (left page)

Sale of merchandise on account

A sales transaction with an agreement that merchandise will be paid for at a later date is called a sale of merchandise on account. A sale of merchandise on account is also known as a charge sale or a credit sale. A person or a business to whom a sale on account is made is called a charge customer.

Single general ledger account for all charge customers. Gift World summarizes in a single general ledger account the total due from all charge customers. This general ledger account is titled Accounts Receivable. Accounts Receivable is an asset account.

Source document for a sale of merchandise on account. The source document for recording the sale of merchandise on account is a sales invoice. A sales invoice also is known as a sales ticket or a sales slip. The sales invoice used by Gift World is shown at the right. Each sales invoice for Gift World is prepared in duplicate. The original copy is used by the accountant as the source document. The carbon copy is given to the charge customer.

Sales invoice

Analyzing a sale of merchandise on account. The transaction for the sales invoice shown above is:

> November 7, 1977. Sold merchandise on account to Medford Interiors, $60.00. Sales Invoice No. 42.

This sale of merchandise on account increases the amount to be collected from customers. The asset account Accounts Receivable has a debit balance. Thus, it is increased on the debit side. Accounts Receivable, therefore, is debited for $60.00.

Accounts Receivable	12
60.00	

Sales	41
	60.00

Chapter 13 describes how Gift World keeps records of amounts to be collected from each charge customer.

		FOR MONTH OF *November* 19 77	PAGE *1*			
5	**6**	**7**	**8**	**9**	**10**	
ACCOUNTS RECEIVABLE		SALES CREDIT	ACCOUNTS PAYABLE		PURCHASES DEBIT	
DEBIT	CREDIT		DEBIT	CREDIT		
		1 432 00				6
60 00				60 00		7
	1 10 00					8
						9

Combination journal with sales of merchandise transactions (right page)

This transaction also increases the balance of the sales account. The revenue account Sales has a credit balance and is increased on its credit side. Sales, therefore, is credited for $60.00.

Recording a sale of merchandise on account. The entry for this sale of merchandise on account is on Line 7 of the combination journal, pages 178 and 179.

The date, 7, is written in the Date column. The amount debited to Accounts Receivable, *$60.00*, is written in the Accounts Receivable Debit column. The amount credited to Sales, *$60.00*, is written in the Sales Credit column. The name of the charge customer, *Medford Interiors*, is written in the Account Title column. The number of the sales invoice, *S42*, is written in the Doc. No. column.

Credit cards and sales of merchandise on account. An embossed plastic plate identifying a customer with a charge account is called a credit card. Before a credit card is issued, the customer's credit rating is checked. When a credit card is used, the card and the sales invoice are placed in a special imprinting device. This device records the customer's name and account number on all copies of the sales invoice. Thus, writing the name and account number on the sales invoice is eliminated.

Company credit card

Some businesses do not issue credit cards. Instead, they may subscribe to a credit card service offered by a bank. The bank (1) issues the credit cards to customers, (2) receives monthly reports from the businesses of their sales to card holders, (3) pays each subscribing business for the purchases of card holders, and (4) bills each credit card holder for any purchases. The card holders then pay the bank for all credit card purchases.

A business subscribing to a bank's credit card service periodically takes all credit card invoices to the bank. The bank credits the business's bank account for the total amount of the invoices less a small charge for the collecting service.

Bank credit card

Gift World has found it necessary to use credit card sales. However, how a business using credit card sales records this data is described in Chapter 26, pages 515 and 516.

Cash received on account

Gift World prepares a receipt when cash is received on account from a customer. The receipts are prenumbered so all receipts can be accounted for. The original copy of the receipt is given to the charge customer.

Source document for cash received on account. The carbon copy of the cash receipt is used as the source document for the cash received on account transaction.

Analyzing cash received on account. Gift World received cash on account from a charge customer:

> November 7, 1977. Received on account from Lavon Starks, $110.00.
> Receipt No. 101.

This cash received on account increases the balance of the asset account Cash. Cash, therefore, is debited for $110.00.

This transaction also decreases the amount to be collected from customers. The asset account Accounts Receivable, therefore, is credited for $110.00.

Cash	11
110.00	

Accounts Receivable	12
	110.00

Recording cash received on account. This transaction is on Line 8 of the combination journal, pages 178 and 179.

The date, 7, is written in the Date column. The amount, *$110.00*, debited to Cash is recorded in the Cash Debit column. The amount, *$110.00*, credited to Accounts Receivable is recorded in the Accounts Receivable Credit column. The name of the charge customer, *Lavon Starks*, is written in the Account Title column. The number of the receipt, *R101*, is written in the Doc. No. column.

Summary of sales of merchandise transactions

A summary of sales of merchandise transactions and the combination journal columns in which they are recorded is below.

	COMBINATION JOURNAL									
	1	2	3	4	5	6	7	8	9	10
	CASH		GENERAL		ACCOUNTS RECEIVABLE		SALES CREDIT	ACCOUNTS PAYABLE		PURCHASES DEBIT
	DEBIT	CREDIT	DEBIT	CREDIT	DEBIT	CREDIT		DEBIT	CREDIT	
Sale of merchandise for cash	X						X			
Sale of merchandise on account					X		X			
Cash received on account	X					X				

Summary of sales of merchandise transactions

JOURNALIZING OTHER TRANSACTIONS

Most merchandising business transactions relate to buying or selling merchandise. However, a merchandising business has other transactions

| CASH | | DATE | ACCOUNT TITLE | Doc. No. | Post. Ref. | GENERAL | |
DEBIT	CREDIT					DEBIT	CREDIT
	4500	8 Delivery Expense	Ck126		4500		9
		8 Supplies	M.76		12600		10
		Martinez Supplies					11
25000		8 Debra Horn, Drawing	Ck127		25000		12
		9 Supplies	M.77		3000		13
		Prepaid Insurance				3000	14

COMBINATION JOURNAL

PAGE /

Combination journal with other
transactions (left page)

that must be recorded. The combination journal also may be used to
record these other transactions as shown above and on page 183.

Cash payment of an expense

Gift World records payments of expenses in the combination journal.
These expense transactions are recorded as in the columnar cash journal
of Rainbow Car Wash, Part 1.

Source document for a cash payment of an expense. The check stub is
the source document for a cash payment of an expense.

Analyzing a cash payment of an expense. Gift World made the following cash payment transaction:

November 8, 1977. Paid delivery expense, $45.00. Check No. 126.

This cash payment increases the delivery expense account. The expense account Delivery Expense has a debit
balance and is increased on its debit side. Delivery Expense, therefore, is debited for $45.00.

This transaction also decreases the balance of the asset
account Cash. Cash, therefore, is credited for $45.00.

Recording a cash payment of an expense. This payment of an expense
is on Line 9 of the combination journal above.

The date, *8*, is written in the Date column. The amount debited to the
delivery expense account, *$45.00*, is written in the General Debit column.
The name of the general ledger account, *Delivery Expense*, is written in
the Account Title column. The amount credited to Cash, *$45.00*, is writ-
ten in the Cash Credit column. The number of the check, *Ck126*, is written in the Doc. No. column.

		FOR MONTH OF *November* 19 77		PAGE *1*		
5	6	7	8	9	10	
ACCOUNTS RECEIVABLE		SALES CREDIT	ACCOUNTS PAYABLE		PURCHASES DEBIT	
DEBIT	CREDIT		DEBIT	CREDIT		
9						9
10						10
11				*12600*		11
12						12
13						13
14						14

Combination journal with other
transactions (right page)

Buying supplies on account

Gift World usually buys supplies for cash. Occasionally, however, some supplies are bought on account.

Source document for buying supplies on account. When Gift World buys supplies on account, it receives an invoice from the seller. This invoice is similar to the purchase invoice received when merchandise is purchased. To distinguish this invoice for supplies from a purchase invoice, Debra Horn, owner of Gift World, attaches a brief note to the invoice. The note tells the accountant that the invoice is for supplies and not for purchases. A form on which a brief interoffice message is written is called a memorandum. Memorandum No. 76 is at the right. The memorandum with its attached invoice is the source document for buying supplies on account. After entries have been made, the memorandums are filed numerically.

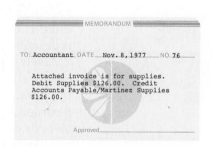

MEMORANDUM

TO: Accountant DATE Nov. 8, 1977 NO. 76

Attached invoice is for supplies.
Debit Supplies $126.00. Credit
Accounts Payable/Martinez Supplies
$126.00.

Approved

Memorandum for
buying supplies on
account

Analyzing buying supplies on account. Gift World bought the following supplies on account:

> November 8, 1977. Bought supplies on account from Martinez Supplies, $126.00. Memorandum No. 76.

Buying supplies on account increases the balance of the supplies account. The asset account Supplies has a debit balance and is increased on the debit side. Supplies, therefore, is debited for $126.00.

Supplies	14
126.00	

This transaction also increases the amount owed to creditors. Therefore, the liability account Accounts Payable is credited for $126.00.

Accounts Payable	21
	126.00

Recording buying supplies on account. This transaction is on Lines 10 and 11 of the combination journal on pages 182 and 183.

The date, *8*, is written in the Date column. Supplies has no special column. Therefore, the amount, *$126.00*, debited to Supplies is recorded in the General Debit column. The title of the account debited, *Supplies*, is written in the Account Title column. The amount, *$126.00*, credited to Accounts Payable is written in the Accounts Payable Credit column on the next line. The name of the creditor, *Martinez Supplies*, is written in the Account Title column and is indented about one-half inch (about 1.3 centimeters). A brace ({) is placed in the Date column to show that both entries on these two lines belong to the same transaction. The number of the memorandum, *M76*, is written in the Doc. No. column.

Changes in capital — cash withdrawals by owner

Changes in the capital account balance are caused by three kinds of entries: (1) the owner invests additional capital, (2) the owner withdraws assets, or (3) the net income or the net loss is recorded.

A cash journal entry recording an additional investment of cash by the owner is on pages 73 and 74. The same procedure is followed to record an additional owner investment in the combination journal. A general journal entry closing the net income or the net loss into the capital account is on page 149. A similar closing entry in the combination journal is described in a later chapter.

Assets taken out of a business for the personal use of the owner are called withdrawals. Withdrawals reduce the amount of capital in the business. Since the capital account has a credit balance, decreases are recorded as debits. Withdrawals could be recorded as debits in the owner's capital account. However, withdrawals normally are recorded in a separate account. Then the total amount of withdrawals for each fiscal period can be determined easily. Gift World records withdrawals in an account titled Debra Horn, Drawing. Because the drawing account shows decreases in capital, the drawing account has a debit balance.

Source document for a cash withdrawal. When Debra Horn withdraws cash from Gift World, a check is written to her for the payment. The check stub of the check is the source document for the transaction.

Analyzing a cash withdrawal. Debra Horn withdrew cash as follows:

November 8, 1977. Debra Horn, owner, withdrew cash, $250.00. Check No. 127.

This cash withdrawal increases the balance of the drawing account. The capital account Debra Horn, Drawing has a debit balance and is increased on its debit side. Debra Horn, Drawing, therefore, is debited for $250.00.

This transaction also decreases the asset account Cash. Cash, therefore, is credited for $250.00.

Recording a cash withdrawal. This cash withdrawal is on Line 12 of the combination journal, pages 182 and 183.

The date, *8*, is written in the Date column. The amount debited to the drawing account, *$250.00*, is written in the General Debit column. The name of the general ledger account, *Debra Horn, Drawing*, is written in the Account Title column. The amount credited to the cash account, *$250.00*, is written in the Cash Credit column. The number of the check, *Ck127*, is written in the Doc. No. column.

Debra Horn, Drawing	32
250.00	

Cash	11
	250.00

Correcting entry

Errors may be made even though care is taken in recording transactions. Simple errors may be corrected by ruling through the incorrect item as described on pages 114 and 115. However, when a transaction has been erroneously recorded in the journal *and* posted to the ledger, an entry to correct the error should be made. A journal entry made to correct an error in the ledger is called a correcting entry.

Source document for a correcting entry. If an accounting error is discovered, the accountant for Gift World prepares a memorandum showing the correction to be made. This memorandum is approved by the owner, Debra Horn. A correcting entry memorandum is shown at the right.

The approved memorandum is the source document for the correcting entry.

MEMORANDUM

TO: Accountant DATE Nov. 9, 1977 NO. 77

Invoice from Martinez Supplies, October 25, 1977, Purchase Invoice No. 20, was for supplies bought on account. Prepaid Insurance was debited in error.

Correcting entry needed to transfer $30.00 from prepaid insurance account to supplies account.

Approved *Debra Horn*

Memorandum for a correcting entry

Analyzing a correcting entry. The accountant for Gift World discovered an error:

> November 9, 1977. *Discovered that supplies bought on October 25 had been recorded and posted in error as a debit to Prepaid Insurance, instead of Supplies, $30.00. Memorandum No. 77.*

To correct the error, the accountant must make an entry to remove $30.00 from the prepaid insurance account. The entry must also add $30.00 to the supplies account.

The asset account Supplies is increased by this correcting entry. Supplies, therefore, is debited for $30.00.

The prepaid insurance account is decreased by this correcting entry. The asset account Prepaid Insurance has a debit balance and is decreased on the credit side. Thus, Prepaid Insurance is credited for $30.00.

Supplies	14
30.00	

Prepaid Insurance	15
	30.00

Recording a correcting entry. The correcting entry is on Lines 13 and 14 of the combination journal, pages 182 and 183.

The date, *9*, is written in the Date column. The amount debited to the supplies account, *$30.00*, is written in the General Debit column. The title of the account, *Supplies*, is written in the Account Title column. The amount credited to the prepaid insurance account, *$30.00*, is written in the General Credit column on the next line. The name of the account, *Prepaid Insurance*, is indented about one-half inch (about 1.3 centimeters) and written in the Account Title column. The source document number, *M77*, is written in the Doc. No. column. A brace is drawn in the Date column to show that both entries on these two lines belong to the same transaction.

Summary of other transactions

A summary of other transactions and the combination journal columns in which they are recorded is below.

	CASH		GENERAL		ACCOUNTS RECEIVABLE		SALES CREDIT	ACCOUNTS PAYABLE		PURCHASES DEBIT
	1	2	3	4	5	6	7	8	9	10
	DEBIT	CREDIT	DEBIT	CREDIT	DEBIT	CREDIT		DEBIT	CREDIT	
Cash payment of an expense	X	X								
Buy supplies on account			X						X	
Change in capital—cash withdrawal by owner	X	X								

COMBINATION JOURNAL

Summary of other transactions

TOTALING AND PROVING THE COMBINATION JOURNAL

The combination journal is totaled and proved when the page is filled and at the end of the fiscal period. The steps are similar to those described in Part 1, pages 77 and 78, for the cash journal of Rainbow Car Wash.

Forwarding the totals of the combination journal

The amount columns are footed, proved, and totaled when a page of the combination journal is filled. The bottom line of the illustration, pages 188 and 189, shows how the totals are prepared for forwarding.

The steps in forwarding totals for a completed page of a combination journal are on the next page.

☐ **1** Pencil foot all amount columns.

☐ **2** Prove that the sum of the debit footings equals the sum of the credit footings.

☐ **3** Write the totals in ink.

☐ **4** Write the date in the Date column.

☐ **5** Write the words *Carried Forward* in the Account Title column.

☐ **6** Place a check mark in the Post. Ref. column to show that none of these totals is to be posted individually.

The illustration on pages 190 and 191 shows how totals brought forward are recorded on the first line of a new page. The steps in recording the totals brought forward to a new page are:

☐ **1** Write the date in the Date column.

☐ **2** Write the words *Brought Forward* in the Account Title column.

☐ **3** Write the totals from the preceding page in each amount column.

> Again prove that the debit totals equal the credit totals to be sure the totals have been forwarded correctly.

☐ **4** Place a check mark in the Post. Ref. column to show that none of these totals is to be posted.

Footing and proving the combination journal at the end of the month

The equality of debits and credits in the combination journal is proved at the end of the month. All columns are footed. Then, if the sum of the debit footings is equal to the sum of the credit footings, the journal totals are proved. For the combination journal, pages 190 and 191, the proof is:

Col. No.	Column	Debit Footings	Credit Footings
1	Cash Debit	$ 8,499.00	
2	Cash Credit		$ 5,755.60
3	General Debit	1,878.60	
4	General Credit		30.00
5	Accounts Receivable Debit	1,092.00	
6	Accounts Receivable Credit		599.00
7	Sales Credit		8,992.00
8	Accounts Payable Debit	2,039.00	
9	Accounts Payable Credit		3,150.00
10	Purchases Debit	5,018.00	
	Totals	$18,526.60	$18,526.60

PAGE /								
			COMBINATION JOURNAL					
1	2					3	4	
CASH		DATE	ACCOUNT TITLE	Doc. No.	Post. Ref.	GENERAL		
DEBIT	CREDIT					DEBIT	CREDIT	
		1977 Nov. 1	Balance on hand $3400.00		✓			1
	50000	1	Rent Expense	Ck123		50000		2
	24800	2	✓	Ck124	✓			3
		3	Lotus Crafts	P21				4
	36000	4	Mac Nary Company	Ck125				5
143200		5	✓	J5	✓			6
		7	Medford Interiors	S42				7
11000		7	Lavon Starks	R101				8
	4500	8	Delivery Expense	Ck126		4500		9
		8	Supplies	M76		12600		10
			Martinez Supplies					11
	25000	8	Debra Horn, Drawing	Ck127		25000		12
		9	Supplies	M77		3000		13
			Prepaid Insurance				3000	14
		9	Lisa Zimmerman	S43				15
		9	Lavon Starks	S44				16
		10	Zane Interiors	S45				17
		10	Mac Nary Company	P22				18
		10	Charles Lebo	S46				19
9500		10	Medford Interiors	R102				20
5800		11	Crater Associates	R103				21
		11	Young's Specialties	P23				22
195800		12	✓	J12	✓			23
	24500	14	Martinez Supplies	Ck128				24
	2500	15	Miscellaneous Expense	Ck129		2500		25
		15	Crater Associates	S47				26
	36000	15	Salary Expense	Ck130		36000		27
6500		16	Lisa Zimmerman	R104				28
	77000	16	Lotus Crafts	Ck131				29
	60000	16	✓	Ck132	✓			30
		17	Zane Interiors	S48				31
		17	Lavon Starks	S49				32
		18	Mac Nary Company	P24				33
6000		19	Medford Interiors	R105				34
183600		19	✓	J19	✓			35
561400	340300	19	Carried Forward		✓	133600	3000	36

Combination journal footed and totaled for forwarding (left page)

These two totals are equal. Therefore, the equality of debits and credits in Gift World's combination journal for November is proved. The next step is to prove cash.

Proving cash with the combination journal

At the end of November, Gift World figures the cash proof as shown at the bottom of the next page.

Divided Column Form

	ACCOUNTS RECEIVABLE		SALES CREDIT	ACCOUNTS PAYABLE		PURCHASES DEBIT	
	DEBIT	CREDIT		DEBIT	CREDIT		
1							1
2							2
3						248 00	3
4					770 00	770 00	4
5				360 00			5
6			1432 00				6
7	60 00		60 00				7
8		110 00					8
9							9
10							10
11					126 00		11
12							12
13							13
14							14
15	65 00		65 00				15
16	30 00		30 00				16
17	61 00		61 00				17
18					264 00	264 00	18
19	478 00		478 00				19
20		95 00					20
21		58 00					21
22					236 00	236 00	22
23			1958 00				23
24				245 00			24
25							25
26	30 00		30 00				26
27							27
28		65 00					28
29				770 00			29
30						600 00	30
31	90 00		90 00				31
32	72 00		72 00				32
33					235 00	235 00	33
34		60 00					34
35	886 00	388 00	1836 00 / 6112 00	1375 00	1631 00	2353 00	35
36	886 00	388 00	6112 00	1375 00	1631 00	2353 00	36

Combination journal footed and totaled for forwarding (right page)

Beginning cash balance
  Line 1, page 1, combination journal (page 188) .... $ 3,400.00
Plus total cash received
  Total of Cash Debit column, Line 23, page 2 (page 190) 8,499.00
Total.. $11,899.00
Less total cash payments
  Total of Cash Credit column, Line 23, page 2 (page 190) 5,755.60
Equals amount of cash that should be on hand .... $ 6,143.40

PAGE 2			COMBINATION JOURNAL				
1	2					3	4
CASH		DATE	ACCOUNT TITLE	Doc. No.	Post. Ref.	GENERAL	
DEBIT	CREDIT					DEBIT	CREDIT
1	561400	340300	1977 Nov. 19 Brought Forward		✓	133600	3000	1

Combination journal footed, totaled, and ruled (left page)

21				30 Mac Nary Company	P28				21
22	133000			30 ✓	J30	✓			22
23	849900	575660		30 Totals			187860	3000	23
	849900	575560					187860	3000	
24									24

The last check written in November, 1977, was Check No. 140. The balance in the checkbook after the last check had been written and after the last deposit was made is $6,143.40. Since this is the same as the balance on hand, page 189, cash is proved.

Ruling the combination journal at the end of the month

The combination journal for Gift World is ruled at the end of the month. The illustration above shows the ruling of the combination journal for November. These ruling procedures are the same as those used by Rainbow Car Wash in Part 1, page 79.

A complete illustration of page 2 of the combination journal for Gift World is shown on pages 208 and 209, Chapter 13.

A complete illustration of page 2 of the combination journal for Gift World is shown on pages 208 and 209, Chapter 13.

Using Business Terms

✦What is the meaning of each of the following?

- merchandising business
- customer
- merchandise
- combination journal
- cost of merchandise
- purchase of merchandise on account

- purchase order
- invoice
- sales invoice
- purchase invoice
- terms of sale
- cash sale

- sale of merchandise on account
- charge customer
- credit card
- memorandum
- withdrawals
- correcting entry

Questions for Individual Study

1. What kind of entry is made to record the beginning cash balance in the combination journal?
2. Which amount columns in the combination journal are used to record a purchase of merchandise for cash?
3. Which amount columns in the combination journal are used to record a purchase of merchandise on account transaction?
4. What is the source document for a journal entry recording a purchase of merchandise on account?

5. Which amount columns in the combination journal are used to record a cash payment on account?
6. Which two accounts are affected by cash sales of merchandise? How?
7. What is the source document for a journal entry for a sale of merchandise on account?
8. Which amount columns in the combination journal are used to record a sale of merchandise on account?
9. Which amount columns are used to record cash received on account?

FOR MONTH OF *November* 19 77 PAGE 2						
ACCOUNTS RECEIVABLE		SALES CREDIT	ACCOUNTS PAYABLE		PURCHASES DEBIT	
DEBIT	CREDIT		DEBIT	CREDIT		
1 88600	38800	611200	137500	163100	235300	1
21				61700	61700	21
22		133000				22
23 109200	59900	899200	203900	315000	501800	23
23 109200	59900	899200	203900	315000	501800	23
24						24

Combination journal footed, totaled, and ruled (right page)

10. Which two accounts are affected by buying supplies on account? How?

11. Which two accounts are affected by a cash withdrawal by the owner? How?

12. How can the combination journal be proved at the end of the month?

CASE 1 George Oxley, an appliance dealer, uses a cash journal and a general journal similar to those in Chapter 6. He asked an accountant to look over his accounting system and recommend changes. The accountant suggests that Mr. Oxley use a combination journal similar to the one in Chapter 12. Which do you think would be better: (a) the cash journal and general journal, or (b) the combination journal? Why?

CASE 2 Jennifer McLain, a high school student, works part-time in Zorba's Clothing Store. After observing several entries in the combination journal, Jennifer asks: "Why do you use the purchase invoice as your source document for recording purchases of merchandise? Then you use a memorandum signed by Mr. Zorba as your source document for recording the entry when supplies are bought. Why don't you use the purchase invoice for both entries?" How will you answer her?

DRILL 12-D 1 Analyzing transactions into debit and credit parts

Instructions: For each of the transactions below and on page 192, prepare two T accounts to show which account in the general ledger is debited and which account is credited. The first transaction is given as an example.

1. Received an additional cash investment from owner, Kent Houk, $1,500.00.
2. Paid November rent, $400.00.
3. Purchased merchandise for cash, $150.00.
4. Paid fire insurance premium, $100.00.
5. Purchased merchandise on account from Perkins Co., $150.00.
6. Bought supplies on account from Auburn Paper Products, $30.00.
7. Bought supplies for cash, $50.00.
8. Paid on account to Perkins Co., $150.00.
9. Discovered that supplies bought last month had been recorded and posted in error as a debit to Prepaid Insurance instead of Supplies, $25.00.
10. Cash sales of merchandise for the week, $600.00.

Cash	
1,500.00	

Kent Houk, Capital	
	1,500.00

11. Sold merchandise on account to Jack Zarn, $60.00.
12. Received on account from Jack Zarn, $60.00.
13. Issued check to owner, Kent Houk, for a cash withdrawal, $150.00.

<table>
<tr><td>**Problem
for
Applying
Concepts**</td><td>**PROBLEM 12-1**   </td><td>Journalizing transactions in a
combination journal</td></tr>
</table>

Olga Koop, a retail florist, completed the transactions below during the month of May of the current year. The cash balance on May 1 was $5,220.00.

Instructions: ◻ **1.** Record the cash balance on hand, May 1, on page 6 of a combination journal like the one on pages 188 and 189.

◻ **2.** Record the following transactions. Source documents are abbreviated as: check, Ck; purchase invoice, P; receipt, R; sales invoice, S; cash register tape, T.

May 1. Paid gas bill for April, $75.00. Ck212. (Miscellaneous Expense)
     1. Received on account from Evan Bale, $105.00. R46.
     2. Paid May rent, $200.00. Ck213.
     3. Sold merchandise on account to Ben Huskey, $55.00. S95.
     3. Cash sales of merchandise for the week, $360.00. T3.
     5. Purchased merchandise on account from Berman, Inc., $200.00. P114.
     6. Paid on account to Heath & Sons, $850.00. Ck214.
     7. Received on account from Tanya Kurtz, $180.00. R47.
     9. Purchased merchandise for cash, $90.00. Ck215.
    10. Cash sales of merchandise for the week, $420.00. T10.
    13. Sold merchandise on account to Earl James, $170.00. S96.
    15. Paid on account to Gordon Brothers, $175.00. Ck216.
    16. Issued check to owner, Olga Koop, for a cash withdrawal, $150.00. Ck217.
    17. Cash sales of merchandise for the week, $525.00. T17.
    19. Purchased merchandise on account from Hopkins Nursery, $500.00. P115.
    21. Paid delivery expense, $50.00. Ck218.
    23. Sold merchandise on account to Floyd Doss, $65.00. S97.
    24. Cash sales of merchandise for the week, $600.00. T24.
    26. Purchased merchandise for cash, $120.00. Ck219.
    27. Paid on account to Green's Garden Center, $250.00. Ck220.
    29. Paid telephone bill, $40.00. Ck221. (Miscellaneous Expense)
    31. Paid delivery expense, $35.00. Ck222.
    31. Paid salary expense, $800.00. Ck223.
    31. Cash sales of merchandise for the week, $420.00. T31.

Instructions: ◻ **3.** Pencil foot the columns of the combination journal and prove the equality of debits and credits.

◻ **4.** Prove cash. The balance on hand shown on the check stub for Check No. 224 is $4,995.00.

◻ **5.** Total and rule the combination journal. Use the illustration on pages 190 and 191 as a guide in ruling.

**MASTERY
PROBLEM 12-M**   Journalizing transactions using two pages of
a combination journal

Lee Coker owns and operates a paint store. The transactions below were completed during November of the current year. The cash balance on November 1 was $1,700.00.

Instructions: □ **1.** Record the cash balance on hand, November 1, on page 10 of a combination journal like the one on pages 188 and 189.

□ **2.** Record the following transactions. Source documents are abbreviated as: check, Ck; memorandum, M; purchase invoice, P; receipt, R; sales invoice, S; cash register tape, T.

Nov. 1. Paid November rent, $250.00. Ck21.
      3. Purchased merchandise for cash, $180.00. Ck22.
      4. Sold merchandise on account to Joan Shelton, $110.00. S71.
      5. Received an additional investment from owner, Lee Coker, $550.00. R103.
      5. Bought supplies on account from Drake Supply Co., $30.00. M12.
      5. Cash sales of merchandise for the week, $600.00. T5.
      8. Purchased merchandise on account from Soper, Inc., $135.00. P40.
      8. Sold merchandise on account to Joan Shelton, $35.00. S72.
      9. Received on account from Richard Hagen, $180.00. R104.
      9. Paid on account to Drake Supply Co., $95.00. Ck23.
      9. Sold merchandise on account to Joan Shelton, $35.00. S73.
     10. Purchased merchandise on account from Ritz Paint Supplies, $120.00. P41.
     12. Cash sales of merchandise for the week, $625.00. T12.
     15. Paid salaries, $105.00. Ck24.
     15. Sold merchandise on account to Alex Penner, $215.00. S74.
     15. Purchased merchandise for cash, $145.00. Ck25.
     16. Received on account from Joan Shelton, $105.00. R105.
     18. Purchased merchandise on account from Masters Company, $150.00. P42.
     19. Paid on account to Soper, Inc., $60.00. Ck26.
     19. Sold merchandise on account to Richard Hagen, $200.00. S75.
     19. Paid electric bill for October, $30.00. Ck27. (Miscellaneous Expense)
     19. Cash sales of merchandise for the week, $860.00. T19.
     20. Purchased merchandise for cash, $60.00. Ck28.
     22. Issued check to owner, Lee Coker, for a cash withdrawal, $60.00. Ck29.
     23. Sold merchandise on account to Richard Hagen, $130.00. S76.
     25. Discovered that supplies bought in September had been recorded and posted in error to Prepaid Insurance, $60.00. M13.
     26. Received on account from Glen Olsen, $75.00. R106.
     26. Sold merchandise on account to Alex Penner, $30.00. S77.
     26. Cash sales of merchandise for the week, $730.00. T26.

Instructions: □ **3.** Prepare page 10 of the combination journal for forwarding. Pencil foot all columns, prove the equality of debits and credits, and record on Line 33 the totals to be carried forward.

□ **4.** Record the totals brought forward on Line 1 of page 11 of the combination journal.

□ **5.** Record on page 11 the transactions listed below.

Nov. 28. Paid on account to Ritz Paint Supplies, $125.00. Ck30.
  29. Paid delivery expenses, $20.00. Ck31.
  29. Bought supplies on account from Drake Supply Co., $110.00. M14.
  29. Paid on account to Masters Company, $150.00. Ck32.
  30. Purchased merchandise for cash, $40.00. Ck33.
  30. Paid salaries, $105.00. Ck34.
  30. Sold merchandise on account to Glen Olsen, $90.00. S78.
  30. Cash sales of merchandise for the week, $410.00. T30.

Instructions: □ **6.** Pencil foot all columns of page 11 of the combination journal and prove the equality of debits and credits.

□ **7.** Prove cash. The check stub for Check No. 35 shows a balance on hand of $4,410.00.

□ **8.** Total and rule page 11 of the combination journal

The combination journal prepared in this problem will be used in Mastery Problem 13-M, Chapter 13.

BONUS Journalizing transactions using two pages of
PROBLEM 12-B a combination journal

Introductory remarks. The ruling of a combination journal can be in different arrangements. For example, the combination journal on pages 188 and 189 is called a divided-column form. The amount columns are divided by the Account Title column. Some of the amount columns are to the left and some are to the right of the Account Title column. Another common pattern is to have *all* amount columns to the right of the Account Title column.

Instructions: □ **1.** Use a combination journal ruled as shown below.

Date	Account Title	Doc. No.	Post. Ref.	General Dr.	General Cr.	Cash Dr.	Cash Cr.	Accounts Payable Dr.	Accounts Payable Cr.	Accounts Receivable Dr.	Accounts Receivable Cr.	Purchases Dr.	Sales Cr.

Instructions: □ **2.** Use the transactions and instructions for Mastery Problem 12-M. Complete all of the instructions using the combination journal shown above.

The combination journal prepared in this problem will be used in Bonus Problem 13-B, Chapter 13.

Posting transactions from a journal to ledger accounts helps sort and summarize the data for future use. In Part 1, Rainbow Car Wash uses only a single ledger. Gift World, however, uses more than one ledger. A ledger that contains all the accounts needed to prepare an income statement and a balance sheet is called a general ledger. Gift World uses a general ledger similar to the ledger used by Rainbow Car Wash.

SUBSIDIARY LEDGERS AND CONTROLLING ACCOUNTS

Frequently accounts that are similar are placed in a separate ledger. For example, a business must keep an individual account for each charge customer to know how much each customer owes. A general ledger can contain an account for each charge customer. However, this makes the general ledger bulky and the trial balance long if a business has many charge customers. These problems can be eliminated by keeping a separate ledger for individual accounts of charge customers.

Subsidiary ledgers

Gift World uses a separate ledger to keep an account for each charge customer. The total amount due from all charge customers is summarized in a single general ledger account, Accounts Receivable. A ledger that is summarized in a single account in the general ledger is called a subsidiary ledger.

Controlling accounts

An account in the general ledger that summarizes all the accounts in a subsidiary ledger is called a controlling account. The separate ledger kept by Gift World for charge customers is a subsidiary ledger. The general ledger account Accounts Receivable is the controlling account. The balance of a controlling account equals the total of all the account balances in the subsidiary ledger.

POSTING TO AN ACCOUNTS RECEIVABLE LEDGER

When the balance of a charge customer's account is changed, the balance of the controlling account Accounts Receivable must be changed. A subsidiary ledger that contains accounts with charge customers only is called an accounts receivable ledger. The relationship between the accounts receivable ledger and accounts receivable account is shown below.

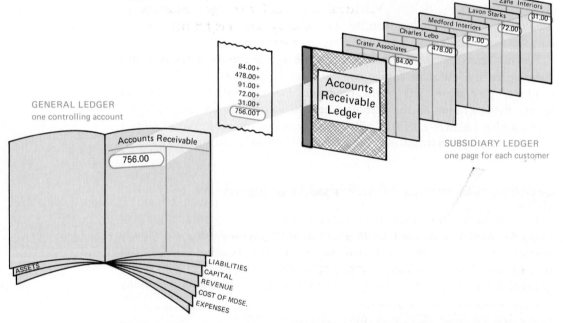

The balances of the customers' accounts in the accounts receivable ledger (a subsidiary ledger) are brought together and summarized in Accounts Receivable (a controlling account in the general ledger).

Accounts receivable ledger form

Gift World uses a three-column account form shown below in the accounts receivable ledger.

Three-column account form used in the accounts receivable ledger

NAME					
ADDRESS					
DATE	ITEM	POST. REF.	DEBIT	CREDIT	DEBIT BALANCE

Each charge customer's account has three amount columns. One column is for debit amounts, one column is for credit amounts, and one column is for the balance. Since accounts receivable are assets and assets have debit balances, the last column is headed Debit Balance. With this third column, the balance of the account can be updated after each posting. Also this ledger form shows at any time how much a customer owes.

Opening new and closing old customer accounts

Each new account is opened by writing the name and address of the customer on the first two lines of the ledger form. The name and address are obtained from the first sales invoice prepared for a charge customer.

Gift World arranges the individual accounts for charge customers alphabetically in a loose-leaf binder. Periodically accounts for new charge customers are added and old accounts are removed from the subsidiary ledger. Therefore, to avoid the difficulty of keeping the accounts in order, the ledger pages are not numbered.

> If a business has many accounts in the accounts receivable ledger, each account may be given a number. The accounts then may be arranged in numerical order. If the accounts are arranged by number, a separate alphabetic card file also must be kept to help locate a customer's account number.

Recording a customer's balance on a new page in the accounts receivable ledger

On November 1, 1977, Gift World prepared a new page for Medford Interiors in the accounts receivable ledger. On that day, the account balance for Medford Interiors was $95.00. The account is shown below.

NAME	Medford Interiors					
ADDRESS	2314 Hillcrest Road, Medford, OR 97501					
DATE	ITEM	POST. REF.	DEBIT	CREDIT	DEBIT BALANCE	
1977 Nov. 1	Balance	✓			95 00	

Opening a new page for a charge customer in the accounts receivable ledger

The name and address of the charge customer are written at the top of the account page. The account balance, *$95.00*, is written in the Debit Balance column. The date, *1977, Nov. 1*, is recorded in the Date column. The word *Balance* is written in the Item column. A check mark is placed in the Post. Ref. column to show that the entry was not posted from the combination journal. This procedure is followed to open a new page in the accounts receivable ledger for any account with a balance.

Posting from the combination journal to the accounts receivable ledger

Each entry in the Accounts Receivable Debit column of the combination journal is an amount to be collected from the customer named in the Account Title column. Each entry in the Accounts Receivable Credit column is an amount that has been collected. Each individual amount listed in these two columns of the combination journal is posted to the proper customer's account in the accounts receivable ledger.

Posting a debit to the accounts receivable ledger. A portion of page 1 of the combination journal for November, 1977, is shown below. The account for Medford Interiors in the accounts receivable ledger is shown after a charge sale entry in the journal has been posted.

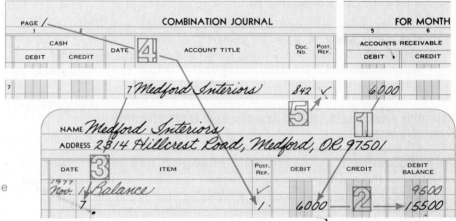

Posting a debit to the accounts receivable ledger

The steps to post this entry in the accounts receivable ledger are:

☐ 1 Write the amount of the sale, *$60.00*, in the Debit column of the account for Medford Interiors.

☐ 2 Add the amount in the Debit column to the amount of the previous balance in the Debit Balance column ($95.00 + $60.00 = $155.00). Write the new balance, *$155.00*, in the Debit Balance column.

☐ 3 Write the date, *7*, in the Date column.

☐ 4 Write the page number of the combination journal, *1*, in the Post. Ref. column of the account.

☐ 5 Place a check mark in the Post. Ref. column of the combination journal to show that the item on Line 7 is posted.

Individual accounts in the accounts receivable ledger do not have page numbers. Therefore, a check mark is used to show that posting is completed. If individual accounts were numbered, the account number would be written in the Post. Ref. column of the combination journal.

Accounts Receivable, the controlling account in the general ledger, also is increased because of this entry. The total of the Accounts Receivable Debit column will be posted to the controlling account Accounts Receivable. Posting column totals is described on page 207.

Posting a credit to the accounts receivable ledger. The same procedure is used to post a credit to the accounts receivable ledger as is used to post a debit. The exceptions are that the amount is entered in the Credit column of the customer's account. Then the credit amount is subtracted from the previous debit balance. The illustration below shows the Lavon Starks account in the accounts receivable ledger after a payment has been received. The entry on Line 8 of the combination journal has been posted. The total of the Accounts Receivable Credit column will be posted to the controlling account Accounts Receivable.

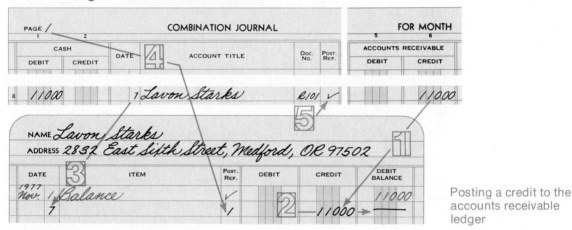

Posting a credit to the accounts receivable ledger

Completed accounts receivable ledger

Gift World posts daily from the combination journal to keep all customer accounts up to date. The column totals in the combination journal, however, are posted at the end of the month.

The volume of work may determine the frequency of posting. Some businesses post daily. Other businesses with less credit sales volume may post weekly. All posting is done at least once a month.

The accounts receivable ledger for Gift World is shown on pages 200 and 201. All postings from the combination journal for November have been completed.

NAME *Crater Associates*
ADDRESS *614 South Main, Medford, OR 97504*

DATE	ITEM	POST. REF.	DEBIT	CREDIT	DEBIT BALANCE
1977 Nov. 1	Balance	✓			58 00
11		1		58 00	—
15		1	30 00		30 00
21		2	84 00		114 00
28		2		30 00	84 00

NAME *Charles Lebo*
ADDRESS *830 Maple Street, Medford, OR 97501*

DATE	ITEM	POST. REF.	DEBIT	CREDIT	DEBIT BALANCE
1977 Nov. 10		1	478 00		478 00

NAME *Medford Interiors*
ADDRESS *2314 Hillcrest Road, Medford, OR 97501*

DATE	ITEM	POST. REF.	DEBIT	CREDIT	DEBIT BALANCE
1977 Nov. 1	Balance	✓			95 00
7		1	60 00		155 00
10		1		95 00	60 00
19		1		60 00	—
30		2	91 00		91 00

NAME *Lavon Starks*
ADDRESS *2832 East Sixth Street, Medford, OR 97502*

DATE	ITEM	POST. REF.	DEBIT	CREDIT	DEBIT BALANCE
1977 Nov. 1	Balance	✓			110 00
7		1		110 00	—
9		1	30 00		30 00
17		1	72 00		102 00
25		2		30 00	72 00

NAME *Zane Interiors*
ADDRESS *518 East, Second, Street, Medford, OR 97501*

DATE	ITEM	POST. REF.	DEBIT	CREDIT	DEBIT BALANCE
1977 Nov. 10		1	61 00		61 00
17		1	90 00		151 00
28		2	31 00		182 00
30		2		151 00	31 00

Accounts receivable ledger

NAME *Lisa Zimmerman*						
ADDRESS *1810 Lindsborg Street, Medford, OR 97502*						

DATE	ITEM	POST. REF.	DEBIT	CREDIT	DEBIT BALANCE
1977 *Nov.* 9		1	6500		6500
16		1		6500	—

Accounts receivable
ledger (concluded)

POSTING TO THE ACCOUNTS PAYABLE LEDGER

A business could include an account for each creditor in its general
ledger. When there are several creditors, it is often easier to have one
controlling account, Accounts Payable, in the general ledger. If a controlling account is used, an account for each creditor is kept in a subsidiary
ledger. The controlling account shows the total amount owed to all creditors. When the balance of a creditor's account is changed, the balance of
the controlling account Accounts Payable must also be changed. A subsidiary ledger that contains accounts with creditors only is called an accounts payable ledger. The relationship between the accounts payable
ledger and the accounts payable account is shown below.

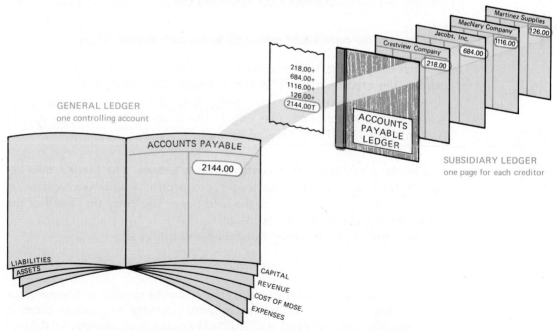

The balances of the individual accounts in the accounts payable ledger
(a subsidiary ledger) are brought together and summarized in Accounts
Payable (a controlling account in the general ledger).

Accounts payable ledger form

The three-column account form below is used in the accounts payable ledger. It is similar to the form used for the accounts receivable ledger. An account payable is a liability and liabilities have credit balances. Therefore, the form used in the accounts payable ledger has a Credit Balance column instead of a Debit Balance column.

Three-column account form used in the accounts payable ledger

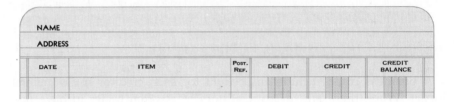

Recording a creditor's balance on a new page in the accounts payable ledger

The procedure is similar for opening a new page in the accounts payable ledger as in the accounts receivable ledger. The balance is recorded in a Credit Balance column instead of a Debit Balance column. The accounts in Gift World's accounts payable ledger are arranged in alphabetic order. The pages, therefore, are not numbered.

Posting from the combination journal to the accounts payable ledger

Each entry in the accounts payable columns of the combination journal affects the creditor named in the Account Title column. Each amount listed in these two columns is posted daily to the proper creditor's account in the accounts payable ledger. The totals of these special amount columns are posted at the end of the month.

Posting a credit to the accounts payable ledger. The Lotus Crafts account in the accounts payable ledger after a purchase of merchandise on account is shown at the top of the next page. The entry on Line 4 of the combination journal has been posted.

The steps to post the entry illustrated on Line 4 are:

☐ 1 Write the amount, *$770.00*, in the Credit column of the account.

☐ 2 Add the amount in the Credit column to the amount of the previous balance in the Credit Balance column. (There is no previous balance; therefore, 0 + $770.00 = $770.00.) Write the new balance, *$770.00*, in the Credit Balance column.

☐ 3 Write the date, *1977, Nov. 3*, in the Date column.

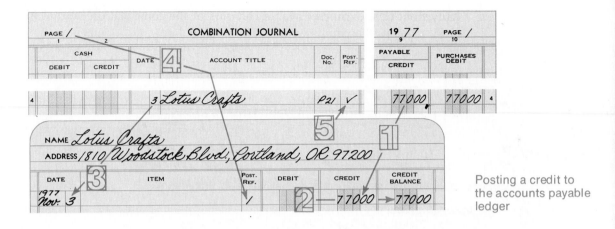

Posting a credit to the accounts payable ledger

☐ 4 Write the page number of the combination journal, *1*, in the Post. Ref. column of the account.

☐ 5 Place a check mark in the Post. Ref. column of the combination journal to show that the posting for this entry has been completed.

Posting a debit to the accounts payable ledger. The same steps are followed to post a debit to a creditor's account as are used to post a credit. The difference is that the amount is entered in the Debit column of the account. Then the debit amount is subtracted from the previous credit balance. Below, the entry on Line 5 of the combination journal for a payment on account is posted to the subsidiary ledger.

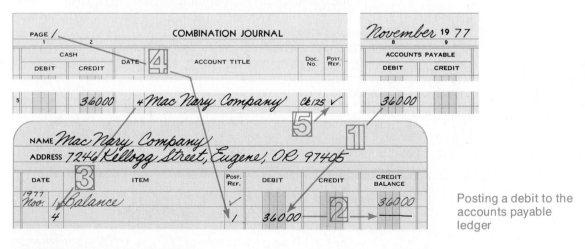

Posting a debit to the accounts payable ledger

Completed accounts payable ledger

Gift World's accounts payable ledger after all posting for November has been completed is illustrated on pages 204 and 205. Gift World posts daily from the Accounts Payable columns of the combination journal in order to keep all accounts with creditors up to date.

NAME *Crestview Company*
ADDRESS *1553 Highland Avenue, Portland, OR 97217*

DATE	ITEM	POST. REF.	DEBIT	CREDIT	CREDIT BALANCE
1977 Nov. 22		2		12400	12400
30		2		9400	21800

NAME *Jacobs, Inc.*
ADDRESS *4020 Thomas Road, Medford, OR 97506*

DATE	ITEM	POST. REF.	DEBIT	CREDIT	CREDIT BALANCE
1977 Nov. 1	Balance	✓			42800
22		2		68400	111200
28		2	42800		68400

NAME *Lotus Crafts*
ADDRESS *1810 Woodstock Blvd, Portland, OR 97200*

DATE	ITEM	POST. REF.	DEBIT	CREDIT	CREDIT BALANCE
1977 Nov. 3		1		77000	77000
16		1	77000		—

NAME *MacNary Company*
ADDRESS *7246 Kellogg Street, Eugene, OR 97405*

DATE	ITEM	POST. REF.	DEBIT	CREDIT	CREDIT BALANCE
1977 Nov. 1	Balance	✓			36000
4		1	36000		—
10		1		26400	26400
18		1		23500	49900
30		2		61700	111600

NAME *Martinez Supplies*
ADDRESS *2701 East Elm, Medford, OR 97503*

DATE	ITEM	POST. REF.	DEBIT	CREDIT	CREDIT BALANCE
1977 Nov. 1	Balance	✓			24500
8		1		12600	37100
14		1	24500		12600

Accounts payable ledger

NAME *Young's Specialties*					
ADDRESS *1636 Knatt Street, Portland, OR 97213*					
DATE	ITEM	POST. REF.	DEBIT	CREDIT	CREDIT BALANCE
1977 *Nov. 11*		1		236 00	236 00
29		2	236 00		

Accounts payable ledger (concluded)

POSTING TO THE GENERAL LEDGER

All transactions of Gift World are recorded in the combination journal. Posting from the combination journal to the general ledger is done periodically throughout the month. However, the posting may be done at least once a month.

General ledger account form

Many businesses, such as Rainbow Car Wash, use a two-column ledger account form in a general ledger. However, Gift World uses the popular four-column ledger account form in the general ledger. The four amount columns are headed: Debit, Credit, Debit Balance, and Credit Balance. The form is shown below.

ACCOUNT					ACCOUNT NO.	
DATE	ITEM	POST. REF.	DEBIT	CREDIT	BALANCE	
					DEBIT	CREDIT

Four-column account form used in the general ledger

The four-column account form shows clearly the amount of each debit and each credit that is posted to the account. As each entry is posted, the amount of the new account balance is recorded in the appropriate Debit or Credit Balance column.

Some businesses using the four-column ledger form determine account balances only after all monthly postings have been completed. Then only the end-of-month balance is recorded in the proper balance column. This is usually done at the time the trial balance is prepared.

Posting from the General columns in the combination journal

Each amount in the General Debit column or the General Credit column in the combination journal is posted individually to the account shown in the Account Title column. Posting the General columns may be done periodically throughout the month. However, all posting is done at least once each month.

Posting a debit to the general ledger. The illustration below shows the rent expense account in the general ledger. The entry on Line 2 of the combination journal has been posted.

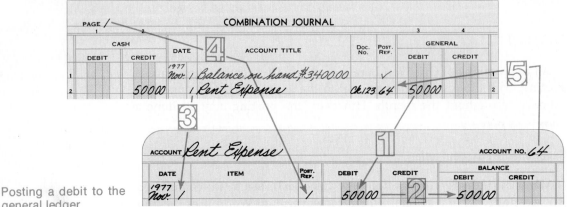

Posting a debit to the general ledger

The steps to post the General Debit amount on Line 2 of the combination journal to the general ledger are:

□ 1 Write the amount, *$500.00*, in the Debit column of the general ledger account Rent Expense.

□ 2 Add the amount in the Debit column to the amount of the previous balance in the Debit Balance column. (There is no previous balance; therefore, 0 + $500.00 = $500.00.) Write the new balance, *$500.00*, in the Debit Balance column.

□ 3 Write the date, *1977, Nov. 1*, in the Date column.

□ 4 Write the page number of the combination journal, *1*, in the Post. Ref. column of the account.

□ 5 Write the number of the rent expense account, *64*, in the Post. Ref. column of the combination journal. Writing the account number in the Post. Ref. column shows that this line in the journal is posted.

Posting a credit to the general ledger. A credit is posted from the General Credit column in the combination journal by entering the amount in the Credit column of the general ledger account shown in the Account Title column. The new balance is figured by deducting the credit from the previous debit balance. Or, if the previous balance is a credit, add the credit to the balance. The prepaid insurance account in the general ledger is shown below after the entry on Line 14 of the combination journal is posted.

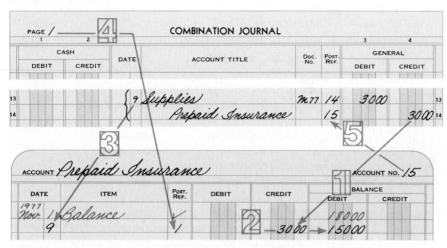

Posting a credit to the general ledger

Posting totals of the special columns in the combination journal

The total of each special column of the combination journal is posted to the account named in the column heading. After each column total is posted, the number of the account is written in parentheses below the column total. The totals of the General columns are not posted because each amount in these columns is posted individually. When totals are not to be posted, a check mark is placed in parentheses below the column total.

The illustrations on pages 208 and 209 show page 2 of the combination journal for November, 1977. All individual items in the General, the Accounts Receivable, and the Accounts Payable columns have been posted. The totals of all special columns also have been posted. Totals of special columns are posted from the combination journal to the general ledger at the end of each month.

The cash account in the general ledger is shown below. The totals of the Cash Debit column and the Cash Credit column for November have been posted.

ACCOUNT	Cash						ACCOUNT NO.	11
						BALANCE		
DATE	ITEM	POST. REF.	DEBIT	CREDIT		DEBIT	CREDIT	
1977 Nov. 1	Balance	✓				3400 00		
30		2	8499 00			11899 00		
30		2		5755 60		6143 40		

Cash account after totals have been posted from combination journal

PAGE 2				COMBINATION JOURNAL					
	1	2						3	4
	CASH		DATE	ACCOUNT TITLE	Doc. No.	Post. Ref.		GENERAL	
	DEBIT	CREDIT						DEBIT	CREDIT
1	561400	340300	*1977* Nov. 19	Brought Forward		✓		133600	3000	1
2			21	Crater Associates	S50	✓				2
3			22	Jacobs, Inc.	P25	✓				3
4			22	Crestview Company	P26	✓				4
5		1400	23	Miscellaneous Expense	Ck133	63		1400		5
6		54000	23	✓	Ck134	✓				6
7	3000		25	Lavon Starks	R106	✓				7
8	134400		26	✓	J26	✓				8
9	3000		28	Crater Associates	R107	✓				9
10		42800	28	Jacobs, Inc.	Ck135	✓				10
11			28	Zane Interiors	S51	✓				11
12		4700	29	Delivery Expense	Ck136	61		4700		12
13		12000	29	Debra Horn, Drawing	Ck137	32		12000		13
14		160	29	Miscellaneous Expense	M78	63		160		14
15		23600	29	Young's Specialties	Ck138	✓				15
16		36000	30	Salary Expense	Ck139	65		36000		16
17		60600	30	✓	Ck140	✓				17
18			30	Crestview Company	P27	✓				18
19			30	Medford Interiors	S52	✓				19
20	15100		30	Zane Interiors	R108	✓				20
21			30	MacNary Company	P28	✓				21
22	133000		30	✓	J30	✓				22
23	849900 575560 849900 575560		30	Totals				187860 187860	3000 3000	23
24	(11)	(11)						(✓)	(✓)	24

Combination journal after posting
has been completed (left page)

Completed general ledger

Gift World's general ledger is shown on pages 209, 210 and 211. All entries in the combination journal for the month of November have been posted.

> No postings appear in Accounts 33, 62, and 66. The transactions for November did not affect these accounts. The use of these three accounts is described in Chapters 15 and 17.

Rainbow Car Wash footed the general ledger accounts, page 108, on the last day of the month. Then the balance was determined for each account. Since the general ledger accounts used by Gift World have balance columns, the accounts do not need to be footed. The account balance for each account is updated each time an entry is posted.

	ACCOUNTS RECEIVABLE		SALES CREDIT	ACCOUNTS PAYABLE		PURCHASES DEBIT	
	5 DEBIT	6 CREDIT	7	8 DEBIT	9 CREDIT	10	
1	886 00	388 00	6112 00	1375 00	1631 00	2353 00	1
2	84 00		84 00				2
3					684 00	684 00	3
4					124 00	124 00	4
5							5
6						540 00	6
7		30 00					7
8			1344 00				8
9		30 00					9
10				428 00			10
11	31 00		31 00				11
12							12
13							13
14							14
15				236 00			15
16							16
17						606 00	17
18				94 00		94 00	18
19	91 00		91 00				19
20		151 00					20
21					617 00	617 00	21
22			1330 00				22
23	1092 00	599 00	8992 00	2039 00	3150 00	5018 00	23
24	(12)	(12)	(41)	(21)	(21)	(51)	24

FOR MONTH OF November 1977 PAGE 2

Combination journal after posting has been completed (right page)

General ledger after combination journal is posted

ACCOUNT **Cash**   ACCOUNT NO. **11**

DATE	ITEM	POST. REF.	DEBIT	CREDIT	BALANCE DEBIT	BALANCE CREDIT
1977 Nov. 1	Balance	✓			3400 00	
30		2	8499 00		11899 00	
30		2		5755 60	6143 40	

ACCOUNT **Accounts Receivable**   ACCOUNT NO. **12**

DATE	ITEM	POST. REF.	DEBIT	CREDIT	BALANCE DEBIT	BALANCE CREDIT
1977 Nov. 1	Balance	✓			263 00	
30		2	1092 00		1355 00	
30		2		599 00	756 00	

ACCOUNT **Merchandise Inventory**   ACCOUNT NO. 13

DATE	ITEM	POST. REF.	DEBIT	CREDIT	BALANCE DEBIT	BALANCE CREDIT
1977 Nov. 1	Balance	✓			784000	

ACCOUNT **Supplies**   ACCOUNT NO. 14

DATE	ITEM	POST. REF.	DEBIT	CREDIT	BALANCE DEBIT	BALANCE CREDIT
1977 Nov. 1	Balance	✓			32000	
8		1	12600		44600	
9		1	3000		47600	

ACCOUNT **Prepaid Insurance**   ACCOUNT NO. 15

DATE	ITEM	POST. REF.	DEBIT	CREDIT	BALANCE DEBIT	BALANCE CREDIT
1977 Nov. 1	Balance	✓			18000	
9		1		3000	15000	

ACCOUNT **Accounts Payable**   ACCOUNT NO. 21

DATE	ITEM	POST. REF.	DEBIT	CREDIT	BALANCE DEBIT	BALANCE CREDIT
1977 Nov. 1	Balance	✓				103300
30		2	203900		100600	
30		2		315000		214400

ACCOUNT **Debra Horn, Capital**   ACCOUNT NO. 31

DATE	ITEM	POST. REF.	DEBIT	CREDIT	BALANCE DEBIT	BALANCE CREDIT
1977 Nov. 1	Balance	✓				1097000

ACCOUNT **Debra Horn, Drawing**   ACCOUNT NO. 32

DATE	ITEM	POST. REF.	DEBIT	CREDIT	BALANCE DEBIT	BALANCE CREDIT
1977 Nov. 8		1	25000		25000	
29		2	12000		37000	

ACCOUNT **Income Summary**   ACCOUNT NO. 33

DATE	ITEM	POST. REF.	DEBIT	CREDIT	BALANCE DEBIT	BALANCE CREDIT

ACCOUNT **Sales**   ACCOUNT NO. 41

DATE	ITEM	POST. REF.	DEBIT	CREDIT	BALANCE DEBIT	BALANCE CREDIT
1977 Nov. 30		2		899200		899200

ACCOUNT **Purchases**   ACCOUNT NO. 51

DATE	ITEM	POST. REF.	DEBIT	CREDIT	BALANCE DEBIT	BALANCE CREDIT
1977 Nov. 30		2	501800		501800	

General ledger after combination journal is posted (continued)

General ledger after combination journal is posted (concluded)

ACCOUNT *Delivery Expense*					ACCOUNT NO. *61*		
DATE	ITEM	POST. REF.	DEBIT	CREDIT	BALANCE		
					DEBIT	CREDIT	
1977 Nov. 8		1	4500		4500		
29		2	4700		9200		

ACCOUNT *Insurance Expense*					ACCOUNT NO. *62*		
DATE	ITEM	POST. REF.	DEBIT	CREDIT	BALANCE		
					DEBIT	CREDIT	

ACCOUNT *Miscellaneous Expense*					ACCOUNT NO. *63*		
DATE	ITEM	POST. REF.	DEBIT	CREDIT	BALANCE		
					DEBIT	CREDIT	
1977 Nov. 15		1	2500		2500		
23		2	1400		3900		
29		2	160		4060		

ACCOUNT *Rent Expense*					ACCOUNT NO. *64*		
DATE	ITEM	POST. REF.	DEBIT	CREDIT	BALANCE		
					DEBIT	CREDIT	
1977 Nov. 1		1	50000		50000		

ACCOUNT *Salary Expense*					ACCOUNT NO. *65*		
DATE	ITEM	POST. REF.	DEBIT	CREDIT	BALANCE		
					DEBIT	CREDIT	
1977 Nov. 15		1	36000		36000		
30		2	36000		72000		

ACCOUNT *Supplies Expense*					ACCOUNT NO. *66*		
DATE	ITEM	POST. REF.	DEBIT	CREDIT	BALANCE		
					DEBIT	CREDIT	

MECHANICAL POSTING TO THE GENERAL LEDGER

Machines can be used to help process accounts receivable and accounts payable transactions. These machines print needed information on business forms. They also are able to add, subtract, multiply, or divide. The picture at the right shows a general-purpose accounting machine.

The general-purpose accounting machine has a movable carriage similar to the one found on a typewriter. The carriage can move back and forth as data are typed or printed on an accounting form. The principles of accounting used with an accounting machine are the same as those used when recording the data manually. The business forms may differ slightly because of the method used to record

Victor Comptometer Corporation

General-purpose accounting machine

the data. For example, in manual data processing the accounts receivable account would appear as shown below.

General ledger account used for processing data manually

The same data recorded by using a general-purpose accounting machine would appear as shown below.

General ledger card used for processing data on a general-purpose accounting machine

Advantages in using a general-purpose accounting machine instead of recording data manually include:

1. Calculations needed to figure the new balance for the customer's accounts are done by the machine. The results of the arithmetic are likely to be more accurate when done by the machine than when done manually by the accountant.
2. The printed copy on the forms is usually clearer to read than when written manually.
3. More legible copies can be made because of machine action.

SUMMARY OF PRINCIPLES OF POSTING FROM THE COMBINATION JOURNAL

A summary of the principles of posting from the cash journal is on pages 96 and 97. Those principles described for Rainbow Car Wash also apply to posting from the combination journal. An additional set of principles guides the posting procedure used when a special amount column and a controlling account are involved.

Posting from general columns

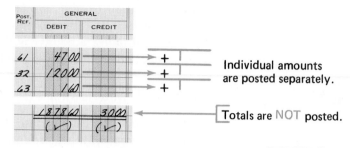

As shown at the right, the individual amounts in the General columns *are* posted separately. The totals of the General columns are *not* posted.

Individual amounts are posted separately.

Totals are NOT posted.

Posting from special columns

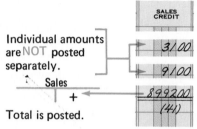

As shown at the right, the totals of special columns *are* posted to the account named in the column heading. The total of the column shown is posted as a credit to the sales account. The individual amounts in special columns are *not* posted separately unless the columns are for a controlling account.

Individual amounts are NOT posted separately.

Total is posted.

Posting from special columns for controlling accounts

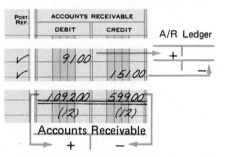

As shown at the right, individual amounts *and* total amounts are posted from special columns for controlling accounts. Individual amounts in the Accounts Receivable Debit and Credit columns *are* posted separately to the proper charge customers' accounts in the accounts receivable ledger. A check mark is placed in the Post. Ref. column of the journal to show that the amount has been posted to the customer's account.

Individual amounts are posted separately to a subsidiary ledger.

Totals are posted to a controlling account.

The total of a special column *is* posted to the controlling account named in the column heading. As shown above, the total of the Accounts Receivable Debit column is posted as a debit to Accounts Receivable in the general ledger. The total of the Accounts Receivable Credit column is posted as a credit to Accounts Receivable in the general ledger. The account number is placed in parentheses under the total of the special column to show the general ledger account to which the total was posted.

The same principles used for the Accounts Receivable columns also apply to the Accounts Payable columns in the combination journal.

PROVING THE ACCURACY OF POSTING

A single error in a ledger account may cause the balance sheet to be out of balance. A single error may cause the profit to be understated or overstated on the income statement. A single error may cause a business to overpay or underpay its creditors. The records must be accurate.

The accountant for Gift World checks many things to assure that the records are accurate. Three of the accuracy checks are: cash proof, agreement of controlling accounts with subsidiary ledgers, and equality of debits and credits in the general ledger.

Proving cash

The way to prove cash is described on pages 188 and 189. After all the posting is completed, the accountant compares the balance of the general ledger cash account with the cash proof. The balance of the cash account on November 30, as shown on page 209, is $6,143.40. The accountant figured the same amount when cash was proved, as shown on pages 188 and 189. The accountant assumes that cash is posted accurately to the cash account.

> The cash proof is important. Because so many transactions affect the cash account, there are many chances to make an error in **Cash**.

Proving the subsidiary ledgers

The balance of the controlling account in the general ledger should equal the sum of the account balances in the corresponding subsidiary ledger.

Proving accounts receivable. A list of customers that shows the balance due from each customer and the total amount due from all customers is called a schedule of accounts receivable. The schedule of accounts receivable is prepared after all posting to the subsidiary ledger is completed. The schedule prepared on November 30, 1977, for Gift World is shown below.

Schedule of accounts
receivable

Gift World		
Schedule of Accounts Receivable		
November 30, 1977		
Crater Associates	8400	
Charles Lebo	47800	
Medford Interiors	9100	
Lavon Starks	7200	
Zane Interiors	3100	
Total Accounts Receivable		75600

The balance of the accounts receivable account in the general ledger, page 209, is $756.00. The total of the schedule of accounts receivable equals the balance of the accounts receivable account in the general ledger. The accounts receivable ledger has been proved.

Proving accounts payable. A list of all creditors that shows the balance owed to each creditor and the total amount owed to all creditors is called a schedule of accounts payable. The schedule of accounts payable is prepared after all posting to the subsidiary ledger is completed. The schedule of accounts payable prepared on November 30, 1977, for Gift World is shown below.

Gift World		
Schedule of Accounts Payable		
November 30, 1977		
Crestview Company	21800	
Jacobs, Inc.	68400	
MacNary Company	111600	
Martinez Supplies	12600	
Total Accounts Payable		214400

Schedule of accounts payable

The balance of the accounts payable account in the general ledger, page 210, is $2,144.00. The total of the schedule of accounts payable and the balance of the accounts payable account in the general ledger agree. The accounts payable ledger has been proved.

Proving equality of debits and credits in the general ledger

For each transaction recorded in a journal, the debits and the credits must be equal. The debits and the credits in the general ledger must also be equal. Before recording a trial balance on a work sheet, the accountant checks the equality of debits and credits in the general ledger. The accountant adds the balances of all accounts with debit balances. Then the accountant adds the balances of all accounts with credit balances. The total of debit balances must equal the total of credit balances. The illustration at the right shows the adding machine tapes prepared for Gift World after all posting is completed for November.

DEBIT BALANCES	CREDIT BALANCES
6,143.40	
756.00	
7,840.00	
476.00	
150.00	
370.00	
5,018.00	
92.00	
40.60	2,144.00
500.00	10,970.00
720.00	8,992.00
22,106.00T	22,106.00T

Adding machine tapes used to prove equality of debits and credits in the general ledger after posting is completed

The totals, $22,106.00, are the same. Therefore, the equality of debits and credits in the general ledger is proved. If the totals do not agree, one or more errors have been made. The accountant must find the errors and correct them before continuing the work.

Recording the trial balance on the work sheet

The trial balance for Gift World on November 30, 1977, is shown at the left in the Trial Balance columns of the work sheet.

	ACCOUNT TITLE	ACCT. No.	TRIAL BALANCE DEBIT	TRIAL BALANCE CREDIT
1	Cash	11	614340	
2	Accounts Receivable	12	75600	
3	Merchandise Inventory	13	784000	
4	Supplies	14	47600	
5	Prepaid Insurance	15	15000	
6	Accounts Payable	21		214400
7	Debra Horn, Capital	31		1097000
8	Debra Horn, Drawing	32	37000	
9	Income Summary	33		
10	Sales	41		899200
11	Purchases	51	501800	
12	Delivery Expense	61	9200	
13	Insurance Expense	62		
14	Miscellaneous Exp.	63	4060	
15	Rent Expense	64	50000	
16	Salary Expense	65	72000	
17	Supplies Expense	66		
18			2210600	2210600

Trial balance

Each account in the general ledger is listed in the trial balance section of the work sheet whether it has a balance or not. All accounts are listed in the same order in which they appear in the general ledger so that accounts will be extended to the Income Statement and Balance Sheet columns with other accounts of like category (assets, liabilities, revenue, expenses). This makes the closing process easier.

This account arrangement also serves as a checklist so that the accountant is sure that all account balances are listed in the trial balance. The completion of the work sheet for Gift World is described in Chapter 15.

STATEMENT OF ACCOUNT

A business normally sends to each charge customer a monthly statement of the amount owed by the customer. The statement may include only the total balance owed. Many businesses, however, include all data about charges to and payments from the customer. A business form that shows the charges to a customer's account, the amounts credited to the account, and the balance of the account is called a statement of account.

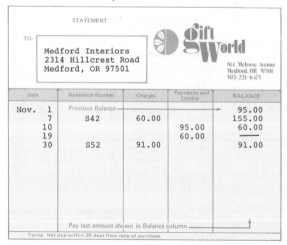

Gift World sends statements of account to charge customers at the end of each month. An example of the statement of account used by Gift World is shown at the left.

A customer should compare a statement of account with personal records. If an error is found on the statement, the business from whom the statement is received should be notified.

Statement of account

Many businesses prepare and mail statements of account to a portion of their charge customers on a specific day during the month. This spreads out the work of preparing the statements over the month. Preparing and mailing statements of account to customers on specific days of each month is called cycle billing. When a business uses cycle billing, a schedule is followed. A cycle billing schedule is shown at the right.

Initial of customers' last names	Date on which statement of account is prepared and mailed
A to D	4th
E to K	10th
L to P	16th
Q to S	22d
T to Z	28th

Cycle billing schedule

If the mailing date comes on Sunday or a holiday, the statements of account are prepared and mailed on the next regular business day.

Many businesses with a small number of accounts receivable do not use cycle billing. All the statements of account are prepared and mailed once each month. Gift World has few accounts receivable; therefore, they mail statements once a month.

✦ What is the meaning of each of the following?

- general ledger
- subsidiary ledger
- controlling account
- accounts receivable ledger

- accounts payable ledger
- schedule of accounts receivable

- schedule of accounts payable
- statement of account
- cycle billing

Using Business Terms

Questions for Individual Study

1. What ledger contains all the accounts needed to prepare the income statement and the balance sheet?
2. What three ledgers does Gift World use?
3. In what ledger should the controlling account for accounts receivable be located?
4. Should a debit entry to an accounts receivable account be added to or subtracted from the previous balance? Why?
5. In what file order are the accounts placed in the accounts receivable ledger? Why?
6. What are the steps in posting from the Accounts Receivable Debit column in the combination journal to the accounts receivable ledger?
7. To what accounts are the individual amounts in the Accounts Payable Debit and Credit columns of the combination journal posted?

8. To what accounts are the individual amounts in the General Debit and Credit columns of the combination journal posted?
9. What are the steps in posting from the General Debit column in the combination journal to the general ledger?
10. What procedure is used in posting the totals of the special columns in the combination journal?
11. Why are the totals of the General Debit and Credit columns of the combination journal not posted at the end of the month?
12. How can the accuracy of the accounts payable subsidiary ledger be proved?
13. How can the equality of debits and credits in the general ledger be proved?
14. Why do some businesses use cycle billing in scheduling the preparation and mailing of their monthly statements of account?

CASE 1 Harry Pate observes his accountant at work and says, "You post each individual account receivable entry in the combination journal. Then you post the total of the accounts receivable columns. You are post-ing these entries twice, which will make the records wrong." The accountant disagrees that the posting procedure is incorrect. Is Mr. Pate or his accountant correct? Why?

CASE 2 The accountant at Coutant's Flower Shop received a call from a customer, Helen Frisch. Miss Frisch stated she had purchased $30.00 worth of flowers on account five weeks ago. She sent a check for $30.00 two weeks ago in payment of the ac-count. Although no additional purchases had been made, she recently received a statement of account that listed her balance due as $60.00. What probably caused this error? When would the accountant probably discover the error?

CASE 3 The accountant of the Silverton Food Market finds that the balance of the controlling account Accounts Payable is $4,290.00. The total shown on the schedule of accounts payable is $5,160.00. What kinds of errors could cause this difference?

DRILL 13-D 1 Analyzing transactions of a merchandising business

Instructions: For each of the transactions below, indicate in T accounts which general ledger account is to be debited and which general ledger account is to be credited. The first transaction is shown as an example.

Purchases	
325.00	

Accounts Payable	
	325.00

1. Purchased merchandise on account from Frontier Company, $325.00.
2. Bought supplies for cash, $268.00.
3. Cash sales for the week, $2,500.00.
4. Received an additional investment from owner George Poole, $2,800.00.
5. Received on account from Ronald Moffitte, $225.00.
6. Paid November rent, $500.00.
7. Sold merchandise on account to John Sampson, $220.00.
8. Paid on account to Lanny Cross, $415.00.
9. Purchased merchandise for cash, $600.00.
10. Bought supplies on account from Herbert Boer, $185.00.
11. Issued check to George Poole, owner, for cash withdrawal, $650.00.
12. Paid telephone bill, $65.00. (Utilities Expense)

The work completed for Drill 13-D 1 will be used to complete Drill 13-D 2.

DRILL 13-D 2 Recording and posting using a combination journal

The solution to Drill 13-D 1 is needed for working Drill 13-D 2.

Instructions: □ **1.** Use a form such as the one shown at the top of the next page. Based on the answers in Drill 13-D 1, indicate by a check mark which amount columns in the combination journal will be used to record the transactions. Transaction 1 is shown as an example.

Transaction	Amount columns in the combination journal									
	Cash		General		Accts. Rec.		Sales Credit	Accts. Pay.		Purchases Debit
	Debit	Credit	Debit	Credit	Debit	Credit		Debit	Credit	
1. Debit amount										✓
Credit amount									✓	

Instructions: □ **2.** Use a form such as the one shown below. For each of the debit amounts and each of the credit amounts shown in your answer to Instruction 1, indicate with a check mark if the amount will be posted separately to the general ledger, to the accounts receivable ledger, to the accounts payable ledger, or not posted separately to any ledger. Transaction 1 is shown as an example.

Transaction	Posted separately to			Not posted separately to any ledger
	General Ledger	Accounts Receivable Ledger	Accounts Payable Ledger	
1. Debit amount				✓
Credit amount			✓	

PROBLEM 13-1   Posting from a combination journal to a general ledger, an accounts receivable ledger, and an accounts payable ledger

Problem for Applying Concepts

If you are not using the workbook correlating with this textbook, complete Review Problem 13-R 1 instead of this problem.

The general ledger, accounts receivable ledger, and accounts payable ledger of Fisher's Store and the combination journal for November are given in the workbook.

Instructions: □ **1.** Post from the combination journal the individual items recorded in the following columns: General Ledger Debit and Credit; Accounts Receivable Debit and Credit; and Accounts Payable Debit and Credit.

□ **2.** Post the totals of the special columns of the combination journal.

□ **3.** Prove cash. The cash balance shown on Check Stub No. 94 is $4,145.00.

□ **4.** Prepare a schedule of accounts receivable similar to the one on page 214. Compare the total of the schedule with the balance of the accounts receivable account in the general ledger. If they are not the same, find and correct the errors.

□ **5.** Prepare a schedule of accounts payable similar to the one on page 215. Compare the total of the schedule with the balance of the accounts payable account in the general ledger. If they are not the same, find and correct the errors.

□ **6.** Prove the equality of debits and credits in the general ledger. On an adding machine or on a separate sheet of paper, add the balances of all accounts with debit balances. Then add the balances of all accounts with credit balances. If the two totals are not the same, find and correct the errors.

□ **7.** Prepare a trial balance, similar to the one shown on page 216 in the Trial Balance columns of a work sheet.

**MASTERY
PROBLEM 13-M** Posting from a combination journal to a general ledger, an accounts receivable ledger, and an accounts payable ledger

The combination journal prepared in Mastery Problem 12-M is needed for Mastery Problem 13-M.

The general ledger, the accounts receivable ledger, and the accounts payable ledger of Coker's Paint are given in the workbook.

Instructions: □ **1.** Using the combination journal prepared in Mastery Problem 12-M, post the individual items recorded in the following columns: General Debit and Credit; Accounts Receivable Debit and Credit; and Accounts Payable Debit and Credit.

□ **2.** Post the totals of the special columns of the combination journal.

□ **3.** Prove cash. The cash balance as shown on the next unused check stub is $4,410.00.

□ **4.** Prepare a schedule of accounts receivable and a schedule of accounts payable. Prove the accuracy of the subsidiary ledgers by comparing the schedule totals with the balances of the controlling accounts in the general ledger.

□ **5.** Prove the equality of debits and credits in the general ledger. On an adding machine or on a separate sheet of paper, add the balances of all accounts with debit balances. Then add the balances of all accounts with credit balances. If the two totals are not the same, find and correct the errors.

□ **6.** Prepare a trial balance in the Trial Balance columns of a work sheet.

**BONUS
PROBLEM 13-B** Posting from a combination journal to a general ledger, an accounts receivable ledger, and an accounts payable ledger

The combination journal prepared in Bonus Problem 12-B is needed for Bonus Problem 13-B.

Instructions: Follow the instructions for Mastery Problem 13-M but use the combination journal prepared in the previous chapter for Bonus Problem 12-B.

The Checking Account and Reconciliation of Bank Statements

14

The asset, cash on hand, includes money present in the place of business as well as money the business has in the bank. Money kept in the place of business or at home is less safe than other assets. This is true because cash can be transferred easily from person to person without its ownership being questioned. Most businesses, therefore, put all cash receipts in a bank and withdraw money or pay bills by writing checks.

Placing all cash receipts in a bank gives additional evidence that the accounting records of a business are accurate. The amount of cash put in the bank will equal the amount of cash received and debited to Cash. The amount of cash withdrawn from the bank account will equal the amount of checks written and credited to Cash.

OPENING A CHECKING ACCOUNT

Placing cash in a bank is called making a deposit. The person or business in whose name cash is deposited is called a depositor. An account with a bank from which a depositor can order payments to others is called a checking account.

Withdrawals from a checking account are made by writing a check. A check is an order in writing, signed by the depositor or authorized person, ordering the bank to pay cash from the depositor's account to a person or business named on the check.

> Sometimes a depositor wishes to deposit cash and leave it for a period of time to earn interest. An account with a bank on which the bank pays interest to the depositor is called a savings account.

The signature card

At the time an account is opened, a depositor indicates on a form those persons authorized to sign checks. A form signed by each individual

Authorized Signatures For:	
GIFT WORLD	Date Opened: Feb. 5, 1976
Address: 814 Melrose Avenue	Checking: X Savings:
Medford, OR 97501	Initial Deposit: $1,500.00
Telephone: 364-9377	Account Number: 68-545-9

CITIZENS STATE BANK
MEDFORD OR 97501

Print Name and Title	Specimen Signature
Debra Horn, Manager	Debra Horn

Signature card for a
checking account

authorized to sign checks on a checking account is called a signature card. A signature card prepared for Gift World is shown at the left. The signature card was prepared by Debra Horn, owner and manager of Gift World.

If more than one person is authorized to sign checks, the signatures of all signers must appear on the signature card. The bank uses the card to verify that authorized signatures are on the checks presented for payment.

The signature card is a safeguard used by the bank to protect against forgeries. Checks must always be signed the same as the depositor or authorized person signed the signature card. If the signature on a check is not the same as one of those on the signature card, the bank may refuse to pay the check. If a business needs to change the persons authorized to sign checks, a new signature card is prepared for the bank.

A signature card is prepared for personal checking accounts as well as for business checking accounts. For a family joint checking account, both husband and wife sign the signature card.

The deposit slip

The business form provided by the bank on which a depositor lists all cash and checks to be deposited is called a deposit slip. The deposit slip is sometimes known as a deposit ticket. Two forms of deposit slips are shown below.

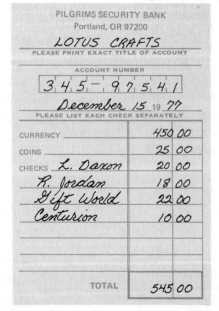

PILGRIMS SECURITY BANK
Portland, OR 97200

LOTUS CRAFTS
PLEASE PRINT EXACT TITLE OF ACCOUNT

ACCOUNT NUMBER

3 4 5 - 9 7 5 4 1

December 15 19 77
PLEASE LIST EACH CHECK SEPARATELY

CURRENCY	450	00
COINS	25	00
CHECKS L. Daxon	20	00
R. Jordan	18	00
Gift World	22	00
Centurion	10	00
TOTAL	545	00

Deposit slip showing checks identified
by person from whom received

CITIZENS
STATE
BANK
MEDFORD, OR 97501

For deposit to the account of

GIFT WORLD
814 Melrose Avenue
Medford, OR 97501

⑆1232⑈0315⑉ 68⑈545⑈09⑈

		96-315 / 1232		
	Date December 9, 19 77			
	Currency		1550	00
	Coin		510	00
	Checks 96-464		64	00
	96-523		48	00
	TOTAL		2172	00

Deposit slip showing checks
identified by ABA numbers

Checks may be listed on a deposit slip (1) by the number of the bank on which the check is drawn, or (2) by the name of the person or business from whom each check was received. A depositor should ask the bank which method is preferred for preparing a deposit slip.

The deposit slip used by a specific bank may differ from the ones shown on page 222. Each bank designs its own form of deposit slip to fit the recording machines the bank uses.

ABA numbers and magnetic ink characters

Identification numbers assigned to banks by the American Bankers Association are called ABA numbers. The ABA numbers are printed on the checks and may be printed on deposit slips. The ABA number for the Security National Bank shown on the check below is $\frac{96\text{-}523}{1232}$.

The ABA number is a code for the following:

(1) The 96 is a number assigned to all banks located in the Medford, Oregon, area.
(2) The 523 is the number assigned to the Security National Bank.
(3) The number under the line, 1232, is a check routing symbol. This number helps the banking system sort the checks and return them to the bank on which each was drawn. This number is not used in listing checks on the deposit slip.

Many banks use automated equipment that can "read" the special numbers printed along the bottom of a check or a deposit slip. Special number characters printed in magnetic ink that can be "read" by automatic machines are known as magnetic ink characters. An abbreviation commonly used for magnetic ink character recognition is MICR. The check shown below has magnetic ink characters preprinted along the bottom.

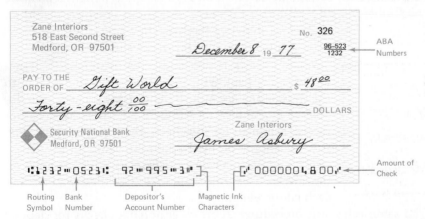

Check with ABA numbers and magnetic ink characters

The magnetic ink characters along the bottom edge of both the deposit slip and the check include the routing symbols, the bank numbers, and the account numbers of the depositors. Banks with MICR equipment print another set of magnetic ink characters on the same line to show the amount of the deposit or the amount of the check. This permits the special equipment to process automatically the deposit slip and the check and to record the amount in the depositor's account.

Receipt for a bank deposit

The bank returns a receipt to the depositor showing the amount of the deposit. The receipt may be a carbon copy of the original deposit slip with the amount imprinted, a stub of the deposit slip with the amount imprinted, or a specially prepared receipt. A few banks prepare the deposit receipt by hand.

The Citizens State Bank uses equipment that prints along the top of the deposit slip: the date of the deposit, the identification of the teller, and the amount of the deposit. A carbon copy of the deposit slip with the amount imprinted is returned to the depositor for a personal record. A receipt for a deposit made by Gift World on December 9, 1977, is at the left.

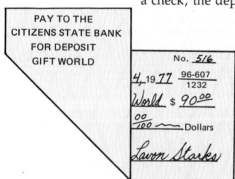

Dec 9 77 D   2172.00

96–315
1232

CITIZENS
STATE
BANK
MEDFORD, OR 97501

CUSTOMER'S RECEIPT

For deposit to the account of

GIFT WORLD
814 Melrose Avenue
Medford, OR 97501

⑆1232⑉0315⑆ 68⑉545⑉09⑈

Date *December 9,* 19 *77*		
Currency	1550	00
Coin	510	00
Checks 96-464	64	00
96-523	48	00
TOTAL	2172	00

Receipt for bank deposit

Endorsing checks

The signature or stamp of the depositor on the back of a check authorizing transfer of ownership is called an endorsement. When depositing a check, the depositor endorses the check. An endorsement is placed on a check as shown at the left. The name is written exactly as it appears on the face of the check.

PAY TO THE
CITIZENS STATE BANK
FOR DEPOSIT
GIFT WORLD

No. *516*

4, 19 *77*   96-607
1232

World $ *90⁰⁰*

⁰⁰/₁₀₀ ⌇⌇⌇ Dollars

Lavon Starks

When a check is deposited, the ownership is transferred to the bank which in turn credits the amount to the depositor's account. By endorsing a check, the depositor guarantees its payment. If the bank does not receive payment for the check, the endorser must then pay the amount of the check to the bank.

The endorsement of a business is often stamped on the checks. This procedure takes less time than writing each endorsement.

Stamped endorsement

The same rules and procedures apply to endorsing checks for deposit to a personal account as apply to endorsing checks for deposit to a business account.

Kinds of endorsements

Different kinds of endorsements serve different purposes. There are four principal forms of endorsements.

Blank endorsement. An endorsement that consists only of the name of the endorser is called a blank endorsement. A lost or stolen check with a blank endorsement can be cashed by the finder or a thief. Therefore, this endorsement should not be placed on a check until the depositor is at the bank to make the deposit or to cash the check.

Blank endorsement

Special endorsement. An endorsement that states to whom the check is to be paid followed by the name of the endorser is called a special endorsement. A special endorsement is also known as an endorsement in full. This endorsement permits the check to be cashed or transferred only on the order of the person or business named in the endorsement.

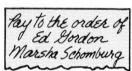

Special endorsement

Restrictive endorsement. An endorsement that restricts further transfers of the check is called a restrictive endorsement. Restrictive endorsements are often used when checks are prepared for deposit.

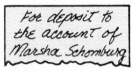

Restrictive endorsement

Qualified endorsement. An endorsement in which the endorser does not accept any responsibility for payment on the check is called a qualified endorsement. If a person or business accepts a check with a qualified endorsement and the bank refuses to cash the check, the owner cannot claim payment from the endorser. However, the owner can claim payment from the original signer of the check.

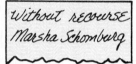

Qualified endorsement

Recording deposits in the checkbook

When a deposit is made, it is recorded on the next unused check stub. The December 9 deposit of Gift World is shown at the right.

> Cash receipts are recorded in the journal for each transaction at the time the cash is received. Therefore, no journal entry is made to record a bank deposit. However, some journals have a special column for recording memorandum entries of bank deposits.

No. **153** Date _____ 19 ___ $ _____
To_____
_____
For_____

	DATE		
BAL. BRO'T. FOR'D.		5978	00
AMT. DEPOSITED	12 9 77	2172	00
TOTAL		8150	00
AMT. THIS CHECK			
BAL. CAR'D. FOR'D			

A deposit recorded on a check stub

WRITING CHECKS

The person who signs the check ordering the bank to pay cash from that person's account or the account of a business is called the drawer. The person or business to whom the bank is ordered to pay the cash is called the payee. The bank on which the check is drawn is called the drawee. Check No. 153 and its stub are on page 226. Gift World is the drawer. Martinez Supplies is the payee. Citizens State Bank is the drawee.

Writing the check stub

Gift World uses check stubs and checks printed by the bank. The number of each check is printed on the check stub and on the check. The consecutive numbers (a) provide an easy means of identification, (b) assure that all checks are accounted for, and (c) are used in filing the checks for future reference.

> Most checks used by businesses are prenumbered as part of the printing process. If not printed on the check stub and check, however, the number should be written in the spaces provided.

The source document for journalizing a cash payment transaction is the check stub for each check issued. The check stub must always be completed before the check is written. The following items are put on the check stub below: the amount of the check, *$12.00*; the date, *December 10, 1977*; the person or business to whom the check is payable (payee), *Martinez Supplies*; and the purpose of the check, *Supplies*. Also, the amount of the check is subtracted from the total on the check stub to determine the balance carried forward. For the check stub below, the calculations are: Total, *$8,150.00*, less the amount of this check, *$12.00*, equals the balance carried forward, *$8,138.00*.

Writing the check

After completing the check stub for Check No. 153, the accountant for Gift World follows these steps to write Check No. 153:

☐ **1** Write the current date on the check, *December 10, 1977*.

☐ **2** Write the name of the payee, *Martinez Supplies*, on the check. If a check is to a business, write the name of the business — not the name of the owner of the business. If a check is to a person instead of a business, write the name of the person.

> A check payable to a married woman should include her given name, not her husband's: Joan Ritson rather than Mrs. Harry Ritson.

Completed
check stub
and check

☐ **3** Write the amount of the check in figures, $12.^{00}. The figures are written close to the printed dollar sign. This makes it difficult to write another figure in front of the first digit to change the amount.

☐ **4** Write the amount of the check in words, *Twelve* $\frac{00}{100}$. This verifies the amount written in figures. The words begin at the extreme left end of the line provided. After the last part of the amount has been written, a line is drawn through the remaining blank space to the printed word *Dollars*. This makes it difficult for anyone to insert additional words or figures and change the amount of the check. If there is a difference between the amount written in figures and the amount written in words, the bank may (a) refuse to pay the check without checking with the depositor, or (b) pay the amount written in words.

> Some businesses use a check-writing machine that perforates the amount into the paper. This perforation makes it difficult to change the amount.

☐ **5** Write in the space provided the purchase invoice number, *P30*, the purpose of the payment, and the amount.

> Some checks show this information on a detachable slip.

☐ **6** Sign the check after the check has been reviewed to see that it is correct. The signature must be written on the check in the same way it was written on the signature card.

Voiding a check

Banks usually refuse to cash an altered check. If an error is made in writing a check, a new check should be written. The check on which the error is made should be filed. Before filing the check, however, it must be voided. Writing the word *Void* across the face of a check and stub to indicate that the check and stub are not to be used is called voiding a check.

So that each check number is shown in the combination journal, a memorandum entry is made for each check that is voided. The memorandum entry consists of: (1) the date in the Date column, (2) the words *Voided check* in the Account Title column, (3) the number of the check in the Doc. No. column, (4) a check mark in the Post. Ref. column, and (5) a small dash in the Cash Credit column to show that no amount is recorded for the entry on this line of the combination journal.

RECONCILING A BANK STATEMENT

The bank keeps a ledger account for each depositor. The deposit slips and checks received at the bank are posted to the depositor's account each business day. The ending balance that appears on the depositor's ledger account is called the bank balance.

The bank statement

A copy of the depositor's ledger account is sent each month by the bank. The copy shows all deposits received, all checks cashed, special charges against the account, and the bank balance. The report the bank sends to a depositor showing the deposits, the withdrawals, and the ending bank balance is called a bank statement. Gift World's bank statement for the period ending December 27, 1977, is shown below.

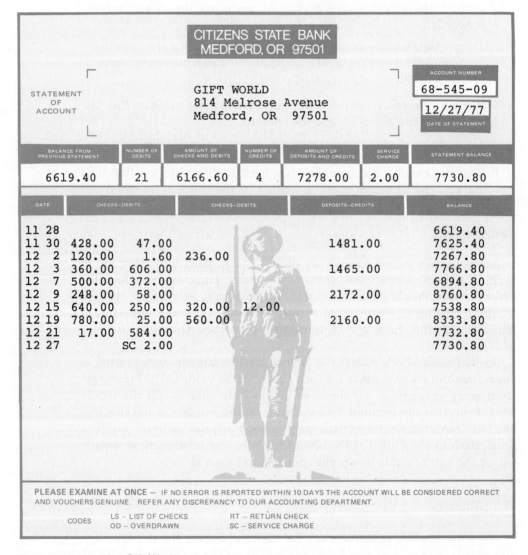

CITIZENS STATE BANK
MEDFORD, OR 97501

STATEMENT
OF
ACCOUNT

GIFT WORLD
814 Melrose Avenue
Medford, OR   97501

ACCOUNT NUMBER
68-545-09

12/27/77

DATE OF STATEMENT

BALANCE FROM PREVIOUS STATEMENT	NUMBER OF DEBITS	AMOUNT OF CHECKS AND DEBITS	NUMBER OF CREDITS	AMOUNT OF DEPOSITS AND CREDITS	SERVICE CHARGE	STATEMENT BALANCE
6619.40	21	6166.60	4	7278.00	2.00	7730.80

DATE	CHECKS–DEBITS		CHECKS–DEBITS		DEPOSITS–CREDITS	BALANCE
11 28						6619.40
11 30	428.00	47.00			1481.00	7625.40
12 2	120.00	1.60	236.00			7267.80
12 3	360.00	606.00			1465.00	7766.80
12 7	500.00	372.00				6894.80
12 9	248.00	58.00			2172.00	8760.80
12 15	640.00	250.00	320.00	12.00		7538.80
12 19	780.00	25.00	560.00		2160.00	8333.80
12 21	17.00	584.00				7732.80
12 27		SC 2.00				7730.80

PLEASE EXAMINE AT ONCE — IF NO ERROR IS REPORTED WITHIN 10 DAYS THE ACCOUNT WILL BE CONSIDERED CORRECT AND VOUCHERS GENUINE. REFER ANY DISCREPANCY TO OUR ACCOUNTING DEPARTMENT.

CODES	LS – LIST OF CHECKS	RT – RETURN CHECK
	OD – OVERDRAWN	SC – SERVICE CHARGE

Bank statement for Gift World

Some banks mail bank statements to all depositors at the end of each month. However, most banks use cycle billing as described in the preceding chapter. This procedure permits the bank to prepare and mail bank statements throughout the month rather than mail all statements at the end of the month.

Checking the accuracy of the bank statement

Banks seldom make errors in their records. However, a check may be charged to a wrong account or a deposit may be credited to a wrong account. If a depositor discovers an error on the bank statement, the bank should be notified at once.

The depositor may make mistakes on the check stubs. The depositor may record the wrong amount or may make a mistake in subtracting the amount of a check from the previous balance or in adding the amount of a deposit.

All checks that have been cashed are sent with the bank statement to the depositor. Checks that have been paid by the bank and returned to the depositor with the bank statement are called canceled checks. Checks that have been issued but not yet cashed at the bank are called outstanding checks.

A deposit that has been made, but which is not shown on the bank statement, is called an outstanding deposit. An outstanding deposit is known also as a deposit in transit. An outstanding deposit is one that has been written on the check stub but has not yet been entered on the bank statement. The deposit will appear on the next bank statement.

Some banks charge a fee for maintaining a checking account. A charge made by a bank for maintaining a checking account is called a bank service charge. The bank deducts the service charge from the checking account. The last line of the bank statement on page 228 shows a service charge of $2.00. This amount has not yet been recorded by the depositor.

The records of the bank and the records of the depositor will not agree if some entries have been made on one but not the other. Good business practice, therefore, requires that the depositor compare private records with those of the bank immediately upon receiving the bank statement. If the bank statement and check stub balances are not the same, the two records must be brought into agreement.

Reconciling the bank statement

The process of bringing the bank balance and the check stub balance into agreement is called reconciling the bank statement. Gift World reconciles the bank statement as soon as it is received. If there are errors on the depositor's record, the check stub record should be corrected. If there are errors on the bank statement, the bank should be notified immediately.

The accountant of Gift World reconciles the bank statement received on December 28, 1977, as follows:

1. Prove cash. (From the journal obtain: beginning cash balance + cash receipts − cash payments = present cash balance. The cash balance according to the journal and the cash balance on the check stub must agree.)
2. Arrange the canceled checks received with the bank statement in check number order. Compare the checks with the check stubs. Place a check mark on the check stub of each check returned with the bank statement. Check stubs with no check mark are for outstanding checks at the time the bank statement was prepared.
3. Prepare a reconciliation of the bank statement. The form of reconciliation used by Gift World is shown and explained below.

Gift World Reconciliation of Bank Statement December 28, 1977			
Balance on Check Stub No. 163, Dec. 28, 1977	8317 10	Balance on bank statement Dec. 27, 1977	7730 80
Deduct:		Add outstanding deposit made Dec. 26	1642 00
Service charge for December	2 00	Total	9372 80
		Deduct outstanding checks	
		No. 160 612.00	
		161 53.00	
		162 2.70	
		163 390.00	
		Total outstanding checks	1057 70
Adjusted check-stub balance Dec. 28, 1977	8315 10	Adjusted bank balance, December 28, 1977	8315 10

a. List the balance shown on the check stub of the last check that had been issued when the bank statement is received. For Gift World on December 28, 1977, this balance on Check Stub No. 163 is $8,317.10.
b. Deduct the amount of the bank service charge. The amount, $2.00, is found on the bank statement. The difference between the check stub balance and the service charge is the adjusted check stub balance, $8,315.10.
c. List the bank statement balance, $7,730.80, shown as the last amount in the Balance column on the bank statement. This amount also appears in the block at the top marked "Statement Balance."
d. Add the amount of any outstanding deposits not listed on the bank statement. The check stub shows that Gift World placed a

deposit of *$1,642.00* in the night depository at the bank on December 26, but this deposit was not listed on the bank statement. When added to the bank statement balance, the total is *$9,372.80*.

  e. List the number and amount of each outstanding check. Four checks are outstanding when Gift World prepared this reconciliation. The total amount of the outstanding checks is *$1,057.70*.

  f. Deduct the amount of the outstanding checks, *$1,057.70*, from the total amount, *$9,372.80*. The difference is the adjusted bank balance, *$8,315.10*.

4. Compare the adjusted check stub balance, *$8,315.10*, with the adjusted bank balance, *$8,315.10*. If the amounts are the same, the bank statement has been reconciled with the checkbook.

Printed form for reconciliation of bank statement

Forms similar to the one above frequently are printed on the back of bank statements. Spaces are provided to complete each step in the bank reconciliation.

Recording a bank service charge in a checkbook

The amount of the adjusted check stub balance is the amount remaining in Gift World's checking account. On the next unused check stub, Check Stub No. 164, Gift World's accountant writes *Less December Service Charge* in the space immediately below "Amount Deposited." The amount of the bank service charge, *$2.00*, is written in the Dollars-Cents columns and deducted from the balance brought forward. The new balance, *$8,315.10*, is recorded on the Total line and brings the check stub into agreement with the bank reconciliation statement.

Check stub showing bank service charge recorded

JOURNAL ENTRIES RELATED TO THE RECONCILED BANK STATEMENT

The bank deducts the bank service charge from the depositor's account as part of the agreement made when the checking account was opened. The bank service charge is one of the few cash payments that is not paid by check and supported by a check stub.

Recording a bank service charge in a journal

After reconciling the bank statement, the depositor makes a journal entry to record the bank service charge. Gift World records the bank service charge as a debit to the miscellaneous expense account.

A portion of the combination journal for Gift World is shown below. The entry is for the bank service charge for December, 1977.

Entry to record bank service charge in combination journal

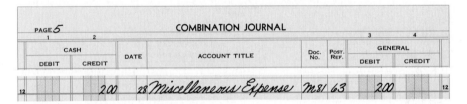

The bank service charge is recorded by writing the date of the entry, *28*, in the Date column. The amount of the service charge, *$2.00*, is written in the General Debit column and in the Cash Credit column. The name of the account, *Miscellaneous Expense*, is written in the Account Title column. The source document is a memorandum approved by Debra Horn, owner, indicating that the charge is correct and should be recorded. The number of the source document, *M81*, is written in the Doc. No. column.

Recording a dishonored check

For a number of reasons, a check may not be accepted by a bank. The amount written on the check may appear to have been altered. The signature may not be the same as that on the signature card. The amount written in figures may not agree with the amount written in words. The check may appear to have been forged. Or, there may be insufficient funds in the drawer's account to pay the check. A check that the bank refuses to pay is called a dishonored check.

If a depositor is notified by the bank that a deposited check has been dishonored, this must be recorded on the depositor's records. In September, 1977, Gift World received a check from Lisa Zimmerman for $20.00 in payment of her account. Later in the month Gift World was notified by its bank that the check from Ms. Zimmerman had been dishonored by her bank. Most banks charge a special fee for handling dishonored checks. Gift World's bank sent a notice that the amount of the dishonored check, $20.00, plus a $2.00 fee, have been deducted from Gift World's checking account. The entry made by Gift World to record the dishonored check and reinstate the $20.00 account receivable plus the expense is shown below.

Entry to record dishonored check in combination journal

The total cost to Gift World, *$22.00*, is recorded in the Accounts Receivable Debit column and in the Cash Credit column. When this entry is posted, Ms. Zimmerman's account is increased $22.00. Now Ms. Zimmerman will be required to pay the original $20.00 plus the $2.00 bank charge. The source document for this entry is a memorandum describing the reason for the entry. The dishonored check is another example of a cash payment that is not supported by a check stub. Gift World's accountant also records this $22.00 deduction on the next unused check stub. This transaction may raise a question about Ms. Zimmerman's future credit. If there is a question, a note about the dishonored check is made in the accounts receivable ledger account for Ms. Zimmerman. This note indicates that care should be taken in granting future requests from her to buy merchandise on account.

✦ What is the meaning of each of the following?

Using Business Terms

- making a deposit
- depositor
- checking account
- savings account
- signature card
- deposit slip
- ABA numbers
- endorsement
- blank endorsement

- special endorsement
- restrictive endorsement
- qualified endorsement
- drawer
- payee
- drawee
- voiding a check
- bank balance

- bank statement
- canceled checks
- outstanding checks
- outstanding deposit
- bank service charge
- reconciling the bank statement
- dishonored check

1. Why is cash less safe than other assets?
2. Why is a depositor required to file a signature card with the bank?
3. How does the bank use the signature card?

4. How may checks be listed on a deposit slip?
5. What is the term used for the special characters printed along the bottom edge of a check or a deposit slip?

Questions for Individual Study

6. How does the bank give its depositors a record of their deposits?
7. Why is a depositor's signature required on the back of checks that are being deposited?
8. What kind of endorsement is often used by a business to prepare checks for deposit to its checking account?
9. What might a bank do if the amount written in figures does not agree with the amount written in words on a check?
10. Why may the balance shown on the bank statement not be the same as

the balance shown on the check stub in the checkbook?
11. What two accounts are affected by the entry to record a bank service charge? How are these two accounts affected?
12. For what reasons may a bank refuse to pay a check?
13. What two entries described in this chapter are treated as cash payments and are supported by memorandums instead of check numbers on the check stubs?

Cases for Management Decision

CASE 1 Audrey Bennett recently opened a checking account for her new appliance store. Ms. Bennett had all six of her employees sign the bank signature card. Is this a good practice? Why or why not?

CASE 2 Max Horton has a personal checking account. He mails money to the bank for deposit when he is unable to get to the bank in person. When the money to be deposited consists of checks, he endorses the checks with a blank endorsement before mailing them to the bank. When Mr. Horton goes to the bank personally to deposit money, he also endorses the checks with a blank endorsement. In which situation is a blank endorsement satisfactory? unsatisfactory? Why?

CASE 3 Joyce Miller, owner and manager of the Sweete Shop, receives a monthly bank statement. She reconciles her bank statements once every three months. Is this a good practice? Why or why not?

CASE 4 Jack Willis sometimes writes checks for which he does not have money in his checking account. He dates the checks for the first of the next month and asks the payee not to cash the check before that date. On the last day of the month, when he receives his pay check, he deposits enough money to equal the total for the checks he has written and postdated. What are the dangers involved in this practice?

CASE 5 Ann Bolser stops by the bank once a week to deposit her weekly receipts. Frequently, she forgets to bring her own deposit slips and borrows a deposit slip from another bank customer. Do you see anything wrong with this practice? Explain.

Drills for Mastering Principles

DRILL 14-D 1   ●   Reconciling a bank statement

On February 2 of the current year, Check Stub No. 211 of W. L. Hipsher's checkbook shows a balance of $426.30. Ms. Hipsher compared the canceled checks accompanying her bank statement with her check stubs. She found that two checks had been issued but not processed: No. 198 for $21.60, and No. 204 for $12.30. The bank statement dated January 31 showed a balance of $456.10 and a service charge of $4.10. Reconcile Ms. Hipsher's bank statement.

DRILL 14-D 2   ●   Reconciling a bank statement

On December 1 of the current year, Check Stub No. 1426 of Carl Alden's checkbook shows a balance of $976.46. In checking his bank statement, Mr. Alden finds that there is a service charge of $3.70. There is an outstanding deposit of $140.15 made on November 30 that was not recorded on the bank statement. The checks issued but not processed by the bank are No. 1392 for $14.12, No. 1409 for $46.40, and No. 1412 for $23.11. The bank statement dated November 30 showed a balance of $916.24. Reconcile Mr. Alden's bank statement.

DRILL 14-D 3 Endorsing checks

Warren Bast prepares and deposits by mail all checks he receives. Write the endorsement that Mr. Bast should use when mailing checks for deposit to his bank.

PROBLEM 14-1 Preparing a deposit slip

On November 10 of the current year Eugenia Young deposited the following items in her checking account (Account No. 148-64530).

Money on hand $473.24

Checks on hand:

George Hansen, drawn on Security National Bank, Medford, OR, ABA number 96-523 .... 125.00

Sally Wehr, drawn on the Citizens State Bank, Medford, OR, ABA number 96-315 .... 42.00

R. A. Mills, drawn on the Citizens State Bank, Medford, OR, ABA number 96-315 .... 102.00

Instructions: Prepare a deposit slip for this deposit. Identify the checks by the ABA numbers.

PROBLEM 14-2 Writing checks and recording a deposit in the checkbook

On the dates shown, Mr. Dale Patton asks you, his accountant, to write and sign the checks listed below and record the deposit in the checkbook.

Instructions: □ **1.** On Check Stub No. 891 record the cash balance brought forward from Check Stub No. 890, $846.20.

□ **2.** Write the checks for the transactions listed below.

Nov. 15. Paid salary to Janice Romero, $300.00. Check No. 891.
16. Paid on account to J. D. Sumner, $76.45. Check No. 892.

□ **3.** Before writing Check No. 893, record on the check stub the deposit of $547.86 made on November 16.

Nov. 17. Issued check to Dale Patton, owner, for cash withdrawal, $120.00. Check No. 893.

PROBLEM 14-3 ○ Reconciling a bank statement for a business

On November 30 of the current year Mary Lane, owner of Lane's Fabric Shop, received the bank statement dated November 28. A comparison of the bank statement with the checkbook of the business revealed the following:

The bank service charge was $3.10. Memorandum No. 46.

The checkbook balance on Check Stub No. 732 at the close of business on November 30 was $754.18.

A deposit had been made on November 30 which did not appear on the bank statement, $190.00.

A check from E. C. Gayle, $18.00, deposited on November 26 was dishonored by the bank. The check was returned and a special handling fee of $2.00 charged to the account of Lane's Fabric Shop. Memorandum No. 47.

The outstanding checks were as follows:

> No. 716, $72.50
> No. 719, $32.40
> No. 731, $83.19

The balance shown on the bank statement was $729.17.

Instructions: □ **1.** Prepare the reconciliation of the bank statement for Lane's Fabric Shop in the same form as shown on page 230.

□ **2.** Record the bank service charge and dishonored check on page 11 of the combination journal.

A BUSINESS SIMULATION
PART 1

QUADRASONICS

ELECTRONIC SOUND EQUIPMENT

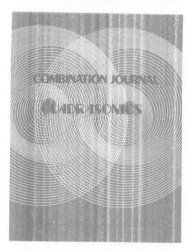

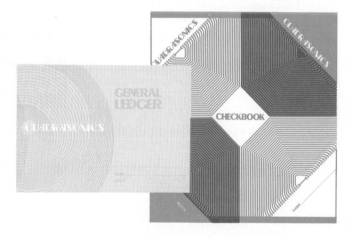

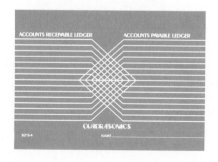

Now that you have learned the basic principles of accounting, you are ready to apply these principles to common business situations that occur in a business simulation. QUADRASONICS is a wholesale dealer in quadraphonic and stereotronic equipment. The source documents and the books used by QUADRASONICS are shown on this page. A pictorial flowchart and a block flowchart of how data are processed in this company are illustrated on the following two pages.

Flowchart of the Partial Accounting Cycle of

QUADRASONICS

PART 1

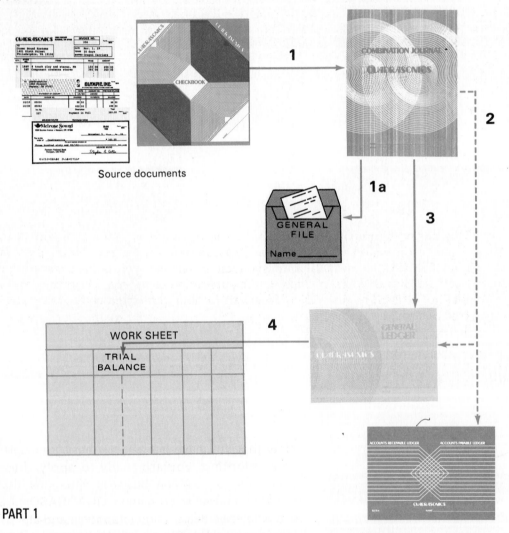

Source documents

PART 1

1   Journalize from the source documents to the combination journal.
1a After journalizing, file the source documents.
2   Post the items to be posted individually to the general ledger and the subsidiary ledgers.
3   Post the column totals to the general ledger.
4   Complete the Trial Balance columns on the work sheet.

Quadrasonics
A Business Simulation
Part 1

PART 1   RECORDING, POSTING, AND PREPARING A TRIAL BALANCE

This business simulation illustrates the entire accounting cycle. The work of a one-month fiscal period is included for Quadrasonics, owned and operated by Janice Ray. The records are those of a wholesale stereo and electronic sound equipment business. However, they illustrate the application of general accounting principles that apply to all businesses. A flowchart for that part of the accounting cycle covered in Part 1 is shown below.

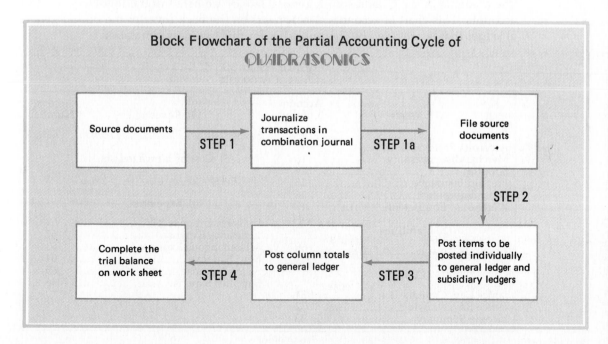

Block Flowchart of the Partial Accounting Cycle of
QUADRASONICS

Only Part 1 of the business simulation is presented at this time. Part 2, the work at the end of the fiscal period, will be completed after the class has studied Chapters 15, 16, and 17.

Required materials

The transactions of this business simulation may be recorded from the narrative of transactions given on pages 242–246. The work may be completed in bound blank books obtainable from the publisher or on unbound sheets of ruled paper. If more realism is desired, a business simulation using incoming and outgoing business papers and bound blank books may be obtained from the publisher.

Model illustrations

The journal and ledgers used in this business simulation are listed below. Also listed are the pages of this textbook on which a similar journal and similar ledgers are illustrated.

Journal and Ledgers	Model Illustrations
Combination Journal	Pages 188 and 189
General Ledger	Page 209
Accounts Receivable Ledger	Page 200
Accounts Payable Ledger	Page 204

Chart of accounts

The accounts in the Quadrasonics general ledger are listed in the following chart of accounts. This chart of accounts also appears on the back cover of the bound general ledger that is provided by the publisher for this business simulation.

QUADRASONICS Chart of Accounts			
(1) Assets	Account Number	**(4) Revenue**	Account Number
Cash	11	Sales	41
Accounts Receivable	12		
Merchandise Inventory	13	**(5) Cost of Merchandise**	
Supplies	14		
Prepaid Insurance	15	Purchases	51
Office Equipment	16		
Warehouse Equipment	17	**(6) Expenses**	
		Delivery Expense	61
(2) Liabilities		Insurance Expense	62
		Miscellaneous Expense	63
Accounts Payable	21	Rent Expense	64
		Salary Expense	65
(3) Capital		Supplies Expense	66
Janice Ray, Capital	31		
Janice Ray, Drawing	32		
Income Summary	33		

Opening a set of books for Quadrasonics

> **NOTE**
>
> If the blank books available from the publisher are used, omit Instructions Nos. 1 through 6. If you are using the set *with* source documents, proceed to envelope No. 1 and follow the instructions given there. If you are using the set *without* source documents, turn to page 242 and begin recording the transactions for November. In the blank books available from the publisher, all accounts in the general ledger, in the accounts receivable ledger, and in the accounts payable ledger have been opened, and the beginning balances have been recorded for you. The journal pages are prenumbered, and the beginning cash balance has been recorded in the combination journal.
>
> If unbound sheets of ruled paper (8½″ × 11″) are used, proceed with Instruction No. 1 given below.

Instructions: 1. Begin numbering the combination journal with page 28, if unbound sheets are used for the journal pages. The combination journal, pages 188 and 189, shows the proper journal column headings.

2. Open the accounts in the general ledger. Open all the accounts that appear in the chart of accounts for Quadrasonics on page 240 in the order in which they are listed. Place four accounts on each sheet. Record the beginning account balances as of November 1 of the current year.

| | Account Balances | |
Balance Sheet Accounts	Debit	Credit
Cash	$ 6,019.80	
Accounts Receivable	6,286.50	
Merchandise Inventory	78,374.40	
Supplies	1,176.00	
Prepaid Insurance	960.00	
Office Equipment	2,160.00	
Warehouse Equipment	6,360.00	
Accounts Payable		$ 6,054.60
Janice Ray, Capital		95,282.10

3. Record the cash balance in the combination journal as a memorandum entry. Use as your guide the illustration on pages 188 and 189. Date the memorandum entry November 1 of the current year.

4. Open an account for each customer in the accounts receivable ledger. The list of customers appears at the top of page 242. Place three accounts on each sheet. Record each customer's beginning balance as of November 1 of the current year.

Customers' Names and Addresses	Account Balances
Audio Sound, 2416 Cherry Avenue, Salem, OR 97302............................	$1,392.30
Electronics, Inc., 38 Princeton Way, Forest Grove, OR 97116...................	552.60
Fisher Stereo, 1534 Alameda Avenue, Klamath Falls, OR 98660	1,251.60
House of Hobbies, 1633 Boone Road, Salem, OR 97305........................	———
Melrose Sound, 1025 Bayview Avenue, Newport, OR 97365	1,104.00
Quad-Phonics, 3840 Kings Highway, Medford, OR 97501	198.00
Record Land, 2618 Seventh Avenue, Eugene, OR 97402	———
Romano's TV, 12 Summit Place, Monmouth, OR 97361...........................	———
Sound, Inc., 7846 Sunnyview Road, Salem, OR 97302...........................	———
Valley Stereo, 9632 East Burnside, Portland, OR 97222...........................	1,626.00
World of Sound, 10 Oxford Road, Albany, OR 97321.............................	162.00

5. Open an account for each creditor in the accounts payable ledger (three accounts to each sheet). Record each creditor's beginning balance as of November 1 of the current year.

Creditors' Names and Addresses	Account Balances
Americo Supplies, 92 Wheeler Street, Salem, OR 97302.........................	———
Cosmo Sound Systems, 1401 Sixth Street, Philadelphia, PA 19106	$1,128.60
Northwest Electronics, 8314 S. W. Canyon Road, Portland, OR 97222.......	2,280.00
Olympic, Inc., 2710 Frontier Road, Nashville, TN 37206........................	———
Reeder's Stereo, 16621 North Rupert Street, Long Beach, CA 90813..........	732.00
Stereo Unlimited, 4682 N. Madison Avenue, Chicago, IL 60610...............	1,914.00
Ultrasonic Equipment, 7816 29th Street, Atlanta, GA 30310	———

Narrative of transactions for November

Instructions: 6. Record the transactions for November 1–4 in the combination journal.

November 1 -1 Sold merchandise on account to Audio Sound, $3,168.00. S121.

-2 Purchased merchandise on account from Cosmo Sound Systems, $12,264.00. P65.

-3 Paid rent for November, $630.00. Ck210.

November 2 -4 Sold merchandise on account to Fisher Stereo, $4,200.00. S122.

-5 Sold merchandise on account to Valley Stereo, $1,536.00. S123.

-6 Paid for new office equipment, $384.00. Ck211.

November 3 -7 Received on account from Valley Stereo, $1,626.00. R178.

-8 Purchased merchandise on account from Northwest Electronics, $1,800.00. P66.

-9 Sold merchandise on account to Sound, Inc., $3,450.00. S124.

November 4 -10 Sold merchandise on account to Record Land, $6,384.00. S125.

-11 Paid on account to Northwest Electronics, $2,280.00. Ck212.

-12 Cash register tape indicates that cash sales for November 1 to 4 were $6,516.90. T4.

Instructions: 7. a. Prove cash. Prove equality of debits and credits in the journal. The cash balance on November 4 is $10,868.70.

b. Post individual items.

8. Record the transactions for November 7–11 in the combination journal.

November 7 -13 Paid on account to Stereo Unlimited, $1,914.00. Ck213.
         -14 Purchased merchandise on account from Olympic, Inc., $11,760.00. P67.
November 8 -15 Paid on account to Reeder's Stereo, $732.00. Ck214.
         -16 Sold merchandise on account to Romano's TV, $3,814.80. S126.
         -17 Sold merchandise on account to Melrose Sound, $4,242.00. S127.
         -18 Sold merchandise on account to Quad-Phonics, $3,480.00. S128.
November 9 -19 Paid telephone bill for October, $51.36. Ck215.
         -20 Bought office supplies on account from Americo Supplies, $162.24. P68.

> See pages 182 and 183 for an illustration of an entry of this type.

November 10 -21 Received on account from Quad-Phonics, $198.00. R179.
         -22 Purchased merchandise on account from Olympic, Inc., $9,360.00. P69.
         -23 Sold merchandise on account to World of Sound, $2,574.00. S129.
November 11 -24 Ms. Ray withdrew cash for personal use, $600.00. Ck216.
         -25 An office memorandum from Ms. Ray indicates that the entry for supplies bought on October 25 was posted incorrectly to Office Equipment instead of Supplies, $162.00. M25.

> See pages 182 and 183 for an illustration of a combination journal entry of this type.

         -26 Cash sales for November 7 to 11 were $7,824.00. T11.

Instructions: **9. a.** Prove cash. Prove equality of debits and credits in the journal. The cash balance on November 11 is $15,593.34.
b. Prepare a cash proof report. Draw a form such as the one below if you are not using the blank books that come with this set. Use November 11 of the current year as the date.

Name_____

QUADRASONICS
Cash Proof Report
November 11, 19--

1. Cash balance at beginning of month .... $_____
2. Plus cash receipts .... _____
3. Total .... $_____
4. Minus cash payments .... _____
5. Cash balance according to journal .... $_____
6. Cash balance according to check stub .... $_____

c. Post individual items.
d. Prepare purchases on account and sales on account report. Draw a form such as the one on page 244 if you are not using the blank books that come with this set. Use November 11 as the date. Use your journal and ledgers to obtain information for items 1 and 2. Find the information for item 3 for (a) Audio Sound, (b) Melrose Sound, and (c) Northwest Electronics.

QUADRASONICS
Purchases on Account and Sales on Account Report
November 11, 19--

1. Number of purchases of   Total
   merchandise on account   _____   amount $ _____

2. Number of sales of   Total
   merchandise on account   _____   amount $ _____

3. Balances shown in the following accounts:

       Accounts   Account Balances

   (a)_____ $ _____
   (b)_____ $ _____
   (c)_____ $ _____

e. Submit the two reports to your instructor.

10. Record the transactions for November 14–18 in the combination journal.

November 14 **-27** Received on account from Melrose Sound, $1,266.00. R180.
      -28 Received on account from World of Sound, $2,736.00. R181.
      -29 Purchased merchandise on account from Ultrasonic Equipment, $13,200.00. P70.
November 15 **-30** Paid salaries for the first half of the month, $1,980.00. Ck217.
      -31 Received on account from Fisher Stereo, $3,000.00. R182.
      -32 Sold merchandise on account to House of Hobbies, $2,280.00. S130.
      -33 Paid for miscellaneous repairs of equipment, $138.00. Ck218.

       Prove the equality of debits and credits before forwarding totals.

November 16 **-34** Received on account from Electronics, Inc., $552.60. R183.
      -35 Paid on account to Olympic, Inc., $11,760.00. Ck219.
      -36 Received on account from Audio Sound, $4,560.30. R184.
      -37 Sold merchandise on account to Record Land, $2,976.00. S131.
November 17 **-38** Sold merchandise on account to Quad-Phonics, $696.00. S132.
      -39 Paid for new warehouse equipment, $1,068.00. Ck220.
      -40 Received from Sound, Inc., on account, $3,450.00. R185.
      -41 Paid Oregon Carriers for delivery service for first half of the month, $456.00. Ck221.
November 18 **-42** Received on account from Record Land, $6,384.00. R186.
      -43 Bought supplies on account from Americo Supplies, $210.00. P71.
      -44 Cash sales for November 14 to 18 were $5,040.00. T18.

Instructions: 11. a. Prove cash. Prove equality of debits and credits in the journal. The cash balance on November 18 is $27,180.24.
    b. Post individual items.

12. Prepare a reconciliation of the bank statement for Quadrasonics. Make a form such as the one on page 230 if you are not using the blank books that come with the set. The data needed are:

a. The November 14 balance on the bank statement is $16,973.70. A deposit of $4,002.00 made on November 14 is not shown on the bank statement. The bank statement shows a service charge of $3.00.

b. When the canceled checks are compared with the check stubs, the following checks issued before November 15 are found to be outstanding: No. 214, $732.00; No. 215, $51.36; No. 216, $600.00.

c. The balance on the check stub on November 14 is $19,595.34.

November 18 **-45** Ms. Ray issued a memorandum requesting that you record the bank service charge in the combination journal, $3.00. M26.

Instructions: 13. Record the transactions for November 21–25 in the combination journal.

November 21 **-46** Paid on account to Cosmo Sound Systems, $13,392.60. Ck222.

-47 Ms. Ray withdrew cash for personal use, $300.00. Ck223.

-48 Received a refund on the repair bill on November 15, $14.40. R187. There was a note on the check stating that a refund was being made because of an error in pricing one of the parts. (Credit Miscellaneous Expense.)

-49 Sold merchandise on account to Valley Stereo, $2,916.60. S133.

November 22 **-50** Received a check on account from Quad-Phonics, $3,480.00. R188.

-51 Purchased merchandise on account from Stereo Unlimited, $8,760.00. P72.

-52 Sold merchandise on account to Melrose Sound, $1,638.00. S134.

-53 Received on account from Romano's TV, $3,814.80. R189.

-54 Purchased merchandise on account from Reeder's Stereo, $11,400.00. P73.

November 23 **-55** Paid on account to Americo Supplies, $162.24. Ck224.

-56 Purchased merchandise on account from Northwest Electronics, $14,640.00. P74.

November 25 **-57** Sold merchandise on account to World of Sound, $4,404.00. S135.

-58 Paid on account to Ultrasonic Equipment, $13,200.00. Ck225.

-59 Cash sales for November 21 to 25, $11,832.00. T25.

Instructions: 14. a. Prove cash. Prove equality of debits and credits in the journal. The cash balance on November 25 is $19,263.60.

b. Post the individual items.

15. Record the transactions for November 28–30 in the combination journal.

November 28 **-60** Sold merchandise on account to Romano's TV, $4,080.00. S136.

-61 Paid gas utility bill for November, $24.00. Ck226.

-62 Sold merchandise on account to Fisher Stereo, $2,160.00. S137.

-63 Received on account from Valley Stereo, $1,536.00. R190.

-64 Received on account from World of Sound, $1,800.00. R191.

-65 Paid the November electricity bill, $65.52. Ck227.

November 29 **-66** Paid the November water bill, $10.92. Ck228.

-67 Received on account from Melrose Sound, $4,080.00. R192.

-68 Ms. Ray withdrew cash for personal use, $540.00. Ck229.

-69 Purchased merchandise on account from Olympic, Inc., $6,840.00. P75.

-70 Paid on account to Northwest Electronics, $16,440.00. Ck230.

-71 Paid cash for merchandise ordered and delivered today, $1,440.00. Ck231.

November 30 -72 Paid salaries for the last half of the month, $1,980.00. Ck232.

-73 Paid Oregon Carriers for delivery service, $468.00. Ck233.

-74 Received on account from Fisher Stereo, $2,451.60. R193.

-75 Cash sales for November 28 to 30 were $8,640.00. T30.

Instructions: 16. a. Prove cash and prepare a cash proof report. (See Instruction 9.) The cash balance on November 30 is $16,802.76.

b. Post the individual items.

c. Prepare a purchases on account and sales on account report for the month of November. (See Instruction 9.) For item 3 find the information for (a) Fisher Stereo, (b) World of Sound, and (c) Olympic, Inc.

d. Submit both reports to your instructor.

17. Total and rule the combination journal. Post totals of the special columns (see illustrations on pages 207–209).

18. Prepare schedules of accounts payable and accounts receivable (see illustration on pages 214 and 215). Compare the schedule totals with the controlling accounts balances in the general ledger.

19. Prepare a trial balance on the work sheet (see illustration on page 216). Use November 30 of the current year as the date. (Only the Trial Balance columns are used at this time. The remaining columns will be completed after you study Chapters 15, 16, and 17.)

Eight-Column Work Sheet with Adjustments 15

The owner or manager of a business must make management decisions and plan for the future operations of the business. Good decision making and future planning depend on periodic information on how well the business is doing. Is a profit being made or is the business losing money? Profit and loss information helps the owner or manager plan the future of the business and make decisions that may increase the profits. Profit and loss information also is needed to prepare required tax reports.

To assist a business in computing the profit or loss, a work sheet is prepared at the end of each fiscal period. A work sheet may be prepared at the end of each month, each three-month period, or each year.

The Rainbow Car Wash, described in Chapter 9, uses a six-column work sheet. However, merchandising businesses like Gift World use an eight-column work sheet.

Some accounts, such as Merchandise Inventory, must be adjusted before the profit is computed. The two additional columns are headed Adjustments Debit and Credit. These two columns provide the space to plan the adjustments required by most businesses. The eight-column work sheet used by Gift World is shown on page 258.

RECORDING THE TRIAL BALANCE ON THE WORK SHEET

At the end of the fiscal period, the accountant first proves the accuracy of the posting as described in Chapter 13. Next the trial balance of the general ledger accounts is entered in the appropriate columns of the work sheet. All the accounts are listed in the order in which they appear in the general ledger even though some may not have balances. Listing all the accounts reduces the possibility of overlooking the need for an adjustment. Also, all the accounts will be listed in the order necessary for preparing the financial statements.

Gift World's trial balance on November 30, 1977, is shown on the partial work sheet below. The following accounts do not show a balance in the Trial Balance columns: Income Summary, Insurance Expense, and Supplies Expense.

	ACCOUNT TITLE	ACCT. No.	TRIAL BALANCE DEBIT	TRIAL BALANCE CREDIT
1	Cash	11	614340	
2	Accounts Receivable	12	75600	
3	Merchandise Inventory	13	784000	
4	Supplies	14	47600	
5	Prepaid Insurance	15	15000	
6	Accounts Payable	21		214400
7	Debra Horn, Capital	31		1097000
8	Debra Horn, Drawing	32	37000	
9	Income Summary	33		
10	Sales	41		899200
11	Purchases	51	501800	
12	Delivery Expense	61	9200	
13	Insurance Expense	62		
14	Miscellaneous Exp.	63	4060	
15	Rent Expense	64	50000	
16	Salary Expense	65	72000	
17	Supplies Expense	66		
18			2210600	2210600
19				

Trial balance entered on a work sheet

NEED FOR ADJUSTING SOME GENERAL LEDGER ACCOUNTS

On any specific day, some general ledger accounts do not show a true, up-to-date balance. This is so even when all of the business transactions for a day or a fiscal period have been journalized and posted. For example, Gift World debits the asset account Supplies each time supplies are bought. It is not practical, however, to credit Supplies each time a piece of wrapping paper or other supply item is used. The balance of the supplies account, therefore, needs to be brought up to date at the end of each fiscal period.

Changes in general ledger accounts that are recorded at the end of a fiscal period to bring the accounts up to date are called adjustments. The general ledger accounts of Gift World that need to be adjusted are Merchandise Inventory, Supplies, and Prepaid Insurance.

The adjustments for the general ledger accounts are first planned in the Adjustments columns of the work sheet. Every adjusting entry has a debit and a credit. Therefore, at least two accounts must be used in each adjustment. The adjustment transfers part or all of the balance of one account to another account. This transfer is planned by writing the debit part in the Adjustments Debit column and the credit part in the Adjustments Credit column.

Adjustments recorded on the work sheet are for planning purposes only. All changes in general ledger accounts result only from posting journal entries. Journal entries made to bring general ledger accounts up to date are called adjusting entries. Planning the adjustments on a work sheet provides a check on the accuracy of the adjusting entries before they are actually recorded in the journal.

The steps to record adjusting entries in the combination journal are described in Chapter 17.

ADJUSTMENTS FOR THE MERCHANDISE INVENTORY ACCOUNT

An itemized list of goods on hand showing their value is called an inventory. An itemized list of goods on hand for resale to customers is called a merchandise inventory. The general ledger account in which merchandise inventory is recorded is titled Merchandise Inventory.

Procedures for taking an inventory are described later in this chapter.

Adjusting the merchandise inventory account affects two financial statements. The correct value of merchandise inventory on hand will be shown on the balance sheet. Also, the cost of merchandise sold will be shown on the income statement.

Gift World prepares financial statements at the end of each month. Therefore, the merchandise inventory account is adjusted at the end of each month. Many businesses, however, make this adjustment only at the end of a fiscal year.

Need for adjusting the merchandise inventory account

The merchandise inventory account of Gift World on November 1, 1977, shows the merchandise on hand to be $7,840.00. When the trial balance is taken on November 30, 1977, the end of a fiscal period, the account shows the same balance, $7,840.00. No entries are made in the merchandise inventory account during the fiscal period to show the changes in inventory resulting from purchases and sales. Therefore, until adjustments are made the merchandise inventory account shows the value of merchandise on hand at the beginning of a fiscal period.

Each purchase increases the amount of merchandise on hand, but all purchases are recorded in the purchases account. Each sale decreases the amount of merchandise on hand, but all sales are recorded in the sales

Merchandise Inventory	13
Nov. 1 Bal. 7,840.00	

account. This plan makes it easier to determine quickly the total purchases and the total sales made during a fiscal period. However, the merchandise inventory account must be brought up to date to show the correct value of merchandise on hand at the end of a fiscal period.

The merchandise inventory and cost of merchandise sold on an income statement

The total original purchase price of all merchandise sold during the fiscal period is called the cost of merchandise sold. Cost of merchandise sold is sometimes known as cost of goods sold or cost of sales. Cost of merchandise sold is computed as follows:

$$
\begin{array}{l}
\text{Beginning Merchandise Inventory} \\
\underline{+ \text{ Purchases}} \\
= \text{Total Merchandise Available to Sell} \\
\underline{- \text{ Ending Merchandise Inventory}} \\
= \text{Cost of Merchandise Sold}
\end{array}
$$

The cost of merchandise sold makes up a large part of the total costs in most retail businesses.

The adjustment for beginning merchandise inventory

The two accounts used to adjust the beginning merchandise inventory are Income Summary and Merchandise Inventory. The T accounts below show the merchandise inventory account and the income summary account before the adjustment is made.

The beginning merchandise inventory, as shown in the merchandise inventory account, is $7,840.00. However, the merchandise inventory account is not up to date. The actual count of goods on November 30 shows that the inventory is valued at $6,280.00. The first step in updating the inventory account is to transfer the beginning inventory to the income summary account. The beginning merchandise inventory, $7,840.00, is credited to Merchandise Inventory and debited to Income Summary as shown in the T accounts at the left.

After the beginning merchandise inventory adjustment is journalized and posted, Merchandise Inventory has a zero balance. The value of the beginning inventory appears as a debit in the income summary account.

BEFORE ADJUSTMENT

Merchandise Inventory	13
Nov. 1 Bal. 7,840.00	

Income Summary	33

AFTER ADJUSTMENT

Merchandise Inventory	13
Nov. 1 Bal. 7,840.00	Nov. 30 (a) 7,840.00

Income Summary	33
Nov. 30 (a) 7,840.00	

The beginning merchandise inventory adjustment on the work sheet

The adjustment for the beginning merchandise inventory is shown in the Adjustments columns of the work sheet on page 251.

	ACCT. NO.	TRIAL BALANCE		ADJUSTMENTS	
ACCOUNT TITLE		DEBIT	CREDIT	DEBIT	CREDIT
1 Cash	11	614340			
2 Accounts Receivable	12	75600			
3 Merchandise Inventory	13	784000			(a) 784000
9 Income Summary	33			(a) 784000	
10					

Work sheet adjustment for the
beginning merchandise inventory

The steps in recording the adjustment for beginning merchandise inventory on the work sheet are:

□ 1 **Debit part of the adjustment.** Write the amount of the beginning merchandise inventory, $7,840.00, in the Adjustments Debit column on the line with the account title Income Summary.

□ 2 **Credit part of the adjustment.** Write the amount of the beginning merchandise inventory, $7,840.00, in the Adjustments Credit column on the line with the account title Merchandise Inventory.

□ 3 **Label the parts of the adjustment.** Write the small letter "a" in parentheses, (a), before the amounts in the Adjustments columns.

A small letter is assigned to each adjustment according to the order in which the adjustments are entered on the work sheet. This labeling helps to locate the two parts of the adjustment when the adjusting entries are made later in the journal.

The adjustment for the ending merchandise inventory

The T accounts show the merchandise inventory account and income summary account before and after the adjustment for the ending merchandise inventory.

The merchandise inventory account is debited for $6,280.00, the value of the ending inventory, and the same amount is credited to the income summary account.

The merchandise inventory account is brought up to date to show the amount of the inventory, $6,280.00, at the end of the fiscal period.

BEFORE ADJUSTMENT

Merchandise Inventory	13
Nov. 1 Bal. 7,840.00	Nov. 30 (a) 7,840.00

Income Summary	33
Nov. 30 (a) 7,840.00	

AFTER ADJUSTMENT

Merchandise Inventory	13
Nov. 1 Bal. 7,840.00	Nov. 30 (a) 7,840.00
30 (b) 6,280.00	

Income Summary	33
Nov. 30 (a) 7,840.00	Nov. 30 (b) 6,280.00

The ending merchandise inventory adjustment on the work sheet

The adjustment for the ending merchandise inventory is shown in the Adjustments columns of the work sheet on page 252.

			1	2	3	4
ACCOUNT TITLE	ACCT. NO.		TRIAL BALANCE		ADJUSTMENTS	
			DEBIT	CREDIT	DEBIT	CREDIT
1 *Cash*	11		6 1 4 3 40			
2 *Accounts Receivable*	12		7 5 6 00			
3 *Merchandise Inventory*	13		7 8 4 0 00		(b) 6 2 8 0 00	(a) 7 8 4 0 00
9 *Income Summary*	33				(a) 7 8 4 0 00	(b) 6 2 8 0 00
10						

Work sheet adjustment for the
ending merchandise inventory

The steps in recording the adjustment for ending merchandise inventory on the work sheet are:

☐ 1 **Debit part of the adjustment.** Write the amount of the ending merchandise inventory, $6,280.00, in the Adjustments Debit column on the line with the account title Merchandise Inventory.

☐ 2 **Credit part of the adjustment.** Write the amount of the ending merchandise inventory, $6,280.00, in the Adjustments Credit column on the line with the account title Income Summary.

☐ 3 **Label the parts of the adjustment.** Write the small letter "b" in parentheses, (b), before the amounts in the Adjustments columns.

ADJUSTMENT FOR THE SUPPLIES ACCOUNT

Each time supplies are purchased, the amount is debited to the asset account Supplies. At the end of a fiscal period, the supplies account shows the beginning inventory plus the supplies bought during the period. The supplies account, however, does not show the cost of supplies used during the period. It is not practical to credit the supplies account each time small quantities of wrapping paper, twine, and other supplies are used.

Need for adjusting the supplies account

The asset account Supplies needs to be brought up to date at the end of a fiscal period. Then the supplies account balance will be the same as the ending inventory of supplies on hand at that time.

Supplies		14
Nov. 1 Bal.	320.00	
8	126.00	
9	30.00	
	476.00	

The supplies account of Gift World on November 30, 1977, is shown at the left. Gift World had a beginning balance of supplies worth $320.00 and bought supplies worth $126.00 and $30.00 during the month. The debit balance at the end of the fiscal period was $476.00, the total amount of supplies available during the period.

The adjustment for supplies

The two accounts used in the adjustment for supplies are Supplies and Supplies Expense. The supplies used during the fiscal period are an expense of the business.

Gift World's supplies and supplies expense accounts are shown in T accounts at the right before and after the adjustment for supplies.

The balance of the supplies account before the adjustment was $476.00. The inventory of supplies on hand on November 30, 1977, was $166.00. The difference between these two amounts, $310.00, is the cost of the supplies used during the month.

The cost of supplies used must be recorded as an expense of the business. Therefore, the cost of supplies used, $310.00, is recorded as a debit to Supplies Expense to show an increase in this expense account.

The cost of supplies used is recorded as a credit to Supplies to show a decrease in this asset account. The total of the debit side, $476.00, less the credit side, $310.00, equals the ending inventory of supplies on hand, $166.00.

BEFORE ADJUSTMENT

Supplies		14
Nov. 1 Bal. 320.00		
8 126.00		
9 30.00		
476.00		

Supplies Expense		66

AFTER ADJUSTMENT

Supplies			14
Nov. 1 Bal. 320.00	Nov. 30 (c)	310.00	
8 126.00			
9 30.00			
476.00			

Supplies Expense		66
Nov. 30 (c) 310.00		

After this adjustment is journalized and posted, the balance of the supplies expense account, $310.00, is the cost of supplies used during the fiscal period. The balance of the supplies account, $166.00, is the value of supplies on hand at the end of the fiscal period.

The supplies adjustment on the work sheet

The adjustment for supplies is shown in the Adjustments columns of the work sheet at the top of page 254.

The steps in recording the adjustment for the supplies account on a work sheet are:

☐ 1 **Debit part of the adjustment.** Write the amount of the supplies expense, *$310.00,* in the Adjustments Debit column on the line with the account title Supplies Expense.

☐ 2 **Credit part of the adjustment.** Write the amount of the supplies expense, *$310.00,* in the Adjustments Credit column on the line with the account title Supplies.

☐ 3 **Label the parts of the adjustment.** Label the two parts of this adjustment with the small letter "c" in parentheses, (c).

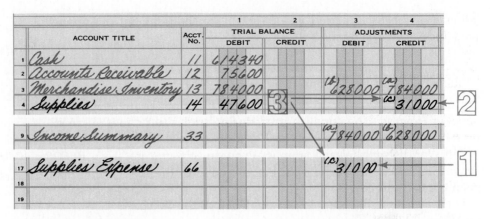

Work sheet adjustment
for supplies used

ADJUSTMENT FOR THE PREPAID INSURANCE ACCOUNT

The cost of insurance premiums paid in advance, and for which the benefits have not yet been received, is called prepaid insurance. The portion of the insurance premiums that has been used up (expired) during the fiscal period is an expense to the business.

Need for adjusting the prepaid insurance account

The prepaid insurance account of Gift World on November 30, 1977, shows it owned $150.00 worth of insurance as of November 1. For every day that passed since that date, the business owns insurance coverage for one day less. Thus, the value of this asset is being reduced constantly. It is not practical, however, to keep this account up to date by making daily entries to record the value of insurance used. Instead, the prepaid insurance account is brought up to date at the end of the fiscal period. Then the balance will show the amount of unused or unexpired insurance.

Prepaid Insurance   15
Nov. 1 Bal. 150.00

The adjustment for prepaid insurance

The two accounts used in the adjustment for prepaid insurance are *Prepaid Insurance* and *Insurance Expense*.

Gift World's prepaid insurance and insurance expense accounts before and after the adjustment for prepaid insurance are shown in T accounts on page 255.

Before the adjustment, the prepaid insurance account has a debit balance of $150.00, dated November 1. This balance is the value of the asset account Prepaid Insurance at the beginning of the fiscal period. No additional insurance premiums were paid during November. A review of the insurance policies showed that as of November 30, $25.00 of the prepaid insurance had expired. Thus, the value of the prepaid insurance at the end of the fiscal period is $125.00. The prepaid insurance account must therefore be adjusted to show its present value. At the same time, the insurance expense must be recorded for the fiscal period.

The amount of the expired insurance, $25.00, is recorded as a debit to Insurance Expense. This entry shows an increase in the balance of this expense account. The amount of the insurance expense, $25.00, is credited to Prepaid Insurance to show a decrease in the balance of this asset account.

After this adjustment is journalized and posted, the prepaid insurance account has a credit of $25.00. This credit represents the deduction for expired insurance for the fiscal period. The new account balance, $125.00, is the value of the asset Prepaid Insurance at the end of the fiscal period. The insurance expense account has a debit balance of $25.00, the insurance expense for the fiscal period.

BEFORE ADJUSTMENT

Prepaid Insurance		15
Nov. 1 Bal. 150.00		

Insurance Expense		62

AFTER ADJUSTMENT

Prepaid Insurance		15
Nov. 1 Bal. 150.00	Nov. 30 (d)	25.00

Insurance Expense		62
Nov. 30 (d) 25.00		

The prepaid insurance adjustment on the work sheet

The adjustment for prepaid insurance is shown in the Adjustments columns of the work sheet below.

	ACCOUNT TITLE	ACCT. NO.	TRIAL BALANCE		ADJUSTMENTS	
			DEBIT	CREDIT	DEBIT	CREDIT
1	Cash	11	614340			
2	Accounts Receivable	12	75600			
3	Merchandise Inventory	13	784000		(b) 628000	(a) 784000
4	Supplies	14	47600			(c) 31000
5	Prepaid Insurance	15	15000			(d) 2500
9	Income Summary	33			(a) 784000	(b) 628000
13	Insurance Expense	62			(d) 2500	
14						

Work sheet adjustment for expired insurance

The steps in recording the adjustment for the prepaid insurance account on a work sheet are:

☐ 1 **Debit part of the adjustment.** Write the amount of the insurance expense, *$25.00*, in the Adjustments Debit column on the line with the account title Insurance Expense.

□ 2 **Credit part of the adjustment.** Write the amount of the insurance expense, $25.00, in the Adjustments Credit column on the line with the account title Prepaid Insurance.

□ 3 **Label the parts of the adjustment.** Label the two parts of this adjustment with the small letter "d" in parentheses, (d).

PROVING THE EQUALITY OF DEBITS AND CREDITS IN THE ADJUSTMENTS COLUMNS OF THE WORK SHEET

After all the adjustments have been recorded on a work sheet, the two Adjustments columns are totaled to prove the equality of debits and credits. The first four amount columns of Gift World's work sheet are shown below after the Adjustments columns have been totaled, proved, and ruled.

	ACCOUNT TITLE	ACCT. No.	TRIAL BALANCE DEBIT	TRIAL BALANCE CREDIT	ADJUSTMENTS DEBIT	ADJUSTMENTS CREDIT
1	Cash	11	614340			
2	Accounts Receivable	12	75600			
3	Merchandise Inventory	13	784000		(b)628000	(a)784000
4	Supplies	14	47600			(c)31000
5	Prepaid Insurance	15	15000			(d)2500
6	Accounts Payable	21		214400		
7	Debra Horn, Capital	31		1097000		
8	Debra Horn, Drawing	32	37000			
9	Income Summary	33			(a)784000	(b)628000
10	Sales	41		899200		
11	Purchases	51	501800			
12	Delivery Expense	61	9200			
13	Insurance Expense	62			(d)2500	
14	Miscellaneous Exp.	63	4060			
15	Rent Expense	64	50000			
16	Salary Expense	65	72000			
17	Supplies Expense	66			(c)31000	
18			2210600	2210600	1445500	1445500
19						
20						
21						

Adjustments columns on work sheet totaled and ruled

The total of the Adjustments Debit column, $14,455.00, is the same as the total of the Adjustments Credit column, $14,455.00. The debits and the credits in the Adjustments columns are proved because the column totals are the same. Single and double lines are then ruled across the Adjustments columns.

STEPS IN COMPLETING THE EIGHT-COLUMN WORK SHEET

Five steps are followed in completing the eight-column work sheet. As you study these steps, check each one with the illustration on page 258.

☐ **1** Extend the balance sheet items to the Balance Sheet columns.

■ Extend balance sheet items not affected by adjustments. If a balance is *not* affected by an adjustment, extend the amount from the Trial Balance column (Column 1 or 2) to the appropriate Balance Sheet column (Column 7 or 8) of the work sheet.

■ Extend balance sheet items affected by adjustments. If a balance in the Trial Balance columns is changed by an adjustment, extend the *adjusted* balance to the appropriate Balance Sheet column.

Adjusted balance sheet items on Gift World's work sheet:

Line 3, Merchandise Inventory:

Trial Balance Debit column......................................	$ 7,840.00
Plus Adjustments Debit column	6,280.00
	$14,120.00
Less Adjustments Credit column..............................	7,840.00
Balance Sheet Debit column	$ 6,280.00

Line 4, Supplies:

Trial Balance Debit column..	$476.00
Less Adjustments Credit column..................................	310.00
Balance Sheet Debit column	$166.00

Line 5, Prepaid Insurance:

Trial Balance Debit column..	$150.00
Less Adjustments Credit column..................................	25.00
Balance Sheet Debit column	$125.00

☐ **2** Extend the revenue, cost, and expense items to the Income Statement columns.

■ Extend income statement items not affected by adjustments. If a balance is *not* affected by an adjustment, extend the amount from the Trial Balance column (Column 1 or 2) to the appropriate Income Statement column (Column 5 or 6) on the work sheet.

■ Extend income statement items affected by adjustments. If a balance in the Trial Balance columns is changed by an adjustment, extend the *adjusted* balance to the appropriate Income Statement column.

Extension of Income Summary is an exception to this procedure. Income Summary, Line 9, has no balance in the Trial Balance columns. The Adjustments Debit column, $7,840.00, the beginning inventory, is extended to the Income Statement Debit column. The Adjustments Credit column, $6,280.00, the ending inventory, is extended to the Income Statement Credit column. Both these amounts are extended because they will be used in preparing the income statement.

Adjusted income statement items on Gift World's work sheet:

Line 13, Insurance Expense:

Trial Balance Debit column... –0–
Plus Adjustments Debit column..................................... $25.00
Income Statement Debit column..................................... $25.00

Line 17, Supplies Expense:

Trial Balance Debit column... –0–
Plus Adjustments Debit column $310.00
Income Statement Debit column..................................... $310.00

Gift World
Work Sheet
For Month Ended November 30, 1977

	ACCT. No.	TRIAL BALANCE DEBIT	TRIAL BALANCE CREDIT	ADJUSTMENTS DEBIT	ADJUSTMENTS CREDIT	INCOME STATEMENT DEBIT	INCOME STATEMENT CREDIT	BALANCE SHEET DEBIT	BALANCE SHEET CREDIT	
1 Cash	11	614340						614340		1
2 Accounts Receivable	12	75600						75600		2
3 Merchandise Inventory	13	784000		(b) 628000	(a) 784000			628000		3
4 Supplies	14	47600			(c) 31000			16600		4
5 Prepaid Insurance	15	15000			(d) 2500			12500		5
6 Accounts Payable	21		214400						214400	6
7 Debra Horn, Capital	31		1097000						1097000	7
8 Debra Horn, Drawing	32	37000						37000		8
9 Income Summary	33			(a) 784000	(b) 628000	784000	628000			9
10 Sales	41		899200				899200			10
11 Purchases	51	501800				501800				11
12 Delivery Expense	61	9200				9200				12
13 Insurance Expense	62			(d) 2500		2500				13
14 Miscellaneous Exp.	63	4060				4060				14
15 Rent Expense	64	50000				50000				15
16 Salary Expense	65	72000				72000				16
17 Supplies Expense	66			(c) 31000		31000				17
18		2210600	2210600	1445500	1445500	1454560	1527200	1384040	1311400	18
19 Net Income						72640			72640	19
20						1527200	1527200	1384040	1384040	20

Completed eight-column work sheet

☐ **3** Calculate the net income on the work sheet.

- Rule a single line across the Income Statement columns and the Balance Sheet columns to indicate addition.

- Add each column and write the totals on the same line as the Trial Balance totals.

- Subtract the smaller total in the Income Statement columns from the larger total, as follows:

  Total of Income Statement Credit column $15,272.00
  Less Total of Income Statement Debit column 14,545.60
  Net income... $ 726.40

☐ **4** Balance and rule the Income Statement columns.

- Write the amount of the net income, $726.40, immediately below the smaller of the two totals in the Income Statement columns.

- Write the words *Net Income* in the Account Title column on the same line as the amount of the net income.

- Total and rule the Income Statement columns.

☐ **5** Balance and rule the Balance Sheet columns.

- Extend the amount of the net income, $726.40, into the Balance Sheet Credit column on the same line with the words *Net Income*. The net income represents an increase in capital.

- Total and rule the Balance Sheet columns. Calculations on the work sheet are considered to be correct since the Balance Sheet Debit and Credit columns are equal.

CALCULATING A NET LOSS ON THE WORK SHEET

If there is a net loss, the total of the Income Statement Debit column will exceed the total of the Income Statement Credit column. An example of net loss is shown on the work sheet below.

	5	6	7	8	
ACCOUNT TITLE	INCOME STATEMENT		BALANCE SHEET		
	DEBIT	CREDIT	DEBIT	CREDIT	
18	4728 00	4428 00	29176 00	29476 00	18
19 *Net Loss*		300 00	300 00		19
20	4728 00	4728 00	29476 00	29476 00	20

Showing net loss on a work sheet

The total of the Income Statement Debit column is larger than the total of the Income Statement Credit column. Therefore, the amount of the net loss, $300.00, is written in the Income Statement Credit column. The amount of the net loss, $300.00, is extended to the Balance Sheet Debit column because it represents a decrease in capital.

TAKING AN INVENTORY

The value of the merchandise and of the supplies on hand at the end of the fiscal period must be determined before the adjustments can be entered on the work sheet.

Physical inventory

An actual count of the items on hand is called a physical inventory. A part of the form used by Gift World to take a physical inventory of merchandise on November 30 is shown below.

Each column of the inventory form is completed as follows:

Item. The name of each item on hand is listed in the Item column.

Stock No. Usually merchandise is ordered by stock number. The stock number is recorded in the Stock No. column as an additional means of identifying the item listed on the inventory.

MERCHANDISE INVENTORY November 30, 1977					
Item	Stock No.	Unit of Count	No. of Units on Hand	Unit Cost Price	Value
Andirons, novelty	CL416	each	10	12.00	$ 120.00
Ashtrays, Venetian glass	TV108	doz.	3	15.00	45.00
Wristwatch, novelty	LR445	each	3	14.40	43.20
Zodiac calendar	MA710	each	25	2.25	56.25
Total					$6,280.00

Inventory record sheet

Unit of Count. The Unit of Count column identifies the way the goods are priced on the supplier's invoice. For example, novelty andirons are priced for each item; ashtrays are priced by the dozen.

No. of Units on Hand. Each item is counted, and the total number of units on hand is recorded in the No. of Units on Hand column.

Unit Cost Price. The amounts in the Unit Cost Price column are taken from the invoices received from the suppliers.

Value. The total value of each kind of item on hand is recorded in the Value column. The No. of Units on Hand times the Unit Cost Price gives the total value of the item on hand.

The Value column is totaled after all items have been entered on the inventory sheet. This total is the amount that appears on the work sheet as the ending merchandise inventory. The inventory record sheet on page 260 shows that the ending merchandise inventory has a total value of $6,280.00.

> A similar type of inventory record sheet may be prepared for taking a physical inventory of the supplies on hand.

Perpetual inventory

An inventory record that shows changes in the amounts on hand as the changes occur is called a perpetual inventory. Other terms used are running inventory and book inventory. When a perpetual inventory is kept, a physical inventory should be taken at least once each year. This will insure that items do not disappear from stock without a record being made on the inventory records.

CENTURY 21 TRANS-VISION® PRESENTATION OF AN EIGHT-COLUMN WORK SHEET

The Century 21 Trans-Vision® insert that follows provides a step-by-step visual review of how to prepare an eight-column work sheet. Follow the directions below in using the insert.

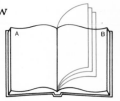

1. Before beginning your study, be sure the pages and transparent overlays are arranged correctly as shown in the illustration at the right.

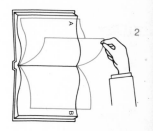

2. Place your book in a horizontal position. Study the steps on page B in preparing the eight-column work sheet. You will be able to read the text through the transparent overlays. When directed in the steps, carefully lift the transparent overlays and apply them over the work sheet as shown at the right.

PREPARING AN EIGHT-COLUMN WORK SHEET

A

To correctly use the Century 21 Trans-Vision® insert, read the steps below. Apply the transparent overlays when directed to do so in the steps.

Gift World
Work Sheet
For Month Ended November 30, 1977

	ACCT. NO.	TRIAL BALANCE DEBIT	TRIAL BALANCE CREDIT	ADJUSTMENTS DEBIT	ADJUSTMENTS CREDIT	INCOME STATEMENT DEBIT	INCOME STATEMENT CREDIT	BALANCE SHEET DEBIT	BALANCE SHEET CREDIT
1 Cash	11	614340							
2 Accounts Receivable	12	75600							
3 Merchandise Inventory	13	784000							
4 Supplies	14	47600							
5 Prepaid Insurance	15	15000							
6 Accounts Payable	21		214400						
7 Debra Horn, Capital	31		1097000						
8 Debra Horn, Drawing	32	37000							
9 Income Summary	33			(a) 784000	(b) 784000				
10 Sales	41		899200						
11 Purchases	51	501800							
12 Delivery Expense	61	9200							
13 Insurance Expense	62								
14 Miscellaneous Exp.	63	4060							
15 Rent Expense	64	50000							
16 Salary Expense	65	72000							
17 Supplies Expense	66								
18		2210600	2210600						

✦ What is the meaning of each of the following?

- adjustments
- adjusting entries
- inventory
- merchandise inventory
- cost of merchandise sold
- prepaid insurance
- physical inventory
- perpetual inventory

1. Why does the owner of a business need to know the amount of profit or loss made by the business?
2. What accounts in the general ledger of Gift World must be adjusted at the end of a fiscal period?
3. Why are the adjustments planned on the work sheet?
4. Why is it necessary to adjust the merchandise inventory account at the end of the fiscal period?
5. If the merchandise inventory account shows a beginning inventory at the end of the fiscal period, what account is debited and what account is credited for the first adjustment? Why?
6. Why is each of the adjustments in the Adjustments columns of the work sheet labeled with a small identifying letter?

7. What account is debited and what account is credited to record the ending merchandise inventory? Why?
8. Why is the supplies account adjusted at the end of the fiscal period?
9. Why is it necessary to adjust the prepaid insurance account at the end of the fiscal period?
10. In adjusting the prepaid insurance account, what account is debited and what account is credited? Why?
11. Both of the adjustments for merchandise inventory on the line with the account title Income Summary are extended to the Income Statement columns of the work sheet. Why?
12. How is a net loss calculated and recorded on a work sheet?
13. How is a physical inventory of merchandise taken?

CASE 1 When Winston King prepared his work sheet at the end of a fiscal period, he made the proper adjustment for the beginning merchandise inventory. However, he forgot to make the adjustment for the ending inventory. Will this have any effect on his calculated net income? What will the effect be?

CASE 2 After completing her work sheet at the end of a fiscal period, Joan West finds that an error was made in taking the supplies inventory. Three boxes of stationery supplies were inadvertently counted twice. The value of the supplies counted twice was $50.00. How does this error affect the amount of net income as calculated on Miss West's work sheet for the fiscal period? How should Miss West correct this error on her work sheet?

CASE 3 The Bast Company paid $480.00 for a year's fire insurance. The company prepares quarterly income statements and balance sheets. However, the accountant prepared an adjusting entry only at the end of the year. Mr. Bast, the owner, thinks the prepaid insurance should be adjusted for each quarter. Who is correct? Why?

CASE 4 Dixie Foster paid $600.00 for a year's insurance on her business. The payment was made on the first business day of the monthly fiscal period starting January 1, 1977. At the end of January, Miss Foster made an adjustment to prepaid insurance, debiting Insurance Expense and crediting Prepaid Insurance for $600.00. What effect will this adjustment have on her net income for each month in 1977?

STEPS IN PREPARING AN EIGHT-COLUMN WORK SHEET

☐ 1 Write the heading and record the trial balance.

☐ 2 Record the beginning merchandise inventory in the Adjustments columns — adjustment (a).

- Write the amount in the Adjustments Debit column on the line with the account title Income Summary.

- Write the amount in the Adjustments Credit column on the line with the account title Merchandise Inventory. *Carefully apply the first overlay.*

☐ 3 Record the ending merchandise inventory in the Adjustments columns — adjustment (b).

- Write the amount in the Adjustments Debit column on the line with the account title Merchandise Inventory.

- Write the amount in the Adjustments Credit column on the line with the account title Income Summary. *Carefully apply the second overlay.*

☐ 4 Record the remaining adjustments in the Adjustments columns — adjustments (c) and (d).

- Write the amount of the supplies adjustment debiting Supplies Expense and crediting Supplies.

- Write the amount of the insurance adjustment debiting Insurance Expense and crediting Prepaid Insurance.

- Rule a single line across both Adjustments columns under the last amount listed.

- Add each Adjustments column and compare the totals.

- Rule double lines below the proving totals of the Adjustments columns. *Carefully apply the third overlay.*

☐ 5 Extend all of the balance sheet items after adjustments into the Balance Sheet columns.

- Extend the amount of each asset after adjustments into the Balance Sheet Debit column (Column 7).

- Extend the amount of each liability, capital, and drawing account after adjustments into the appropriate Balance Sheet column (Column 7 or 8).

☐ 6 Extend all of the income statement items after adjustments into the Income Statement columns.

- Extend both adjustments to Income Summary for beginning and ending merchandise inventory to the respective Income Statement columns (Columns 5 and 6).

- Extend the amount of revenue into the Income Statement Credit column (Column 6).

- Extend the amount of purchases and each expense after adjustments into the Income Statement Debit column (Column 5).

☐ 7 Total the Income Statement columns and the Balance Sheet columns.

- Rule a single line across the Income Statement columns and the Balance Sheet columns.

- Add each column and write the totals on the same line as the Trial Balance totals.

☐ 8 Figure and record the net income (or the net loss).

- Subtract the smaller total in the Income Statement columns from the larger total.

- Write the amount of the net income (or the net loss) immediately below the smaller of the two totals.

- Write the words *Net Income (or Net Loss)* in the Account Title column on the same line as the amount of the net income (or the net loss).

- Rule a single line across the Income Statement columns. Add and write the proving totals on the next line.

☐ 9 Extend the net income (or the net loss) to the Balance Sheet columns.

- Extend the net income into the Balance Sheet Credit column (or net loss into the Balance Sheet Debit column).

- Rule a single line across the Balance Sheet columns. Add and write the proving totals on the next line.

☐ 10 Rule double lines below the proving totals of the Income Statement columns and the Balance Sheet columns.

DRILL 15-D 1 Adjusting the merchandise inventory account

Beginning and ending inventories for four businesses are given below.

Instructions: For each of the businesses listed in the chart shown at the right, state the adjustments that are needed to bring the merchandise inventory account up to date.

Business	Beginning Merchandise Inventory	Ending Merchandise Inventory
A	$ 7,840.00	$8,360.00
B	none	4,200.00
C	10,640.00	9,120.00
D	2,392.00	none

DRILL 15-D 2 Adjusting the supplies and prepaid insurance accounts

The data given in the chart below are related to the preparation of work sheets for two businesses:

Business	Trial Balance Debit Column	End-of-Period Information
A	Supplies .... $360.00 Prepaid Insurance 480.00	Supplies on hand .... none Insurance remaining........ $440.00
B	Supplies .... $810.00 Prepaid Insurance 60.00	Supplies on hand .... $280.00 Insurance has expired at end of period

Instructions: From the data given above, determine the following for each business firm:

1. The amount of the adjustment needed to bring the supplies account and the prepaid insurance account up to date.

2. The Adjustments column in which the amount should be recorded to show the change in the supplies account.

3. The Adjustments column in which the amount should be recorded to show the change in the prepaid insurance account.

4. The balance of the supplies account that will be extended to the Balance Sheet Debit column.

5. The balance of the prepaid insurance account that will be extended to the Balance Sheet Debit column.

DRILL 15-D 3 Extensions on the work sheet

The partial work sheet showing the Trial Balance columns and the Adjustments columns after all adjustments have been recorded is illustrated at the top of the following page.

	Account Title	Acct. No.	Trial Balance		Adjustments	
			Debit	Credit	Debit	Credit
1	Cash	11	3 720 00			
2	Accounts Receivable	12	815 00			
3	Merchandise Inventory	13	8 640 00		(b) 7 680 00	(a) 8 640 00
4	Supplies	14	430 00			(c) 130 00
5	Prepaid Insurance	15	300 00			(d) 50 00
6	Accounts Payable	21		2 220 00		
7	K. E. Bost, Capital	31		10 220 00		
8	K. E. Bost, Drawing	32	480 00			
9	Income Summary	33			(a) 8 640 00	(b) 7 680 00
10	Sales	41		9 890 00		
11	Purchases	51	6 300 00			
12	Delivery Expense	61	150 00			
13	Insurance Expense	62			(d) 50 00	
14	Miscellaneous Expense	63	85 00			
15	Rent Expense	64	360 00			
16	Salary Expense	65	1 050 00			
17	Supplies Expense	66			(c) 130 00	
18			22 330 00	22 330 00	16 500 00	16 500 00

Instructions: □ **1.** On a separate eight-column work sheet form, enter the trial balance and the adjustments shown above.

□ **2.** Extend the balance sheet items to the Balance Sheet columns of the work sheet.

□ **3.** Extend the income statement items to the Income Statement columns of the work sheet.

□ **4.** Complete the work sheet as follows:
  a. Add the Income Statement columns and the Balance Sheet columns.
  b. Calculate and record the net income or net loss.
  c. Total and rule the Income Statement columns and the Balance Sheet columns.

Problem
for
Applying
Concepts

PROBLEM 15-1 ● Work sheet for an appliance store

On December 31 of the current year, the end of a fiscal period of one year, the accounts and their balances in the general ledger of Whitley Appliances and the list of inventories appear as shown at the top of the next page.

Instructions: Prepare an eight-column work sheet for Whitley Appliances. Use as your guide the eight-column work sheet illustrated on page 261A.

Account Title	Acct. No.	Account Balance
Cash...	11	$ 9,194.92
Accounts Receivable	12	11,903.80
Merchandise Inventory................................	13	29,218.30
Supplies..	14	3,465.10
Prepaid Insurance.......................................	15	1,177.00
Accounts Payable	21	7,421.68
D. R. Whitley, Capital	31	46,829.26
D. R. Whitley, Drawing	32	7,010.00
Income Summary..	33	———
Sales..	41	113,851.10
Purchases..	51	84,430.20
Delivery Expense..	61	702.72
Insurance Expense	62	———
Miscellaneous Expense	63	840.00
Rent Expense	64	6,480.00
Salary Expense	65	13,680.00
Supplies Expense..	66	———

Inventories, December 31

Merchandise inventory................................	$ 35,412.00
Supplies inventory..	1,113.02
Value of insurance policies..........................	586.00

The solution to Problem 15-1 will be needed for Problem 16-1 in the next chapter. If it is collected by your teacher at this time, it will be returned to you before it is needed in Chapter 16.

MASTERY PROBLEM 15-M   ● **Work sheet for a hardware store**

Mr. Joe Stallard started his business, Stallard's Hardware, on October 1 of the current year. At that time he had no merchandise inventory. On December 31 of the current year, the end of a quarterly fiscal period, the general ledger accounts and their balances and the list of inventories appear as shown below and on page 266.

Account Title	Acct. No.	Account Balance
Cash...	11	$ 5,434.80
Accounts Receivable	12	819.84
Merchandise Inventory................................	13	———
Supplies..	14	149.52
Prepaid Insurance.......................................	15	90.00
Accounts Payable	21	4,378.80
Joe Stallard, Capital....................................	31	6,429.40
Joe Stallard, Drawing	32	720.00
Income Summary..	33	———
Sales..	41	20,419.10
Purchases..	51	19,950.16

Account Title	Acct. No.	Account Balance
Delivery Expense...	61	1,107.74
Insurance Expense...	62	——
Miscellaneous Expense......................................	63	115.24
Rent Expense..	64	1,200.00
Salary Expense..	65	1,640.00
Supplies Expense...	66	——

Inventories, December 31

Merchandise inventory..	$ 2,880.00
Supplies inventory...	122.00
Value of insurance policies...	60.00

Instructions: Prepare an eight-column work sheet for Stallard's Hardware. Use as your guide the eight-column work sheet shown on page 261A.

**BONUS
PROBLEM 15-B** ● Work sheet for a florist shop

On March 31 of the current year, the end of a fiscal period of one month, the accounts and their balances in the general ledger of Maree's Flower Shop and the list of inventories appear as shown below.

Account Title	Acct. No.	Account Balance
Cash...	11	$ 6,242.10
Accounts Receivable	12	3,266.08
Merchandise Inventory..	13	12,929.20
Supplies...	14	358.50
Prepaid Insurance..	15	500.00
Accounts Payable	21	4,776.30
Maree Burk, Capital..	31	14,644.30
Maree Burk, Drawing..	32	750.00
Income Summary..	33	——
Sales..	41	13,158.00
Purchases..	51	7,074.85
Advertising Expense...	61	125.00
Delivery Expense..	62	114.42
Insurance Expense	63	——
Miscellaneous Expense	64	138.45
Rent Expense..	65	480.00
Salary Expense	66	600.00
Supplies Expense..	67	——

Inventories, March 31

Merchandise inventory..	$11,674.20
Supplies inventory...	264.30
Value of insurance policies...	352.00

Instructions: Prepare an eight-column work sheet for Maree's Flower Shop. Use as your guide the eight-column work sheet shown on page 261A.

Financial Statements for a Merchandising Business

16

One of the main purposes for keeping financial records is to report the financial progress and condition of a business. The journals and ledgers are used to record, classify, and sort data about financial transactions. The work sheet is used to organize and summarize the financial data about the operation of a business. All of these activities are done, however, so that the financial progress and condition of the business can be reported. Most businesses report their progress and condition by preparing three financial statements: (1) the income statement, (2) the capital statement, and (3) the balance sheet.

INCOME STATEMENT

An income statement reports the revenue, the cost of merchandise sold, the expenses of operating the business, and the net income. Normally an owner compares the current income statement with income statements for previous fiscal periods to determine if net income is increasing or decreasing. The owner also may determine if the costs and expenses are reasonable when compared to the total revenue.

Preparing the income statement for a merchandising business

Data in the Account Title column and the Income Statement columns of the work sheet are used to prepare the income statement. A partial work sheet of Gift World for the month ended November 30, 1977, is shown on page 268.

The complete work sheet for Gift World is on page 261A.

The income statement for a merchandising business has three main sections: (1) revenue section, (2) cost of merchandise sold section, and (3) expenses section. The income statement for Gift World is on page 269.

ACCOUNT TITLE	ACCT. No.	INCOME STATEMENT DEBIT	INCOME STATEMENT CREDIT
Gift World			
Work Sheet			
For Month Ended November 30, 1977		5	6
9 *Income Summary*	33	784000	628000
10 *Sales*	41		899200
11 *Purchases*	51	501800	
12 *Delivery Expense*	61	9200	
13 *Insurance Expense*	62	2500	
14 *Miscellaneous Exp.*	63	4060	
15 *Rent Expense*	64	50000	
16 *Salary Expense*	65	72000	
17 *Supplies Expense*	66	31000	
18		1454560	1527200
19 *Net Income*		72640	
20		1527200	1527200
21			
22			
23			
24			
25			

Partial work sheet showing Income Statement columns

The steps in preparing the income statement for Gift World are:

☐ **1** Write the heading of the income statement on three lines.

☐ **2** Prepare the revenue section. Use the data from the Income Statement Credit column of the work sheet.

- Write the name of this section, *Revenue*, at the extreme left of the wide column on the first line.

- Write the title of the revenue account, *Sales*, on the next line, indented about one-half inch (about 1.3 centimeters).

- Write the balance of the sales account, *$8,992.00*, in the second amount column. This amount is the total of the revenue section.

   If there is more than one source of revenue, each revenue account title is listed in the wide column indented about one-half inch (about 1.3 centimeters). The balance of each account is written in the first amount column. The words *Total Revenue* are written in the wide column on the next line below the last revenue account title. The total amount of revenue is written in the second amount column.

Gift World Income Statement For Month Ended November 30, 1977			
Revenue:			
Sales			899200
Cost of Merchandise Sold:			
Merchandise Inventory, Nov. 1, 1977	784000		
Purchases	501800		
Total Cost of Mdse. Available for Sale	1285800		
Less Mdse. Inventory, Nov. 30, 1977	628000		
Cost of Merchandise Sold		657800	
Gross Profit on Sales		241400	
Expenses:			
Delivery Expense	9200		
Insurance Expense	2500		
Miscellaneous Expense	4060		
Rent Expense	50000		
Salary Expense	72000		
Supplies Expense	31000		
Total Expenses		168760	
Net Income		72640	

Income statement for a merchandising business

☐ 3 Prepare the cost of merchandise sold section. Use the data from the Income Statement columns of the work sheet.

The cost of merchandise sold is determined as follows:

Beginning merchandise inventory, November 1, 1977 .... $ 7,840.00
 (*This amount is shown as a debit to Income Summary in the Income Statement Debit column of the work sheet.*)
Plus purchases made during the fiscal period 5,018.00

 (*This amount is shown as a debit to Purchases in the Income Statement Debit column of the work sheet.*)
Equals total cost of merchandise available for sale during the
 fiscal period.. $12,858.00
Less ending merchandise inventory, November 30, 1977 .... 6,280.00
 (*This amount is shown as a credit to Income Summary in the Income Statement Credit column of the work sheet.*)
Equals cost of merchandise sold during the fiscal period............ $ 6,578.00

The cost of merchandise sold section is entered on the income statement as follows:

■ Write the name of this section, *Cost of Merchandise Sold*, at the extreme left of the wide column.

- Indent one-half inch (about 1.3 centimeters) and write in the wide column items needed to figure cost of merchandise sold. Write the amount of each item in the first amount column.

- Write the amount of the cost of merchandise sold, *$6,578.00*, in the second amount column.

☐ **4** Figure the gross profit on sales. The revenue that a merchandising business earns from operations before expenses are deducted is called gross profit on sales.

- Write the words *Gross Profit on Sales* on the next line at the extreme left of the wide column.

- Subtract the cost of merchandise sold, *$6,578.00*, from the total revenue, *$8,992.00*, to find the gross profit on sales, *$2,414.00*. Write the amount of the gross profit on sales, *$2,414.00*, in the second amount column.

☐ **5** Prepare the expenses section. Use the data from the Income Statement Debit column of the work sheet.

- Write the name of this section, *Expenses*, at the extreme left of the wide column.

- Indent about one-half inch (about 1.3 centimeters) and list the expense account titles in the order in which they appear on the work sheet. Write the amount of each expense account balance in the first amount column.

- Write the words *Total Expenses* in the wide column on the next line below the last expense account title. Total the individual expenses and write the total, *$1,687.60*, in the second amount column on the total line.

☐ **6** Figure the net income.

- Write the words *Net Income* on the next line at the extreme left of the wide column.

- Subtract the total expenses, *$1,687.60*, from the gross profit on sales, *$2,414.00*, to find the net income, *$726.40*. Write this amount in the second amount column on the net income line.

- Compare the amount of net income figured on the income statement, *$726.40*, with the amount on the work sheet, *$726.40*. The two amounts must be the same.

- Rule double lines across both amount columns on the income statement to show that the statement has been completed.

Income statement showing a net loss

When the expenses of a business are greater than the gross profit on sales, the difference is called net loss. For example, the partial income statement below shows a loss of $300.00 for the fiscal period.

Gross Profit on Sales		120000
Expenses:		
Miscellaneous Expense	9000	
Postage Expense	15000	
Rent Expense	40000	
Salary Expense	80000	
Supplies Expense	6000	
Total Expenses		150000
Net Loss		30000

Partial income statement showing a net loss

The net loss is found by subtracting the gross profit on sales, $1,200.00, from the total expenses, $1,500.00. The difference, $300.00, is written in the second amount column on the line with the words *Net Loss*.

CAPITAL STATEMENT

The amount of net income earned by the business is important to the owner. The owner also is interested in changes that occur in the capital during the fiscal period. A financial statement that summarizes the changes in capital during a fiscal period is called a capital statement. An owner of a business can review the capital statement to determine if and why the capital is increasing or decreasing. Changes in the amount of capital occur:

1. When additional capital is invested.
2. When cash, merchandise, or other assets are withdrawn.
3. When the business earns a profit or incurs a loss from its operation.

Preparing the capital statement

Data needed to prepare the capital statement of Gift World are obtained from the capital account in the general ledger and from the Balance Sheet columns of the work sheet. Data from the general ledger capital account include (1) the beginning balance of capital and (2) additional investments made during the fiscal period. Data from the work sheet include (1) the withdrawals during the fiscal period and (2) the net income or net loss for the fiscal period.

The general ledger capital account for Debra Horn, owner of Gift World, is shown at the top of page 272.

ACCOUNT *Debra Horn, Capital*					ACCOUNT NO. *31*	
DATE	ITEM	POST. REF.	DEBIT	CREDIT	BALANCE DEBIT	CREDIT
1977 *Nov.* 1	*Balance*	✓				*1097000*

Debra Horn did not invest any additional capital during November, 1977. Therefore, the beginning and ending balances of the capital account are the same as recorded in the trial balance on the work sheet. If an additional investment had been made during the month, the ending balance on November 30 would have been greater than the beginning balance.

The portions of the work sheet needed to prepare the capital statement are shown below.

	ACCOUNT TITLE	ACCT. NO.	7 BALANCE SHEET DEBIT	8 CREDIT	
1	*Cash*	*11*	*614340*		1
2	*Accounts Receivable*	*12*	*75600*		2
3	*Merchandise Inventory*	*13*	*628000*		3
4	*Supplies*	*14*	*16600*		4
5	*Prepaid Insurance*	*15*	*12500*		5
6	*Accounts Payable*	*21*		*214400*	6
7	*Debra Horn, Capital*	*31*		*1097000*	7
8	*Debra Horn, Drawing*	*32*	*37000*		8
18			*1384040*	*1311400*	18
19	*Net Income*			*72640*	19
20			*1384040*	*1384040*	20
21					21

Partial work sheet showing Balance Sheet columns

The capital statement prepared for Gift World on November 30, 1977, is shown below.

Gift World
Capital Statement
For Month Ended November 30, 1977

Debra Horn, Capital, November 1, 1977		*1097000*
Net Income for November, 1977	*72640*	
Less Withdrawals for November, 1977	*37000*	
Net Increase in Capital		*35640*
Debra Horn, Capital, November 30, 1977		*1132640*

Capital statement

The steps in preparing the capital statement for Gift World are:

☐ 1 Write the heading of the capital statement on three lines as shown.

☐ 2 Write the words *Debra Horn, Capital, November 1, 1977* at the extreme left of the wide column. Write the amount of the beginning capital, *$10,970.00*, in the second amount column on the same line. This amount is obtained from the capital account in the general ledger.

☐ 3 Calculate the net increase in capital.

■ Write the words *Net Income for November, 1977* at the extreme left of the wide column. On the same line write the amount of net income for November, *$726.40*, in the first amount column. This amount is obtained from the work sheet.

■ Write the words *Less Withdrawals for November, 1977* at the extreme left of the wide column. On the same line write the withdrawals for the month, *$370.00*, in the first amount column. This amount is obtained from the balance sheet debit column of the work sheet.

■ Write the words *Net Increase in Capital* at the extreme left of the wide column. Subtract the withdrawals, *$370.00*, from the net income, *$726.40*. On the same line write the amount, *$356.40*, in the second amount column.

☐ 4 Write the words *Debra Horn, Capital, November 30, 1977* at the extreme left of the wide column. On the same line write the total, *$11,326.40*, in the second amount column. (The beginning capital, *$10,970.00*, plus the net increase, *$356.40*.)

☐ 5 Make sure that all figures on the capital statement have been transferred correctly from the capital account and the work sheet to the capital statement. Recheck the addition and the subtraction. Rule double lines across both amount columns on the capital statement to show that the statement has been completed.

> In some businesses the data on the capital statement may be included as part of the balance sheet. An example of this method of reporting changes in the capital account is shown on page 138.

Preparing a capital statement with an additional investment and with a net loss

On August 31, 1977, the capital account of H. O. Holder showed that he had invested additional capital of $250.00 during August. In addition, his work sheet, page 259, showed a net loss of $300.00. The net loss of

$300.00 was also shown on his income statement, page 271. The capital statement prepared for Mr. Holder is shown below.

H. O. Holder Capital Statement For Month Ended August 31, 1977			
H. O. Holder, Capital, August 1, 1977	3 2 3 8 00		
Plus Additional Investment	2 5 0 00		
Total		3 4 8 8 00	
Net Loss for August, 1977	3 0 0 00		
Plus Withdrawals for August, 1977	1 0 0 00		
Net Decrease in Capital		4 0 0 00	
H. O. Holder, Capital, August 31, 1977		3 0 8 8 00	

Capital statement showing an additional investment and a net loss

BALANCE SHEET

An owner must make many management decisions about the business. Some of these decisions can best be made after the owner has determined the amount of the assets, liabilities, and capital. The owner obtains some of the data needed by inspecting the general ledger accounts. The data may be found on the work sheet. However, the data are more convenient to use when they are reported on a single financial statement. The balance sheet reports the assets, liabilities, and current capital of a business.

Two forms of balance sheet

The balance sheet may be prepared in one of two forms: (1) account form or (2) report form. In the account form, the assets are listed on the left-hand side and the liabilities and capital are listed on the right-hand side. The account form of balance sheet, used by Rainbow Car Wash, is on page 137.

A balance sheet with the assets, liabilities, and capital listed in a vertical arrangement is called the report form of balance sheet. Gift World uses the report form of balance sheet.

Report form of balance sheet

The report form of balance sheet prepared by Gift World on November 30, 1977, is shown on the next page. The portion of the work sheet used in preparing the balance sheet is on page 272.

Gift World
Balance Sheet
November 30, 1977

Assets		
Cash	614340	
Accounts Receivable	75600	
Merchandise Inventory	628000	
Supplies	16600	
Prepaid Insurance	12500	
Total Assets		1347040
Liabilities		
Accounts Payable		214400
Capital		
Debra Horn, Capital		1132640
Total Liabilities and Capital		1347040

Report form of balance sheet

The steps in preparing the balance sheet are:

☐ 1 Write the heading of the balance sheet on three lines.

☐ 2 Prepare the assets section of the balance sheet. Use the data in the Balance Sheet Debit column of the work sheet.

- ■ Write the section title, *Assets*, in the middle of the wide column.

- ■ Write the title of each asset account at the extreme left of the wide column. Write the balance of each asset account in the first amount column.

- ■ Write the words *Total Assets* on the next line at the extreme left of the wide column. Total the individual assets and write the total, $13,470.40, in the second amount column on the total line.

- ■ Rule double lines across both amount columns.

☐ 3 Prepare the liabilities section of the balance sheet. Use the data in the Balance Sheet Credit column of the work sheet.

- ■ Write the title of the section, *Liabilities*, in the middle of the wide column.

- ■ Write the title of the liability account, *Accounts Payable*, at the extreme left of the wide column. Write the account balance, $2,144.00, in the second amount column. This amount is written in the second column because it is also the total of the liabilities section.

If there is more than one liability, each liability account title is listed at the extreme left of the wide column. The balance of each account is written in the first amount column. The words *Total Liabilities* are written in the wide column below the last liability account title. The individual liability account balances are totaled, and the total amount of liabilities is written in the second amount column.

☐ 4 Prepare the capital section of the balance sheet. Use the data in the capital statement.

- Write the section title, *Capital*, in the middle of the wide column.

- Write the account title, *Debra Horn, Capital*, at the extreme left of the wide column. On the same line write the amount of current capital, *$11,326.40*, in the second amount column. This amount is taken from the last line of the capital statement shown at the bottom of page 272.

☐ 5 Total the liabilities and capital section of the balance sheet.

- Write the words *Total Liabilities and Capital* at the extreme left of the wide column. Total the amounts in the second amount column and write the total, *$13,470.40*, in the second amount column on the total line.

- Compare the total amount of assets and the total amount of liabilities and capital. Since these two amounts, *$13,470.40*, are the same, the balance sheet is assumed to be correct.

- Rule double lines across both amount columns to show that the balance sheet has been completed.

Supporting schedules for the balance sheet

A report prepared to give details about an item on a principal financial statement is called a supporting schedule. A supporting schedule is sometimes known as a supplementary report or an exhibit.

Two supporting schedules are prepared by Gift World to accompany the balance sheet: (1) a schedule of accounts receivable and (2) a schedule of accounts payable. The balance sheet shows only the total amount of accounts receivable. The account balance of each charge customer is not shown. When this detailed information is desired, a supporting schedule of accounts receivable is usually prepared. The balance sheet also shows only the total amount of accounts payable. When information about the account balance of each creditor is desired, a supporting schedule of accounts payable is prepared. These supporting schedules for Gift World on November 30, 1977, are shown on pages 214 and 215.

REPORTING BUSINESS INCOME OR LOSS ON FEDERAL INCOME TAX RETURNS

Income tax laws require each individual who owns a business to report the details of the business operations as part of the owner's personal income tax return. Miss Horn is required to submit with her personal income tax return a special form known as Schedule C, Form 1040, Profit or (Loss) From Business or Profession.

Much of the information needed for filling out Schedule C, Form 1040, is on the annual income statement of the business. A part of Schedule C, Form 1040, completed by Debra Horn for Gift World is shown on page 279. This schedule was prepared from information on the annual income statement below.

Gift World		
Income Statement		
For Year Ended December 31, 1977		
Revenue:		
Sales..		$86,749.00
Cost of Merchandise Sold:		
Merchandise Inventory, January 1, 1977	$ 5,925.00	
Purchases...	55,283.00	
Total Cost of Merchandise Available for Sale........	$61,208.00	
Less Merchandise Inventory, December 31, 1977...	6,197.00	
Cost of Merchandise Sold................................		55,011.00
Gross Profit on Sales...		$31,738.00
Expenses:		
Delivery Expense..	$ 1,824.00	
Insurance Expense..	192.00	
Miscellaneous Expense...................................	454.00	
Rent Expense..	6,000.00	
Salary Expense..	9,840.00	
Supplies Expense..	3,155.00	
Total Expenses		21,465.00
Net Income..		$10,273.00

Annual income statement used
for data on Schedule C, Form 1040

The procedure for completing Schedule C, Form 1040, for Gift World is as follows:

- The name and social security number of the owner of Gift World are written at the top of the schedule.

- **Line A.** Gift World is a retail business engaged in selling specialty gift items. Therefore, the word *Retail* is written on Line A to indicate the principal business activity. The product is described by writing the word *Gifts*.

- **Lines B and C.** The name of the business, Gift World, and the employer's identification number, 76-7832168, are written on these lines.

  > Each employer subject to social security taxes is assigned an identification number by the federal government. The Internal Revenue Service files all records for Gift World under this identification number, 76-7832168.

- **Line D.** The business address of Gift World is written on Line D.

- **Line E.** On this line Miss Horn indicates that the accrual method of accounting is used by Gift World.

  > The method of accounting that includes (1) all revenue earned during a fiscal period and (2) all expenses incurred during the fiscal period is called the accrual basis of accounting.
  >
  > The method of accounting that includes (1) only revenue received during a fiscal period and (2) only expenses paid during a fiscal period is called the cash basis of accounting.
  >
  > Federal and state income tax laws permit the filing of income tax returns either on the accrual basis or the cash basis. These two accounting methods are further discussed in a later chapter.

- **Line 1.** These amounts are copied directly from the annual income statement.

- **Line 2.** The amount is taken from Schedule C-1, Line 8.

- **Line 3.** The amount is figured as instructed on Schedule C. The gross profit on Schedule C is compared with the gross profit shown on the annual income statement. The two amounts must agree.

- **Line 4.** All revenue amounts listed on the income statement other than from "sales" are totaled and written on Line 4.

- **Line 5.** Amounts on Lines 3 and 4 are added and listed on Line 5.

- **Line 6 through 18.** All of these amounts are taken directly from the annual income statement.

- **Line 19.** "Other business expenses" are the business expenses that are not listed on Lines 6 through 18. These amounts are obtained from the annual income statement. The total of all the expenses listed on Line 19, $5,433.00, is written on Line 19(k).

- **Line 20.** All the amounts on Lines 6 through 19 are added. The total, $21,465.00, is written on Line 20. This total must agree with the total expenses shown on the annual income statement.

- **Line 21.** The net profit is obtained by subtracting the amount on Line 20 from the amount on Line 5. The net profit on Schedule C, Form

Profit or (Loss) From Business or Profession

SCHEDULE C (Form 1040)
Department of the Treasury
Internal Revenue Service

(Sole Proprietorship)
Partnerships, Joint Ventures, etc., Must File Form 1065.
► Attach to Form 1040.   ► See Instructions for Schedule C (Form 1040).

1977

Name(s) as shown on Form 1040	Social security number
Debra Horn	372 : 34 : 0261

A Principal business activity (see Schedule C Instructions) ► Retail .... product ► Gifts ....

B Business name ► Gift World .... C Employer identification number ► 76-7832168 ....

D Business address (number and street) ► 813 Melrose Avenue ....

   City, State and ZIP code ► Medford, OR 97501 ....

C

E Indicate method of accounting: (1) ☐ Cash (2) ☒ Accrual (3) ☐ Other ► ....   Yes | No

F Were you required to file Form W-3 or Form 1096 for 1977? (see Schedule C Instructions) . . . . | X

   If "Yes," where filed ► ....

G Was an Employer's Quarterly Federal Tax Return, Form 941, filed for this business for any quarter in 1977? . . . .   X |

H Method of inventory valuation ► First in, First out .... Was there any substantial change in
   the manner of determining quantities, costs, or valuations between the opening and closing inventories? (If "Yes," attach explanation) . . | X

Income

1 Gross receipts or sales $86,749.00 Less: returns and allowances $.................. Balance ►	1	86,749	00
2 Less: Cost of goods sold and/or operations (Schedule C-1, line 8)	2	55,011	00
3 Gross profit	3	31,738	00
4 Other income (attach schedule)	4		
5 **Total income** (add lines 3 and 4)	5	31,738	00

Deductions

6 Depreciation (explain in Schedule C-3)	6		
7 Taxes on business and business property (explain in Schedule C-2)	7		
8 Rent on business property	8	6,000	00
9 Repairs (explain in Schedule C-2)	9		
10 Salaries and wages not included on line 3, Schedule C-1 (exclude any paid to yourself) .	10	9,840	00
11 Insurance	11	192	00
12 Legal and professional fees	12		
13 Commissions	13		
14 Amortization (attach statement)	14		
15 (a) Pension and profit-sharing plans (see Schedule C Instructions)	15(a)		
(b) Employee benefit programs (see Schedule C Instructions)	(b)		
16 Interest on business indebtedness	16		
17 Bad debts arising from sales or services	17		
18 Depletion	18		
19 Other business expenses (specify):			
(a) Delivery Expense 1,824 00			
(b) Miscellaneous Expense 454 00			
(c) Supplies Expense 3,155 00			
(d)			
(e)			
(f)			
(g)			
(h)			
(i)			
(j)			
(k) Total other business expenses (add lines 19(a) through 19(j))	19(k)	5,433	00
20 **Total deductions** (add lines 6 through 19(k))	20	21,465	00
21 Net profit or (loss) (subtract line 20 from line 5). Enter here and on Form 1040, line 28. **ALSO** enter on Schedule SE, line 5(a)	21	10,273	00

SCHEDULE C-1.—Cost of Goods Sold and/or Operations (See Schedule C Instructions for Line 2)

1 Inventory at beginning of year (if different from last year's closing inventory, attach explanation) . . .	1	5,925	00
2 Purchases $55,323.00 Less: cost of items withdrawn for personal use $ 40.00 ...... Balance ►	2	55,283	00
3 Cost of labor (do not include salary paid to yourself)	3		
4 Materials and supplies	4		
5 Other costs (attach schedule)	5		
6 Total of lines 1 through 5	6	61,208	00
7 Less: Inventory at end of year	7	6,197	00
8 Cost of goods sold and/or operations. Enter here and on line 2 above	8	55,011	00

Schedules C and C-1, Form 1040, Profit
or (Loss) From Business or Profession

1040, $10,273.00, should agree with the net income shown on the annual income statement.

Schedule C-1, Cost of Goods Sold and/or Operations, is completed as follows:

■ **Line 1.** The amount of the beginning inventory is obtained from the income statement.

■ **Line 2.** These two amounts must be obtained directly from the purchases account in the general ledger. When the merchandise used by the proprietor is withdrawn, the remainder, $55,283.00, should agree with the amount of purchases shown on the annual income statement.

■ **Lines 3, 4, 5, and 6.** Gift World has no amounts for Lines 3, 4, and 5. The amount for Line 6 is figured according to the instructions on Schedule C-1.

■ **Line 7.** The amount of the ending merchandise inventory is taken from the annual income statement.

■ **Line 8.** The amount is computed by deducting the amount in Line 7 from the amount in Line 6. The amount is also entered on Line 2 of Schedule C.

> The terms *net profit* and *net income* are often used interchangeably. *Net profit* is used on government forms while *net income* is generally preferred among accountants.

The data reported on Schedule C, Form 1040, are almost identical with the data on the income statement of a business. The federal government requires information to be summarized in specific classifications, as shown on Lines 1 to 21 of Schedule C. Therefore, a business should keep its accounting records so that the required data are readily available. Many accounting policies and practices result from government regulations for reporting data.

Using Business Terms

✦ What is the meaning of each of the following?

- gross profit on sales
- capital statement
- report form of balance sheet
- supporting schedule
- accrual basis
- cash basis

Questions for Individual Study

1. What is one of the main purposes for keeping financial records?
2. What are the three most common financial statements of a business?
3. What can an owner learn by comparing income statements of the business for two or more fiscal periods?
4. Where is the information that is needed to prepare the income statement?
5. What are the three major sections of an income statement for a merchandising business?
6. How is the cost of merchandise sold calculated?

7. How can the accuracy of the amount of net income figured on the income statement be checked?
8. Where does one get the information that is needed to prepare the capital statement?
9. How does the report form of balance sheet differ from the account form of balance sheet?

10. Where does one get the information needed to prepare the balance sheet?
11. What information is shown on a schedule of accounts payable that does not appear on the balance sheet?
12. Where does Debra Horn obtain the data needed to complete Schedules C and C-1 of Form 1040?

CASE 1 Sue Marsh owns an art supplies store. The store is on a yearly fiscal period. At the end of a year, a public accountant is employed to assist Miss Marsh in preparing a work sheet and financial statements and completing other end-of-fiscal-period work. At the end of each month during the year, Miss Marsh prepares a work sheet for herself to determine if the business is making a net income or a net loss for that month. The public accountant suggests that Miss Marsh also prepare monthly financial statements. Miss Marsh believes, however, that the monthly work sheet is sufficient to determine how the business is doing. Do you agree with Miss Marsh or with the accountant? Why?

CASE 2 Roger Wenman and Jean Burk, co-owners of a photographic store, differed as to the financial statement that is most important to them. Mr. Wenman believes the income statement is most important; Miss Burk believes the balance sheet is most important. Who is correct? Explain.

CASE 3 Mr. Joe Garrison, owner of Joe's Malt Shop, analyzes his income statement for October and compares it with his income statement for the same month a year ago. He notes that his sales this year are 15% higher than a year ago. He also notes that his expenses have increased nearly 20%. What points should Mr. Garrison consider in deciding whether the increase in expenses is justified?

CASE 4 Ms. Jane Wade inspected her balance sheet for the current fiscal year. The amount of capital at the end of the fiscal year was $11,280.00. The balance sheet at the end of the previous fiscal year showed the capital to be $9,762.00. What might have caused the increase in the capital of Ms. Wade?

DRILL 16-D 1 Figuring the cost of merchandise sold

The data given below have been taken from the work sheets for three businesses.

		Income Statement	
		Debit	Credit
Business 1.	Purchases............................	$ 6,768.00	
	Income Summary..................	7,320.00	$ 5,880.00
Business 2.	Purchases............................	14,400.00	
	Income Summary..................	15,724.00	——
Business 3.	Purchases............................	10,030.00	
	Income Summary..................	——	7,322.00

Instructions: Figure the cost of merchandise sold for each of the businesses.

DRILL 16-D 2 Figuring the net income or net loss

The data given below have been taken from the work sheets for three businesses.

		Income Statement	
		Debit	Credit
Business 1.	Income Summary.................	$ 6,000.00	$ 3,600.00
	Sales..................................		9,000.00
	Purchases...........................	4,200.00	
	Total Expenses	840.00	
Business 2.	Income Summary.................	9,600.00	4,800.00
	Sales..................................		10,800.00
	Purchases...........................	4,800.00	
	Total Expenses	1,200.00	
Business 3.	Income Summary.................	1,800.00	2,400.00
	Sales..................................		9,600.00
	Purchases...........................	8,880.00	
	Total Expenses	2,040.00	

Instructions: For each of the businesses, figure the following: (a) cost of merchandise sold, (b) gross profit on sales, and (c) net income or net loss.

DRILL 16-D 3 Figuring the present capital

The data given below have been taken from the capital accounts and the work sheets for four businesses.

	Business 1	Business 2	Business 3	Business 4
Beginning capital...............................	$14,880.00	$ 8,940.00	$10,260.00	$12,600.00
Net income.......................................	3,120.00	1,800.00	———	———
Net loss...	———	———	550.00	1,920.00
Additional investment.........................	———	———	2,400.00	1,200.00
Withdrawals.....................................	———	540.00	———	240.00

Instructions: Figure the current capital for each of the businesses.

PROBLEM 16-1 Financial reports for an appliance store (net income; no additional investment)

The work sheet completed in Problem 15-1 is needed for this problem. If the work sheet has not been returned to you, complete Review Problem 16-R 1.

Instructions: ▢ **1.** Prepare an income statement similar to the one on page 269.

▢ **2.** Prepare a capital statement similar to the one shown on page 272. Mr. D. R. Whitley did not invest any additional capital in the business during the year.

▢ **3.** Prepare a balance sheet in report form similar to the one shown on page 275.

PROBLEM 16-2   Federal income tax returns for an
appliance store

Instructions: □ **1.** Prepare a Schedule C, Form 1040, Profit or (Loss) From Business or Profession and Schedule C-1, similar to the ones shown on page 279. Prepare the schedule for Mr. D. R Whitley from the financial statements in Problem 16-1.

MASTERY   Work sheet and financial statements for a
PROBLEM 16-M   furniture store (net loss; additional
investment)

The account balances and the inventories on January 31 of the current year for Romero's, a furniture store, are below:

Account Title	Acct. No.	Debit Balance	Credit Balance
Cash...	11	$ 5,498.00	
Accounts Receivable	12	6,064.00	
Merchandise Inventory...........................	13	10,625.00	
Supplies..	14	388.00	
Prepaid Insurance..................................	15	720.00	
Accounts Payable	21		$ 7,386.00
Jose Romero, Capital...............................	31		15,587.00
Jose Romero, Drawing.............................	32	800.00	
Income Summary:...................................	33	——	
Sales..	41		20,160.00
Purchases...	51	15,294.00	
Delivery Expense....................................	61	360.00	
Insurance Expense..................................	62	——	
Miscellaneous Expense............................	63	504.00	
Rent Expense..	64	720.00	
Salary Expense	65	2,160.00	
Supplies Expense....................................	66	——	

Inventories, January 31:	Merchandise inventory	$9,108.00
	Supplies inventory...	209.00
	Value of insurance policies...	660.00

Instructions: □ **1.** Prepare an eight-column work sheet similar to the one shown on page 261A.

□ **2.** Prepare an income statement similar to the one shown on page 269.

□ **3.** Prepare a capital statement similar to the one shown on page 274. Mr. Romero made an additional capital investment of $600.00 during the month. He had a beginning capital of $14,987.00.

□ **4.** Prepare a balance sheet similar to the one shown on page 275.

**BONUS
PROBLEM 16-B**

Work sheet and financial statements for an
auto supply store (net income; additional
investment)

The account balances and the inventories on March 31 of the current year, the
end of a quarterly fiscal period, for Cawley's Auto Supply are:

Account Title	Acct. No.	Debit Balance	Credit Balance
Cash..	11	$ 6,505.32	
Accounts Receivable	12	3,823.52	
Merchandise Inventory...	13	22,849.82	
Supplies..	14	312.00	
Prepaid Insurance..	15	540.00	
Accounts Payable	21		$ 4,820.00
Isaac Cawley, Capital	31		27,766.57
Isaac Cawley, Drawing	32	720.00	
Income Summary..	33	——	——
Sales..	41		18,358.14
Purchases...	51	14,758.40	
Delivery Expense..	61	325.65	
Insurance Expense	62	——	
Rent Expense..	63	525.00	
Supplies Expense..	64	——	
Wages Expense	65	585.00	

Inventories, March 31: Merchandise inventory $21,886.50
Supplies inventory.. 168.00
Value of insurance policies 340.00

Instructions: ☐ **1.** Prepare an eight-column work sheet similar to the one shown
on page 261A.

☐ **2.** Prepare an income statement similar to the one shown on page 269.

☐ **3.** Prepare a capital statement similar to the one shown on page 274. Mr. Cawley
made an additional capital investment of $4,200.00 on March 5 of the current year.

☐ **4.** Prepare a balance sheet similar to the one shown on page 275.

Adjusting and Closing Entries for a Merchandising Business

17

An accountant uses the work sheet (1) to plan the adjustments to the general ledger accounts and (2) to assemble the data needed for preparing the income statement and balance sheet. However, the accounts are changed only by posting journal entries. The Adjustments columns of the work sheet contain the data for journalizing the adjusting entries. The Income Statement columns contain the data for making the journal entries that close the revenue, cost, and expense accounts.

ADJUSTING ENTRIES

Each adjustment in the Adjustments columns of the work sheet must be recorded in a journal and posted to general ledger accounts. Gift World's four adjusting entries are shown in the work sheet, page 261A.

Adjusting entry for beginning merchandise inventory

The partial work sheet below shows the adjustment for the beginning merchandise inventory for Gift World on November 30, 1977. The debit and the credit parts of this adjustment are identified by the letter (a).

ACCOUNT TITLE	Acct. No.	TRIAL BALANCE		ADJUSTMENTS	
		DEBIT	CREDIT	DEBIT	CREDIT
₃ Merchandise Inventory	13	784000			(a) 784000
₉ Income Summary	33			(a) 784000	

Partial work sheet showing adjustment for beginning merchandise inventory

The adjusting entry for the beginning merchandise inventory for Gift World is shown in the combination journal, page 286. The general ledger accounts affected by this entry also are shown.

285

Journal entry to adjust beginning merchandise inventory

General ledger accounts after posting the adjusting entry for beginning merchandise inventory

The words *Adjusting Entries* are written in the middle of the Account Title column of the combination journal on the line before the first adjusting entry. This heading explains all of the adjusting entries that follow, therefore indicating a source document is unnecessary.

The adjusting entry for beginning merchandise inventory debits Income Summary and credits Merchandise Inventory for $7,840.00. This entry transfers the beginning balance of the merchandise inventory account to the debit side of the income summary account.

After the adjusting entry is posted, the debit balance in the merchandise inventory account is canceled by the credit entry. The merchandise inventory account then has a zero balance.

Adjusting entry for ending merchandise inventory

The partial work sheet below shows the adjustment for the ending merchandise inventory for Gift World on November 30, 1977. The debit and the credit parts of this adjustment are identified by the letter (b).

Partial work sheet showing adjustment for ending merchandise inventory

The adjusting entry for the ending merchandise inventory for Gift World is shown below in the combination journal. The accounts in the general ledger affected by this entry also are shown.

Journal entry to adjust ending merchandise inventory

General ledger accounts after posting the adjusting entry for ending merchandise inventory

The adjusting entry for ending merchandise inventory debits Merchandise Inventory and credits Income Summary for $6,280.00. This adjusting entry records the amount of the ending merchandise inventory as a debit to the merchandise inventory account. Now the asset account is up to date. This entry also records the ending merchandise inventory as a credit to the income summary account.

After the adjusting entry is posted, the merchandise inventory account has a debit balance of $6,280.00. This figure is the amount of merchandise inventory at the end of the fiscal period.

Adjusting entry for supplies

The partial work sheet at the top of the next page shows the adjustment for supplies for Gift World on November 30, 1977. The debit and the credit parts of the adjustment are identified by the letter (c).

Partial work sheet
showing adjustment
for supplies

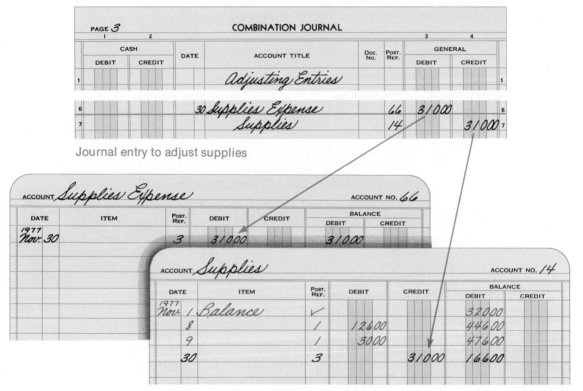

			1	2	3	4
ACCOUNT TITLE	ACCT. No.	TRIAL BALANCE		ADJUSTMENTS	
		DEBIT	CREDIT	DEBIT	CREDIT
₄ *Supplies*	14	476 00			(a) 310 00
₁₇ *Supplies Expense*	66			(a) 310 00	

The entry to record this adjustment for supplies is shown below. Also, the accounts in the general ledger affected by this entry are shown.

PAGE *3*   COMBINATION JOURNAL

	CASH		DATE	ACCOUNT TITLE	Doc. No.	Post. Ref.	GENERAL	
	DEBIT	CREDIT					DEBIT	CREDIT
1				*Adjusting Entries*				
6			30	*Supplies Expense*		66	310 00	
7				*Supplies*		14		310 00

Journal entry to adjust supplies

ACCOUNT *Supplies Expense*   ACCOUNT NO. *66*

DATE	ITEM	Post. Ref.	DEBIT	CREDIT	BALANCE	
					DEBIT	CREDIT
1977 Nov. 30		3	310 00		310 00	

ACCOUNT *Supplies*   ACCOUNT NO. *14*

DATE	ITEM	Post. Ref.	DEBIT	CREDIT	BALANCE	
					DEBIT	CREDIT
1977 Nov. 1	*Balance*	✓			320 00	
8		1	126 00		446 00	
9		1	30 00		476 00	
30		3		310 00	166 00	

General ledger accounts after posting
the adjusting entry for supplies

The debit to Supplies Expense for $310.00 is the expense resulting from the use of supplies during the fiscal period. The credit to Supplies for $310.00 is the decrease in the balance of this asset account.

After the adjusting entry for supplies is posted, the supplies expense account has a debit balance of $310.00. This is the amount of expense for supplies used during the fiscal period. The supplies account has a debit balance of $166.00, the amount of the supplies inventory at the end of the fiscal period.

Adjusting entry for prepaid insurance

The partial work sheet below shows the adjustment for prepaid insurance for Gift World on November 30, 1977. The debit and the credit parts of the adjustment are identified by the letter (*d*).

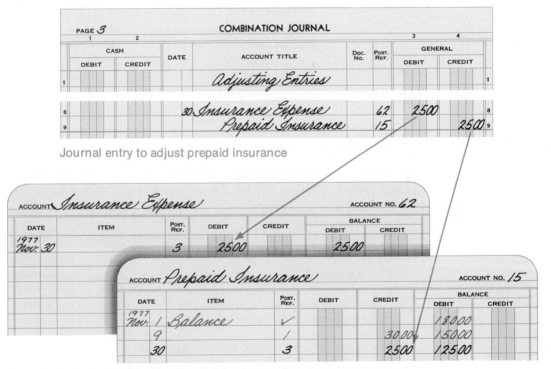

Partial work sheet showing adjustment for prepaid insurance

Journal entry to adjust prepaid insurance

General ledger accounts after posting the adjusting entry for prepaid insurance

The entry to record this adjustment for prepaid insurance is illustrated below. Also, the accounts in the general ledger affected by this entry are shown.

The debit to Insurance Expense for $25.00 is the expense resulting from the insurance expired during the fiscal period. The credit to Prepaid Insurance for $25.00 is the decrease in the balance of this asset account.

After the adjusting entry for prepaid insurance is posted, the insurance expense account has a debit balance of $25.00. This is the amount of expense for insurance during the fiscal period. The prepaid insurance account has a debit balance of $125.00. This is the amount of the prepaid insurance at the end of the fiscal period.

Complete journal entries for adjustments

The illustration below shows all four of the adjusting entries made by Gift World on November 30, 1977.

PAGE *3*				COMBINATION JOURNAL					3	4
	1	2								
	CASH		DATE	ACCOUNT TITLE	Doc. No.	Post. Ref.	GENERAL			
	DEBIT	CREDIT					DEBIT	CREDIT		
1				*Adjusting Entries*					1
2			1977 nov. 30	*Income Summary*		33	7 8 40 00		2
3				*Mdse. Inventory*		13		7 8 40 00	3
4			30	*Merchandise Inventory*		13	6 28 00		4
5				*Income Summary*		33		6 28 00 0	5
6			30	*Supplies Expense*		66	3 1 0 00		6
7				*Supplies*		14		3 1 0 00	7
8			30	*Insurance Expense*		62	25 00		8
9				*Prepaid Insurance*		15		25 00	9

Adjusting entries for Gift World

CLOSING ENTRIES

Gift World uses closing entries to prepare the general ledger for the next fiscal period. Closing entries are prepared at the end of each fiscal period for the following reasons:

1. To clear the revenue, the cost, and the expense accounts by transferring their balances to the income summary account.

> After these account balances are cleared, amounts of the next fiscal period are clearly separated from amounts of past fiscal periods. Each revenue, cost, and expense account begins a new fiscal period with a zero balance.

2. To bring the owner's capital account up to date.

   a. A journal entry is made to record the net income (or net loss) in the capital account. The balance of the income summary account is equal to the net income (or the net loss) for the fiscal period.
   b. A journal entry is made to transfer the balance of the drawing account to the capital account.

The data to record the closing entries are obtained from the Income Statement columns and the Balance Sheet columns of the work sheet.

Closing Entry No. 1 — closing income statement accounts with credit balances

The portion of Gift World's work sheet needed to make the first two closing entries is at the right.

The data for Closing Entry No. 1 are taken from the Income Statement Credit column of the work sheet. Sales is the only account balance in the Income Statement Credit column of Gift World's work sheet. The entry in the combination journal of Gift World to close the revenue account Sales is shown below.

The words *Closing Entries* are written in the middle of the Account Title column of the combination journal immediately above the first closing entry. This is the explanation for all of the closing entries that follow. A source document is not indicated when journalizing closing entries.

	ACCOUNT TITLE	ACCT. NO.	INCOME STATEMENT	
			DEBIT	CREDIT
10	Sales	41		8992 00
11	Purchases	51	5018 00	
12	Delivery Expense	61	92 00	
13	Insurance Expense	62	25 00	
14	Miscellaneous Exp.	63	40 60	
15	Rent Expense	64	500 00	
16	Salary Expense	65	720 00	
17	Supplies Expense	66	310 00	
18			14545 60	15272 00
19	Net Income		726 40	
20			15272 00	15272 00
21				

Partial work sheet showing revenue, cost, and expense accounts balances

COMBINATION JOURNAL — PAGE 3

CASH		DATE	ACCOUNT TITLE	Doc. No.	Post. Ref.	GENERAL	
DEBIT	CREDIT					DEBIT	CREDIT
11			Closing Entries				
12			30 Sales		41	8992 00	
13			Income Summary		33		8992 00

Sales			41	Income Summary			33
Closing	8,992.00	Balance	8,992.00	Beg. Inv.	7,840.00	End. Inv.	6,280.00
						Revenue	8,992.00

Journal entry to close the revenue account

After Gift World's Closing Entry No. 1 is posted, the sales account has a zero balance. The balance of the sales account, $8,992.00, has been transferred as a credit to the income summary account.

Closing Entry No. 2 — closing income statement accounts with debit balances

The data for Closing Entry No. 2 are taken from the Income Statement Debit column of the partial work sheet above. All account balances in the

Income Statement Debit column of the work sheet are closed with one journal entry. The income summary account is debited for the total of these account balances. Each account with a debit balance in the Income Statement Debit column is credited for the amount of its balance. The entry in the combination journal to close the cost and expense accounts is shown below.

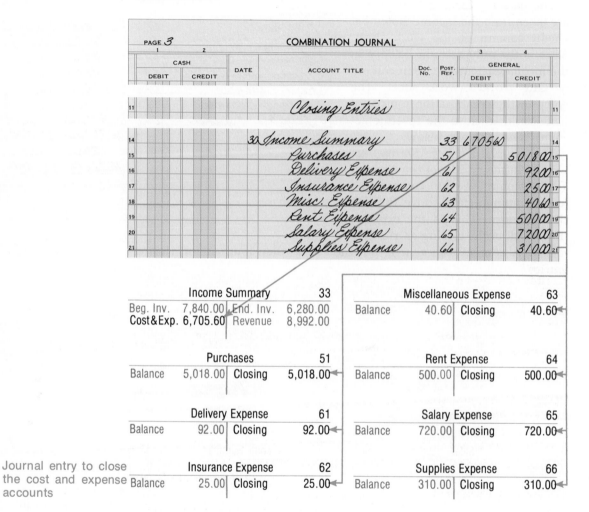

Journal entry to close the cost and expense accounts

After Closing Entry No. 2 is posted, the cost and expense accounts have zero balances. The total of these account balances, $6,705.60, is posted as a debit to the income summary account.

After Closing Entries Nos. 1 and 2 are posted, the credit balance of the income summary account, $726.40, is the amount of net income. This is the same amount shown on Line 19 of the work sheet, page 261A. When the net income (or net loss) is the same in both places, Closing Entries Nos. 1 and 2 are assumed to be correct.

Closing Entry No. 3 — recording net income (or net loss) in the capital account

The credit balance of the income summary account, $726.40, is closed into the capital account. The data for this closing entry are obtained from the Net Income line of the work sheet, page 261A. Closing Entry No. 3 is recorded in the combination journal of Gift World as shown below.

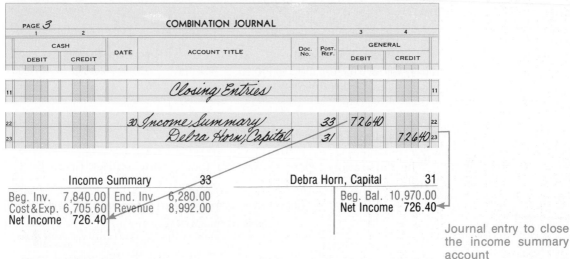

Journal entry to close the income summary account

After Closing Entry No. 3 is posted, the income summary account has a zero balance. The net income, $726.40, has been recorded as a credit in the capital account.

> If a business has a net loss, the income summary account has a debit balance. The capital account would then be debited and the income summary account credited for the amount of the net loss.

Closing Entry No. 4 — closing drawing account into owner's capital account

Withdrawals by the owner decrease capital. At the end of the fiscal period, the balance of the drawing account is closed into the owner's capital account. The work sheet for Gift World, page 261A, shows that the drawing account, Line 8, has a debit balance of $370.00. The closing entry to transfer the balance of the drawing account to the capital account is shown in the combination journal on the next page.

After Closing Entry No. 4 is posted, the drawing account has a zero balance. The debit of $370.00 in the capital account shows the decrease in capital because of the withdrawals.

The credit balance of Debra Horn's capital account on November 30, 1977, $11,326.40, is her new capital at the end of this fiscal period. This amount is the same as the capital shown in the capital statement, page 272. The capital account has been brought up to date.

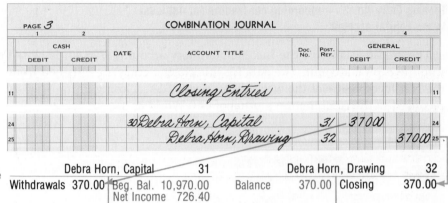

Journal entry to close
the owner's drawing
account

Debra Horn, Capital	31		Debra Horn, Drawing	32
Withdrawals 370.00	Beg. Bal. 10,970.00		Balance 370.00	Closing 370.00
	Net Income 726.40			

Complete closing entries

The illustration below shows the four closing entries made by Gift
World on November 30, 1977.

COMBINATION JOURNAL — PAGE 3

		Date	Account Title	Doc. No.	Post. Ref.	General Debit	General Credit	
11			Closing Entries					11
12		30	Sales	41		8992 00		12
13			Income Summary	33			8992 00	13
14		30	Income Summary	33		6705 60		14
15			Purchases	51			5018 00	15
16			Delivery Expense	61			92 00	16
17			Insurance Expense	62			25 00	17
18			Misc. Expense	63			40 60	18
19			Rent Expense	64			500 00	19
20			Salary Expense	65			720 00	20
21			Supplies Expense	66			310 00	21
22		30	Income Summary	33		726 40		22
23			Debra Horn, Capital	31			726 40	23
24		30	Debra Horn, Capital	31		370 00		24
25			Debra Horn, Drawing	32			370 00	25

Closing entries for
Gift World

CHECKING THE ACCURACY OF THE GENERAL LEDGER AFTER ADJUSTING AND CLOSING ENTRIES HAVE BEEN POSTED

The Rainbow Car Wash in Part 1 uses a two-column ledger account
form. At the end of each fiscal period, the general ledger accounts are

footed, ruled, and balanced. This balancing prepares the accounts for the new fiscal period as described on pages 152 and 153.

Gift World uses a four-column general ledger account form with separate columns for Debit Balance and Credit Balance. Each time an entry is posted to a general ledger account, the account balance is figured and recorded in the appropriate balance column. When an account is closed, a short line is drawn in both the Debit and Credit Balance columns. Each general ledger account shows its current balance at all times. For this reason, there is no need to foot, rule, and balance the general ledger accounts of Gift World. The ending balance for one fiscal period is the beginning balance for the new fiscal period.

Completed general ledger

After the adjusting and closing entries have been posted, the general ledger appears as shown below and on pages 296 and 297.

General ledger of Gift World after posting of closing entries

ACCOUNT **Cash**   ACCOUNT NO. *11*

DATE	ITEM	POST. REF.	DEBIT	CREDIT	BALANCE DEBIT	BALANCE CREDIT
1977 Nov. 1	Balance	✓			340000	
30		2	849900		1189900	
30		2		575560	614340	

ACCOUNT **Accounts Receivable**   ACCOUNT NO. *12*

DATE	ITEM	POST. REF.	DEBIT	CREDIT	BALANCE DEBIT	BALANCE CREDIT
1977 Nov. 1	Balance	✓			26300	
30		2	109200		135500	
30		2		59900	75600	

ACCOUNT **Merchandise Inventory**   ACCOUNT NO. *13*

DATE	ITEM	POST. REF.	DEBIT	CREDIT	BALANCE DEBIT	BALANCE CREDIT
1977 Nov. 1	Balance	✓			784000	
30		3		784000	—	—
30		3	628000		628000	

ACCOUNT **Supplies**   ACCOUNT NO. *14*

DATE	ITEM	POST. REF.	DEBIT	CREDIT	BALANCE DEBIT	BALANCE CREDIT
1977 Nov. 1	Balance	✓			32000	
8		1	12600		44600	
9		1	3000		47600	
30		3		31000	16600	

ACCOUNT **Prepaid Insurance**   ACCOUNT NO. 15

DATE		ITEM	POST. REF.	DEBIT	CREDIT	BALANCE DEBIT	BALANCE CREDIT
1977 Nov.	1	Balance	✓			18000	
	9		1		3000	15000	
	30		3		2500	12500	

ACCOUNT **Accounts Payable**   ACCOUNT NO. 21

DATE		ITEM	POST. REF.	DEBIT	CREDIT	BALANCE DEBIT	BALANCE CREDIT
1977 Nov.	1	Balance	✓				103300
	30		2	203900		100600	
	30		2		315000		214400

ACCOUNT **Debra Horn, Capital**   ACCOUNT NO. 31

DATE		ITEM	POST. REF.	DEBIT	CREDIT	BALANCE DEBIT	BALANCE CREDIT
1977 Nov.	1	Balance	✓				1097000
	30		3		72640		1169640
	30		3	37000			1132640

ACCOUNT **Debra Horn, Drawing**   ACCOUNT NO. 32

DATE		ITEM	POST. REF.	DEBIT	CREDIT	BALANCE DEBIT	BALANCE CREDIT
1977 Nov.	8		1	25000		25000	
	29		2	12000		37000	
	30		3		37000	—	—

ACCOUNT **Income Summary**   ACCOUNT NO. 33

DATE		ITEM	POST. REF.	DEBIT	CREDIT	BALANCE DEBIT	BALANCE CREDIT
1977 Nov.	30		3	784000		784000	
	30		3		628000	156000	
	30		3		899200		743200
	30		3	670560			72640
	30		3	72640		—	—

ACCOUNT **Sales**   ACCOUNT NO. 41

DATE		ITEM	POST. REF.	DEBIT	CREDIT	BALANCE DEBIT	BALANCE CREDIT
1977 Nov.	30		2		899200		899200
	30		3	899200		—	—

General ledger of Gift World after posting of closing entries (continued)

ACCOUNT *Purchases*   ACCOUNT NO. *51*

DATE	ITEM	POST. REF.	DEBIT	CREDIT	BALANCE DEBIT	BALANCE CREDIT
1977 Nov. 30		2	5018 00		5018 00	
30		3		5018 00	—	

ACCOUNT *Delivery Expense*   ACCOUNT NO. *61*

DATE	ITEM	POST. REF.	DEBIT	CREDIT	BALANCE DEBIT	BALANCE CREDIT
1977 Nov. 8		1	45 00		45 00	
29		2	47 00		92 00	
30		3		92 00	—	—

ACCOUNT *Insurance Expense*   ACCOUNT NO. *62*

DATE	ITEM	POST. REF.	DEBIT	CREDIT	BALANCE DEBIT	BALANCE CREDIT
1977 Nov. 30		3	25 00		25 00	
30		3		25 00	—	—

ACCOUNT *Miscellaneous Expense*   ACCOUNT NO. *63*

DATE	ITEM	POST. REF.	DEBIT	CREDIT	BALANCE DEBIT	BALANCE CREDIT
1977 Nov. 15		1	25 00		25 00	
23		2	14 00		39 00	
29		2	1 60		40 60	
30		3		40 60	—	—

ACCOUNT *Rent Expense*   ACCOUNT NO. *64*

DATE	ITEM	POST. REF.	DEBIT	CREDIT	BALANCE DEBIT	BALANCE CREDIT
1977 Nov. 1		1	500 00		500 00	
30		3		500 00	—	

ACCOUNT *Salary Expense*   ACCOUNT NO. *65*

DATE	ITEM	POST. REF.	DEBIT	CREDIT	BALANCE DEBIT	BALANCE CREDIT
1977 Nov. 16		1	360 00		360 00	
30		2	360 00		720 00	
30		3		720 00	—	

ACCOUNT *Supplies Expense*   ACCOUNT NO. *66*

DATE	ITEM	POST. REF.	DEBIT	CREDIT	BALANCE DEBIT	BALANCE CREDIT
1977 Nov. 30		3	310 00		310 00	
30		3		310 00	—	—

General ledger of Gift World after posting of closing entries (concluded)

The income statement accounts (revenue, cost, and expense accounts) have zero balances. Since they have zero balances as a result of closing entries, they are said to be "closed." The balance sheet accounts (asset, liability, and capital accounts) show balances as of November 30, 1977. Because they have balances, they are said to be "open." The balances in the balance sheet accounts agree with the amounts shown on the balance sheet, page 275. The balances shown in the general ledger accounts as of November 30, 1977, will be the beginning balances for December 1, 1977. Unless a new page is being opened for an account, it is unnecessary to write in the beginning balance for December 1, 1977.

Post-closing trial balance

A post-closing trial balance is taken after adjusting and closing entries have been posted. The purpose of the post-closing trial balance is to prove the equality of debits and credits in the general ledger. The post-closing trial balance prepared for Gift World on November 30, 1977, is shown below.

ACCOUNT TITLE	ACCT. NO.	DEBIT	CREDIT
Cash	11	614340	
Accounts Receivable	12	75600	
Merchandise Inventory	13	628000	
Supplies	14	16600	
Prepaid Insurance	15	12500	
Accounts Payable	21		214400
Debra Horn, Capital	31		1132640
		1347040	1347040

Gift World
Post-Closing Trial Balance
November 30, 1977

Post-closing trial balance

The general ledger accounts that have balances are listed on the post-closing trial balance. Only the balance sheet accounts remain open. The accounts are listed in the same order as they appear in the general ledger. Accounts with zero balances are closed and are not listed on the post-closing trial balance. Accounts that are closed are the revenue, cost, and expense accounts; the owner's drawing account; and the income summary account.

The account balances on the post-closing trial balance agree with the balances shown on the balance sheet on page 275. Also, on the post-closing trial balance, the debit balance total, $13,470.40, is the same as the credit balance total, $13,470.40. The equality of debits and credits in the general ledger is proved. The general ledger is ready for the next fiscal period.

SUMMARY OF THE ACCOUNTING CYCLE FOR A MERCHANDISING BUSINESS

The accounting cycle contains the same basic steps for a merchandising business as it does for a service business. Minor variations occur when subsidiary ledgers are kept and a capital statement is prepared. The steps in the accounting cycle for Rainbow Car Wash are shown in the flowchart on page 157. The following flowchart shows the steps in the accounting cycle for Gift World.

Flowchart of the steps in the accounting cycle of Gift World

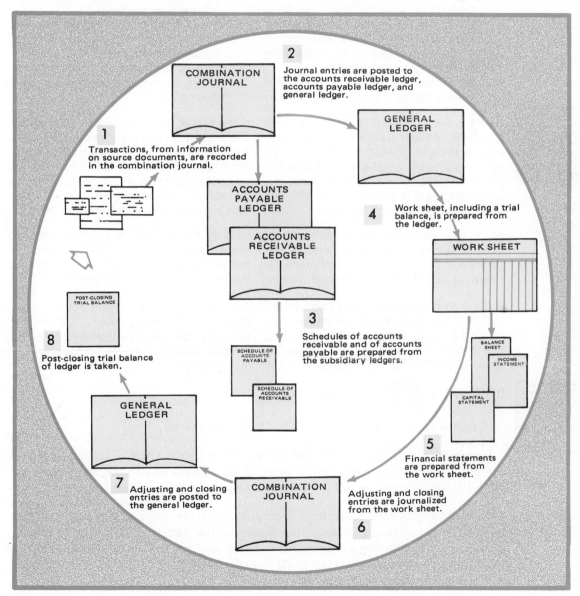

1. How are account balances in the general ledger changed?
2. Where is the information found for journalizing the adjusting entries?
3. Why are the adjustments that are planned on the work sheet recorded as entries in a journal?
4. Where is the explanation for the adjusting entries written in the combination journal?
5. What effect does the adjustment for beginning merchandise inventory have on the general ledger accounts?
6. What effect does the adjustment for ending merchandise inventory have on the general ledger accounts?
7. What does the amount represent that is recorded as a credit to the supplies account by an adjusting entry in the journal?
8. What does the amount represent that is recorded as a credit to the prepaid insurance account by an adjusting entry?
9. Why are closing entries needed at the end of a fiscal period?
10. From what columns of the work sheet is the information obtained for making the entries to close revenue, cost, and expense accounts?
11. How are the general ledger accounts affected by the closing entry to close the sales account?
12. Why is the drawing account transferred to the capital account by a closing entry?

CASE 1 Sarah Crowell prepares a work sheet and financial statements for her business at the end of each month. However, she uses a yearly fiscal period ending December 31. Ms. Crowell's father helps her check her records and suggests that she should make adjusting and closing entries at the end of each month at the same time she prepares her work sheet and financial statements. Ms. Crowell decides that this is not necessary and that she only needs to make the adjusting and closing entries at the end of each fiscal year. Do you agree with Ms. Crowell or with her father? Why?

CASE 2 George Rowe had a debit balance of $480.00 in the supplies account on January 1. On January 31, Mr. Rowe made the following adjusting entry to record supplies used of $160.00. Debit Supplies $160.00; credit Supplies Expense $160.00. What effect will this adjusting entry have on the net income? On the balance sheet? Why?

CASE 3 Two businesses have been following different accounting practices. You have been asked to determine which practice is correct. Tom Rains first closes the drawing account to the capital account, then he closes the income summary account. Glenn Hadley closes the income summary account first, then he closes the drawing account. Which practice is correct? Explain.

DRILL 17-D 1   Adjusting entries

A partial work sheet of Gale Stein is shown on page 301.

Instructions: □ **1.** On a separate sheet of paper, prepare a T account for each account shown on the partial work sheet. If the account has a balance listed in the Trial Balance columns, record the balance on the proper side of the T account.

□ **2.** In the appropriate T accounts, record the debit amount and the credit amount for each of the following adjustments shown on the partial work sheet: (a) the adjusting entry for the beginning merchandise inventory; (b) the adjusting entry for the ending merchandise inventory; (c) the adjusting entry for supplies; (d) the adjusting entry for prepaid insurance.

Account Title	Trial Balance		Adjustments	
	Debit	Credit	Debit	Credit
Merchandise Inventory....	11 900 00		(b) 5 800 00	(a) 11 900 00
Supplies........................	462 00			(c) 142 00
Prepaid Insurance...........	112 00			(d) 32 00
Income Summary............			(a) 11 900 00	(b) 5 800 00
Insurance Expense..........			(d) 32 00	
Supplies Expense............			(c) 142 00	

DRILL 17-D 2 Adjusting entries

Data are shown below for three businesses. These data are related to adjustments needed at the end of a fiscal period.

Business	Account Title	Account Balance in General Ledger	Ending Inventories
1............	Merchandise Inventory	$11,200.00	$10,500.00
	Supplies	700.00	200.00
	Prepaid Insurance	250.00	130.00
2............	Merchandise Inventory	$ 9,030.00	$ 9,940.00
	Supplies	430.00	120.00
	Prepaid Insurance	390.00	240.00
3............	Merchandise Inventory	$14,700.00	$13,020.00
	Supplies	870.00	390.00
	Prepaid Insurance	760.00	630.00

Instructions: □ **1.** On a separate sheet of paper, open the following six T accounts for each of the three businesses: Merchandise Inventory, Supplies, Prepaid Insurance, Income Summary, Insurance Expense, and Supplies Expense. Record the account balance on the proper side of each T account.

□ **2.** In the appropriate T accounts, record for each company the debit and credit amounts for each of the following: (a) the adjusting entry for beginning merchandise inventory; (b) the adjusting entry for ending merchandise inventory; (c) the adjusting entry for supplies, (d) the adjusting entry for prepaid insurance.

DRILL 17-D 3 Closing entries

A partial work sheet for Anna Tsung is shown on page 302.

Instructions: □ **1.** On a separate sheet of paper, prepare a T account for each account on the partial work sheet. In each T account, record on the appropriate side the amount that is shown in the Income Statement or Balance Sheet columns.

□ **2.** In the appropriate T accounts, record the debit amount and the credit amount for each of the following: (a) the closing entry to close the revenue account; (b) the closing entry to close the cost account and the expense accounts; (c) the closing entry to record net income (or loss) in the capital account; (d) the closing entry to transfer the balance of the drawing account to the capital account.

Account Title	Income Statement		Balance Sheet	
	Debit	Credit	Debit	Credit
Anna Tsung, Capital				13 600 00
Anna Tsung, Drawing............			400 00	
Income Summary...................	6 400 00	5 600 00		
Sales....................................		6 200 00		
Purchases............................	3 300 00			
Insurance Expense.................	40 00			
Miscellaneous Expense...........	60 00			
Rent Expense.......................	320 00			
Salary Expense.....................	580 00			
Supplies Expense..................	70 00			
	10 770 00	11 800 00	17 830 00	16 800 00
Net Income..........................	1 030 00			1 030 00
	11 800 00	11 800 00	17 830 00	17 830 00

PROBLEM 17-1 ○ Work at the end of the fiscal period

If you are not using the workbook correlating with this textbook, complete Review Problem 17-R 1.

The ledger accounts of DuBois Jewelers as of April 30 of the current year, the end of a monthly fiscal period, are given in the workbook.

Instructions: ☒ 1. Prepare a trial balance in the Trial Balance columns of a work sheet. List each account title whether it has a balance or not.

☒ 2. Complete the work sheet. Use the following data about inventories on April 30: Merchandise inventory, $12,216.50; supplies inventory, $190.00; value of insurance policies, $224.00. Compare your work sheet with the one shown on page 261A.

☒ 3. Prepare an income statement from the information on the work sheet. Compare your income statement with the one shown on page 269.

☒ 4. Prepare a capital statement from the information on the work sheet and in the capital account. Compare your capital statement with the one shown on page 272.

☒ 5. Prepare a balance sheet in report form from the information on the work sheet. Compare your balance sheet with the one shown on page 275.

☒ 6. On page 2 of the combination journal record the adjusting entries shown in the Adjustments columns of the work sheet. Compare your work with the adjusting entries shown on page 290.

☒ 7. Record in the combination journal the closing entries from the information on the work sheet. Compare your closing entries with the ones shown on page 294.

☒ 8. Post the adjusting entries and the closing entries to the general ledger.

☒ 9. Prepare a post-closing trial balance. Compare your post-closing trial balance with the one shown on page 298.

QUADRASONICS

ELECTRONIC SOUND EQUIPMENT

WORK SHEET				
	TRIAL BALANCE	ADJUST-MENTS	INCOME STATE-MENT	BALANCE SHEET

CAPITAL STATEMENT		

INCOME STATEMENT		

BALANCE SHEET		

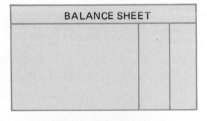

POST-CLOSING TRIAL BALANCE		

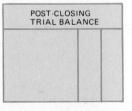

You have learned in Chapters 15, 16, and 17 how to use an eight-column work sheet in preparing financial statements and for making adjusting and closing entries. The general ledger and the business forms discussed in those chapters are shown on this page. You are now ready to apply the principles you have learned in completing the work at the end of the fiscal period for the QUADRASONICS business simulation. An expanded flowchart of the accounting cycle of QUADRASONICS is shown on the next two pages. A block flowchart of the accounting cycle is shown on page 306.

303

Flowchart of the Accounting Cycle of QUADRASONICS

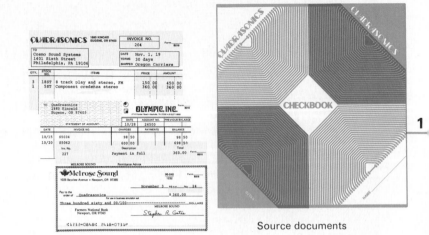

Source documents

PART I

1   Journalize from source documents in the combination journal.
1a   After journalizing, file the source documents.
2   Post items to be posted individually to the general ledger and subsidiary ledgers.
3   Post column totals to the general ledger.
4   Complete the trial balance columns on the work sheet.

PART II

5   Enter adjustments and complete the work sheet.
6   Prepare the financial statements.
7   Journalize the adjusting and closing entries from the work sheet.
8   Post the adjusting and closing entries to the general ledger.
9   Prepare a post-closing trial balance from the general ledger.

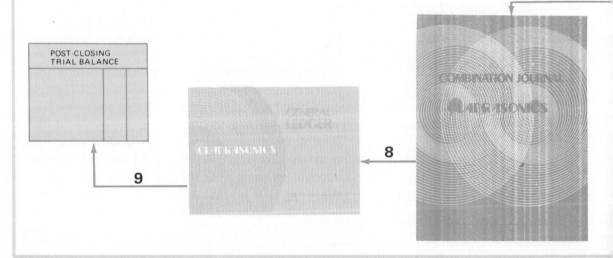

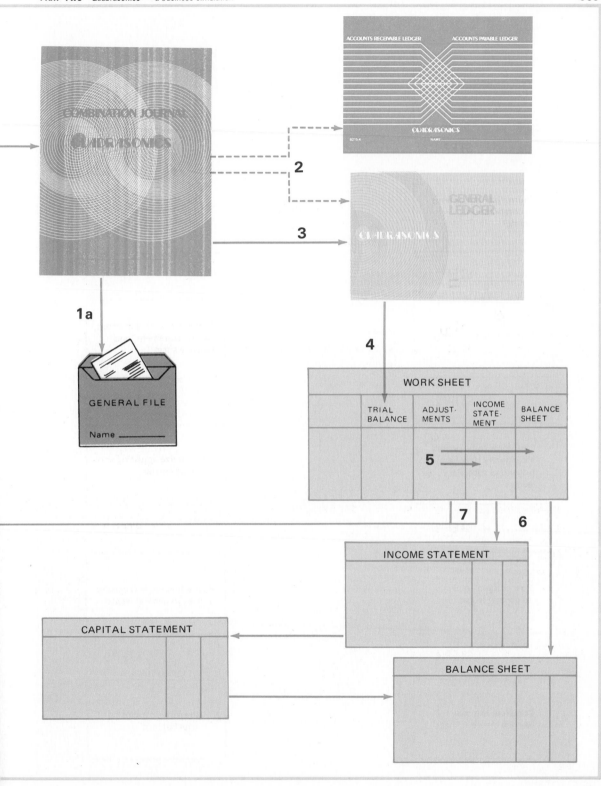

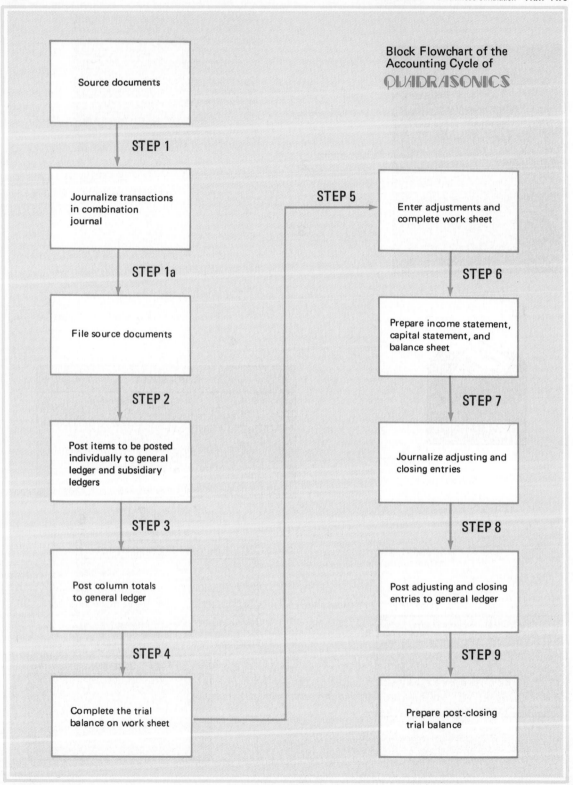

Block Flowchart of the
Accounting Cycle of
QUADRASONICS

Source documents

STEP 1

Journalize transactions
in combination
journal

STEP 1a

File source documents

STEP 2

Post items to be posted
individually to general
ledger and subsidiary
ledgers

STEP 3

Post column totals
to general ledger

STEP 4

Complete the trial
balance on work sheet

STEP 5

Enter adjustments and
complete work sheet

STEP 6

Prepare income statement,
capital statement, and
balance sheet

STEP 7

Journalize adjusting and
closing entries

STEP 8

Post adjusting and closing
entries to general ledger

STEP 9

Prepare post-closing
trial balance

Quadrasonics
A Business Simulation
Part 2

PART 2 WORK AT THE END OF THE FISCAL PERIOD

Now you are to complete the work at the end of a fiscal period for Quadrasonics. For this work you will need all the records that you completed for the month of November in Part 1 of this business simulation.

Instructions: **1.** Complete the eight-column work sheet, using the following data as of November 30 for adjustments. Compare your work with the work sheet on page 261A.

Merchandise inventory	$84,960.00
Supplies inventory	1,200.00
Value of insurance policies	768.00

2. Prepare an income statement from the information given on the work sheet. Compare your work with the income statement illustrated on page 269.

3. Prepare a capital statement from the information given on the work sheet. Compare your work with the capital statement illustrated on page 272.

4. Prepare a balance sheet from the information given on the work sheet. Compare your work with the balance sheet illustrated on page 275.

5. Record in the General columns of the combination journal the adjusting entries planned on the work sheet. Compare your work with the adjusting entries on page 290.

6. Record in the General columns of the combination journal the closing entries from the information shown in the Income Statement and Balance Sheet columns of the work sheet. Compare your work with the closing entries on page 294.

7. Post the adjusting entries and the closing entries.

Since accounts with balance-column ruling are used in the general ledger, there is no need to rule and balance the accounts. When an account is closed, draw a short line in both the Debit and Credit Balance columns.

8. Prepare a post-closing trial balance. Compare your work with the post-closing trial balance illustrated on page 298.

9. Present all books, statements, and schedules to your instructor for approval.

AUTOMOTIVE SUPPL

WAYSIDE *furniture*

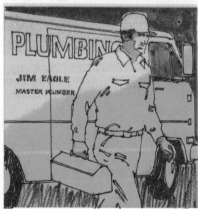

PLUMBIN

JIM EAGLE
MASTER PLUMBER

AN INTRODUCTION TO AUTOMATED DATA PROCESSING

EVERY BUSINESS PROCESSES DATA. Some form of data processing system is used by all businesses to report their daily operations. The primary goal of any data processing system is to obtain accurate, up-to-date facts as quickly and as economically as possible. An increasing number of businesses are using the computer to process accounting data. Regardless of the type of data processing system being used, the basic accounting principles remain the same.

AUTOMATED DATA PROCESSING IS FASTER THAN MANUAL PROCESSING. In Part 3 of this textbook, we will learn how *Wayside Furniture* uses an automated accounting system by studying (a) the basic concepts of automated data processing; (b) how a business converts from a manual to an automated accounting system; (c) how to prepare the necessary forms to prepare data for computer processing; (d) how a computer center prepares accounting data for computer processing; and (e) how accounting data flows through a computer system and back to the business.

WAYSIDE FURNITURE
CHART OF ACCOUNTS
GENERAL LEDGER

Account Number	(10000) ASSETS	Account Number	(40000) REVENUE
11000	Cash	41000	Sales
12000	Accounts Receivable		
13000	Merchandise Inventory		(50000)
14000	Supplies		COST OF MERCHANDISE
15000	Prepaid Insurance	51000	Purchases
	(20000) LIABILITIES		(60000) EXPENSES
21000	Accounts Payable	61000	Delivery Expense
		62000	Insurance Expense
	(30000) CAPITAL	63000	Miscellaneous Expense
31000	Richard Davis, Capital	64000	Rent Expense
32000	Richard Davis, Drawing	65000	Salary Expense
33000	Income Summary	66000	Supplies Expense

CHART OF ACCOUNTS
SUBSIDIARY LEDGERS

Accounts Receivable		Accounts Payable	
Customer Number	Customer Name	Creditor Number	Creditor Name
10020	Bruce Abbot	20020	Allen Manufacturing Co.
10040	Charles Adams	20040	Bonnell Furniture Supply
10060	John Alexander	20060	Callison Mattresses
10080	Mary Austin	20080	Jackson Supply Co.
10100	Dale Backus	20100	Johnson Electrical
10120	Robert Bailey	20120	Trower Sofas
10140	Samuel Bailey	20140	Weidman Furniture
10160	Raymond Barton	20160	Zant Manufacturing
10180	John Bishop	20180	Zeigler Furniture Co.
10200	Roger Bland		
10220	Donald Carr		
10240	Nancy Clay		
10260	Bonnie Devine		
10280	Douglas Dickerson		
10300	Jeffrey Fortino		
10320	Charles Fox		
10340	Erma Jefferson		
10360	Benny Lopez		
10380	Ronald Lutz		
10400	Earl Moore		
10420	Rosemary Render		
10440	Douglas Roper		
10460	Nancy Taylor		
10480	Scott Wilson		
10500	George Zolte		

The charts of accounts for the general ledger and for the subsidiary ledgers of Wayside Furniture are illustrated above for ready reference as you study Part 3.

Data Processing Systems

18

As described in earlier chapters, business decisions are based on information that has been gathered and reported. Current, correct, and complete data about all aspects of a business are vital to wise choices of action. As businesses have become larger, the methods and machines used to collect data have become more complicated. The result has been the development of various systems of collecting and processing data.

DATA PROCESSING SYSTEMS

The recording, classifying, sorting, calculating, summarizing, reporting, and storing of data is known as data processing. The procedures, forms, and machines used to provide data when needed are called a data processing system. A data processing system includes the handling of *all* the facts of a business. There are many different kinds of data. One of the most important kinds of data in any business is financial data — such as the data which have been processed in previous chapters.

Goals in a data processing system

Richard Davis operates a retail store known as Wayside Furniture. The store sells a full line of household furniture. A monthly rent is paid for the use of building and fixtures. Mr. Davis wants to improve his whole data processing system. He wants the work done faster and less expensively, and he also wants to be free to spend more time in his store. He decides to gather information about data processing systems in general.

Mr. Davis found that the basic principles in planning for an automated data processing system were similar to those he had followed in planning his current manual system. For example, planning for a data processing system consists of (1) setting goals — deciding what is to be processed and reported, and (2) establishing procedures and determining the equipment needed to process the data. Mr. Davis had such goals for keeping his old records.

Mr. Davis also found that in the automated data processing system, accuracy in every detail is as important as in a smaller manual system. The results in any data processing system can be only as accurate as the information put into the system. If incorrect facts are put into a data processing system, incorrect facts will be reported. For example, assume that an accountant has transposed an amount from $18.90 to $19.80 when journalizing a sale. The incorrect $19.80 put into the system will result in incorrect facts being reported on the trial balance and on the financial statements.

Established procedures for recording, processing, and reporting the facts must also be followed. Even if the information put into a system is accurate but the procedures are not followed accurately, the results will be incorrect. For example, if an accountant fails to record the general ledger account number in the Post. Ref. column of the journal, the same entry may be posted twice. This incorrect procedure will result in inaccurate data in the general ledger because of the duplicate posting. Accuracy in every detail is essential in processing data. This is equally true in all types of data processing systems.

Procedures and equipment in a data processing system

Data processing systems can be classified in many ways. One way to classify these systems is according to the procedures and equipment used to process data. The two most common types of data processing systems are (1) manual data processing, and (2) automated data processing.

Mr. Davis has been processing his financial data manually, keeping his books according to the accounting principles presented in this book. A data processing system, even though using automated equipment, usually will have some procedures done manually.

Phases of a data processing system

Mr. Davis found in his study of data processing systems that there was a new vocabulary with which he had to become familiar. In many instances the new words referred to old procedures with which he was already familiar. This was particularly true when he looked at the way a data processing system is organized.

A data processing system consists of four phases — input, processing, storage, and output. These four phases are illustrated on page 313.

Data that are received for processing and put into a system are called input. Input may be the data on purchase invoices, sales invoices, memorandums, and other business forms. Working with data according to precise procedures is called processing. Filing or holding data until they

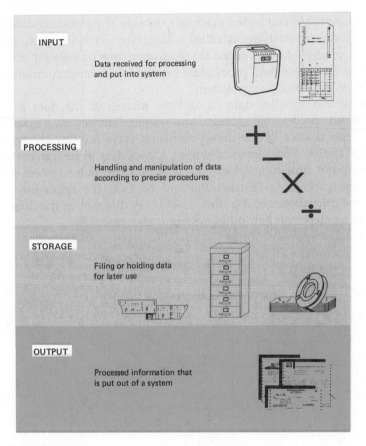

INPUT

Data received for processing
and put into system

PROCESSING

Handling and manipulation of data
according to precise procedures

STORAGE

Filing or holding data
for later use

OUTPUT

Processed information that
is put out of a system

Phases of a data pro-
cessing system

are needed is called storage. Storage may involve the use of filing cabinets or other devices. The information produced by a data processing
system is called output. Examples of output are facts about assets, liabilities, capital, revenue, and expenses reported on financial statements.
Output can also be printed on forms such as checks and invoices. Output
may be facts that will be used for further processing.

AUTOMATED DATA PROCESSING USED IN ACCOUNTING

The manual system may not be adequate to keep up with the work to
be done. This may be true when the total amount of data in the complete
data processing system is large or efficiency needs to be improved. Mr.
Davis found this to be true of Wayside Furniture. Under these circumstances, equipment and procedures must be found that will process data
more rapidly and efficiently.

The process by which work is done mostly by machines with a minimum amount of human effort is called automation. A system using automated machines to process data is called an automated data processing
(ADP) system.

A group of interconnected machines capable of processing data according to stored instructions is called a computer. A system using a computer to process data is called an electronic data processing (EDP) system. The electronic data processing system is the most common type of automated data processing system.

A computer handles data in all four phases of the data processing cycle: input, processing, storage, and output. The separate machines for the various phases of the data processing cycle are linked together by electrical cables. This electrical wiring allows data to be transferred from one computer unit to another. The unit of a computer system that performs the processing instructions and controls the other machines is called the central processing unit or CPU. A diagram of the flow of data through an electronic computer system is shown below.

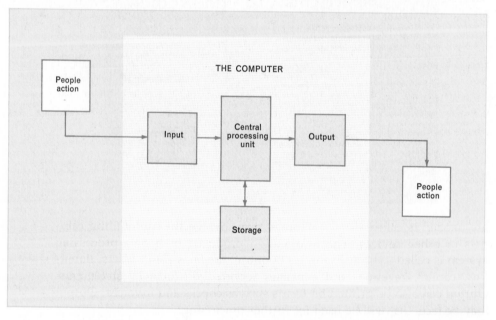

Diagram of data flow in an electronic computer system

The arrows in the diagram show the direction in which data flow in a computer system. The arrows with points at each end indicate that data can flow in either direction.

Before data can be processed by a computer, the following people action is necessary:

1. Management problems and the goals for which processed data are needed must be recognized and fully described.
2. Flowcharts are prepared showing the sequence of the steps for each job to be processed.
3. Instructions are written for the computer.
4. Data (input) to be processed are checked for accuracy.
5. Input is converted into a form that can be processed by machines.

After data have been processed by the computer and the output is available, people action is again necessary:

1. The output must be inspected.
2. The output must be given to people who can interpret and use it.

PLANNING A PROGRAM FOR A COMPUTER

Before data can be processed by a computer, step-by-step instructions for doing each job must be prepared. A set of instructions followed by a computer to process data is called a computer program. The term "program" may also describe a set of step-by-step instructions for processing data by manual means. For example, on pages 9–10 is a program for preparing a balance sheet. A person who prepares a computer program is called a programmer.

The programming of a computer is a detailed procedure that calls for special training in electronic data processing. While it is helpful for a computer programmer to understand the principles of accounting, such understanding is not essential to program the computer. However, the accountant for a business using an electronic data processing system needs to understand the basic concepts of a computer system.

AUTOMATED ACCOUNTING FOR A MERCHANDISING BUSINESS

After getting facts about automated data processing, Mr. Davis decided to change his manual accounting system to an automated accounting system. He determined that more complete accounting information could be obtained by using an automated system. Also, the new system will allow him to spend more time in the operation of the store.

Wayside Furniture does not have the amount of data needed to justify the cost of automated equipment. Therefore, Mr. Davis will use the services of a computer service center.

The computer service center

For many years automated data processing systems were used only by larger businesses. The high cost of computers made it impossible for smaller businesses to go beyond manual systems. Today, however, automated data processing systems are also available for use by the smaller firms. Mr. Davis found that computer services could be purchased for a fee based on the amount and type of data processed. A business established for the purpose of providing computer services for a fee is called a computer service center. A computer service center is also known as a computer service bureau or a business service bureau.

Services provided for small businesses. The processing of accounting data for small businesses is one of the most important services provided by a computer service center. Accounting services are also provided to professional people such as doctors, dentists, and lawyers. Computer service centers provide services such as: assisting with design of business forms, converting input data into machine-readable form, preparing computer programs for the processing of data, and producing output reports from the input data.

Services provided for large businesses. Businesses with their own computer systems will often use a computer service center. Most businesses have peak periods of business activity. By using the services of a computer service center during these peak periods, businesses may avoid installing costly, new and larger machines. Businesses planning to install their own equipment or convert to a larger computer may use the services of a computer center for a short period of time. These businesses need computer time to test their programs and refine their use. If the computer programs are written and tested, the business can change to the new or larger system as soon as the machines are installed.

Using a computer service center does not eliminate the accountant's need to master basic accounting knowledge. People working with the financial data of a business still must know accounting principles. Accounting principles do not change. Only the tools and methods change. The computer performs only the routine and repetitive operations.

Chart of accounts in an automated data processing system

In working with the computer service center, Mr. Davis was first asked to submit a list of his accounts. The name of each account had meaning for Mr. Davis. However, machines are designed to work more efficiently with numbers. All of Wayside Furniture's account names, therefore, had to be converted to numbers with which machines can work.

The numbering system used for the chart of accounts for an automated accounting system must provide for (1) a numeric sequence within each division, (2) a proper order within each division, and (3) enough digits to allow the addition of new accounts. Businesses that use an ADP system will normally use at least a five-digit account number. Each business numbers its accounts according to its particular needs. Wayside Furniture uses a five-digit account number. A part of the chart of accounts is shown at the top of the next page.

The accounts in the beginning chart of accounts are assigned account numbers by thousands within each division. For example, the cash account is assigned the account number 11000; the accounts payable account, 21000. The complete chart of accounts for Wayside Furniture is shown on page 310.

WAYSIDE FURNITURE CHART OF ACCOUNTS GENERAL LEDGER	
Account <u>Number</u> (10000) ASSETS	Account <u>Number</u> (20000) LIABILITIES
11000 Cash 12000 Accounts Receivable 13000 Merchandise Inventory 14000 Supplies 15000 Prepaid Insurance	21000 Accounts Payable

Partial chart of accounts for the general ledger of Wayside Furniture

New accounts that are added as the last account in a division are assigned the next one-thousand number. If a new account Office Equipment had to be added to the assets division following Prepaid Insurance (Account Number 15000), the new account number would be 16000.

New accounts that are added between two existing accounts are assigned the unused middle number. For example, if a new account Store Equipment had to be inserted between Prepaid Insurance (Account Number 15000) and Office Equipment (16000), the new account number would be 15500. The order of assigning new account numbers between two existing accounts is illustrated below.

Existing Account Numbers	Assignment of One New Account Number	Additional Account Numbers Available
15000		15001–15449
	←————————15500	
16000		15501–15999

The numbering procedures for new accounts, described above, keep the chart of accounts in numeric sequence. By always assigning the unused middle number to new accounts that are inserted between two existing accounts, there will be sufficient remaining numbers available for new accounts. For example, the illustration above shows that after assigning a new account number for Store Equipment, the numbers 15001–15449 and 15501–15999 are still available. If a new account Delivery Equipment is added between Prepaid Insurance and Store Equipment, the account number 15250 would be assigned.

Prepaid Insurance	15000
DELIVERY EQUIPMENT	15250
Store Equipment	15500

In an automated accounting system, accounts in the subsidiary ledgers also are assigned account numbers. A partial chart of accounts for the subsidiary ledgers of Wayside Furniture is shown on the next page.

The complete chart of accounts for the subsidiary ledgers of Wayside Furniture is given on page 310.

CHART OF ACCOUNTS WAYSIDE FURNITURE SUBSIDIARY LEDGERS			
Accounts Receivable		Accounts Payable	
Customer Number	Customer Name	Creditor Number	Creditor Name
10020	Bruce Abbot	20020	Allen Manufacturing Co.
10040	Charles Adams	20040	Bonnell Furniture Supply
10060	John Alexander	20060	Callison Mattresses
10080	Mary Austin	20080	Jackson Supply Co.

Partial chart of accounts for the subsidiary ledgers of Wayside Furniture

The numbering system for the accounts in the subsidiary ledger must be designed so that new accounts can be inserted in alphabetic order. The first digit identifies the division in which the controlling account appears in the general ledger. The 1 shows that the account is an asset, and the 2 shows that the account is a liability. The numbers are assigned by twenties to each customer name in the accounts receivable ledger and to each creditor name in the accounts payable ledger. This procedure makes it possible to assign numbers to new accounts that will fall in between these numbers. In this way, the accounts will be in alphabetic order when arranged by number.

A five-digit customer number is used in this discussion for simplicity. A six-digit or larger numbering system may be required to handle a large volume of subsidiary accounts.

The order of assigning new customer numbers for the subsidiary ledgers is the same as for the general ledger. New accounts to be inserted between two existing accounts are also assigned the unused middle number.

Dale Aaron	10020
Beth Adams	10030
Charles Agee	10040

For example, the customer number 10020 has been used for the Dale Aaron account in the accounts receivable ledger of the Hobson Company. The number 10040 has been used for the Charles Agee account. To add a new account, Beth Adams, the customer number 10030 is assigned.

If there is not an exact middle number available, the number closest to the middle is used. To illustrate, the middle number between 10020 and 10025 is 10022.5. The number 10022.5 contains six digits and cannot be used in a five-digit numbering system.

Dale Aaron	10020
Carol Abner	10022
Gordon Acton	10025
Beth Adams	10030

Therefore, either 10022 or 10023 could be used. The illustration at the left shows that customer number 10020 has been assigned to the Dale Aaron account. The number 10025 has been used for the Gordon Acton account. To add a new account, Carol Abner, the customer number 10022 is assigned. The number 10023 also could have been used.

Chart of accounts setup

The first chart of accounts, page 310, shows the divisions of all balance sheet and income statement accounts. The chart further lists all accounts within each division in the same order as they will appear on the balance sheet and income statement. The second chart of accounts, page 310, shows the names of the accounts in the subsidiary ledgers. The chart also lists the names in alphabetic order — the same order as they will appear on the subsidiary schedules. In a manual data processing system, the accountant prepares all reports by hand. In an ADP system, the reports are prepared by automated machines. Therefore, both charts of accounts must be converted to a coded form that can be read and processed by automated equipment.

Before data from the charts of accounts are converted into machine-readable form, a special form is prepared. The form shows the division names, the account titles, and the arrangement of the data on the reports. A form used in an ADP system to describe the data from the charts of accounts and the arrangement of these data on the reports is called a chart of accounts setup form.

Setup for general ledger chart of accounts. The data from the general ledger chart of accounts for Wayside Furniture are recorded by Mr. Davis on the chart of accounts setup form shown on page 320.

This preprinted form is supplied by the computer service center.

Steps in preparing the chart of accounts setup form. The chart of accounts setup form for Wayside Furniture is prepared as follows:

1. Write the name of the business in the space provided.
2. Write the client number, *230,* in the space provided. The client number is assigned by the computer service center and will be used on all data transmitted to the center.
3. Write the account number or division number obtained from the charts of accounts, page 310. All division names and account titles must be identified by numbers in numeric sequence.
4. Write the data type code. The code *1* is used when the code is for a division name, and the code *2* is used when the code refers to an account title in the general ledger. A code *3* is used when the code is for a name in a subsidiary ledger.
5. Write the division names and the account titles just as they will appear on the output.

    Wayside Furniture uses the report form of balance sheet, page 275, with the division names centered over the account titles. The computer program used to process the data from the chart of accounts setup form provides for a maximum of 25 positions (characters and spaces). The position of the division names is determined as follows: (a) determine the maximum number of positions

An introduction to automated data processing **PART THREE**

available, (b) count the number of letters in the name and subtract the number of letters in the name from 25, (c) divide the difference by 2, and (d) round to the nearest whole number and place the first character at that point.

The location of the division name ASSETS is figured as follows:

a. The number of positions available on a line..........................25
b. *Less* the number of letters in the name (Assets) 6

    Remainder 19

c. *Divide* remainder by 2 .... 9.5
d. Round to nearest whole number; this is the position on the line for writing the first letter of the name 10

On Line 1 of the form below the word *Assets* is centered starting in space 10.

On the income statement the division names are not centered but are aligned at the left. On the form below the account title **Sales**, Line 14, is indented three spaces from the division name **Revenue**, Line 13.

CHART OF ACCOUNTS SETUP

NAME OF BUSINESS *Wayside Furniture*   CLIENT NUMBER 230

	Acct. No.	Data Type	Description
1	10000	1	ASSETS
2	11000	2	CASH
3	12000	2	ACCOUNTS RECEIVABLE
4	13000	2	MERCHANDISE INVENTORY
5	14000	2	SUPPLIES
6	15000	2	PREPAID INSURANCE
7	20000	1	LIABILITIES
8	21000	2	ACCOUNTS PAYABLE
9	30000	1	CAPITAL
10	31000	2	RICHARD DAVIS, CAPITAL
11	32000	2	RICHARD DAVIS, DRAWING
12	33000	2	INCOME SUMMARY
13	40000	1	REVENUE
14	41000	2	SALES
15	50000	1	COST OF MERCHANDISE
16	51000	2	PURCHASES
17	60000	1	EXPENSES
18	61000	2	DELIVERY EXPENSE
19	62000	2	INSURANCE EXPENSE
20	63000	2	MISCELLANEOUS EXPENSE
21	64000	2	RENT EXPENSE
22	65000	2	SALARY EXPENSE
23	66000	2	SUPPLIES EXPENSE
38			
39			
40			

DATA TYPE

1 = DIVISION NAME

2 = ACCOUNT TITLE GENERAL LEDGER

3 = NAME SUBSIDIARY LEDGER

PREPARED BY

Richard Davis

Chart of accounts setup form for general ledger chart of accounts

Setup for subsidiary ledgers chart of accounts. The same chart of accounts setup form is used for subsidiary ledger accounts as was used for general ledger accounts. The data from the subsidiary ledgers chart of accounts are recorded by Mr. Davis on the chart of accounts setup form that follows:

CHART OF ACCOUNTS SETUP

NAME OF BUSINESS _Wayside Furniture_   CLIENT NUMBER _230_

	Acct. No.	Data Type	Description
1	10020	3	BRUCE ABBOT
2	10040	3	CHARLES ADAMS
3	10060	3	JOHN ALEXANDER
4	10080	3	MARY AUSTIN
5	10100	3	DALE BACKUS
6	10120	3	ROBERT BAILEY
7	10140	3	SAMUEL BAILEY
8	10160	3	RAYMOND BARTON
9	10180	3	JOHN BISHOP
10	10200	3	ROGER BLAND
11	10220	3	DONALD CARR
12	10240	3	NANCY CLAY
13	10260	3	BONNIE DEVINE
14	10280	3	DOUGLAS DICKERSON
15	10300	3	JEFFREY FORTINO
16	10320	3	CHARLES FOX
17	10340	3	ERMA JEFFERSON
18	10360	3	BENNY LOPEZ
19	10380	3	RONALD LUTZ
20	10400	3	EARL MOORE
21	10420	3	ROSEMARY RENDER
22	10440	3	DOUGLAS ROPER
23	10460	3	NANCY TAYLOR
24	10480	3	SCOTT WILSON
25	10500	3	GEORGE ZOLTE
26	20020	3	ALLEN MANUFACTURING CO.
27	20040	3	BONNELL FURNITURE SUPPLY
28	20060	3	CALLISON MATTRESSES
29	20080	3	JACKSON SUPPLY CO.
30	20100	3	JOHNSON ELECTRICAL
31	20120	3	TROWER SOFAS
32	20140	3	WEIDMAN FURNITURE
33	20160	3	ZANT MANUFACTURING
34	20180	3	ZEIGLER FURNITURE CO.

DATA TYPE

1 = DIVISION NAME
2 = ACCOUNT TITLE GENERAL LEDGER
3 = NAME SUBSIDIARY LEDGER

PREPARED BY
Richard Davis

Chart of accounts setup form for subsidiary ledgers chart of accounts

The steps in preparing the chart of accounts setup form for the subsidiary ledgers are the same as those used when preparing the general ledger setup form. The customer and creditor numbers and names are obtained from the chart of accounts, page 310. The computer service center will produce as output a schedule of accounts receivable and a schedule of accounts payable. There are no division names shown on the schedule of accounts receivable, page 214, and the schedule of accounts payable, page 215. Therefore, Mr. Davis uses a data type code 3 for all subsidiary ledger accounts.

Adding new accounts to the general ledger and subsidiary ledgers. The chart of accounts setup form is also used to describe new accounts that are added to either the general ledger or subsidiary ledgers. For example, a new account Delivery Equipment would be included on the chart of accounts setup form as follows:

CHART OF ACCOUNTS SETUP

NAME OF BUSINESS *Wayside Furniture*   CLIENT NUMBER 230

Acct. No.	Data Type	DESCRIPTION
1 15250	2	DELIVERY EQUIPMENT

DATA TYPE		PREPARED BY
1 = DIVISION NAME	3 = NAME SUBSIDIARY LEDGER	*Richard Davis*
2 = ACCOUNT TITLE GENERAL LEDGER		

Chart of accounts setup form to add
a new account to the general ledger

The account number is determined by the procedures described on page 317.

To add the accounts of Larry Caldwell and Mary Malloy to the accounts receivable subsidiary ledger, the chart of accounts setup form would be prepared as shown below.

CHART OF ACCOUNTS SETUP

NAME OF BUSINESS *Wayside Furniture*   CLIENT NUMBER 230

Acct. No.	Data Type	DESCRIPTION
1 10210	3	LARRY CALDWELL
2 10390	3	MARY MALLOY

DATA TYPE		PREPARED BY
1 = DIVISION NAME	3 = NAME SUBSIDIARY LEDGER	*Richard Davis*
2 = ACCOUNT TITLE GENERAL LEDGER		

Chart of accounts setup form to add
new accounts to the subsidiary ledgers

The account number is determined by the procedure described on page 318.

Recording the chart of accounts for computer processing. The completed chart of accounts setup forms for Wayside Furniture are sent to the computer service center. At the computer service center the data from the setup forms are converted into machine-readable form. This procedure is described in Chapter 19.

✦ What is the meaning of each of the following?

- data processing system
- input
- processing
- storage
- output

- automation
- automated data processing (ADP) system
- computer
- electronic data processing (EDP) system

- central processing unit (CPU)
- computer program
- programmer
- computer service center
- chart of accounts setup form

1. What is data processing?
2. What is one of the most important kinds of data in any business?
3. What is involved in planning for a data processing system?
4. What are the two most common types of data processing systems?
5. What are the four phases of a data processing system?
6. Give some examples of input.
7. Give some examples of output.
8. What is the most common type of automated data processing system?
9. What people action is necessary before a computer can process data?
10. What people action is necessary after a computer has processed data?

11. What are the services that are provided for small businesses by the computer service center?
12. Why doesn't the use of a computer service center for the processing of accounting data eliminate the need for the accountant to master basic accounting principles?
13. What must be provided for in the numbering system used for the chart of accounts for an ADP system?
14. In the numbering system for automated accounting, how are new accounts assigned numbers between two existing accounts?

CASE 1 Sally Fortino, accountant for American Trucking Company, has been told to design a numbering system for the chart of accounts in the subsidiary ledgers in preparation for automated data processing. Miss Fortino does not understand why an account number must be assigned to each account appearing in the subsidiary ledgers. How would you explain the need for assigning an account number to each account in the subsidiary ledgers?

CASE 2 Harold Salem uses a manual accounting system with a two-digit account number assigned to all accounts in the general ledger. He is planning to change to an automated accounting system. He plans to continue to use a two-digit account number. What problems, if any, will a two-digit account number create in an automated accounting system?

CASE 3 Mary Fox owns and operates a ladies apparel store called Fashion Corner. She uses a manual accounting system and does all of the accounting herself. The demands of the business have been taking more and more of her time. Consequently, she has been having difficulty finding time to run an efficient accounting system. A local computer service center has approached her about automating her accounting system. She has also considered hiring an accountant. What factors should Mary Fox consider in making her decision to either automate her accounting system or hire an accountant?

Drills for Mastering Principles

DRILL 18-D 1 Adding new accounts to the general ledger

This drill is planned to give you practice in assigning account numbers to new accounts being added to the general ledger chart of accounts.

Account Number	Account Title
13000	Merchandise Inventory
———	Store Supplies
14000	Office Supplies
15000	Prepaid Insurance
———	Store Equipment
15250	Office Equipment
61000	Advertising Expense
———	Delivery Expense
61500	Insurance Expense
———	Office Supplies Expense
63000	Salary Expense
———	Store Supplies Expense
64000	Utilities Expense

Instructions: ☐ **1.** On a sheet of paper, rule a form similar to the one illustrated at the left. Write the headings as shown on the illustration. In the Account Title column, copy all the account titles (including those to be added) in the order given in the illustration. In the Account Number column, copy the account numbers provided for the existing accounts.

☐ **2.** Assign an account number to those accounts that have a blank in the Account Number column illustrated at the left. Use the "unused middle number" method of assigning new account numbers explained on page 317.

DRILL 18-D 2 Adding new accounts to the subsidiary ledger

This drill is planned to give you practice in assigning customer numbers to new accounts being added to the accounts receivable chart of accounts.

Customer Number	Customer Name
10020	Joyce Ablet
———	George Adams
10030	Leonard Adams
10040	John Adkins
———	Charles Alexander
———	Mary Allison
10050	Loren Anderson
10060	Rodney Anthony
———	Susan Arnold
10065	Kay Arthur
10070	Nancy Atkins
———	Warren Atkins
10080	LeRoy Austin

Instructions: ☐ **1.** On another sheet of paper, prepare a form similar to the one at the left. Copy the customers' names and numbers from the illustration.

☐ **2.** Assign a customer number to those accounts that have a blank in the Customer Number column in the illustration at the left. Use the "unused middle number" method of assigning new account numbers to subsidiary ledger accounts, explained on page 318.

PROBLEM 18-1 ## Chart of accounts setup form for a general ledger

The general ledger chart of accounts for the Crestline Department Store is given below.

Account Number	(10000) ASSETS	Account Number	(40000) REVENUE
11000	Cash	41000	Sales
12000	Accounts Receivable		
13000	Merchandise Inventory		(50000) COST OF MERCHANDISE
14000	Store Supplies	51000	Purchases
15000	Prepaid Insurance		
	(20000) LIABILITIES		(60000) EXPENSES
21000	Accounts Payable	61000	Insurance Expense
		62000	Miscellaneous Expense
	(30000) CAPITAL	63000	Rent Expense
31000	Harold Garner, Capital	64000	Salary Expense
32000	Harold Garner, Drawing	65000	Store Supplies Expense
33000	Income Summary		

Instructions: Prepare a chart of accounts setup form for the general ledger chart of accounts given above. Use as a guide the chart of accounts setup form, page 320.

PROBLEM 18-2 ## Chart of accounts setup form for a subsidiary ledger

The chart of accounts for the accounts receivable and the accounts payable subsidiary ledgers of the Crestline Department Store is given below.

Customer Number	Customer Name	Creditor Number	Creditor Name
10020	Helene Abler	20020	Addison Fabric Supply
10040	Keith Allen	20040	Albers Manufacturing Co.
10060	Robert Bauer	20060	Collins Ladies Apparel
10080	Gloria Bell	20080	Durfee, Inc.
10100	Richard Bridges	20100	Fryman Clothiers
10120	Donald Carson	20120	Multiline Distributors
10140	Patricia Davis	20140	United Shoes
10160	John Foley	20160	Westline Men's Wear
10180	Nancy Ford	20180	Zant Manufacturing
10200	Albert Goodwin		
10220	Robert Klein		
10240	Susan Klein		
10260	James McGuire		
10280	Diane Trost		
10300	Donald Wixson		

Instructions: Prepare a chart of accounts setup form for the accounts receivable and accounts payable subsidiary ledgers chart of accounts illustrated above. Use as your model the chart of accounts setup form on page 321.

MASTERY
PROBLEM 18-M Adding new accounts to the general
ledger chart of accounts

The general ledger chart of accounts for the Myers Automotive Supply is given below. New accounts that are being added to the general ledger appear in their proper order within each division.

Account Number	(10000) ASSETS	Account Number	(40000) REVENUE
11000	Cash	41000	Sales
12000	Accounts Receivable		
13000	Merchandise Inventory		**(50000)**
			COST OF MERCHANDISE
——	Store Supplies (New Account)	51000	Purchases
——	Office Supplies (New Account)		
			(60000) EXPENSES
14000	Prepaid Insurance	61000	Advertising Expense
——	Store Equipment	62000	Insurance Expense
	(New Account)	63000	Miscellaneous Expense
——	Office Equipment		
	(New Account)	——	Office Supplies Expense
			(New Account)
	(20000) LIABILITIES		
21000	Accounts Payable	64000	Rent Expense
		65000	Salary Expense
	(30000) CAPITAL		
31000	John Myers, Capital	——	Store Supplies Expense
32000	John Myers, Drawing		(New Account)
33000	Income Summary		

Instructions: □ **1.** Assign account numbers to the new accounts illustrated above. Use the "unused middle number" method described on page 317.

□ **2.** Prepare a chart of accounts setup form that describes the *new* accounts for automated data processing. Follow the procedures described on page 322.

□ **3.** On a sheet of paper prepare a new chart of accounts for the general ledger. Follow the form illustrated above. Include the new accounts with their respective account numbers.

The chart of accounts prepared in Instruction 3 will be needed to complete Mastery Problems 19-M and 20-M, Chapters 19 and 20.

BONUS
PROBLEM 18-B Adding new accounts to the
subsidiary ledger

The chart of accounts for the accounts receivable subsidiary ledger for the Myers Automotive Supply is given on the next page.

Instructions: □ **1.** Assign customer numbers to the new accounts listed at the top of the next page. The accounts for these new customers are being added to the accounts receivable ledger that is shown at the right. Use the "unused middle number" method.

Allen Abbey	James Gorthy
Gary Anderson	Louis Gray
Floyd Baker	John Martin
Donald Barr	George Mason
Susan Goodrich	Carl Woods

Customer Number	Customer Name
10020	Charlotte Abbey
10040	Paul Acker
10060	Leonard Adams
10080	Jerald Ambler
10100	Joan Bailey
10120	William Bell
10140	Thomas Carter
10160	Kathy Clark
10180	Judy Decker
10200	John Fleming
10220	Gregg Ford
10240	Arthur Hamilton
10260	Diane Hanson
10280	Dale Jarrett
10300	David Kizer
10320	Mary Malloy
10340	Thomas Nash
10360	Steve Pruden
10380	Lewis Walters

□ **2.** Prepare a chart of accounts setup form that describes the new accounts for automated data processing. Follow the procedures described on page 322.

□ **3.** On a sheet of paper prepare a new chart of accounts for the accounts receivable subsidiary ledger. Include the new accounts with their respective account numbers.

   The chart of accounts prepared in Instruction 3 will be needed to complete Bonus Problem 19-B and Mastery Problem 20-M, Chapters 19 and 20.

19

Automated Accounting Systems: Processing the Chart of Accounts and the Opening Entry

Chapter 18 described the procedures followed by Mr. Davis, owner of Wayside Furniture, to prepare for automated data processing. The first thing Mr. Davis did was to assign new account numbers for all accounts in his general ledger and subsidiary ledgers. He then prepared and sent to the computer service center the chart of accounts setup forms which described the accounts for computer processing.

THE AUTOMATED DATA PROCESSING CYCLE

The flow of data through a data processing system follows a set of procedures. A complete set of procedures followed in a data processing system is called a data processing cycle. For example, the complete set of manual accounting procedures described in Part 2 for Gift World represents a data processing cycle. Because primarily manual methods were followed, the system used by Gift World is known as a manual data processing cycle.

The complete set of procedures followed when automated equipment is used in a data processing system is called an automated data processing cycle. In an automated data processing cycle, the data flow through the system with a minimum of human effort.

In his study of data processing, Mr. Davis found that different materials and devices were used for the various phases of the automated data processing cycle. He also learned that the phases of the automated data processing cycle follow the same basic accounting principles as the manual data processing cycle.

INPUT MEDIA AND DEVICES

Mr. Davis found that the automated accounting cycle uses the same types of source documents as the manual accounting cycle. In an automated accounting cycle, the data for the chart of accounts are entered on a chart of accounts setup form. To prepare the data on the chart of accounts setup form for computer processing, the data must be converted to machine-readable form. The form of the data prepared for processing by automated equipment is called input media.

Punched cards

Computers use many kinds of input media. One of the most common ways of converting data into a coded form that can be processed by automated equipment is by using a card. Holes are punched in a card in certain places. The placement of the holes forms a code. A card in which holes have been punched to represent data is called a punched card.

The card on page 330 is divided into 80 vertical columns. The very small numbers at the top and bottom of the card identify each of these 80 columns. Each of the columns contains the digits 0 through 9. Thus, each vertical column has 10 numbered positions on it. Each horizontal line of numbered positions across the card is referred to as a row. Thus, there is a *zero row*, a *1 row*, a *2 row*, etc. Data are punched into the card by punching a hole in one or more numbered positions in a single vertical column on the card for numbers, letters of the alphabet, and some special characters. A machine used to make holes in a card to represent data is known as a card punch machine or a keypunch machine. The illustration below shows one kind of card punch machine.

Recording data in a punched card

Data may be punched into a card according to a code. The code is set up by the placement of the holes. Most card punch machines print the interpretation of the code at the top edge of the card as it is being punched.

The code for numbers is easily read. If a hole is punched in the 4 row, it stands for the number 4. If the number 10 is to be punched, the digit 1 is punched in one column and the digit 0 is punched in the next column.

To record alphabetic data, two holes are punched in the same column. Two additional unnumbered rows are used — the 11 and 12 positions. The 11, 12, and 0 rows are known as the zone punching area. Each letter of the alphabet is recorded by punching a hole in one of the three zone areas and a hole in one of the rows numbered 1 to 9 of

Courtesy of IBM

Card punch

the same column. The letter A is punched by placing a hole in the 12 row and a hole in the 1 row of the same column.

Special characters are punched into a card using one, two, and sometimes three positions in a column. Some characters, such as the dollar sign and decimal point, are omitted to save space when cards are punched.

The standard punched card code

The illustration below shows the complete code for punching numbers, the alphabet, and special characters on a card.

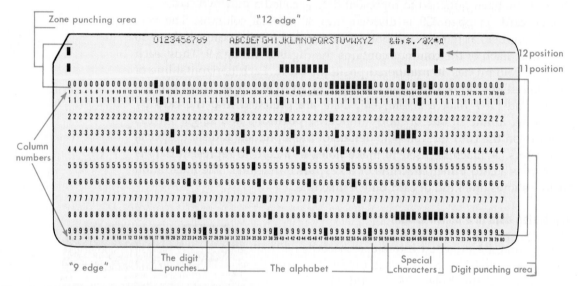

Standard code for punched cards

Numbers	Alphabetic characters			Special characters	
Digit punch	12 punch	11 punch	0 punch	12 punch only	&
only	and	and	and	12 punch, 3, 8	.
0				12 punch, 4, 8	□
1	1-A	1-J		11 punch only	–
2	2-B	2-K	2-S	11 punch, 3, 8	$
3	3-C	3-L	3-T	11 punch, 4, 8	*
4	4-D	4-M	4-U	0 punch, 1	/
5	5-E	5-N	5-V	0 punch, 3, 8	,
6	6-F	6-O	6-W	0 punch, 4, 8	%
7	7-G	7-P	7-X	3, 8	#
8	8-H	8-Q	8-Y	4, 8	@
9	9-I	9-R	9-Z		

Only punches based on the code for numbers, the alphabet, and special characters can be "read" by automated equipment. Any other punches in the card cannot be read. For example, if a hole were punched in the 7 row and another hole were punched in the 9 row of Column 12 of a data card, the machine would not be able to read the data in Column 12. These two punches do not represent any of the numbers, letters of the alphabet, or special symbols.

The 96-column punched card

Another type of punched card that is used as input media is the 96-column card. The card is one-third the size of the standard 80-column card but will hold 20 percent more information. The 96-column card is prepared on a special type of card punch that punches round holes. The code arrangement is different from the standard card code. Illustrated below is a 96-column card with its two sections.

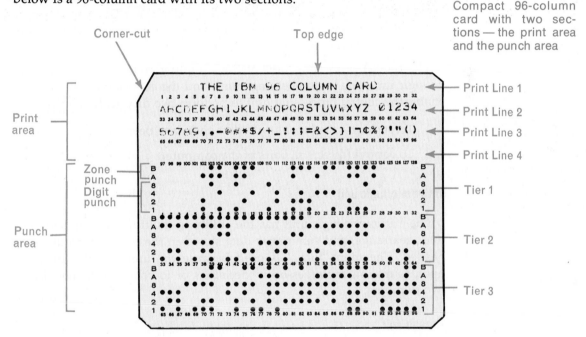

Compact 96-column card with two sections — the print area and the punch area

The equipment used by the computer service center uses the 80-column punched card as the input media for Wayside Furniture.

Assuring the accuracy of punched cards

The accuracy of the output depends on the accuracy of the person punching the cards. Checking the accuracy of data in any form is called verifying. A machine that is used to determine if the data are accurately punched into cards is known as a verifier. A verifier has much the same appearance as a card punch. A card punch machine punches holes in the card, and a verifier "reads" the holes to assure that the correct data are punched in the card.

Card reader

Card readers

An input device for reading the data on punched cards into the CPU (central processing unit) and storage units of a computer is known as a card reader. The card reader is linked to and controlled by the instructions in the computer program located in the CPU. As the punched card is the most popular type of input media, most computer systems will have a card reader.

CENTRAL PROCESSING UNIT

Central processing unit

Between the input and the output of any processing job, the data entered into the system are processed. While all of the units in an electronic data processing system combine to form a computer, the central processing unit is often referred to as the "computer."

The central processing unit of the computer consists of the arithmetic/logic unit, the internal storage unit, and the control unit. These units enable the central processing unit to perform two distinct functions:

1. To perform calculations with data that have been stored.

2. To control (direct) all parts of the computer.

Arithmetic/logic unit

The arithmetic/logic unit has the ability to multiply, divide, add, subtract, rearrange, and summarize data stored in the computer in the order needed. The term "logic" is used because the unit can also be called upon to make simple yes-or-no decisions or to compare the equality of two numbers.

Storage unit

The unit within the central processing unit in which data are stored is known as internal storage. Sometimes the internal storage ability of a computer is referred to as its "memory." Once the data have been stored in the computer, the computer can "remember" them until they are erased or replaced with new data. The data can be recalled from the computer's "memory" as often as needed during processing.

Control unit

All of the steps in any data processing system must be controlled. The control unit within the central processing unit tells each of the other parts of the computer what do do, when to do it, and how to do it. The computer does this by means of a computer program that is fed into the computer as input data.

A computer, like any other machine, must also be controlled externally by a human operator. The operator can start and stop the computer by pushing a button. He can communicate with the computer by means of a special typewriter known as a console typewriter.

STORAGE MEDIA AND DEVICES

The internal storage of a computer is normally not sufficient to hold at one time all the data to be processed. As a result, the capacity of the computer is expanded by adding external storage devices. Storage units attached to and under the control of the central processing unit are known as auxiliary storage. Data may be transferred from auxiliary storage to the central processing unit as needed during processing. The use of auxiliary storage devices, such as magnetic disk drives and magnetic tape drives, greatly increases a computer's data processing capability.

Magnetic disk pack and disk drive

The computer service center that processes data for Wayside Furniture uses magnetic disks as its form of auxiliary storage. Disk packs come in different sizes. Each of the disks looks something like a phonograph record. The amount of data that can be stored on a disk pack depends on the size of the pack. Most packs will store several million characters. The packs can be removed from the disk drive. Therefore, there is no limit to the amount of data that can be stored on magnetic disk packs. More storage can be made possible by simply adding new packs.

Disk pack

Courtesy of IBM

Disk drive

A magnetic disk drive is the storage device that is used for placing data on or reading data from disk packs. The magnetic disk drive is linked to and controlled by the central processing unit. Data are read from the disk pack at a high speed.

Magnetic tape and magnetic tape drive

Some computer systems use magnetic tape for auxiliary storage. The magnetic tape that is used with a computer for auxiliary storage is similar to that used on common tape recorders. The tape surface can be magnetized to represent data.

The magnetic tape drive "senses" magnetized spots on the tape and in turn creates electronic impulses to correspond to the data recorded.

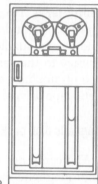

Magnetic tape   Magnetic tape drive

OUTPUT MEDIA AND DEVICES

The end result of processing data by a computer is the output of the computer. Computers use different kinds of output devices to prepare the different kinds of output media.

Printers

The output device that produces the results of processed data in human-readable form is called a printer. The printer is the most common output device of computers handling accounting data. The output of the computer in human-readable form is called the printout.

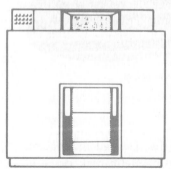

Printer

The printer is connected to and controlled by the central processing unit. The printout can be on a wide variety of forms and paper sizes. The printing unit can print data at high speeds because an entire line is printed at one time instead of a single character at a time as done on a typewriter. The printer, which may be capable of printing words and numbers as fast as 2,000 lines a minute, is at the left.

Console typewriters

The console typewriter functions on a small scale as an output device for use in the printout of special information. The device may also be used as a relatively minor input device of a computer.

Console typewriter

Photo courtesy of Control Data Corporation

Visual display unit

The cathode-ray tube, similar to the picture tube found in home television sets, has become a common output device in some computer systems. A cathode-ray tube can be connected to a computer. Instead of printing output, the "picture tube" displays letters and numbers processed by the computer. Information will appear on the tube until a change is directed by the computer. If the information shown is to be made permanent, the display can be recorded on microfilm or on photographic paper.

Visual display unit

THE AUTOMATED ACCOUNTING CYCLE

The automated accounting cycle for Wayside Furniture requires the same basic steps that were used in the manual accounting cycle. Only the tools and procedures are different.

Recording the chart of accounts for the general ledger

Using the general ledger chart of accounts setup form for Wayside Furniture, page 320, the computer service center punches one card for each line. The punched cards for all of the general ledger accounts of Wayside Furniture are shown on page 336.

The computer service center decides how the data will be arranged on the punched cards. All punched cards contain the client number, 230, the account number, and the division name or account title as described on the chart of accounts setup form at the top of page 320. Note that the spacing of the division names and account titles on the punched cards is exactly the same as the spacing described on the chart of accounts setup form.

The location of the information on the punched cards must be consistent from card to card. That is, if the account number is to be punched in card columns 4–8 in one card, the account number must also be punched in the same location in all remaining cards. The punched card columns reserved for the recording of specific information, such as the account number, are called fields. A field may vary in length from one column to several columns, depending on the specific information desired. The punched card fields for the general ledger chart of accounts follow:

Card Columns 1–3 ....Client Number
Card Columns 4–8 ....Account Number
Card Column 9...........................Data Type
Card Columns 10–35 ....Division Name or Account Title

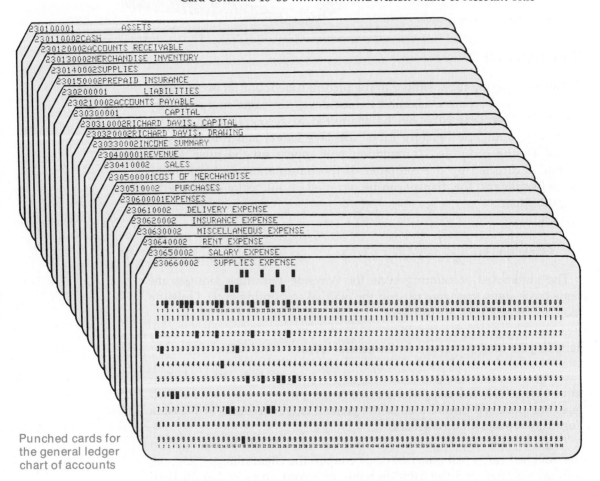

Punched cards for the general ledger chart of accounts

Recording the chart of accounts for the subsidiary ledgers

The data from the chart of accounts setup form for the subsidiary ledgers, page 321, are used to record the accounts of Wayside Furniture. One card is punched for each line on the setup form. The data are punched in the same card fields as the cards punched for the general ledger chart of accounts. The punched cards for all of the subsidiary ledger accounts of Wayside Furniture are shown on page 337.

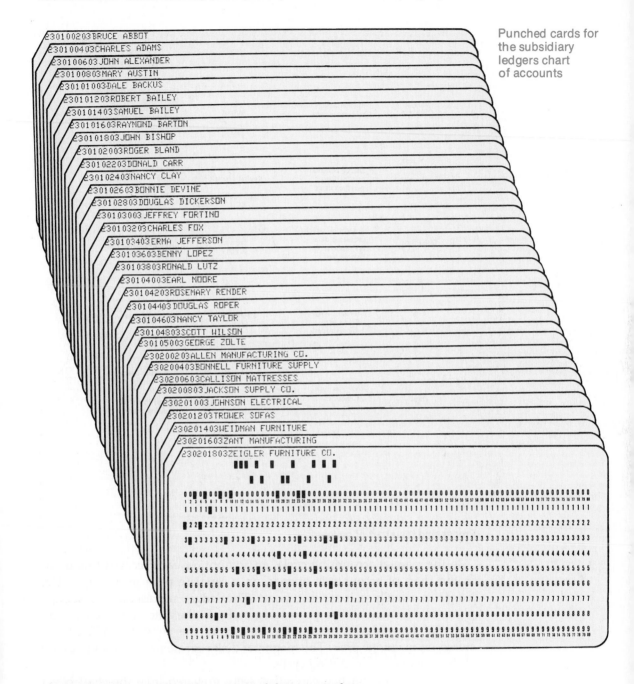

Punched cards for the subsidiary ledgers chart of accounts

Flowcharting the procedures for automated data processing

A chart that uses symbols to show the sequence of steps necessary to complete all or part of a data processing system is called a system flowchart. The standard symbols commonly used in business to prepare system flowcharts are given on page 338.

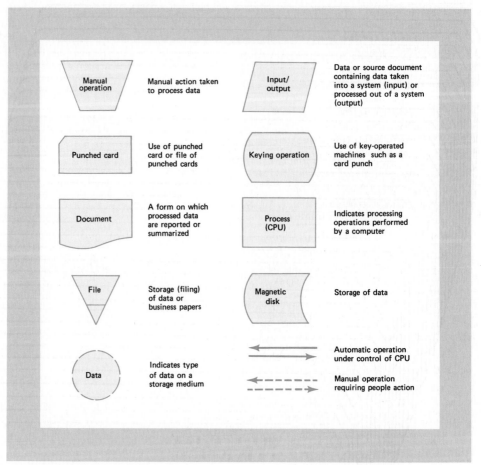

Flowchart symbols

Processing the chart of accounts

In the manual accounting cycle, an account for each account title listed in the chart of accounts is opened on a separate page in a ledger. The ledger is usually a loose-leaf book. The ledger represents the storage phase of the manual data processing cycle. In the automated accounting cycle for Wayside Furniture, the data from the chart of accounts are stored on magnetic disk. The magnetic disk represents the storage phase of the automated accounting cycle.

Data from the punched cards that were prepared from the chart of accounts setup forms, pages 320–321, must be read by the computer system before the data can be stored on magnetic disk. This procedure requires computer processing. When computer processing is needed, a computer program is used to provide the processing instructions to the central processing unit (CPU). Several computer programs are needed for the different parts of the automated accounting cycle. These programs are stored in auxiliary storage until needed for processing. Magnetic disks are a common type of auxiliary storage media for computer programs.

The flowchart at the right illustrates the sequence of steps for processing the chart of accounts for Wayside Furniture. Human assistance is required in automated systems. The direction arrow with a broken line indicates that the data flow requires a manual operation. For example, the punched cards from the chart of accounts must be manually inserted into the card reader. The direction arrow with a solid line shows that the data flow is automatic and under the control of the stored computer program. The steps in processing the chart of accounts for Wayside Furniture are described below. The numbers in the steps correspond to the numbers on the flowchart, at the right.

(1) The computer operator manually places the punched cards in the card reader and starts the computer system. (2) The CPU reads the computer program stored on magnetic disk and transfers the instructions to the internal storage area of the CPU. (3) The data from the punched cards are read and transferred to the internal storage area of the CPU. (4) After being read, the punched cards are manually removed from the card reader and filed in a punched card file. (5) The CPU, according to the instructions in the stored computer program, performs the following: (5a) Transfers the data for each account to magnetic disk; (5b) Arranges and transfers the data for the computer printouts to the printer. (6) The computer printout of the chart of accounts for the general ledger is prepared. (7) The computer printout of the chart of accounts for the accounts receivable subsidiary ledger is prepared. (8) The computer printout of the chart of accounts for the accounts payable subsidiary ledger is prepared. (9) An accuracy check is made by comparing the data on the printouts with the data on the chart of accounts setup form. (10) After accuracy has been determined, the computer printouts are sent to Wayside Furniture.

At Wayside Furniture the computer printouts are checked for accuracy and then filed for future reference. Copies of the computer printouts are shown on pages 340–341.

```
                        WAYSIDE FURNITURE
                        CHART OF ACCOUNTS
                         GENERAL LEDGER

                      CLIENT NUMBER 230
             ACCOUNT
             NUMBER                           DESCRIPTION

              10000                         ASSETS
              11000               CASH
              12000               ACCOUNTS RECEIVABLE
              13000               MERCHANDISE INVENTORY
              14000               SUPPLIES
              15000               PREPAID INSURANCE
              20000                      LIABILITIES
              21000               ACCOUNTS PAYABLE
              30000                       CAPITAL
              31000               RICHARD DAVIS, CAPITAL
              32000               RICHARD DAVIS, DRAWING
              33000               INCOME SUMMARY
              40000               REVENUE
              41000                  SALES
              50000               COST OF MERCHANDISE
              51000                  PURCHASES
              60000               EXPENSES
              61000                  DELIVERY EXPENSE
              62000                  INSURANCE EXPENSE
              63000                  MISCELLANEOUS EXPENSE
              64000                  RENT EXPENSE
              65000                  SALARY EXPENSE
              66000                  SUPPLIES EXPENSE
```

Computer printout of the chart of accounts for the general ledger

The opening entry

Mr. Davis closed the books for his manual accounting system on August 31, 1977. He changed to the automated data processing system on September 1. The balance for each account in the general ledger and for each account in the subsidiary ledgers is used for the opening entry for the automated data processing system for Wayside Furniture.

The source documents for the opening entry. The August 31, 1977, balance sheet of Wayside Furniture, page 342, is the source document for the opening entry for all accounts in the general ledger.

The schedules of accounts receivable and accounts payable for August 31, 1977, are the source documents for the opening entry for all accounts in the subsidiary ledgers. The two schedules are shown on page 342.

```
                         WAYSIDE FURNITURE
                         CHART OF ACCOUNTS
                         ACCOUNTS RECEIVABLE

                         CLIENT NUMBER 230


           CUSTOMER                              CUSTOMER
            NUMBER                                 NAME

            10020                            BRUCE ABBOT
            10040                            CHARLES ADAMS
            10060                            JOHN ALEXANDER
            10080                            MARY AUSTIN
            10100                            DALE BACKUS
            10120                            ROBERT BAILEY
            10140                            SAMUEL BAILEY
            10160                            RAYMOND BARTON
            10180                            JOHN BISHOP
            10200                            ROGER BLAND
            10220                            DONALD CARR
            10240                            NANCY CLAY
            10260                            BONNIE DEVINE
            10280                            DOUGLAS DICKERSON
            10300                            JEFFREY FORTINO
            10320                            CHARLES FOX
            10340                            ERMA JEFFERSON
            10360                            BENNY LOPEZ
            10380                            RONALD LUTZ
            10400                            EARL MOORE
            10420                            ROSEMARY RENDER
            10440                            DOUGLAS ROPER
            10460                            NANCY TAYLOR
            10480                            SCOTT WILSON
            10500                            GEORGE ZOLTE
```

Computer printout of the chart of accounts for the accounts receivable subsidiary ledger

```
                         WAYSIDE FURNITURE
                         CHART OF ACCOUNTS
                         ACCOUNTS PAYABLE


                         CLIENT NUMBER 230


           CREDITOR                             CREDITOR
            NUMBER                                NAME

            20020                           ALLEN MANUFACTURING CO.
            20040                           BONNELL FURNITURE SUPPLY
            20060                           CALLISON MATTRESSES
            20080                           JACKSON SUPPLY CO.
            20100                           JOHNSON ELECTRICAL
            20120                           TROWER SOFAS
            20140                           WEIDMAN FURNITURE
            20160                           ZANT MANUFACTURING
            20180                           ZEIGLER FURNITURE CO.
```

Computer printout of the chart of accounts for the accounts payable subsidiary ledger

Wayside Furniture
Balance Sheet
August 31, 1977

Assets		
Cash	683500	
Accounts Receivable	1264000	
Merchandise Inventory	8600000	
Supplies	96000	
Prepaid Insurance	38000	
Total Assets		10681500
Liabilities		
Accounts Payable		1643000
Capital		
Richard Davis, Capital		9038500
Total Liabilities and Capital		10681500

Balance sheet of Wayside Furniture

Wayside Furniture
Schedule of Accounts Receivable
August 31, 1977

Bruce Abbot	174000	
Mary Austin	76000	
Dale Backus	260000	
Donald Carr	26000	
Nancy Clay	3800	
Charles Fox	16000	
Erma Jefferson	1600	
Benny Lopez	106300	
Ronald Lutz	124000	
Earl Moore	63500	
Rosemary Render	78500	
Douglas Roper	220000	
Nancy Taylor	114300	
Total Accounts Receivable		1264000

Schedule of accounts receivable for Wayside Furniture

Wayside Furniture
Schedule of Accounts Payable
August 31, 1977

Bonnell Furniture Supply	608000	
Callison Mattresses	73500	
Johnson Electrical	98000	
Trower Sofas	486000	
Weidman Furniture	293000	
Zant Manufacturing	84500	
Total Accounts Payable		1643000

Schedule of accounts payable for Wayside Furniture

The journal entry transmittal. When Mr. Davis started Wayside Furniture, he recorded his opening entry in a general journal. In an automated data processing system, Mr. Davis learned that punched cards represent the journal of a manual data processing system. Therefore, punched cards are prepared for the account balances of each account listed on the balance sheet and of each account listed on the subsidiary schedules.

The computer service center could punch the data for the opening entry directly from the source documents. However, the center prefers that all original source documents be retained in the client's accounting office. Therefore, Mr. Davis was instructed to write the data for the opening entry on a form supplied by the computer service center. Entries for transactions will also be written on a similar form. A special form used for the recording of accounting transactions for an automated data processing system is called a journal entry transmittal. A journal entry transmittal is also known as a transaction transmittal. The form of the journal entry transmittal is shown below.

Journal entry transmittal form

In learning how to prepare the journal entry transmittal form, Mr. Davis found that the form resembled the journal that he had been using in his manual accounting system. He also discovered that the columns on the journal entry transmittal form allow him to record all business transactions. Special columns are provided on which to enter source document numbers. For transactions based on memorandums, no source document number is entered. The journal entry transmittal form will be the only form required to journalize business transactions.

Mr. Davis found one feature of the journal entry transmittal form that was different from the journal that he had been using. This feature involved the need for special totals to be computed before submitting the form to the computer service center. Mr. Davis was familiar with the need to compute the total of debits and the total of credits to establish the equality of debits and credits. However, he had never computed the total of account numbers. He learned that the special totals were used to check the accuracy of the punched cards that are prepared from the data recorded on the journal entry transmittal form. A sum of numbers used to check the accuracy of punched cards is called a control total. A control total is also known as a hash total.

Mr. Davis also learned that the arrangement of the columns on the journal entry transmittal form had special meaning. The order of the data on the journal entry transmittal form is the same as the order of the data on the punched cards.

The advantages of using a journal entry transmittal form are:

1. All source documents are kept in the client's accounting department. This method reduces the possibility of transactions being lost.
2. Card punching is faster. The card punch operator reads the data from single sheets with the data arranged in the same order as the punched cards. Source documents vary in size and arrangement.
3. Better accuracy is maintained through the control totals. The totals are checked to see that no entries have been omitted or incorrectly punched.

Journalizing the opening entry. The completed journal entry transmittal form for the opening entry of Wayside Furniture is illustrated on page 345.

The steps followed in recording the opening entry on the journal entry transmittal form are:

1. Write the client number, 230.
2. Write the numeric date, 09/01/77.
3. Write the page number of the form and the total number of pages that are included for the transmittal data, 1,1.
4. Write the account number for each account in the general ledger and subsidiary ledgers that had a balance after the books were closed on August 31, 1977. These accounts are listed on the balance sheet and schedules of accounts on page 342.
5, 6, 7, 8. Leave blank for opening entry. These columns are used only for recording daily transactions as described in Chapter 20.
9. Write the words "Opening Entry." Comments in this space alert the computer service center about the type of transactions being submitted.
10. Write the debits and the credits in the appropriate columns.
11. Add the debit entries and record the sum in the space provided.
12. Add the credit entries and record the sum in the space provided.

> Note that the sum of debit entries and the sum of credit entries are not equal. The unequal debits and credits are a result of recording both the general ledger accounts and the subsidiary ledger accounts at the same time. The unequal balances on the journal entry transmittal do not cause unequal debits and credits in

the general ledger. The general ledger and subsidiary ledgers are stored in different locations on magnetic disk storage. The total of the account balances in the subsidiary ledgers still equals the respective controlling accounts in the general ledger.

13. Add all the account numbers and record the sum in the space provided.

JOURNAL ENTRY TRANSMITTAL

CLIENT NUMBER _230_   DATE _09/01/77_   PAGE _1_ OF _1_ PAGES

	Acct. No.	Check No.	Purch. No.	Sales No.	Rcpt. No.	COMMENTS	DEBIT	CREDIT	
1	11000					Opening Entry	6835 00		1
2	12000						12640 00		2
3	13000						86000 00		3
4	14000						960 00		4
5	15000						380 00		5
6	21000							16430 00	6
7	31000							90385 00	7
8	10020						1740 00		8
9	10080						760 00		9
10	10100						2600 00		10
11	10220						260 00		11
12	10240						38 00		12
13	10320						160 00		13
14	10340						16 00		14
15	10360						1063 00		15
16	10380						1240 00		16
17	10400						635 00		17
18	10420						785 00		18
19	10440						2200 00		19
20	10460						1143 00		20
21	20040							6080 00	21
22	20060							735 00	22
23	20100							980 00	23
24	20120							4860 00	24
25	20140							2930 00	25
26	20160							845 00	26
27									27
28									28
29									29
30									30

SUM OF DEBIT ENTRIES	**11** 119455 00	PREPARED BY
SUM OF CREDIT ENTRIES	**12** 123245 00	_Richard Davis_
SUM OF ACCOUNT NUMBERS	**13** 371,400	

Journal entry transmittal for opening entry

Recording the opening entry for computer processing

The completed journal entry transmittal form for the opening entry is sent to the computer service center. At the center the data from the journal entry transmittal, page 345, are used to record the opening entry for Wayside Furniture. One card is punched for each line on the transmittal. The same rule applies to transaction cards as applied to chart of accounts cards. The location of the information on the punched cards must again be consistent from card to card. The punched cards for the opening entry are shown below.

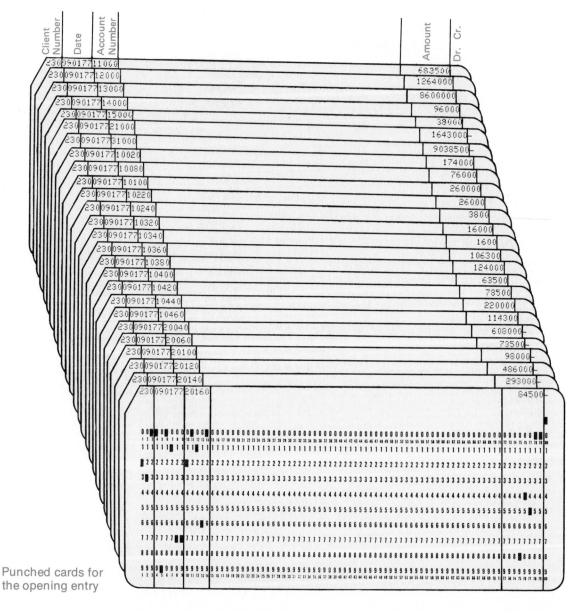

Punched cards for
the opening entry

The punched card fields for the opening entry cards follow:

Card Columns 1–3   Client Number   Card Columns 72–79 Amount
Card Columns 4–9   Date   Card Column 80   Debit/Credit
Card Columns 10–14 Account Number

Note that the amount field (card columns 72–79) is the same for both debits and credits. This is accomplished by designating the status of the amount field in card column 80. If the amount is a debit, card column 80 is left blank. If the amount is a credit, a dash (—) is punched in card column 80.

Processing the opening entry

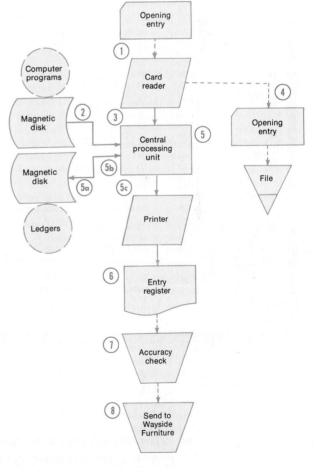

The data from the punched cards that were prepared from the journal entry transmittal form, page 345, are read and processed by the computer system. The flowchart at the right illustrates the steps necessary to process the opening entry.

(1) The computer operator manually places the punched cards in the card reader and starts the computer system. (2) The CPU reads the computer program stored on magnetic disk and transfers the instructions to the internal storage area of the CPU. (3) The data from the punched cards are read and transferred to the internal storage area of the CPU. (4) After being read, the punched cards are manually removed from the card reader and filed in a punched card file. (5) The CPU, according to instructions in the stored computer program, performs the following: (5a) Posts the account balances for the opening entry to magnetic disk; (5b) Transfers the data for each account to the internal storage area of the CPU; (5c) Transfers the data for each account to the printer. (6) A computer printout of the account number, description, and account balance for each account from the general ledger and subsidiary ledgers is prepared. A computer printout of the transaction data that are entered into a computer system is called an entry register. An entry register is also known as a transaction register. (7) An accuracy check is made by comparing the data and control totals on the entry register with the data and control

totals on the journal entry transmittal form. (8) After accuracy has been determined, the entry register for the opening entry is sent to Wayside Furniture.

At Wayside Furniture the entry register for the opening entry is checked for accuracy and then filed for future reference. A copy of the entry register is shown below.

```
                        WAYSIDE FURNITURE
                         ENTRY REGISTER
                          OPENING ENTRY

    CLIENT NUMBER 230                               DATE    09/01/77

      ACCOUNT
      NUMBER           DESCRIPTION           DEBIT            CREDIT

       11000    CASH                      $  6,835.00
       12000    ACCOUNTS RECEIVABLE         12,640.00
       13000    MERCHANDISE INVENTORY       86,000.00
       14000    SUPPLIES                       960.00
       15000    PREPAID INSURANCE              380.00
       21000    ACCOUNTS PAYABLE                            $16,430.00
       31000    RICHARD DAVIS, CAPITAL                       90,385.00
       10020    BRUCE ABBOT                  1,740.00
       10080    MARY AUSTIN                    760.00
       10100    DALE BACKUS                  2,600.00
       10220    DONALD CARR                    260.00
       10240    NANCY CLAY                      38.00
       10320    CHARLES FOX                    160.00
       10340    ERMA JEFFERSON                  16.00
       10360    BENNY LOPEZ                  1,063.00
       10380    RONALD LUTZ                  1,240.00
       10400    EARL MOORE                     635.00
       10420    ROSEMARY RENDER                785.00
       10440    DOUGLAS ROPER                2,200.00
       10460    NANCY TAYLOR                 1,143.00
       20040    BONNELL FURNITURE SUPPLY                      6,080.00
       20060    CALLISON MATTRESSES                             735.00
       20100    JOHNSON ELECTRICAL                             980.00
       20120    TROWER SOFAS                                  4,860.00
       20140    WEIDMAN FURNITURE                             2,930.00
       20160    ZANT MANUFACTURING                             845.00


             SUM OF DEBIT ENTRIES        $119,455.00
             SUM OF CREDIT ENTRIES                        $123,245.00
             SUM OF ACCOUNT NUMBERS         371,400
```

Entry register for opening entry

SUMMARY OF STEPS IN PREPARING FOR AUTOMATED DATA PROCESSING

The steps followed by Mr. Davis and the computer service center in preparing for automated data processing of the accounting data of Wayside Furniture are summarized on page 349. Steps 1 and 2 were described in Chapter 18. Steps 3–6 were described in Chapter 19.

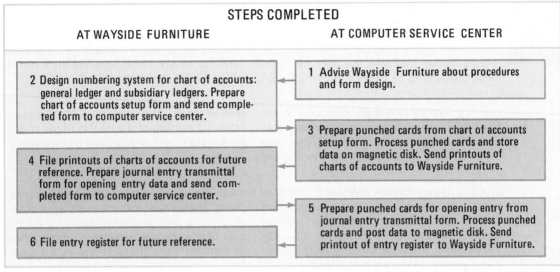

STEPS COMPLETED

AT WAYSIDE FURNITURE   AT COMPUTER SERVICE CENTER

1 Advise Wayside Furniture about procedures and form design.

2 Design numbering system for chart of accounts: general ledger and subsidiary ledgers. Prepare chart of accounts setup form and send completed form to computer service center.

3 Prepare punched cards from chart of accounts setup form. Process punched cards and store data on magnetic disk. Send printouts of charts of accounts to Wayside Furniture.

4 File printouts of charts of accounts for future reference. Prepare journal entry transmittal form for opening entry data and send completed form to computer service center.

5 Prepare punched cards for opening entry from journal entry transmittal form. Process punched cards and post data to magnetic disk. Send printout of entry register to Wayside Furniture.

6 File entry register for future reference.

Flowchart of steps in preparing for automated data processing

Using Business Terms

✦ What is the meaning of each of the following?

- data processing cycle
- automated data processing cycle
- input media
- punched card

- verifying
- printout
- fields
- system flowchart

- journal entry transmittal
- control total
- entry register

Questions for Individual Study

1. What is the most common way of converting data into a coded form that can be processed by automated equipment?
2. How are data punched into the card?
3. What is the name of the machine that is used to make holes in a card?
4. What is the name of the machine that is used to determine if the data are accurately punched into cards?
5. What is the name of the input device that is used for reading data on punched cards into the CPU and storage units of a computer?
6. What are the two distinct functions performed by the CPU?
7. Why is the term "logic" used in the name of the arithmetic/logic unit?
8. What unit within the CPU tells each of the other parts of the computer what to do, when to do it, and how to do it?
9. How is the storage capacity of the computer expanded?

10. Why is there no limit to the amount of data stored on magnetic disk?
11. What is the name of the output device that produces the results of processed data in human-readable form?
12. Computer programs are commonly stored on what type of auxiliary storage?
13. How does the printing of a printer compare to that of a typewriter?
14. What is the source document for the opening entry for the accounts in the general ledger?
15. What are the source documents for the opening entry for all accounts in the subsidiary ledgers?
16. The journal entry transmittal form resembles what form commonly used in a manual accounting system?
17. What are the advantages of using a journal entry transmittal form?
18. How are debit and credit amounts designated in the punched card?

Cases for Management Decision

CASE 1 John Munford, owner and operator of Superior Hardware Company, uses the services of a computer service center to process his accounting data. The computer service center prepares the data for computer processing by punching cards for all business transactions. Mr. Munford is considering installing his own card punch machine to prepare the data for machine processing. What factors should Mr. Munford consider before deciding whether or not to install a card punch machine?

CASE 2 The local electric company in the town where the Johnson family lives sends to its customers a monthly bill that is a punched card with data about the amount printed on it. The customer, Mr. Dawson, returns a portion of the card with his check. What data might be punched on the card?

CASE 3 Helen Tilman owns and operates a family shoe store. She has her accounting data processed by a computer service center. The source documents for daily transactions are sent directly to the computer service center each morning. Recently, one set of transactions got lost in the mail. The source documents were never located. The loss of these transactions created serious problems in accounting for the data that were lost. How could the method of sending daily transactions to the computer service center be improved?

Drills for Mastering Principles

DRILL 19-D 1 Analyzing punched cards

Instructions: Turn to page 330 in your textbook and answer the following questions about punched cards:

1. The punched card is divided into how many vertical columns?
2. Each vertical column has how many numbered positions?
3. What are the numbered positions across the card called?
4. What type of data may be punched into cards?
5. To punch the number 13658, how many columns would be used?
6. How many holes are punched in each column to record an alphabetic character?
7. What are the two unnumbered rows on a card called?
8. What rows make up the zone punching area of the card?

DRILL 19-D 2 Reading punched cards

Instructions: Refer to the standard punched card code on page 330 and answer the following questions about the punched card at the right.

1. What numeric number is punched in card columns 1–6?

2. What name is punched in card columns 7–18?

PROBLEM 19-1 ### Recording the opening entry in an automated system

The balance sheet and the subsidiary schedules of the Crestline Department Store for October 31, 1977, are shown below.

Crestline Department Store Balance Sheet October 31, 1977		
Assets		
Cash............................	2 560 00	
Accounts Receivable	1 840 00	
Merchandise Inventory..	31 000 00	
Store Supplies..............	160 00	
Prepaid Insurance.........	485 00	
Total Assets		36 045 00
Liabilities		
Accounts Payable		3 640 00
Capital		
Harold Garner, Capital..		32 405 00
Total Liab. and Cap.		36 045 00

Crestline Department Store Schedule of Accounts Receivable October 31, 1977		
Helene Abler	93 00	
Keith Allen...................	36 00	
Gloria Bell	145 00	
Donald Carson	18 00	
John Foley	364 00	
Nancy Ford..................	585 00	
Robert Klein	88 00	
Susan Klein	283 00	
James McGuire.............	196 00	
Diane Trost..................	20 00	
Donald Wixson	12 00	
Total Accts. Receivable..		1 840 00

Instructions: Record the opening entry for the Crestline Department Store, Client No. 382, on a journal entry transmittal form. Use November 1, 1977, as the date of the opening entry. The account numbers are given in the chart of accounts illustrated in Problems 18-1 and 18-2, Chapter 18, page 325. Use as your model the journal entry transmittal illustrated on page 345.

Crestline Department Store Schedule of Accounts Payable October 31, 1977		
Addison Fabric Supply..	985 00	
Collins Ladies Apparel ..	88 00	
Durfee, Inc.	1 360 00	
Fryman Clothiers..........	146 00	
Multiline Distributors ...	550 00	
United Shoes	325 00	
Zant Manufacturing	186 00	
Total Accounts Payable..		3 640 00

MASTERY PROBLEM 19-M ### Recording the opening entry for a general ledger

The chart of accounts prepared in Mastery Problem 18-M is needed to complete Mastery Problem 19-M.

The balance sheet of the Myers Automotive Supply for December 31, 1977, is shown on page 352.

Instructions: Record the opening entry for the Myers Automotive Supply, Client No. 423, on a journal entry transmittal form. Use January 1, 1978, as the date of the opening entry. Use the account numbers from the chart of accounts prepared in Mastery Problem 18-M.

Myers Automotive Supply Balance Sheet December 31, 1977					
Assets					
Cash	3	140	00		
Accounts Receivable	1	620	00		
Merchandise Inventory	26	000	00		
Store Supplies		340	00		
Office Supplies		280	00		
Prepaid Insurance		390	00		
Store Equipment	2	400	00		
Office Equipment	1	600	00		
Total Assets				35	770	00
Liabilities					
Accounts Payable				2	360	00
Capital					
John Myers, Capital				33	410	00
Total Liabilities and Capital				35	770	00

BONUS PROBLEM 19-B   ## Recording the opening entry for a subsidiary ledger

The chart of accounts prepared in Bonus Problem 18-B is needed for Bonus Problem 19-B.

The schedule of accounts receivable of the Myers Automotive Supply for December 31, 1977, is shown below.

Instructions: Record the opening entry for the Myers Automotive Supply, Client No. 423, on a journal entry transmittal form. Use January 1, 1978, as the date of the opening entry for the accounts receivable subsidiary ledger. Use the account numbers from the chart of accounts prepared in Bonus Problem 18-B.

Myers Automotive Supply Schedule of Accounts Receivable December 31, 1977					
Charlotte Abbey	38	00			
Leonard Adams	116	00			
Jerald Ambler	62	00			
Joan Bailey	12	00			
Judy Decker	316	00			
John Fleming	134	00			
Gregg Ford	92	00			
Dale Jarrett	64	00			
David Kizer	19	00			
John Martin	430	00			
Thomas Nash	110	00			
Steve Pruden	86	00			
Lewis Walters	26	00			
Carl Woods	115	00			
Total Accounts Receivable			1	620	00

Automated Accounting Systems: Processing Transactions and End-of-Fiscal-Period Work

20

After the chart of accounts and opening entry have been recorded and processed, Mr. Davis submits data about Wayside Furniture's daily transactions to the computer service center. The daily transactions are processed by the computer system at the computer service center. Mr. Davis also lets the computer service center know the types of end-of-fiscal-period reports he wants prepared.

PROCESSING TRANSACTIONS

All accounting transactions are submitted to the computer service center for recording and processing.

Journalizing daily transactions

The methods of journalizing daily transactions for an automated data processing system vary depending on the nature of the business. Wayside Furniture uses the following methods.

Grouping of transactions. Mr. Davis journalizes all daily transactions on a journal entry transmittal form. Transactions are manually arranged by categories or groups before the journal entries are made. For example, cash payments are in one group and cash receipts in another group. Likewise, purchases of merchandise on account and sales of merchandise on account are arranged in separate groups. The arranging of transactions by similar groups is called batching. The batching procedure reduces the number of journal entries. For example, five cash payment transactions could require five cash credit entries. With the batching procedure, the five cash payments transactions are entered as one combined entry.

353

Cash payments. Mr. Davis writes checks for all cash payments. At the end of each day, Mr. Davis records on a journal entry transmittal form all cash payments for the day. He totals the amount of cash payments for the day on an adding machine. The following cash payments were made on September 1, 1977.

> September 1, 1977. Summary of cash payments for the day:
> Paid cash for September rent, $600.00. Check No. 820.
> Paid cash for telephone bill, $73.00. Check No. 821.
> Paid cash on account to Bonnell Furniture Supply, $1,500.00. Check No. 822.
> Paid cash on account to Callison Mattresses, $735.00. Check No. 823.
> Paid cash on account to Johnson Electrical, $980.00. Check No. 824.

The day's cash payments for Wayside Furniture are summarized on lines 1–6 of the journal entry transmittal form shown below.

JOURNAL ENTRY TRANSMITTAL

CLIENT NUMBER _230_   DATE _09|01|77_   PAGE _1_ OF _1_ PAGES

	Acct. No.	Check No.	Purch. No.	Sales No.	Rcpt. No.	COMMENTS	DEBIT	CREDIT	
1	64000	820				Daily Transactions	600 00		1
2	63000	821					73 00		2
3	20040	822					1500 00		3
4	20060	823					735 00		4
5	20100	824					980 00		5
6	11000							3888 00	6

Cash payments summarized on journal entry transmittal form

Only one combined entry is made for the total of all cash payments for a single day.

Cash receipts. When a charge customer pays all or part of an account, a receipt is prepared in duplicate. A machine that is used to record in handwritten form the information about a business transaction is called an autographic register. The receipt for cash received on account is recorded by Wayside Furniture on an autographic register.

The register has two printed rolls of paper with a carbon sheet between the rolls. Thus, a carbon copy is made of each receipt written. The original copy is given to the person making the payment. The carbon copy, kept by Wayside Furniture, is the source document for the cash received on account transaction.

Krauth & Benninghofen Corp.

Autographic register

Wayside Furniture uses a cash register on which to record all cash sales. The cash register prints a tape showing the amount of each individual cash sale made. At the end of each day, the total of the cash sales for the day shown on the cash register tape is recorded on the autographic register. The copy from the autographic register is the source document for total cash sales for the day.

At the end of each day, Mr. Davis enters on the journal entry transmittal form all cash receipts for the day. Mr. Davis runs a total of all cash receipts for the day on an adding machine. The following cash receipts transactions were made on September 1.

> September 1, 1977. Summary of cash receipts for the day:
> Received on account from Bruce Abbot, $125.00. Receipt No. 513.
> Received on account from Nancy Clay, $38.00. Receipt No. 514.
> Received on account from Earl Moore, $635.00. Receipt No. 515.
> Cash sales for the day, $1,325.00. Receipt No. 516.

The day's cash receipts for Wayside Furniture are summarized on lines 7–11 of the journal entry transmittal form shown below.

JOURNAL ENTRY TRANSMITTAL

CLIENT NUMBER _230_   DATE _09/01/77_   PAGE _1_ OF _1_ PAGES

	Acct. No.	Check No.	Purch. No.	Sales No.	Rcpt. No.	COMMENTS	DEBIT	CREDIT	
7	11000						212300		7
8	10020				513			12500	8
9	10240				514			3800	9
10	10400				515			63500	10
11	41000				516			132500	11

Cash receipts summarized on journal entry transmittal form

Only one combined entry is made for the total of all cash receipts for a single day.

Purchases of merchandise on account. The purchase invoice is used as the source document for the journal entry for a purchase of merchandise on account. When Wayside Furniture receives a purchase invoice, the date and a number are stamped in the upper right-hand corner. The number automatically changes each time the stamp is used. The consecutive numbers are used to identify all purchase invoices.

At the end of each day, Mr. Davis records on the journal entry transmittal form all purchases of merchandise on account for the day. Mr. Davis totals all purchases on account on an adding machine. The following purchases of merchandise on account were made on September 1.

September 1, 1977. *Summary of purchases of merchandise on ac-*
count for the day:
Purchased merchandise on account from Allen
Manufacturing Co., $625.00. Purchase Invoice
No. 217.
Purchased merchandise on account from Jackson
Supply Co., $268.00. Purchase Invoice No. 218.
Purchased merchandise on account from Zant
Manufacturing, $430.00. Purchase Invoice No.
219.

The day's purchases of merchandise on account are summarized on
lines 12–15 of the journal entry transmittal form below.

One combined entry is made for the total of all purchases of merchandise on account for a single day.

Purchases of mer-
chandise on account
summarized on jour-
nal entry transmittal
form

JOURNAL ENTRY TRANSMITTAL

CLIENT NUMBER *230*   DATE *09 / 01 / 77*   PAGE *1* OF *1* PAGES

	Acct. No.	Check No.	Purch. No.	Sales No.	Rcpt. No.	COMMENTS	DEBIT	CREDIT	
12	51000						1 32300		12
13	20020		217					62500	13
14	20080		218					26800	14
15	20160		219					43000	15

Sales of merchandise on account. A sales invoice is used by Wayside
Furniture for all sales on account. At the end of each day, Mr. Davis
records on the journal entry transmittal form all sales of merchandise on
account for the day. He totals all sales invoices for the day on an adding
machine. The following sales of merchandise on account were made on
September 1.

September 1, 1977. *Summary of sales of merchandise on account for*
the day:
Sold merchandise on account to Charles Adams,
$98.00. Sales Invoice No. 644.
Sold merchandise on account to Mary Austin,
$169.00. Sales Invoice No. 645.
Sold merchandise on account to Erma Jefferson,
$149.00. Sales Invoice No. 646.
Sold merchandise on account to Douglas Roper,
$63.00. Sales Invoice No. 647.

The day's sales of merchandise on account are summarized on lines
16–20 of the journal entry transmittal form at the top of page 357.

One combined entry is made for the total of all sales of merchandise on
account for a single day.

Recording the control totals. After all transactions for the day have
been recorded on the journal entry transmittal form, Mr. Davis computes

JOURNAL ENTRY TRANSMITTAL

CLIENT NUMBER 230   DATE 09/01/77   PAGE 1 OF 1 PAGES

	Acct. No.	Check No.	Purch. No.	Sales No.	Rcpt. No.	Comments	Debit	Credit	
16	10040			644			9800		16
17	10080			645			16900		17
18	10340			646			14900		18
19	10440			647			6300		19
20	41000							47900	20

Sales of merchandise on account summarized on journal entry transmittal form

the control totals on an adding machine. The control totals are used to check the equality of debits and credits. The totals are also used by the computer service center to check the accuracy of the punched cards that are prepared from the journal entry transmittal form. The completed journal entry transmittal form for September 1, 1977, is shown below.

JOURNAL ENTRY TRANSMITTAL

CLIENT NUMBER 230   DATE 09/01/77   PAGE 1 OF 1 PAGES

	Acct. No.	Check No.	Purch. No.	Sales No.	Rcpt. No.	Comments	Debit	Credit	
1	64000	820				Daily Transactions	60000		1
2	63000	821					7300		2
3	20040	822					150000		3
4	20060	823					73500		4
5	20100	824					98000		5
6	11000							388800	6
7	11000						212300		7
8	10020			513				12500	8
9	10240			514				3800	9
10	10400			515				63500	10
11	41000			516				132500	11
12	51000						132300		12
13	20020	217						62500	13
14	20080	218						26800	14
15	20160	219						43000	15
16	10040			644			9800		16
17	10080			645			16900		17
18	10340			646			14900		18
19	10440			647			6300		19
20	41000							47900	20

SUM OF DEBIT ENTRIES	781300	PREPARED BY
SUM OF CREDIT ENTRIES	781300	Richard Davis
SUM OF ACCOUNT NUMBERS	474,020	

Journal entry transmittal form for daily transactions

Recording the daily transactions for computer processing

Mr. Davis sends the completed journal entry transmittal form to the computer service center each morning. The form includes a record of all business activity from the previous day. The data from the journal entry transmittal form are used to record the daily transactions of Wayside Furniture. One card is punched for each line on the journal entry transmittal form. The punched cards for the daily transactions of Wayside Furniture for September 1, 1977, are shown below.

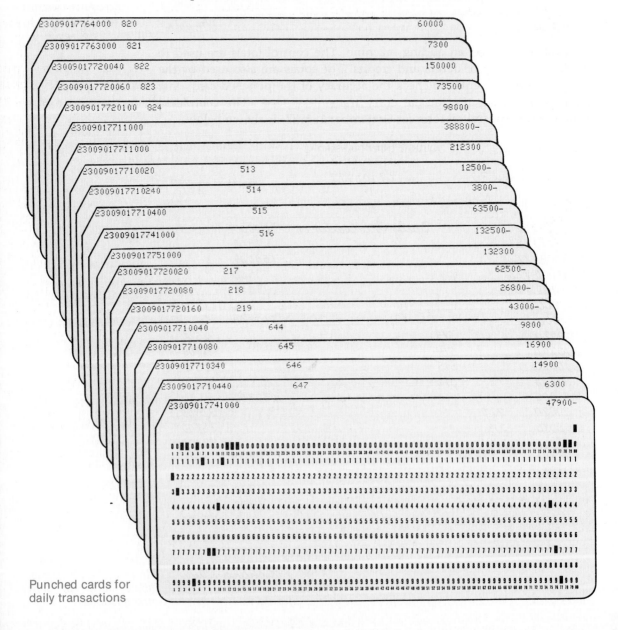

Punched cards for daily transactions

The fields on the daily transaction punched cards are:

Card Columns		Card Columns	
1–3	Client Number	25–29	Sales Number
4–9	Date	30–34	Receipt Number
10–14	Account Number	72–79	Amount
15–19	Check Number	80	Debit/Credit
20–24	Purchase Number		

Processing the daily transactions

The flowchart below illustrates the sequence of steps necessary to process the daily transactions of Wayside Furniture for September 1, 1977. The steps in processing the daily transactions are also described below. The numbers in the steps correspond to the numbers on the flowchart.

(1) The computer operator manually places the punched cards in the card reader and starts the computer system. (2) The CPU (central processing unit) reads the computer program stored on magnetic disk and transfers the instructions to the internal storage area of the CPU. (3) The data from the punched cards are read and transferred to the internal storage area of the CPU. (4) After being read, the punched cards are manually removed from the card reader and filed in a punched card file. (5) The CPU, according to instructions in the stored computer program, performs the following: (5a) Posts the daily transactions to the ledgers stored on magnetic disk; (5b) Computes and arranges the data for the entry register; (5c) Transfers the data for the entry register to the printer. (6) The entry register is printed. (7) An accuracy check is made by comparing the data and control totals on the entry register with the data and control totals on the journal entry transmittal. (8) After accuracy has been determined, the entry register for the daily transactions is sent to Wayside Furniture.

At Wayside Furniture the entry register is inspected and filed for future reference. The entry register is shown on page 360.

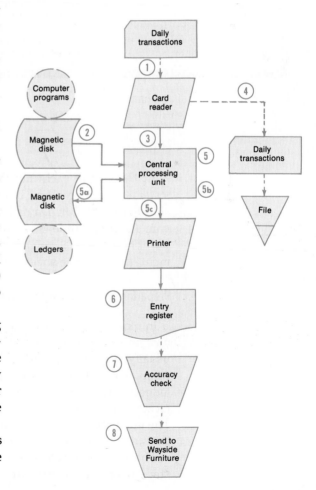

```
                              WAYSIDE FURNITURE
                              ENTRY REGISTER
                              DAILY TRANSACTIONS

CLIENT NUMBER 230                                               DATE    09/01/77

ACCT.  CK.  PURCH. SALES RCPT.                                          ACCOUNT
 NO.   NO.   NO.   NO.   NO.        DESCRIPTION      DEBIT     CREDIT    BALANCE

64000  820                     RENT EXPENSE        $  600.00          $   600.00
63000  821                     MISCELLANEOUS EXPENSE    73.00              73.00
20040  822                     BUNNELL FURNITURE SUPPLY 1,500.00        4,580.00
20060  823                     CALLISON MATTRESSES      735.00         ---------
20100  824                     JOHNSON ELECTRICAL       980.00         ---------
11000                          CASH                           $3,888.00 2,947.00
11000                          CASH                   2,123.00          5,070.00
10020              513         BRUCE ABBOT                      125.00  1,615.00
10240              514         NANCY CLAY                        38.00  ---------
10400              515         EARL MOORE                       635.00  ---------
41000              516         SALES                          1,325.00  1,325.00-
51000                          PURCHASES            1,323.00            1,323.00
20020  217                     ALLEN MANUFACTURING CO.         625.00    625.00-
20080  218                     JACKSON SUPPLY CO.              268.00    268.00-
20160  219                     ZANT MANUFACTURING             430.00   1,275.00-
10040         644              CHARLES ADAMS           98.00              98.00
10080         645              MARY AUSTIN            169.00             929.00
10340         646              ERMA JEFFERSON         149.00             165.00
10440         647              DOUGLAS ROPER           63.00           2,263.00
41000                          SALES                           479.00  1,804.00-

                        SUM OF DEBIT ENTRIES      $7,813.00
                        SUM OF CREDIT ENTRIES                $7,813.00
                        SUM OF ACCOUNT NUMBERS      474,020
```

Entry register for daily transactions

PROCESSING THE END-OF-FISCAL-PERIOD WORK

At the end of each monthly fiscal period, the schedules and financial statements are prepared by the computer service center and sent to Wayside Furniture. Mr. Davis instructed the computer service center to prepare (1) a schedule of accounts receivable and a schedule of accounts payable, (2) a trial balance, (3) an income statement, (4) a capital statement, (5) a balance sheet, and (6) a post-closing trial balance.

Preparing the subsidiary schedules

In manual accounting the accounts receivable and the accounts payable data are stored in the subsidiary ledgers. The subsidiary ledgers are usually kept in a loose-leaf book. In automated accounting the accounts receivable and the accounts payable data are also stored in the subsidiary ledgers. However, the subsidiary ledgers in automated accounting are located in the auxiliary storage media connected to the computer system. The magnetic disk used by the computer service center stores the data for the subsidiary ledgers of Wayside Furniture.

The flowchart at the top of the next page illustrates the sequence of steps necessary to prepare the schedule of accounts receivable and the schedule of accounts payable for Wayside Furniture.

(1) The computer operator starts the computer system. (2) The CPU reads the computer program stored on magnetic disk and transfers the instructions to the internal storage area of the CPU. (3) The CPU, according to instructions in the stored computer program, performs the following: (3a) Reads and transfers the data from magnetic disk to the internal storage area of the CPU; (3b) Computes and arranges the data for the schedules; (3c) Transfers the data for the schedules to the printer. (4) The schedule of accounts receivable is printed. (5) The schedule of accounts payable is printed. (6) The computer printouts of the subsidiary schedules are sent to Wayside Furniture.

At Wayside Furniture the subsidiary schedules are analyzed for management decisions and filed for future reference. The subsidiary schedules are shown below and on page 362.

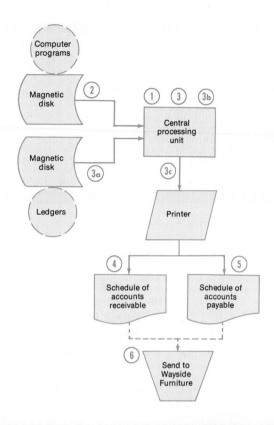

```
                       WAYSIDE FURNITURE
               SCHEDULE OF ACCOUNTS RECEIVABLE
                     SEPTEMBER 30, 1977

     BRUCE ABBOT                          $ 1,616.00
     CHARLES ADAMS                          1,265.00
     JOHN ALEXANDER                           186.00
     MARY AUSTIN                              540.00
     DALE BACKUS                            1,093.00
     ROBERT BAILEY                            245.00
     SAMUEL BAILEY                          2,475.00
     RAYMOND BARTON                           890.00
     JOHN BISHOP                              525.00
     ROGER BLAND                              539.00
     DONALD CARR                              263.00
     BONNIE DEVINE                            285.00
     DOUGLAS DICKERSON                        565.00
     JEFFREY FORTINO                          280.00
     BENNY LOPEZ                              900.00
     RONALD LUTZ                            1,100.00
     ROSEMARY RENDER                          700.00
     DOUGLAS ROPER                          2,150.00
     NANCY TAYLOR                           1,043.00
     GEORGE ZOLTE                           2,217.00

     TOTAL ACCOUNTS RECEIVABLE             $18,877.00
```

Schedule of accounts receivable

```
                              WAYSIDE FURNITURE
                         SCHEDULE OF ACCOUNTS PAYABLE
                            SEPTEMBER 30, 1977

        ALLEN MANUFACTURING CO.                      $ 1,461.00
        BONNELL FURNITURE SUPPLY                       4,580.00
        CALLISON MATTRESSES                              683.00
        JACKSON SUPPLY CO.                             1,860.00
        TROWER SOFAS                                   3,280.00
        WEIDMAN FURNITURE                              1,859.00
        ZANT MANUFACTURING                               978.00
        ZEIGLER FURNITURE CO.                          4,265.00

        TOTAL ACCOUNTS PAYABLE                       $18,966.00
```

Schedule of accounts payable

Preparing the trial balance

The trial balance provides the proof of the equality of debits and credits in the general ledger. In manual accounting the general ledger data are stored in a loose-leaf book similar to the books used to store the data for the subsidiary ledgers. The general ledger data for Wayside Furniture are stored on magnetic disks at the computer service center.

The trial balance is recorded directly on the work sheet in a manual accounting system. In an automated accounting system, the work sheet

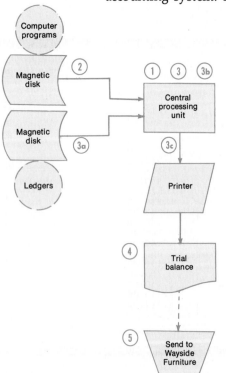

is not required. All computations are done by the computer according to instructions in the stored computer program. However, the trial balance is still needed to prove the equality of debits and credits in the general ledger and to plan the adjusting entries. The flowchart at the left illustrates the sequence of steps for processing the trial balance of Wayside Furniture.

(1) The computer operator starts the computer system. (2) The CPU reads the computer program stored on magnetic disk and transfers the instructions to the internal storage area of the CPU. (3) The CPU, according to instructions in the stored computer program, performs the following: (3a) Reads and transfers the data from magnetic disk to the internal storage area of CPU; (3b) Computes and arranges data for the trial balance; (3c) Transfers the data for the trial balance to the printer. (4) The trial balance is printed. (5) The trial balance is sent to Wayside Furniture.

At Wayside Furniture the trial balance is used to plan the adjusting entries and then filed for future reference. The computer printout of the trial balance is illustrated below.

```
                          WAYSIDE FURNITURE
                            TRIAL BALANCE
                    FOR MONTH ENDED SEPTEMBER 30, 1977


        11000  CASH                       $  8,650.00
        12000  ACCOUNTS RECEIVABLE          18,877.00
        13000  MERCHANDISE INVENTORY        86,000.00
        14000  SUPPLIES                      1,220.00
        15000  PREPAID INSURANCE               380.00
        21000  ACCOUNTS PAYABLE                            $ 18,966.00
        31000  RICHARD DAVIS, CAPITAL                        90,385.00
        32000  RICHARD DAVIS, DRAWING        1,000.00
        41000  SALES                                         26,039.00
        51000  PURCHASES                     9,360.00
        61000  DELIVERY EXPENSE                235.00
        63000  MISCELLANEOUS EXPENSE           116.00
        64000  RENT EXPENSE                    600.00
        65000  SALARY EXPENSE                8,952.00

               TOTALS                     $135,390.00      $135,390.00
```

Trial balance

Journalizing the adjusting entries

The computer does not have the ability to make the decisions needed to plan adjusting entries. Therefore, after examining the trial balance and determining ending inventories, Mr. Davis recorded the necessary adjusting entries on the journal entry transmittal form below.

JOURNAL ENTRY TRANSMITTAL

CLIENT NUMBER 230   DATE 09/30/77   PAGE 1 OF 1 PAGES

	Acct. No.	Check No.	Purch. No.	Sales No.	Rcpt. No.	COMMENTS	DEBIT	CREDIT	
1	33000					Adjusting Entries	8600000		1
2	13000							8600000	2
3	13000						8338200		3
4	33000							8338200	4
5	66000						28000		5
6	14000							28000	6
7	62000						9500		7
8	15000							9500	8

SUM OF DEBIT ENTRIES	16975700	PREPARED BY
SUM OF CREDIT ENTRIES	16975700	Richard Davis
SUM OF ACCOUNT NUMBERS	249,000	

Journal entry transmittal form for adjusting entries

The completed transmittal form is sent to the computer service center where the adjusting entries are converted to machine-readable form.

Recording the adjusting entries for computer processing

One card is punched for each line on the journal entry transmittal form. The information in the Comments column is not punched. It is included to alert the computer service center about the type of transactions that are being submitted. The punched cards for the adjusting entries for Wayside Furniture are shown below.

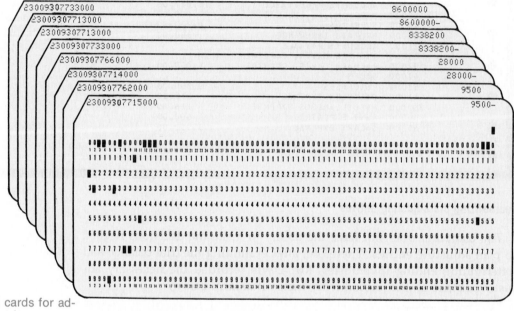

Punched cards for adjusting entries

Preparing the financial statements

In manual accounting the financial statements are prepared from the completed worksheet. In automated accounting the financial statements are prepared by the computer system after the adjusting entries have been processed. The flowchart on page 365 shows the sequence of steps necessary to prepare the financial statements for Wayside Furniture.

The steps for processing the entry register and the financial statements are as follows:

(1) The computer operator manually places the punched cards in the card reader and starts the computer system. (2) The CPU reads the computer program stored on magnetic disk and transfers the instructions to the internal storage area of the CPU. (3) The data from the punched cards are read and transferred to the internal storage area of the CPU. (4) After being read, the punched cards are manually removed from the card reader and filed in a punched card file. (5) The CPU, according to instructions in the stored computer program, performs the following: (5a) Posts

the adjusting entries to the general ledger; (5b) Computes and arranges the data for the entry register; (5c) Transfers the data for the entry register to the printer. (6) The entry register is printed. (7) An accuracy check is made by comparing the data and control totals on the entry register with the data and control totals on the journal entry transmittal form. After accuracy has been determined, the computer operator starts the computer. (8) The CPU computes, arranges, and transfers the data for the financial statements to the printer. (9) The income statement is printed. (10) The capital statement is printed. (11) The balance sheet is printed. (12) The computer printouts are sent to Wayside Furniture.

At Wayside Furniture the computer printouts are inspected to determine the necessary closing entries and to make management decisions. The computer printouts are then filed for future reference. The computer printout of the entry register is shown below. The income statement and the capital statement are shown on page 366; the balance sheet is shown on page 367.

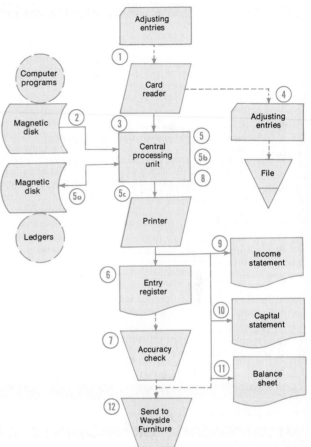

WAYSIDE FURNITURE
ENTRY REGISTER
ADJUSTING ENTRIES

CLIENT NUMBER 230   DATE   09/30/77

ACCOUNT NUMBER	DESCRIPTION	DEBIT	CREDIT
33000	INCOME SUMMARY	$ 86,000.00	
13000	MERCHANDISE INVENTORY		$ 86,000.00
13000	MERCHANDISE INVENTORY	83,382.00	
33000	INCOME SUMMARY		83,382.00
66000	SUPPLIES EXPENSE	280.00	
14000	SUPPLIES		280.00
62000	INSURANCE EXPENSE	95.00	
15000	PREPAID INSURANCE		95.00
	SUM OF DEBIT ENTRIES	$169,757.00	
	SUM OF CREDIT ENTRIES		$169,757.00
	SUM OF ACCOUNT NUMBERS	249,000	

Entry register for adjusting entries

```
                           WAYSIDE FURNITURE
                            INCOME STATEMENT
                    FOR MONTH ENDED SEPTEMBER 30, 1977

      REVENUE
        SALES                                                    $26,039.00

      COST OF MERCHANDISE SOLD
        MERCHANDISE INVENTORY, SEPTEMBER 1        $86,000.00
        PURCHASES                                   9,360.00
        TOTAL COST OF MERCHANDISE AVAILABLE FOR SALE $95,360.00
        LESS MERCHANDISE INVENTORY, SEPTEMBER 30   83,382.00
        COST OF MERCHANDISE SOLD                                 11,978.00

      GROSS PROFIT ON SALES                                     $14,061.00

      EXPENSES
        DELIVERY EXPENSE                          $    235.00
        INSURANCE EXPENSE                               95.00
        MISCELLANEOUS EXPENSE                          116.00
        RENT EXPENSE                                   600.00
        SALARY EXPENSE                               8,952.00
        SUPPLIES EXPENSE                               280.00
        TOTAL EXPENSES                                           10,278.00

      NET INCOME                                               $  3,783.00
```

Income statement

```
                           WAYSIDE FURNITURE
                            CAPITAL STATEMENT
                    FOR MONTH ENDED SEPTEMBER 30, 1977


      RICHARD DAVIS, CAPITAL, SEPTEMBER 1, 1977                 $90,385.00
      NET INCOME FOR SEPTEMBER, 1977            $ 3,783.00
      LESS WITHDRAWALS FOR SEPTEMBER, 1977        1,000.00

      NET INCREASE IN CAPITAL                                    2,783.00

      RICHARD DAVIS, CAPITAL, SEPTEMBER 30, 1977               $93,168.00
```

Capital statement

```
                    WAYSIDE FURNITURE
                      BALANCE SHEET
                   SEPTEMBER 30, 1977

            ASSETS
    CASH                                    $ 8,650.00
    ACCOUNTS RECEIVABLE                      18,877.00
    MERCHANDISE INVENTORY                    83,382.00
    SUPPLIES                                    940.00
    PREPAID INSURANCE                          285.00

    TOTAL ASSETS                                         $112,134.00

            LIABILITIES
    ACCOUNTS PAYABLE                                     $ 18,966.00

            CAPITAL
    RICHARD DAVIS, CAPITAL                                93,168.00

    TOTAL LIABILITIES AND CAPITAL                        $112,134.00
```

Balance sheet

Journalizing the closing entries

The computer program used for Wayside Furniture does not include the instructions necessary to make the closing entries. Therefore, Mr. Davis recorded the closing entries on the journal entry transmittal form shown below.

JOURNAL ENTRY TRANSMITTAL

CLIENT NUMBER _230_   DATE _09/30/77_   PAGE _1_ OF _1_ PAGES

	Acct. No.	Check No.	Purch. No.	Sales No.	Rcpt. No.	COMMENTS	DEBIT	CREDIT	
1	41000					Closing Entries	2603900		1
2	33000							2603900	2
3	33000						1963800		3
4	51000							936000	4
5	61000							23500	5
6	62000							9500	6
7	63000							11600	7
8	64000							60000	8
9	65000							895200	9
10	66000							28000	10
11	33000						378300		11
12	31000							378300	12
13	31000						100000		13
14	32000							100000	14

SUM OF DEBIT ENTRIES	5046000
SUM OF CREDIT ENTRIES	5046000
SUM OF ACCOUNT NUMBERS	666,000

PREPARED BY _Richard Davis_

Journal entry transmittal form for closing entries

The completed journal entry transmittal form is sent to the computer service center where the entries are converted to machine-readable form.

Recording the closing entries for computer processing. One card is punched for each line on the journal entry transmittal form. The punched cards for the closing entries of Wayside Furniture for the month ended September 30, 1977, are shown below.

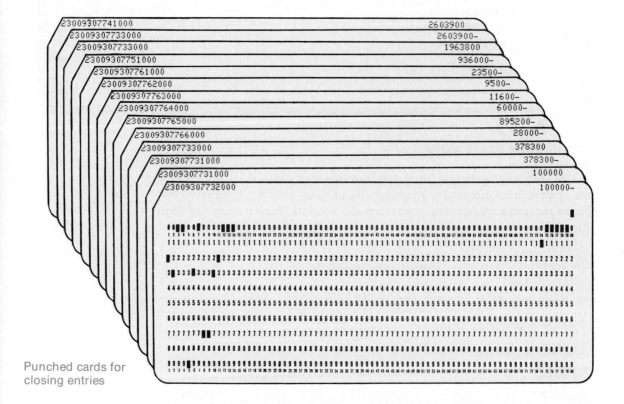

Punched cards for
closing entries

Preparing the post-closing trial balance. In manual accounting the post-closing trial balance is prepared from the general ledger. In automated accounting the post-closing trial balance is prepared by the computer system from data on the magnetic disks used for the general ledger. The flowchart shown at the top of the next page illustrates the processing procedures necessary to prepare the post-closing trial balance for Wayside Furniture.

The steps in processing the post-closing trial balance are as follows:

(1) The computer operator manually places the punched cards in the card reader and starts the computer system. (2) The CPU reads the computer program stored on magnetic disk and transfers the instructions to the internal storage area of the CPU. (3) The data from the punched cards are read and transferred to the internal storage area of the CPU. (4) After

being read the punched cards are manually removed from the card reader and filed in a punched card file. (5) The CPU, according to instructions in the stored computer program, performs the following: (5a) Posts the closing entries to the general ledger; (5b) Computes and arranges the data for the entry register; (5c) Transfers the data for the entry register to the printer. (6) The entry register is printed. (7) An accuracy check is made by comparing the data and control totals on the entry register with the data and control totals on the journal entry transmittal form. After accuracy has been determined, the computer operator starts the computer. (8) The CPU computes, arranges, and transfers the data for the post-closing trial balance to the printer. (9) The post-closing trial balance is printed. (10) The computer printouts are sent to Wayside Furniture.

At Wayside Furniture the computer printouts are inspected and analyzed for management decisions and then filed for future reference. The computer printout of the post-closing trial balance is shown below. The computer printout of the entry register is shown on page 370.

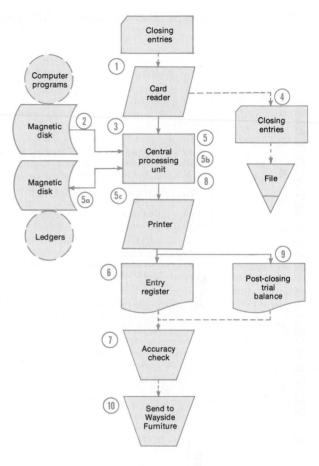

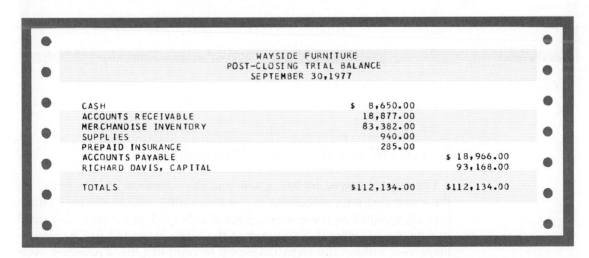

WAYSIDE FURNITURE POST–CLOSING TRIAL BALANCE SEPTEMBER 30,1977		
CASH	$ 8,650.00	
ACCOUNTS RECEIVABLE	18,877.00	
MERCHANDISE INVENTORY	83,382.00	
SUPPLIES	940.00	
PREPAID INSURANCE	285.00	
ACCOUNTS PAYABLE		$ 18,966.00
RICHARD DAVIS, CAPITAL		93,168.00
TOTALS	$112,134.00	$112,134.00

Post-closing trial balance

```
                        WAYSIDE FURNITURE
                         ENTRY REGISTER
                         CLOSING ENTRIES

CLIENT NUMBER 230                                        DATE    09/30/77

        ACCOUNT
        NUMBER          DESCRIPTION              DEBIT            CREDIT

         41000      SALES                     $26,039.00
         33000      INCOME SUMMARY                            $26,039.00
         33000      INCOME SUMMARY            19,638.00
         51000      PURCHASES                                   9,360.00
         61000      DELIVERY EXPENSE                              235.00
         62000      INSURANCE EXPENSE                              95.00
         63000      MISCELLANEOUS EXPENSE                         116.00
         64000      RENT EXPENSE                                  600.00
         65000      SALARY EXPENSE                              8,952.00
         66000      SUPPLIES EXPENSE                              280.00
         33000      INCOME SUMMARY             3,783.00
         31000      RICHARD DAVIS, CAPITAL                      3,783.00
         31000      RICHARD DAVIS, CAPITAL     1,000.00
         32000      RICHARD DAVIS, DRAWING                      1,000.00


                    SUM OF DEBIT ENTRIES      $50,460.00
                    SUM OF CREDIT ENTRIES                     $50,460.00
                    SUM OF ACCOUNT NUMBERS      666,000
```

Entry register for closing entries

SUMMARY OF STEPS FOR THE COMPLETE AUTOMATED ACCOUNTING SYSTEM OF WAYSIDE FURNITURE

The steps followed by Mr. Davis and the computer service center for the automated data processing of the accounting data of Wayside Furniture are outlined in the chart on page 371. Steps 1 and 2 were described in Chapter 18. Steps 3–6 summarize the steps presented in Chapter 19. Steps 7–17 outline the steps necessary to complete the accounting cycle and are described in Chapter 20.

STEPS COMPLETED

AT WAYSIDE FURNITURE	AT COMPUTER SERVICE CENTER

2 Design numbering system for chart of accounts: general ledger and subsidiary ledgers. Prepare chart of accounts setup form and send completed form to computer service center.

1 Advise Wayside Furniture about procedures and form design.

3 Prepare punched cards from chart of accounts setup form. Process punched cards and store data on magnetic disk. Send printouts of charts of accounts to Wayside Furniture.

4 File printouts of charts of accounts for future reference. Prepare journal entry transmittal form for opening entry data and send completed form to computer service center.

5 Prepare punched cards for opening entry from journal entry transmittal form. Process punched cards and post data to magnetic disk. Send printout of entry register to Wayside Furniture.

6 File entry register for future reference.

7 Prepare journal entry transmittal form for daily transactions. Send daily to computer service center.

8 Prepare punched cards for daily transactions from journal entry transmittal form. Process punched cards daily to up date ledgers and post to magnetic disk. Send printout of entry register to Wayside Furniture.

9 File entry register daily for future reference.

11 Inspect printouts for data needed in making management decisions. File computer printouts for future reference.

10 Prepare subsidiary schedules at the end of the fiscal period from data stored on magnetic disk. Send printouts to Wayside Furniture.

13 Inspect printout for data needed in planning adjusting entries. Prepare journal entry transmittal for adjusting entries and send completed form to computer service center. File computer printout for future reference.

12 Prepare trial balance from data stored on magnetic disk. Send printout to Wayside Furniture.

14 Prepare punched cards for adjusting entries from journal entry transmittal form. Process punched cards to produce entry register, income statement, capital statement, and balance sheet. Send printouts to Wayside Furniture.

15 Inspect printouts for data needed in determining closing entries and making management decisions. Prepare journal entry transmittal for closing entries and send completed form to computer service center. File computer printouts for future reference.

16 Prepare punched cards for closing entries from journal entry transmittal form. Process punched cards to produce entry register and post-closing trial balance. Send printouts to Wayside Furniture.

17 Inspect printouts for data needed in making management decisions. File computer printouts for future reference. Post-closing trial balance shows beginning balances in ledger for next fiscal period.

Flowchart of steps for the complete automated accounting system

Using Business Terms

✦ What is the meaning of each of the following?

- batching
- autographic register

Questions for Individual Study

1. What form is used to record the daily transactions in an automated accounting system?
2. Why does the batching procedure reduce the number of journal entries?
3. What is the source document for cash received on account?
4. What is the source document for purchases of merchandise on account?
5. What is the source document for sales of merchandise on account?
6. How often is the journal entry transmittal sent to the computer service center for the recording of daily transactions for computer processing?

7. Where are the subsidiary ledgers stored in an automated accounting system?
8. Why does the automated accounting system not require a work sheet?
9. How is the trial balance used in an automated accounting system?
10. How are the financial statements prepared in an automated accounting system?
11. How is the post-closing trial balance prepared in an automated accounting system?

Cases for Management Decision

CASE 1 Pauline Murphy owns and operates a chain of four gift shops known as Quality Gifts. One store is located in the downtown shopping area and three stores are located in suburban shopping centers. A computer system is installed in the downtown store. All four stores use a journal entry transmittal form to journalize daily transactions for computer processing. Each morning a record of the business transactions from the previous day is delivered to the data processing department of the downtown store. The design of the automated accounting system does not provide for a way to distinguish in which store the business transactions occur. All transactions are combined, punched cards are prepared, and the data are processed as though only one store was involved. Miss Murphy feels a need to be able to analyze business activity by store. What changes might be made to the input media so that transactions could be identified by store?

CASE 2 Melvin Young owns and operates the Central Tire Supply. The business has a large amount of data to process daily. Therefore, a computer system is installed within the firm to process the accounting data. The manager of the data processing center was asked recently to explain to the accounting staff why the total of account numbers was necessary on the journal entry transmittal. How would you explain the importance of the "Sum of Account Numbers" as a control total?

CASE 3 Richard Westbrook uses an automated accounting system. A journal entry transmittal form is used to journalize daily transactions for computer processing. The sum of debits, the sum of credits, and the sum of account numbers are used as control totals. Comparisons of the control listing printed by the computer and the control totals recorded on the journal entry transmittal have been checked out. However, a number of errors have been found in balances of the accounts in the accounts receivable subsidiary ledger. What may be causing the problem?

DRILL 20-D 1 Analyzing the completed journal entry transmittal

Instructions: Turn to the completed journal entry transmittal form for the journalizing of daily transactions, page 357. Answer the following questions:

1. How many combined entries were recorded on the journal entry transmittal of the Wayside Furniture for September 1, 1977?
2. How many sales on account were made on September 1?
3. How many checks were written on September 1?
4. Why are account titles omitted from the journal entry transmittal form?
5. Why is there only one entry to Cash for entries 1–5 shown on lines 1–5?
6. How many transactions involve general ledger accounts?
7. How many transactions involve subsidiary ledger accounts?
8. Did the cash account increase or decrease as a result of the transactions for September 1?

DRILL 20-D 2 Analyzing a systems flowchart

Instructions: Refer to page 359 in your textbook which shows and explains the flowchart for processing daily transactions. Answer the following questions:

1. Why is the line broken in Step 4?
2. Why does Step 2 show a different symbol than Step 4 when both steps involve storage?
3. In what steps does the actual processing take place?
4. What step transfers a computer program to the CPU's internal storage area?
5. In what step is a document printed?
6. What people action takes place in Step 7?

PROBLEM 20-1 Journalizing transactions using a journal entry transmittal

Mr. Harold Garner, owner and operator of the Crestline Department Store, completed the following transactions on November 1, 1977. Mr. Garner arranges all transactions by groups before recording the entries.

Instructions: ▫ **1.** Record on a journal entry transmittal form the transactions listed by groups below and on page 374. Use the account numbers from the chart of accounts for Crestline Department Store illustrated in Problems 18-1 and 18-2, Chapter 18, page 325. Client No. 382.

November 1, 1977. Summary of cash payments for the day:
        Paid cash for November rent, $580.00. Ck623.
        Paid cash for electricity, $93.00. Ck624.
        Paid cash for store supplies, $38.00. Ck625.
        Paid cash on account to Durfee, Inc., $1,360.00. Ck626.
        Paid cash on account to United Shoes, $325.00. Ck627.

November 1, 1977. Summary of cash receipts for the day:
> Received on account from Helene Abler, $93.00. R316.
> Received on account from Keith Allen, $36.00. R317.
> Received on account from Susan Klein, $283.00. R318.
> Cash sales for the day, $1,980.00. R319.

November 1, 1977. Summary of purchases of merchandise on account for the day:
> Purchased merchandise on account from Addison Fabric Supply, $236.00. P716.
> Purchased merchandise on account from Fryman Clothiers, $960.00. P717.

November 1, 1977. Summary of sales of merchandise on account for the day:
> Sold merchandise on account to Robert Bauer, $43.00. S844.
> Sold merchandise on account to Donald Carson, $103.00. S845.
> Sold merchandise on account to Robert Klein, $78.00. S846.
> Sold merchandise on account to Diane Trost, $116.00. S847.

Instructions: □ 2. Compute and enter the control totals.

PROBLEM 20-2 Recording the adjusting entries using a journal entry transmittal

On October 31 of the current year, the end of a fiscal period, the beginning and ending inventories and the value of the prepaid insurance of the Crestline Department Store, Client No. 382, appear as shown below.

	Beginning Balance	Ending Balance
Merchandise Inventory	$3,100.00	$2,980.00
Store Supplies	160.00	125.00
Prepaid Insurance	485.00	436.50

Instructions: □ 1. On a journal entry transmittal form, enter the adjusting entries needed to bring the inventory, supplies, and insurance accounts up to date.

□ 2. Compute and enter the control totals on the journal entry transmittal form.

Optional Problems

MASTERY PROBLEM 20-M Journalizing transactions using a journal entry transmittal

The chart of accounts prepared in Mastery Problem 18-M and Bonus Problem 18-B is needed to complete Mastery Problem 20-M.

John Myers owns and operates the Myers Automotive Supply. The following transactions were completed on January 4, 1978. Mr. Myers arranges all transactions by groups before recording the entries on the journal entry transmittal form.

Instructions: □ **1.** Record the transactions listed by groups below on a journal entry transmittal form. Use the account numbers from the chart of accounts prepared in Problems 18-M and 18-B, Chapter 18. Client No. 423.

January 4, 1978. Summary of cash payments for the day:
        Paid cash for January rent, $450.00. Ck914.
        Paid cash for advertising expense, $63.00. Ck915.
        Paid cash for store supplies, $33.00. Ck916.
        Paid cash for office supplies, $76.00. Ck917.
        Paid cash for purchases of merchandise, $358.00. Ck918.

January 4, 1978. Summary of cash receipts for the day:
        Received on account from Charlotte Abbey, $38.00. R631.
        Received on account from Leonard Adams, $116.00. R632.
        Received on account from John Fleming, $134.00. R633.
        Received on account from Thomas Nash, $55.00. R634.
        Received on account from Carl Woods, $115.00. R635.
        Cash sales for the day, $1,693.00. R636.

January 4, 1978. Summary of sales of merchandise on account for the day:
        Sold merchandise on account to Allen Abbey, $39.00. S803.
        Sold merchandise on account to Paul Acker, $65.00. S804.
        Sold merchandise on account to Kathy Clark, $26.00. S805.
        Sold merchandise on account to John Martin, $118.00. S806.
        Sold merchandise on account to Louis Gray, $104.00. S807.

Instructions: □ **2.** Compute and record the control totals.

**BONUS
PROBLEM 20-B** Preparing a systems flowchart

Steven Mack owns and operates a plumbing supply company. Mr. Mack is converting his manual accounting system to an automated accounting system. The following steps have been completed in preparation for the new system:

1. Mr. Mack designed a new numbering system for his chart of accounts.
2. Mr. Mack prepared a chart of accounts setup form.
3. Mr. Mack sent the completed chart of accounts setup form to the data processing department.
4. The data processing department prepared the punched cards for the chart of accounts.

Instructions: Prepare a systems flowchart that describes the above four steps. Use five symbols, three of which are to be identical. Refer to the flowchart symbols illustrated on page 338.

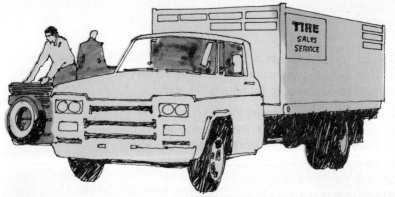

JOHNSTONE
ORCHARD
→

SOCIAL SECU
509-28-
Rich

PAYROLL SYSTEMS

BUSINESSES WITH EMPLOYEES HAVE PAYROLLS.
Businesses are required by law to keep accurate payroll
records and to prepare government reports related to
payroll records. In small businesses, the accountant does
all of the work. In larger businesses, payroll clerks do most
of the routine work. Many businesses also use automated
equipment to prepare some of their payroll records.

PAYROLL RECORDS ARE ESSENTIAL. Every payroll
system includes the same basic payroll records:
(a) employees' pay; (b) employee and employer taxes;
(c) general ledger accounts related to payroll transactions;
and (d) government reports related to payroll. In Part 4 of
this textbook, we shall study the payroll system used by
Johnstone Orchard, a small merchandising business. Also
included is a study of how payroll records may be handled
by automated equipment and by the use of a pegboard.

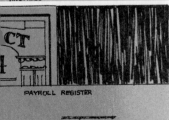

JOHNSTONE ORCHARD
CHART OF ACCOUNTS

(2) LIABILITIES	Account Number
Employees Income Tax Payable	22
FICA Tax Payable	23
Federal Unemployment Tax Payable	24
State Unemployment Tax Payable	25
Hospital Insurance Premiums Payable	26
United Fund Donations Payable	27
U.S. Savings Bonds Payable	28

(6) EXPENSES

Payroll Taxes Expense	64
Salary Expense	65

Payroll accounts of Johnstone Orchard

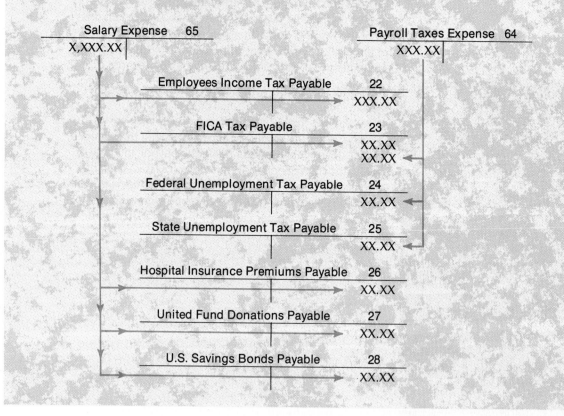

The payroll accounts for Johnstone Orchard are illustrated above
for ready reference as you study Part 4 of this textbook.

Payroll Records

A business periodically pays its employees for their services. The amount of money paid to an employee is known as a wage or a salary. The period covered by the wage or salary payment is called a pay period. Not all businesses base their wage payments on the same length of time. The pay period may be weekly, biweekly, semimonthly, or monthly. The same basic procedure is used for computing the wage or salary regardless of the length of the pay period.

A list of employees that shows payments due them for a pay period is called a payroll. Various methods of doing payroll work are used by different companies. The method used depends on the number of employees, the type of office equipment available, and the amount of time required to do the work. Employees are entitled to receive their salary as close as possible to the end of a pay period. The use of machines speeds the preparation of payroll records and payroll checks. Therefore, many businesses use automated data processing equipment to prepare payrolls. As a result, payroll work that formerly required days to do by hand can now be done in a few hours by machine. The basic accounting principles are the same regardless of whether manual or automated methods are used.

PAYROLL TAXES

Taxes based on the payroll of a business are called payroll taxes. A business is required by law to withhold certain payroll taxes from the salaries paid to employees. A business itself is also required to pay certain payroll taxes. All payroll taxes are based on the earnings of the employees. Accurate and detailed payroll records, therefore, are very important. Errors in payroll records could cause incorrect payments of the payroll taxes. A business that underpays taxes may have to pay a penalty for failure to pay taxes on time.

Employees' income tax

A business is required to withhold federal income tax levied upon its employees' salaries. The business must also forward the tax withheld to the government. Each qualified person supported by the employee, including the employee, entitles the worker to a reduction in the amount of income tax to be paid. For example, a married man supporting a wife and two children pays less income tax than a single person with the same weekly earnings. A deduction for each qualified person supported by a taxpayer is called an exemption. One exemption is allowed for the employee, one exemption for a spouse, and one exemption for each additional person who qualifies as a dependent. Additional exemptions are given for those over 65 years of age and for blindness.

The number of exemptions a worker declares and the marital status of the worker affect the amount that is deducted each pay period for income tax. Whenever a business employs a new worker, that person must report the number of exemptions and the marital status to the employer. The worker does this by filling out and signing Form W-4, Employee's Withholding Allowance Certificate. The Form W-4 for John C. Arthur is shown below and indicates that he is single and claims one exemption for himself.

Form W-4, Employee's Withholding Allowance Certificate

The law requires that each employer have on file a properly filled out Form W-4 for each employee. A revised form should be filed with the employer if the number of exemptions or the marital status changes. The accountant uses the information from the completed Form W-4 when figuring the income tax to be withheld each pay period.

Federal income tax is withheld from employees' earnings in all 50 states. Employers are required in some states also to withhold state or city income taxes from employees' pay. State and local income tax rates vary. Therefore, the employer must be familiar with tax regulations in the community.

Payroll taxes withheld represent a liability for the employer until payment is made. The payment of federal taxes may be made to a district internal revenue service center or to a bank that is authorized to receive such funds for the government.

Some employees may be exempt from having federal taxes withheld from their wages. An example would be a part-time worker, such as a student employed during a vacation period. The employee must certify that no income tax was paid in the prior year and none is expected to be paid for the current year. This is done by filling out a withholding exemption certificate, Form W-4E, which is shown below.

Form W-4E

The employer is not required to withhold federal income tax for employees who have on file a Form W-4E. However, other payroll taxes must still be withheld.

Employees' and employers' social security taxes

All the taxes imposed under the social security laws are called social security taxes. The social security laws of our federal government provide:

1. Old-age, survivors, and disability insurance benefits for qualified employees and their wives or husbands, widows or widowers, dependent children, and parents.
2. Grants to states that provide benefits for persons temporarily unemployed and for certain relief and welfare purposes, such as aid to the blind.
3. Payments to the aged for the costs of certain hospital and related services. The federal health insurance program, designed for people who have reached age 65, is popularly called medicare.

FICA tax. The social security tax paid to the federal government by both employees and employers for use in paying old-age, survivors, disability insurance benefits, and health insurance benefits (medicare) is called FICA tax. FICA is the abbreviation for the Federal Insurance Contributions Act. The FICA tax is based on the amount of wages paid to employees. Employers are required to withhold FICA tax from each employee up to a specified amount of wages paid in the calendar year. Employers must also pay the same rate of FICA tax on the total taxable payroll as each employee pays on a salary.

> The tax bases and the tax rates for social security are set by Congress and may be changed at any time by an act of Congress. Changes are made frequently. Regardless of changes in tax bases and tax rates, the accounting principles involved are the same. Therefore, for purposes of illustration, a rate of 6% on a maximum annual salary of $15,000.00, or a maximum annual FICA tax of $900.00, will be assumed for all payroll calculations in this textbook.

Federal unemployment tax. The tax assessed by the federal government for paying state and federal administrative expenses for the unemployment program is called the federal unemployment tax. This tax is paid entirely by the employer.

State unemployment tax. The tax assessed by the state for paying benefits to unemployed workers is called state unemployment tax. This tax is usually paid by the employer although employee payroll deductions are made in certain states. The Social Security Act specifies certain standards for unemployment compensation laws. Therefore, there is a high degree of uniformity in the state unemployment laws and their requirements. But the details of state unemployment laws do differ. Because of these differences, employers should become familiar with the requirements of the states in which they operate.

Retention of records. The employer is required to keep all payroll records showing payments and deductions. Some records must be kept longer than others. Records pertaining to social security tax payments and deductions should be retained for four years. There are variations in the length of time state unemployment tax payment records should be retained. The period of time is set by state law and varies from state to state, but it is at least four years in every state.

Obtaining a social security card and an account number

Every employee in an occupation covered by the social security laws is required to have a social security number. If a new employee does not have a social security number, the worker must obtain one. An application for a new social security number is shown on page 383.

ID	CN	DO	234	

APPLICATION FOR A SOCIAL SECURITY NUMBER

See Instructions on Back.   Print in Black or Dark Blue Ink or Use Typewriter.

— DO NOT WRITE IN THE ABOVE SPACE —

1 *Print* FULL NAME YOU WILL USE IN WORK OR BUSINESS
(First Name) Nathaniel   (Middle Name or Initial – if none, draw line ___) A.   (Last Name) Gordon

2 *Print* FULL NAME GIVEN YOU AT BIRTH
Nathaniel Alphonso Gordon

6 YOUR DATE OF BIRTH   (Month) (Day) (Year) 1/15/62

3 PLACE OF BIRTH
(City) Cincinnati   (County if known) Hamilton   (State) Ohio

7 YOUR PRESENT AGE (Age on last birthday) 15

4 MOTHER'S FULL NAME AT HER BIRTH (Her maiden name)
Laura Lee Harris

8 YOUR SEX   MALE ☒   FEMALE ☐

5 FATHER'S FULL NAME (Regardless of whether living or dead)
Christopher Jennings Gordon

9 YOUR COLOR OR RACE   WHITE ☐   NEGRO ☒   OTHER ☐

10 HAVE YOU EVER BEFORE APPLIED FOR OR HAD A SOCIAL SECURITY, RAILROAD, OR TAX ACCOUNT NUMBER?   NO ☒   DON'T KNOW ☐   YES ☐   (If "YES" Print STATE in which you applied and DATE you applied and SOCIAL SECURITY NUMBER if known)

11 YOUR MAILING ADDRESS   (Number and Street, Apt. No., P.O. Box, or Rural Route) 16 Lakeview Terrace   (City) Orange   (State) Texas   (Zip Code) 77630

12 TODAY'S DATE 6/1/77

14 NOTICE: Whoever, with intent to falsify his or someone else's true identity, willfully furnishes or causes to be furnished false information in applying for a social security number, is subject to a fine of not more than $1,000 or imprisonment for up to 1 year, or both.

Sign YOUR NAME HERE (Do Not Print)

13 TELEPHONE NUMBER 382-7220   *Nathaniel Alphonso Gordon*

TREASURY DEPARTMENT Internal Revenue Service   FORM SS-5 (2-73)   ☐ RESCREEN   ☒ ASSIGN   ☐ DUP ISSUED   Return completed application to nearest SOCIAL SECURITY ADMINISTRATION OFFICE

Form SS-5, Application for a Social Security Number

The application form may be obtained from any local office of the Social Security Administration and from some post offices. The form should be sent to the nearest field office of the Social Security Administration. A social security card is issued to anyone upon request without charge. Every person seeking a job should obtain a social security card in advance. Having a card simplifies making application for employment. A social security card is shown at the right.

A person who loses a social security card may apply for a new card. On the application blank the person lists the social security number, if known, in Item 10. A new card is issued with the same account number. Each person should have only one account number. An employee having more than one account number may not receive all the benefits to which a person is entitled at retirement.

SOCIAL SECURITY
276-54-1610
THIS NUMBER HAS BEEN ESTABLISHED FOR
Nathaniel A. Gordon
Nathaniel A. Gordon
SIGNATURE

Social security card

If an employee's name is changed by court order or by marriage, the Social Security Administration should be notified of the change. The account number will not be changed. A form for reporting the change in name may be obtained from a social security field office.

Need for social security account number

Each employer must have a social security identification number which appears on state and federal tax reports. The employer is also required to list the social security number of each employee from whom a tax deduction is made.

Social security account numbers of individuals are used in many ways. Banks are required to furnish the federal government with a list of interest payments of $10.00 or more giving the names and social security numbers of the payees. Social security numbers are shown on drivers' licenses in some states and on both personal and business income tax returns. They are used as student identification numbers at some universities and as serial numbers to identify members of the armed forces.

PREPARING THE PAYROLL

The first requirement of an adequate payroll record system is an accurate record of the time each employee has worked. There are several methods of keeping time records. Time cards and time sheets are used most frequently.

Payroll time sheet

Firms with only a few employees usually do not find the use of a time clock economical. A time sheet showing the hours worked is maintained by a supervisor who has knowledge of absences or tardiness of the employees. Some businesses record only the total hours worked each day while others record the exact time the employee arrives and leaves. Time sheets provide the information required by law about the hours worked by each employee. At the end of each pay period the time sheet is submitted to the payroll clerk. The time sheet is used as the basic source of data for the preparation of the payroll.

Payroll time card

Many companies have a time clock which their employees use to record times of arrival and departure. These times are imprinted by the

Time clock

Courtesy of the Cincinnati Time Recorder Company

time clock on a time card. Using a time clock to record the time on the time card is known as ringing in and ringing out. Each employee has his or her name on a card in a rack beside the time clock. The employee rings in when arriving and rings out when leaving. Executives usually are not required to ring in and ring out since their pay is not affected by brief absences from the office.

The Johnstone Orchard, a small company selling fresh citrus fruits, uses a time clock to record the time of arrival and departure of each employee each day. The time card for John C. Arthur, a shipping clerk, for the week ending June 24 is shown on page 385.

Analyzing the payroll time card

At the top of the card is Mr. Arthur's employee number. The use of a number makes it easier for Mr. Arthur to place his time card in the rack in its proper place rather than if his card were filed alphabetically. Below the payroll number are his name, his social security number, and the date of the payroll period.

For recording the time, there are three sections — Morning, Afternoon, and Overtime — with an In and an Out under each section. When Mr. Arthur reported for work on Monday, he inserted the card in the slot in the time clock, which recorded his time of arrival as 7:56. The other entries on this line indicate that he rang out for lunch at 12:00 and in at 12:55 and that he left for the day at 5:02. On Thursday he worked 3⅓ hours overtime, as shown on the line for Thursday.

EMPLOYEE NO. 6							
NAME John C. Arthur							
SOC. SEC. NO. 143-05-0832							
WEEK ENDING June 24, 1977							

MORNING		AFTERNOON		OVERTIME		HOURS	
IN	OUT	IN	OUT	IN	OUT	REG	OT
7:56	12:00	12:55	5:02			8	
7:50	12:01	12:59	5:07			8	
7:51	12:01	12:50	5:04			8	
7:58	12:02	1:01	5:03	6:00	9:20	8	3⅓
8:00	12:05	12:58	5:06			8	

	HOURS	RATE	AMOUNT
REGULAR	40	4.00	160.00
OVERTIME	3⅓	6.00	20.00
TOTAL HOURS	43⅓	TOTAL EARNINGS	180.00

Payroll time card

At the end of the week, the payroll clerk entered in the Hours column the number of hours of regular time and the number of hours of overtime worked each day. Each firm has its own rules regarding deductions for tardiness. The payroll clerk must know these rules in order to make the proper deductions if employees are late or if they leave early.

Determining each employee's total earnings from the time card

Each employee's hours of work and earnings are calculated by the payroll clerk as follows:

☐ 1 Examine the time card for tardiness and early departure and make the necessary notations.

> Mr. Arthur's working day is from 8:00 a.m. to 5:00 p.m. with a one-hour lunch period from 12:00 noon until 1:00 p.m. He reported to work one minute late on Thursday afternoon. Deductions are not made by Johnstone Orchard for such short periods of tardiness.

☐ 2 Extend the regular hours into the Hours Reg. column.

> The regular hours for Mr. Arthur are 8 hours each day Monday through Friday.

☐ 3 Calculate the number of hours of overtime for each day and enter the amount in the Hours OT column.

> Mr. Arthur worked from 6:00 p.m. to 9:20 p.m. on Thursday, so 3⅓ hours are recorded in the OT column.

☐ 4 Add the regular hours and the overtime hours separately and enter the two totals in the spaces provided at the bottom of the card.

□ 5 Enter the rates for regular time and overtime and calculate the regular and overtime earnings.

Mr. Arthur is paid one and one-half times his regular rate for overtime work.

□ 6 Add the Hours column to find the total hours and the Earnings column to find the total earnings. The total of the Earnings column is recorded in the payroll register.

The total pay due for the pay period before deductions is called total earnings. Total earnings are sometimes known as gross pay or gross earnings.

□ 7 File the time cards.

The payroll register

A business form on which the entire payroll is recorded is called a payroll register. The payroll register of the Johnstone Orchard for the week ending June 24 is shown below. All the information about the payroll is recorded on this form — the total earnings from the time cards; amounts deducted for taxes, hospital insurance premiums, savings bonds, and United Fund contributions; total deductions; net pay; and the check number of each payroll check.

PAYROLL REGISTER

WEEK ENDED *June 24, 1977*   DATE OF PAYMENT *June 24, 1977*

EMPL. NO.	EMPLOYEE'S NAME	MARITAL STATUS	NO. OF EXEMPTIONS	TOTAL EARNINGS	DEDUCTIONS						NET PAY	CK. NO.
					INCOME TAX	FICA TAX	HOSP. INS.	OTHER		TOTAL		
1	6 Arthur, John C.	S	1	18000	3080	1080	950	B 475		5585	12415	733
2	11 Austin, Ellen R.	M	3	16250	1720	975	1200			3895	12355	734
3	4 Blake, Charles A.	M	2	13800	1510	828	1200			3538	10262	735
4	1 Cardoni, Henry L.	M	2	17600	2110	1056	1200	B 475 UF 200		5041	12559	736
5	8 Diaz, Mary M.	S	1	17850	2870	1071	950	B 475		5366	12484	737
6	3 Figg, Richard R.	S	1	19000	3290	1140	950	B 475		5855	13145	738
7	14 Garcia, Leslie A.	M	4	18300	1810	1098	1200	B 475		4583	13717	739
8	12 Irwin, Linda T.	S	1	12600	1870	756	950			3576	9024	740
9	5 Lemon, Ronald B.	M	2	13800	1510	828	1200	UF 300		3838	9962	741
10	7 Martinez, Mary S.	M	1	14600	1900	876	1200	UF 200		4176	10424	742
11	9 Rose, Daniel C.	S	1	11200	1550	672	950			3172	8028	743
12	2 Stewart, Roy W.	M	4	19300	1970	1158	1200			4328	14972	744
13	10 Vanquez, Stella J.	M	1	14275	1820	857	1200			3877	10398	745
14	13 Zelty, Alvin B.	M	3	11500	960	690	1200	UF 200		3050	8450	746
15	Totals			218075	27970	13085	15550	UF 900 B 2375		59880	158195	
16												
17												
18												
19												
20												
21												
22												

OTHER DEDUCTIONS: B — U.S. SAVINGS BONDS;   GI — GROUP INSURANCE;   UF — UNITED FUND

Payroll register

The employee number, name, marital status, and number of exemptions claimed are listed in the payroll register for each employee who has performed work during the pay period. The amount of total earnings from the time card is written in the Total Earnings column of the payroll register opposite the employee's name.

Calculating the Deductions section of the payroll register. The Deductions section of the payroll register is used to record the various amounts deducted from the employees' earnings. Certain payroll taxes must be deducted to comply with government regulations. In addition, some companies deduct amounts for hospitalization and group insurance premiums, retirement plans, union dues, U.S. savings bonds, or contributions to the United Fund. These deductions will vary from one company to another depending on policies established by the management.

☐ **1** The Income Tax column is used to record the amount of income tax withheld from each employee's earnings. This amount is determined from tables furnished by the government that take into account the amount of wages earned, the marital status, and the number of exemptions claimed. Portions of tables showing the tax to be withheld based on weekly earnings for married and for single persons are on page 390. These are the tables that were available when materials for this textbook were prepared.

To determine the income tax for John C. Arthur on the $180.00 he earned, the table on page 390 for single persons is used. The proper wage bracket is from $180.00 to $190.00. The income tax to be withheld is the amount shown on this line under the column for one withholding exemption, $30.80.

Income tax tables are also available for daily, biweekly, semi-monthly, and monthly pay periods.

☐ **2** The FICA Tax column is used to record the amount deducted for social security tax. There are two ways to calculate this amount — by referring to a tax table supplied by the government or by multiplying the total earnings by the tax rate.

☐ **3** The Hosp. Ins. column is used to record hospital insurance premiums. Since most employees of Johnstone Orchard subscribe to hospitalization insurance through the company to take advantage of the lower group rate, a special column is used for these deductions. The hospital insurance premium is deducted only once each month.

☐ **4** The Other column is used to list amounts withheld for which no special column is provided. These are voluntary deductions requested by the employee. The entries in this column are identified by code letters. B is used to identify amounts withheld for the purchase of U.S. Savings Bonds. UF is used to identify amounts withheld for contributions to the United Fund. The different items in this column are sorted and classified, and a separate total is shown for each different type of deduction.

☐ 5 The Total column is used to record the total deductions. All the deductions for each employee are added crosswise, and the total is recorded in the Total column.

Completing the payroll register. The Net Pay section is used to record the amount due each employee and the number of the payroll check issued. The net pay is calculated by subtracting the amount of each employee's total deductions from the employee's total earnings.

After the net pay has been recorded for each employee, each of the amount columns is totaled. The accuracy of these additions is verified by subtracting the total of the Total Deductions column from the total of the Total Earnings column. The result should equal the total of the Net Pay column. If the totals do not agree, the errors must be found and corrected. After the totals are proved, a double rule is drawn below the totals across all the amount columns.

Before each check is written for the amount of net pay, the manager or some person designated by the manager examines the payroll computations and approves the payroll. After each check is written, the check number is recorded in the Ck. No. column. This completes the payroll register.

The employee's earnings record

The business form showing details of all items affecting payments made to each employee is called an employee's earnings record. This information is recorded each pay period. The record includes total earnings, deductions for income tax and social security tax and other deductions authorized by the employee, net pay, and accumulated earnings for the calendar year.

Keeping the employee's earnings record

The Johnstone Orchard keeps all of the employee's earnings records on cards. There is one card for each calendar quarter of the year. The quarterly totals are used in the preparation of reports required by the government. At the end of the quarter, the total of the Total Earnings column for each quarter is carried forward to the Accumulated Earnings section on the card for the following quarter. Therefore, the Accumulated Earnings column always reflects the total earnings of the employee from the beginning of the year.

After the payroll register has been prepared and the pay checks written, the payroll data for each employee are recorded on the employee's earnings record. These records are subject to inspection by government officials and must be kept up to date at all times.

Analyzing the employee's earnings record. The employee's earnings record for Mr. Arthur is shown below for the second quarter of 1977. His name is entered at the top of his earnings record, together with his employee number and his social security number.

The amount columns of the employee's earnings record, except for the Accumulated Earnings column, are the same as the amount columns of the payroll register. The amounts opposite the employee's name on the payroll register are recorded in the corresponding columns of the employee's earnings record. The pay period ending June 24 is the thirteenth week in the second quarter. Mr. Arthur's earnings and deductions for that week are therefore entered on Line 13 of his earnings record. The total earnings are then added to the total of Accumulated Earnings on Line 12 to get the new total for the year. This is sometimes known as year-to-date earnings.

EARNINGS RECORD FOR QUARTER ENDING *June 30, 1977*

LAST NAME: *Arthur* FIRST: *John* MIDDLE INITIAL: *C*
EMPLOYEE NO. *6* MARITAL STATUS *S* EXEMPTIONS *1*
SOCIAL SECURITY NO. *143-05-0832*
POSITION *Shipping Clerk*

| Pay Period | | Total Earnings | Deductions | | | | | Net Pay | Accumulated Earnings |
Week No.	Week Ended		Income Tax	FICA Tax	Hosp. Ins.	Other	Total		
									2048 00
1	4/1	16000	2660	960		B 475	4095	11905	220800
2	4/8	16000	2660	960		B 475	4095	11905	236800
3	4/15	16800	2660	1008		B 475	4143	12657	253600
4	4/22	16200	2660	972	950	B 475	5057	11143	269800
5	4/29	17000	2870	1020		B 475	4365	12635	286800
6	5/6	16600	2660	996		B 475	4131	12469	303400
7	5/13	16000	2660	960		B 475	4095	11905	319400
8	5/20	16000	2660	960		B 475	4095	11905	335400
9	5/27	16200	2660	972	950	B 475	5057	11143	351600
10	6/3	16800	2660	1008		B 475	4143	12657	368400
11	6/10	16000	2660	960		B 475	4095	11905	384400
12	6/17	16400	2660	984		B 475	4119	12281	400800
13	6/24	18000	3080	1080	950	B 475	5585	12415	418800
QUARTERLY TOTALS		214000	35210	12840	2850	86175	57075	156925	

Employee's earnings record

The Accumulated Earnings column shows the earnings for Mr. Arthur since the first of the year. The first entry in this column, $2,048.00, is the total amount of his earnings brought forward from his earnings record for the first quarter. The amounts in the Accumulated Earnings column supply an up-to-date reference for seeing when an employee's earnings have reached an amount beyond which certain payroll taxes do not apply. For example, employers do not have to pay state and federal unemployment taxes on the wages of an employee whose earnings for a year have reached a specified amount. Also, the maximum amount on which FICA taxes are paid is determined by law.

The Quarterly Totals line provides space for the totals for the quarter. These totals are needed to prepare reports required by the government.

INCOME TAX WITHHOLDING TABLES

SINGLE Persons—WEEKLY Payroll Period

And the wages are—		And the number of withholding allowances claimed is—										
At least	But less than	0	1	2	3	4	5	6	7	8	9	10 or more
		The amount of income tax to be withheld shall be—										
$100	$105	$16.50	$13.40	$10.40	$7.80	$5.20	$2.80	$.80	$0	$0	$0	$0
105	110	17.50	14.50	11.50	8.70	6.10	3.50	1.50	0	0	0	0
110	115	18.60	15.50	12.50	9.60	7.00	4.40	2.20	.10	0	0	0
115	120	19.60	16.60	13.60	10.50	7.90	5.30	2.90	.80	0	0	0
120	125	20.70	17.60	14.60	11.60	8.80	6.20	3.60	1.50	0	0	0
125	130	21.70	18.70	15.70	12.60	9.70	7.10	4.50	2.20	.20	0	0
130	135	22.80	19.70	16.70	13.70	10.70	8.00	5.40	2.90	.90	0	0
135	140	23.80	20.80	17.80	14.70	11.70	8.90	6.30	3.70	1.60	0	0
140	145	24.90	21.80	18.80	15.80	12.80	9.80	7.20	4.60	2.30	.30	0
145	150	25.90	22.90	19.90	16.80	13.80	10.80	8.10	5.50	3.00	1.00	0
150	160	27.50	24.50	21.40	18.40	15.40	12.30	9.50	6.90	4.30	2.00	0
160	170	29.60	26.60	23.50	20.50	17.50	14.40	11.40	8.70	6.10	3.50	1.40
170	180	31.70	28.70	25.60	22.60	19.60	16.50	13.50	10.50	7.90	5.30	2.80
180	190	33.80	30.80	27.70	24.70	21.70	18.60	15.60	12.60	9.70	7.10	4.50
190	200	35.90	32.90	29.80	26.80	23.80	20.70	17.70	14.70	11.70	8.90	6.30
200	210	38.10	35.00	31.90	28.90	25.90	22.80	19.80	16.80	13.80	10.70	8.10
210	220	40.40	37.10	34.00	31.00	28.00	24.90	21.90	18.90	15.90	12.80	9.90
220	230	42.70	39.30	36.10	33.10	30.10	27.00	24.00	21.00	18.00	14.90	11.90
230	240	45.10	41.60	38.30	35.20	32.20	29.10	26.10	23.10	20.10	17.00	14.00
240	250	47.80	43.90	40.60	37.30	34.30	31.20	28.20	25.20	22.20	19.10	16.10

MARRIED Persons—WEEKLY Payroll Period

And the wages are—		And the number of withholding allowances claimed is—										
At least	But less than	0	1	2	3	4	5	6	7	8	9	10 or more
		The amount of income tax to be withheld shall be—										
$100	$105	$14.10	$11.80	$9.50	$7.20	$4.90	$2.80	$.80	$0	$0	$0	$0
105	110	14.90	12.60	10.30	8.00	5.70	3.50	1.50	0	0	0	0
110	115	15.70	13.40	11.10	8.80	6.50	4.20	2.20	.10	0	0	0
115	120	16.50	14.20	11.90	9.60	7.30	5.00	2.90	.80	0	0	0
120	125	17.30	15.00	12.70	10.40	8.10	5.80	3.60	1.50	0	0	0
125	130	18.10	15.80	13.50	11.20	8.90	6.60	4.30	2.20	.20	0	0
130	135	18.90	16.60	14.30	12.00	9.70	7.40	5.10	2.90	.90	0	0
135	140	19.70	17.40	15.10	12.80	10.50	8.20	5.90	3.60	1.60	0	0
140	145	20.50	18.20	15.90	13.60	11.30	9.00	6.70	4.40	2.30	.30	0
145	150	21.30	19.00	16.70	14.40	12.10	9.80	7.50	5.20	3.00	1.00	0
150	160	22.50	20.20	17.90	15.60	13.30	11.00	8.70	6.40	4.10	2.00	0
160	170	24.10	21.80	19.50	17.20	14.90	12.60	10.30	8.00	5.70	3.40	1.40
170	180	26.00	23.40	21.10	18.80	16.50	14.20	11.90	9.60	7.30	5.00	2.80
180	190	28.00	25.20	22.70	20.40	18.10	15.80	13.50	11.20	8.90	6.60	4.30
190	200	30.00	27.20	24.30	22.00	19.70	17.40	15.10	12.80	10.50	8.20	5.90
200	210	32.00	29.20	26.30	23.60	21.30	19.00	16.70	14.40	12.10	9.80	7.50
210	220	34.40	31.20	28.30	25.40	22.90	20.60	18.30	16.00	13.70	11.40	9.10
220	230	36.80	33.30	30.30	27.40	24.50	22.20	19.90	17.60	15.30	13.00	10.70
230	240	39.20	35.70	32.30	29.40	26.50	23.80	21.50	19.20	16.90	14.60	12.30
240	250	41.60	38.10	34.60	31.40	28.50	25.60	23.10	20.80	18.50	16.20	13.90

Section of income tax withholding tables for weekly pay period

PAYING THE PAYROLL

Some firms pay their employees in cash. This practice is usually followed when the employees find it difficult to reach a bank to have their checks cashed. However, most businesses find that paying their employees by check is more convenient.

Paying the payroll by check

The Johnstone Orchard pays its employees by check. Mr. Johnstone uses a special payroll check form that has a detachable stub on which are recorded the amounts deducted. The employee detaches the stub for a record of deductions and cash received.

The information for the payroll checks is taken from the payroll register. A payroll check for the pay period ending June 24 is shown below.

	JOHNSTONE ORCHARD							733

JOHNSTONE ORCHARD
ORANGE, TX 77630

June 24 19 77   88-21 / 1131   733

PAY TO THE ORDER OF John C. Arthur $124.15

One hundred twenty-four 15/00 ----------------------------------- DOLLARS

ORANGE CITIZENS BANK
Orange, TX 77630

JOHNSTONE ORCHARD
Romero Johnstone

⑈1131⑈002⑈790⑈01363⑈

STATEMENT OF EMPLOYEE EARNINGS AND PAYROLL DEDUCTIONS

PERIOD ENDING	HOURS	EARNINGS REG.	EARNINGS O.T.	TOTAL EARNINGS	INCOME TAX	FICA TAX	HOSP. INS.	U.S. SAVINGS BONDS	OTHER	NET PAY
6/24/77	43⅓	160.00	20.00	180.00	30.80	10.80	9.50	4.75		124.15

JOHNSTONE ORCHARD

Payroll check with detachable stub

After the payroll register is completed, a check for the amount of the total payroll is drawn on Johnstone Orchard's regular checking account and deposited in a separate bank account. Only the check drawn for the total payroll is recorded in the combination journal. Detailed data about the payroll are obtained from the payroll register.

Paying the payroll in cash

When the payroll is to be paid in cash, the payroll clerk must obtain the cash from the bank in the proper denominations in order to have the necessary change for each pay envelope. Therefore, the payroll clerk prepares a payroll change sheet.

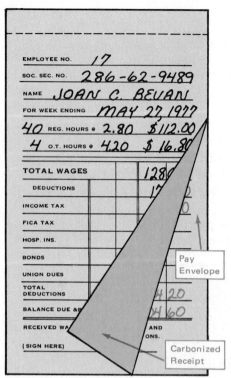

EMPLOYEE NO.	*17*		
SOC. SEC. NO.	*286-62-9489*		
NAME	*JOAN C. BEVAN*		
FOR WEEK ENDING	*MAY 27, 1977*		
40 REG. HOURS ● *2.80*	*$112.00*		
4 O.T. HOURS ● *4.20*	*$16.80*		
TOTAL WAGES		*128.8(*	
DEDUCTIONS		*17*	
INCOME TAX			*0*
FICA TAX			
HOSP. INS.			
BONDS			
UNION DUES			
TOTAL DEDUCTIONS		*4.20*	
BALANCE DUE &P		*4.60*	
RECEIVED WA		AND ONS.	
(SIGN HERE)			

Pay Envelope

Carbonized Receipt

Combination payroll
envelope and
receipt

The payroll change sheet lists each employee and the total pay due each. There is also an amount column for each denomination of bill and coin that will be required. In these columns are listed the quantity of each denomination of bill and coin necessary for each individual's pay envelope. The columns are then totaled to determine how many bills and coins of each denomination to requisition from the bank. These forms are not shown since most businesses today pay their employees by check. After the cash is received from the bank, each employee's pay is placed in a separate envelope along with a payroll receipt similar to the one at the left.

Since more time is required to requisition change and prepare pay envelopes for cash payment and there is more chance for error and theft, most employers prefer to pay by check.

Payroll receipt

When the payroll check has an itemized stub, a separate payroll receipt is not necessary. The gross pay, deductions, and net pay are itemized on the check stub. However, when the payroll is paid by cash, a separate receipt giving this information is prepared. The employer keeps one copy and the employee receives a copy for a record.

Sometimes the payroll receipt is a stub attached to the pay envelope. The one shown above has been prepared in this way. When the stub is torn off for the company's records, a duplicate copy is on the pay envelope for the employee's records. The information for the receipt is obtained from the payroll register. Some companies require the employee to sign the receipt.

Self-processed pay checks

Some businesses use self-processed pay checks to save time and effort for the payroll department. The payroll must still be computed, but individual checks are not written and do not have to be distributed. The payroll bank account is no longer necessary. Therefore, a reconciliation of this account is not required.

Under this system the payroll department prepares the payroll register and a statement of earnings and deductions for each employee. The employees' statements are given to them on payday so they can compare them with the amount of the payroll deposit. The company furnishes the bank a copy of the payroll register along with a check for the amount of the total payroll. The bank credits the individual employee's checking account at the bank. The employee may withdraw cash from the bank by writing a check.

Payroll accounting using a pegboard

A special board used to write the same information at one time on several separate kinds of forms held in place by a number of pegs is called a pegboard. The pegboard is also known as an accounting board. One form of a pegboard is shown below.

A pegboard

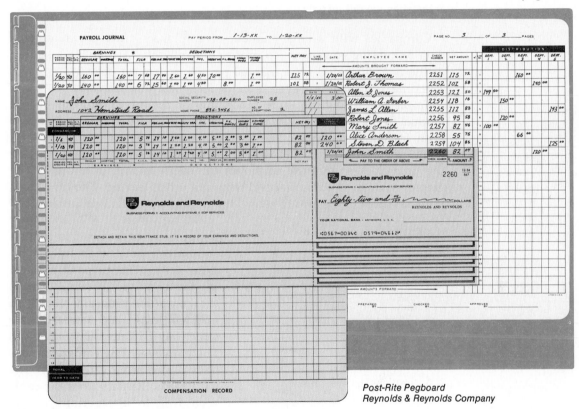

Post-Rite Pegboard
Reynolds & Reynolds Company

The name of the pegboard comes from the pegs along one side of the board. The forms used with this device have holes punched along one side. Each of the forms is placed on the pegs so that the line on each form on which data are to be written is aligned one below the other.

When a payroll is recorded, a page of the payroll register is attached to the pegboard. Next, the employee's earnings record is properly positioned on top of the payroll register page. Then, the check is positioned on top of both of these sheets. Thus, as each payroll check is written, the same data also are recorded on the employee's earnings record and on the payroll register. The data are written only once, but they are recorded on three different records at the same time. The procedure of producing more than one copy of the same data in only one writing is called the write-it-once principle.

The pegboard has two major purposes: (1) to provide a solid writing base for writing on the forms by hand, and (2) to provide a means of holding several forms in alignment while data are being recorded in the proper space on each form with one writing.

Automating payroll records

Companies with a large number of employees often use automated data processing equipment to process payroll data. A time clock similar to the one illustrated for a manual payroll system on page 384 is used. The time card used, however, is in the form of a punched card.

Employees follow the same procedure for ringing in and out as in a manual data processing system. A time card is prepared in punched card form for each employee. The punched time card has the employee's name and number punched into it. The punched card is placed beside the time clock so that the employee can see it to ring in and out. The employee rings in on arrival and rings out when leaving. The time clock punches holes in the card to record the time of arrival and departure.

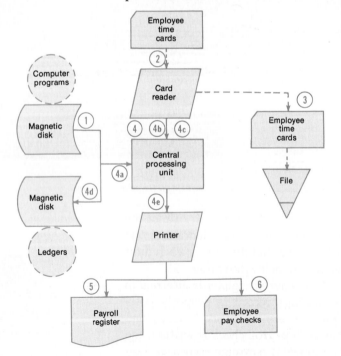

The flowchart at the left shows the procedures required to process the payroll time cards by a computer system. The steps in processing the data are: (1) The CPU reads the computer program stored on magnetic disks and stores the instructions in internal storage. (2) The employee time cards are manually placed in the card reader. The CPU reads the data from the cards according to instructions in the stored computer program. The data are stored in internal storage. (3) Employee time cards are manually removed from the card reader and filed. (4) The CPU reads the instructions in the stored computer program and does the following: (4a) Reads the payroll data and accumulated earnings data for each employee from magnetic disks. The payroll data include the name, employee number, rate of pay, and voluntary deductions. The accumulated earnings data include the totals of all earnings and deductions from previous pay periods; (4b) Computes the data for the payroll register; (4c) Adds the data for the current pay period to the accumulated data from the previous pay periods; (4d) Transfers the totals from 4c to disk storage. These totals will be used for processing the payroll for the next payroll period and for processing an employee's earnings record at the end of the quarter; (4e) Arranges the data in an order for printing the output and transfers the results to the printer. (5) The payroll register is printed. (6) The employee pay checks are printed. The pay checks are in the form of punched cards.

✦What is the meaning of each of the following?

Using
Business
Terms

- pay period
- payroll
- payroll taxes
- exemption
- social security taxes
- medicare
- FICA tax
- federal unemployment tax
- state unemployment tax
- total earnings
- payroll register
- employee's earnings record
- pegboard
- write-it-once principle

Questions
for
Individual
Study

1. What determines the method used for doing payroll work?
2. Why is it necessary for a business to keep accurate payroll records?
3. How does an employer collect for the federal government the income tax of the employees?
4. How does an employer know how many exemptions each employee is entitled to?
5. Give an example of an employee entitled to a withholding exemption.
6. How are tax bases and tax rates for social security changed?
7. How long must records pertaining to social security tax payments and deductions be retained?
8. How does a person obtain a social security card?
9. What are the principal types of information recorded on the time card illustrated on page 385?
10. How many hours of overtime did John C. Arthur work according to his time card on page 385?
11. How is the amount of income tax withheld from an employee's wages determined?
12. What is the main purpose of the Accumulated Earnings column on the employee's earnings record?
13. What is the difference between the time card used in a manual payroll system and the time card used in an automated payroll system?
14. How are paychecks prepared in an automated payroll system?

Cases for
Management
Decision

CASE 1 The Valley Insurance Company has a clerical office staff of 23 employees. A handwritten time card is currently being used to record arrival and departure time for each employee. The accountant suggests that a time clock be installed to record the arrival and departure times. The office manager believes that the present system is satisfactory. Do you agree with the accountant or with the office manager? Give your reasons.

CASE 2 The Doyle Department Store is now paying its 18 employees in cash every two weeks. The accountant has recently talked with a representative of a business forms manufacturing company, who has recommended that the store pay its employees by check. The payroll clerk, too, feels that this would be a desirable change in the payroll accounting system. What factors should the accountant investigate before making a recommendation to management that the present system of paying employees be changed?

DRILL 21-D 1   Determining payroll income tax withholdings

This drill is planned to give you practice in determining the federal income tax that must be withheld from employees' gross pay for each payroll period. The marital status, number of exemptions, and total earnings for five employees on the weekly payroll of July 15, 1977, are shown below.

Employee's Name	Marital Status	Number of Exemptions	Total Earnings
1. Ann Bulger	S	1	$125.00
2. Charles Burch	M	3	123.00
3. Irwin Daniels	M	2	134.00
4. Karen Holmes.......	S	1	115.00
5. Mary Laurence......	M	2	135.00

Instructions: □ **1.** On a sheet of paper number from 1 to 5.

□ **2.** Determine the income tax that must be withheld for each of the five employees. Use the income tax withholding tables on page 390.

DRILL 21-D 2   Figuring total weekly earnings for employees

The information listed below is taken from the time cards for each employee.

Employee Number	Hours worked Regular	Hours worked Overtime	Pay Rate	Amount of pay Regular	Amount of pay Overtime	Total Earnings
1	40	2	$4.00	$160.00	$12.00	$172.00
2	40	6	4.25			
3	35	0	3.50			
4	40	3	4.50			
5	40	0	4.50			

Instructions: For each employee, figure the amount of regular pay, overtime pay, and total earnings. The amounts for Employee Number 1 are given as an example. Overtime hours are paid at one and one-half times the regular pay rate.

PROBLEM 21-1   Applying for a social security account number

If the workbook correlating with this textbook is not available, this problem may be omitted.

Instructions: Fill in the application for a social security account number given in the workbook. Use your own personal data. Compare your application with the illustration on page 383.

PROBLEM 21-2   Using payroll time cards

If the workbook correlating with this textbook is not available, complete Review Problem 21-R 1 instead of this problem.

Instructions: ◻ **1.** Complete the time cards given in the workbook.

◻ **2.** Record the time cards in a payroll register similar to the one on page 386 of the textbook. The date of payment is April 22.

◻ **3.** Use the income tax withholding tables on page 390 to find the income tax deduction for each employee. Deduct 6% of each employee's total earnings for FICA taxes.

PROBLEM 21-3   Preparing an employee's earnings record

The total earnings of Marcia Higgins for the 13 weeks in the quarterly period October through December of the current year are given below, together with the deductions for hospitalization insurance.

Week Ended	Total Earnings	Deductions	Week Ended	Total Earnings	Deductions
10/7	$140.00	$9.50	11/25	$139.76	
10/14	138.00		12/2	130.00	
10/21	139.76		12/9	130.00	$9.50
10/28	134.88		12/16	123.50	
11/4	136.00	9.50	12/23	125.00	
11/11	130.00		12/30	136.00	
11/18	144.64				

Instructions: Prepare an employee's earnings record, similar to the one on page 389, for Marcia Higgins for the fourth quarter of the current year. Additional data needed to complete the record are as follows:

(1) Miss Higgins' time card number is 38.
(2) Miss Higgins' social security number is 286-05-1609.
(3) Miss Higgins' position is that of secretary.
(4) Miss Higgins' accumulated earnings for the first three quarters of the current year amount to $4,757.04.
(5) In addition to her deductions for hospitalization insurance, the following deductions for taxes should be made:
    (a) A deduction is to be made from her total earnings each week for her income tax withheld. Miss Higgins claims only one withholding exemption for herself. Use the weekly income tax withholding table on page 390 to obtain each of her weekly income tax deductions.
    (b) A deduction of 6% of her total earnings each week is to be made for FICA taxes.

PROBLEM 21-4 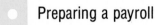 Preparing a payroll

Midway Supply Company pays its employees by check. For each pay period the payroll clerk prepares a payroll register showing the total earnings, the deductions, and the net pay of each employee.

A part of the payroll register for the week ended March 18 of the current year is given below. This portion of the payroll register shows the number, the name, the marital status, the number of exemptions, the total earnings, and other deductions of each employee.

						PAYROLL REGISTER				
Week Ended March 18, 19—							Date of Payment			
							Deductions			
No.	Employee's Name	Marital Status	Number of Exemptions	Total Earnings		Income Tax	FICA Tax	Hosp. Ins.	Other	
3	Barry, John.............	S	1	138.00					B 6.00	
1	Benson, Harold.......	M	3	118.00						
2	Clark, George	S	1	106.00						
10	Calvin, Sarah..........	M	4	112.00					UF 3.00	
7	Deters, Nancy.........	S	1	108.00					B 2.00	
4	French, O. D.	M	3	122.00					UF 2.00	
5	Heaton, Ruth..........	M	2	103.00						
9	Lawton, Paul..........	M	4	102.00						
8	Manning, Helen......	S	1	106.00						
6	Riley, R. C.	M	4	136.00					B 9.00	

Other Deductions: B — Bonds, UF — United Fund

Instructions: □ **1.** Prepare a payroll register similar to the one illustrated on page 386. The date of payment is March 21. Payroll checks, beginning with the one for Mr. Barry on Line 1, are numbered consecutively. Mr. Barry's payroll check is No. 268.

□ **2.** Use the income tax withholding tables on page 390 to find the income tax deduction for each employee. Deduct 6% of each employee's total earnings for FICA taxes.

□ **3.** Prepare a check for the total amount of the net pay. Make the check payable to *Payroll Account*, and sign your name as treasurer of the company. This check will be deposited in a separate bank account against which all payroll checks will be drawn.

□ **4.** Prepare payroll checks for John Barry and Harold Benson. Sign your name as treasurer of the company.

MASTERY
PROBLEM 21-M   Preparing a payroll

A part of a payroll register for the week ended July 22 of the current year, showing the number, the name, the marital status, the number of exemptions, the total earnings, and other deductions of each employee, is given below.

	PAYROLL REGISTER							
Week Ended July 22, 19—					Date of Payment			
						Deductions		
No.	Employee's Name	Marital Status	Number of Exemptions	Total Earnings	Income Tax	FICA Tax	Hosp. Ins.	Other
6	Burke, Elsie............	S	1	113.00				B 4.00
5	Carter, Nancy.........	S	1	103.40				
4	Decker, Bruce.........	M	2	130.00			3.30	
14	Faulkner, G. T.	M	4	112.00				
2	Hafner, Louise........	M	3	118.50				
15	Lincoln, Thomas	M	4	140.00			3.60	
9	Malloy, Martha	M	2	116.00				
7	Norton, Joan	S	1	108.00				B 2.00
13	Powell, Audrey.......	S	1	113.00				
1	Sherman, Judith......	M	3	106.80				B 3.50
11	Sikes, Fred.............	M	2	118.60			3.30	
8	Taylor, Donald........	M	2	132.40			3.30	
12	Voight, Ellen	S	1	108.00				
3	Ward, Marie...........	S	1	116.30				B 5.00
10	Ziegler, L. R.	M	3	115.20				

Other Deductions: B — Bonds

Instructions: ☐ **1.** Prepare a payroll register similar to the one illustrated on page 386. The date of payment is July 25. Begin with Check No. 582.

☐ **2.** Use the income tax withholding tables on page 390 to find the income tax deduction for each employee. Deduct 6% of each employee's total earnings for FICA taxes.

BONUS
PROBLEM 21-B   Computing piecework wages

Introductory remarks. Production workers in factories are frequently paid on the basis of the number of units they produce. This is known as the piecework incentive wage plan. Most piecework wage plans include a guaranteed hourly rate to employees regardless of the number of units they produce. This guaranteed hourly rate is known as the base rate.

Time and motion study engineers usually determine the standard time required for producing a single unit. For example, if the time studies determine that 6 minutes is the standard time required to produce a unit, then the standard rate for one hour would be 10 units (60 minutes ÷ 6 minutes = 10 units per hour). If the worker's base pay is $2.80 per hour, the piece rate is 28¢ ($2.80 ÷ 10 units = 28¢ per unit). Therefore, the worker who produces 10 or less units per hour is paid the base pay, $2.80 per hour. But for every unit in excess of 10 that the worker produces each hour, the worker is paid 28¢ in addition to the base pay.

The Youngstown Manufacturing Company has a crew of three working in the welding department and a crew of three working in the assembly department. Standard production for the welding department is 12 units per hour per worker. Standard production for the assembly department is 8 units per hour per worker. Each of the workers in both departments worked 8 hours a day during the first week in October. Payroll records for the week ended October 7 show the following data:

No.	Worker	Marital Status	No. of Exemptions	Guaranteed Hourly Rate	Units Produced					Weekly Total
					M	Tu	W	Th	F	
	Welding Department:									
W3	Sara Bradshaw	S	1	$2.80	96	93	95	105	98	487
W8	Arthur Drake	M	4	2.80	90	93	96	98	96	473
W6	Roy White	M	3	2.80	106	103	117	108	102	536
	Assembly Department:									
A14	Mark Fender	M	2	2.40	70	66	66	71	73	346
A6	Larry Griffin	S	1	2.40	74	70	68	68	70	350
A9	Jenny Klein	M	3	2.40	66	69	63	65	72	335

There is a piecework incentive rate for the welding department of 23¢ per unit and for the assembly department of 30¢ per unit.

Instructions: □ **1.** Prepare a payroll register similar to the one illustrated on page 386. The date of payment is October 10. Begin with Check No. 743.

□ **2.** Use the income tax withholding tables on page 390 to find the income tax deduction for each employee. Deduct 6% of each employee's total earnings for FICA taxes. None of the employees had "Other" deductions.

Payroll Accounts, Taxes, and Reports

22

The payroll register is used to summarize the payroll data for each pay period. The payroll register is the source document for journalizing the payroll entry.

JOURNALIZING THE PAYROLL IN THE COMBINATION JOURNAL

A portion of the payroll register of Johnstone Orchard for the week ended June 24 is shown below.

PAYROLL REGISTER

WEEK ENDED *June 24, 1977* DATE OF PAYMENT *June 24, 1977*

	EMPL. NO.	EMPLOYEE'S NAME	MARITAL STATUS	NO. OF EXEMPTIONS	TOTAL EARNINGS	DEDUCTIONS: INCOME TAX	FICA TAX	HOSP. INS.	OTHER	TOTAL	NET PAY	CK. NO.	
1	6	Arthur, John C.	S	1	180 00	30 80	10 80	9 50	B 4 75	55 85	124 15	733	1
13	10	Vanquez, Stella J.	M	1	142 75	18 20	8 57	12 00		38 77	103 98	745	13
14	13	Zolty, Alvin B.	M	3	115 00	9 60	6 90	12 00	UF 2 00	30 50	84 50	746	14
15		Totals			2180 75	279 70	130 85	155 50	B 23 75 UF 9 00	598 80	1581 95		15
16													16
17													17

OTHER DEDUCTIONS: B — U.S. SAVINGS BONDS; GI — GROUP INSURANCE; UF — UNITED FUND

Payroll register

Analyzing the debits and the credits in the payroll register

The debits and the credits based on the column totals of the payroll register are summarized in the T accounts at the top of page 402.

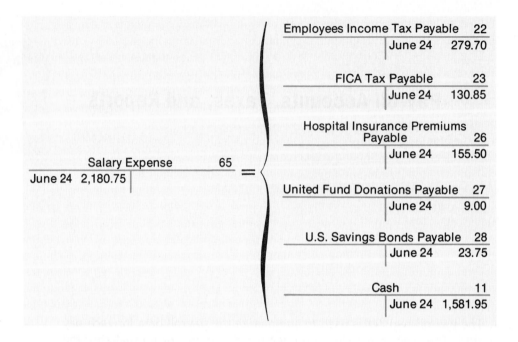

The total of the Total Earnings column, $2,180.75, is the salary expense for the period. Salary Expense is therefore debited for this amount.

The total of the Income Tax column, $279.70, is the amount withheld from the employees' salaries for federal income tax. The amount withheld is a liability of the business until the tax is paid to the government. Employees Income Tax Payable is credited for $279.70 to record this liability.

The total of the FICA Tax column, $130.85, is the amount withheld from salaries of employees for FICA tax. The amount withheld is a liability of the business until the tax is paid the government. To record this liability, FICA Tax Payable is credited for $130.85.

The total of the Hosp. Ins. column, $155.50, is the amount withheld from salaries to apply on the insurance premium. The amount withheld is a liability of the business until the premium is paid to the insurance company. Hospital Insurance Premiums Payable is credited for $155.50 to record this liability.

The Other column of the Deductions section may contain more than one total. In the payroll register shown on page 401 there are two types of other deductions for which there is no special column.

The $23.75 total in the Other column is the amount withheld from salaries of employees who wish to have U.S. Savings Bonds purchased for them. The total of $9.00, also in the Other column, is the amount withheld from salaries to apply on the pledges that employees have made to the annual United Fund drive. Until these amounts have been paid by the employer, they are liabilities of the business. To record these two liabilities, United Fund Donations Payable is credited for $9.00 and U.S. Savings Bonds Payable is credited for $23.75.

The total of the Net Pay column, $1,581.95, the amount of cash paid to employees, is credited to Cash.

The payroll entry in the combination journal

The payroll check was issued on June 24. The entry made in the combination journal to record the totals of the June 24 payroll register is shown below.

PAGE *12*   COMBINATION JOURNAL

CASH DEBIT	CASH CREDIT	DATE	ACCOUNT TITLE	Doc. No.	Post. Ref.	GENERAL DEBIT	GENERAL CREDIT	
	1581 95	24	Salary Expense	ck721		2180 75		11
			Empl. Income Tax Pay.				279 70	12
			FICA Tax Payable				130 85	13
			Hosp. Ins. Prem. Pay.				155 50	14
			U. Fund Donations Pay.				9 00	15
			U.S. Savings Bonds Pay.				23 75	16
								17
								18

Entry to record the payroll

The amount of the Salary Expense, $2,180.75, is written in the General Debit column. The credit to Cash, $1,581.95, is written in the Cash Credit column. The amounts of the two tax liabilities and the other liabilities are written in the General Credit column.

POSTING THE PAYROLL ENTRY FROM THE COMBINATION JOURNAL

The amounts recorded in the General Debit and General Credit columns of the combination journal are posted individually to the accounts in the general ledger. After the payroll entry of June 24 is posted, the five liability accounts and the salary expense account appear as shown below and on the next page.

ACCOUNT *Employees Income Tax Payable*   ACCOUNT NO. *22*

DATE	ITEM	Post. Ref.	DEBIT	CREDIT	BALANCE DEBIT	BALANCE CREDIT
24		12		279 70		1298 50

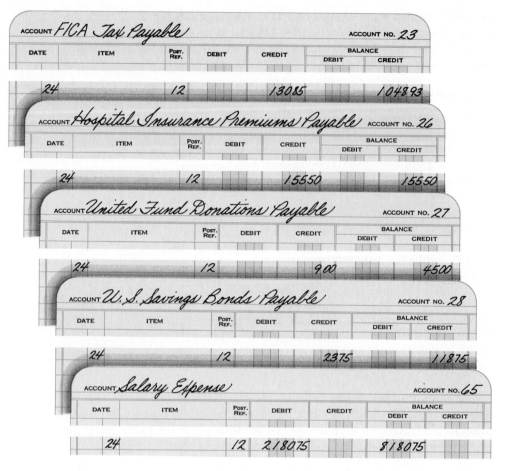

The credit to Cash, $1,581.95, is not posted separately to the cash account. The amount is included with the Cash Credit column total of the combination journal that is posted at the end of the month.

JOURNALIZING THE EMPLOYER'S PAYROLL TAXES

Employers must pay to the government the taxes they withhold from their employees' earnings. Most employers must pay several payroll taxes of their own. The employer's payroll taxes are expenses of the business.

The employer's FICA tax

The employer's share of the FICA tax is computed at the same rate and on the same earnings used in figuring the employees' FICA tax.

The Johnstone Orchard withheld $130.85 in FICA tax from the pay of its employees for the pay period ended June 24, 1977. The amount,

$130.85, was obtained by totaling the FICA Tax column of the payroll register. The employer's FICA tax is figured by multiplying the tax rate by the Total Earnings column. Thus, for the pay period ended June 24, the employer's FICA tax is $130.85 ($2,180.75 × 6%).

Sometimes there is a difference of a few cents between the total employer's FICA tax and the total employees' FICA tax. This difference is caused by the rounding of fractional cents when making the calculations. The employees' tax is based on the taxable amount earned by each employee during the pay period. The employer's tax is based on the total taxable wages paid to all employees during the pay period. In the case above there is no difference.

The FICA tax of Johnstone Orchard, $130.85, is included in a combined journal entry illustrated on page 406.

The employer's federal unemployment tax

Under the provisions of the federal and the state unemployment insurance laws, employers are required to pay taxes that are used for unemployment compensation. The unemployment taxes are based on the taxable amount of the total salaries. In most states these taxes are levied on the employers only.

Under the federal unemployment insurance law, employers are required also to pay an unemployment tax to the federal government. The federal unemployment tax rate is 3.28%, but the employer is allowed to deduct a tax credit of up to 2.7% for unemployment tax paid to the state. The effective federal unemployment tax rate in most states is, therefore, .58% on the first $4,200.00 earned by each employee.

No employee on Johnstone Orchard's payroll of June 24 had yet earned $4,200.00 in 1977. Thus, the federal unemployment tax to be paid by Johnstone Orchard on the total wages of $2,180.75 is .58% of this amount, or $12.65. The federal unemployment tax expense is recorded in the combined journal entry shown on page 406.

> The federal and the state unemployment tax rates do not change as frequently as the FICA tax rate. Therefore, the effective tax rates for federal and state unemployment taxes at the time this book was written are used throughout the book.

The employer's state unemployment tax

Under the state unemployment compensation laws, employers are required to pay contributions into state unemployment compensation funds at a basic rate of 2.7% of the taxable wages. The taxable wages for unemployment taxes in most states consist of the first $4,200.00 earned by each employee. No employee on Johnstone Orchard's payroll of June 24 had yet earned $4,200.00 in 1977. Thus, the state unemployment tax is

2.7% of the total earnings of $2,180.75, or $58.88. The entry for state unemployment tax is included in the combined entry shown below.

Recording the employer's payroll taxes

The Johnstone Orchard's payroll taxes for the payroll period ended June 24, 1977, amount to: FICA tax, $130.85; federal unemployment tax, $12.65; and state unemployment tax, $58.88. The payroll clerk records these three expenses in a combined entry as shown below.

Combined entry for employer's payroll taxes

			COMBINATION JOURNAL				
PAGE 12							
1	2					3	4
CASH		DATE	ACCOUNT TITLE	DOC. No.	POST. REF.	GENERAL	
DEBIT	CREDIT					DEBIT	CREDIT
17		24	Payroll Taxes Expense	M 44		202 38		17
18			FICA Tax Payable				130 85	18
19			Fed. Unempl. Tax Pay.				12 65	19
20			State Unempl. Tax Pay.				58 88	20
21								21

Payroll Taxes Expense is debited for $202.38 to record the total of the employer's payroll taxes expense. The three credits in this combination entry record the three different liabilities resulting from the June 24 payroll as follows: FICA Tax Payable, $130.85; Federal Unemployment Tax Payable, $12.65, State Unemployment Tax Payable, $58.88.

> The use of one tax expense account for recording all of the employer's payroll taxes is a common practice. If a breakdown is ever needed of the amounts of the different payroll taxes, the amounts can be obtained from the payroll tax liability accounts.
>
> Some businesses use a separate expense account for each kind of employer's payroll tax. When this is done, the single account, **Payroll Taxes Expense**, is replaced with expense accounts such as **FICA Tax Expense**, **Federal Unemployment Tax Expense**, and **State Unemployment Tax Expense**.

POSTING THE PAYROLL ENTRY FOR THE EMPLOYER'S PAYROLL TAXES

After the entry for the employer's payroll taxes is posted, the four accounts involved appear as shown on page 407.

The debit of $202.38 to Payroll Taxes Expense is the total employer's payroll taxes expense for the week ended June 24. Offsetting this $202.38 debit are credits totaling $202.38 in the three liability accounts as follows: FICA Tax Payable, $130.85; Federal Unemployment Tax Payable, $12.65; State Unemployment Tax Payable, $58.88.

ACCOUNT *FICA Tax Payable*					ACCOUNT NO. *23*	
DATE	ITEM	POST. REF.	DEBIT	CREDIT	BALANCE DEBIT	BALANCE CREDIT
24		*12*		*13085*		*104893*
24		*12*		*13085*		*117978*

ACCOUNT *Federal Unemployment Tax Payable*					ACCOUNT NO. *24*	
DATE	ITEM	POST. REF.	DEBIT	CREDIT	BALANCE DEBIT	BALANCE CREDIT
24		*12*		*1265*		*14115*

ACCOUNT *State Unemployment Tax Payable*					ACCOUNT NO. *25*	
DATE	ITEM	POST. REF.	DEBIT	CREDIT	BALANCE DEBIT	BALANCE CREDIT
24		*12*		*5888*		*76963*

ACCOUNT *Payroll Taxes Expense*					ACCOUNT NO. *64*	
DATE	ITEM	POST. REF.	DEBIT	CREDIT	BALANCE DEBIT	BALANCE CREDIT
24		*12*	*20238*		*101190*	

The FICA tax payable account has two credits. The first credit, $130.85, is the employer's liability for the amount of FICA tax withheld from the *employees'* wages for the week ended June 24. This amount was posted from the entry that recorded the payroll. The second credit, $130.85, is the *employer's* FICA tax. This amount was posted from the journal entry that recorded the employer's liability for his share of the FICA tax.

AUTOMATING THE JOURNALIZING AND POSTING OF PAYROLL ACCOUNTS AND TAXES

In an automated data processing system, the data for the general ledger accounts are normally stored on magnetic disk storage. The punched time cards used for payroll accounting described in Chapter 21, page 394, represent the journal of a manual data processing system. The posting to the general ledger accounts on magnetic disk storage is done at the same time that the payroll register and the payroll checks are being prepared, pages 394–395. This procedure is accomplished through instructions in the stored computer program.

PAYING THE WITHHOLDING TAXES AND
THE PAYROLL TAXES

At the end of each quarter of the year, every employer must pay to the government the amount of the income tax and FICA tax withheld from employees. In addition, each employer must pay a FICA tax equal to that withheld from the employees. If the employer owes less than $200.00 a quarter, the payment is sent with the quarterly federal tax return, Form 941. However, if the employer owes more than $200.00 but less than $2,000.00 by the end of any month, monthly deposits are required. For the first two months of the quarter, the tax must be deposited by the 15th of the following month. Monthly deposits are not required until the employer's accumulated tax liability is $200.00 or more. If the employer owes $150.00 for the first month of the quarter, no deposit is made. However, if the employer also owes $150.00 for the second month, a deposit for the first two months must be made. The deposit is required because the employer's accumulated tax liability is more than $200.00.

Those employers who owe $2,000.00 or more by the 7th, 15th, 22d, or last day of a month must deposit the tax within three banking days after those dates. Businesses in this bracket are permitted to estimate their tax. If the deposit is 90% of the tax actually owed, there is no penalty for underdeposit. Any balance due at the end of the quarter must be paid by the end of the following month. If an overpayment is made, it is deducted from the next deposits.

Tax deposits are made in certain banks authorized to accept these payments for the federal government or in the Federal Reserve bank that serves the district in which the business is located. The deposit is recorded on Form 501 which is forwarded to the bank with the payment. A record of the deposit is on the stub of Form 501 and is retained by the employer for his records. This information will be needed to complete the employer's quarterly tax return.

Paying the liability for employees' income tax and for FICA tax

The Johnstone Orchard withheld $1,018.80 for income tax from its employees' salaries for May. The liability for FICA tax for May is $918.08. This amount includes both the employer's share and the amounts withheld from employees as recorded in the general ledger. The total FICA tax and income tax for May is $1,936.88. A monthly deposit is required since this is over $200.00 but less than $2,000.00. The federal tax deposit is therefore made on June 15 as shown at the top of the next page.

After the tax deposit is prepared, Check No. 698 is issued for the amount of the deposit, $1,936.88. An entry is then made in the combination journal to record the payment of the liabilities for Employees Income

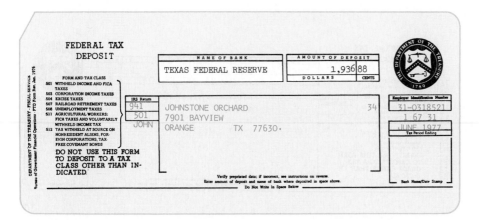

Tax Payable and FICA Tax Payable for the month of May. The entry to record this payment is shown below.

PAGE *11*			COMBINATION JOURNAL					
1	2					3	4	
CASH		DATE	ACCOUNT TITLE	Doc. No.	Post. Ref.	GENERAL		
DEBIT	CREDIT					DEBIT	CREDIT	
	1936 88	*15 Employees Income Tax Pay. ck 698*				*1018 80*		10
		FICA Tax Payable				*918 08*		11
								12
								13

The liability accounts Employees Income Tax Payable and FICA Tax Payable are debited to record the decreases in these liabilities. The cash account is credited to record the decrease in the asset Cash.

Paying the liability for federal unemployment tax

The federal unemployment tax is payable annually on or before January 31 of the following year if the annual tax is $100.00 or less. If the annual tax is over $100.00, quarterly deposits are required by the end of the month following the end of the quarter. No deposit is required until the calendar quarter in which the accumulated tax exceeds $100.00. Deposits are made each quarter after that period.

Since the federal unemployment tax for Johnstone Orchard at the end of March amounted to $141.15, a quarterly deposit was required by April 30. A deposit must be made each quarter but no report is due until the end of the year. The deposit for federal unemployment tax is similar to the one required for income tax and FICA tax. The same form is used but with different identifying numbers inserted in the IRS Return section. The federal unemployment tax deposit made by Johnstone Orchard on April 30 for the first quarter is shown at the top of page 410.

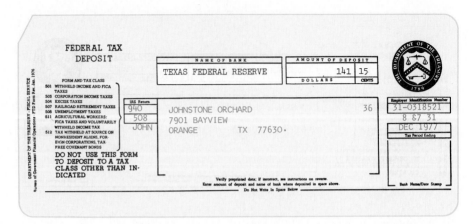

After the tax deposit was prepared, Check No. 471 was issued for the amount of the deposit, $141.15. The check stub is the source document for the journal entry. The entry in the combination journal to record this payment of the liability for Federal Unemployment Tax Payable on April 30 is shown below.

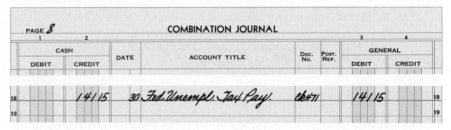

Entry to record payment for liability for federal unemployment tax

The liability account Federal Unemployment Tax Payable is debited to record the decrease in this liability. The cash account is credited to record the decrease in the asset Cash. The same procedure is followed each quarter when the deposit is made.

Paying the liability for state unemployment taxes

State requirements vary for reporting and paying the state unemployment taxes. The forms used for reporting this tax also vary from state to state. Therefore, the form sent in with the quarterly payment of the state unemployment tax is not shown. In general, employers are required to pay the state unemployment tax during the month following each calendar quarter. The accountant should be familiar with the requirements of the state in which the business operates.

The state unemployment tax for Johnstone Orchard for the second quarter of 1977 amounted to $769.63. On July 31, Check No. 810 was issued in payment of this liability. The entry in the combination journal to record this payment of the liability for State Unemployment Tax Payable on July 31 is shown at the top of the next page.

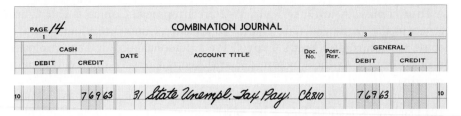

CASH		DATE	ACCOUNT TITLE	Doc. No.	Post. Ref.	GENERAL	
DEBIT	CREDIT					DEBIT	CREDIT
10	769 63	31	State Unempl. Tax Pay.	Ck810		769 63		10

(PAGE 14 — COMBINATION JOURNAL)

Entry to record payment of liability for state unemployment tax

The liability account State Unemployment Tax Payable is debited to record the decrease in this liability. The cash account is credited to record the decrease in the asset Cash.

This payment covers the state unemployment tax based on the payrolls of April, May, and June. The same procedure is followed each time a payment is made.

PAYROLL TAX REPORTS

Some payroll tax reports and tax returns are submitted quarterly and others are submitted annually. The most important of these are illustrated and discussed on the following pages.

Employer's annual report to employees of taxes withheld

Each employer who is required to withhold income tax and FICA tax from employees' wages must furnish each employee with an annual statement. This statement shows the employee's total year's earnings and the amounts withheld for taxes. This report is prepared on Form W-2 obtained from the District Director of the Internal Revenue Service.

The employer is required to furnish Form W-2 to each employee for the previous calendar year's earnings on or before January 31. If the employee terminates employment prior to the end of the year, Form W-2 must be furnished to the employee within 30 days.

The Form W-2 prepared by Johnstone Orchard for John C. Arthur for the year 1977 is shown below.

Wage and Tax Statement   1977

Johnstone Orchard 7901 Bayview Orange, TX 77630	Type or print EMPLOYER'S name, address, ZIP code and Federal identifying number.	Copy B To be filed with employee's FEDERAL tax return
		Employer's State identifying number 31-0318521

Employee's social security number	1 Federal income tax withheld	2 Wages, tips, and other compensation	3 FICA employee tax withheld	4 Total FICA wages
143-05-0832	962.00	8,560.00	513.60	
Type or print Employee's name, address, and ZIP code below.	5 Was employee covered by a qualified pension plan, etc.? No	6	7	
John C. Arthur 812 Twin Hills Drive Orange, TX 77630	8 State or local tax withheld	9 State or local wages	10 State or locality	
	11 State or local tax withheld	12 State or local wages	13 State or locality	

Form W-2   This information is being furnished to the Internal Revenue Service.   Department of the Treasury—Internal Revenue Service

Form W-2, Wage and Tax Statement

Four copies (A to D) of Form W-2 are prepared. Copies B and C are given to the employee. The employee attaches Copy B to a personal income tax return and keeps Copy C for a personal record. The employer sends Copy A to the government and keeps Copy D for the business records.

The employer's quarterly federal tax return

Each employer who withholds income taxes and FICA taxes from employees' wages must file a quarterly report of these withholdings with the Internal Revenue Service on Form 941. The quarterly federal tax return for the calendar quarter ending June 30, 1977, which was prepared by Johnstone Orchard is illustrated on page 413.

This quarterly return must be filed by the last day of the month following the end of the calendar quarter if payment is sent in with the report. If the company owes less than $200.00 for the quarter, payment may be sent with the report instead of deposits being made each month. If the company owes $200.00 or more in any month of the quarter, a deposit must be made. If deposits have been made for the first two months of the quarter and the balance due for the third month is less than $200.00, the payment may be sent in with the report at the end of the month.

If deposits have been made on time for each of the three months in the quarter and no additional payment is due with the return, an additional ten days is allowed for submitting the quarterly return. Since Johnstone Orchard made deposits on time for each of the three months in the second quarter which ended June 30, 1977, its quarterly federal tax return is due by August 10, 1977.

The employees' earnings records, described in Chapter 21, contain data on taxable wages that are required for the quarterly federal tax return, Form 941. After an employee's wages exceed $15,000.00, deductions for the FICA tax are no longer made. However, if an employee received any taxable wages during the quarter, the employee must be listed on the employer's tax return for that quarter.

The data for completing Schedule B are obtained from the stubs of the monthly tax deposits on Form 501. The date and amount of each deposit must be included on Schedule B.

The employer's annual transmittal of income and tax statements

Form W-3, Transmittal of Income and Tax Statements, is sent to the Internal Revenue Service along with Copy A of all W-2 forms furnished to employees. On Form W-3 the employer indicates the number of and the kind of forms being sent. The W-2 forms provide for a comparison of the total income tax and FICA tax withheld as reported on all W-2 forms and the total amount of income tax and FICA tax withheld as reported on the employer's four quarterly tax returns, Form 941. The transmittal form

Form **941** (Rev. July 1977) Department of the Treasury Internal Revenue Service	Employer's Quarterly Federal Tax Return	

Schedule A—Quarterly Report of Wages Taxable under the Federal Insurance Contributions Act—FOR SOCIAL SECURITY

List for each nonagricultural employee the WAGES taxable under the FICA which were paid during the quarter. If you pay an employee more than $15,000 in a calendar year report only the first $15,000 of such wages. In the case of "Tip Income" see instructions on page 4. IF WAGES WERE NOT TAXABLE UNDER THE FICA MAKE NO ENTRIES IN ITEMS 1 THROUGH 9 AND 14 THROUGH 18.

SSA Use Only

1. Total pages of this return including this page and any page of Form 941a ▶ 1	2. Total number of employees listed ▶ 14	3. (First quarter only) Number of employees (except household) employed in the pay period including March 12th ▶	31-0318521

4. EMPLOYEE'S SOCIAL SECURITY NUMBER	5. NAME OF EMPLOYEE (Please type or print)	6. TAXABLE FICA WAGES Paid to Employee in Quarter (Before deductions) Dollars Cents	7. TAXABLE TIPS REPORTED (See page 4) Dollars Cents
000 00 0000			
143 05 0832	John C. Arthur	2,140.00	
157 16 3844	Ellen R. Austin	2,430.75	

If you need more space for listing employees, use Schedule A continuation sheets, Form 941a.
Totals for this page—Wage total in column 6 and tip total in column 7 ▶ | 28,600.80

8. TOTAL WAGES TAXABLE UNDER FICA PAID DURING QUARTER. $ 28,600.80 ◁

9. TOTAL TAXABLE TIPS REPORTED UNDER FICA DURING QUARTER. $ None ◁

Name (as distinguished from trade name): Johnstone Orchard Date quarter ended: June 30, 1977
Trade name, if any Employer Identification No. 31-0318521
Address and ZIP code: 7901 Bayview, Orange, TX 77630

Name (as distinguished from trade name): Johnstone Orchard Date quarter ended: June 30, 1977
Trade name, if any
Address and ZIP code: 7901 Bayview, Orange, TX 77630

10. Total Wages And Tips Subject To Withholding Plus Other Compensation ▶	28,600 80
11. Amount Of Income Tax Withheld From Wages, Tips, Annuities, etc. (See instructions)	3,860 45
12. Adjustment For Preceding Quarters Of Calendar Year	None
13. Adjusted Total Of Income Tax Withheld ▶	3,860 45
14. Taxable FICA Wages Paid (Item 8) . $ 28,600.80 multiplied by 12% =TAX	3,432 10
15. Taxable Tips Reported (Item 9) . $ multiplied by 5.85%=TAX	None
16. Total FICA Taxes (Item 14 plus Item 15)	3,432 10
17. Adjustment (See instructions)	None
18. Adjusted Total Of FICA Taxes ▶	3,432 10
19. Total Taxes (Item 13 plus Item 18)	7,292 55
20. TOTAL DEPOSITS FOR QUARTER (INCLUDING FINAL DEPOSIT MADE FOR QUARTER) AND OVERPAYMENT FROM PREVIOUS QUARTER LISTED IN SCHEDULE B (See instructions on page 4)	7,292 55
21. Undeposited Taxes Due (Item 19 Less Item 20—This Should Be Less Than $200). Pay To Internal Revenue Service And Enter Here ▶	None

22. If Item 20 is More Than Item 19, Enter Excess Here ▶ $ And Check If You Want It □ Applied To Next Return, Or □ Refunded.
23. If not liable for returns in the future write "FINAL" (See instructions) ▶ Date final wages paid ▶

Under penalties of perjury, I declare that I have examined this return, including accompanying schedules and statements, and to the best of my knowledge and belief it is true, correct and complete.
Date August 8, 1977 Signature Romero Johnstone Title (Owner, etc) Owner

Form 941, Employer's Quarterly Federal Tax Return — Page 1

SCHEDULE B—RECORD OF FEDERAL TAX DEPOSITS

Deposit period ending:	A. Tax liability for period	B. Amount deposited	C. Date of deposit
Overpayment from previous quarter			
First month of quarter — 1st through 7th day			
8th through 15th day			
16th through 22d day			
23d through last day			
1 First month total	2,086.86	2,086.86	5-15-77
Second month of quarter — 1st through 7th day			
8th through 15th day			
16th through 22d day			
23d through last day			
2 Second month total	1,936.88	1,936.88	6-15-77
Third month of quarter — 1st through 7th day			
8th through 15th day			
16th through 22d day			
23d through last day			
3 Third month total	3,268.81	3,268.81	7-15-77
4 Total for quarter (total of items 1, 2, and 3)	7,292.55	7,292.55	
5 Final deposit made for quarter. (Enter zero if the final deposit made for the quarter is included in item 4.)	0		
6 Total deposits for quarter (total of items 4 and 5)—enter here and in item 20, page 1	7,292.55		

Form 941, Employer's Quarterly Federal Tax Return, Schedule B and W-2 forms must be filed on or before February 28 of each year. The Form W-3 prepared by Johnstone Orchard is shown below.

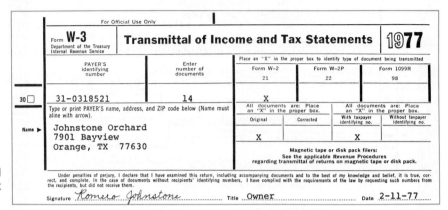

Form W-3, Transmittal of Income and Tax Statements

Instead of sending the actual W-2 forms with Form W-3, the employer may report the information on magnetic tape or magnetic disks. Before using this method, however, the employer must receive permission from the Internal Revenue Service Center.

Questions for Individual Study

1. What is the source document for journalizing the payroll entry for each payroll period?
2. The total earnings of the employees for the week ending June 24, 1977, as illustrated in the payroll register on page 386, amounted to $2,180.75. However, the total amount actually paid to the employees was $1,581.95. What causes the difference between these two amounts?
3. What payroll taxes must the employer pay?
4. Why does the account FICA Tax Payable illustrated on page 407 show two credit entries on the same date?

5. When an automated data processing system is used, how is the payroll entry journalized and posted?
6. When is an employer required to deposit withholdings in an authorized bank?
7. What two payroll tax liabilities are paid with one check and recorded as a combined entry?
8. How frequently must employers pay their federal unemployment tax?
9. What statement is the employer required to furnish each employee at the end of the year?
10. When is the employer's quarterly federal tax return filed?

Cases for Management Decision

CASE 1 The Jackson Supply Company is required to pay taxes under the Federal Insurance Contributions Act and the Federal Unemployment Tax Act. The company is also subject to a state unemployment tax of 2.7%. The general manager of the company has estimated that the total payroll for 1977 which will be subject to the FICA tax is $80,000.00. It is estimated that 50 percent of the total payroll for 1977 will be subject

to federal and state unemployment taxes. The general manager has asked you, the payroll clerk, the following questions:

(a) What is the estimated total amount of payroll taxes expense the company will be required to pay in 1977?
(b) What percentage of the estimated payroll will the company be required to pay in payroll taxes expense in 1977?

CASE 2 The Blackstone Company has a weekly payroll of $8,000.00 with the following deductions: employees' income tax, $688.00; FICA tax, $479.98; union dues, $57.98.

The company's liabilities for payroll taxes are as follows: FICA tax, 6%; federal unemployment tax, .58%; state unemployment tax, 2.7%.

What entry should the payroll clerk make in the combination journal to record (a) the payment of the payroll and the amounts withheld, and (b) the liability of the company for payroll taxes? (c) Explain the difference between the total of FICA taxes deducted from the employees' earnings and the employer's liability for FICA tax.

DRILL 22-D 1 Analyzing payroll transactions

Instructions: □ **1.** Open the following accounts in T-account form: Cash, Employees Income Tax Payable, FICA Tax Payable, Federal Unemployment Tax Payable, State Unemployment Tax Payable, Payroll Taxes Expense, Salary Expense.

□ **2.** Use the T accounts to analyze the following transactions.

July 31. Paid monthly payroll, $1,260.50, covering salary expense of $1,550.00 less a deduction of $196.50 for employees' income tax and a deduction of $93.00 for FICA tax.

31. Recorded employer's payroll taxes as follows: FICA tax, 6%; federal unemployment tax, .58%; state unemployment tax, 2.7%.

Aug. 10. Deposited with the bank the amount of the liabilities for the month of July for employees' income tax payable, $196.50, and for FICA tax payable, $186.00; total deposit, $382.50.

PROBLEM 22-1 Recording payrolls and payroll taxes

The totals of the payroll register of Malloy Tire Service for the week ended July 22 are given below:

No.	Employee's Name	Marital Status	Exemp-tions	Total Earnings	Deductions				Net Pay	
					Income Tax	FICA Tax	Other	Total	Amount	Check No.
	Totals........			1340 00	114 38	80 40		194 78	1145 22	

The employer's liabilities for payroll taxes include the following: FICA tax, 6%; federal unemployment tax, .58%; state unemployment tax, 2.7%.

Instructions: □ **1.** Record the payroll and withholdings in a combination journal (page 7). The payroll was paid by Check No. 628 on July 22 of the current year.

□ **2.** Record the employer's share of payroll taxes in the combination journal. M71.

PROBLEM 22-2 Recording payroll transactions

Jane Archer, owner of a stationery store, completed the payroll transactions given below.

Feb. 28. Paid monthly payroll, $1,583.08, covering salary expense of $1,896.00 less a deduction of $199.16 for employees' income tax and a deduction of $113.76 for FICA tax. Ck148.

28. Recorded the employer's payroll taxes at the following rates: FICA tax, 6%; federal unemployment tax, .58%; state unemployment tax, 2.7%. M22.

Mar. 10. Deposited the amount of the liabilities for the month of February for employees' income tax payable, $199.16, and for FICA tax payable, $227.52; total deposit, $426.68. Ck163.

31. Paid monthly payroll, $1,530.36, covering salary expense of $1,903.00 less a deduction of $258.46 for employees' income tax and a deduction of $114.18 for FICA tax. Ck205.

31. Recorded the employer's payroll taxes at the same rates as in February. M25.

Apr. 15. Deposited the amount of the liabilities for the month of March for employees' income tax payable, $258.46, and for FICA tax payable, $228.36; total deposit, $486.82. Ck238.

30. Paid the amount of the liability for state unemployment tax for January, February, and March, $163.32. Ck249.

Instructions: Record the transactions on page 18 of a combination journal. Use the current year in the date.

**MASTERY
PROBLEM 22-M** Recording and posting
payroll transactions

Valdez's Nursery completed the payroll transactions given on page 417 during the period January 1 to February 5. Valdez's Nursery is liable for payroll taxes at the following rates: FICA tax, 6%; federal unemployment tax, .58%; state unemployment tax, 2.7%. It is also liable for the purchase of U.S. Savings Bonds for employees as the accumulated withholdings for each particular employee reach the necessary amount.

Instructions: □ **1.** Open the accounts given on page 417 and record the balances as of January 1 of the current year. Allow ten lines for the FICA tax payable account and five lines for each of the other accounts.

□ **2.** Record the selected transactions given on page 417. Use page 28 of a combination journal.

□ **3.** After recording each transaction in the combination journal, post the individual items recorded in the General Debit and General Credit columns.

Account Title	Acct. No.	Credit Balance
Employees Income Tax Payable........................	22	$324.60
FICA Tax Payable	23	238.00
Federal Unemployment Tax Payable	24	38.50
State Unemployment Tax Payable.....................	25	206.50
U.S. Savings Bonds Payable	26	116.00
Payroll Taxes Expense	64	——
Salary Expense...	65	——

Transactions

Jan. 7. Paid weekly payroll, $650.00 (less deductions: employees' income tax, $87.30; FICA tax, $39.00; U.S. Savings Bonds, $42.00). Ck58.

   7. Recorded the employer's payroll tax liabilities. M14.

   12. Paid deposit for December liabilities (employees' income tax and FICA tax), $562.60. Ck83.

   12. Paid federal unemployment tax for the quarter ended December 31, $38.50. Ck84.

   12. Paid state unemployment tax for the quarter ended December 31, $206.50. Ck85.

   12. Purchased six U.S. Savings Bonds at $18.75 each for employees, $112.50. Ck86.

   14. Paid weekly payroll, $625.00 (less deductions: employees' income tax, $79.60; FICA tax, $37.50; U.S. Savings Bonds, $48.00). Ck103.

   14. Recorded the employer's payroll tax liabilities. M17.

   21. Paid weekly payroll, $680.00 (less deductions: employees' income tax, $98.30; FICA tax, $40.80; U.S. Savings Bonds, $48.00). Ck116.

   21. Recorded the employer's payroll tax liabilities. M19.

   28. Paid weekly payroll, $630.00 (less deductions: employees' income tax, $81.60; FICA tax, $37.80; U.S. Savings Bonds, $48.00). Ck133.

   28. Recorded the employer's payroll tax liabilities. M23.

Feb. 1. Purchased nine U.S. Savings Bonds at $18.75 each for employees, $168.75. Ck139.

   3. Paid deposit for January liabilities (employees' income tax and FICA tax), $657.00. Ck153.

**BONUS
PROBLEM 22-B**

Recording and posting
payroll transactions

Taylor Sporting Goods completed the payroll transactions given on page 418 during the period January 1 to April 15. Taylor Sporting Goods is liable for payroll taxes at the following rates: FICA tax, 6%; federal unemployment tax, .58%; and state unemployment tax, 2.7%. It is also liable for the purchase of U.S. Savings Bonds for employees as the accumulated withholdings for an employee reach the necessary amount.

Instructions: □ **1.** Open the accounts given at the top of the next page and record the balances as of January 1 of the current year.

Account Title	Acct. No.	Credit Balance
Employees Income Tax Payable.........................	22	$334.68
FICA Tax Payable	23	383.40
Federal Unemployment Tax Payable	24	56.74
State Unemployment Tax Payable......................	25	288.36
U.S. Savings Bonds Payable	26	187.50
Payroll Taxes Expense	64	——
Salary Expense..	65	——

Instructions: □ **2.** Record the following selected transactions on page 26 of a combination journal.

□ **3.** After recording each transaction in the combination journal, post the individual items recorded in the General Debit and Credit columns.

Jan. 2. Paid for U.S. Savings Bonds for employees (10 bonds at $18.75 each), $187.50. Ck108.
   15. Deposited the amount of the liabilities for the month of December for employees' income tax payable and FICA tax payable, $718.08. Ck118.
   15. Paid the federal unemployment tax for the quarter ended December 31, $56.74. Ck119.
   15. Paid the state unemployment tax for the quarter ended December 31, $288.36. Ck120.
   31. Paid monthly payroll, $2,852.42, covering salary expense of $3,590.00 less a deduction of $334.68 for employees' income tax, a deduction of $215.40 for FICA tax, and $187.50 for U.S. Savings Bonds deductions. Ck133.
   31. Recorded the employer's payroll tax liabilities. M51.
Feb. 2. Paid for U.S. Savings Bonds for employees, $187.50. Ck136.
   15. Deposited the amount of the liabilities for the month of January for employees' income tax payable and FICA tax payable, $765.48. Ck143.
   28. Paid monthly payroll, $2,835.76, covering salary expense of $3,560.00 less a deduction of $323.14 for employees' income tax, a deduction of $213.60 for FICA tax, and $187.50 for U.S. Savings Bonds deductions. Ck163.
   28. Recorded the employer's payroll tax liabilities. M54.
Mar. 1. Paid for U.S. Savings Bonds for employees, $187.50. Ck172.
   15. Deposited the amount of the liabilities for the month of February for employees' income tax payable and FICA tax payable, $750.34. Ck182.
   31. Paid monthly payroll, $2,894.68, covering salary expense of $3,640.00 less a deduction of $339.42 for employees' income tax, a deduction of $218.40 for FICA tax, and $187.50 for U.S. Savings Bonds deductions. Ck209.
   31. Recorded the employer's payroll tax liabilities. M59.
Apr. 1. Paid for U.S. Savings Bonds for employees, $187.50. Ck213.
   15. Deposited the amount of the liabilities for the month of March for employees' income tax payable and FICA tax payable, $776.22. Ck228.
   15. Paid state unemployment tax for the quarter ended March 31, $291.33. Ck229.

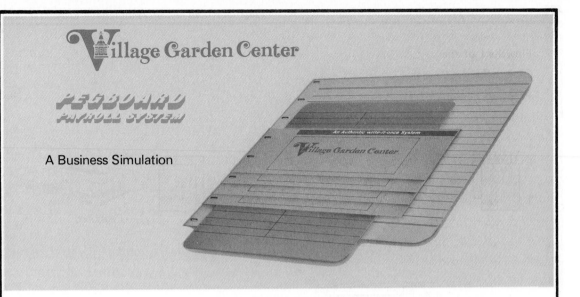

Village Garden Center

PEGBOARD PAYROLL SYSTEM

A Business Simulation

An Authentic write-it-once System

Village Garden Center

Employee's earnings record → ← Payroll checks

Payroll register

Pegboard →

An Authentic
Write-it-once System

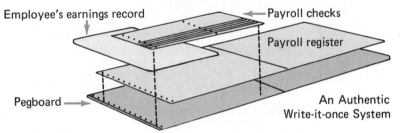

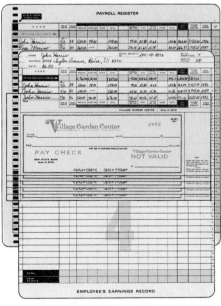

The VILLAGE GARDEN CENTER Pegboard Payroll System provides experience in preparing records using a pegboard and no-carbon-required forms. When data are entered on the statement of earnings and deductions stub on the check, the employee's earnings record and the payroll register are simultaneously prepared. Posting is eliminated in this system. A pictorial and symbolic flowchart are shown on pages 420 and 421.

(The narrative is provided in the set available from the publisher.)

419

Flowchart of the

𝒱illage 𝒢arden 𝒞enter

Pegboard Payroll System

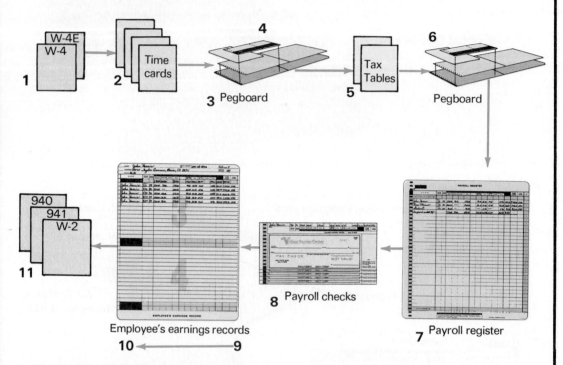

4

6

W-4E
W-4

1

Time cards

2

3 Pegboard

Tax Tables

5

Pegboard

940
941
W-2

11

Employee's earnings records

10 ◄———— **9**

8 Payroll checks

7 Payroll register

1 Prepare the necessary forms for new employees.
2 Complete time cards by entering summary data.
3 Assemble forms on pegboard: checks with earnings and deductions stubs, employee's earnings records, and payroll register. All records will be completed with one writing.
4 Record the time card summary data on the statement of earnings and deductions stubs of the checks on the pegboard.
5 Determine the appropriate deductions using tax tables and figure net pay.
6 Record the deductions and net pay on the statement of earnings and deductions stubs.
7 Total, prove, rule, and file the payroll register. File the employee's earnings records.
8 Separate, write, and sign the paychecks.

AT THE END OF THE QUARTER
9 Total and prove the employee's earnings records for the quarter.

AT THE END OF THE FOURTH QUARTER ONLY
10 Total and prove the employee's earnings records for the end of the quarter and year-to-date.
11 Prepare the quarterly reports and annual reports including: Form W-2, Employees' Wage and Tax Statements; Form 941, Employer's Quarterly Federal Tax Return; and Form 940, Employer's Annual Federal Unemployment Tax Return.

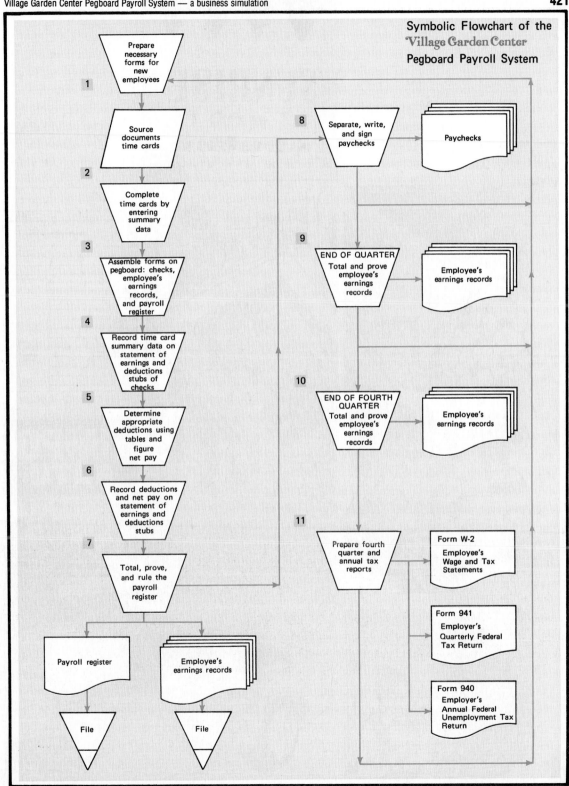

Symbolic Flowchart of the Village Garden Center Pegboard Payroll System

1 Prepare necessary forms for new employees

2 Source documents time cards

3 Complete time cards by entering summary data

4 Assemble forms on pegboard: checks, employee's earnings records, and payroll register

5 Record time card summary data on statement of earnings and deductions stubs of checks

6 Determine appropriate deductions using tables and figure net pay

7 Record deductions and net pay on statement of earnings and deductions stubs

Total, prove, and rule the payroll register

Payroll register — File

Employee's earnings records — File

8 Separate, write, and sign paychecks → Paychecks

9 END OF QUARTER Total and prove employee's earnings records → Employee's earnings records

10 END OF FOURTH QUARTER Total and prove employee's earnings records → Employee's earnings records

11 Prepare fourth quarter and annual tax reports

Form W-2 Employee's Wage and Tax Statements

Form 941 Employer's Quarterly Federal Tax Return

Form 940 Employer's Annual Federal Unemployment Tax Return

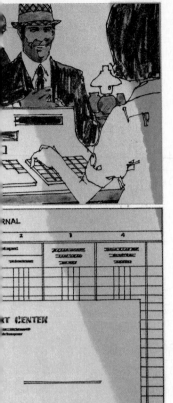

THE ACCOUNTING CYCLE USING SPECIAL JOURNALS

SPECIAL JOURNALS IMPROVE EFFICIENCY. As a business expands it may find that a single combination journal is not sufficient. The most frequently used special columns of the combination journal are separated into two or more special journals. Special journals save time because more than one person can journalize and post at the same time. The number and the kinds of special journals used depend on the nature of the business and the accounts in its ledger.

SPECIAL JOURNALS VARY IN DESIGN. The *Sunrise Art Center* uses the special journals described in Chapters 23 and 24. The *Import Auto Company* uses a cash register system described in Chapter 25. The cash register system combines the use of a cash register with procedures involving special journals.

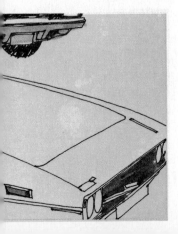

SUNRISE ART CENTER
CHART OF ACCOUNTS

(1) ASSETS

	Account Number
Cash	11
Accounts Receivable	12
Merchandise Inventory	13
Supplies	14
Prepaid Insurance	15

(2) LIABILITIES

Accounts Payable	21
Employees Income Tax Payable	22
FICA Tax Payable	23
Federal Unemployment Tax Payable	24
State Unemployment Tax Payable	25
United Fund Donations Payable	26

(3) CAPITAL

S. G. Justin, Capital	31
S. G. Justin, Drawing	32
Income Summary	33

(4) REVENUE

	Account Number
Sales	41
Sales Returns and Allowances	41.1
Sales Discount	41.2

(5) COST OF MERCHANDISE

Purchases	51
Purchases Returns and Allowances	51.1
Purchases Discount	51.2

(6) EXPENSES

Delivery Expense	61
Insurance Expense	62
Miscellaneous Expense	63
Payroll Taxes Expense	64
Rent Expense	65
Salary Expense	66
Supplies Expense	67

The chart of accounts for Sunrise Art Center is shown above for ready reference as you study Part 5 of this textbook.

Special Journals: Purchases and Cash Payments; Four-Column General Journal

23

The combination journal is often used when a small number of transactions can be recorded by one accountant. The combination journal is not practical when more than one accountant is needed. In such cases, it is customary to use several journals. Some journals may be used to record only one kind of transaction. A journal in which only one kind of business transaction is recorded is called a special journal.

The Sunrise Art Center, an arts and craft store, uses five journals to record its transactions: (1) purchases journal — for all purchases of merchandise on account, (2) cash payments journal — for all cash payments, (3) sales journal — for all sales of merchandise on account, (4) cash receipts journal — for all cash receipts, and (5) general journal — for all other transactions.

The purchases journal, cash payments journal, and general journal used by Sunrise Art Center are described in this chapter. The sales journal, cash receipts journal, and additional uses of the general journal are described in Chapter 24.

PURCHASES JOURNAL

A special journal used to record only purchases of merchandise on account is called a purchases journal.

Form of purchases journal

The purchases journal used by Sunrise Art Center is on page 426. In the purchases journal a purchase of merchandise on account can be recorded on one line. Each amount recorded in the single amount column is both a debit to Purchases and a credit to Accounts Payable. The names of both general ledger accounts are listed in the column heading.

425

Journalizing a purchase of merchandise on account in a purchases journal

The source document for recording the purchase of merchandise on account is the purchase invoice received from a creditor. The Sunrise Art Center dates, numbers, and checks its purchase invoices in the same way as shown on page 174 for Gift World.

The Sunrise Art Center made the following purchase of merchandise on account:

> December 1, 1977. Purchased merchandise on account from Acker Company, $624.00. Purchase Invoice No. 147.

In this transaction, Purchases is debited for $624.00, and Accounts Payable is credited for $624.00. The creditor's account, Acker Company, in the accounts payable ledger, also is credited for $624.00. The entry to record this transaction in the purchases journal is shown below.

	DATE	ACCOUNT CREDITED	PURCH. NO.	POST. REF.	PURCHASES, DR. ACCTS. PAY. CR.	
	PURCHASES JOURNAL				PAGE *12*	
1	*1977 Dec. 1*	*Acker Company*	*147*		*624 00*	1
2						2
3						3

Purchase of merchandise on account
recorded in purchases journal

The date, *1977, Dec. 1*, is written in the Date column. The amount of the invoice, *$624.00*, is written in the amount column. The name of the creditor, *Acker Company*, is written in the Account Credited Column. The number of the invoice, *147*, is written in the Purch. No. column. (Only purchase invoice numbers are recorded in this column. Therefore, it is not necessary to use an identifying letter with the invoice number.)

Each purchase of merchandise on account is recorded in the purchases journal in the same way. The illustration on page 428 shows the completed purchases journal of Sunrise Art Center for December.

Posting the purchases journal to the accounts payable ledger

Each amount in the amount column of the purchases journal is posted individually as a credit to a creditor's account in the accounts payable ledger. This procedure is the same as posting from the Accounts Payable Credit column of the combination journal described on pages 202 and 203 of Chapter 13.

The Sunrise Art Center posts daily to the accounts payable ledger. In this way, each creditor's account shows an up-to-date balance at all times. The illustration below shows the posting of the entry on Line 1 of the purchases journal.

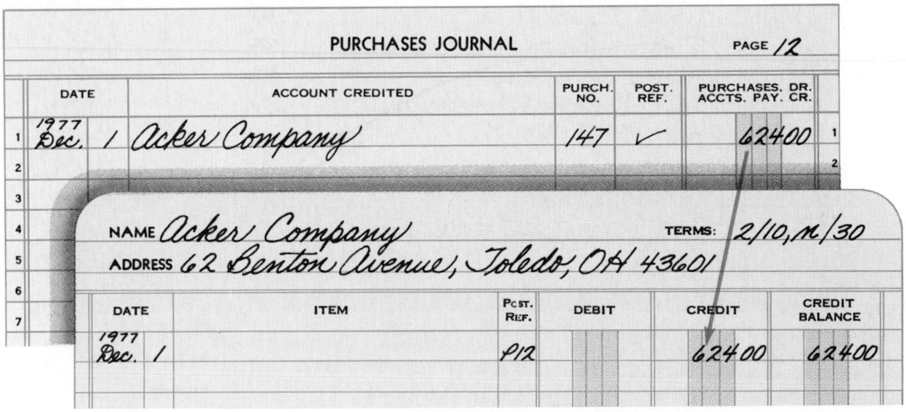

Posting from the purchases journal to the accounts payable ledger

The terms 2/10, n/30 in the account heading will be explained later in the chapter.

The completion of posting is shown by writing *P12* in the Post. Ref. column of the subsidiary ledger account. A check mark is placed in the Post. Ref. column of the purchases journal to show completion of the posting of this line.

When more than one journal is used, a letter is used to show the journal from which the posting is made. *P* is the letter used for the purchases journal.

Posting the totals of the purchases journal to the general ledger

The purchases journal is totaled and ruled at the end of the month. A single line is drawn across the amount column under the last amount recorded, and the column is added. The total is written directly below the single line as shown in the illustration on page 428.

The date of the last day of the month, *31*, is written in the date column. The word *Total* is written in the Account Credited column. Double lines are ruled across the amount column under the total amount.

The total of the purchases journal is posted twice: (1) as a debit to the general ledger account Purchases; and (2) as a credit to the general ledger account Accounts Payable. The illustration, page 428, shows the purchases journal and the two general ledger accounts after posting is completed.

PURCHASES JOURNAL   PAGE *12*

	DATE	ACCOUNT CREDITED	PURCH. NO.	POST. REF.	PURCHASES. DR. ACCTS. PAY. CR.	
1	*1977* Dec. 1	Acker Company	147	✓	62400	1
2	2	Byers & Sons	148	✓	12000	2
3	5	Mike Flanagan Company	149	✓	54000	3
4	9	Minor Company	150	✓	49200	4
5	14	Keith Dunham & Company	151	✓	13200	5
6	21	Van Fleet Mills	152	✓	75600	6
7	26	Minor Company	153	✓	58800	7
8	27	Byers & Sons	154	✓	45900	8
9	30	McxGuire Art Company	155	✓	8400	9
10	31	Total			379500	10
11					(51)(21)	11

Purchases journal totaled, ruled, and posted

ACCOUNT *Purchases*   ACCOUNT NO. *51*

DATE	ITEM	POST. REF.	DEBIT	CREDIT	BALANCE DEBIT	BALANCE CREDIT
1977 Dec. 1		CP16	21000		21000	
15		J15		7500	13500	
31		P12	379500		393000	

ACCOUNT *Accounts Payable*   ACCOUNT NO. *21*

DATE	ITEM	POST. REF.	DEBIT	CREDIT	BALANCE DEBIT	BALANCE CREDIT
1977 Dec. 1	Balance	✓				58200
12		J15		16000		74200
31		P12		379500		453700

General ledger accounts after posting from purchases journal

After the total of the purchases journal is posted to Purchases, the account number, *51*, is written in parentheses under the total in the purchases journal. After this same total is posted to Accounts Payable, the account number, *21*, is also written in parentheses under the total in the purchases journal. The total is posted as both a debit and a credit. Thus, the equality of debits and credits in the general ledger is maintained.

Summary of journalizing and posting from a purchases journal

(1) The Sunrise Art Center records all purchases of merchandise on account in a one-column purchases journal. (2) The items in the amount column are posted daily to the accounts payable ledger. (3) At the end of the month, the total of the purchases journal is posted to two general

ledger accounts: Purchases is debited; Accounts Payable is credited. The flowchart below shows this procedure.

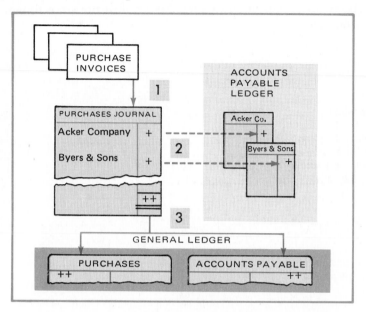

Flowchart showing journalizing and posting purchases of merchandise on account using a special purchases journal

CASH PAYMENTS JOURNAL

A special journal in which only cash payments transactions are recorded is called a cash payments journal.

Form of cash payments journal

The cash payments journal used by Sunrise Art Center is shown on page 430. This five-column cash payments journal has special amount columns for transactions that occur frequently. For example, Sunrise Art Center makes frequent payments to creditors. Thus, there is a special amount column for Accounts Payable Debit. Transactions that do not occur often, such as the monthly payment of rent, are recorded in the General columns.

Journalizing cash payments in a cash payments journal

All cash payments made by Sunrise Art Center are recorded in the cash payments journal. The source document for each cash payment is a check stub in the checkbook.

Most cash payments are for (1) expenses, (2) cash purchases, (3) payment of creditors, (4) withdrawals of cash by the owner, and (5) payroll transactions. Examples of entries for these transactions are shown in the illustration below.

	DATE	ACCOUNT TITLE	CHECK No.	POST. REF.	GENERAL DEBIT	GENERAL CREDIT	ACCOUNTS PAYABLE DEBIT	PURCHASES DISCOUNT CREDIT	CASH CREDIT	
1	1977 Dec. 1	Rent Expense	243		50000				50000	1
2	1	Purchases	244		21000				21000	2
3	5	McGuire Art Company	245				25200		25200	3
4	7	S. G. Justin, Drawing	246		45000				45000	4
5	7	Employees Income Tax Pay.	247		7860				16500	5
6		FICA Tax Payable			8640					6
7										7
8										8
9										9
10										10

CASH PAYMENTS JOURNAL — PAGE 16

Cash payments recorded in a five-column cash payments journal

On Line 1 is an entry to pay the rent for December, 1977. On Line 2 is an entry for a cash purchase. Line 3 shows a payment on account to a creditor. Line 4 shows a cash withdrawal. Lines 5 and 6 show the deposit for payroll liabilities. These entries are similar to the ones made for the same transactions in the combination journal.

Discounts and terms of sale

The total amount shown on an invoice is not always the amount that the buyer will pay. Discounts and terms of sale affect the amount to be paid.

Trade discount. Many businesses print price lists and catalogs that show prices greater than those the customer will actually pay. A manufacturer's or a wholesaler's catalog price that is subject to a reduction is called a list price. A reduction in the list price granted to customers is called a trade discount.

When a trade discount is granted, the seller's invoice shows the actual amount charged after the trade discount has been deducted from the list price. Only the net amount of the invoice is used in a journal entry. The invoice is recorded by both the seller and buyer at the same amount. No journal entry is made to show the amount of the trade discount.

Terms of sale. The agreement between a buyer and a seller as to payment for merchandise is called the terms of sale. If payment is to be made immediately, the terms of sale are said to be *cash* or *net cash*. A sale for which a buyer is allowed a period of time before payment must be made is called a credit sale. The credit period of a sale usually begins with the date of the invoice. The credit period may be for 30 days, 60 days, or any agreed-upon length of time. The terms of a credit sale are usually stated on the invoice sent to a buyer by a seller.

Cash discount. For a credit sale, a buyer is expected to pay the seller within the credit period agreed upon. To encourage a buyer to make payment before the end of this period, a seller may allow a deduction from the amount of the invoice. A deduction that a seller allows on the amount of an invoice to encourage a buyer to make prompt payment is called a cash discount.

A cash discount is usually stated as a percentage that can be deducted from the amount of the invoice. For example, the terms of sale on an invoice may be written as *2/10, n/30*. These terms are commonly read *two ten, net thirty*. The term *two ten* means that a buyer may deduct 2% of the invoice amount if payment is made within 10 days from the date of the invoice. The term *net thirty* means that if an invoice is not paid within 10 days, the buyer is required to pay the total amount within 30 days.

A business also may indicate the date for full payment of an invoice as *EOM*. This means that full payment is expected not later than the *end of the month*. If the terms are stated as *1/10, n/30 EOM*, a 1% discount may be taken if the invoice is paid within 10 days after the end of the month in which the invoice is dated. The full amount of the invoice must be paid on or before 30 days after the end of the month.

Purchases discount. A cash discount on purchases taken by a buyer is called a purchases discount. When a buyer takes advantage of a purchases discount, he pays less than the purchase price recorded on his books. Therefore, a purchases discount is a deduction from purchases. Purchases discounts are recorded by a buyer in a general ledger account titled Purchases Discount.

In the general ledger of Sunrise Art Center, Purchases Discount is given the account number 51.2. The purchases discount account is in the cost of merchandise division of the general ledger, as shown in the chart of accounts, page 424.

> The account number of the purchases discount account, *51.2*, indicates that the balance of this account is deducted from the balance of the account with the number *51, Purchases*. Therefore the purchases discount account is often called a minus purchases account. In this text, the balance of any account whose number contains a decimal is a deduction from the balance of the account having the same number without the decimal. (The account numbered *51.1, Purchases Returns and Allowances*, is discussed on page 436.) Many variations in the system of numbering accounts are used in business.

Journalizing a cash payment on account with a purchases discount

The Sunrise Art Center tries to pay all creditors in time to take the purchases discount. This policy reduces the cost of merchandise purchased by the Center.

The Sunrise Art Center made the following payment on account:

> *December 8, 1977. Paid on account to Acker Company, $611.52, for Purchase Invoice No. 147, for $624.00 less a 2% discount of $12.48. Check No. 249.*

GENERAL LEDGER

Accounts Payable		21
Dec. 8	624.00	

	Cash		11
		Dec. 8	611.52

Purchases Discount		51.2
	Dec. 8	12.48

ACCOUNTS PAYABLE LEDGER

	Acker Company		
Dec. 8	624.00	Dec. 1	624.00

Accounts Payable is debited for the amount of the purchase invoice, $624.00. This debit decreases the amount owed to creditors. This amount, $624.00, also is debited to the account of Acker Company in the accounts payable ledger. This shows that Purchase Invoice No. 147 has been paid in full.

Cash is credited for the amount of the check, $611.52.

Purchases Discount is credited for the amount of the purchases discount, $12.48. The balance of the purchases discount account is a deduction on the income statement from the balance of the purchases account. The purchases account has a debit balance. Therefore, to show a deduction from Purchases the purchases discount account has a credit balance.

The entry for this payment on account with a purchases discount is shown in the cash payments journal below.

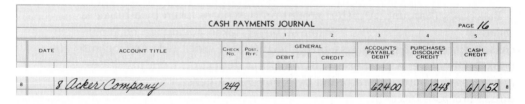

Payment on account with purchases discount recorded in cash payments journal

The amount of the purchase invoice, *$624.00*, is written in the Accounts Payable Debit column. The amount of the purchases discount, *$12.48*, is written in the Purchases Discount Credit column. The amount of cash paid, *$611.52*, is written in the Cash Credit column. The name of the creditor, *Acker Company*, is written in the Account Title column. The total of the two credits ($12.48 + $611.52) is $624.00 and is equal to the one debit of $624.00.

Purchases discounts are recorded frequently by Sunrise Art Center. Therefore, a special amount column for Purchases Discount Credit is provided in the cash payments journal.

Posting the cash payments journal

Each amount in the Accounts Payable Debit column is posted individually as a debit to the accounts payable ledger account named in the Account Title column. A check mark is placed in the Post. Ref. column of the cash payments journal to indicate the completion of the posting. This posting is done daily by Sunrise Art Center.

Each amount in the General Debit and the General Credit columns is posted individually to the general ledger account named in the Account Title column. The account number is written in the Post. Ref. column of the cash payments journal to indicate the completion of the posting. This posting is done periodically during the month.

> In the Post. Ref. columns of the ledger accounts, the source of the postings is indicated by writing the journal page; in this case, CP16. CP is the abbreviation for *cash payments journal*.

At the end of the month, the cash payments journal is footed and the equality of debits and credits is proved. The cash payments journal is then totaled and ruled as shown below.

The total of each special column in the cash payments journal is posted to the account named in the column heading. The completion of the posting of each special column total is shown by writing the number of the account in parentheses below the column total. The totals of the General columns are not posted. Each amount in these columns was posted individually to a general ledger account. To indicate that these totals are not to be posted, a check mark is placed in parentheses below each column total.

					CASH PAYMENTS JOURNAL					PAGE 16	
					1	2	3	4	5		
	DATE	ACCOUNT TITLE	CHECK No.	POST. REF.	GENERAL DEBIT	GENERAL CREDIT	ACCOUNTS PAYABLE DEBIT	PURCHASES DISCOUNT CREDIT	CASH CREDIT		
1	1977 Dec. 1	Rent Expense	243	65	50000				50000	1
2	1	Purchases	244	51	21000				21000	2
3	5	McGuire Art Company	245	✓			25200		25200	3
4	7	S.L. Justin, Drawing	246	32	45000				45000	4
5	7	Employees Income Tax Pay.	247	22	7860				16500	5
6		FICA Tax Payable		23	8640					6
7	8	Supplies	248	14	2600				2600	7
8	8	Acker Company	249	✓			62400	1248	61152	8
23	30	Salary Expense	258	66	36000				29910	23
24		Employees Income Tax Pay.		22		3930				24
25		FICA Tax Payable		23		2160				25
26	30	Delivery Expense	259	61	8400				8400	26
27	31	Totals			272056	52576	270600	3372	486708	27
28					(✓)	(✓)	(21)	(51.2)	(11)	28

Cash payments journal totaled, ruled, and posted

Summary of journalizing and posting cash payments using a cash payments journal

(1) The Sunrise Art Center records all cash payments in a five-column cash payments journal. (2) The individual items in the Accounts Payable Debit column are posted daily to the accounts payable ledger. (3) The individual items in the General Debit and Credit columns are posted often during the month to the general ledger. (4) At the end of the month, the totals of the special columns — Accounts Payable Debit, Purchases Discount Credit, and Cash Credit — are posted to the general ledger. The flowchart below shows this procedure.

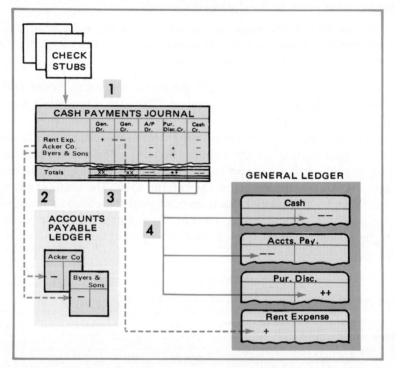

Flowchart showing journalizing and posting of cash
payments using a special cash payments journal

AUTOMATED DATA PROCESSING FOR PURCHASES AND CASH PAYMENTS

The use of special journals for recording purchases and cash payments is one way to expand and improve an accounting system. Another way a business may expand and improve its accounting system is through automated data processing procedures. The same basic accounting principles apply regardless of whether manual or automated methods are used.

Both the manual and the automated data processing systems allow for more than one accounting clerk to work on the books at the same time. Only the form used to journalize the data differs between the two systems. In a manual system the accounting clerk records the data on a form designed for the type of data being recorded. For example, purchases are recorded in a purchases journal and cash payments are recorded in a cash payments journal. In an ADP system the accounting clerks record the data on a journal entry transmittal form that is designed to be used for all types of data. One accounting clerk may record all purchases on one journal entry transmittal form, and another accounting clerk may record all cash payments on a separate journal entry transmittal form. Even though two different types of data are recorded, the layout and design of the transmittal forms are the same.

In a manual data processing system, the data from the special journals are manually posted to the general ledger. In an ADP system, the journal entry transmittal forms are sent to the data processing department of the business or to a computer service center. The data are converted to punched cards which serve as input media to the computer system. The computer will "post" the data to the general ledger according to the program stored in the computer. The general ledger data are commonly stored on magnetic disk storage in an ADP system.

The methods of journalizing and posting purchases and cash payments for an automated data processing system are described for Wayside Furniture in Chapter 20. Pages 355–356 show the journalizing of purchases, and page 354 shows journalizing for cash payments. Page 359 shows the procedures for posting to the general ledger and subsidiary ledgers in an ADP system.

FOUR-COLUMN GENERAL JOURNAL

Sunrise Art Center uses special journals to record transactions for purchases of merchandise on account, cash payments, sales of merchandise on account, and cash receipts. All other kinds of transactions are recorded in a four-column general journal.

Form of four-column general journal

The general journal used by Sunrise Art Center is shown on page 437. This four-column general journal differs from the two-column general journal in Chapter 2, page 18, in two ways: (1) the four-column general journal has two special amount columns (Accounts Payable Debit and Accounts Receivable Credit), and (2) the two debit columns are at the left of the Date column. The two credit columns are at the right of the Post. Ref. column.

Most of the transactions of Sunrise Art Center are recorded in the special journals. However, there are other kinds of transactions that belong in the general journal. Three of these transactions are: (1) purchases returns and allowances, (2) supplies bought on account, and (3) withdrawal of merchandise by the owner for personal use.

> Other transactions recorded in the general journal by Sunrise Art Center are described in Chapter 24.

Purchases returns and allowances

The buyer of merchandise may be allowed a reduction in an account for the return of part or all of the merchandise purchased. Merchandise returned by a buyer for credit is called a purchases return.

A buyer may also be allowed a reduction in an account by the seller if the merchandise received was inferior in quality or was damaged when received. In this situation, the merchandise is often retained by the buyer. Credit allowed for merchandise that is not completely satisfactory, but that is not returned, is called a purchases allowance.

A purchases return or allowance should be confirmed in writing. The details may be stated in a letter or on a form. A form, prepared by the buyer, containing a record of the amount of the debit taken by the buyer for returns, allowances, and similar items is called a debit memorandum. It is called a *debit* memorandum because the amount is a deduction (debit) from the liability account Accounts Payable.

The buyer may use a copy of the debit memorandum as the source document for journalizing a purchases returns and allowances transaction. However, the buyer may wait for written confirmation from the seller and use that as the source document. The Sunrise Art Center issues a debit memorandum for each purchases return or allowance and uses the form as the source document. In this way the transaction can be recorded immediately without waiting for written confirmation from the seller. The original of the debit memorandum is sent to the creditor, and the carbon copy is kept by Sunrise Art Center. The form of debit memorandum used by Sunrise Art Center is shown at the left.

Purchases returns and allowances are a decrease in the purchases. Some businesses credit the purchases account for the amount of the purchases return or allowance. However, it is better to credit these amounts to a separate account with the title Purchases Returns and Allowances. In this way, a business can see how large its purchases returns and allowances are. Also, the business can see if purchases returns and allowances

DEBIT MEMORANDUM   NO. 18

ART CENTER 1312 MILLS STREET PORTLAND, OR 97230

TO   Mike Flanagan Co.
     133 Elm Street   DATE December 8, 1977
     Lincoln, NB 68527

               WE DEBIT YOUR ACCOUNT AS FOLLOWS:

| 7 | #621 Paint-by-Number Kits, your Invoice No. 88613, are being returned by parcel post. Our order specified #721 kits. | 2.00 | 14.00 |

Debit memorandum

are increasing or decreasing from year to year. If the amounts are very large, one account may be kept for purchases returns and another account for purchases allowances. Usually it is satisfactory to combine the two in one account.

The Sunrise Art Center has few purchases returns and few purchases allowances. Therefore, it uses a single account title Purchases Returns and Allowances to record both. The purchases returns and allowances account is placed in the cost of merchandise division of the general ledger as shown in the chart of accounts, page 424. The account is numbered 51.1 to show that the balance of this minus purchases account is a deduction from the balance of account number 51, Purchases.

Journalizing a purchases returns and allowances transaction in a four-column general journal

The Sunrise Art Center recorded the following purchases returns and allowances transaction:

> *December 8, 1977. Returned merchandise to Mike Flanagan Company, $14.00, Debit Memorandum No. 18.*

The source document for this particular purchases return is a debit memorandum.

The amount owed to a creditor is decreased by this transaction. Accounts Payable is debited for the amount of the return, *$14.00*. The same amount is also debited to the account of Mike Flanagan Company in the accounts payable ledger. The purchases returns and allowances account, a minus purchases account, has a credit balance. Therefore, the purchases returns and allowances account is increased on the credit side. Since this transaction increases the purchases returns and allowances account, Purchases Returns and Allowances is credited for *$14.00*.

The entry to record this purchases returns and allowances transaction in a four-column general journal is:

GENERAL LEDGER

Accounts Payable			21
Dec. 8	14.00	Dec. 1 Bal.	582.00

Purchases Returns and Allowances			51.1
		Dec. 8	14.00

ACCOUNTS PAYABLE LEDGER

Mike Flanagan Company			
Dec. 8	14.00	Dec. 1 Bal.	330.00
		5	540.00

				GENERAL JOURNAL				PAGE *15*	
1 ACCOUNTS PAYABLE DEBIT	**2** GENERAL DEBIT	DATE		ACCOUNT TITLE	POST. REF.	**3** GENERAL CREDIT	**4** ACCOUNTS RECEIV. CREDIT		
1400		*Dec.* 8	*Mike Flanagan Company*						1
			Purchases Ret. & Allow.		1400			2
			Debit Memo. No. 18.					3
								4

Purchases returns and allowances transaction recorded in a four-column general journal

The date, *1977, Dec. 8*, is written in the Date column. The amount of the debit, *$14.00*, is written in the Accounts Payable Debit column. The name of the creditor, *Mike Flanagan Company*, is written in the Account Title column. The amount of the credit, *$14.00*, is written in the General Credit column on the next line. The account to be credited, *Purchases Returns and Allowances*, is written in the Account Title column. This account title is indented one-half inch (about 1.3 centimeters). The source document for the entry, *Debit Memo. No. 18*, is written on the next line and is indented another half inch (about 1.3 centimeters).

Journalizing a buying of supplies on account transaction in a four-column general journal

The Sunrise Art Center may buy supplies on account. Supplies are not merchandise. Only merchandise purchased on account is recorded in the purchases journal. Therefore, the buying on account of any item that is not merchandise is recorded in the general journal.

The Sunrise Art Center received an invoice for supplies bought on account as follows:

December 12, 1977. Bought supplies on account from Kelso Supply Company, $160.00. Memorandum No. 109.

GENERAL LEDGER

	Supplies		14
Dec. 1 Bal.	240.00		
12	160.00		

	Accounts Payable		21
		Dec. 1 Bal.	582.00
		12	160.00

ACCOUNTS PAYABLE LEDGER

Kelso Supply Company	
	Dec. 12 160.00

The source document for this transaction is the memorandum prepared by the owner of Sunrise Art Center. The invoice received from Kelso Supply Company is attached to the memorandum.

This transaction increases the balance of the supplies account. Supplies is debited for $160.00.

The amount owed to a creditor is increased by this transaction. Therefore, Accounts Payable is credited for $160.00. The same amount also is credited to the account of Kelso Supply Company in the accounts payable ledger.

The entry to record this transaction in a four-column general journal is shown below.

Buying of supplies on account transaction recorded in a four-column general journal

The amount of the debit, *$160.00*, is written in the General Debit column. The account to be debited, *Supplies*, is written in the Account Title column. The amount of the credit, *$160.00,* is written on the next line in the General Credit column. The accounts to be credited, *Accounts Payable/Kelso Supply Co.,* are written in the Account Title column. These accounts are indented one-half inch (about 1.3 centimeters). The source document, *Memorandum No. 109,* is written on the next line and is indented another half inch (about 1.3 centimeters).

> Both the controlling account, **Accounts Payable**, and the creditor's name, *Kelso Supply Company*, are written in the Account Title column. The credit amount is posted to both of these accounts. A diagonal line is placed between the two account titles to separate them clearly. A diagonal line is also placed in the Post. Ref. column to show that the credit amount is posted to two accounts.

Journalizing a withdrawal of merchandise transaction in a four-column general journal

When an owner takes merchandise out of the business for personal use, the transaction is called a withdrawal of merchandise. Withdrawals of merchandise decrease the amount of merchandise purchased for sale to customers. Therefore, the *cost* price of merchandise withdrawn is deducted from the balance of the purchases account.

On December 15, the owner of Sunrise Art Center withdrew a motorized gem-cutting machine from the merchandise on hand.

> *December 15, 1977. S. G. Justin, owner, withdrew merchandise for personal use, $75.00. Memorandum No. 110.*

The source document for this transaction is a memorandum prepared by the owner.

All withdrawals, both cash and merchandise, decrease capital. Decreases in capital are debits to the capital account. However, withdrawals are recorded in a separate drawing account. For this transaction, the drawing account is debited for $75.00. This debit increases the balance of the account.

S. G. Justin, Drawing	32
Dec. 15 75.00	

The balance side of the purchases account is the debit side. This transaction decreases the balance of the purchases account. Therefore, **Purchases** is credited for $75.00.

The entry to record this transaction in a four-column general journal is shown on the next page.

Purchases	51
	Dec. 15 75.00

The amount of the debit, *$75.00,* is written in the General Debit column. The account to be debited, *S. G. Justin, Drawing,* is written in the Account Title column. The amount of the credit, *$75.00,* is written in the General Credit column on the next line. The account to be credited, *Purchases,* is written in the Account Title column and indented one-half inch (about 1.3 centimeters). The source document, *Memorandum No. 110,* is written on the next line and indented another half inch (about 1.3 centimeters).

Withdrawal of merchandise transaction
recorded in a four-column general journal

Posting the four-column general journal

Each individual amount in the Accounts Payable Debit column of a general journal is posted separately to the accounts payable ledger. Each individual amount in the Accounts Receivable Credit column is posted separately to the accounts receivable ledger. A check mark is placed in the Post. Ref. column of the general journal to show that posting has been completed. Individual posting from the Accounts Payable and Accounts Receivable columns is done daily by Sunrise Art Center.

> In the Post. Ref. columns of the ledger accounts, the source of the posting is shown by writing the journal page. In this transaction, J15 is written in the Post. Ref. column of the ledger account. J is the abbreviation for *general journal*.

Each individual amount in the General Debit and Credit columns is posted separately to the general ledger account named in the Account Title column. The account number is written in the Post. Ref. column to indicate that posting is completed. Individual posting from the General columns is done periodically during the month.

A portion of the four-column general journal used by Sunrise Art Center for December is shown on the next page. The general journal has been posted and the account numbers written in the Post. Ref. column.

The $160.00 amount on Line 5 in the General Credit column is posted twice. It is posted to the credit of the accounts payable account. It is also posted to the credit of the Kelso Supply Company account in the accounts payable ledger. The account number of the accounts payable account, 21, is written at the left of the diagonal line in the Post. Ref. column. A check mark is placed at the right of the diagonal line to show the completion of posting to the subsidiary ledger.

At the end of the month, the four-column general journal is footed. The equality of debits and credits is proved. The general journal is then totaled and ruled as shown on page 441.

1	2				3	4	
ACCOUNTS PAYABLE DEBIT	GENERAL DEBIT	DATE	ACCOUNT TITLE	POST. REF.	GENERAL CREDIT	ACCOUNTS RECEIV. CREDIT	
1400		*19̇77* Bi. 8	*Mike Flanagan Company*	√			1
			Purchases Ret. & Allow.	51.1	1400		2
			Debit Memo. No. 18.				3
	16000	12	*Supplies*	14			4
			Accts. Pay. / Kelso Supply Co.	21/√	16000		5
			Memorandum No. 109.				6
	7500	15	*S. G. Justin, Drawing*	32			7
			Purchases	51	7500		8
			Memorandum No. 110.				9
	2712	30	*Payroll Taxes Expense*	64			24
			FICA Tax Payable	23	2160		25
			Fed. Unemploy. Tax Pay.	24	180		26
			State Unemploy. Tax Pay.	25	372		27
			Memorandum No. 121.				28
1400 1400	46488 46488	31	*Totals*		35323 35323	12560 12560	29
(21)	(√)				(√)	(12)	30
							31

GENERAL JOURNAL   PAGE *15*

Four-column general journal totaled, ruled, and posted

The use of the Accounts Receivable Credit column of the general journal is described in Chapter 24.

The totals of the two special columns, Accounts Payable Debit and Accounts Receivable Credit, are posted to the accounts listed in the column heading. The number of the account is placed in parentheses below the column total. The totals of the General columns are not posted. Each amount in these columns was posted individually during the month. A check mark is placed in parentheses below each general column total. The check mark shows that these totals were not posted.

TRANSPORTATION CHARGES ON MERCHANDISE PURCHASED

As a convenience to a customer, a seller often pays the transportation charges on merchandise at the time it is shipped. When this is done, the transportation charges are included on the invoice and become part of the total of the invoice. If a seller pays the transportation charges and includes them on the invoice, the buyer debits the entire amount of the invoice, including the transportation charges, to the purchases account. Transportation charges on incoming shipments are a part of the total cost of purchases. If transportation costs are included on an invoice, the discount (if any) is not allowed on this portion of the invoice.

Sometimes the transportation charges on purchases are paid by a buyer directly to the transportation company. When a buyer pays the transportation charges, the buyer debits Purchases for the amount of the charges. Some businesses prefer to record the transportation charges in a separate account titled *Transportation on Purchases* or *Freight In*. When either of these accounts is used, it is classified as a cost of merchandise account and is added to Purchases on the income statement.

Using Business Terms

✦ What is the meaning of each of the following?

- special journal
- purchases journal
- cash payments journal
- list price
- trade discount

- terms of sale
- credit sale
- cash discount
- purchases discount

- purchases return
- purchases allowance
- debit memorandum
- withdrawal of merchandise

Questions for Individual Study

1. When is it more practical to use separate special journals instead of a combination journal?
2. How is the equality of debits and credits kept in a purchases journal with only one amount column?
3. To what accounts are the separate items in the amount column of the purchases journal, page 426, posted?
4. To what two accounts in the general ledger is the total of the amount column of the purchases journal on page 428 posted?
5. Why is a cash discount sometimes offered to a person who has purchased merchandise on account?
6. What is meant by terms of sale 2/10, n/30?
7. Why is the purchases discount account given an account number with a decimal, such as 51.2?

8. When Sunrise Art Center issues a check on account with a discount, what account is debited and what accounts are credited?
9. What column totals are posted from the cash payments journal shown on page 433?
10. Why are the totals of the other columns in the cash payments journal *not* posted?
11. What accounts are debited and credited by the buyer to record a purchases returns and allowances transaction?
12. When supplies are bought on account, why is the entry made in the general journal instead of the purchases journal?
13. What is meant by the posting reference P6? CP14? J10?
14. What column totals are posted from the general journal on page 441?

Cases for Management Decision

CASE 1 Lee Kelley owns and manages a paint store. She has been using separate special journals in keeping her financial records. A friend has suggested that Ms. Kelley would ease her work if she used only a combination journal. What should Ms. Kelley consider in making a decision either to stay with the special journals or to change to a combination journal?

CASE 2 The Regency Gift Store uses a cash payments journal similar to the one shown on page 433. One difference is that it has a special amount column titled *Rent Expense Debit*. A recently employed accountant says that the column is not needed. The owner insists that the column is needed. With whom do you agree? Why?

CASE 3 William Casey owns and runs Willie's Taco Wagon. He buys all his food and supplies from one business. Does he need to keep an accounts payable ledger? Under what circumstances might he want to keep an accounts payable ledger? Why?

DRILL 23-D 1 Analyzing transactions affecting purchases and cash payments

Drill for Mastering Principles

If you are not using the workbook with this textbook, prepare on a sheet of paper a form similar to the one shown below.

Trans. No.	(a) Account Debited	(b) Account Credited	(c) Journal in Which Recorded	(d) and (e) Name of Amount Column Used in Journal	
				For Amount Debited	For Amount Credited
1	Rent Expense	Cash	Cash Payments	General Debit	Cash Credit

Instructions: For each of the following transactions: (a) Write the name of the account(s) debited. (b) Write the name of the account(s) credited. (c) Write the name of the journal in which the transaction is recorded. (d) and (e) Write the names of the amount column(s) in the journal in which the debit and credit amounts will be recorded. (Transaction No. 1 is given as an example in the form above.)

1. Paid cash for February rent.
2. Purchased merchandise on account from Carter's Store.
3. Paid cash on account to Carter's Store; no discount.
4. Paid cash for purchases of merchandise.
5. Paid cash for cleaning of store windows. (Miscellaneous Expense)
6. The owner, Mary Lewis, withdrew merchandise for personal use.
7. Paid cash for supplies.
8. Bought supplies on account from Talbott Company.
9. The owner, Mary Lewis, withdrew cash for personal use.
10. Paid cash on account to McGuire Company for a purchase invoice less the amount of a discount.
11. Paid cash for weekly payroll less deductions for employees' income tax and FICA Tax.
12. Issued a debit memorandum to Carter's Store.

PROBLEM 23-1 Journalizing and posting transactions affecting purchases and cash payments

Problem for Applying Concepts

Instructions: □ **1.** Open the creditors' accounts given on page 444 in the accounts payable ledger of the Wheatland Wholesale Company. Record the balances as of March 1 of the current year.

Creditor	Terms of Sale	Account Balance
Burkhardt Company, Portland, OR 97202	n/30	$ 145.00
James Leland Company, Salem, OR 97301	1/10, n/30	———
Rush Company, Tacoma, WA 98403	n/30	1,380.00
Tyrone Supply Company, Portland, OR 97203	1/10, n/30	540.00
Zackary & Sons, Eugene, OR 97401	2/10, n/30	———

Instructions: □ **2.** Open the following accounts in the general ledger of the Wheatland Wholesale Company. Record the balances as of March 1 of the current year. (Only those general ledger accounts needed in this problem are included in the following list.)

Account Title	Acct. No.	Account Balance	Account Title	Acct. No.	Account Balance
Cash................................	11	$11,200.00	Manny Wheatland,		
Supplies..........................	14	442.20	Drawing.......................	32	——
Accounts Payable	21	2,065.00	Purchases.........................	51	——
Employees Income Tax			Purchases Ret. & Allow.	51.1	——
Payable........................	22	76.32	Purchases Discount...........	51.2	——
FICA Tax Payable	23	99.84	Delivery Expense..............	61	——
Federal Unemployment Tax			Miscellaneous Expense......	63	——
Payable........................	24	24.00	Payroll Taxes Expense	64	——
State Unemployment Tax			Rent Expense	65	——
Payable........................	25	51.84	Salary Expense.................	66	——

Instructions: □ **3.** The following transactions affecting purchases and cash payments were completed by the Wheatland Wholesale Company during March of the current year. Record these transactions in a purchases journal, a general journal, and a cash payments journal similar to those illustrated in this chapter. Use page 6 for each journal. Source documents are abbreviated as: check, Ck; memorandum, M; purchase invoice, P; debit memorandum, DM.

March 1. Purchased merchandise on account from Rush Company, $960.00. P73.

   1. Paid March rent, $400.00. Ck132.

   3. Returned merchandise to Rush Company, $60.00. DM14.

   4. Purchased merchandise on account from James Leland Company, $936.00. P74.

   Posting. Post the items that are to be posted individually. Post from the journals in this order: purchases journal, general journal, and cash payments journal.

   7. Bought supplies on account from Burkhardt Company, $126.00. M19.

   9. Paid on account to Tyrone Company, $534.60, covering P70 for $540.00 less a 1% cash discount of $5.40. Ck133.

   10. Issued check to Manny Wheatland, the owner, for a cash withdrawal for personal use, $150.00. Ck134.

March 11. Deposited February liabilities for employees' income tax payable, $76.32, and for FICA tax payable, $99.84; total deposit, $176.16. Ck135.

Posting. Post the items that are to be posted individually.

14. Purchased merchandise for cash, $210.00. Ck136.

14. Paid on account to James Leland Company, $926.64, covering P74 for $936.00 less a 1% discount of $9.36. Ck137.

15. Purchased merchandise on account from Zackary & Sons, $1,632.00. P75.

15. Paid semimonthly payroll, $413.04, covering salary expense of $480.00 less deductions for employees' income tax, $38.16, and for FICA tax, $28.80. Ck138.

15. Recorded employer's payroll taxes as follows: FICA tax, $28.80; federal unemployment tax, $2.78; state unemployment tax, $12.96; total payroll taxes expense, $44.54. M20.

19. Purchased merchandise on account from James Leland Company, $1,134.00. P76.

Posting. Post the items that are to be posted individually.

21. Paid on account to Rush Company, $1,320.00, for March 1 balance of $1,380.00 less DM14 for $60.00; no discount. Ck139.

22. Paid miscellaneous expense, $18.00. Ck140.

22. Paid on account to Burkhardt Company, $145.00; no discount. Ck141.

22. Paid delivery expense, $36.00. Ck142.

23. Purchased merchandise on account from Tyrone Company, $600.00. P77.

24. Manny Wheatland, the owner, withdrew merchandise for personal use at cost, $50.00. M21.

25. Paid on account to Zackary & Sons, $1,599.36, covering P75 for $1,632.00 less a 2% discount of $32.64. Ck143.

25. Purchased merchandise on account from Rush Company, $395.00. P78.

Posting. Post the items that are to be posted individually.

28. Paid on account to Burkhardt Company, $126.00; no discount, Ck144.

28. Purchased merchandise on account from Zackary & Sons, $472.00. P79.

29. Paid on account to James Leland Company, $1,122.66, covering P76 for $1,134.00 less a 1% discount of $11.34. Ck145.

29. Purchased merchandise on account from James Leland Company, $432.00. P80.

30. Paid miscellaneous expense, $49.00. Ck146.

30. Returned merchandise to James Leland Company, $144.00. DM15.

31. Paid semimonthly payroll, $413.04, covering salary expense of $480.00 less deductions for employees' income tax, $38.16, and for FICA tax, $28.80. Ck147.

31. Recorded employer's payroll taxes as follows: FICA tax, $28.80; federal unemployment tax, $2.78; state unemployment tax, $12.96; total payroll taxes expense, $44.54. M22.

31. Issued check to Manny Wheatland, the owner, for a cash withdrawal for personal use, $500.00. Ck148.

Posting. Post the items that are to be posted individually.

Instructions: □ **4.** Total and rule the purchases journal. Post the total. Compare your work with the purchases journal shown on page 428.

□ **5.** Foot, prove, total, and rule the general journal. Post the totals of the special columns. Compare your work with the general journal shown on page 441.

□ **6.** Foot, prove, total, and rule the cash payments journal. Post the totals of the special columns. Compare your work with the cash payments journal shown on page 433.

□ **7.** Prepare a schedule of accounts payable similar to the one shown on page 215. Compare the schedule total with the balance of the accounts payable account in the general ledger. The total and the balance should be the same.

Optional
Problems

**MASTERY
PROBLEM 23-M** Journalizing and posting transactions
affecting purchases and cash payments

Instructions: □ **1.** As of May 1 of the current year, Dawson Hardware had the following accounts payable. Open an account and record the balance for each of the creditors.

Creditor	Terms of Sale	Account Balance
John Battle Company, Helena, MT 59601	1/10, n/30	$144.00
Naylor Company, Billings, MT 59101	n/30	280.00
O'Brien Supply Company, Park City, MT 59063	n/30	——
Weber Sales, Inc., Great Falls, MT 59401	2/10, n/30	588.00

Instructions: □ **2.** Open the following accounts in the general ledger of Dawson Hardware. Record the balances as of May 1 of the current year. (Only those general ledger accounts needed in this problem are included.)

Account Title	Acct. No.	Account Balance	Account Title	Acct. No.	Account Balance
Cash............................	11	$7,350.00	Bud Dawson, Drawing	32	——
Supplies.........................	14	148.32	Purchases........................	51	——
Accounts Payable	21	1,012.00	Purchases Returns and Al-		
Employees Income Tax			lowances	51.1	——
Payable........................	22	132.60	Purchases Discount...........	51.2	——
FICA Tax Payable	23	99.84	Delivery Expense..............	61	——
Federal Unemployment Tax			Miscellaneous Expense	63	——
Payable.......................	24	43.20	Payroll Taxes Expense	64	——
State Unemployment Tax			Rent Expense	65	——
Payable.......................	25	77.76	Salary Expense	66	——

Instructions: □ **3.** The following transactions affecting purchases and cash payments were completed by Dawson Hardware during May of the current year. Record these transactions on page 10 of a purchases journal, on page 3 of a general journal, and on page 7 of a cash payments journal similar to those shown in this chapter. Source documents are abbreviated as: check, Ck; memorandum, M; purchase invoice, P; debit memorandum, DM.

May 2. Paid May rent, $450.00. Ck51.
   2. Bud Dawson, the owner, withdrew merchandise for personal use at cost, $144.00. M19.
   2. Returned merchandise to Naylor Company, $60.00. DM8.
   3. Paid on account to John Battle Company, $142.56, covering P50 for $144.00 less a 1% cash discount of $1.44. Ck52.
   4. Purchased merchandise on account from Weber Sales, Inc., $252.00. P52.
   5. Purchased merchandise on account from John Battle Company, $198.00. P53.
   6. Paid on account to Weber Sales, Inc., $576.24, covering P51 for $588.00 less a 2% discount of $11.76. Ck53.

   Posting. Post the items that are to be posted individually. Post from the journals in this order: purchases journal, general journal, and cash payments journal.

   9. Paid on account to Naylor Company, $220.00, covering P49 for $280.00 less DM8 for $60.00; no discount. Ck54.
   9. Paid cash for delivery expense, $18.00. Ck55.
   10. Bought supplies on account from O'Brien Supply Company, $90.00. M20.
   12. Purchased merchandise on account from Naylor Company, $297.00. P54.
   13. Paid on account to Weber Sales, Inc., $246.96, covering P52 for $252.00 less a 2% discount of $5.04. Ck56.
   13. Paid on account to John Battle Company, $196.02, covering P53 for $198.00 less a 1% discount of $1.98. Ck57.

   Posting. Post the items that are to be posted individually.

   16. Returned merchandise to Naylor Company, $38.00. DM9.
   17. Purchased merchandise on account from Weber Sales, Inc., $284.00. P55.
   17. Deposited the amount of April liabilities for employees' income tax payable, $132.60, and for FICA tax payable, $99.84; total deposit, $232.44. Ck58.
   17. Paid liability for state unemployment tax, $77.76. Ck59.
   18. Purchased merchandise on account from John Battle Company, $262.80. P56.
   20. Paid on account to O'Brien Supply Company, $90.00; no discount. Ck60.
   20. Paid on account to Naylor Company, $259.00, covering P54 for $297.00 less DM9 for $38.00; no discount. Ck61.

   Posting. Post the items that are to be posted individually.

   23. Bought supplies on account from O'Brien Supply Company, $140.00. M21.
   24. Paid miscellaneous expenses, $57.00. Ck62.
   25. Purchased merchandise on account from Naylor Company, $114.00. P57.
   28. Paid on account to John Battle Company, $260.17, covering P56 for $262.80 less a 1% discount of $2.63. Ck63.

May 31. Paid monthly payroll, $833.95, covering salary expense of $1,040.00 less deductions for employees' income tax, $143.65, and for FICA tax, $62.40. Ck64.

31. Recorded employer's payroll taxes: FICA tax, $62.40; federal unemployment tax, $6.03; state unemployment tax, $28.08; total payroll taxes expense, $96.51. M22.

31. Issued check to Bud Dawson, the owner, for a cash withdrawal for personal use, $250.00. Ck65.

Posting. Post the items that are to be posted individually.

Instructions: ☐ **4.** Total and rule the purchases journal. Post the total.

☐ **5.** Foot, prove, total, and rule the general journal. Post the totals of the special columns.

☐ **6.** Foot, prove, total, and rule the cash payments journal. Post the totals of the special columns.

☐ **7.** Prepare a schedule of accounts payable similar to the one shown on page 215. Compare the schedule total with the balance of the accounts payable account in the general ledger. The total and the balance should be the same.

BONUS PROBLEM 23-B   Journalizing transactions in a combined purchases-cash payments journal

The accountant for Dawson Hardware has suggested that time could be saved if the purchases journal and the cash payments journal were combined into one journal. He suggests using a journal such as the one below.

PURCHASES — CASH PAYMENTS JOURNAL

				General		Purchases	Accounts Payable		Purchases Discount	Cash
				1	2	3	4	5	6	7
Date	Account Title	Doc. No.	Post. Ref.	Debit	Credit	Purchases Debit	Debit	Credit	Credit	Credit

Bud Dawson, owner, has asked the accountant to show him how it would appear after transactions have been recorded in the journal shown above.

Instructions: ☐ **1.** Use page 8 of a journal like the one shown above, and page 11 of a four-column general journal like the one shown on page 441. Journalize the transactions given in Instruction 3, Mastery Problem 23-M, page 447.

☐ **2.** Foot, prove, total, and rule the combined purchases-cash payments journal. Foot, prove, total, and rule the four-column general journal.

☐ **3.** Do you agree with the accountant that the combined purchases-cash payments journal used in this problem saves time in journalizing and posting? Why?

Special Journals: Sales and Cash Receipts

24

The Sunrise Art Center uses five journals: purchases journal and cash payments journal — described in Chapter 23; sales journal and cash receipts journal — described in this chapter; and four-column general journal — described in Chapter 23 and in this chapter.

SALES JOURNAL

A special journal used to record only sales of merchandise on account is called a sales journal. The sales journal used by Sunrise Art Center is on page 450. A sales journal sometimes is known as a sales book or a sales register.

Form of sales journal

The sales journal used by Sunrise Art Center has columns in which a sale on account can be recorded on one line. An amount recorded in the single amount column is both a debit to Accounts Receivable and a credit to Sales. Both account titles are listed in the column heading.

Journalizing a sale on account in a sales journal

The Sunrise Art Center prepares a sales invoice in duplicate for each sale of merchandise on account. The carbon copy is given to the charge customer. The original copy is used by Sunrise Art Center as the source document for recording sales of merchandise on account transactions. The sales invoice used by Sunrise Art Center is similar to the one on page 179.

On December 2, Sunrise Art Center made the following sale of merchandise on account:

December 2, 1977. Sold merchandise on account to Steven Eby, $180.00. Sales Invoice No. 166.

449

Accounts Receivable is debited and Sales is credited for $180.00. The customer's account, Steven Eby, in the accounts receivable ledger, is also debited for $180.00. This sale of merchandise on account is shown in the sales journal below.

Sale of merchandise on account recorded in the sales journal

The date, *1977, Dec. 2*, is written in the Date column. The amount of the sale, *$180.00*, is written in the amount column. The name of the charge customer, *Steven Eby*, is written in the Account Debited column. The number of the sales invoice, *166*, is written in the Sale No. column. A check mark is placed on the sales invoice at the right of the customer's name. This check mark shows that the invoice has been recorded in the sales journal.

Each sale of merchandise on account is recorded in the sales journal in this same way. The completed sales journal of Sunrise Art Center for December is on the opposite page.

Posting from the sales journal to the accounts receivable ledger

Each entry in the sales journal is an amount to be collected from a charge customer. Each entry in the sales journal is posted individually to the accounts receivable ledger. The procedure for posting is the same as posting the Accounts Receivable Debit column of the combination journal. This procedure is described on page 198 of Chapter 13.

The Sunrise Art Center posts daily from the sales journal to the accounts receivable ledger. This daily posting keeps each customer's account balance up to date at all times. The illustration below shows Line 1 on page 15 of the sales journal posted to the accounts receivable ledger.

Posting from the sales journal to the accounts receivable ledger

The completion of posting is indicated by placing *S15* in the Post. Ref. column of the subsidiary ledger account. A check mark is also placed in the Post. Ref. column of the sales journal.

> *S* is the abbreviation for *sales* journal.

Posting the totals of the sales journal to the general ledger

At the end of the month, the sales journal is totaled and ruled. A single line is drawn across the amount column under the last amount. The column is added and the total is written below the single line as shown below. The last day of the month, *31*, is placed in the Date column. The word *Total* is written in the Account Debited column. Then double lines are ruled across the amount column under the total.

The total of the sales journal is posted twice to the general ledger: (1) as a debit to the accounts receivable account, and (2) as a credit to the sales account. The sales journal of Sunrise Art Center after posting for December is completed is shown below.

SALES JOURNAL   PAGE *15*

	DATE	ACCOUNT DEBITED	SALE NO.	POST. REF.	ACCTS. REC. DR. SALES CR.	
1	1977 Dec. 2	Steven Eby	166	✓	180 00	1
2	5	Allen Kinder	167	✓	42 00	2
3	8	William Levi	168	✓	138 00	3
4	9	Sharon Oren	169	✓	78 00	4
5	13	L. G. Imhoff	170	✓	324 00	5
6	13	B. J. Milford	171	✓	390 00	6
7	15	W. V. Huber	172	✓	432 00	7
8	19	Sharon Oren	173	✓	153 00	8
9	22	William Levi	174	✓	342 00	9
10	24	B. J. Milford	175	✓	234 00	10
11	27	Sharon Oren	176	✓	270 00	11
12	29	Charles Joris	177	✓	337 00	12
13	31	Total			2920 00	13
14					(12) (41)	14

Sales journal totaled, ruled, and posted

ACCOUNT *Accounts Receivable*   **ACCOUNT NO.** *12*

DATE	ITEM	POST. REF.	DEBIT	CREDIT	BALANCE DEBIT	CREDIT
1977 Dec. 1	Balance	✓			1209 00	
31		S15	2920 00		4129 00	

ACCOUNT *Sales*   **ACCOUNT NO.** *41*

DATE	ITEM	POST. REF.	DEBIT	CREDIT	BALANCE DEBIT	CREDIT
1977 Dec. 31		S15		2920 00		2920 00

General ledger accounts after posting the total from the sales journal

After the sales journal total is posted as a debit to Accounts Receivable, the account number, *12*, is placed in parentheses under the total in the sales journal. This same total also is posted as a credit to Sales, and the account number, *41*, is placed in parentheses under the total. The total is posted both as a debit and as a credit. This maintains the equality of debits and credits in the general ledger.

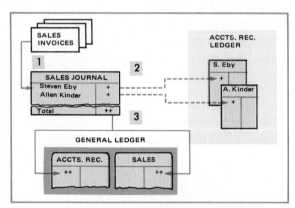

Flowchart showing journalizing and posting of sales on account using a special sales journal

Summary of journalizing and posting sales on acccunt using a sales journal

(1) The Sunrise Art Center records all sales on account in a one-column sales journal. (2) The individual items in the sales journal are posted daily. The items are posted to the individual accounts for charge customers in the accounts receivable ledger. (3) At the end of the month, the total of the amount column is posted to Accounts Receivable as a debit and to Sales as a credit. The flowchart that is illustrated at the left shows this procedure.

CASH RECEIPTS JOURNAL

A special journal in which only cash receipts transactions are recorded is called a cash receipts journal. The cash receipts journal used by Sunrise Art Center is on the next page.

Form of cash receipts journal

The six-column cash receipts journal of Sunrise Art Center has special amount columns for those kinds of transactions that occur most often. For example, Sunrise Art Center has many transactions in which cash is received from charge customers. There is a special amount column for Accounts Receivable Credit. Additional investments by the owner do not occur very often. Therefore, no special amount column is provided for a credit to the capital account. Investments by the owner are recorded in the General Credit column of the cash receipts journal.

Journalizing cash receipts in a cash receipts journal

Cash is most often received from customers on account and from cash sales. Every cash receipt is recorded in the cash receipts journal. The source document for all cash receipts except cash sales is a receipt. The source document for cash sales is a cash register tape. Sometimes cash is received from other sources, such as an additional investment by the owner. These three types of cash receipt transactions are on Lines 2, 3, and 4 of the cash receipts journal below.

					GENERAL		SALES CREDIT	ACCOUNTS RECEIVABLE CREDIT	SALES DISCOUNT DEBIT	CASH DEBIT	
	DATE	ACCOUNT TITLE	Doc. No.	Post. Ref.	DEBIT	CREDIT					
1	1977 Dec. 1	Balance on hand, $3,100.00		✓							1
2	1	William Levi	R151					36600		36600	2
3	3	✓	73	✓			103000			103000	3
4	5	S. G. Justin, Capital	R152			100000				100000	4

CASH RECEIPTS JOURNAL   PAGE 17

Cash receipts transactions recorded in a cash receipts journal

Line 1 shows a memorandum entry for the beginning cash balance. As explained on page 68, Chapter 6, this memorandum entry makes the beginning cash balance readily available for proving cash at any time during the month.

Line 2 shows a receipt of cash from a customer; Line 3 shows cash sales for the week. The entries to record these transactions in the cash receipts journal are similar to the entries explained in Chapter 12, pages 177–181.

Line 4 shows an additional investment of cash by the owner. The entry on this line is similar to the entry explained in Chapter 6, page 73.

Sales discount

A cash discount on sales granted to a customer by the seller is called a sales discount. Sales discounts are granted to encourage prompt payment. Sunrise Art Center sells to charge customers on terms of 1/10, n/30.

When a sales discount is granted, the seller receives less than the sale price recorded at the time of the sale. A sales discount reduces the revenue from sales. Sales discounts are recorded by Sunrise Art Center in the general ledger account Sales Discount. The number of this account is 41.2. The decimal number shows that the balance of the sales discount account is a deduction from the balance of account number 41, Sales. The sales discount account is often known as a minus sales account. The sales discount account is in the revenue section of the general ledger, as shown in the chart of accounts, page 424.

Journalizing a cash receipt on account with a sales discount

The Sunrise Art Center received the following cash on account:

December 5, 1977. Received on account from Steven Eby, $142.56 for Sales Invoice No. 149, $144.00 less 1% discount, $1.44. Receipt No. 153.

GENERAL LEDGER

Cash   11

Dec. 1 Bal. 3,100.00
    5   142.56

Sales Discount   41.2

Dec. 5   1.44

Accounts Receivable   12

Dec. 1 Bal. 1,209.00 | Dec. 5   144.00

ACCOUNTS RECEIVABLE LEDGER

Steven Eby

Dec. 1 Bal.   144.00 | Dec. 5   144.00

Cash is debited for the amount received, $142.56. Sales Discount is debited for the amount of the discount, $1.44. The balance of Sales Discount is a deduction on the income statement from Sales. The sales account has a credit balance. The sales discount account has a debit balance.

Accounts Receivable is credited for the amount of the sales invoice, $144.00. This entry decreases the amount to be collected from charge customers. The account of Steven Eby in the accounts receivable ledger also is credited for $144.00.

The entry for this cash receipt on account with a sales discount is shown below.

					GENERAL		SALES CREDIT	ACCOUNTS RECEIVABLE CREDIT	SALES DISCOUNT DEBIT	CASH DEBIT	
					1	2	3	4	5	6	
	DATE	ACCOUNT TITLE	Doc. No.	Post. Ref.	DEBIT	CREDIT					
5	5	Steven Eby		✓53				14400	144	14256	5
6											6
7											7

CASH RECEIPTS JOURNAL   PAGE 17

Cash receipt on account with sales discount recorded in a cash receipts journal

Sales discounts are recorded often by Sunrise Art Center. Therefore, the cash receipts journal has a special amount column for Sales Discount Debit.

The amount of the sales invoice, *$144.00*, is written in the Accounts Receivable Credit column. The amount of the sales discount, *$1.44*, is written in the Sales Discount Debit column. The amount of cash received, *$142.56*, is written in the Cash Debit column. The name of the charge customer, *Steven Eby*, is written in the Account Title column. The total of the two debits ($1.44 + $142.56), $144.00, is equal to the one credit, $144.00.

Posting from the cash receipts journal

Each amount in the Accounts Receivable Credit column is posted to an individual account in the accounts receivable ledger. A check mark is placed in the Post. Ref. column of the cash receipts journal. The check mark shows that posting is completed for the line in the journal with an amount in the Accounts Receivable Credit column. The Sunrise Art Center does this posting daily.

Each amount in the General Debit and Credit columns is posted to the general ledger. The account number is written in the Post. Ref. column of the journal when each item is posted. The Sunrise Art Center posts items in the General Debit and Credit columns often during the month.

CR17 is placed in the Post. Ref. column of the ledger accounts. CR is the abbreviation for *cash receipts* journal.

At the end of a month, the cash receipts journal is footed, and the equality of debits and credits is proved. Cash is then proved. The cash proof for Sunrise Art Center at the end of December is:

Beginning cash balance, December 1, 1977 (Line 1 of the cash receipts journal, below	$ 3,100.00
Plus total cash received (total of Cash Debit column, cash receipts journal, below...	7,793.96
Total...	$10,893.96
Less total cash payments (total of Cash Credit column, cash payments journal, page 433	4,867.08
Equals cash balance, December 31, 1977.................................	$ 6,026.88

The check-stub balance after the last check (Check No. 259) was written is $6,026.88. The balance on the check stub agrees with the balance figure above; therefore, cash is proved.

After cash is proved, the cash receipts journal is totaled and ruled as shown below. The total of each special column is posted to the account listed in the column heading. The posting reference is written in parentheses below the column total. The totals of the General columns are not posted because each amount in these two columns is posted separately to a general ledger account. A check mark is placed in parentheses below each General column total.

CASH RECEIPTS JOURNAL — PAGE 17

	DATE	ACCOUNT TITLE	Doc. No.	Post. Ref.	GENERAL DEBIT	GENERAL CREDIT	SALES CREDIT	ACCOUNTS RECEIVABLE CREDIT	SALES DISCOUNT DEBIT	CASH DEBIT	
1	1977 Dec. 1	Balance on hand, $3,100.00		✓							1
2	1	William Levi	R151	✓				36600		36600	2
3	3	✓	J3	✓			103000			103000	3
4	5	S. G. Justin, Capital	R152 31			100000				100000	4
5	5	Steven Eby	R153	✓				14400	144	14256	5
6	7	L. G. Imhoff	R154	✓				11500	115	11385	6
19	29	Sharon Oren	R165	✓				7800	78	7722	19
20	30	✓	J30	✓			46800			46800	20
21	31	Totals				100000	466453	214400	1457	779396	21
22						(✓)	(44)	(12)	(41.2)	(11)	22

Cash receipts journal totaled, ruled, and posted

The use of the General Debit column of the cash receipts journal is described in later chapters.

Summary of journalizing and posting cash receipts using a cash receipts journal

(1) The Sunrise Art Center records cash receipts in a six-column cash receipts journal. (2) Each item in the Accounts Receivable Credit column is posted daily to the accounts receivable ledger. (3) Each item in the General Debit and Credit columns is posted often during the month to the general ledger. (4) The totals of the special columns are posted at the end of the month to the general ledger accounts. The flowchart below shows this procedure.

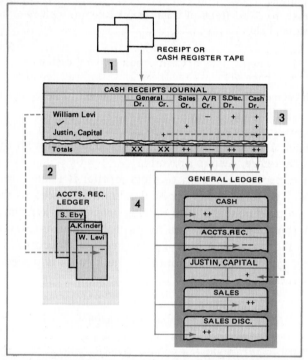

Flowchart showing journalizing and posting of cash receipts using a special cash receipts journal

FOUR-COLUMN GENERAL JOURNAL

As described in Chapter 23, special transactions related to purchases are recorded in a four-column general journal by Sunrise Art Center. The Sunrise Art Center also records special transactions related to sales in its four-column general journal:

(1) Sales returns and allowances.
(2) Correcting entries affecting charge customers' accounts but not the controlling account.

Sales returns and allowances

Most businesses that sell goods can expect to have some of the goods returned as unsatisfactory. The customer may decide not to keep the purchase. The customer may have received the wrong style, the wrong size, or damaged goods. The customer may return the goods to the seller and ask to receive credit on account or to be given a cash refund. The return of goods for which the customer is allowed credit on account or given a cash refund is called a sales return.

The seller may grant credit to a customer without asking for the return of the damaged or imperfect goods. Credit given to a customer for part of the sales price of goods when the goods are not returned, is called a sales allowance. An allowance might also be given because of a shortage in a shipment.

When a sales return or a sales allowance is granted, the seller usually informs the buyer in writing. A form showing the amount of credit granted by the seller for returns, allowances, and similar items is called a credit memorandum. It is called a *credit* memorandum because the asset account, Accounts Receivable, is decreased. Decreases in asset accounts are recorded as credits.

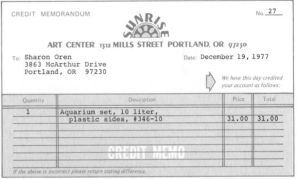

The Sunrise Art Center issues a credit memorandum in duplicate for each sales return or sales allowance. The carbon copy is given to the customer. The original copy is used by Sunrise Art Center as the source document for the transaction. The form of credit memorandum used by Sunrise Art Center is shown above.

Credit memorandum

Sales returns and sales allowances decrease the amount of sales. Some businesses debit the sales account for the amount of a return or allowance. However, most businesses debit these amounts to a separate account. The title of the account used by Sunrise Art Center is *Sales Returns and Allowances*. A separate account is used to show how large the amount of sales returns and allowances has become. The business can see if the returns and allowances are increasing or decreasing from one year to the next. If the amounts are very large, one account may be kept for sales returns and another account for sales allowances. The Sunrise Art Center has few sales returns and allowances, so a single account is used.

The sales returns and allowances account is placed in the revenue division of the general ledger. This is shown in the chart of accounts, page 424. The sales returns and allowances account is numbered 41.1. The number shows that the balance of this minus sales account, like Sales Discount, is a deduction from account number 41, Sales.

Journalizing a sales returns and allowances transaction in a four-column general journal

The Sunrise Art Center recorded the following transaction:

December 19, 1977. Granted credit to Sharon Oren for merchandise returned by her, $31.00. Credit Memorandum No. 27.

GENERAL LEDGER

Sales Returns and Allowances	41.1
Dec. 19 31.00	

Accounts Receivable	12
Dec. 1 Bal. 1,209.00	Dec. 19 31.00

ACCOUNTS RECEIVABLE LEDGER

Sharon Oren

Dec. 1 Bal. 120.00	Dec. 19 31.00
9 78.00	
19 153.00	

The sales returns and allowances account is a minus sales account. It has a debit balance. The sales returns and allowances account increases on the debit side. Because this transaction increases the balance of the account, Sales Returns and Allowances is debited for $31.00.

The amount to be collected from the charge customer is decreased. Therefore, Accounts Receivable is credited for the amount of the return, $31.00. The same amount is also credited to Sharon Oren's account in the accounts receivable ledger.

The entry in the four-column general journal for this transaction is:

Sales returns and allowances transaction recorded in a four-column general journal

The debit, *$31.00*, is written in the General Debit column. The account to be debited, *Sales Returns and Allowances*, is written in the Account Title column. The credit, *$31.00*, is written in the Accounts Receivable Credit column on the next line. The name of the charge customer, *Sharon Oren*, is written in the Account Title column indented about one-half inch (about 1.3 centimeters). The source document, *Credit Memo. No. 27*, is then written on the next line and indented another half inch (about 1.3 centimeters).

Journalizing a correcting entry affecting only charge customers' accounts

Sometimes errors are made in recording or posting data to subsidiary ledgers that do not affect the controlling account in the general ledger. For example, if a sale on account is charged to the wrong charge customer, the column total posted from the sales journal to the general ledger is correct. The accounts receivable account shows the correct balance. However, two of the charge customers' accounts in the accounts receivable ledger show incorrect balances. To correct this error, only the subsidiary ledger accounts need to be corrected.

The Sunrise Art Center discovered and corrected the following error:

December 20, 1977. Discovered that a sale on account to Walter Bohn on November 29 was incorrectly charged to Russell Bohr, $28.00. Memorandum No. 112.

The source document for this correcting entry is a memorandum prepared by the accountant and approved by the owner.

The total of the amount column in the sales journal, posted November 30, is correct. No correction is needed for this amount. The correcting entry involves only subsidiary ledger accounts. The Walter Bohn account is debited for $28.00 to record the charge sale in the correct account. The Russell Bohr account is credited for $28.00 to cancel the incorrect entry.

ACCOUNTS RECEIVABLE LEDGER

Walter Bohn

| Dec. 20 | 28.00 | | |

Russell Bohr

| Nov. 29 | 28.00 | Dec. 20 | 28.00 |

The entry in the four-column general journal for this correcting entry is:

Correcting entry for posting error recorded in a four-column general journal

The amount of the debit, *$28.00*, is written in the General Debit column. The name of the charge customer, *Walter Bohn*, is written in the Account Title column. The amount of the credit, *$28.00*, is written in the

General Credit column on the next line. The name of the charge customer, *Russell Bohr*, is written in the Account Title column indented about one-half inch (about 1.3 centimeters). The source document, *Memorandum No. 112*, is written on the next line and indented another half inch (about 1.3 centimeters).

Posting transactions affecting sales from a four-column general journal

The posting of a four-column general journal is described in Chapter 23, pages 440–441. The two general journal entries described in this chapter are posted in the same way.

In the sales returns and allowances entry on page 458, the amount in the General Debit column, Line 15, is posted to the general ledger. The amount in the Accounts Receivable Credit column, Line 16, is posted to the accounts receivable ledger.

In the correcting entry on page 459, Lines 18 and 19, both amounts are written in General columns. The amounts in the General Debit and General Credit columns are posted to the subsidiary ledger.

At the end of the month, the total of the Accounts Receivable Credit column in the four-column general journal is posted as described in Chapter 23, page 441.

Summary of journalizing and posting miscellaneous entries using a four-column general journal

(1) The Sunrise Art Center records all miscellaneous entries affecting accounts receivable in a four-column general journal. These entries include sales returns and allowances and correcting entries affecting subsidiary ledger accounts only. (2) Each item in the Accounts Receivable Credit column is posted daily to the accounts receivable ledger. (3) Items in the General Debit and Credit columns are posted often during the month to the general ledger and the subsidiary ledger. (4) The total of the Accounts Receivable Credit column is posted to the general ledger at the end of the month. The flowchart illustrated on the opposite page shows this procedure.

ORDER OF POSTING FROM SPECIAL JOURNALS

Items affecting customers' or creditors' accounts are posted often during the month. Some businesses do this posting daily so that the balances of these accounts in the subsidiary ledgers will always be up to date. Items affecting general ledger accounts are posted less often during the month. All items, including the totals of special columns, must be posted before a trial balance is prepared.

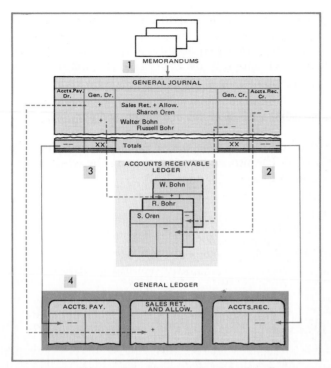

Flowchart showing journalizing and posting of miscellaneous entries affecting accounts receivable using a four-column general journal

It is usually best to post the journals in the following order: (1) sales journal, (2) purchases journal, (3) general journal, (4) cash receipts journal, and (5) cash payments journal. This order of posting helps put the debits and credits in the accounts in the order in which the transactions occurred.

AUTOMATED DATA PROCESSING FOR SALES AND CASH RECEIPTS

The same procedures used for the journalizing and posting of purchases and cash payments, Chapter 23, pages 429 and 434, apply to the processing of sales and cash receipts. In a manual data processing system using special journals, sales are recorded in a sales journal; cash receipts, in a cash receipts journal. In an automated data processing system, sales and cash receipts are recorded on journal entry transmittal forms.

The journalizing and posting of sales and cash receipts transactions in an ADP system are described for Wayside Furniture in Chapter 20. Page 356 shows journalizing of sales, and page 354 shows journalizing of cash receipts. Page 359 shows the posting to a general ledger and subsidiary ledgers.

WORK AT THE END OF THE FISCAL PERIOD

The Sunrise Art Center prepares a work sheet and financial statements at the end of each monthly fiscal period. The Center also records and posts adjusting and closing entries at the end of a fiscal period.

Work sheet including cash discounts and returns and allowances

The work sheet below was prepared by Sunrise Art Center on December 31, 1977. The procedure for preparing the work sheet is similar to that described in Chapter 15, page 261B.

Sunrise Art Center
Work Sheet
For Month Ended December 31, 1977

	ACCOUNT TITLE	ACCT. NO.	TRIAL BALANCE DEBIT	TRIAL BALANCE CREDIT	ADJUSTMENTS DEBIT	ADJUSTMENTS CREDIT	INCOME STATEMENT DEBIT	INCOME STATEMENT CREDIT	BALANCE SHEET DEBIT	BALANCE SHEET CREDIT	
1	Cash	11	602688						602688		1
2	Accounts Receivable	12	185940						185940		2
3	Merchandise Inventory	13	739500		(b)687000	(a)739500			687000		3
4	Supplies	14	40800			(c)25100			15700		4
5	Prepaid Insurance	15	25200			(d)8400			16800		5
6	Accounts Payable	21		181700						181700	6
7	Employees Income Tax Pay.	22		7860						7860	7
8	FICA Tax Payable	23		8640						8640	8
9	Fed. Unemploy. Tax Pay.	24		1080						1080	9
10	State Unemploy. Tax Pay.	25		2232						2232	10
11	United Fund Donat. Pay.	26		4787						4787	11
12	S. G. Justin, Capital	31		1237800						1237800	12
13	S. G. Justin, Drawing	32	55000						55000		13
14	Income Summary	33			(a)739500	(b)687000	739500	687000			14
15	Sales	41		758453				758453			15
16	Sales Returns + Allow.	41.1	12600				12600				16
17	Sales Discount	41.2	1456				1456				17
18	Purchases	51	393000				393000				18
19	Purchases Ret. + Allow.	51.1		1440				1440			19
20	Purchases Discount	51.2		3372				3372			20
21	Delivery Expense	61	19340				19340				21
22	Insurance Expense	62			(d)8400		8400				22
23	Miscellaneous Expense	63	4416				4416				23
24	Payroll Taxes Expense	64	5424				5424				24
25	Rent Expense	65	50000				50000				25
26	Salary Expense	66	72000				72000				26
27	Supplies Expense	67			(c)25100		25100				27
28			2207364	2207364	1460000	1460000	1331236	1450265	1563128	1444099	28
29	Net Income						119029			119029	29
30							1450265	1450265	1563128	1563128	30

Work sheet of Sunrise Art Center

The work sheet includes the four new accounts described in Chapters 23 and 24: Sales Returns and Allowances, Sales Discount, Purchases Returns and Allowances, and Purchases Discount. The balances of the sales returns and allowances account and the sales discount account are deductions from Sales. These two debit balances are extended to the Income Statement Debit columns of the work sheet. The balances of the purchases returns and allowances account and the purchases discount account are deductions from Purchases. These two credit balances are extended to the Income Statement Credit column of the work sheet.

Income statement including cash discounts and returns and allowances

The income statement below is prepared from the Income Statement Debit and Credit columns of the work sheet, page 462.

Sunrise Art Center
Income Statement
For Month Ended December 31, 1977

Revenue:			
Sales		758453	
Less Sales Returns + Allow.	12600		
Sales Discount	1456	14056	
Net Sales			744397
Cost of Merchandise Sold:			
Mdse. Inventory, Dec. 1, 1977		739500	
Purchases	393000		
Less Purchases Ret. + Allow. 14.40			
Purchases Discount 33.72	4812		
Net Purchases		388188	
Total Cost of Mdse. Avail. for Sale		1127688	
Less Mdse. Inventory, Dec. 31, 1977		687000	
Cost of Merchandise Sold			440688
Gross Profit on Sales			303709
Operating Expenses:			
Delivery Expense		19340	
Insurance Expense		8400	
Miscellaneous Expense		4416	
Payroll Taxes Expense		5424	
Rent Expense		50000	
Salary Expense		72000	
Supplies Expense		25100	
Total Operating Expenses			184680
Net Income			119029

Income statement including cash discounts and returns and allowances

The total sales less sales returns and allowances and sales discount is called net sales. The total purchases less purchases returns and allowances and purchases discount is called net purchases. Each of the expenses is listed on the income statement under the heading *Operating Expenses*. Any expenses incurred in the normal operations of a business, other than the cost of goods sold, are called operating expenses.

> Some businesses treat Sales Discount as an expense instead of as a deduction from sales. They also treat Purchases Discount as revenue instead of as a deduction from purchases. When this is done, Sales Discount is not considered to be a regular operating expense. Neither is Purchases Discount considered to be a regular operating source of revenue. Instead, these items are reported at the bottom of the income statement under the separate headings *Other Expense* and *Other Revenue*.

Closing entries including cash discounts and returns and allowances

The closing entries made from the work sheet, page 462, are similar to the closing entries described in earlier chapters. On December 31, 1977, Sunrise Art Center makes the closing entries shown below.

	ACCOUNTS PAYABLE DEBIT	GENERAL DEBIT	DATE	ACCOUNT TITLE	POST. REF.	GENERAL CREDIT	ACCOUNTS RECEIV. CREDIT	
	1	2				3	4	
1				*Closing Entries*				1
2		758453	1977 Dec. 31	Sales				2
3		1440		Purchases Returns & Allow.				3
4		3372		Purchases Discount				4
5				Income Summary		763265		5
6		591736	31	Income Summary				6
7				Sales Returns & Allow.		12600		7
8				Sales Discount		1456		8
9				Purchases		393000		9
10				Delivery Expense		19340		10
11				Insurance Expense		8400		11
12				Miscellaneous Expense		4416		12
13				Payroll Taxes Expense		5424		13
14				Rent Expense		50000		14
15				Salary Expense		72000		15
16				Supplies Expense		25100		16
17		119029	31	Income Summary				17
18				S. G. Justin, Capital		119029		18
19		55000	31	S. G. Justin, Capital				19
20				S. G. Justin, Drawing		55000		20
21								21
22								22
23								23
24								24

GENERAL JOURNAL   PAGE 16

Closing entries recorded in a four-column general journal

TRANSPORTATION CHARGES ON MERCHANDISE SOLD

Transportation charges for delivering merchandise may be paid by the seller. When the seller agrees to pay the transportation charges, the shipping terms are called FOB destination. The letters *FOB* stand for *free on board*. The cost of delivering merchandise is debited to an account titled *Delivery Expense* or *Freight Out*. When Sunrise Art Center pays a transportation company for delivering goods, Delivery Expense is debited and Cash is credited.

When the buyer agrees to pay the transportation charges, the shipping terms are called FOB shipping point. In most instances, the customers of Sunrise Art Center pay the transportation charges. Therefore, Sunrise Art Center has few cash payment transactions for transportation charges.

✦ What is the meaning of each of the following?

Using Business Terms

- sales journal
- cash receipts journal
- sales discount
- sales return
- sales allowance
- credit memorandum
- net sales
- net purchases
- operating expenses
- FOB destination
- FOB shipping point

Questions for Individual Study

1. What is the source document used by Sunrise Art Center for a sale of merchandise on account?
2. What two general ledger accounts are affected by a sale on account? In what way?
3. When only one amount column is used in a sales journal, how is the equality of debits and credits maintained in the general ledger?
4. What is the source document used by Sunrise Art Center for a cash received on account transaction?
5. What is the source document used by Sunrise Art Center for cash received for a cash sales transaction?
6. Why is a sales discount given to customers of Sunrise Art Center?
7. Why did Sunrise Art Center give the account number 41.2 to the sales discount account?
8. What accounts are affected when cash is received on account and a cash discount is taken? How are the accounts affected?
9. In the cash receipts journal, page 455, which column totals are posted?
10. In the cash receipts journal, page 455, which column totals are *not* posted? Why not?
11. What is the source document used by Sunrise Art Center for a sales returns and allowances transaction?
12. What accounts in the general ledger are affected by a sales returns and allowances transaction? How are the accounts affected?
13. In what order should special journals be posted? Why?
14. How does Sunrise Art Center show the sales returns and allowances account and the sales discount account on an income statement?
15. Why does Sunrise Art Center rarely make an entry for shipping costs of merchandise sold on account?

Cases for Management Decision

CASE 1 Manning Office Supply Company does not allow cash discounts to customers. Several customers report that other office supply companies in the city do allow a cash discount if payment is made on account within 10 days. Mr. Manning, the owner, does not want to start the practice of giving cash discounts and lose this revenue. His sales manager says that the company should give them. Who is correct?

CASE 2 Melba's Gift Shop receives a check from a charge customer to be applied on account. The original sale was made on May 5, 1977, with terms of 2/10, n/30. The check was received from the charge customer on May 16, 1977, a Monday. The postmark on the envelope was May 13, 1977, a Friday. The owner of the Gift Shop tells the accountant not to grant a sales discount to this customer because payment was not received within the 10 days allowed for the discount. The accountant suggests that the sales discount should be allowed. Who is right?

CASE 3 The Burns Sweeper Shop uses a four-column general journal similar to the one shown on page 464. The accountant for the shop urges the owner to adopt a five-column general journal. The new journal would be similar to the one shown on page 464 except it would have a special column titled Sales Returns and Allowances Debit. Under what circumstances would it be acceptable to use this additional special column in a general journal?

Drills for
Mastering
Principles

DRILL 24-D 1 Analyzing the recording of transactions affecting sales and cash receipts

Instructions: □ **1.** If you are not using the workbook correlating with this textbook, prepare on a separate sheet of paper a form similar to the one that is shown below.

Trans. No.	(a) Account Debited	(b) Account Credited	(c) Journal in Which Recorded	(d) Name of Amount Column Used in Journal	
				For Amount Debited	For Amount Credited
1	Cash	A. R. Wells, Capital	Cash Receipts	Cash Debit	General Credit

Instructions: □ **2.** For each of the following transactions: (a) Write the name of the account(s) debited. (b) Write the name of the account(s) credited. (c) Write the name of the journal in which the transaction would be recorded. (d) Write the names of the amount columns in the journal in which the debit and credit amounts will be recorded. Transaction No. 1 is shown as an example.

1. Received cash from A. R. Wells, the owner, as an additional investment.
2. Sold merchandise on account to D. L. Blaser.
3. Received cash on account from Edward Bloom; no discount deducted.
4. Issued a credit memorandum to D. L. Blaser for merchandise that was returned by him.
5. Recorded cash sales for the week as shown on the cash register tape.
6. Received cash on account from E. W. Jackson less discount.
7. Discovered and corrected a posting error of the previous month in which a sale that was made to B. Y. Summers was incorrectly posted to the B. Y. Sumptner account.

DRILL 24-D 2   ## Analyzing the recording of transactions in special journals

Instructions: Indicate how the following transactions would be recorded in special journals. Follow Instructions 1 and 2 in Drill 24-D 1.

1. Paid cash for August rent.
2. Received cash from Dorothy Downs, the owner, as an additional investment.
3. Sold merchandise on account to Eileen Denton.
4. Recorded cash sales for the week as shown on the cash register tape.
5. Paid cash for merchandise purchased today.
6. Received cash on account from Mrs. Edna Knoll; no discount deducted.
7. Paid cash on account to Cascade Company for invoice less discount.
8. Issued a debit memorandum to Dunlap Corporation for merchandise returned to it.
9. Received cash on account from Paul Wesley less discount.
10. Purchased merchandise on account from Cannan Company.
11. Issued a credit memorandum to Eileen Denton for merchandise returned by her.
12. Bought supplies on account from Georgia Supply Company.
13. The owner, Dorothy Downs, withdrew merchandise for personal use.
14. The owner, Dorothy Downs, withdrew cash for personal use.
15. Discovered and corrected a posting error of the previous month in which a sale made to D. L. Grant was incorrectly posted to the J. C. Grantly account.

PROBLEM 24-1   ## Journalizing and posting transactions affecting sales and cash receipts

Problems for Applying Concepts

Instructions: □ **1.** Open the following charge customers' accounts in the accounts receivable ledger of the Draper Equipment Company. Record each account balance as of June 1 of the current year. Terms of sale for all charge customers are 1/10, n/30.

Charge Customer	Account Balance
Baldwin, Inc., 905 Center Street, Denver, CO 80206	——
Boyd & Sons, 2293 Memorial Drive, Denver, CO 80205	$223.00
Charles Carter, 131 Madison Avenue, Denver, CO 80209	240.00
Oscar Mount, 425 High Street, Denver, CO 80206	144.00
J. T. Orbock, 5318 Bell Place, Denver, CO 80206	——
Raymond O'Rourck, 3310 Ash Street, Golden, CO 80401	348.00
S. G. Schultz, 1623 Baker Street, Denver, CO 80215	——

Instructions: □ **2.** Open the following accounts in the general ledger of the Draper Equipment Company. Record the balances as of June 1 of the current year. (Only those general ledger accounts needed in this problem are included in the list.)

Account Title	Acct. No.	Account Balance
Cash...	11	$ 4,200.00
Accounts Receivable	12	955.00
Lee Draper, Capital..	31	18,000.00
Sales...	41	——
Sales Returns and Allowances.....................................	41.1	——
Sales Discount..	41.2	——

Instructions: □ **3.** The following transactions affecting sales and cash receipts were completed by the Draper Equipment Company during June of the current year. Record these transactions in a sales journal (page 6), a general journal (page 10), and a cash receipts journal (page 8) like those illustrated in this chapter. Source documents are abbreviated as: memorandum, M; receipt, R; sales invoice, S; cash register tape, T; credit memorandum, CM.

June 1. Recorded the cash balance on June 1 as a memorandum entry in the cash receipts journal, $4,200.00.

  1. Sold merchandise on account to Boyd & Sons, $234.00. S86.

  2. Received on account from Oscar Mount, $142.56, covering S83 for $144.00 less a 1% discount of $1.44. R122.

  2. Received on account from Charles Carter, $240.00, covering S77 for $240.00; no discount. R123.

  3. Sold merchandise on account to S. G. Schultz; $244.20. S87.

  3. Discovered that a sale on account to Baldwin, Inc., on May 28 (S84) was incorrectly posted to the account of Boyd & Sons, $223.00. M51.

  4. Cash sales for the week, $1,218.00. T4.

   Posting. Post the items that are to be posted individually. Post from the journals in this order: sales journal, general journal, and cash receipts journal.

  6. Sold merchandise on account to J. T. Orbock, $90.00. S88.

  7. Received on account from Baldwin, Inc., $220.77, covering S84 for $223.00 less a 1% discount of $2.23. R124.

  8. Granted credit to S. G. Schultz for merchandise returned by him, $24.00. CM18.

  9. Received on account from Boyd & Sons, $231.66, covering S86 for $234.00 less a 1% discount of $2.34. R125.

  11. Cash sales for the week, $1,366.00. T11.

   Posting. Post the items that are to be posted individually.

  13. Sold merchandise on account to Charles Carter, $134.40. S89.

  15. Sold merchandise on account to Raymond O'Rourck, $72.00. S90.

  16. Received on account from J. T. Orbock, $89.10, covering S88 for $90.00 less a 1% discount of $0.90. R126.

  17. Granted credit to Raymond O'Rourck as an allowance on damaged merchandise, $12.00. CM19.

  18. Cash sales for the week, $1,186.80. T18.

   Posting. Post the items that are to be posted individually.

June 20. Sold merchandise on account to Baldwin, Inc., $180.00. S91.
   22. Received on account from Charles Carter, $133.06, covering S89 for $134.40 less a 1% discount of $1.34. R127.
   24. Granted credit to Baldwin, Inc., for merchandise returned by them, $36.00. CM20.
   25. Cash sales for the week, $1,517.86. T25.

   Posting. Post the items that are to be posted individually.

   27. Sold merchandise on account to Oscar Mount, $270.00. S92.
   28. Received on account from Raymond O'Rourck, $348.00, covering S85 for $348.00; no discount. R128.
   29. Received cash from the owner, Lee Draper, as an additional investment in the business, $750.00. R129.
   30. Cash sales for the week, $914.40. T30.

   Posting. Post the items that are to be posted individually.

Instructions: □ **4.** Total and rule the sales journal. Post the total. Compare your work with the sales journal shown on page 451.

□ **5.** Foot, prove, total, and rule the general journal. Post the totals of the special columns. Compare your work with the general journal shown on page 441.

□ **6.** Foot the cash receipts journal and prove the equality of debits and credits.

□ **7.** Prove cash. The total of the Cash Credit column of the cash payments journal for the Draper Equipment Company is $9,390.72. The cash balance on hand on June 30 is $3,167.49.

□ **8.** Total and rule the cash receipts journal. Post the totals of the special columns. Compare your work with the cash receipts journal shown on page 455.

□ **9.** Prepare a schedule of accounts receivable. Compare the schedule total with the balance of the accounts receivable account in the general ledger. The total and the balance should be the same.

PROBLEM 24-2 Preparing an income statement; recording closing entries including cash discounts and returns and allowances

Portions of the work sheet for Men's Town, a men's clothing store owned and operated by Donald Frisch, for the monthly fiscal period ended April 30 of the current year are shown on the next page.

Instructions: □ **1.** Prepare an income statement similar to the one shown on page 463.

□ **2.** Record the four closing entries on page 6 of a four-column general journal, using the illustration on page 464 as a model.

Men's Town
Work Sheet
For Month Ended April 30, 19—

Account Title	Acct. No.	Income Statement		Balance Sheet	
		Debit	Credit	Debit	Credit
Donald Frisch, Capital	31				8 641 20
Donald Frisch, Drawing	32			1 080 00	
Income Summary	33	7 529 40	6 408 96		
Sales	41		18 276 48		
Sales Returns and Allowances	41.1	293 28			
Sales Discount	41.2	196 67			
Purchases	51	11 484 36			
Purchases Returns and Allowances	51.1		81 00		
Purchases Discount	51.2		165 72		
Insurance Expense	61	115 20			
Miscellaneous Expense	62	244 50			
Rent Expense	63	480 00			
Salary Expense	64	1 260 00			
Supplies Expense	65	455 55			
		22 058 96	24 932 16	13 826 94	10 953 74
Net Income		2 873 20			2 873 20
		24 932 16	24 932 16	13 826 94	13 826 94

The Accounting Cycle
Using Special Journals

Your goals in working Project 3 are to review the use of special journals and to review the steps in an accounting cycle. You will:

1. Open a new set of books if you are not using the workbook.
2. Record and post transactions for one month.
3. Prepare a work sheet and the financial statements.
4. Record and post adjusting and closing entries.
5. Prepare a post-closing trial balance.

Open a
new set of books
if you are not using
the workbook

↓

Record and post
transactions
for one month

↓

Prepare a work sheet
and the
financial statements

↓

Record and post
adjusting and closing
entries

↓

Prepare a post-closing
trial balance

EVANS COMPANY

Evans Company sells fancy candy and related products. The company is located in a large shopping center. The company also sells candy products in bulk to a few other retail stores. The Evans Company uses the chart of accounts on page 472.

The Evans Company uses the following journals and ledgers:

Similar to the
illustration on

Sales journal	page 451
Purchases journal	page 428
General journal	page 441
Cash receipts journal	page 455
Cash payments journal	page 433
Accounts receivable ledger with three-column ruling	page 450
Accounts payable ledger with three-column ruling	page 427
General ledger with four-column ruling	page 428

EVANS COMPANY
Chart of Accounts

(1) Assets	Account Number	(4) Revenue	Account Number
Cash	11	Sales	41
Accounts Receivable	12	Sales Returns and Allowances	41.1
Merchandise Inventory	13	Sales Discount	41.2
Supplies	14		
Prepaid Insurance	15	**(5) Cost of Merchandise**	
(2) Liabilities		Purchases	51
		Purchases Returns and Allowances	51.1
Accounts Payable	21	Purchases Discount	51.2
Employees Income Tax Payable	22		
FICA Tax Payable	23	**(6) Expenses**	
Federal Unemployment Tax Payable	24	Hospital Insurance Expense	61
State Unemployment Tax Payable	25	Insurance Expense	62
Hospital Insurance Premiums Payable	26	Miscellaneous Expense	63
		Payroll Taxes Expense	64
(3) Capital		Rent Expense	65
		Salary Expense	66
Paul Evans, Capital	31	Supplies Expense	67
Paul Evans, Drawing	32		
Income Summary	33		

Opening the books

If you are using the workbook, omit Instructions 1 to 6. These instructions have been completed for you. Turn to page 474 and begin with Instruction 7. If you are not using the workbook, begin with Instruction 1.

Instructions: 1. Place the following page numbers on the five journals: Sales journal, page 21; purchases journal, page 12; general journal, page 46; cash receipts journal, page 33; and cash payments journal, page 41.

2. Open the following charge customers' accounts in the accounts receivable ledger. Allow five lines for each account. Record the balances as of December 1 of the current year. The terms of sale for all charge sales are 2/10, n/30.

Charge Customer	Debit Balance
Atkins Market, 1214 Main Street, Concord, NH 03301	$648.90
Candies, Inc., 69 Bellevue Avenue, Concord, NH 03302	554.70
Castle Candy Corner, 763 Oak Avenue, Concord, NH 03302	817.80
Fischer's Pharmacy, 125 Fourth Street, Concord, NH 03301	764.70
Neighborhood Shoppe, 5134 Memorial Avenue, Concord, NH 03303	514.32

Instructions: 3. Open the following creditors' accounts in the accounts payable ledger. Allow five lines for each account. Record the balances as of December 1 of the current year.

Creditors	Terms of Sale	Credit Balance
Ebright Candies, Inc., 418 Robbins Avenue, Atlanta, GA 30304	1/10, n/30	$1,104.70
Newcomb Supply Company, 712 Mulberry Street, Louisville, KY 40202	n/30	131.04
Phillips Candies Corporation, 542 Mill Run Road, Cincinnati, OH 45216	1/30, n/60	———
Thrift Products, Inc., 988 Milborn Road, Lexington, KY 40508	2/10, n/30	1,156.50
Urban Candy Company, 4026 Petty Road, Nashville, TN 37215	2/10, n/30	396.85

Instructions: 4. Open an account in the general ledger for each of the accounts shown on the chart of accounts on the opposite page. Allow six lines for each account.

5. Record in the general ledger accounts the following account balances as of December 1 of the current year.

Account Title	Debit Balance	Credit Balance
Cash...	$ 8,677.38	———
Accounts Receivable	3,300.42	———
Merchandise Inventory..	24,505.68	———
Supplies..	1,518.84	———
Prepaid Insurance...	828.00	———
Accounts Payable	———	$ 2,789.09
Employees Income Tax Payable...................................	———	248.32
FICA Tax Payable	———	262.88
Federal Unemployment Tax Payable	———	26.36
State Unemployment Tax Payable................................	———	122.80
Hospital Insurance Premiums Payable	———	151.20
Paul Evans, Capital...	———	37,848.08
Paul Evans, Drawing...	11,790.00	———
Sales...	———	95,706.89
Sales Returns and Allowances....................................	785.52	———
Sales Discount..	918.00	———
Purchases..	51,517.04	———
Purchases Returns and Allowances..............................	———	650.16
Purchases Discount...	———	1,027.68
Hospital Insurance Expense..	491.40	———
Miscellaneous Expense	2,918.27	———
Payroll Taxes Expense	2,234.51	———
Rent Expense	3,993.00	———
Salary Expense...	25,355.40	———

Instructions: 6. Record a memorandum entry in the cash receipts journal for the cash balance on December 1 of the current year.

Journalizing business transactions

Instructions: 7. Record the following transactions for December of the current year. Source documents are abbreviated as: check, Ck; memorandum, M; purchase invoice, P; receipt, R; sales invoice, S; cash register tape, T; credit memo, CM; debit memo, DM.

December   1. Paid December rent, $363.00. Ck330.

      1. Received on account from Atkins Market, $635.92, covering S77 for $648.90 less a 2% discount of $12.98. R77.

      1. Purchased merchandise on account from Phillips Candies Corporation, $2,728.32. P66.

      2. Granted credit to Candies, Inc., for merchandise returned, $50.00. CM58.

      2. Received on account from Castle Candy Corner, $801.44, covering S78 for $817.80 less a 2% discount of $16.36. R78.

      3. Sold merchandise on account to Neighborhood Shoppe, $385.62. S82.

      3. Paid on account to Ebright Candies, Inc., $1,093.65, covering P62 for $1,104.70 less a 1% discount of $11.05. Ck331.

      3. Cash sales for the week, $834.96. T3.

Posting. Post the items that are to be posted individually. Post the journals in the following order: Sales journal, purchases journal, general journal, cash receipts journal, and cash payments journal.

December   5. Returned merchandise to Phillips Candies Corporation, $60.00. DM13.

      6. Paid on account to Thrift Products, Inc., $1,133.37, covering P63 for $1,156.50 less a 2% discount of $23.13. Ck332.

      7. Received on account from Neighborhood Shoppe, $504.03, covering S79 for $514.32 less a 2% discount of $10.29. R79.

      7. Purchased merchandise on account from Urban Candy Company, $2,239.44. P67.

      8. Sold merchandise on account to Castle Candy Corner, $265.80. S83.

      8. Paid on account to Urban Candy Company, $388.91, covering P64 for $396.85 less a 2% discount of $7.94. Ck333.

      9. Received on account from Candies, Inc., $494.61, for balance due on S80 of $504.70 less a 2% discount of $10.09. R80.

> S80 was for $554.70, but CM58 for $50.00 was deducted. The balance on which the discount was figured is $504.70.

    10. Cash sales for the week, $3,763.56. T10.

Posting. Post the items that are to be posted individually from the five journals.

December 12. Purchased merchandise on account from Thrift Products, Inc., $2,443.80. P68.

    12. Paid the liabilities owed for employees' income tax payable, $248.32, and for FICA tax payable, $262.88; total, $511.20. Ck334.

December 12. Paid the liability for hospital insurance premiums payable, $151.20. Ck335.

> This liability is the total of hospital insurance premiums withheld from employees' wages during previous months plus the employer's share of the cost of the hospital insurance program.
>
> Evans Company has a group hospital insurance plan in which the company pays a portion of each employee's monthly premium. When the payment of the payroll is recorded, the amount of the premiums deducted from employees' wages is credited to Hospital Insurance Premiums Payable. When the payroll expenses for the employer are recorded, the amount of the employer's share is debited to Hospital Insurance Expense and credited to Hospital Insurance Premiums Payable. The balance of the account, Hospital Insurance Premiums Payable, is paid once every three months to the local Hospital Care agency.

  13. Paid miscellaneous expense, $163.34. Ck336.

  13. Bought supplies for cash, $33.00. Ck337.

  13. Received on account from Neighborhood Shoppe, $377.91, covering S82 for $385.62 less a 2% discount of $7.71. R81.

  14. Sold merchandise on account to Fischer's Pharmacy, $105.00. S84.

  14. Issued a check to Paul Evans, the owner, for a cash withdrawal for personal use, $25.00. Ck338.

  15. Paid semimonthly payroll, $921.72, for salary expense of $1,137.00 less deductions for employees' income tax, $128.16, for FICA tax, $68.22, and for hospital insurance premiums, $18.90. Ck339.

  15. Recorded employer's payroll taxes and hospital insurance costs for the December 15 payroll: FICA tax, $68.22; federal unemployment tax, $6.59; state unemployment tax, $30.70; hospital insurance expense, $18.90. M54.

> Make one combined entry: Debit Payroll Taxes Expense for the total of the three payroll taxes; debit Hospital Insurance Expense for the employer's share of the premiums; credit the three payroll liability accounts and Hospital Insurance Premiums Payable.

  16. Paid on account to Urban Candy Company, $2,194.65, covering P67 for $2,239.44 less a 2% discount of $44.79. Ck340.

  16. Received on account from Fischer's Pharmacy, $764.70, covering S73 for $764.70; no discount. R82.

  17. Received on account from Castle Candy Corner, $260.48, covering S83 for $265.80 less a 2% discount of $5.32. R83.

  17. Cash sales for the week, $2,698.56. T17.

Posting. Post the items that are to be posted individually from the five journals.

December 19. The owner, Paul Evans, withdrew merchandise at cost for personal use, $14.40. M55.

  19. Sold merchandise on account to Candies, Inc., $696.00. S85.

  20. Paid on account to Thrift Products, Inc., $2,394.92, covering P68 for $2,443.80 less a 2% discount of $48.88. Ck341.

  21. Paid on account to Newcomb Supply Company, $131.04; no discount. Ck342.

December 22. Purchased merchandise on account from Ebright Candies, Inc., $1,120.00. P69.
   23. Purchased merchandise for cash, $150.00. Ck343.
   24. Sold merchandise on account to Castle Candy Corner, $258.36. S86.
   24. Cash sales for the week, $4,040.60. T24.

Posting. Post the items that are to be posted individually from the five journals.

December 27. Bought supplies on account from Newcomb Supply Company, $587.70. M56.
   27. Sold merchandise on account to Atkins Market, $456.00. S87.
   28. Purchased merchandise on account from Urban Candy Company, $865.08. P70.
   29. Received on account from Candies, Inc., $682.08, covering S85 for $696.00 less a 2% discount of $13.92. R84.
   29. Paid on account to Phillips Candies Corporation, $2,641.64, for the balance due on P66 of $2,668.32 less a 1% cash discount of $26.68. Ck344.

> The amount of P66 was $2,728.32, but DM13 for $60.00 was deducted. The balance of the invoice to which the discount applied was $2,668.32.

   30. Received cash from Paul Evans, the owner, as an additional investment in the business, $1,000.00. R85.
   30. Sold merchandise on account to Neighborhood Shoppe, $984.80. S88.
   31. Paid semimonthly payroll, $921.72, for salary expense of $1,137.00 less deductions for employees' income tax, $128.16, for FICA tax, $68.22, and for hospital insurance premiums, $18.90. Ck345.
   31. Recorded employer's payroll taxes and hospital insurance costs for the December 31 payroll: FICA Tax, $68.22; federal unemployment tax, $6.59; state unemployment tax, $30.70; hospital insurance expense, $18.90. M57.
   31. Cash sales for the week, $2,721.72. T31.

Posting. Post the items that are to be posted individually from the five journals.

Work at the end of the month

Instructions: **8.** Total and rule the sales journal and the purchases journal. Post the totals.

9. Foot, prove, total, and rule the general journal. Post the totals of each of the special columns.

10. Foot the cash receipts journal and the cash payments journal. Prove the equality of debits and credits for the column totals in each journal.

11. Prove cash using as your guide the steps described on page 455. The bank balance according to the last check stub is $15,039.59.

12. Total and rule the cash receipts journal and the cash payments journal. Post the special columns in each journal.

13. Prepare a schedule of accounts receivable and of accounts payable. Compare the schedule totals with the balances of the controlling accounts in the general ledger.

Work at the end of the fiscal year

Instructions: **14.** Prepare an eight-column work sheet for the fiscal year ended December 31 of the current year. Use the illustration of a work sheet, page 462, as your guide. Data needed for the adjustments are:

Merchandise inventory, December 31	$25,657.56
Supplies inventory, December 31	703.68
Value of insurance policies, December 31	300.00

15. Prepare an income statement for the year ended December 31. (The beginning merchandise inventory on January 1 was $24,505.68.)

16. Prepare a capital statement for the year ended December 31. Data needed to prepare this statement are:

   a. There were no additional investments in the business during the first 11 months of the year. Therefore, the December 1 balance in the capital account is also the January 1 balance.
   b. The additional investment in the business during December is recorded in the capital account.
   c. The net income for the year is taken from the work sheet prepared in Instruction 14 above.
   d. The amount of withdrawals is the balance of the owner's drawing account shown on the work sheet.

17. Prepare a balance sheet as of December 31.

18. Record the adjusting and closing entries on page 47 of the general journal. Post these entries to the general ledger accounts.

19. Prepare a post-closing trial balance.

25

A Cash Register System and Petty Cash

Many businesses use machines to speed the recording of daily transactions. A machine that is used to speed the recording of sales and cash transactions is known as a cash register.

Cash registers are available on which it is possible (1) to record the amount of a sale of merchandise on account or for cash; (2) to record the kind of merchandise sold; (3) to print a receipt for the customer; (4) to figure the amount of change due a customer; and (5) to keep a record of each transaction on paper tape inside the register.

Stores with a large volume of sales may use cash registers to produce tape records that can be processed on automated data processing equipment. Data recorded on these tape records can be used in a number of ways. The data can be used to analyze sales by the type of merchandise sold, to update inventory records, and to post customers' accounts.

THE CASH REGISTER USED BY IMPORT AUTO COMPANY

Edward Burl owns and operates Import Auto Company that sells automobile parts, accessories, tires, and batteries. Sales are made to individuals, local service stations, and some garages. Most sales are for cash.

Import Auto Company is a self-service store. A customer selects the merchandise and takes it to the checkout counter where the cashier records the sale on a cash register. The cash register on page 479 is similar to the one used by Import Auto Company. The cash register records each transaction on a paper tape inside the machine, supplies a printed receipt for customers, and has a conveniently organized money drawer.

Cash registers are available in many models to meet the needs of different types of businesses. The kind and the number of keys on a cash register depend upon the needs of a particular business and its accounting system. In general, the keys on most cash registers are similar to those on the one used by Import Auto Company.

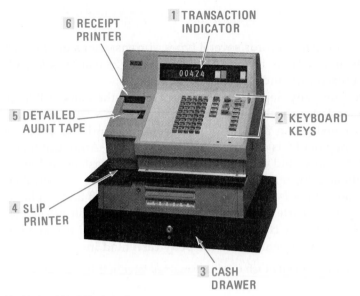

6 RECEIPT PRINTER

1 TRANSACTION INDICATOR

00424

5 DETAILED AUDIT TAPE

2 KEYBOARD KEYS

4 SLIP PRINTER

3 CASH DRAWER

The National Cash Register Company

A cash register

1. The transaction indicator shows the kind and the amount of each transaction as it is entered on the cash register.
2. The keyboard keys are used to record the details of each transaction.
3. The cash drawer is used to sort and store money during the business day.
4. The slip printer is used to print selected data on business forms inserted in the cash register.
5. The detailed audit tape is a paper tape on which all transactions recorded on the cash register are automatically printed.
6. The receipt printer provides a printed record of the transaction that is given to the customer as a receipt.

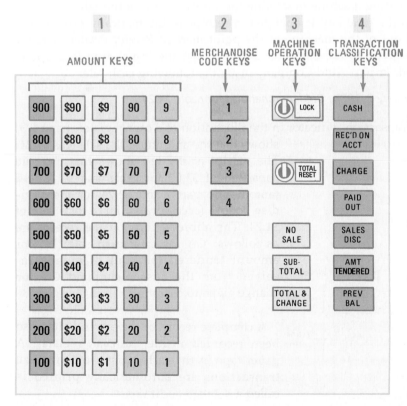

1	2	3	4
AMOUNT KEYS	MERCHANDISE CODE KEYS	MACHINE OPERATION KEYS	TRANSACTION CLASSIFICATION KEYS

900	$90	$9	90	9	1	LOCK	CASH
800	$80	$8	80	8	2		REC'D ON ACCT
700	$70	$7	70	7	3	TOTAL RESET	CHARGE
600	$60	$6	60	6	4		PAID OUT
500	$50	$5	50	5		NO SALE	SALES DISC
400	$40	$4	40	4		SUB-TOTAL	AMT TENDERED
300	$30	$3	30	3		TOTAL & CHANGE	PREV BAL
200	$20	$2	20	2			
100	$10	$1	10	1			

1. The amount keys are used to record the amount of each transaction.
2. The merchandise code keys are used to identify the kind of merchandise sold. Import Auto Company uses four merchandise code keys: 1 — automobile parts; 2 — accessories; 3 — tires; and 4 — batteries.
3. The machine operation keys are used to activate the cash register and make it record the transaction.
4. The transaction classification keys are used to record the nature of a transaction.

Key arrangement on a cash register

RECORDING TRANSACTIONS IN A CASH REGISTER SYSTEM

Import Auto Company records several types of transactions on the cash register. These transactions include (1) cash sales, (2) charge sales, (3) cash received on account, and (4) small cash payments.

Import Auto Company deposits all cash receipts in the bank. All large payments are made by check. Small cash payments, however, are made from the cash register. An amount of cash kept on hand and used for making small payments is called petty cash. Import Auto Company maintains a petty cash fund of $200.00 in order to have cash available for small payments and for making change. At the beginning of each day, $50.00 in bills and coins is taken from the petty cash fund and is placed in the cash register for use in making change and small cash payments. At the end of the day, any change left over from this amount is taken out of the cash register and is returned to the petty cash fund in the safe.

The handling of a petty cash fund is explained later in this chapter.

Recording a cash sale on a cash register

When several items are sold to a customer, the amount and the kind of each item are recorded on the cash register. The cash register operates like an adding machine in totaling the various items of the sale.

When the total key is operated, a receipt is automatically printed and pushed out of the machine at the point marked *Receipt Printer*. The receipt is given to the customer as proof that the transaction is properly recorded. Import Auto Company made the following cash sale:

January 3, 1977. Sold merchandise for cash, $4.24.

Receipt for a cash sale

The transaction indicator in the illustration of a cash register, page 479, shows that the amount of the sale was $4.24. The receipt at the left shows that the sale consisted of $2.00 for merchandise code 1 (automobile parts) and $2.24 for merchandise code 2 (accessories), for a total sale of $4.24. The abbreviations on the receipt are as follows: CA for total cash sale; AT for amount tendered (amount of money received from the customer); and CG for change given to customer.

A complete record of the cash sale has also been recorded inside the cash register. A paper tape in the cash register on which all transactions are automatically printed is called a detailed audit tape.

```
IMPORT

A

AUTO
COMPANY

                          ┌─ Amounts
          $002.00–1  ┐
          $002.24–2  ┘ ─ Mdse.
          $004.24CA  ┐
          $010.00AT  ├ Trans-
JAN 3 77 001  $005.76CG  ┘   action
```

Date

Trans. No.

Recording a charge sale on a cash register

January 3, 1977. Sold   merchandise   on   account   to George Alcott, $28.20.

For this sale on account, the cashier at the checkout counter prepares the sales slip illustrated at the right. An original and a carbon copy are made.

When the items on the sales slip have been recorded on the cash register, the cashier inserts both copies of the sales slip in the slip printer of the cash register. The date, the transaction number, the total amount of the charge sale, and the transaction classification (CH for charge sale) are printed across the top of both copies of the sales slip. The data about the transaction are also recorded on the detailed audit tape inside the cash register.

The original copy of the sales slip is given to the customer. The duplicate copy is kept by Import Auto Company for its records.

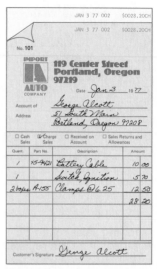

> The system used by Import Auto Company for keeping records of its charge customers is described later in this chapter.

Sales slip in duplicate showing a charge sale recorded on a cash register

Recording cash received on account on a cash register

Import Auto Company makes all sales to charge customers on terms of 1/10, n/30. The 1% sales discount is offered to encourage early payment of charge accounts. In the transaction below, payment was received within the 10-day period.

January 3, 1977. Received cash on account from Allen Towers, $14.85, for sale on December 27, 1976, $15.00 less a 1% discount, $0.15.

For this transaction, the cashier prepares a sales slip in duplicate as shown at the right. Both copies of the sales slip are inserted into the slip printer of the cash register. The previous balance owed by the charge customer, $15.00, the sales discount, $0.15, and the amount of cash received, $14.85, are printed across the top of both copies of the sales slip. The cash register also records this data on the detailed audit tape inside the machine.

The original copy of the sales slip is given to the customer as his receipt. The carbon copy is kept by Import Auto Company for its records.

Sales slip showing cash received on account recorded on a cash register

Recording sales returns and allowances on account on a cash register

Sales slip showing sales return on account recorded on a cash register

Import Auto Company granted the following credit:

January 3, 1977. Granted credit to John Barton, a charge customer, for merchandise returned, $13.20.

The cashier prepares a sales slip and records it on the cash register as shown at the left. The cash register used by Import Auto Company has no special transaction key for sales returns and allowances on account. Therefore, the cashier uses the NO SALE (NS) key for this transaction. The data are printed on the detailed audit tape, but the amount is not accumulated by the cash register.

All sales slips are recorded on the cash register in order to validate them with the line printed across the top. Sales slips for sales returns and allowances on account are validated on the cash register even though the total is not accumulated.

The original copy of the sales slip is given to the customer. The duplicate copy is kept by Import Auto Company as the source document for an entry in the general journal.

Recording cash payments on a cash register

Import Auto Company makes all large cash payments by check. However, the cashier is authorized to make small payments up to $5.00 each from the change in the cash register. Each time a cash payment is made from the cash register, the cashier prepares a paid-out voucher and records the payment on the cash register. A form that provides written authority for a business transaction is called a voucher.

Paid-out voucher

One kind of voucher is a petty cash voucher. The handling of the petty cash fund is described later in this chapter.

January 3, 1977. Paid a cash refund for merchandise returned by a cash customer, $3.76.

For this cash payment, the cashier prepares a paid-out voucher as shown at the left. The date, the transaction number, the amount of the cash payment, and the transaction classification (PO for paid out) are printed across the top of the paid-out voucher. The same information is also printed on the detailed audit tape inside the cash register.

CASH REGISTER TOTALS AND CASH PROOF

Each time a transaction is recorded on the cash register, the details are printed on the detailed audit tape inside the register. The cash register acts as an adding machine and accumulates totals for the various types of transactions.

Obtaining cash register totals

The cash register used by Import Auto Company accumulates the total for each of the following types of transactions: (1) cash sales, (2) charge sales, (3) cash received on account, (4) sales discount, and (5) cash paid out. The total sales for each of the four kinds of merchandise sold are also accumulated.

At the end of each day, the cashier uses the cash register to print the totals on the detailed audit tape inside the machine. At the same time the data are printed on a separate cash proof form that the cashier inserts into the slip printer on the cash register. A form on which cash register totals are recorded is called a cash proof and balances slip.

The slip for January 3 totals is on page 484. When the totals are printed, the cash register is automatically cleared so that none of the amounts will be added to the transactions for the following day.

Completing the cash proof and balances slip

To prove cash, the cashier completes the cash proof and balances slip as follows:

☐ **1** Writes on Line 1 of the cash proof and balances slip the amount of change that was placed in the cash register at the beginning of the day, $50.00.

☐ **2** (a) Removes the paid-out vouchers from the cash register and totals them. On January 3, 1977, the total of all paid-out vouchers is $18.60.

(b) Compares the total of the paid-out vouchers, $18.60, with the amount printed on Line 2 of the cash proof and balances slip, $18.60. The two amounts should be the same.

(c) Deducts the total amount paid out, $18.60, from the amount of change, $50.00, and writes the difference, $31.40, on Line 3 as the balance of change.

(d) Removes $31.40 from the cash register and returns it to the petty cash fund in the office safe along with the paid-out vouchers.

☐ **3** Counts the actual money remaining in the cash register drawer and writes this amount on Line 7 of the cash proof and balances slip. On January 3, 1977, the actual money in the cash drawer is $1,109.58.

CASH PROOF AND BALANCES SLIP

	Items	Accounts		Register Proof and Balances	
			CHANGE FROM CASH DRAWER		
1	Change to be Accounted for				$50.00
2	Less Paid Out		JAN 3 77 321	$0018.60PO	
3	Balance of Change				31 40
			CASH PROOF		
4	Cash Sales		JAN 3 77 322	$0877.38CA	
5	Received on Account		JAN 3 77 323	$0233.20RC	
6	Total Received		JAN 3 77 324	$1110.58TL	
7	Cash in drawer by actual count	Debit Cash			1109 58 [7]
8	Cash Short	Debit Cash Short and Over			1 00 [1]
9	Cash Over	Credit Cash Short and Over			[2]
			SALES PROOF		
10	Code 1 – Auto Parts		JAN 3 77 325	$0527.30–1	
11	Code 2 – Accessories		JAN 3 77 326	$0112.98–2	
12	Code 3 – Tires		JAN 3 77 327	$0210.00–3	
13	Code 4 – Batteries		JAN 3 77 328	$0330.00–4	
14	Total Sales	Credit Sales	JAN 3 77 329	$1180.28TL [3]	
15	Cash Sales		JAN 3 77 330	$0877.38CA	
16	Charge Sales	Debit Accounts Receivable	JAN 3 77 331	$0302.90CH [4]	
17	Total Sales		JAN 3 77 332	$1180.28TL	
			RECEIVED ON ACCOUNT		
18	Total Accounts Receivable	Credit Accounts Receivable	JAN 3 77 333	$0234.72PB [5]	
19	Less Sales Discounts	Debit Sales Discount	JAN 3 77 334	$0001.52SD [6]	
20	Received on Account		JAN 3 77 335	$0233.20RC	

RECORD IN JOURNAL COLUMN NO.

Date _January 3, 1977_   Cashier's Signature _Alice Sellers_

Cash proof and balances slip

□ 4 Compares the total receipts printed on Line 6, $1,110.58, with the actual cash in the drawer written on Line 7, $1,109.58. These two amounts should be the same. However, on January 3 the amount of cash in the drawer (Line 7) is $1.00 less than the amount of total receipts printed by the cash register (Line 6). There is $1.00 less in the cash drawer than there should be. When the cash on hand is less than the amount shown by the records, the amount of the difference is called cash short. The cashier writes the amount of cash short, $1.00, on Line 8 of the cash proof and balances slip.

If the actual amount in the cash drawer is greater than the amount printed by the cash register, there will be more cash in the drawer than there should be. When the cash on hand is greater than the amount shown by the records, the amount of the difference is called cash over. The amount of cash over would be written on Line 9 of the cash proof and balances slip.

☐ 5 Compares the total sales (sum of sales of all kinds of merchandise) printed on Line 14, $1,180.28, with the total sales (sum of cash and charge sales) printed on Line 17, $1,180.28. The two amounts should be the same.

☐ 6 Compares the total amount received on account printed on Line 20, $233.20, with the amount printed on Line 5, $233.20. The two amounts should be the same. The total amount credited to Accounts Receivable (Line 18) less the total sales discount (Line 19) should equal the amount received on account (Line 20).

☐ 7 Prepares a deposit slip for the cash remaining in the cash drawer, $1,109.58 (Line 7 of the cash proof and balances slip). Gives the deposit slip and the cash to the accountant to be checked and deposited in the bank.

☐ 8 Removes the detailed audit tape from the cash register, attaches it to the cash proof and balances slip, and gives both forms to the accountant. The accountant, after checking the forms, uses the cash proof and balances slip as the source document for the necessary journal entry. The detailed audit tape is filed for future reference if questions arise about amounts shown on the cash proof and balances slip.

Cash short and over account

When cash is short or over, the error is caused by mistakes in recording transactions on the cash register or by mistakes in making change. A careful cashier usually does not have cash short or cash over at the end of a day. The cashier for Import Auto Company, for example, had cash short on only two business days in the entire month of December, 1977. At no time was there cash over.

The amount of cash short or cash over is recorded in a general ledger account with the title Cash Short and Over. Cash short is an expense and is debited to this account. Cash over is revenue and is credited to this account. Past records show that if the cash short and over account for Import Auto Company has a balance at the end of a fiscal period, it is usually a small debit balance. For this reason, Import Auto Company places the cash short and over account in the expenses section of its general ledger.

USING SPECIAL JOURNALS IN A CASH REGISTER ACCOUNTING SYSTEM

Import Auto Company records transactions in three special journals and a four-column general journal listed on page 486.

1. Purchases journal similar to the one on page 428.
2. Cash payments journal similar to the one on page 433.
3. Combined cash receipts-sales journal described in this chapter.
4. Four-column general journal similar to the one on page 441.

The procedures for using the purchases journal, cash payments journal, and general journal are described in Chapters 23 and 24. The procedures for recording transactions in the combined cash receipts-sales journal are described in this chapter.

Cash receipts-sales journal

The combined cash receipts-sales journal used by Import Auto Company is shown below.

| | | | | GENERAL | | SALES | ACCOUNTS RECEIVABLE | | SALES | CASH |
DATE	ACCOUNT TITLE	DOC. NO.	POST. REF.	1 DEBIT	2 CREDIT	3 CREDIT	4 DEBIT	5 CREDIT	6 DISCOUNT DEBIT	7 DEBIT
1977 Jan. 1	Balance on hand, $2341.72		✓							
3	Cash Short and Over	CB3	61	100		118028	30290	23472	152	110958
4	Edward Burl, Capital	R1	31		100000					100000
4	✓	084	✓			113833	25830	24468	240	112231
5	✓	085	✓			84450	11940	13584	136	85958
31	✓	CB31	✓			76974	27060	19530	150	49294
31	Totals			180	130959	1365267	371865	365078	3452	4885803
				(✓)	(✓)	(44)	(13)	(13)	(41.2)	(11)

Cash receipts-sales journal
used by Import Auto Company

The combined journal above has the features of a cash receipts journal, page 455, and a sales journal, page 451, all in one journal. The data used by Import Auto Company for recording cash receipts and sales are taken from the cash proof and balances slip. All the data from the cash proof and balances slip can be recorded in the single, combined cash receipts-sales journal rather than dividing the entry between two journals.

Recording data from the cash proof and balances slip in the cash receipts-sales journal

The data on daily cash proof and balances slips are recorded daily in the cash receipts-sales journal by Import Auto Company. The data can be recorded on a single line as shown on Lines 2, 4, 5, and 30 above.

The entry on Line 2 of the journal is for the cash proof and balances slip, page 484. In making the entry, the accountant for Import Auto Company goes down the Accounts column on the cash proof and balances slip to determine the accounts affected. The amounts for the accounts are shown in the amount column at the right of the slip. The journal column number in which to record each amount is shown in the right margin of the cash proof and balances slip.

The cash receipts-sales journal of Import Auto Company has no special column in which to record amounts affecting the cash short and over account. Therefore, the amount of cash short, $1.00, is written in the General Debit column and the account title is written in the Account Title column. The source document for the entry, CB3, is written in the Doc. No. column.

> The abbreviation CB indicates the cash proof and balances slip as the source document.

After the entry is recorded, the accountant checks the equality of debits and credits in the entry. The accountant prepared a check on the equality of debits and credits for the entry on Line 2 of the journal, page 486, as follows:

Journal Col. No.	Account Debited or Credited	Debit Amount	Credit Amount
7	Cash	$1,109.58	
1	Cash Short and Over	1.00	
3	Sales		$1,180.28
4	Accounts Receivable	302.90	
5	Accounts Receivable		234.72
6	Sales Discount	1.52	
	Totals	$1,415.00	$1,415.00

The entry on Line 4 of the journal, page 486, shows the data recorded for the cash proof and balances slip of January 4. There is no cash short or cash over on January 4. Therefore, no entry is required in the General columns of the journal. A check mark is placed in the Account Title column to show that no account title needs to be written for this entry. A check mark is also placed in the Post. Ref. column to show that no item on this line needs to be posted individually.

Import Auto Company has few cash receipts that are not recorded on the cash register. For this reason, most of the entries in the cash receipts-sales journal are based on the cash proof and balances slip. Other kinds of cash receipt entries are also recorded in the cash receipts-sales journal in the same manner as described in Chapter 24. The entry on Line 3 of the journal, page 486, shows an additional investment by the owner.

Posting the cash receipts-sales journal

The cash receipts-sales journal of Import Auto Company is posted in the same way as other special journals. However, individual amounts in the Accounts Receivable Debit and Credit columns are not posted. Import Auto Company uses the duplicate sales slips themselves as its accounts receivable ledger, as described on page 489. This eliminates the need for posting to subsidiary accounts with customers.

During the month, the individual amounts in the General Debit and Credit columns are posted to the general ledger at frequent intervals. At the end of the month, the columns of the cash receipts-sales journal are footed, proved, totaled, and ruled. The totals of the special columns are then posted to the general ledger.

Recording sales returns and allowances on account in the general journal

The cash register used by Import Auto Company does not total amounts for sales returns and allowances on account. For this reason, each sales return or sales allowance transaction with a charge customer is recorded separately in the general journal. The duplicate copy of the sales slip showing the amount of the sales return or allowance is the source document for the entry in the general journal. The slip on page 482 showing the sales return by John Barton is recorded in the general journal as follows:

ACCOUNTS PAYABLE DEBIT	GENERAL DEBIT	DATE	ACCOUNT TITLE	POST. REF.	GENERAL CREDIT	ACCOUNTS RECEIV. CREDIT	
	1320	*1977* Jan. 3	Sales Returns + Allowances				1
			John Barton	✓		1320	2
			Sales Slip No. 103.				3
							4
							5
							6

Entry to record a sales returns and allowances transaction
in the general journal of Import Auto Company

On Line 1, Sales Returns and Allowances is debited for $13.20 in the General Debit column. On Line 2, Accounts Receivable is credited for $13.20 in the Accounts Receivable Credit column. No posting is made to individual charge customers' accounts. However, the name of the customer, John Barton, is written on the second line for identification purposes only. A check mark is placed in the Post. Ref. column to show that no individual posting is required.

> Since Import Auto Company uses sales slips as its accounts receivable ledger, no individual posting to a customer's account is required from any of the journals.

SUBSIDIARY LEDGERS IN A CASH REGISTER ACCOUNTING SYSTEM

The same subsidiary ledgers can be used with a cash register accounting system as used with any other system.

Accounts payable ledger

Import Auto Company uses a loose-leaf subsidiary ledger for its accounts payable. The three-column account form is used in this ledger. The forms and the ways of handling the ledger are the same as described in Chapter 13 for Gift World and in Chapter 23 for Sunrise Art Center.

Accounts receivable ledger

Import Auto Company does not use the three-column account form in its accounts receivable ledger. Instead, the Company uses copies of the sales slips prepared for each sale of merchandise on account. The Company also uses a small cabinet in which to file the slips. This file cabinet is the accounts receivable ledger for Import Auto Company.

Guide cards for all charge customers are arranged in alphabetical order in the accounts receivable file. Each sales slip is filed behind the customer's guide card, with the latest slip in front. The balance of each individual account can be figured at any time by totaling the customer's unpaid sales slips.

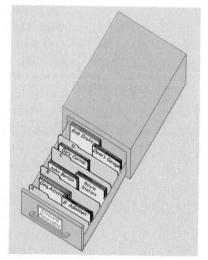

Accounts receivable file

Sales on account. Each time a sale on account is made, a sales slip is prepared and is recorded on the cash register. The carbon copies of the sales slips for sales on account are sent daily to the accountant. At the end of the day the accountant totals all the sales slips for sales on account and compares the total amount with the amount shown on Line 16 of the cash proof and balances slip. On January 3, 1977, the accountant's total of sales slips for sales on account is $302.90, the same as the amount shown on Line 16 of the cash proof and balances slip, page 484. The accountant makes this check to prove the accuracy of the data on the cash proof and balances slip and on the sales slips for sales on account.

Each sales slip for a sale on account is then filed in the accounts receivable file immediately behind the individual customer's guide card.

Sales returns and allowances on account. Each time credit is granted to a charge customer for a sales return or allowance, a sales slip for sales returns and allowances on account is prepared in duplicate by the cashier and is recorded on the cash register. The carbon copies are sent daily to the accountant.

Each sales slip for sales returns and allowances on account is recorded in the general journal as described on page 488 and is then filed in the accounts receivable file.

At the time the sales slip for sales returns and allowances is filed, it is stapled to the sales on account slip to which it applies. For example, the sales slip for the sales return shown on page 482 is for a return of merchandise sold on December 29, 1976. The sales slip for this sales return is stapled to the December 29 sales on account slip, and the set of two slips is filed behind Mr. Barton's guide card in the accounts receivable ledger.

Cash received on account. Each time a charge customer pays an amount he owes to Import Auto Company, a sales slip for cash received on account is prepared and is recorded on the cash register. The carbon copies of the sales slips for cash received on account are sent daily to the accountant. At the end of the day the accountant totals all the sales slips for cash received on account and compares the totals with the amounts shown on Lines 18, 19, and 20 of the cash proof and balances slip received from the cashier. On January 3, 1977, the totals of the sales slips for cash received on account are:

Total credit to Accounts Receivable	$234.72	(compare with Line 18)
Less debit to Sales Discount	− 1.52	(compare with Line 19)
Total cash received on account	$233.20	(compare with Line 20)

Each cash received on account slip is stapled to the charge sales slip (or slips) to which it applies. The set of paid slips is then filed alphabetically by the name of the customer in a "paid" file for future reference. In this way, the accounts receivable file contains only the unpaid sales slips for each customer.

Preparing a schedule of accounts receivable. At the end of each fiscal period, Import Auto Company prepares a schedule of accounts receivable. The form used is similar to the one in Chapter 13, page 214. The names of the charge customers to be listed are taken from the name guides in the accounts receivable file. The amount to be listed for each customer is figured by totaling all the unpaid sales slips minus any returns and allowances filed behind the customer's name guide. The total shown on the completed schedule is compared with the balance of the accounts receivable account in the general ledger. The total and the balance should be the same.

Advantages of using sales slips as an accounts receivable ledger

The advantages in using sales slips as an accounts receivable ledger are:

- **1.** The accountant uses the sales slips related to charge sales to recheck the accuracy of the amounts shown on the cash proof and balances slip. In this way, the figures are checked by both the cashier and the accountant. Greater accuracy is assured when more than one person checks the records.

■ **2.** The charge sales and the cash received on account transactions do not have to be recorded individually in journals. This saves time in recording. It also saves space in the cash receipts-sales journal.

■ **3.** Separate postings from a journal to the accounts receivable ledger do not have to be made. This saves time and decreases the chance of making mistakes in posting.

> As the number of charge customers increases, greater savings of time will be possible. However, when a very large number of charge customers' accounts are being kept, most businesses will use special accounting machines or data processing equipment to assist in keeping the records.

AUTOMATION AND A CASH REGISTER SYSTEM

As the volume of retail business has grown, business has looked for improved equipment to speed the recording, sorting, and reporting of financial data. One way to speed the procedures is to use cash registers that are part of an automated data processing system.

In one type of automated cash register system, a credit card is used to record a customer's account number on the cash register. At the time of the sale, the credit card is inserted into the cash register. The account number from the card is printed on the detailed audit tape inside the register. The data are printed in a special set of characters known as optical type. The illustration below shows optical type as it might appear on a cash register tape.

Customer's credit card

The National Cash Register Company

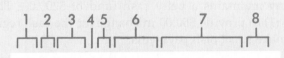	1 Register Number
	2 Date
	3 Transaction Number
	4 Control Symbols
	5 Classification and/or Department Number
	6 Amount
	7 Account Number
	8 Control Symbols

153≦170323 d800045.67012345 43210 0 4|
153≦170323 d800056.78012345 43210 0 3|
153≦170323 d800067.89012345 43210 0 2|
153≦170323 d800078.90012345 43210 0 3|

1 2 3 4 5   6   7   8

Data printed in optical type on a cash register tape

At the end of a business day, the tape is removed from the cash register and sent to the data processing center or department. The optical type data on the cash register tape are "read" by special data processing equipment and converted to input media that can be processed by automated machines. The data on input media are then read into the computer and the records are updated.

Data may also be sent from some cash registers directly to the computer at the time the transaction is recorded on the cash register. This is accomplished by having the cash register connected to the computer system by telephone wires. As a transaction is being entered on the cash register, the data are sent over the telephone lines to the computer. Records may then be updated instantly. By using telephone wires to send data to the computer, the cash register does not have to be in the same room, same building, or even in the same town. Therefore, several retail stores can have cash registers connected to the same computer. This is particularly helpful for a business with stores or branches and a centralized accounting department.

PETTY CASH FUND

Most businesses have some small payments that are best paid in cash instead of by check. Examples are small payments for postage due, for deliveries by special messenger, for buying small amounts of supplies, and for small refunds to cash customers. Making such payments in cash avoids the issuing of checks for small amounts. It also makes it possible to pay for services or goods in small amounts where it is not desirable to open a separate charge account with a creditor.

Using a petty cash fund enables a business to follow the common practice of depositing *all* cash receipts in the bank and of making *all* withdrawals of such cash by writing checks. When this is done, the monthly bank statements may be used to prove the cash records of the business and to give a double check on their accuracy.

Import Auto Company maintains a petty cash fund of $200.00. This petty cash fund is used (1) to provide $50.00 in change for the cash register each day and (2) to make small cash payments.

Establishing a petty cash fund

When the petty cash fund for Import Auto Company was established in 1970, Mr. Burl decided that $200.00 would be sufficient for the needs of his business. He drew a check for $200.00 payable to Petty Cash, cashed the check, and placed the $200.00 in a petty cash box in the office safe. The check stub is used as the source document for the entry in the cash payments journal in which Petty Cash is debited for $200.00 and Cash is credited for $200.00.

The petty cash money is kept separate from all other cash. The petty cash money is often kept in a small box in the office safe. One person is usually responsible for making all petty cash payments. The entry to establish a petty cash fund is:

CASH PAYMENTS JOURNAL										PAGE 5	
				1		2	3	4		5	
DATE	ACCOUNT TITLE	CHECK No.	POST. REF.	GENERAL			ACCOUNTS PAYABLE DEBIT	PURCHASES DISCOUNT CREDIT		CASH CREDIT	
				DEBIT	CREDIT						
1970 May 1	Petty Cash	41	12	200 00						200 00	1

ACCOUNT Petty Cash							ACCOUNT NO. 12	
DATE	ITEM	POST. REF.	DEBIT	CREDIT	BALANCE			
					DEBIT		CREDIT	
1970 May 1		CP5	200 00		200 00			

Recording a petty cash fund

This entry, when posted, transfers $200.00 from the cash account to the new asset account, Petty Cash. The petty cash account is placed immediately after the cash account in the general ledger. The petty cash account is given account number 12 to show that it is the second asset account.

Making payments from a petty cash fund

The cashier for Import Auto Company removes $50.00 in bills and coins from the petty cash box at the beginning of each day. This money is placed in the cash register for use in making change and small cash payments. The cashier is authorized to make cash payments of not more than $5.00 for a single payment. Petty cash payments in excess of $5.00 must have the manager's approval.

Each time a payment is made from the petty cash fund, a paid-out voucher is prepared showing (a) to whom payment is made; (b) reason for payment; (c) how much is paid; (d) the account debited; and (e) the signature of the person receiving the money. The paid-out form used by Import Auto Company is shown on page 482.

At the end of each day, all paid-out vouchers are removed from the cash register, totaled, and placed in the petty cash box. At all times the sum of the paid-out vouchers plus the amount of money remaining in the petty cash box should equal the original amount of the petty cash fund. For example, on January 3, paid-out vouchers totaling $18.60, and the remaining change, $31.40, are returned to the petty cash box. The total of these two, $50.00 ($18.60 + $31.40), equals the amount of change placed in the cash register for use on January 3.

Also, at the end of each day *all* the paid-out vouchers in the petty cash box are added and *all* the money in the box is counted. The total of all

paid-out vouchers plus the money in the petty cash box must equal
$200.00, the total amount placed in the petty cash fund originally.

Replenishing a petty cash fund

After many small cash payments have been made from petty cash, little
actual money will remain in the petty cash box. It is then necessary to
replenish the amount of cash in the fund. Import Auto Company replenishes its petty cash fund when the amount of actual money on hand in
the petty cash box is reduced to $75.00. This policy assures that the
$50.00 needed each day for change will be available.

Import Auto Company replenishes its petty cash fund as follows:

REQUEST TO REPLENISH PETTY CASH FUND	
PAYMENTS	
Account	Amount
Supplies	43.61
Sales Returns and Allowances	28.50
Delivery Expense	47.40
Miscellaneous Expense	12.49
Total needed to replenish	132.00

Date   Jan. 24 19 77   *Alice Sellers*
                                    Cashier

Check No. issued   35   Date   Jan. 24 19 77
Accountant _____ *Jim Smith*

Report used for replenishing
a petty cash fund

☐ **1** The cashier prepares a request to replenish
the petty cash fund. The form at the left
shows this report as prepared on January 24,
1977. The cashier sorts the paid-out vouchers according to the name of the account to
be charged. The vouchers for each account
are then totaled and the account titles and
the amounts are recorded on the form as
shown at the left. After signing the form, the
cashier gives this report to the accountant.

☐ **2** The accountant issues a check for the
amount needed to replenish the petty cash
fund, $132.00. The accountant signs the form
at the bottom after filling in the number of
the check issued and the date.

☐ **3** The accountant makes a summary entry in the cash payments journal for the check written to replenish the petty cash fund. Each account listed on the report is debited for the amount shown on the
report, and Cash is credited for the total amount of the check written. The summary entry for the replenishment of the petty cash
fund is recorded in the cash payments journal as follows:

CASH PAYMENTS JOURNAL   PAGE 2

	DATE	ACCOUNT TITLE	CHECK NO.	POST. REF.	GENERAL DEBIT	GENERAL CREDIT	ACCOUNTS PAYABLE DEBIT	PURCHASES DISCOUNT CREDIT	CASH CREDIT	
12	24	Supplies	35		4361				132 00	12
13		Sales Returns + Allowances			28 50					13
14		Delivery Expense			4740					14
15		Miscellaneous Expense			12 49					15
16										16

Entry to replenish a petty cash fund

□ 4 The check written to replenish petty cash is given to the cashier. The cashier cashes the check and places the money in the petty cash box. The total amount of cash in the box after the fund has been replenished is again $200.00 ($68.00 cash that remained in the box plus the $132.00 cash received from the check to replenish the fund).

□ 5 The accountant files all the paid-out vouchers and the summary form for payments from the petty cash fund showing the money needed to replenish the petty cash fund. These forms are filed in a folder labeled "Petty Cash Paid Out."

Replenishing the petty cash fund at the end of each fiscal period

The petty cash fund is replenished at the end of each fiscal period regardless of the amount of money remaining in the petty cash fund on that date. The paid-out vouchers in the petty cash box represent transactions that have not yet been journalized and posted. If the petty cash fund is not replenished at the end of each fiscal period, (a) the balance of Petty Cash in the general ledger is not an accurate statement of cash on hand, (b) the balance sheet is not an accurate statement of assets, and (c) the income statement is not an accurate statement of expenses.

Import Auto Company replenishes its petty cash fund at the end of each fiscal period so that all its petty cash payments will be recorded before the financial statements are prepared. The procedure for replenishing petty cash on the last day of a fiscal period is the same as the procedure used for replenishing the petty cash fund when it is low.

Balance of the petty cash account

Unless the petty cash fund has been permanently increased or decreased, the balance of the petty cash account is always the original amount of the fund. For Import Auto Company, the balance of the petty cash account is $200.00. No part of the entry to replenish the petty cash fund is posted to the petty cash account in the general ledger. The check issued to replenish the petty cash fund does not change the balance of the petty cash account. Neither do the amounts paid out from the petty cash fund affect the balance of the petty cash account.

The balance of the petty cash account in the general ledger changes only when it is decided to increase or decrease the size of the petty cash fund. For example, if Import Auto Company decided to increase the petty cash fund from $200.00 to $250.00, it would issue a check payable to Petty Cash for the additional $50.00. The entry to record this addition would be similar to the entry made when the petty cash fund was established: Petty Cash would be debited and Cash would be credited. The debit to Petty Cash would increase the balance of the petty cash account in the general ledger.

SUMMARY OF PROCEDURES FOR USING A CASH REGISTER ACCOUNTING SYSTEM

The summary illustration below shows the procedures used by Import Auto Company in its cash register accounting system. The yellow blocks on the diagram represent the documents or the reports prepared on the cash register.

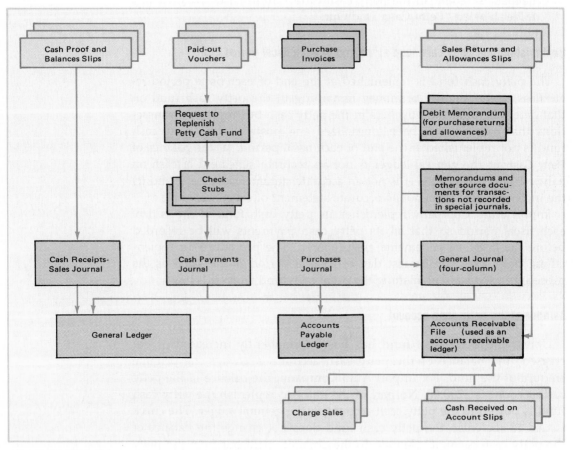

Summary illustration showing recording and
posting procedures in a cash register system

The charge sales slips and the cash received on account slips are not used as source documents for entries in a journal. The totals from these slips are accumulated by the cash register as the slips are recorded on the cash register. At the end of the day, the cash register is used to print a cash proof and balances slip. The cash proof and balances slip is used as the source document for the daily entry in the cash receipts-sales journal.

The cash register does not accumulate totals for sales returns and allowances. Therefore, the duplicate copies of the sales returns and allowances slips are the source documents for these entries in the general journal.

No posting is required from any journal to the accounts receivable file, which serves as the accounts receivable ledger. The charge sales slips are filed in the accounts receivable file according to the name of the charge customer. The cash received on account slips with the appropriate charge sales slips attached are filed alphabetically in a "paid" file. Using the slips as the accounts receivable ledger saves the time needed to keep data about transactions affecting the accounts of charge customers.

Except for the entry to replenish petty cash, the entries made in the cash payments journal and the purchases journal are the same as those described in Chapter 23 for Sunrise Art Center.

Using Business Terms

✦ What is the meaning of each of the following?

- petty cash
- detailed audit tape
- voucher
- cash proof and balances slip
- cash short
- cash over

Questions for Individual Study

1. What five kinds of operations may be performed by cash registers?
2. Why does Import Auto Company prepare sales slips in duplicate?
3. When the cashier for Import Auto Company makes a small cash payment from money in the cash register, what record is prepared?
4. How does the cashier for Import Auto Company prove cash?
5. Why is a combined cash receipts-sales journal used by Import Auto Company?
6. How does the accountant know what data to record from the cash proof and balances slip?
7. In what form does Import Auto Company keep its accounts receivable ledger?
8. How can Import Auto Company determine a charge customer's account balance?
9. What are the advantages of using an accounts receivable file such as the one kept by Import Auto Company?
10. How does the use of a cash register tape printed with optical type characters help when a business uses a computer?
11. What entry is made to establish a petty cash fund?
12. What entry is made by Import Auto Company on January 24 to replenish petty cash?
13. Why should petty cash always be replenished at the end of a fiscal period?

Cases for Management Decision

CASE 1 Doris Calloway owns a dress shop. She uses a simple cash register that records cash transactions on a detailed audit tape inside the register. The register also prints a paper tape receipt for each cash sale. Mrs. Calloway keeps her accounts receivable ledger on three-column ledger account forms. She pays a public accountant to check her records and to prepare end-of-fiscal-period reports for her. The accountant has suggested that she adopt a cash register system similar to the one described for Import Auto Company in Chapter 25. Mrs. Calloway has objected to the plan because she believes it will cost more money to operate the system with a new cash register. Do you agree with Mrs. Calloway or with the accountant? Why?

CASE 2 Curtis Welman operates a small neighborhood grocery store. He has a petty cash fund of $40.00. He uses the fund to make change each day and to make small cash payments. Mr. Welman replenishes the petty cash fund whenever it is all used. A friend, who is an accountant, suggests that Mr. Welman should have a larger petty cash fund. The accountant also suggests that Mr. Welman replenish the petty cash fund before it is completely used. Do you agree with Mr. Welman's procedures or with those suggested by his friend? Why?

CASE 3 Mickey Jamison owns a hardware and lumber business. He sells primarily to home owners, and he sells on a cash basis only. He does not sell any merchandise on account. Mr. Jamison has his accounting records kept by an accounting service which uses a computer. The accounting service suggests that Mr. Jamison would reduce costs by installing cash registers that print optical type characters on the cash register tapes. How would the use of these cash registers reduce costs for Mr. Jamison? Should he make the change?

Drill for Mastering Principles

DRILL 25-D 1 Replenishing the petty cash fund

Petty cash is replenished for the amounts and on the dates shown in the table below:

Example: March 4 entry

Supplies
22.00|

Sales Returns and Allowances
30.10|

Advertising Expense
5.50|

Delivery Expense
13.75|

Miscellaneous Expense
21.60|

Cash
| 92.95

Total   Total
debits, $92.95 = credits, $92.95

Date on which replenished	Total of Paid-out Vouchers for				
	Supplies	Sales Returns and Allowances	Advertising Expense	Delivery Expense	Miscellaneous Expense
March 4	$22.00	$30.10	$5.50	$13.75	$21.60
March 11	25.57	28.50	9.70	14.74	10.96
March 21	18.43	49.47	2.91	28.42	2.42
March 31	7.76	67.60	7.26	8.24	1.00

Instructions: □ **1.** For each of the dates shown above, prepare T accounts for the six accounts affected by the entry to replenish the petty cash fund. Record the amounts on the debit or credit side of each T account to show how the account is affected. The T accounts for the March 4 entry are shown at the left.

□ **2.** Check the equality of debits and credits for each entry.

Problems for Applying Concepts

PROBLEM 25-1 Establishing, proving, and replenishing the petty cash fund

Betty Horton owns and operates a retail store. On February 1 of the current year, Miss Horton issued and cashed Check No. 65 for $150.00 to establish a petty cash fund. During the month of February, the cashier made payments from the petty cash fund and on February 28 submitted the report shown at the right.

Instructions: □ **1.** Record on page 10 of a cash payments journal like the one on page 493 the issuance of Check No. 65, February 1, to establish the petty cash fund.

□ **2.** Prove the petty cash fund. At the end of the month of February, the amount of money actually left in the petty cash fund is $100.62.

□ **3.** Record in the cash payments journal the issuance of Check No. 98 to replenish the petty cash fund on February 28.

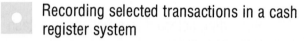

REQUEST TO REPLENISH PETTY CASH FUND	
PAYMENTS	
Account	Amount
Supplies	15.00
Sales Returns and Allowances	2.88
Delivery Expense	21.60
Miscellaneous Expense	9.90
Total needed to replenish	49.38

Date __Feb. 28__ 19 77   *Jane Demerest*
                                          Cashier

Check No. issued _____   Date _____ 19 ____

Accountant _____

PROBLEM 25-2   Recording selected transactions in a cash register system

If you are not using the workbook correlating with this textbook, complete Review Problem 25-R 1 instead of Problem 25-2.

On September 17 of the current year, the cashier for the Dawson Grocery Store prepared on the cash register the cash proof and balances slip given in the workbook. The following data were also obtained on the same date:

Money from petty cash fund placed in cash register
at beginning of the day for making change .... $ 75.00

Paid-out vouchers for the following amounts are in
the cash register drawer......................................   3.19
                                                                 4.88
                                                                 4.90
                                                                 1.47

Actual amount of money counted in the cash drawer
before the money for change is taken out 1,341.10

Sales Slip No. 89 for a sales return on account made
out to Mrs. Henry Carlton is in the cash register
drawer..   8.76

Instructions: □ **1.** Complete the cash proof and balances slip for September 17 as follows:

a. Record on Line 1 the amount of change placed in the cash register at the beginning of the day.

b. Total the paid-out vouchers and compare the total with the amount printed on Line 2.

c. Subtract Line 2 from Line 1 and record the balance of change on Line 3.

d. Determine the amount of money that remains in the cash drawer after the balance of change has been removed. Record this amount on Line 7.

e. Compare the amounts on each of the following pairs of lines. The amounts on each pair of lines should be the same. If the amounts are not the same, record the cash short or the cash over on the appropriate line.

Lines 6 and 7; Lines 14 and 17; Lines 5 and 20; Lines 4 and 15.

Instructions: □ **2.** On page 11 of a cash receipts-sales journal similar to the one on page 486, make the entry to record the data from the completed cash proof and balances slip for September 17.

□ **3.** Check the equality of debits and credits in the journal entry made for Instruction 2.

□ **4.** On page 8 of a four-column general journal similar to the one on page 488, record the entry for the sales returns and allowances slip for Mrs. Carlton.

Optional
Problems

MASTERY PROBLEM 25-M Recording selected transactions in a cash register system

If you are not using the workbook correlating with this textbook, Omit Problem 25-M.

On June 10 of the current year, the cashier of Sewing Center prepared a cash proof and balances slip as shown in the workbook. The following data were also obtained on the same date:

Money from the petty cash fund placed in the cash register at the beginning of the day for making change...	$ 60.00
Paid-out vouchers for the following amounts are in the cash register drawer..	2.04
	3.21
	4.18
	1.00
	2.55
Actual count of money in cash drawer *before* the money for change is taken out..............................	1,056.65
Sales Slip No. 876 for a sales return on account made out to Betty Edwards is in the cash register drawer ..	7.58

Instructions: □ **1.** Complete the cash proof and balances slip for June 10 following the procedures listed in Instruction 1 of Problem 25-2.

□ **2.** On page 8 of a cash receipts-sales journal similar to the one on page 486, make the entry to record the data from the completed cash proof and balances slip for June 10.

□ **3.** Check the equality of the debits and credits in the journal entry made in Instruction 2.

□ **4.** On page 5 of a four-column general journal similar to the one on page 488, make the entry to record the sales returns and allowances slip for Miss Edwards.

BONUS Recording selected transactions in a
PROBLEM 25-B   cash register system

On May 7 of the current year, the detailed audit tape for Casey's Toy Shop was as shown below.

The cash register used by Casey's Toy Shop does not have a slip printer on it. For this reason, the cashier cannot print a cash proof and balances slip.

In addition to the detailed audit tape, the cashier reports the following:

Money taken from the cash drawer and deposited was $2,002.82.
Paid-out vouchers for the day totaled $28.77.
Money placed in the cash drawer at the beginning of the day from the petty cash fund was $100.00.
Amount of money taken from the cash drawer at the end of the day and returned to the petty cash fund was $71.23.
Two sales slips for sales returns on account were:
   Sales Slip No. 343, Albert Downey, $16.50.
   Sales Slip No. 350, Carl Manning, $10.73.

May 7—428	$00028.77	—PO
May 7—429	$01761.38	—CA
May 7—430	$00240.24	—RC
May 7—431	$00900.24	—1
May 7—432	$00182.93	—2
May 7—433	$00471.68	—3
May 7—434	$00250.91	—4
May 7—435	$00044.38	—CH
May 7—436	$00002.43	—SD

Instructions: □ **1.** Use a blank cash proof and balances slip similar to the one on page 484. Enter the data given on the detailed audit tape above on the proper lines of the cash proof and balances slip.

□ **2.** Complete the cash proof and balances slip for May 7.

□ **3.** On page 6 of a cash receipts-sales journal similar to the one on page 486, make the entry to record the data from the completed cash proof and balances slip for May 7. Check the equality of debits and credits in the journal entry.

□ **4.** On page 5 of a four-column general journal similar to the one on page 488, make one combined entry to record the two sales returns and allowances on account slips.

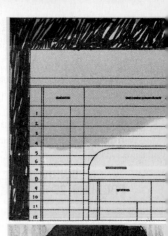

PHILLIPS

PAPER PRODUCTS

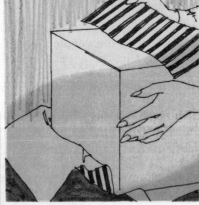

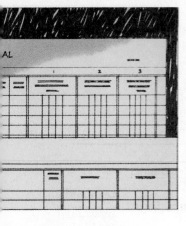

ACCOUNTING FOR SALES TAX, BAD DEBTS, AND DEPRECIATION

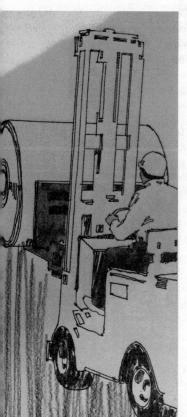

MANY BUSINESSES HAVE SPECIAL TRANSACTIONS.
Special business transactions are related to sales, purchases, accounts receivable, and plant assets. These transactions are in addition to the normal purchases and sales transactions. Specific ledger accounts and special attention to these additional transactions are needed to maintain complete and accurate records. Some of the special transactions are: recording of sales taxes, ledgerless accounting, bad debts expense, and buying or disposing of plant assets.

RECORDING PROCEDURES FOR SPECIAL TRANSACTIONS VARY. How *Phillips Paper Products* journalizes and posts special transactions is described in Part 6. The use of special journals and specific ledger accounts for these special transactions is described.

PHILLIPS PAPER PRODUCTS

CHART OF ACCOUNTS

Balance Sheet Accounts

(1) ASSETS	Account Number
11 Current Assets	
Cash	111
Petty Cash	112
Accounts Receivable	113
Allowance for Uncollectible Accounts	113.1
Merchandise Inventory	114
Supplies	115
Prepaid Insurance	116
12 Plant Assets	
Delivery Equipment	121
Accumulated Depreciation — Delivery Equipment	121.1
Store Equipment	122
Accumulated Depreciation — Store Equipment	122.1

(2) LIABILITIES	
21 Current Liabilities	
Accounts Payable	211
Employees Income Tax Payable	212
FICA Tax Payable	213
Federal Unemployment Tax Payable	214
State Unemployment Tax Payable	215
Sales Tax Payable	216

(3) CAPITAL	
Jerry Phillips, Capital	311
Jerry Phillips, Drawing	312
Income Summary	313

Income Statement Accounts

(4) OPERATING REVENUE	Account Number
Sales	411
Sales Returns and Allowances	411.1

(5) COST OF MERCHANDISE	
Purchases	511
Purchases Returns and Allowances	511.1
Purchases Discount	511.2

(6) OPERATING EXPENSES	
Bad Debts Expense	611
Delivery Expense	612
Depreciation Expense — Delivery Equipment	613
Depreciation Expense — Store Equipment	614
Insurance Expense	615
Miscellaneous Expense	616
Payroll Taxes Expense	617
Rent Expense	618
Salary Expense	619
Supplies Expense	620

(7) OTHER REVENUE	
Gain on Plant Assets	711

(8) OTHER EXPENSE	
Loss on Plant Assets	811

The chart of accounts for Phillips Paper Products is illustrated above for ready reference as you study Part 6 of this textbook.

Sales Tax and Other Sales and Purchases Systems

26

The laws of most states and some cities require a retailer to collect a tax from customers at the time each taxable sale is made. A tax levied on a sale of goods is called a sales tax. Sales tax rates usually are stated as a percentage of sales. The kinds of goods taxed and the tax rates vary from state to state and from city to city.

SALES TAX

At regular intervals, the retailer is required to file reports with the proper government unit and to pay the amount of sales tax collected. Because of the tax reports, every business that collects sales tax needs accurate records of the amount of tax collected. The tax records need to show:

1. Total cash sales and total charge sales on which sales tax has been collected.
2. Total amount of sales tax due to the government.

Charge sales with sales tax

Phillips Paper Products operates in a state with a 5% sales tax rate. When the company sells taxable merchandise, the customer is charged for the amount of the sale plus the sales tax. Phillips Paper Products uses a sales journal, a purchases journal, a general journal, a cash receipts journal, and a cash payments journal.

Phillips Paper Products made the following charge sale:

October 3, 1977. Sold merchandise on account to Oliver Evans $100.00 plus sales tax, $5.00. Sales Invoice No. 610.

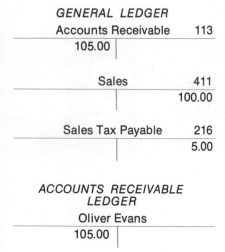

GENERAL LEDGER

Accounts Receivable	113
105.00	

Sales	411
	100.00

Sales Tax Payable	216
	5.00

ACCOUNTS RECEIVABLE LEDGER

Oliver Evans

105.00	

Accounts Receivable is debited for $105.00, the amount of the sale plus the sales tax. Sales is credited for $100.00, the amount of the sale. Sales Tax Payable is credited for $5.00, the amount of the tax on this sale. The amount of sales tax charged each customer is a liability because Phillips Paper Products owes the tax to the state government.

Oliver Evans' account in the accounts receivable ledger is also debited for the $105.00.

The account numbers in the general ledger (113, 411, and 216) contain three digits. Many businesses, especially those with a large number of accounts, use account numbers with three or four digits. Each business numbers its accounts according to its particular needs. The chart of accounts for Phillips Paper Products is on page 504.

The sales journal used by Phillips Paper Products has three amount columns: Accounts Receivable Debit, Sales Credit, and Sales Tax Payable Credit.

					1	2	3	
SALES JOURNAL							PAGE 16	
	DATE	ACCOUNT DEBITED	SALE NO.	POST. REF.	ACCOUNTS RECEIVABLE DEBIT	SALES CREDIT	SALES TAX PAYABLE CREDIT	
1	1977 Oct. 3	Oliver Evans	610	✓	10500	10000	500	1
2	4	James Kane	611	✓	10080	9600	480	2
3	4	Martin Wilson	612	✓	8694	8280	414	3
29	28	Francis Cox	638	✓	22502	21430	1072	29
30	31	Irving Lake	639	✓	20160	19200	960	30
31	31	Totals			880426 838501 880426	838501	41925 41925	31
32					(113)	(411)	(216)	32
33								33

Sales journal with Sales Tax Payable Credit column

The entry on Line 1 of the sales journal is for the charge sale to Oliver Evans. Accounts Receivable in the general ledger and Oliver Evans' account in the subsidiary ledger are debited for $105.00, the total amount to be collected. Sales is credited for $100.00, the amount of the sale. Sales Tax Payable is credited for $5.00, the amount of the sales tax.

The individual amounts in the Accounts Receivable Debit column are posted daily to the accounts receivable ledger. A check mark is placed in the Post. Ref. column of the journal immediately after each of these amounts is posted.

At the end of the month, the equality of debits and credits in the journal is proved. The totals of the special columns are then posted to the general ledger. As each total is posted, the account number is placed in parentheses below the total.

Cash sales with sales tax

Phillips Paper Products enters each cash sale on a cash register. At the end of the day, the totals from the cash register for all cash sales and sales tax are recorded in a cash receipts journal.

The cash register tape of Phillips Paper Products on October 3 shows the following summary information:

Total cash sales		Sales tax (5%)		Total cash received
$150.00	+	$7.50	=	$157.50

October 3, 1977. Cash sales, $150.00, plus sales tax, $7.50. Cash Register Tape No. T3.

Cash is debited for $157.50, the total amount of cash received. Sales is credited for $150.00, the amount of merchandise sold. Sales Tax Payable is credited for $7.50, the amount of sales tax collected.

The amount of sales tax collected from all customers is a liability because Phillips Paper Products owes this amount to the state government.

The cash receipts journal used by Phillips Paper Products has a special amount column in which to record the amount of sales tax collected on cash sales.

Cash	111
157.50	

Sales	411
	150.00

Sales Tax Payable	216
	7.50

	DATE	ACCOUNT TITLE	Doc. No.	Post. Ref.	GENERAL DEBIT	GENERAL CREDIT	SALES CREDIT	SALES TAX PAYABLE CREDIT	ACCOUNTS RECEIVABLE CREDIT	CASH DEBIT	
1	*1977 Oct. 1*	*Balance on hand, $4,323.27*		✓							1
2	3	✓	T3	✓			15000	750		15750	2
29	28	*James Kane*	R319	✓					10080	10080	29
30	28	✓	T28	✓			29030	1452		30482	30
31	31	✓	T31	✓			18640	932		19572	31
32	31	*Totals*			12240	28621	943531	47177	436813	1443902	32
33					(✓)	(✓)	(411)	(216)	(113)	(111)	33
34											34

Cash receipts journal with Sales Tax Payable Credit column

The entry on Line 2 of the cash receipts journal above records the total cash sales for October 3. Cash is debited in the Cash Debit column, $157.50. Sales is credited in the Sales Credit column, $150.00. Sales Tax Payable is credited in the Sales Tax Payable Credit column, $7.50. A check mark is placed in the Account Title column and in the Post. Ref. column.

> After the posting from all journals has been completed for a month, the sales tax payable account shows the total amount of sales tax owed to the government for both cash and charge sales.

Cash receipts on account with sales tax

Phillips Paper Products records the receipt of cash on account in its cash receipts journal.

> *October 28, 1977. Received on account from James Kane, in payment of Sales Invoice No. 611, $100.80. Receipt No. 319.*

The entry on Line 29 of the cash receipts journal is for the receipt of cash from James Kane. Cash is debited for the full amount received, $100.80. Accounts Receivable and the customer's account are credited for the same amount, $100.80. No entry is required for the sales tax because the tax was recorded when the sale was entered in the sales journal. (This sale is shown on Line 2 of the sales journal, page 506.)

The individual amounts in the Accounts Receivable Credit column of the cash receipts journal, page 507, are posted to customers' accounts daily. The individual amounts in the General Debit and Credit columns are posted frequently during the month.

At the end of the month, cash is proved and the equality of debits and credits in the cash receipts journal is verified. The totals of the special columns are then posted to the general ledger.

Paying sales tax owed to the government

Sales tax collected by the retailer must be paid to the proper government unit. In many states the sales tax collected on cash sales and on charge sales is paid to the state each month. In other states, the payment is made quarterly.

> *October 28, 1977. Paid sales tax collected during September to the State Tax Commission, $797.88. Check No. 445.*

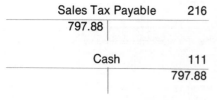

Sales Tax Payable is debited for the amount of the tax paid, $797.88. Cash is credited for the same amount.

The cash payments journal used by Phillips Paper Products is shown on the next page. Since the company pays the amount of sales tax collected only once a month, a special column for Sales Tax Payable Debit is not needed.

The entry in the cash payments journal to record the payment of sales tax collected during September is shown on Line 29. Sales Tax Payable is debited for $797.88. The account title is written in the Account Title column. The amount is written in the General Debit column. Cash is credited for $797.88 by writing the amount in the Cash Credit column.

The individual amounts in the Accounts Payable Debit column of the cash payments journal are posted daily to the creditors' accounts. The individual amounts in the General Debit and Credit columns are posted frequently during the month.

					GENERAL		ACCOUNTS PAYABLE DEBIT	PURCHASES DISCOUNT CREDIT	CASH CREDIT	
	DATE	ACCOUNT TITLE	CHECK No.	POST. REF.	DEBIT	CREDIT				
1	1977 Oct. 3	Rent Expense	417	618	28000				28000	1
2	4	Miscellaneous Expense	418	616	4000				4000	2
3	4	J. C. Towne	419	✓			33200	664	32536	3
29	28	Sales Tax Payable	445	216	79788				79788	29
30	28	Marsh & Co.	446	✓			62065		62065	30
31	31	Supplies	447	115	860				3880	31
32		Delivery Expense		612	375					32
33		Miscellaneous Expense		616	2645					33
34	31	Totals			624979		1032607	14606	1642980	34
35					(✓)		(211)	(511.2)	(111)	35
36										36

CASH PAYMENTS JOURNAL PAGE 10

At the end of the month, cash is proved and the equality of debits and credits in the cash payments journal is verified. The totals of the special columns are then posted to the general ledger.

Cash payments journal with sales tax entry

Sales returns and allowances with sales tax

When merchandise is returned, the customer is entitled to a credit for both the amount of merchandise returned and the sales tax on that amount. Similarly, if an allowance is granted on merchandise sold to a customer, the credit must include the sales tax on the allowance.

In a charge sale on October 3, Oliver Evans' account was debited for $105.00. The charge was for $100.00 sales and $5.00 sales tax. On October 12, Mr. Evans returned part of the merchandise.

October 12, 1977. Granted credit to Oliver Evans for merchandise he returned, $50.00, plus sales tax, $2.50. Credit Memorandum No. 31.

Mr. Evans is entitled to a credit of $50.00 for the merchandise returned. He is also entitled to a credit of $2.50 for the sales tax on the returned merchandise. The total credit is $52.50.

Sales Returns and Allowances is debited for $50.00, the amount of merchandise returned. Sales Tax Payable is debited for $2.50, the amount of tax on the returned merchandise. Accounts Receivable is credited for $52.50, and Mr. Evans' account is also credited for $52.50.

The entry to record Oliver Evans' return of merchandise is shown on Lines 12–15 of the four-column general journal on page 510.

Sales Returns and Allowances is debited for $50.00 in the General Debit column. Sales Tax Payable is debited for

GENERAL LEDGER

Sales Returns and Allowances 411.1
50.00

Sales Tax Payable 216
2.50

Accounts Receivable 113
52.50

ACCOUNTS RECEIVABLE LEDGER

Oliver Evans
Bal. 105.00   52.50

$2.50 in the General Debit column. Oliver Evans is credited for $52.50 in the Accounts Receivable Credit column.

ACCOUNTS PAYABLE DEBIT	GENERAL DEBIT	DATE	ACCOUNT TITLE	POST. REF.	GENERAL CREDIT	ACCOUNTS RECEIV. CREDIT	
			GENERAL JOURNAL			PAGE *10*	
					3	4	
1	2						
12	5000	12	*Sales Returns + Allowances*	411.1			12
13	250		*Sales Tax Payable*	216			13
14			*Oliver Evans*	✓		5250	14
15			*Credit Memo: No. 31.*				15
16	9938	24	*M. R. Waltz*	✓			16
17			*M. L. Watts*	✓	9938		17
18			*Memorandum No: 116.*				18
39	~~81192~~ ~~135215~~ 81192 135215	31	*Totals*		~~115215~~ 115215	~~101192~~ 101192	39
40	(211) (✓)				(✓)	(113)	40

Four-column general journal with sales tax entry and correcting entry

A correcting entry with sales tax

A correcting entry that affects only accounts in a subsidiary ledger is recorded in a general journal. For example, on October 24, Phillips Paper Products discovered that a charge sale had been recorded incorrectly in its charge customers' accounts.

> October 24, 1977. Discovered that Sales Invoice No. 607 to M. R. Waltz on September 28 was incorrectly posted to the account of M. L. Watts, $99.38. Memorandum No. 116.

The posting of Sales Invoice No. 607 from the sales journal was in error. The account of M. L. Watts was debited for $99.38 when the account of M. R. Waltz should have been debited.

The entry on Lines 16–18 of the general journal above shows the correcting entry for this error. M. R. Waltz is debited for $99.38 in the General Debit column to charge his account for the sale. M. L. Watts is credited for $99.38 in the General Credit column to remove the incorrect charge from his account. No entry is made for the sales tax of $4.73 because it was correctly recorded and posted at the time of the sale. The correcting entry is recorded only in the General columns because the accounts receivable account in the general ledger is not affected.

The individual amounts in the Accounts Payable Debit column and the Accounts Receivable Credit column of the general journal are posted daily. The individual amounts in the General columns are posted frequently during the month. At the end of the month, the equality of debits and credits in the general journal is proved. Then the totals of the two special columns are posted to the general ledger.

INVOICES USED AS JOURNALS AND LEDGERS

Some accounting systems use duplicate copies of source documents as a journal, as a subsidiary ledger, or as both. Using copies of source documents as a journal is called journalless accounting. Using copies of source documents as a subsidiary ledger is called ledgerless accounting. The use of source documents in this way reduces the possibility of error in recording and posting transactions, and it also reduces accounting costs.

Sales invoices used as a sales journal

Some businesses use a file of all charge sales invoices as a sales journal. These businesses post directly from the sales invoices to the customers' accounts. At the end of the month, the sales invoices for the month are totaled and the total is recorded as a single entry in the general journal.

When sales invoices are used as a sales journal, the following is done:

1. Post the total of each sales invoice directly to the debit side of the proper customer's account in the accounts receivable ledger. Write the number of the sales invoice in the Post. Ref. column of the customer's account. Place a check mark at the right of the customer's name on each sales invoice to show that it been posted. File all charge sales invoices for the month in numeric order in a special file. This file is used as a sales journal.

2. At the end of the month, total all charge sales invoices in the sales file to obtain the total amount of all sales on account for the month. If the business collects a sales tax, three totals must be figured: (a) the total sales price on all invoices, (b) the total sales tax on all invoices, and (c) the total amount of all invoices including the sales tax. The sales invoices shown below have been totaled to obtain the three totals.

Sales invoices with adding machine tapes showing (a) the total sales price on all these invoices, (b) the total sales tax on all these invoices, and (c) the total amount of all charge sales invoices for the month.

Sales

```
  8 5 1 4  < +
    8 2 5  < +
  1 6 8 0  < +
  4 2 0 0  < +
  2 4 9 5  < +
  5 3 4 0  < +
1 2 3 0 0  < +
  7 6 4 3  < +

4 2 9 9 7  < T
```

(a)

Sales Tax

```
  4 2 6  < +
   4 1  < +
   8 4  < +
  2 1 0  < +
  1 2 5  < +
  2 6 7  < +
  6 1 5  < +
  3 8 2  < +

2 1 5 0  < T
```

(b)

Accounts Receivable

```
  8 9 4 0  < +
    8 6 6  < +
  1 7 6 4  < +
  4 4 1 0  < +
  2 6 2 0  < +
  5 6 0 7  < +
1 2 9 1 5  < +
  8 0 2 5  < +

4 5 1 4 7  < T
```

(c)

3. Record one entry in the general journal for all sales on account for the month. The general journal below shows the entry for the sales invoices illustrated on page 511.
4. Post the general journal entry to the three general ledger accounts: Accounts Receivable, Sales, and Sales Tax Payable.

			GENERAL JOURNAL			PAGE *16*
1	2				3	4
ACCOUNTS PAYABLE DEBIT	GENERAL DEBIT	DATE	ACCOUNT TITLE	POST. REF.	GENERAL CREDIT	ACCOUNTS RECEIV. CREDIT
33	451 47	30	*Accounts Receivable*			33
34			*Sales*		429 97	34
35			*Sales Tax Payable*		21 50	35
36			*Total sales on*			36
37			*account for April Sales*			37
38			*Invoices Nos. 267-274.*			38

Entry to record total monthly sales on account when sales invoices serve as a sales journal

Sales invoices used as an accounts receivable ledger

Some businesses use charge sales invoices both as a sales journal and as an accounts receivable ledger. In such journalless and ledgerless systems, sales invoices are prepared in triplicate. One copy is given to the customer, one copy is used with other sales invoices as a sales journal, and one copy is used with other sales invoices as an accounts receivable ledger.

Carbon copies of all charge sales invoices are placed in a separate folder for each customer. The folders are kept in alphabetic order in an accounts receivable file similar to the one described in Chapter 25. The sales invoices are filed daily so that the customers' accounts will always be up to date.

All sales invoices for each customer are filed together in a folder with the latest invoice at the front of the folder. Whenever payment is received, the file copy of the invoice is marked *Paid* and placed in a "paid" file. The total amount due from any customer can be determined by adding the unpaid sales invoices in that customer's accounts receivable folder. Any credit memorandums for returns or allowances are attached to the sales invoice to which they apply. The credit memorandums are deducted in determining the amount due.

Purchase invoices used as a purchases journal

Some businesses file copies of all purchase invoices for purchases on account in one place and use the file of invoices as a purchases journal.

These businesses post directly from the purchase invoices to the creditors' accounts in the accounts payable ledger.

When purchase invoices are used as a purchases journal, the following is done:

1. Number and verify each invoice as it is received.
2. Post the total of each invoice directly to the creditor's account in the accounts payable ledger. Write the number of the purchase invoice in the Post. Ref. column of the creditor's account. Place a check mark at the right of the creditor's name on the invoice to show that it has been posted. File all purchase invoices received during the month in a file in numeric order. This file of purchase invoices serves as the purchases journal.

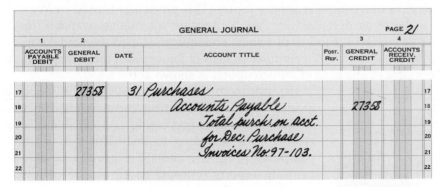

Purchase invoices with an adding machine tape showing the total purchases on account for the month

3. At the end of the month, total all purchase invoices in the purchases file to obtain the amount of all merchandise purchased on account during the month. The purchase invoices in the illustration above have been totaled at the end of December.
4. Record one entry in the general journal for all invoices for purchases on account during the month. The general journal below shows the December, 1977, entry to record the purchase invoices above.

ACCOUNTS PAYABLE DEBIT	GENERAL DEBIT	DATE	ACCOUNT TITLE	POST. REF.	GENERAL CREDIT	ACCOUNTS RECEIV. CREDIT	
			GENERAL JOURNAL			PAGE 21	
	273.58	31	Purchases				
			Accounts Payable		273.58		
			Total purch. on acct.				
			for Dec. Purchase				
			Invoices No. 97-103.				

Entry to record total monthly purchases on account when purchase invoices serve as a purchases journal

5. Post the general journal entry to the two general ledger accounts: Purchases and Accounts Payable.

Purchase invoices used as an accounts payable ledger

Copies of all purchase invoices for purchases on account are placed in a file with a separate folder for each creditor. The folders are kept in

Accounts payable file

alphabetic order in an accounts payable file similar to the one shown at the left.

The purchase invoices are filed daily to keep the accounts payable file up to date. All invoices for the creditor are filed in a folder with the latest invoice at the front. Whenever an invoice is paid, the file copy of the invoice is marked *Paid* and is filed in a "paid" file. The total amount owed to any creditor can be determined by adding all the "unpaid" invoices still in that creditor's folder in the accounts payable file. Any debit memorandums for returns or allowances are attached to the invoices to which they apply. The debit memorandums are deducted from the amount of the invoices in figuring the amount yet to be paid to a creditor.

USING PUNCHED CARDS TO AUTOMATE THE ACCOUNTS RECEIVABLE AND ACCOUNTS PAYABLE LEDGERS

An automated data processing system using magnetic disk storage for the accounts receivable and accounts payable ledgers is described in Chapter 20. Many businesses are not large enough to justify the cost of a full-scale computer system with auxiliary storage devices. Businesses of this type may still have a need to automate their accounting system to improve the efficiency and to lower the cost. One alternative is to use the services of a computer service center. This procedure is used by Wayside Furniture as described in Part 3. Another alternative available to the small business is to install a small scale punched card oriented computer system. This type of computer system is known as a minicomputer. An example of one kind of minicomputer is shown at the left.

Courtesy of IBM

The minicomputer is composed of (1) a card reader capable of reading input from punched cards, (2) a central processing unit capable of processing data according to instructions in a stored computer program, and (3) a printer capable of printing reports (output) based on the results of processing. Punched cards are the media for storage.

When using the minicomputer for an automated data processing system, the accounting clerk has the same responsibility as when a full-scale computer system is being used. Transaction data for accounts receivable and accounts payable are first recorded on a journal entry transmittal form. The journal entry transmittal forms are then sent to the data processing department where punched cards are prepared. Rather than entering the punched cards into the computer system, which was necessary when magnetic disk storage was used, the cards are stored in a file. The punched card file is used as the accounts receivable and accounts payable ledgers.

To process the schedule of accounts receivable and the schedule of accounts payable, the data are processed by the CPU according to instructions in the stored computer program.

CREDIT CARD SALES

To speed the handling of sales on account, some businesses issue credit cards to approved charge customers. The major gasoline companies and many of the national or regional department store chains issue their own credit cards. Other businesses may subscribe to one or more of the credit card systems operated by banks or other agencies.

Recording charge sales with a business' own credit card system

When a business issues its own credit cards, the business usually handles credit card sales as regular charge sales. If the business wanted to know how much of its charge sales are on regular charge and how much are on credit cards, the business might keep a separate account for credit card sales. However, this would increase the amount of work involved.

Recording charge sales with an outside credit card system

When a business subscribes to a credit card system, the charge sales invoices are deposited with the bank or agency running the system. The business is given cash for the invoices and the bank or agency assumes the responsibility for collecting the amount due. Because the business immediately gets cash for charge sales, the sales are recorded as cash sales instead of charge sales. The bank or agency charges the business a fee for the service. The fee is usually based on a percentage of the credit card sales accepted from the business.

Kitner's Gift Shop subscribes to a bank credit card system. The bank investigates persons or businesses who apply, and if the applicant's credit rating is good, a credit card is issued. The customer presents the credit card at Kitner's Gift Shop (or at any business that accepts the card) when merchandise is bought on account.

When a credit card sale is made at Kitner's Gift Shop, a sales invoice is prepared and the credit card used to imprint the customer's name and credit card number. The invoices are prepared in triplicate: one copy for the customer, one for Kitner's Gift Shop, and one for the bank.

At the end of the week, Kitner's Gift Shop totals all the credit card invoices for the week. The invoices are deposited with the bank, which increases the balance of Kitner's checking account by this total minus the service fee. Credit card sales are therefore recorded as cash sales at the time the invoices are deposited at the bank.

> *February 17, 1978. Credit card sales for the week, $963.50, plus sales tax, $48.18, less credit card fee, $45.09, net cash, $966.59. Credit Card Summary Sheet No. CS17.*

The entry to record the February 17 deposit of credit card sales invoices is: debit Cash, $966.59; debit Credit Card Fee Expense, $45.09; credit Sales Tax Payable, $48.18; and credit Sales, $963.50. This one entry in the cash receipts journal records all the credit card sales made by Kitner's Gift Shop for the week ending February 17, 1978.

In some credit card systems, the business deposits all the credit card invoices and gets full credit for the deposit. At the end of the month, the bank includes the credit card fee expense on the bank statement. When the bank statement is received, the business makes an entry to record the credit card expense.

Using Business Terms

✦ What is the meaning of each of the following?

- sales tax
- journalless accounting
- ledgerless accounting

Questions for Individual Study

1. How are sales tax rates stated?
2. Why is sales tax collected from a customer a liability of the seller?
3. What accounts are affected by the entry on Line 1 of the sales journal, page 506, to record a charge sale with sales tax? How are they affected?
4. What accounts are affected by the entry on Line 2 of the cash receipts journal, page 507, to record the daily cash sales with sales tax? How are the accounts affected?
5. On Line 29 of the cash receipts journal, page 507, why is no amount recorded for Sales Tax Payable?
6. Why is Sales Tax Payable debited when a customer returns merchandise for credit?
7. When sales invoices are used as a sales journal, how are entries made in charge customers' accounts?

8. When sales invoices are used as an accounts receivable ledger, how are data about charge sales determined for making an entry in a journal? Which journal?
9. When a business uses purchase invoices as an accounts payable ledger, how can the business determine how much is owed to a specific creditor?
10. When using a minicomputer as described on pages 514 and 515, how does a business know how much is owed to each charge customer?
11. How does a business record credit card sales when the business issues its own credit cards?
12. How does a business record credit card sales when the business subscribes to an outside credit card system? What accounts are affected and how?

Cases for Management Decision

CASE 1 Phillips Paper Products writes the names of accounts in the Account Title columns of its various journals. The Allison Company uses account numbers instead of account titles in the Account Title columns of its journals. What are the advantages and disadvantages of each system?

CASE 2 Phillips Paper Products uses a sales journal to record its sales on account. Owens Company uses one copy of sales in- voices as its sales journal and another copy as its accounts receivable ledger. What are the advantages of each plan?

DRILL 26-D 1 The effect of sales tax transactions on accounts

Instructions: □ **1.** Open the following accounts in T-account form: *General Ledger:* Cash, Accounts Receivable, Sales Tax Payable, Sales. *Accounts Receivable Ledger:* J. Cassady, L. Haynes.

□ **2.** Use T accounts to analyze the effect of the following transactions. In addition to the sales price listed in each of these transactions, there is a 5% sales tax to be added to each sale.

1. Sold merchandise for cash, $48.00.
2. Sold merchandise on account to J. Cassady, $26.00.
3. Sold merchandise on account to L. Haynes, $21.00.
4. Sold merchandise for cash, $516.00.
5. Received payment in full for J. Cassady account.
6. Sold merchandise on account to L. Haynes, $192.00.
7. Sold merchandise for cash, $252.00.
8. Received payment in full for L. Haynes' account.
9. Sold merchandise on account to J. Cassady, $370.00.
10. Issued a check to the state in full payment of all sales tax payable.

Instructions: □ **3.** Prove the equality of debits and credits in the general ledger by preparing a trial balance.

PROBLEM 26-1 Recording sales tax transactions in special journals

Instructions: □ **1.** Record the following selected transactions completed by Vogue Appliances during January of the current year. Use page 12 of a sales jour- nal, page 18 of a general journal, page 10 of a cash receipts journal, and page 10 of a cash payments journal. The journals are similar to those illustrated in Chapter 26. Source documents are abbreviated as: check, Ck; memorandum, M; receipt, R; sales invoice, S; cash register tape, T; credit memorandum, CM.

Jan. 1. Record the cash balance on January 1 as a memorandum entry in the cash receipts journal, $2,464.66.
      3. Received on account from Fred Meany, $88.00. R1.
      3. Sold merchandise on account to Jamie Hunt, $46.00, plus sales tax of $2.30. S101.
      5. Sold merchandise on account to Ted Meeks, $77.00, plus sales tax of $3.85. S102.
      8. Cash sales for January 1 to 8, $660.00, plus sales tax of $33.00. T8.

Jan. 8. Discovered that S96 to Jeanne Stoval on December 27 was incorrectly posted to the account of Jean Stobal, $13.86. M3.

10. Received on account from Ken Cruiz, $165.00. R2.

10. Paid sales tax collected during December to the State Tax Commission,
$225.00. Ck469.

15. Cash sales for January 9 to 15, $900.00, plus sales tax of $45.00. T15.

15. Received cash for office supplies sold to accommodate a local merchant,
$9.00. R3.

> Sales tax is not collected in this state on an accommodation sale.

17. Sold merchandise on account to Ken Cruiz, $192.00, plus sales tax of $9.60.
S103.

18. Received on account from Ted Meeks, $80.85. R4.

19. Granted credit to Jamie Hunt for merchandise returned by him on S101,
$19.20, plus sales tax of $0.96. CM31.

22. Cash sales for January 16 to 22, $816.00, plus sales tax of $40.80. T22.

24. Received on account from Steve Adler, $139.20. R5.

29. Cash sales for January 23 to 29, $960.00, plus sales tax of $48.00. T29.

29. Received on account from Jamie Hunt, $28.14, covering S101 for $48.30,
less CM31 for $20.16. R6.

31. Sold merchandise on account to A. K. Bary, $264.00, plus sales tax of
$13.20. S104.

31. Sold merchandise on account to Ted Meeks, $96.00, plus sales tax of $4.80.
S105.

31. Cash sales for January 30 to 31, $36.00, plus sales tax of $1.80. T31.

Instructions: □ 2. Foot, prove, total, and rule the journals.

PROBLEM 26-2 Using sales invoices as a sales journal and as an accounts receivable ledger

*If you are not using the workbook correlating with this textbook, complete Review Problem 26-R 1
instead of this problem.*

Abbie Klein, who operates Abbie's Antique Shop, uses sales invoices both as a
sales journal and as an accounts receivable ledger. The sales invoices for charge
sales in the month of May of the current year are given in the workbook.

Using sales invoices as a sales journal

Instructions: □ 1. Carefully tear apart the 16 sales invoices in the workbook and
arrange them in numerical order.

□ 2. Add the amounts on the 16 sales invoices and obtain separate totals for the (a)
total sales price of all merchandise on all invoices, (b) total sales tax (figured at 4%)
on all invoices, and (c) grand total of all invoices.

□ 3. Record the total monthly sales on account in a general journal (page 5) like the
one shown in Chapter 26.

Using sales invoices as accounts receivable ledger

Instructions: ◻ **4.** Sort the 16 sales invoices by name of customer, putting all sales invoices for one customer together. Then arrange the file of invoices so that those for the customers are in alphabetical order.

◻ **5.** Prepare a schedule of accounts receivable as of May 31 of the current year.

MASTERY PROBLEM 26-M   Figuring and recording sales tax transactions in special journals

Instructions: ◻ **1.** Record the following selected transactions completed by Harris Hobby Shop during August of the current year. Use page 8 of a sales journal, page 3 of a general journal, page 9 of a cash receipts journal, and page 10 of a cash payments journal. Source documents are abbreviated as: check, Ck; memorandum, M; receipt, R; sales invoice, S; cash register tape, T; credit memorandum, CM.

The amount of sales tax is *not* included in the sales on account transactions. The tax rate in this state is 5%. Figure the tax on each sale on account and add the tax to the amount of each invoice.

Aug. 1. Record the cash balance on August 1 as a memorandum entry in the cash receipts journal, $2,099.16.
    2. Sold merchandise on account to Betty Fox, $19.20. S305.
    3. Received on account from Casey Toll, $75.60. R163.
    4. Sold merchandise on account to Ted Barr, $28.00. S306.
    5. Discovered that S292 to Morey Pazol, July 23, was incorrectly posted to the account of Larry Pound, $25.00, plus sales tax. M14.
    6. Cash sales for August 1 to 6, $600.00, plus sales tax of $30.00. T6.
    9. Received on account from D. Cohn, $84.00. R164.
    11. Paid sales tax collected during July to the State Tax Commission, $148.60. Ck204.
    12. Sold merchandise on account to Joe Amber, $57.60. S307.
    13. Cash sales for August 7 to 13, $576.00, plus sales tax of $28.80. T13.
    15. Received cash for office supplies sold to accommodate a neighboring merchant, $12.00. R165. (No sales tax on this accommodation sale.)
    16. Sold merchandise on account to Louis Lancer, $18.00. S308.
    17. Received on account from Betty Fox, $20.16. R166.
    19. Granted credit to Joe Amber for merchandise returned by him on S307, $10.00, plus sales tax of $0.50. CM27.
    20. Cash sales for August 14 to 20, $650.40, plus sales tax of $32.52. T20.
    23. Sold merchandise on account to Nancy Oliver, $9.60. S309.
    25. Received on account from Joe Amber, $49.98, for S307 less CM27. R167.
    29. Sold merchandise on account to Richard Boyer, $73.00. S310.
    31. Cash sales for August 21 to 31, $738.00, plus sales tax of $36.90. T31.

Instructions: ◻ **2.** Foot, prove, total, and rule the journals.

BONUS Recording sales tax as part of
PROBLEM 26-B   total sales

Charlene Baker owns a shop that sells ready-made draperies. The shop is located
in a state that imposes a sales tax of 4% on all merchandise sold by Miss Baker. To
save time, Miss Baker records only the total of each sales invoice which includes the
amount for the merchandise and the amount for the 4% sales tax. At the end of a
fiscal period, Miss Baker makes an adjusting entry to separate the total amount of
sales tax from the sales account and record it in a sales tax payable account.

Instructions: ◻ **1.** Use a cash receipts journal (page 8) with the following amount
columns: General Debit, General Credit, Sales Credit, Accounts Receivable Credit,
Cash Debit; and a sales journal (page 6) with a single amount column: Accounts
Receivable Debit/Sales Credit. Record the following selected transactions completed
by Miss Baker during June of the current year. Source documents are abbreviated
as: sales invoice, S; cash register tape, T.

June   3. Sold draperies on account to Jon Wisher, total sale, $239.20. S169.

       (Note: The amount of merchandise sold is $230.00. The 4% sales tax is
       $9.20. The total for the sale is $239.20.)

      4. Cash sales for the week ending June 4, $1,435.20. T4.

       (Note: The amount of merchandise sold for cash is $1,380.00. The 4% sales
       tax is $55.20. Total for cash sales is $1,435.20)

      9. Sold draperies on account to Wilber Amsterdam, total sale, $287.04. S170.
    11. Cash sales for the week ending June 11, $1,406.50. T11.
    13. Sold draperies on account to April Wilson, total sale, $215.28. S171.
    17. Sold draperies on account to Marva Jones, total sale, $75.35. S172.
    18. Cash sales for the week ending June 18, $1,293.98. T18.
    25. Cash sales for the week ending June 25, $1,306.92. T25.
    29. Sold draperies on account to Donna Stoval, total sale, $79.12. S173.
    30. Cash sales for partial week ending June 30, $746.81. T30.

Instructions: ◻ **2.** Foot, prove, total, and rule the sales and cash receipts journals. Post the total of the Sales Credit column from both journals to the sales account.

◻ **3.** Figure the amount of the sales tax payable as follows: (a) Balance of the sales
account *divided* by 104% *equals* the amount of sales for June. (b) Balance of the sales
account *minus* the amount of sales for June *equals* sales tax payable for June.

◻ **4.** Record in a general journal (page 3) an adjusting entry to debit Sales and
credit Sales Tax Payable for the amount of sales tax payable for June.

Uncollectible Accounts and Valuation of Accounts Receivable

27

Phillips Paper Products sells merchandise for cash and on account. Most of its sales on account are made to small businesses. Before Phillips Paper Products extends credit to potential customers, the customers' credit ratings are obtained from local credit bureaus. Wholesalers and manufacturers may obtain credit ratings from the financial reports submitted by potential customers and from national credit agencies such as Dun & Bradstreet.

> Dun & Bradstreet, Inc., publishes a credit-rating book containing data about the financial condition of businesses throughout the United States. This reference book is available to a business subscribing for it.

VALUATION OF ACCOUNTS RECEIVABLE

Even though a business is careful in extending credit to charge customers, there are sometimes accounts receivable that cannot be collected. Accounts receivable that cannot be collected are called uncollectible accounts. Uncollectible accounts are sometimes known as bad debts. If a business fails to collect from a charge customer, the business incurs an operating expense. The expense caused by uncollectible accounts is called bad debts expense.

Uncollectible accounts

A business must determine that an account receivable is uncollectible before a bad debt expense is actually recorded. Sometimes this is several months or more after the date on which the sale is made. During the time that this uncollectible amount is carried on the books, the value of accounts receivable is overstated. Also, the expense resulting from uncollectible accounts is not recorded. A business should estimate the amount of its bad debts expense at the end of each fiscal period. This amount should be recorded to prevent the overstatement of the value of accounts receivable on the balance sheet. The estimated bad debts expense also should be recorded so that it is included on the income statement for the fiscal period in which the charge sale is made.

Book value of accounts receivable

To show the value of accounts receivable on a balance sheet, the estimated value of uncollectible accounts is subtracted from the balance of the accounts receivable account. The difference between the balance of Accounts Receivable and the total of estimated uncollectible accounts is called the book value of accounts receivable.

On December 31, 1977, Phillips Paper Products has a balance in the accounts receivable account of $8,900.00. This balance includes some accounts receivable that will prove to be uncollectible. If, therefore, Phillips Paper Products lists on its balance sheet the value of accounts receivable as $8,900.00, the value of this asset will be overstated. The company must find the estimated book value of accounts receivable in order to report this asset more accurately on the balance sheet.

Valuation accounts

Phillips Paper Products has no way of knowing for sure which charge customers will fail to pay in the future. Since the company does not know which customers will not pay, specific customers' accounts cannot be credited as uncollectible. Neither can the accounts receivable account in the general ledger be credited. The balance of Accounts Receivable, a controlling account, has to equal the sum of the balances of the customers' accounts in the subsidiary ledger. However, the company should record an *estimated* bad debts expense. Phillips Paper Products, therefore, makes an adjusting entry by crediting the estimated total value of uncollectible accounts to an account titled Allowance for Uncollectible Accounts. The same amount is debited to an expense account titled Bad Debts Expense.

> Allowance for Bad Debts or Allowance for Doubtful Accounts are account titles sometimes used instead of Allowance for Uncollectible Accounts. Until recent years, this account was sometimes known as Reserve for Bad Debts. However, the American Institute of Certified Public Accountants recommends that the word "allowance" rather than "reserve" be used in the account title.

An account used in figuring the book value of the asset to which it is related is called a valuation account. Allowance for Uncollectible Accounts is a valuation account used to determine the book value of accounts receivable. The balance of a valuation account always has a credit balance because it is a deduction from the balance of an asset account. A valuation account is sometimes known as a minus asset account or a contra asset account.

A valuation account is numbered the same as the asset account to which it applies, followed by a decimal point and a number. For example, Phillips Paper Products' accounts receivable account is numbered 113. Allowance for Uncollectible Accounts is numbered 113.1.

ESTIMATING BAD DEBTS EXPENSE BASED ON CHARGE SALES

The ledger of Phillips Paper Products shows a balance of $8,900.00 for Accounts Receivable at the end of the annual fiscal period, December 31, 1977. Phillips Paper Products estimates that some of the individual accounts will eventually prove to be uncollectible. As a result, the $8,900.00 debit balance in Accounts Receivable overstates the value of this asset.

Phillips Paper Products has learned from published reports that bad debts expense in stores of this type usually amounts to about ½% (.005) of the total charge sales for a fiscal year. The company's total charge sales for the fiscal year are $90,530.00. The company, therefore, *estimates* that $452.65 ($90,530.00 × .005) of its accounts receivable will be bad debts expense for this fiscal year.

RECORDING THE ESTIMATED BAD DEBTS EXPENSE

Before an estimate of bad debts expense is journalized, an adjustment is planned on a work sheet.

Analyzing adjustment for bad debts expense

The adjustment for bad debts expense of Phillips Paper Products, December 31, 1977, is shown in the T accounts at the right.

Bad Debts Expense is debited for $452.65 to show the increase in the balance of this expense account.

Allowance for Uncollectible Accounts is credited for $452.65 to show the increase in the balance of this valuation account. The balance of this account is the estimated amount of accounts receivable that will be uncollectible.

Bad Debts Expense	611
452.65	

Allowance for Uncollectible Accounts	113.1
	452.65

Recording adjustment for bad debts expense on a work sheet

At the end of the fiscal period, December 31, 1977, the accountant for Phillips Paper Products plans the adjustment for bad debts expense on a work sheet. This adjustment is shown in the Adjustments columns, Lines 4 and 26, of the partial work sheet below.

ACCOUNT TITLE	ACCT. No.	TRIAL BALANCE		ADJUSTMENTS		INCOME STATEMENT		BALANCE SHEET	
		DEBIT	CREDIT	DEBIT	CREDIT	DEBIT	CREDIT	DEBIT	CREDIT
1 *Cash*	111	617650						617650		1
2 *Petty Cash*	112	10000						10000		2
3 *Accounts Receivable*	113	890000						890000		3
4 *Allow. for Uncoll. Accts.*	113.1				(a) 45265				45265	4
26 *Bad Debts Expense*	611			(a) 45265		45265				26

Phillips Paper Products Work Sheet For Year Ended December 31, 1977

Partial work sheet showing adjustment
for bad debts expense

Debit part of adjustment. As shown on Line 26 of the partial work sheet above, Bad Debts Expense is debited for $452.65 in the Adjustments Debit column. The amount is extended to the Income Statement Debit column.

Credit part of the adjustment. As shown on Line 4 of the partial work sheet above, Allowance for Uncollectible Accounts is credited for $452.65 in the Adjustments Credit column. This amount is extended to the Balance Sheet Credit column.

This is the first year that Phillips Paper Products has sold merchandise on account. Allowance for Uncollectible Accounts has no balance in the Trial Balance Credit column. When the allowance account has a previous balance, the amount of the adjustment is added to the previous balance. The new balance is then extended to the Balance Sheet Credit column.

Journalizing the adjustment for bad debts expense

The data needed to journalize the adjustment for bad debts expense are obtained from the Adjustments columns of the work sheet. The adjusting entry in the general journal is shown below:

ACCOUNTS PAYABLE DEBIT	GENERAL DEBIT	DATE	ACCOUNT TITLE	POST. REF.	GENERAL CREDIT	ACCOUNTS RECEIV. CREDIT	
			Adjusting Entries				1
	45265	1977 Dec. 31	*Bad Debts Expense*				2
			Allow. for Uncoll. Accts.		45265		3
							4
							5
							6

GENERAL JOURNAL   PAGE *13*

Adjusting entry for
estimated bad debts
expense

Posting the adjustment for bad debts expense

Accounts Receivable, Allowance for Uncollectible Accounts, and Bad Debts Expense appear as shown below after the adjustment is posted.

ACCOUNT *Accounts Receivable* ACCOUNT NO. *113*

DATE	ITEM	POST. REF.	DEBIT	CREDIT	BALANCE DEBIT	BALANCE CREDIT
1977 Dec. 1	Balance	✓			836079	
31		S20	704056		1540135	
31		CR22		650135	890000	

ACCOUNT *Allowance for Uncollectible Accounts* ACCOUNT NO. *113.1*

DATE	ITEM	POST. REF.	DEBIT	CREDIT	BALANCE DEBIT	BALANCE CREDIT
1977 Dec. 31		J13		45265		45265

ACCOUNT *Bad Debts Expense* ACCOUNT NO. *611*

DATE	ITEM	POST. REF.	DEBIT	CREDIT	BALANCE DEBIT	BALANCE CREDIT
1977 Dec. 31		J13	45265		45265	

General ledger accounts after the adjusting entry for estimated bad debts expense is posted

The accounts receivable account has a debit balance of $8,900.00, the total amount due from charge customers. Allowance for Uncollectible Accounts has a credit balance of $452.65 on December 31, 1977. The account number *113.1* shows that the balance of this valuation account is to be subtracted from the balance of account No. 113 on the balance sheet. The balance of the bad debts expense account is $452.65, the estimated bad debts expense for the fiscal period ended December 31, 1977.

Phillips Paper Products figures the book value of its accounts receivable on December 31, 1977, as:

Balance of accounts receivable account............................	$8,900.00
Less allowance for uncollectible accounts.........................	452.65
Equals book value of accounts receivable.........................	$8,447.35

WRITING OFF AN ACTUAL UNCOLLECTIBLE ACCOUNT RECEIVABLE

Canceling the balance of a charge customer's account because the customer cannot or will not pay is called writing off an account. When a customer's account is determined to be uncollectible, a journal entry is made.

Analyzing an entry to write off an uncollectible account

The accountant for Phillips Paper Products learned that the past-due account of J. R. West cannot be collected.

January 3, 1978. Wrote off past-due account of J. R. West as uncollectible, $48.00. Memorandum No. 164.

GENERAL LEDGER

Allowance for
Uncollectible Accounts   113.1

48.00	Bal.	452.65

Accounts Receivable   113

Bal.	8,900.00	48.00

ACCOUNTS RECEIVABLE LEDGER

J. R. West

Bal.	48.00	48.00

The entry to write off this uncollectible account is analyzed in the T accounts at the left.

Allowance for Uncollectible Accounts is debited for $48.00 to reduce the balance of this account. This specific amount of the allowance is no longer an *estimate;* it is an actual amount.

Accounts Receivable is credited for $48.00 to reduce the balance due from charge customers. The new balance of the accounts receivable account is $8,852.00.

J. R. West's account in the accounts receivable ledger is also credited for $48.00. This entry cancels the debit balance of his account; his account is written off.

Journalizing the entry to write off an uncollectible account

The entry to write off the account of J. R. West is shown in the general journal below.

				GENERAL JOURNAL			PAGE *15*
	1	2			3	4	
	ACCOUNTS PAYABLE DEBIT	GENERAL DEBIT	DATE	ACCOUNT TITLE	POST. REF.	GENERAL CREDIT	ACCOUNTS RECEIV. CREDIT
16		48.00	3	*Allow. for Uncollectible Accts.*				16
17				*J. R. West*			48.00	17
18				*Memorandum No. 164.*				18
19								19
20								20
21								21

Entry to write off an uncollectible account when
Allowance for Uncollectible Accounts is used

Allowance for Uncollectible Accounts is debited for $48.00 in the General Debit column. Accounts Receivable and J. R. West are both credited for $48.00 by writing the customer's name in the Account Title column and writing the amount, $48.00, in the Accounts Receivable Credit column.

Posting an entry to write off an uncollectible account

After the journal entry to write off an uncollectible account, page 526, is posted, Allowance for Uncollectible Accounts in the general ledger appears as shown below.

ACCOUNT *Allowance for Uncollectible Accounts*					ACCOUNT NO. *113.1*		
DATE	ITEM	POST. REF.	DEBIT	CREDIT	BALANCE		
					DEBIT	CREDIT	
1977 *Dec. 31*		*J13*		*45265*		*45265*	
1978 *Jan. 3*		*J15*	*4800*			*40465*	

Allowance for Uncollectible Accounts in the general ledger
after the entry writing off an uncollectible account is posted

The credit to Accounts Receivable will be posted as part of the Accounts Receivable Credit column total. After the credit to J. R. West's account is posted, his account appears as shown below.

NAME *J. R. West*				TERMS *n/30*		
ADDRESS *504 Main Street, Dayton, OH 45409*						
DATE	ITEM	POST. REF.	DEBIT	CREDIT	DEBIT BALANCE	
1977 *May 15*		*S7*	*4800*		*4800*	
1978 *Jan. 3*	*Written off*	*J15*		*4800*	—	

Customer's account in the accounts receivable ledger after the
entry writing off the account as uncollectible is posted

REPORTING UNCOLLECTIBLE ACCOUNTS ON THE FINANCIAL STATEMENTS

Phillips Paper Products obtains the data about uncollectible accounts needed for its financial statements from the work sheet of December 31, 1977.

Bad debts expense on an income statement

Bad Debts Expense, listed in the operating expenses section, is shown on the partial income statement on page 528.

Phillips Paper Products Income Statement For Year Ended December 31, 1977			
Gross Profit on Operations			6613506
Operating Expenses:			
Bad Debts Expense		45265	
Delivery Expense		162540	
Salary Expense		348 28 00	
Supplies Expense		50050	
Total Operating Expenses			4996254

Bad debts expense on an income statement

Allowance for uncollectible accounts on a balance sheet

Phillips Paper Products lists the following on its balance sheet: (1) the balance of Accounts Receivable, (2) the balance of Allowance for Uncollectible Accounts, and (3) the book value of accounts receivable. This is shown on the partial balance sheet below.

Phillips Paper Products Balance Sheet December 31, 1977			
Assets			
Current Assets:			
Cash		617650	
Petty Cash		10000	
Accounts Receivable	890000		
Less Allow. for Uncoll. Accts.	45265	844735	
Merchandise Inventory		4231700	
Supplies		18950	
Prepaid Insurance		22400	
Total Current Assets			5745435

Allowance for uncollectible accounts on a balance sheet

The total amount due from customers, *$8,900.00*, is written in the first column of the balance sheet on the line with Accounts Receivable. *Less Allowance for Uncollectible Accounts* is written on the next line, indented one-half inch (about 1.3 centimeters). The amount, *$452.65*, is written below the $8,900.00. The difference between the two amounts, *$8,447.35*, is written in the second amount column on the same line as the amount of allowance. The amount, $8,447.35, is the book value of accounts receivable on December 31, 1977.

Classifying current assets on a balance sheet

As shown in the chart of accounts, page 504, Phillips Paper Products classifies its assets in two categories: Current Assets and Plant Assets. These categories are based on the length of time the assets will be in use. Cash and other assets that will be turned into cash or quickly consumed (usually within a year) in the operation of a business are called current assets. Current assets include such things as cash, accounts receivable, merchandise inventory, supplies, and prepaid insurance.

A business owning both current assets and plant assets usually lists them under separate headings on a balance sheet. Phillips Paper Products does this as shown on the balance sheet in Chapter 28, page 549.

Each of the current asset accounts is listed on the balance sheet under the heading *Current Assets*. The usual order for listing current asset accounts is to start with Cash and to follow with the other current assets. The other current assets are often listed in the order that they can be most readily turned into cash.

Plant assets are described in Chapters 28 and 29.

OTHER METHODS OF ESTIMATING BAD DEBTS EXPENSE

Phillips Paper Products estimates its bad debts expense as a percentage of the charge sales for a fiscal period. Other businesses may estimate their bad debts expense in the same way, or by using (1) a percentage of the net sales, (2) a percentage of the balance of the accounts receivable account at the end of a fiscal period, or (3) a percentage of the amount past due from customers. In any case, a business should use the method that results in the most accurate estimate of its actual bad debts expense over the years. The debit to Bad Debts Expense should be about the same amount that experience shows actually does become uncollectible.

Estimating bad debts expense based on net sales

Mr. Betterman, a wholesale hardware merchant, has found from past experience that his bad debts expense usually amounts to about $\frac{1}{2}\%$ (.005) of his net sales for a fiscal period. Mr. Betterman's net sales for the quarterly period ended December 31, 1978, were $24,270.40. He estimates that $121.35 ($24,270.40 × .005) will be bad debts expense. Once the amount of bad debts expense has been estimated, Mr. Betterman records this expense on a work sheet in the same manner as described for Phillips Paper Products.

Estimating bad debts expense based on the balance in the accounts receivable account

Tatum Company knows from past experience that about 1% of the balance in its accounts receivable account at the end of a fiscal period will be uncollectible. If the balance of its accounts receivable account is $250,000.00, the bad debts will be $2,500.00 ($250,000.00 × .01). This amount, $2,500.00, should be the credit balance of Allowance for Uncollectible Accounts.

The accountant for Tatum Company subtracts the balance shown in Allowance for Uncollectible Accounts, $450.00, from the amount that should be the balance, $2,500.00. The difference, $2,050.00, is the bad debts expense for the current fiscal period. An adjusting entry is planned on the work sheet to debit Bad Debts Expense for $2,050.00 and to credit Allowance for Uncollectible Accounts for the same amount. This method of estimating bad debts expense is based on figuring first what the allowance should be rather than estimating what the expense should be.

Estimating bad debts expense based on how long customers have owed amounts for charge sales

Some businesses find that the longer a customer's account is overdue, the more likelihood that the amount will be uncollectible. To estimate what amount owed by charge customers may become uncollectible, a business using this method analyzes each customer's account. Analyzing accounts receivable according to when they are due is called aging accounts receivable. For example, Mantow Lumber Company prepares a list of customers' accounts to show how much of each account is six months or more past due. Past experience shows them that 75% of amounts past due for six months or more will be uncollectible.

The Mantow Lumber Company finds from aging its accounts receivable that $6,000.00 is six months or more past due. The estimated uncollectible amount is $4,500.00 ($6,000.00 × .75). Allowance for Uncollectible Accounts should have a credit balance of $4,500.00. If the balance of the allowance account is $320.00, an adjustment is made to debit Bad Debts Expense for $4,180.00 and credit Allowance for Uncollectible Accounts for the same amount. The new balance of Allowance for Uncollectible Accounts will be $4,500.00 ($320.00 + $4,180.00).

Estimating bad debts expense based on the aging of accounts receivable requires more time than is true of the other methods. For this reason, many businesses prefer to use one of the other methods.

Direct write-off method of handling uncollectible accounts

Some businesses have relatively few uncollectible accounts. Therefore, they record bad debts expense only when it is actually known that an account will be uncollectible. This is done by debiting Bad Debts Expense and crediting Accounts Receivable and the customer's account at the time the uncollectible account becomes known.

Recording bad debts expense only at the time a customer's account is actually known to be uncollectible is called the direct write-off of uncollectible accounts. The direct write-off method is simple and acceptable for a business with few uncollectible accounts receivable. In some cases, however, the method fails to charge the bad debts expense to the fiscal period in which the debt occurred. Thus, for that fiscal period (1) the value of Accounts Receivable is overstated on the balance sheet, and (2) the amount of net income is overstated on the income statement.

AUTOMATED DATA PROCESSING FOR VALUATION OF ACCOUNTS RECEIVABLE

The best method of estimating bad debts expense often depends on the size and the type of business. Another factor that helps determine which method to use is the type of data processing system. For example, the calculations necessary to age accounts receivable usually makes this method impractical for a business using a manual data processing system. For a business using an automated data processing system, however, aging accounts receivable is a commonly used method.

When an automated data processing system is used, a report is printed that shows the status of each customer's account in the accounts receivable ledger. A list of charge customers that shows the balance due from each, the current charges (those made in the last 30 days), and the amounts due over 30 days is called a schedule of accounts receivable by age. A computer printout of a schedule of accounts receivable by age is shown below.

CUSTOMER NUMBER	CUSTOMER NAME	DATE OF LAST PAYMENT	BALANCE DUE	DUE FOR LESS THAN 30 DAYS	ACCOUNTS PAST DUE		
					30-59 DAYS	60-89 DAYS	90 DAYS AND OVER
10040	RICHARD ADAMS	11-03-77	180.75	70.00	110.75		
10085	MARY ADKINS	11-12-77	68.00			35.00	33.00
10235	ROBERT ZIMMERMAN	11-15-77	143.66	38.50	105.16		
	TOTALS		26,435.77*	20,698.85*	3,218.43*	1,835.85*	682.64*

SCHEDULE OF ACCOUNTS RECEIVABLE BY AGE
NOVEMBER 30, 1977

Computer printout of a schedule of accounts receivable by age

Past experience with bad debts expense helps determine which past due amounts are likely to be uncollectible. For the schedule of accounts receivable by age shown on page 531, the business has learned that 10% of the accounts past due for 90 days or more, and 3% of the accounts past due 60–89 days will become uncollectible. The amount that should be the balance of Allowance for Uncollectible Accounts is figured as follows:

Number of Days Past Due	Amount Past Due	Percentage	Estimated Uncollectible Amounts
60–89 days	$1,835.85	3%	$ 55.08
90+ days	682.64	10%	68.26
Total			$123.34

The current balance of Allowance for Uncollectible Accounts is $21.95; therefore the estimated bad debts expense is $101.39 ($123.34 − $21.95). An adjustment is planned on the journal entry transmittal form to debit Bad Debts Expense and to credit Allowance for Uncollectible Accounts for $101.39. After the adjustment is journalized and posted, the balance of Allowance for Uncollectible Accounts is $123.34 ($21.95 + $101.39).

Using Business Terms

✦ What is the meaning of each of the following?

- uncollectible accounts
- bad debts expense
- book value of accounts receivable
- valuation account
- writing off an account
- current assets
- aging accounts receivable
- direct write-off of uncollectible accounts
- schedule of accounts receivable by age

Questions for Individual Study

1. When does an account receivable become a bad debts expense?
2. Why is it desirable for a business to estimate and record the amount of its bad debts expense?
3. How is the book value of accounts receivable figured?
4. Why is the amount of estimated bad debts expense credited to Allowance for Uncollectible Accounts rather than to Accounts Receivable?
5. Why is Allowance for Uncollectible Accounts called a valuation account?
6. When is a customer's account written off?
7. Why is Allowance for Uncollectible Accounts debited when a customer's account is written off?

8. What entry was made in the general journal, page 526, to write off the customer's account?
9. In what section of the partial income statement, page 528, is Bad Debts Expense listed?
10. What is the correct order for listing current assets on a balance sheet?
11. When the direct method of writing off an uncollectible account is used, what entry is made to record bad debts expense?
12. What four bases for estimating bad debts expense are described in this chapter?
13. Why do most businesses not estimate bad debts expense based on a schedule of accounts receivable by age?

CASE 1 Mr. Willard Stovall credits Accounts Receivable for the amount of estimated bad debts expense at the end of each fiscal period. Mr. Orval Downey credits Allowance for Uncollectible Accounts for the amount of estimated bad debts expense at the end of each fiscal period. Is Mr. Stovall or Mr. Downey using the best method? Why?

CASE 2 Mr. Neuman Watson owns and operates a small parking lot. He rents some spaces by the month. His monthly customers usually pay him at the end of each month. Mr. Watson does not record a bad debts expense at the end of each fiscal year. He has engaged an accountant to help him prepare financial statements at the end of the current fiscal year. The accountant advises Mr. Watson to make an adjustment to record an estimated amount for bad debts expense. Mr. Watson does not want to do this because he believes that all his customers will eventually pay him what they owe. Do you agree with the procedures suggested by the accountant or by Mr. Watson? Why?

DRILL 27-D 1 Figuring bad debts expense

The accounting records of three hardware stores show the following summary information for the fiscal period ending December 31 of the current year:

Store	Total Net Sales	Total Charge Sales	Balance in Accounts Receivable Account
1	$30,678.00	$11,892.10	$ 1,149.50
2	51,454.70	24,585.00	10,850.95
3	41,679.00	21,132.40	6,776.00

Instructions: Figure the *bad debts expense* for each of these stores under the following conditions:

Store 1 estimates its bad debts expense based on ¼% (.0025) of its total *net sales*.

Store 2 estimates its bad debts expense based on 2% of its total *charge sales*.

Store 3 estimates its allowance for uncollectible accounts based on 3% of the balance in the accounts receivable account. (The December 31 balance in Allowance for Uncollectible Accounts is $15.13.)

DRILL 27-D 2 Figuring bad debts expense based on aging accounts receivable

A schedule of accounts receivable by age was prepared at the end of a fiscal period. A partial illustration of the schedule is shown on page 534.

Instructions: □ **1.** For each of the time periods, figure the amount estimated to be uncollectible (for example, .5% of the total $969.00).

Name of Customer	Balance Owed	Amount Owed for			
		Less than 30 days	30–59 days	60–89 days	90 days and over
Joseph Sanford	$ 85.00	$ 85.00	—	—	—
Ruth Zimmerman	240.00	200.00	$ 20.00	$ 20.00	—
Totals	$2,934.00	$1,438.00	$969.00	$227.00	$300.00
Percent of total estimated to be uncollectible	—	—	.5%	10%	50%

Instructions: □ **2.** Figure the total amount estimated to be uncollectible.

□ **3.** The balance of Allowance for Uncollectible Accounts is $37.29 before the end of fiscal period adjustment is made. What is the amount of bad debts expense that will be used in making this adjustment?

Problems for Applying Concepts

PROBLEM 27-1   Recording transactions with bad debts expense

W. M. Ellison, owner of Ellison Art Supplies, records his transactions in special journals. In his general ledger he maintains accounts for Allowance for Uncollectible Accounts and Bad Debts Expense. At the beginning of the current year, the credit balance of Allowance for Uncollectible Accounts was $94.91. Selected transactions affecting uncollectible accounts are given below.

Instructions: □ **1.** Record all the necessary entries for the following transactions on page 19 of a four-column general journal like the one on page 526.

Feb.   7 Wrote off past-due account of Albert Pole as uncollectible, $59.76. M16.

Mar. 31 *End of first quarterly fiscal period.* Make adjusting entry for estimated bad debts expense. Increase allowance for uncollectible accounts by ½% of the total charge sales for the first quarterly fiscal period, $11,834.88.

May   14 Wrote off past-due account of Ralph Mailer as uncollectible, $42.00. M28.

June 30 *End of second quarterly fiscal period.* Make adjusting entry for estimated bad debts expense. Increase allowance for uncollectible accounts by ½% of the total charge sales for the fiscal period, $9,914.58.

Aug. 13 Wrote off past-due account of Marta Kelso as uncollectible, $44.30. M51.

Sept. 30 *End of third quarterly fiscal period.* Make adjusting entry for estimated bad debts expense. Increase allowance for uncollectible accounts by ½% of total charge sales for the fiscal period, $10,116.24.

Dec. 30 Wrote off past-due accounts for two customers as uncollectible: Ralph Jost, $72.67; Anna Vannetta, $15.00. M108. (Make one combined entry, debiting Allowance for Uncollectible Accounts for the total.)

Dec. 31 *End of fourth quarterly fiscal period.* Make adjusting entry for estimated bad debts expense. Increase allowance for uncollectible accounts by ½% of total charge sales for the fiscal period, $12,579.00.

Instructions: □ **2.** Foot, prove, total, and rule the general journal.

PROBLEM 27-2   Work at the end of a fiscal period with bad debts expense

A portion of a trial balance for Martha's Boutique is shown below.

Martha's Boutique
Trial Balance
December 31, 1977

Account Title	Acct. No.	Debit	Credit
Cash	111	4 543 14	
Petty Cash	112	150 00	
Accounts Receivable	113	22 095 52	
Allowance for Uncollectible Accounts	113.1		69 36
Merchandise Inventory	114	10 047 00	
Supplies	115	244 80	
Prepaid Insurance	116	367 20	
Income Summary	313		
Bad Debts Expense	611		
Insurance Expense	612		
Supplies Expense	618		

Instructions: □ **1.** Enter the information above in the Trial Balance columns of an eight-column work sheet for the fiscal year ended December 31, 1977.

□ **2.** Make the adjustments in the Adjustments columns of the work sheet. Use the following additional data:

Additional allowance for uncollectible accounts, ½% of total charge sales, $21,027.10.
Merchandise inventory, December 31, $9,516.60.
Supplies inventory, December 31, $89.25.
Value of insurance policies, December 31, $244.80.

□ **3.** Extend all amounts to their appropriate columns in the Income Statement or Balance Sheet columns of the work sheet.

□ **4.** Record the adjusting entries on page 23 of a general journal like the one on page 524.

Optional
Problems   **MASTERY**   Recording transactions with bad
       PROBLEM 27-M   debts expense

Jacob Wasson, in his business, records transactions in special journals. In his general ledger he has these accounts: Allowance for Uncollectible Accounts and Bad Debts Expense. On January 1 of the current year, the credit balance of Allowance for Uncollectible Accounts was $73.50. Selected transactions affecting uncollectible accounts are given below.

Instructions: □ **1.** Record all the necessary entries for the following selected transactions on page 49 of a general journal like the one on page 526.

Feb. 18 Wrote off past-due account of Willie Baumgarten as uncollectible, $55.88. M117.

Mar. 31 *End of the first quarterly fiscal period.* Make adjusting entry for estimated bad debts expense. Increase allowance for uncollectible accounts by ½% (.005) of the total net sales for the first quarterly fiscal period, $13,611.05.

Apr. 11 Wrote off past-due account of Milton Hamilton as uncollectible, $73.65. M193.

June 30 *End of the second quarterly fiscal period.* Make adjusting entry for estimated bad debts expense. Increase allowance for uncollectible accounts by ½% (.005) of the total net sales for the second quarterly fiscal period, $15,285.41.

July 20 Wrote off past-due account of Carol Brandt as uncollectible, $81.05. M226.

Sept. 30 *End of third quarterly fiscal period.* Make adjusting entry for estimated bad debts expense. Increase allowance for uncollectible accounts by ½% (.005) of the total net sales for the third quarterly fiscal period, $14,070.73.

Dec. 31 Wrote off past-due accounts of three customers as uncollectible: Andy Dunkin, $27.60; Sally Moses, $47.33; Steve Patterson, $2.40. M423. (Make one combined entry, debiting Allowance for Uncollectible Accounts for the total.)

Dec. 31 *End of the fourth quarterly fiscal period.* Make adjusting entry for estimated bad debts expense. Increase allowance for uncollectible accounts by ½% (.005) of the total net sales for the fourth quarterly fiscal period, $18,016.12.

Instructions: □ **2.** Foot, prove, total, and rule the general journal.

       BONUS   Recording the collection of accounts
       PROBLEM 27-B   previously written off

Introductory remarks: Occasionally a customer's account that has been written off as uncollectible is later collected. When this happens, the customer's account is first reinstated by a general journal entry debiting Accounts Receivable and the customer's account, and crediting Allowance for Uncollectible Accounts. Second, an entry is made debiting Cash and crediting Accounts Receivable and the customer's account. These two entries provide a complete record of what has happened to the customer's account.

If only part of an old debt is collected, only the actual amount received should be used in each transaction, rather than writing into the account the full amount previously charged off as uncollectible.

Instructions: □ **1.** During 1977, Jerry Lake completed several transactions affecting bad debts. These selected transactions are given below. Record these transactions on page 12 of a general journal like the one on page 526, and on page 16 of a cash receipts journal like the one on page 507.

Mar. 9 Wrote off past due account of Karl Roth as uncollectible, $44.00. M33.

May 23 Received 50% of the $382.80 owed by Steven Dudley. Mr. Dudley has been declared bankrupt, so the remainder of the amount owed by Mr. Dudley is written off as uncollectible. R138 and M52.

June 2 Received full payment of $22.00 for Wilma Auterson's account. Ms. Auterson's account had been written off on February 19, 1976, as uncollectible. R147 and M57.

June 29 Wrote off past-due account of Barry Wilson as uncollectible, $137.28. M61.

Sept. 24 Received a payment from the receiver in bankruptcy for Benjamin Cranston in final settlement of his account, $38.50. His account balance was $66.00 when it had been written off on March 31, 1977. R221 and M84.

Dec. 15 Received a partial payment on account from Karl Roth, $22.00. His check was accompanied by a letter promising to pay the balance of his account by December 31. His account had been written off on March 9. R373 and M113.

Instructions: □ **2.** Foot, prove, total, and rule both journals.

28

Plant Assets and Depreciation

Assets that will be used for a number of years in a business are called plant assets. Examples of plant assets are delivery equipment, store equipment, office equipment, buildings, and land.

> Until recent years, plant assets were known as fixed assets. However, the American Institute of Certified Public Accountants recommends the word "plant" rather than "fixed" be used in the account title.

Plant assets such as delivery trucks, machinery, display cases, tables, typewriters, and desks are called equipment. Some businesses record the cost of all equipment in one asset account titled Equipment. Other businesses prefer to record the various kinds of equipment in separate plant asset accounts such as Delivery Equipment and Office Equipment.

RECORDING THE BUYING OF PLANT ASSETS

Plant assets may be bought either for cash or on account. When a plant asset is bought, it is recorded at the cost price. On July 5, 1977, Phillips Paper Products bought a new cash register for $1,500.00. A cash register is considered to be store equipment. The entry to record this transaction is shown in the cash payments journal below.

				1	2	3	4	5
				GENERAL		ACCOUNTS PAYABLE DEBIT	PURCHASES DISCOUNT CREDIT	CASH CREDIT
	DATE	ACCOUNT TITLE	CHECK No.	POST. REF.	DEBIT	CREDIT				
2	5	Store Equipment	318		1500 00				1500 00

CASH PAYMENTS JOURNAL   PAGE 7

Entry to record the buying of a plant asset

Phillips Paper Products has a separate asset account for store equipment. Store Equipment is debited for the cost of the cash register, and Cash is credited. After the entry is posted, the store equipment account in the general ledger appears as shown on page 539.

ACCOUNT *Store Equipment*					ACCOUNT NO. *122*		
DATE	ITEM	POST. REF.	DEBIT	CREDIT	BALANCE		
					DEBIT	CREDIT	
1977 *Jan. 1*	*Balance*	✓			*488000*		
July 5		*CP7*	*150000*		*638000*		

A plant asset account in the general ledger

The January 1 balance of Store Equipment is the original cost of equipment on hand that date. The debit balance of Store Equipment always shows the original cost of all store equipment owned.

WHAT IS DEPRECIATION?

A bicycle bought for $65.00 in December is not worth $65.00 twelve months later. Similarly, a plant asset of any kind bought in July for $1,000.00 is not worth $1,000.00 at the end of the year. Plant assets such as store equipment decrease in value because of wear and because new models become available. The decrease in the value of a plant asset because of use and the passage of time is called depreciation. Land, because of its permanent nature, is generally not subject to depreciation.

The amount by which a plant asset depreciates is an expense of the business. The plant asset is used to operate the business and earn revenue. Therefore, the expense of depreciation should be recorded in each fiscal period that the plant asset is used to earn revenue. If depreciation is not recorded, the income statement will not contain all the expenses of the business. Therefore, the net income will be overstated.

Income tax laws allow a business to deduct depreciation as an expense in figuring net income. If depreciation expenses are not included on the income tax reports, a business will pay more income tax than required.

DETERMINING THE AMOUNT OF DEPRECIATION EXPENSE

A business that buys a plant asset normally expects to use the asset for a number of years. When a plant asset is no longer useful or it needs to be replaced, the asset must be traded in, sold, or discarded.

Original cost, salvage value, and estimated life of plant assets

Before recording the depreciation expense of a plant asset, an accountant must know how to figure the expense. To figure depreciation expense, the accountant must know:

1. The original cost.
2. The amount the business estimates will be received when disposing of the plant asset.
3. The estimated useful life of the plant asset.

Original cost. The original cost of a plant asset is obtained from the seller's invoice. The cost is debited to the appropriate plant asset account. The cost of the new cash register bought by Phillips Paper Products is $1,500.00.

Estimated salvage value. The amount that the owner expects to receive when disposing of a plant asset is called the estimated salvage value. The estimated salvage value is also known as the trade-in value or the scrap value. The original cost minus the estimated salvage value equals the total estimated depreciation of a plant asset.

Phillips Paper Products estimates that at the end of the useful life of the new cash register, it will have a salvage value of $250.00. The total amount of the estimated depreciation for the cash register is figured as:

Original cost	minus	Estimated salvage value	equals	Amount of estimated depreciation
$1,500.00	−	$250.00	=	$1,250.00

Estimated useful life. Income tax laws require that the total amount of depreciation expense be distributed over the estimated useful life of a plant asset. When a plant asset is bought, it is not possible to know exactly how long it will be useful. Therefore, the number of years of useful life must be estimated.

The Internal Revenue Service issues guidelines giving the estimated life of many common plant assets. From these guidelines, Phillips Paper Products determines that the estimated useful life of a cash register is 10 years.

Figuring depreciation expense for a fiscal period

Phillips Paper Products figures the annual depreciation expense for the cash register as follows:

Amount of estimated depreciation	divided by	Years of estimated useful life	equals	Annual estimated depreciation expense
$1,250.00	÷	10	=	$125.00

Since Phillips Paper Products bought the cash register in July, one-half year has passed by the end of the fiscal period, December 31, 1977. Therefore, only one half of the annual depreciation, $62.50, is charged as an expense for the year 1977.

Charging an *equal* amount of depreciation expense for a plant asset each year of its estimated useful life is called the straight-line method of depreciation. There are other methods of figuring and charging depreciation expense. However, the straight-line method is widely adopted because it is simple to use.

Book value of a plant asset

The original cost of a plant asset minus the total amount of its recorded depreciation is called the book value of a plant asset. The table below shows the estimated depreciation expense and book value of the cash register for its estimated useful life.

Cash Register	Recorded Depreciation for Each Year	Total Recorded Depreciation	Book Value
Original Cost, July 5, 1977.....................			$1,500.00
One-half Year, ending 12/31/77............	$ 62.50	$ 62.50	1,437.50
One Year, ending 12/31/78	125.00	187.50	1,312.50
One Year, ending 12/31/79	125.00	312.50	1,187.50
One Year, ending 12/31/80	125.00	437.50	1,062.50
One Year, ending 12/31/81	125.00	562.50	937.50
One Year, ending 12/31/82	125.00	687.50	812.50
One Year, ending 12/31/83	125.00	812.50	687.50
One Year, ending 12/31/84	125.00	937.50	562.50
One Year, ending 12/31/85	125.00	1,062.50	437.50
One Year, ending 12/31/86	125.00	1,187.50	312.50
One-half Year, ending 6/30/87..............	62.50	1,250.00	250.00

The book value of the cash register at the end of the first half of 1987 is $250.00. This amount is the salvage value that Phillips Paper Products estimates the cash register will be worth at the end of ten years.

PLANT ASSET RECORDS

For a business to determine quickly the total amount of depreciation expense to be charged to each fiscal period, accurate records must be kept for each plant asset. The accounting form on which a business records data about each plant asset is called a plant asset record.

When Phillips Paper Products buys the cash register on July 5, 1977, a plant asset record is prepared as shown on the next page. The plant asset record includes (1) a complete description of the asset, including the serial number; (2) the date the asset was bought; (3) the cost; (4) the estimated useful life; (5) the estimated salvage value; and (6) the annual amount of depreciation expense.

At the end of the first fiscal period, December 31, 1977, the cash register had been owned for one-half year. Therefore, the amount of depreciation expense for 1977, $62.50, is recorded in the Accumulated Depreciation column. Since there was no previous depreciation on the cash register, the amount, $62.50, is deducted from the book value, $1,500.00, at the beginning of the fiscal period. The new book value at the end of the fiscal period, $1,437.50, is recorded in the Book Value column.

				PLANT ASSET RECORD				ACCOUNT NO. 122		

ITEM **Cash register**   GENERAL LEDGER ACCOUNT **Store Equipment**

SERIAL NO. **46947**   DESCRIPTION **Model KR 15**

FROM WHOM PURCHASED **Scott Equipment Company, Cleveland, Ohio**

ESTIMATED LIFE **10 years** ESTIMATED SALVAGE OR TRADE-IN VALUE **250.00** DEPRECIATION PER YEAR **125.00**

DATE			EXPLANATION	ASSET			ACCUMULATED DEPRECIATION			BOOK VALUE
MO.	DAY	YR.		DR.	CR.	BAL.	DR.	CR.	BAL.	
7	5	77		1,500.00		1,500.00				1,500.00
12	31	77						62.50	62.50	1,437.50
12	31	78						125.00	187.50	1,312.50
12	31	79						125.00	312.50	1,187.50

Plant asset record

At the close of each fiscal period, each plant asset record is brought up to date. The depreciation expense for that period is recorded and the new book value of the asset is figured.

VALUATION OF PLANT ASSETS

Three general ledger accounts are used to record data about each kind of plant asset: (1) An asset account (such as Delivery Equipment) is used to record the original cost price of the asset; (2) A valuation account (such as Accumulated Depreciation — Delivery Equipment) is used to record the total estimated amount of depreciation to date; and (3) An expense account (such as Depreciation Expense — Delivery Equipment) is used to record the annual amount of depreciation expense.

Plant asset accounts

Phillips Paper Products uses two plant asset accounts: Delivery Equipment and Store Equipment. The appropriate plant asset account is debited for the cost price when equipment is bought. The account is credited for the cost price when equipment is disposed of. Therefore, the balance of the plant asset account always shows the cost price of all equipment in current use.

Accumulated depreciation accounts

The valuation account to which the estimated amount of depreciation is credited is titled Accumulated Depreciation. The name of the equipment account is added to the title, such as Accumulated Depreciation — Delivery Equipment. Phillips Paper Products uses two accumulated depreciation accounts: (1) Accumulated Depreciation — Delivery Equipment, and (2) Accumulated Depreciation — Store Equipment.

The account titles Allowance for Depreciation or Reserve for Depreciation are sometimes used instead of Accumulated Depreciation.

The debit balance of each plant asset account continues to show the original cost of the asset in use. The credit balance of the accumulated depreciation account shows the estimated decrease in value of the asset because of depreciation. The difference between the balance of the two accounts is the book value of the plant asset. Accumulated depreciation accounts are known as valuation accounts, like Allowance for Uncollectible Accounts, or minus asset accounts.

Depreciation expense accounts

The amount of estimated depreciation of plant assets is an operating expense of the business. Phillips Paper Products uses two depreciation expense accounts: (1) Depreciation Expense — Delivery Equipment, and (2) Depreciation Expense — Store Equipment. The estimated amounts of depreciation for each fiscal period are debited to these accounts.

ADJUSTMENTS FOR DEPRECIATION

At the end of the fiscal period, December 31, 1977, Phillips Paper Products refers to each plant asset record and figures the amount of estimated depreciation for each asset. Next, the total amount of estimated depreciation expense is figured for all plant assets of the same kind. According to the plant asset records, the total estimated depreciation for each kind of plant asset at the end of the fiscal period is:

Kind of equipment	Estimated depreciation expense this year	Previous balance of accumulated depreciation	New balance of accumulated depreciation
Delivery equipment	$1,650.00	$1,072.50	$2,722.50
Store equipment	360.14	272.80	632.94

The book values of delivery equipment and store equipment, December 31, 1977, are:

Kind of equipment	Balance of asset account	less	Total accumulated depreciation	equals	Book value 12/31/77
Delivery equipment	$9,284.00	–	$2,722.50	=	$6,561.50
Store equipment	6,380.00	–	632.94	=	5,747.06

The book value of each kind of plant asset that a business owns is figured in the same way as described above.

Analyzing the adjustment for estimated depreciation

To record the estimated depreciation expense for the year, an adjusting entry is made. The adjustment for estimated depreciation of delivery equipment is shown in the T accounts at the left.

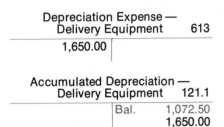

Depreciation Expense — Delivery Equipment is debited for $1,650.00 to show the increase in the balance of this expense account. The balance of this account is the estimated depreciation expense for the current fiscal period.

Accumulated Depreciation — Delivery Equipment is credited for $1,650.00 to show the increase in the balance of this valuation account. This account's new balance, $2,722.50, is the total accumulated depreciation on all delivery equipment at the end of the current fiscal period.

The same kind of adjusting entry is made to record the estimated depreciation expense for store equipment, $360.14. Depreciation Expense — Store Equipment is debited for $360.14, and Accumulated Depreciation — Store Equipment is credited for the same amount.

Adjustments for depreciation on a work sheet

Phillips Paper Products plans the adjustments for estimated depreciation expense in the Adjustments columns of a work sheet. The December 31, 1977, adjustment for depreciation of delivery equipment is shown on Lines 9 and 28 of the work sheet, page 545. The adjustment for depreciation of store equipment is shown on Lines 11 and 29.

The accounts Gain on Plant Assets (Line 36) and Loss on Plant Assets (Line 37) are described in Chapter 29.

Adjustment for depreciation of delivery equipment. On Line 28, Depreciation Expense — Delivery Equipment is debited for $1,650.00 in the Adjustments Debit column. On Line 9, Accumulated Depreciation — Delivery Equipment is credited for $1,650.00 in the Adjustments Credit column. The debit amount, $1,650.00, is extended to the Income Statement Debit column. The credit amount, $1,650.00, is added to the credit balance of this valuation account, $1,072.50. The total accumulated depreciation of delivery equipment, $2,722.50, is extended to the Balance Sheet Credit column.

Adjustment for depreciation of store equipment. On Line 29, Depreciation Expense — Store Equipment is debited for $360.14 in the Adjustments Debit column. On Line 11, Accumulated Depreciation — Store Equipment is credited for $360.14 in the Adjustments Credit column. The debit amount, $360.14, is extended to the Income Statement Debit column. The credit amount, $360.14, is added to the credit balance of this valuation account, $272.80. The total accumulated depreciation of store equipment, $632.94, is extended to the Balance Sheet Credit column.

Phillips Paper Products
Work Sheet
For Year Ended December 31, 1977

	ACCOUNT TITLE	ACCT. NO.	TRIAL BALANCE DEBIT	TRIAL BALANCE CREDIT	ADJUSTMENTS DEBIT	ADJUSTMENTS CREDIT	INCOME STATEMENT DEBIT	INCOME STATEMENT CREDIT	BALANCE SHEET DEBIT	BALANCE SHEET CREDIT	
1	Cash	111	617650						617650		1
2	Petty Cash	112	10000						10000		2
3	Accounts Receivable	113	890000						890000		3
4	Allow. for Uncoll. Accts.	113.1				(a) 45265				45265	4
5	Merchandise Inventory	114	3872605		(c) 4231700	(b) 3872605			4231700		5
6	Supplies	115	69000			(d) 50050			18950		6
7	Prepaid Insurance	116	75400			(e) 53000			22400		7
8	Delivery Equipment	121	928400						928400		8
9	Accum. Depr.-Del. Equip.	121.1		107250		(f) 165000				272250	9
10	Store Equipment	122	638000						638000		10
11	Accum. Depr. Store Equip.	122.1		27280		(g) 36014				63294	11
12	Accounts Payable	211		463710						463710	12
13	Employees Income Tax Pay.	212		17177						17177	13
14	FICA Tax Payable	213		10227						10227	14
15	Federal Unempl. Tax Pay.	214		1475						1475	15
16	State Unempl. Tax Pay.	215		7980						7980	16
17	Sales Tax Payable	216		118209						118209	17
18	Jerry Phillips, Capital	311		5627721						5627721	18
19	Jerry Phillips, Drawing	312	900000						900000		19
20	Income Summary	313			(b) 3872605	(c) 4231700	3872605	4231700			20
21	Sales	411		11915255				11915255			21
22	Sales Returns + Allow.	411.1	94280				94280				22
23	Purchases	511	5832354				5832354				23
24	Purchases Ret. & Allow.	511.1		124620				124620			24
25	Purchases Discount	511.2		141170				141170			25
26	Bad Debts Expense	611			(a) 45265		45265				26
27	Delivery Expense	612	162540				162540				27
28	Depr. Expense-Del. Equip.	613			(f) 165000		165000				28
29	Depr. Expense-Store Equip.	614			(g) 36014		36014				29
30	Insurance Expense	615			(e) 53000		53000				30
31	Miscellaneous Expense	616	240375				240375				31
32	Payroll Taxes Expense	617	261210				261210				32
33	Rent Expense	618	500000				500000				33
34	Salary Expense	619	3482800				3482800				34
35	Supplies Expense	620			(d) 50050		50050				35
36	Gain on Plant Assets	711		40700				40700			36
37	Loss on Plant Assets	811	28160				28160				37
38			18602774	18602774	8453634	8453634	14823653	16453445	8257100	6627308	38
39	Net Income						1629792			1629792	39
40							16453445	16453445	8257100	8257100	40

Work sheet with adjustments for depreciation

Recording adjustments for estimated depreciation

The data needed to journalize the adjustments for estimated depreciation expense are obtained from the Adjustments columns of the work sheet. The two adjusting entries for Phillips Paper Products are shown in the general journal below.

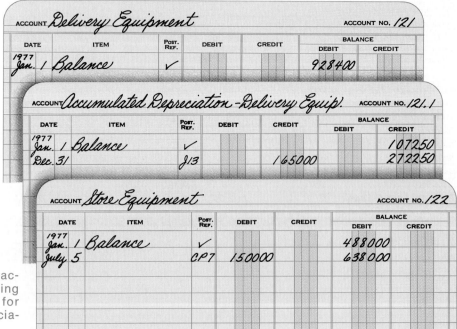

Adjusting entries to record depreciation

Posting the adjustments for estimated depreciation

When the adjusting entries are posted from the general journal the plant asset accounts, accumulated depreciation accounts, and depreciation expense accounts appear as shown below and on page 547.

General ledger accounts after posting the adjustments for estimated depreciation expense

Delivery Equipment and Store Equipment have debit balances showing the cost price of equipment. The two valuation accounts Accumulated Depreciation — Delivery Equipment and Accumulated Depreciation — Store Equipment have credit balances showing the total accumulated depreciation recorded to date. Depreciation Expense — Delivery Equipment and Depreciation Expense — Store Equipment have debit balances showing the estimated depreciation expense for the current fiscal period.

REPORTING PLANT ASSETS AND DEPRECIATION ON FINANCIAL STATEMENTS

Accumulated depreciation accounts are minus asset accounts. Each accumulated depreciation account is listed on the balance sheet immediately following the plant asset account to which it applies. Depreciation expense accounts are listed with the operating expenses on the income statement.

Depreciation expense on the income statement

Phillips Paper Products prepares its income statement from data on a work sheet. The balance of each depreciation expense account is listed in the operating expense section of the partial income statement shown on page 548.

Phillips Paper Products Income Statement For Year Ended December 31, 1977		
Gross Profit on Operations		66 135 06
Operating Expenses:		
Bad Debts Expense	452 65	
Delivery Expense	1 625 40	
Depr. Exp.–Delivery Equip.	1 650 00	
Depreciation Exp.–Store Equip.	360 14	
Insurance Expense	530 00	
Miscellaneous Expense	2 403 75	
Payroll Taxes Expense	2 612 10	
Rent Expense	5 000 00	
Salary Expense	34 828 00	
Supplies Expense	500 50	
Total Operating Expenses		49 962 54

Depreciation expense on an income statement

Accumulated depreciation on the balance sheet

Phillips Paper Products prepares a balance sheet from data on a work sheet. In the plant assets section are listed data for each type of plant asset: (1) the original cost, (2) the accumulated depreciation, and (3) the book value. The plant assets section is shown on the balance sheet, December 31, 1977, at the top of the next page.

In the plant assets section of the balance sheet, the original cost of each type of plant asset is shown in the first amount column. The accumulated depreciation of each type of plant asset is written immediately under the original cost of the asset and is subtracted. The difference between the two amounts is the book value and is written in the second amount column. The book values are totaled, and the sum of the book values for all plant assets is written in the third amount column.

A business having several plant assets might prefer to list them on the balance sheet in a compact fashion as shown at the bottom of page 549.

Classifying assets on the balance sheet

As shown in the balance sheet, page 549, Phillips Paper Products classifies assets according to the length of time they will be used in the operation of the business. Assets that will be used within a relatively short time, usually a year, are listed under the heading *Current Assets*. The current assets are totaled to find the *Total Current Assets*, and this amount is entered in the third amount column.

Phillips Paper Products
Balance Sheet
December 31, 1977

Assets			
Current Assets:			
Cash		617650	
Petty Cash		10000	
Accounts Receivable	890000		
Less Allow. for Uncoll. Accts.	45265	844735	
Merchandise Inventory		4231700	
Supplies		18950	
Prepaid Insurance		22400	
Total Current Assets			5745435
Plant Assets:			
Delivery Equipment	928400		
Less Accum. Depr.-Del. Equip.	272250	656150	
Store Equipment	638000		
Less Accum. Depr.-Store Equip.	63294	574706	
Total Plant Assets			1230856
Total Assets			6976291
Liabilities			
Current Liabilities:			
Accounts Payable		463710	
Employees Income Tax Pay.		17177	
FICA Tax Payable		10227	
Federal Unempl. Tax Pay.		1475	
State Unempl. Tax Payable		7980	
Sales Tax Payable		118209	
Total Current Liabilities			618778
Capital			
Jerry Phillips, Capital			6357513
Total Liabilities and Capital			6976291

Balance sheet showing plant assets and accumulated depreciation

SOUND-MATIC COMPANY
Balance Sheet
June 30, 1977

Assets				
Total Current Assets				$41,250.00
	Cost	Accumulated Depreciation	Book Value	
Plant Assets:				
Delivery Equipment	$ 7,535.77	$ 2,904.00	$ 4,631.77	
Office Equipment	3,280.00	973.50	2,306.50	
Factory Equipment	29,742.20	16,557.12	13,185.08	
Buildings	60,000.00	20,000.00	40,000.00	
Land	22,100.00	----	22,100.00	
Total Plant Assets	$122,657.97	$40,434.62		82,223.35

Section of a balance sheet showing five plant assets in compact form

Assets to be used for a number of years are listed on the balance sheet under the heading *Plant Assets*. The plant assets are totaled to find the *Total Plant Assets*. This amount is entered in the third amount column.

The Total Current Assets and the Total Plant Assets are then added to obtain the *Total Assets*. This amount is entered in the third amount column, and double lines are ruled across all the amount columns.

> Current assets are usually listed in the order in which they can most readily be turned into cash. The order of listing plant assets is not uniform in practice. One common method is to list those with the shortest life first.

Classifying liabilities on a balance sheet

Phillips Paper Products classifies liabilities as well as assets on a balance sheet. The liabilities are classified according to the length of time until they are due. Liabilities due within a relatively short time, usually within a year, are called current liabilities. Examples of current liabilities are: Accounts Payable, Employees Income Tax Payable, FICA Tax Payable, Federal Unemployment Tax Payable, State Unemployment Tax Payable, and Sales Tax Payable.

As shown in the chart of accounts, page 504, all the liabilities of Phillips Paper Products are listed as current liabilities because they fall due within a year. The balance sheet, page 549, shows the correct way of preparing the liabilities section when all liabilities are current liabilities.

Liabilities that are not due for a number of years in the normal operation of a business are called long-term liabilities. An example of a long-term liability is Mortgage Payable. Long-term liabilities are sometimes known as fixed liabilities. Phillips Paper Products does not have any long-term liabilities.

> Liabilities are commonly arranged on the balance sheet according to the order in which they fall due.

When a business has both current liabilities and long-term liabilities, it is customary to list them on the balance sheet in separate sections. The liabilities section of the balance sheet for Sound-matic Company illustrated below shows both current liabilities and long-term liabilities.

Total Assets				$123,473.35
Liabilities				
Current Liabilities:				
Accounts Payable			$4,785.00	
Sales Tax Payable			925.19	
Total Current Liabilities				$18,425.00
Long-term Liabilities:				
Mortgage Payable				33,000.00
Total Liabilities				$51,425.00

Liabilities section of a balance sheet showing current and long-term or fixed liabilities

✦ What is the meaning of each of the following?

- plant assets
- equipment
- depreciation
- estimated salvage value
- straight-line method of depreciation
- book value of a plant asset
- plant asset record
- current liabilities
- long-term liabilities

1. Why are most plant assets worth less than their original cost after they have been used for a fiscal period?
2. If the expense of using a plant asset is not recorded, how will this omission affect the total expenses of the business? How will this omission affect the net income for the period?
3. What three things must an accountant know about a plant asset in order to figure its depreciation expense?
4. On the plant asset record, page 542, how is the book value figured at the end of a fiscal period?

5. Why is the amount of depreciation of a plant asset credited to an accumulated depreciation account rather than to the plant asset account?
6. Why is the accumulated depreciation account called a valuation account?
7. On the work sheet, page 545, what accounts are debited and credited in planning the adjustments for estimated depreciation of delivery equipment?
8. What is the usual order for listing assets on a balance sheet?
9. What is the usual order for listing liabilities on a balance sheet?

CASE 1 Jack Palmer, owner of a small business, does not record depreciation expense. Mr. Palmer says that he does not make actual cash payments for deprecia-tion; therefore, he should not record the expense until a payment is made. What is wrong with Mr. Palmer's viewpoint?

CASE 2 The Speedi-Delivery Service has more business than can be handled with the present number of trucks it owns. The Service is investigating the cost of buying an additional truck. One truck dealer suggests a small truck costing $5,000.00. The useful life of the truck is estimated to be 5 years with an estimated salvage value of $900.00. Another truck dealer suggests a larger truck with about twice the capacity of the smaller truck. The cost price is $8,500.00, with a useful life of 6 years, and estimated salvage value of $1,100.00. Which truck would you suggest the Speedi-Delivery Service buy? Why?

DRILL 28-D 1 Figuring depreciation expense

Instructions: Using the straight-line method described on page 540, find the amount of annual depreciation for each of the following plant assets.

Plant Asset	Original Cost	Estimated Salvage Value	Estimated Life
1	$ 2,650.00	$ 450.00	4 years
2	700.00	100.00	5 years
3	600.00	none	3 years
4	7,000.00	1,600.00	20 years
5	29,040.00	2,400.00	8 years
6	12,800.00	800.00	16 years

DRILL 28-D 2 Figuring book value of a plant asset

Instructions: For each of the following plant assets, find (a) the total amount of estimated depreciation and (b) the book value as of December 31, 1977. Compute the time of depreciation to the nearest number of months.

Plant Asset	Date Bought	Original Cost	Estimated Salvage Value	Estimated Life
1	Dec. 31, 1973	$1,500.00	$ 50.00	5 years
2	July 1, 1974	4,460.00	300.00	10 years
3	Jan. 3, 1975	1,165.00	250.00	20 years
4	Nov. 1, 1975	150.00	20.00	4 years
5	Jan. 2, 1976	812.35	none	10 years
6	Dec. 1, 1977	300.00	60.00	8 years

Problems for Applying Concepts

PROBLEM 28-1 Figuring and recording depreciation expense

Jason Butler bought the following office equipment during the first two years he was in business:

Office Equipment	Date Bought	Original Cost	Estimated Salvage Value	Estimated Life
1	Jan. 6, 1976	$ 448.00	$180.00	10 years
2	July 1, 1976	88.00	none	4 years
3	Mar. 1, 1977	79.00	none	5 years
4	July 2, 1977	517.00	none	10 years
5	Nov. 1, 1977	1,056.00	66.00	5 years
6	Dec. 1, 1977	1,600.40	200.00	10 years

Instructions: □ **1.** Record on page 14 of a general journal the adjusting entry for the total depreciation expense for the year ended December 31, 1976. Compute the time of depreciation to the nearest number of months.

□ **2.** Record the adjusting entry for the total depreciation expense for the year ended December 31, 1977.

PROBLEM 28-2 Work at the end of a fiscal period including depreciation expense

A partial trial balance of Concord Building Supplies is shown at the top of the next page. The accounts for depreciation of plant assets are illustrated on this partial trial balance.

Instructions: □ **1.** Record the information in the Trial Balance columns of an eight-column work sheet for the year ended December 31, 1977.

Concord Building Supplies
Trial Balance
December 31, 1977

Delivery Equipment..	17 380 00	
Accumulated Depreciation — Delivery Equipment		9 680 00
Store Equipment	7 150 00	
Accumulated Depreciation — Store Equipment..........		2 056 00
Depreciation Expense — Delivery Equipment.............		
Depreciation Expense — Store Equipment.................		

Instructions: ☐ **2.** Record on the work sheet the adjustments for estimated depreciation for the year, using the following additional data:

Annual depreciation of delivery equipment $3,960.00
Annual depreciation of store equipment............................. 423.50

☐ **3.** Extend all amounts to their appropriate columns in the Income Statement or Balance Sheet columns on the work sheet.

☐ **4.** Journalize the adjusting entries on page 19 of a general journal.

☐ **5.** Prepare the plant assets section of a balance sheet.

**MASTERY
PROBLEM 28-M**   Figuring and journalizing depreciation
expense; finding book value
of plant assets

Malcom Printing Service purchased the following items of equipment during the first two years the business existed:

Equipment	Date Bought	Original Cost	Estimated Salvage Value	Estimated Life
1	Jan. 3, 1976	$ 264.00	$ 50.00	10 years
2	July 1, 1976	320.00	none	10 years
3	Apr. 2, 1977	700.00	100.00	5 years
4	Sept. 1, 1977	5,328.00	500.00	10 years
5	Nov. 1, 1977	72.00	none	8 years
6	Dec. 1, 1977	519.00	50.00	7 years

Malcom Printing Service uses only one plant asset account in its general ledger. This plant asset account is titled Printing Equipment.

Instructions: ☐ **1.** Record on page 18 of a general journal the adjusting entry for the total depreciation expense for the year ended December 31, 1976. Compute the time of depreciation to the nearest number of months.

☐ **2.** Record the adjusting entry for the total depreciation expense for the year ended December 31, 1977.

☐ **3.** Find the book value as of December 31, 1977, for each item of equipment.

BONUS PROBLEM 28-B ## Figuring depreciation expense using the declining-balance method

Federal income tax regulations permit a business to use the straight-line method of figuring depreciation as described in this chapter. The regulations also permit a business to use the *declining-balance method of figuring depreciation*. Under the declining-balance method of figuring depreciation, the depreciation rate is twice what the rate would be under the straight-line method. The rate is applied to the *book value* of the plant asset at the *beginning* of each fiscal period.

A delivery truck was bought on January 7, 1976, for $2,000.00, with an estimated life of 10 years. The rate of depreciation under the straight-line method would be 10% per year. Therefore, the rate under the declining-balance method is 20%. Under the declining-balance method, the remaining book value at the end of the tenth year will be approximately the estimated salvage value of the truck.

Instructions: Using a chart similar to the one below, figure the book value at the beginning of each of the 10 years of useful life, the amount of annual depreciation for each year, the accumulated depreciation at the end of each year, and the book value at the end of each year. (The book value at the end of one year is the book value for the beginning of the next year.) Figures for the first two years are given as examples.

Year	Book value at beginning of year	Rate of depreciation	Annual depreciation this year	Accumulated depreciation at end of year	Book value at end of year
1976	$2,000.00	20%	$400.00	$400.00	$1,600.00
1977	1,600.00	20%	320.00	720.00	1,280.00

Disposing of Plant Assets

29

When a plant asset is no longer useful, the asset may be sold, traded in on a new asset, or discarded as worthless. Plant assets may wear out from use or may become outdated because newer models are available. Usually a business will consider a plant asset as worthless when the expense of selling it is greater than the salvage value.

DISCARDING A PLANT ASSET

A plant asset that is of no further use to the business and cannot be sold or traded is often discarded. When a discarded plant asset has no book value, the plant asset account is credited for the original cost of the item. At the same time, the accumulated depreciation account is debited for the total accumulated depreciation of the item being discarded. When the plant asset has a book value at the time it is discarded, the business incurs a loss.

Discarding a plant asset that has no book value

Phillips Paper Products discarded the following plant asset that has no book value.

> *August 2, 1977. Discarded a display rack bought on January 10, 1975, for $50.00. Memorandum No. 80.*

After the additional depreciation on this display rack for 1977 is recorded, the plant asset record shows no book value for the asset. The analysis of this transaction to discard a plant asset with no book value is shown in the T accounts on page 556.

Accumulated Depreciation —
Store Equipment   122.1

50.00	

Store Equipment   122

	50.00

Accumulated Depreciation — Store Equipment is debited for $50.00 to show the decrease in the balance of this valuation account. This amount represents the total depreciation recorded on the display rack when it is discarded.

Store Equipment is credited for $50.00 to show the decrease in the balance of this plant asset account. This amount cancels the original cost, $50.00, debited to the store equipment account when the display rack was bought.

The general journal entry to record the discarding of the display rack is shown below.

Entry to record the discarding of a plant asset that has no book value

ACCOUNTS PAYABLE DEBIT	GENERAL DEBIT	DATE	ACCOUNT TITLE	POST. REF.	GENERAL CREDIT	ACCOUNTS RECEIV. CREDIT
	50 00	1977 Aug. 2	Accum. Depr.-Store Equip.			
			Store Equipment		50 00	
			Memorandum No. 80.			

GENERAL JOURNAL   PAGE 8

Discarding a plant asset that has a book value

Phillips Paper Products discarded the following plant asset that had a book value:

> November 17, 1977. Discarded a cabinet bought on January 10, 1969, for $120.00. Memorandum No. 123.

Recording depreciation for part of a fiscal year. Depreciation on the discarded cabinet was last recorded on December 31, 1976. The depreciation of the cabinet for the eleven months from January 1 to November 17, 1977, needs to be recorded.

> When a plant asset is disposed of during a fiscal period, the time of depreciation is usually figured to the nearest number of months. Thus, a plant asset disposed of during the first half of a month need not have any depreciation charged to it for that month. A plant asset disposed of during the last half of a month should have a full month's depreciation expense recorded.

The general journal entry to record the depreciation on the discarded cabinet is shown on page 557.

The plant asset record form showed that the accumulated depreciation recorded on December 31, 1976, totaled $96.00. Annual depreciation is $12.00. The depreciation for the eleven-month period is $11.00. After the entry above is posted, the accumulated depreciation for the discarded cabinet is $107.00 ($96.00 *plus* $11.00). The book value of the discarded cabinet is $13.00 (original cost, $120.00 *minus* accumulated depreciation, $107.00).

		GENERAL JOURNAL			PAGE //	
1	2			3	4	
ACCOUNTS PAYABLE DEBIT	GENERAL DEBIT	DATE	ACCOUNT TITLE	POST. REF.	GENERAL CREDIT	ACCOUNTS RECEIV. CREDIT
18	1100	17	Depr. Expense -Store Equip.			18
19			Accum. Depr.-Store Equip.		1100	19
20			Memorandum No. 123.			20

Entry to record estimated depreciation for part of a fiscal period

Recording the discarding of a plant asset with a book value. The analysis of this transaction is shown in the T accounts at the right. Accumulated Depreciation — Store Equipment is debited for $107.00. Loss on Plant Assets is debited for $13.00 (the loss that results from discarding a plant asset with a book value). Store Equipment is credited for the original cost of the cabinet, $120.00.

The general journal entry to record the discarding of this cabinet is shown below.

Accumulated Depreciation — Store Equipment	122.1
107.00	

Loss on Plant Assets	811
13.00	

Store Equipment	122
	120.00

		GENERAL JOURNAL			PAGE //	
1	2			3	4	
ACCOUNTS PAYABLE DEBIT	GENERAL DEBIT	DATE	ACCOUNT TITLE	POST. REF.	GENERAL CREDIT	ACCOUNTS RECEIV. CREDIT
21	10700	17	Accum. Depr.- Store Equip.			21
22	1300		Loss on Plant Assets			22
23			Store Equipment		12000	23
24			Memorandum No. 123.			24

Entry to record the discarding of a plant asset that has a book value

Gain or loss on disposal of plant assets

A plant asset's book value is an estimate of its actual value. The actual value is determined only when a plant asset is disposed of. If the actual value of a plant asset is *more* than its book value, the total asset value of the business is greater than shown on the records. For example, a plant asset with a book value of $90.00 is sold for $105.00. The difference between the book value and the actual value is $15.00. The $15.00 is the amount of increase in the value of this plant asset. The amount of increase in value that occurs when a plant asset is disposed of is called gain on plant assets.

If the actual value of a plant asset is *less* than its book value, that plant asset is worth less than is shown on the records. For example, a plant asset with a book value of $75.00 is sold for $40.00. The difference between the book value and the actual value is $35.00. The $35.00 is the amount of decrease in the value of this plant asset. The amount of decrease in value that occurs when a plant asset is disposed of is called loss on plant assets.

Gains or losses on plant assets must be shown as separate items on income tax returns and on income statements. Therefore, separate accounts are used in the general ledger to record the gains or losses on plant assets. The revenue account Gain on Plant Assets is used to record gains. The expense account Loss on Plant Assets is used to record losses.

GAIN ON SALE OF A PLANT ASSET

Phillips Paper Products sold the following fixed asset:

> *May 3, 1977. Received cash, $395.00, from the sale of a showcase bought on January 8, 1975, for $500.00. Memorandum No. 53 and Receipt No. 115.*

The plant asset record for the showcase is shown below.

		PLANT ASSET RECORD		ACCOUNT NO. 122

ITEM __Showcase__   — GENERAL LEDGER ACCOUNT __Store Equipment__

SERIAL NO. __GT 708-2__   DESCRIPTION __Excel Glass Top Two-Section__

FROM WHOM PURCHASED __Howe Office Supplies, Cleveland, Ohio__

ESTIMATED LIFE __5 years__   ESTIMATED SALVAGE OR TRADE-IN VALUE __50.00__   DEPRECIATION PER YEAR __90.00__

DATE			EXPLANATION	ASSET			ACCUMULATED DEPRECIATION			BOOK VALUE
MO.	DAY	YR.		DR.	CR.	BAL.	DR.	CR.	BAL.	
1	8	75		500.00		500.00				500.00
12	31	75						90.00	90.00	410.00
12	31	76						90.00	180.00	320.00

Recording depreciation for part of a fiscal period

The showcase was sold on May 3, 1977. Depreciation was recorded only to December 31, 1976. The depreciation of the showcase for the four-month period, January 1, 1977, to May 3, 1977, needs to be recorded. One third of the annual depreciation is $30.00.

The general journal entry to record the depreciation of the showcase for one third of a year is shown below.

Entry to record estimated depreciation for part of a fiscal period

		GENERAL JOURNAL				PAGE *5*
1	2				3	4
ACCOUNTS PAYABLE DEBIT	GENERAL DEBIT	DATE	ACCOUNT TITLE	POST. REF.	GENERAL CREDIT	ACCOUNTS RECEIV. CREDIT
	30 00	*1977 May 3*	*Depr. Expense – Store Equip.*			
			Accum. Depr. – Store Equip.		30 00	
			Memorandum No. 53.			

After the journal entry is recorded and posted, the plant asset record is brought up to date. The depreciation for the four months, $30.00, is recorded on the plant asset record. The plant asset record then shows the total accumulated depreciation of $210.00. The cost of the showcase, $500.00, less the accumulated depreciation, $210.00, equals the book value, $290.00, on May 3, 1977.

Recording a gain on the sale of a plant asset

The showcase was sold for $395.00, which is $105.00 more than the book value, $290.00. Thus, the assets of the business increased by $105.00. The analysis of this transaction is shown in the T accounts at the right.

Cash is debited for $395.00 to show the increase in the balance of this asset account.

Accumulated Depreciation — Store Equipment is debited for $210.00 to show the decrease in the balance of this valuation account. This amount is the total depreciation recorded for the showcase at the time of its sale.

Cash	111
395.00	

Accumulated Depreciation — Store Equipment	122.1
210.00	

Store Equipment	122
	500.00

Gain on Plant Assets	711
	105.00

> When a plant asset is disposed of, a record of the estimated accumulated depreciation of that asset is no longer needed. Therefore, the amount of estimated accumulated depreciation is removed from the accumulated depreciation account. The remaining balance of the account represents the estimated depreciation of the plant assets still owned by the business.

Store Equipment is credited for $500.00 to show the decrease in the balance of this plant asset account. This amount cancels the original cost of $500.00 debited to the store equipment account when the showcase was bought.

Gain on Plant Assets is credited for $105.00 to show the increase in the balance of this revenue account. This amount is the excess of the sale price of the showcase over its book value.

> When the amount received from the sale of a plant asset is more than its book value, it means that too much depreciation expense has been recorded in previous fiscal periods. This also means that in previous fiscal periods, the net income has been understated. The Internal Revenue Service requires that an adjustment of net income be made. The gain on plant assets account is used to show this adjustment as revenue for the fiscal period in which the plant asset is disposed of.

The entry in the cash receipts journal to record the sale of a showcase by Phillips Paper Products is shown on the next page.

After the journal entry is recorded, an entry is also made on the plant asset record to show that the asset has been disposed of. The plant asset record is then removed from the file of plant assets still in use.

	CASH RECEIPTS JOURNAL								PAGE 8
				1	2	3	4	5	6
DATE	ACCOUNT TITLE	Doc. No.	Post. Ref.	GENERAL		SALES CREDIT	SALES TAX PAYABLE CREDIT	ACCOUNTS RECEIVABLE CREDIT	CASH DEBIT
				DEBIT	CREDIT				
16	3 Accum. Depr.-Store Equip.	R115		210 00					395 00
17	Store Equipment				500 00				
18	Gain on Plant Assets				105 00				

Entry to record the sale of a
plant asset at a gain

LOSS ON SALE OF A PLANT ASSET

Phillips Paper Products sold the following plant asset:

*July 6, 1977. Received cash, $750.00, from the sale of a delivery trailer
bought on January 6, 1975, for $1,000.00. Memorandum
No. 68 and Receipt No. 182.*

The plant asset record for the delivery trailer is shown below.

PLANT ASSET RECORD   ACCOUNT NO. 121

ITEM Delivery trailer _____ GENERAL LEDGER ACCOUNT Delivery Equipment

SERIAL NO. SL-7605-B ____ DESCRIPTION Tully-Mason Two-Wheel

FROM WHOM PURCHASED Frazier Trucks, Cleveland, Ohio

ESTIMATED LIFE 10 years ESTIMATED SALVAGE OR TRADE-IN VALUE 200.00 DEPRECIATION PER YEAR 80.00

DATE			EXPLANATION	ASSET			ACCUMULATED DEPRECIATION			BOOK VALUE
MO.	DAY	YR.		DR.	CR.	BAL.	DR.	CR.	BAL.	
1	6	75		1,000.00		1,000.00				1,000.00
12	31	75						80.00	80.00	920.00
12	31	76						80.00	160.00	840.00

Recording depreciation for part of a fiscal period

Depreciation for a six-month period, January 1, 1977, to July 6, 1977,
must be recorded. Six months is one half of a year. Therefore, one half of
the annual depreciation, $40.00, is recorded.

The general journal entry to record the depreciation of the delivery
trailer for six months is shown at the top of the next page.

The plant asset record is brought up to date by recording the depreciation of $40.00 for one-half year. The plant asset record then shows the
total accumulated depreciation of $200.00. The amount of the accumulat-
ed depreciation, $200.00, is subtracted from the cost of the trailer,
$1,000.00, to find the book value, $800.00, on July 6, 1977.

			GENERAL JOURNAL			PAGE 7	
						3	4
1	2						
ACCOUNTS PAYABLE DEBIT	GENERAL DEBIT	DATE	ACCOUNT TITLE	POST. REF.	GENERAL CREDIT	ACCOUNTS RECEIV. CREDIT	
4000		*1977* July 6	Depr. Exp. - Delivery Equip.				1
			Accum. Depr. - Del. Equip.		4000		2
			Memorandum No. 68.				3

Entry to record estimated depreciation for part of a fiscal period

Recording a loss on the sale of a plant asset

The trailer was sold for $50.00 less than its book value. Therefore, the assets of the business decreased $50.00. The analysis of this transaction is shown in the T accounts at the right.

Cash is debited for $750.00 to show the increase in the balance of this asset.

Accumulated Depreciation — Delivery Equipment is debited for $200.00 to show the decrease in the balance of this valuation account. The amount, $200.00, is the total depreciation recorded on the trailer at the time of its sale.

Loss on Plant Assets is debited for $50.00 to show the increase in the balance of this expense account. This amount is the excess of the book value of the trailer over its sale price.

Cash	111
750.00	

Accumulated Depreciation — Delivery Equipment	121.1
200.00	

Loss on Plant Assets	811
50.00	

Delivery Equipment	121
	1,000.00

> In previous fiscal periods, an insufficient amount of depreciation expense was recorded. This resulted in the overpayment of income tax. Income tax regulations permit the business to record this loss when the asset is sold.

Delivery Equipment is credited for $1,000.00 to show the decrease in the balance of this plant asset account. This amount cancels the original cost, $1,000.00, debited to the delivery equipment account when the trailer was bought.

The entry in the cash receipts journal to record the sale of the delivery trailer is shown below.

						CASH RECEIPTS JOURNAL					PAGE 12	
						1	2	3	4	5	6	
DATE		ACCOUNT TITLE	Doc. No.	Post. Ref.	GENERAL DEBIT	GENERAL CREDIT	SALES CREDIT	SALES TAX PAYABLE CREDIT	ACCOUNTS RECEIVABLE CREDIT	CASH DEBIT		
6	Accum. Depr. - Delivery Equip.	R132		20000						75000		8
	Loss on Plant Assets			5000								9
	Delivery Equipment				100000							10

Entry to record the sale of a plant asset at a loss

TRADING IN A PLANT ASSET

A common practice is to trade in a used plant asset for another similar plant asset. For example, a business may trade in a used typewriter for a new typewriter. Income tax regulations do not allow a business to show a gain or a loss when one plant asset is traded in for another similar plant asset. The new plant asset is recorded at an amount equal to the sum of cash actually paid plus the book value of the used plant asset that was traded in.

Phillips Paper Products replaced a used plant asset as follows.

> *February 21, 1977. Bought a new delivery truck for $2,500.00 cash plus the trade-in of a used delivery truck with a book value of $3,975.00. Memorandum No. 11 and Check No. 107.*

The plant asset record for the used delivery truck immediately before the trade-in transaction is shown below.

PLANT ASSET RECORD — ACCOUNT NO. 121

ITEM Delivery truck — GENERAL LEDGER ACCOUNT Delivery Equipment
SERIAL NO. KM 567009 — DESCRIPTION Almo Side Panel
FROM WHOM PURCHASED Ames Motors, Cleveland Ohio
ESTIMATED LIFE 4 years — ESTIMATED SALVAGE OR TRADE-IN VALUE 1,500.00 — DEPRECIATION PER YEAR 1,350.00

DATE MO. DAY YR.	EXPLANATION	ASSET DR.	CR.	BAL.	ACCUMULATED DEPRECIATION DR.	CR.	BAL.	BOOK VALUE
1 5 75		6,900.00		6,900.00				6,900.00
12 31 75						1,350.00	1,350.00	5,550.00
12 31 76						1,350.00	2,700.00	4,200.00

Recording depreciation for part of a fiscal period

The delivery truck is traded on February 21. A journal entry is needed to record the depreciation for the two-month period, January 1, 1977, to February 21, 1977. The amount of depreciation for the two months (one sixth of a year), is $225.00.

The general journal entry to record the depreciation for two months is shown below.

GENERAL JOURNAL — PAGE 2

ACCOUNTS PAYABLE DEBIT	GENERAL DEBIT	DATE	ACCOUNT TITLE	POST. REF.	GENERAL CREDIT	ACCOUNTS RECEIV. CREDIT
	225 00	1977 Feb. 21	Depr. Exp.-Delivery Equip.			
			Accum. Depr.-Del. Equip.		225 00	
			Memorandum No. 11.			

Entry to record estimated depreciation for part of a fiscal period

The plant asset record is brought up to date by recording the depreciation for two months. The plant asset record then shows a total accumulated depreciation of $2,925.00. The cost of the used delivery truck, $6,900.00, less the total accumulated depreciation, $2,925.00, equals the book value, $3,975.00, on February 21, 1977.

Recording the trading in of a plant asset

The cost price to be recorded for the new truck is:

Book value of used truck traded in............................... $3,975.00
Plus the cash payment for new truck 2,500.00

Equals the cost price of the new truck $6,475.00

The new truck is recorded at a cost price of $6,475.00 regardless of the advertised price of the new truck.

The analysis of this transaction to record the trading in of a plant asset is shown in the T accounts at the right.

Delivery Equipment is debited for $6,475.00 to show the increase in the balance of this plant asset account. This amount is the cost price of the new truck.

Accumulated Depreciation — Delivery Equipment is debited for $2,925.00 to show the decrease in the balance of this valuation account. This amount is the total depreciation recorded on the used truck at the time of the trade-in.

Delivery Equipment	121
6,475.00	6,900.00

Accumulated Depreciation — Delivery Equipment	121.1
2,925.00	

Cash	111
	2,500.00

Delivery Equipment is credited for $6,900.00 to show the decrease in the balance of this plant asset account. This amount cancels the original cost of $6,900.00 debited to the delivery equipment account when the truck was bought in 1975.

Cash is credited for $2,500.00 to show the decrease in the balance of this asset account. This amount is the cash payment made to complete the buying of a new truck.

The entry in the cash payments journal to record the buying of a new truck with a trade-in is shown below.

Entry to record the trade-in of a plant asset

CASH PAYMENTS JOURNAL — PAGE 2

DATE	ACCOUNT TITLE	CHECK No.	POST. REF.	GENERAL DEBIT	GENERAL CREDIT	ACCOUNTS PAYABLE DEBIT	PURCHASES DISCOUNT CREDIT	CASH CREDIT
21	Delivery Equipment	107		647500				250000
	Accum. Depr.-Del. Equip.			292500				
	Delivery Equipment				690000			

OTHER REVENUE AND OTHER EXPENSES
ON THE INCOME STATEMENT

A business may have revenue and expenses that do not result directly from the regular operations of the business. These nonoperating revenue and expense items are classified separately on the income statement. The income statement of Phillips Paper Products shown below includes the nonoperating revenue account Gain on Plant Assets and the nonoperating expense account Loss on Plant Assets.

Phillips Paper Products				
Income Statement				
For Year Ended December 31, 1977				
Operating Revenue:				
Sales			11915255	
Less Sales Returns + Allow.			94280	
Net Sales				11820975
Cost of Merchandise Sold:				
Mdse. Inventory, Jan. 1, 1977			3872605	
Purchases		5832354		
Less: Purch. Ret. + Allow. 1,246.20				
Purchases Discount 1,411.70		265790		
Net Purchases			5566564	
Total Cost of Mdse. Avail. for Sale			9439169	
Less Mdse. Inventory, Dec. 31, 1977			4231700	
Cost of Merchandise Sold				5207469
Gross Profit on Operations				6613506
Operating Expenses:				
Bad Debts Expense			45265	
Delivery Expense			162540	
Depr. Exp. - Delivery Equip.			165000	
Depreciation Exp. - Store Equip.			36014	
Insurance Expense			53000	
Miscellaneous Expense			240375	
Payroll Taxes Expense			261210	
Rent Expense			500000	
Salary Expense			3482800	
Supplies Expense			50050	
Total Operating Expenses				4996254
Income from Operations				1617252
Other Revenue:				
Gain on Plant Assets			40700	
Other Expense:				
Loss on Plant Assets			28160	
Net Addition				12540
Net Income				1629792

Income statement showing Other Revenue and Other Expense

The differences between this income statement and those shown previously in this text are:

Line 1. The more complete title *Operating Revenue* is used instead of *Revenue.* The more complete title distinguishes sales revenue from other revenue shown on Line 28.

Line 27. The gross profit on operations minus the operating expenses is given the title *Income from Operations.* This title distinguishes between revenue from the regular operations of the business and the net income after other revenue and other expense are included.

Lines 28 and 29. Phillips Paper Products is not in business to make a profit on the sale of its plant assets. A gain on the disposal of a plant asset is not, therefore, considered part of the regular operating revenue. The revenue account Gain on Plant Assets is listed separately on the income statement under the heading *Other Revenue.*

Lines 30 and 31. A business sometimes will have an expense that is not an operating expense of the business. The expense account Loss on Plant Assets is an example of a nonoperating expense. The account is listed on the income statement under the heading *Other Expense.*

The chart of accounts for Phillips Paper Products, page 504, shows the location of Other Revenue and Other Expense accounts in the general ledger.

Lines 32 and 33. The amount by which the Other Revenue exceeds the Other Expense is labeled *Net Addition* on the income statement. The Net Addition is added to the Income from Operations, Line 27. The sum is the *Net Income,* Line 33, of the business for the fiscal period.

When Other Revenue is less than Other Expense, the difference is labeled *Net Subtraction.* This amount is subtracted from the Income from Operations as shown below.

Income from Operations		6,219.65
Other Revenue:		
Gain on Plant Assets	178.39	
Other Expense:		
Loss on Plant Assets	252.35	
Net Subtraction		73.96
Net Income		6,145.69

Partial income statement showing Other Revenue less than Other Expense

Closing entries for accounts classified as Other Revenue and Other Expense

Accounts classified as Other Revenue and Other Expense are closed into Income Summary. These accounts are closed in the same manner and at the same time as are the operating revenue and operating expense accounts.

**Using
Business
Terms**
✦ What is the meaning of each of the following?

       • gain on plant assets   • loss on plant assets

**Questions
for
Individual
Study**

1. What are three ways to dispose of plant assets?
2. What accounting record contains the data needed by an accountant to determine whether there is a gain or loss when disposing of a plant asset?
3. When a plant asset is disposed of during a fiscal period, why is depreciation recorded before the entry is journalized showing disposition of the plant asset?
4. When can the actual value of a plant asset be determined?
5. What is the name of the account in which the increases in the value of a plant asset are recorded at the time of disposal?
6. What is the name of the account in which decreases in the value of a plant asset are recorded at the time of disposal?
7. What determines the amount that will be debited to the accumulated depreciation account when a plant asset is disposed of?

8. What determines the amount to be credited to the plant asset account when a plant asset is disposed of?
9. What effect would it have on the financial records if the depreciation for part of a year, as described in question 3, were not recorded?
10. When cash and a used plant asset are given in payment for a new plant asset of a similar kind, what amount is debited to the equipment account for the new plant asset?
11. Why is revenue from sales listed under the heading Operating Revenue on the income statement of Phillips Paper Products, page 564?
12. Under what heading on an income statement is Gain on Plant Assets listed?
13. Under what heading on an income statement is Loss on Plant Assets listed?
14. Why is Loss on Plant Assets not listed under operating expenses on the income statement?

**Cases for
Management
Decision**

CASE 1 Jamie Watson operates a pizza shop. He has a small, used car he uses for making deliveries. In his accounting records, he does not record depreciation on the car at the end of each fiscal period. An accountant advises him to make an adjustment for depreciation.

Mr. Watson says that he does not make the entries because he has only the one plant asset. The amount of depreciation expense for each year is small. He plans to record his gain or loss on the car when he disposes of it. Which is the better plan? Why is it better?

CASE 2 When Joseph Bower disposes of plant assets in his business, he usually records a large gain on the asset. This has been true for the past ten years. Mr. Bower thinks that this gain results because the price of most items, including used plant

assets, is increasing every year. Mrs. Bower, however, suggests that he may not be figuring the amount of depreciation expense correctly. With whom do you agree? Why?

CASE 3 Martha Mount decides to discard a filing cabinet used in her business. The plant asset records show that the accumulated depreciation is the same as the original cost price of the cabinet. Ms. Mount contends that because the cabinet has no

book value, one amount off-sets the other. Therefore, no entry is necessary to record the disposing of the cabinet. A friend recommends that an entry should be made to write off the values related to the filing cabinet. With whom do you agree? Why?

DRILL 29-D 1 Figuring gain or loss on plant assets

Instructions: For each of the following plant assets, figure (a) the accumulated depreciation, (b) the book value, and (c) the amount of the gain or loss when disposed of.

Item	Date of Purchase	Original Cost	Estimated Salvage Value	Estimated Life	Date of Disposal	Disposition
1	Jan. 2, 1974	$350.00	$ 50.00	5 years	Jan. 6, 1978	Sold for $ 80.00
2	July 2, 1974	242.00	50.00	4 years	Jan. 8, 1978	Sold for $ 80.00
3	July 5, 1972	600.00	200.00	10 years	Apr. 3, 1978	Sold for $300.00
4	Apr. 28, 1972	150.00	none	5 years	Mar. 27, 1978	Discarded
5	Oct. 1, 1970	800.00	none	8 years	Mar. 31, 1978	Discarded
6	May 1, 1975	650.00	50.00	10 years	Oct. 30, 1978	Sold for $480.00

DRILL 29-D 2 Figuring cost price for trade in of plant assets

Instructions: For each of the following plant assets, figure (a) the book value of the item traded in, and (b) the cost price of the new item bought.

Item	Original Cost of Used Item	Accumulated Depreciation Recorded on Used Item	Cash Payment
1	$ 6,000.00	$2,400.00	$3,000.00
2	10,000.00	7,000.00	6,000.00
3	4,000.00	1,600.00	2,600.00

PROBLEM 29-1 Buying and disposing of plant assets

Instructions: □ **1.** Open the following accounts in the general ledger of Rosemary Young who owns and manages a millinery shop. Record the balances as of January 1 of the current year.

Delivery Equipment...	121	$7,200.00
Accumulated Depreciation — Delivery Equipment	121.1	4,300.00
Store Equipment	122	6,000.00
Accumulated Depreciation — Store Equipment...................	122.1	2,400.00
Depreciation Expense — Delivery Equipment.....................	613	——
Depreciation Expense — Store Equipment.........................	614	——
Gain on Plant Assets	711	——
Loss on Plant Assets..	811	——

Instructions: □ **2.** Record the following transactions selected from those completed by Miss Young during the current year. Use a cash receipts journal (page 26), a cash payments journal (page 25), and a general journal (page 21) like those shown in this chapter. Post from the General columns of the three journals after *each* entry is recorded. Source documents are abbreviated as: check, Ck; memorandum, M; receipt, R.

Jan.   3. Bought new display case, $700.00. Ck206.

Jan.   5. Discarded table (store equipment) that originally cost $100.00 and that has a book value of $10.00. M26.

Apr.   7. Received cash, $20.00, from sale of a showcase that originally cost $250.00 and that has a book value on January 1 of $100.00. Additional depreciation for the period January 1 to April 7 is $10.00. R241 and M37.

May 19. Bought a mirror table (store equipment) for $300.00. Ck429.

July   3. Bought a new truck for $4,000.00 cash plus trade-in of a used truck. Original cost value of the used truck is $4,800.00. Annual depreciation on the used truck is $900.00. Accumulated depreciation recorded on the used truck on January 1 of the current year is $2,950.00. M84 and Ck543.

  (a) Record depreciation for the current year to June 30 on used truck.

  (b) Record the purchase of the new truck and the trade-in of the used truck.

July   6. Received cash, $25.00, from sale of sewing machine that originally cost $180.00 and that has a book value of $15.00. R278.

Dec. 31. Record estimated depreciation for the year based on the following: depreciation expense for delivery equipment, $850.00; depreciation expense for store equipment, $670.00.

PROBLEM 29-2 Work at the end of a fiscal period

If you are not using the workbook correlating with this textbook, complete Review Problem 29-R 1 instead of this problem.

The trial balance of the general ledger of Mercer's Household Supplies as of December 31 of the current year is shown on the work sheet in the workbook.

Instructions: □ 1. Complete the eight-column work sheet for the fiscal year ended December 31 of the current year. Additional data needed are:

  Allowance for Uncollectible Accounts should equal ½% of the balance of the accounts receivable account.
  Merchandise Inventory, $17,762.00.
  Supplies Inventory, $358.00.
  Value of insurance policies, $360.00.
  Annual depreciation of equipment, $729.50.

□ 2. Prepare an income statement, a capital statement, and a balance sheet.

□ 3. Record the adjusting entries and the closing entries on page 12 of a four-column general journal.

MASTERY
PROBLEM 29-M Buying and disposing of plant assets

Instructions: □ 1. Open the following accounts in the general ledger of Dunham Company. Record the account balances as of January 1 of the current year.

Delivery Equipment...	121	$5,600.00
Accumulated Depreciation — Delivery Equipment	121.1	2,805.00
Store Equipment	122	3,580.00
Accumulated Depreciation — Store Equipment...................	122.1	1,890.00
Depreciation Expense — Delivery Equipment....................	613	——
Depreciation Expense — Store Equipment........................	614	——
Gain on Plant Assets...	711	——
Loss on Plant Assets..	811	——

Instructions: ◻ **2.** Record the following transactions selected from those completed during the current year. Use a cash receipts journal (page 10), a cash payments journal (page 12), and a general journal (page 8) like those shown in this chapter. Post from the General columns of the three journals after *each* entry is recorded. Source documents are abbreviated as: check, Ck; memorandum, M; receipt, R.

Jan. 2. Bought store equipment, $410.00. Ck174.

Jan. 3. Discarded store equipment that originally cost $175.00 and that has a book value of $25.00. M2.

Jan. 10. Bought a new delivery truck, $5,800.00. Ck182.

Jan. 12. Received cash, $45.00, from sale of store equipment that originally cost $100.00 and that has a book value of $35.00. R43.

June 30. Bought new cash register for $930.00 cash plus trade-in of used cash register that originally cost $1,000.00. Depreciation on used cash register is $90.00 a year; accumulated depreciation to January 1 of current year is $675.00. M68 and Ck309.

Nov. 13. Received cash, $10.00, from sale of delivery equipment that originally cost $137.00 and that has a book value of $15.00 as of January 1. Annual depreciation on equipment is $24.00. R250 and M96.

Dec. 31. Record depreciation expense for the year: depreciation on delivery equipment, $1,360.00; depreciation on store equipment, $455.00.

BONUS
PROBLEM 29-B Buying and disposing of plant assets

Instructions: ◻ **1.** Open the following accounts in the ledger of Karl Mickleson:

Delivery Equipment..	121
Accumulated Depreciation — Delivery Equipment	121.1
Office Equipment	122
Accumulated Depreciation — Office Equipment.................................	122.1
Income Summary..	313
Depreciation Expense — Delivery Equipment.....................................	613
Depreciation Expense — Office Equipment..	614
Gain on Plant Assets	711
Loss on Plant Assets...	811

◻ **2.** Record the following selected transactions in a cash receipts journal (page 10), a cash payments journal (page 15), and a general journal (page 23). Source documents are abbreviated as: check, Ck; memorandum, M; receipt, R.

Jan.   3, 1977. Bought a used delivery truck, $2,300.00, with an estimated trade-in value of $500.00 and estimated life of 2 years. Ck8.

Jan.   6, 1977. Bought a used adding machine, $75.00, with no estimated trade-in value and an estimated life of 5 years. Ck13.

Dec. 31, 1977. Made adjusting entries to record depreciation for the year.

    Instructions: ◻ **3.** Post the entries for 1977 to the accounts opened in the ledger.

◻ **4.** Make an entry to close the depreciation expense accounts on December 31, 1977. Post the closing entry.

◻ **5.** Record the following selected transactions.

Jan. 10, 1978. Discarded as useless the adding machine bought on January 6, 1977. M3.

Jan. 11, 1978. Bought a new adding machine, $700.00, with estimated trade-in value of $50.00 and estimated life of 10 years. Ck22.

July   3, 1978. Sold delivery truck bought January 3, 1977, for $700.00 cash.
        (a) Record the depreciation for the current year to July 3. M70.
        (b) Record the sale of the truck. R115.

July   3, 1978. Bought a new delivery truck, $5,500.00, with an estimated trade-in value of $750.00 and an estimated life of 5 years. Ck151.

Dec. 28, 1978. Traded in the delivery truck bought on July 3, 1978, for a newer model at a cost price of $700.00 cash plus the book value of the used truck.
        (a) Record the depreciation from July 3 to December 28 of the current year. M126.
        (b) Record the purchase of the new truck and the trade-in of the used truck. The new truck is estimated to have a trade-in value of $925.00 and a useful life of 5 years. Ck302.

Dec. 31, 1978. Made adjusting entries to record the depreciation expense for the year.

    Instructions: ◻ **6.** Post the entries for 1978.

◻ **7.** Make an entry to close the revenue and the expense accounts on December 31, 1978. Post the closing entry.

New Horizons

Select Camping Gear
A Business Simulation

Special Journals
New Horizons

B225-2   Name

Checkbook
New Horizons

B225-4   NAME

GENERAL LEDGER
New Horizons

B225-3

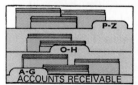

P-Z
O-H
A-G
ACCOUNTS RECEIVABLE

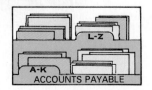

L-Z
A-K
ACCOUNTS PAYABLE

Files

You have learned the principles of accounting for a variety of transactions and the use of special journals for recording them. You are ready to apply these principles to realistic situations included in the NEW HORIZONS business simulation. NEW HORIZONS uses the books shown above in its cash register accounting system. A pictorial flowchart of the accounting cycle for NEW HORIZONS is shown on the next two pages. A block flowchart and a symbolic flowchart are shown on pages 574 and 575.

(The narrative is provided in the set available from the publisher.)

Flowchart of the
Accounting Cycle of

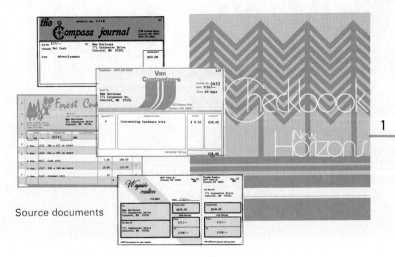

Source documents

1   Journalize from the source documents to the appropriate special journal.
1a-b After journalizing, file the source documents, the sales slips, and the purchase invoices in
     the appropriate files.
2   Post the items to be posted individually to the general ledger.
3   Post the column totals to the general ledger.
4   Prepare schedules of accounts receivable and accounts payable.
5   Complete the trial balance columns on the work sheet.
6   Enter the adjustments and complete the work sheet.
7   Prepare the financial statements.
8   Journalize the adjusting and closing entries from the work sheet.
9   Post the adjusting and closing entries to the general ledger.
10   Prepare a post-closing trial balance from the general ledger.

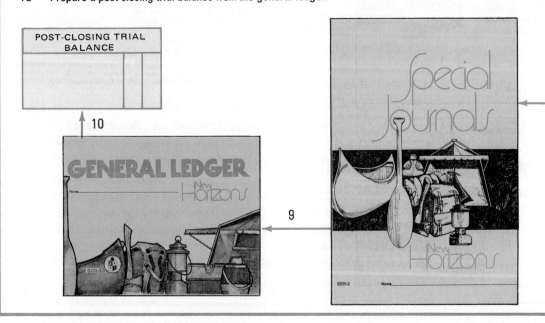

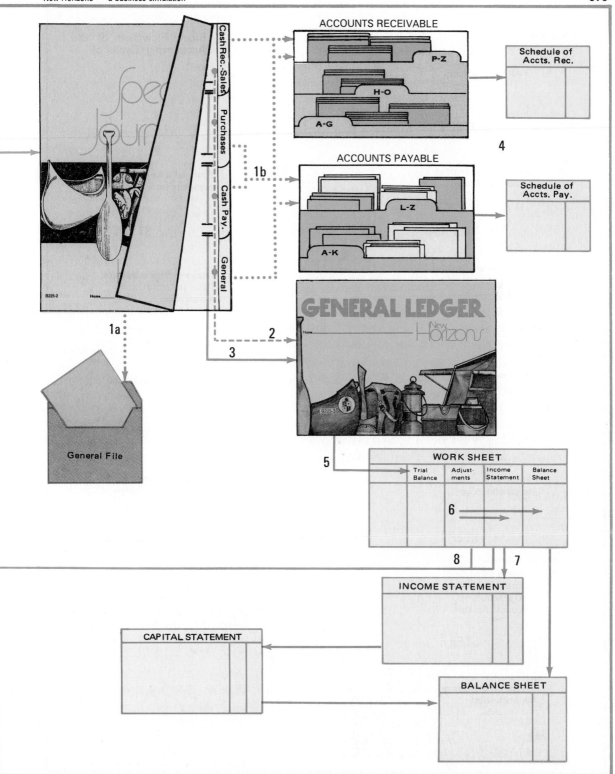

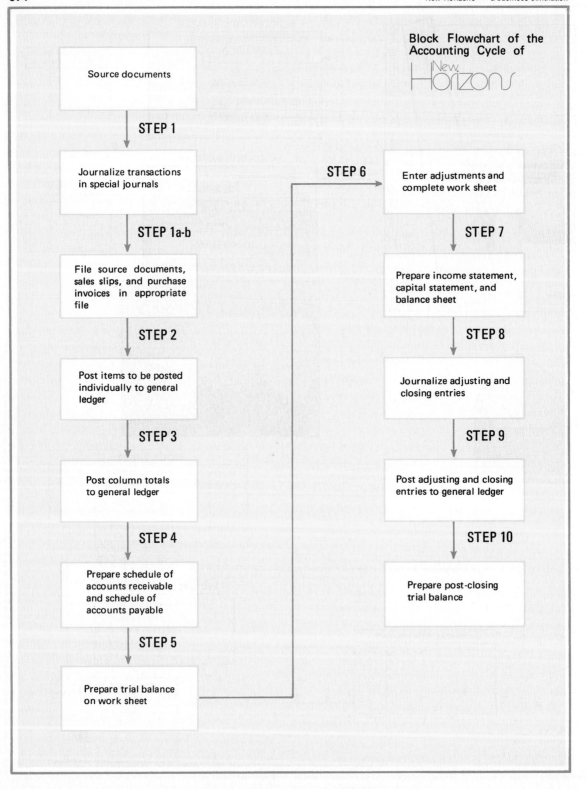

Block Flowchart of the Accounting Cycle of New Horizons

Source documents

STEP 1

Journalize transactions in special journals

STEP 1a-b

File source documents, sales slips, and purchase invoices in appropriate file

STEP 2

Post items to be posted individually to general ledger

STEP 3

Post column totals to general ledger

STEP 4

Prepare schedule of accounts receivable and schedule of accounts payable

STEP 5

Prepare trial balance on work sheet

STEP 6

Enter adjustments and complete work sheet

STEP 7

Prepare income statement, capital statement, and balance sheet

STEP 8

Journalize adjusting and closing entries

STEP 9

Post adjusting and closing entries to general ledger

STEP 10

Prepare post-closing trial balance

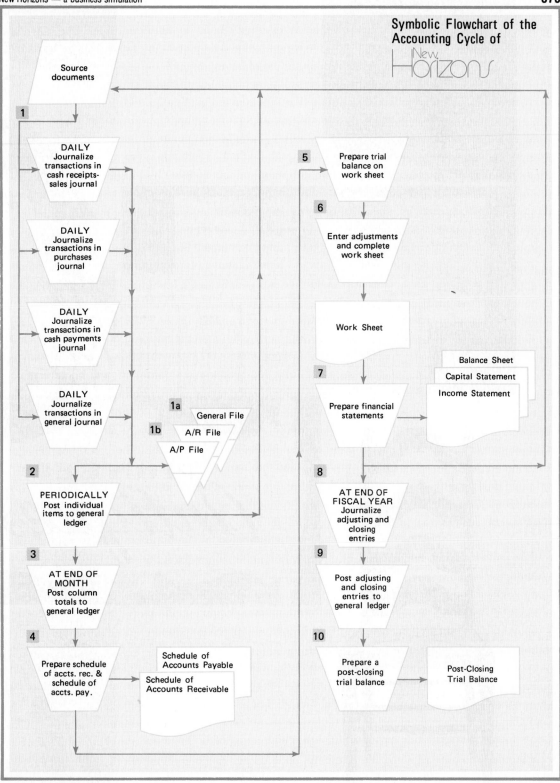

Symbolic Flowchart of the Accounting Cycle of
New Horizons

Source documents

1

DAILY Journalize transactions in cash receipts-sales journal

DAILY Journalize transactions in purchases journal

DAILY Journalize transactions in cash payments journal

DAILY Journalize transactions in general journal

1a General File

1b A/R File

A/P File

2 PERIODICALLY Post individual items to general ledger

3 AT END OF MONTH Post column totals to general ledger

4 Prepare schedule of accts. rec. & schedule of accts. pay.

Schedule of Accounts Payable

Schedule of Accounts Receivable

5 Prepare trial balance on work sheet

6 Enter adjustments and complete work sheet

Work Sheet

7 Prepare financial statements

Balance Sheet

Capital Statement

Income Statement

8 AT END OF FISCAL YEAR Journalize adjusting and closing entries

9 Post adjusting and closing entries to general ledger

10 Prepare a post-closing trial balance

Post-Closing Trial Balance

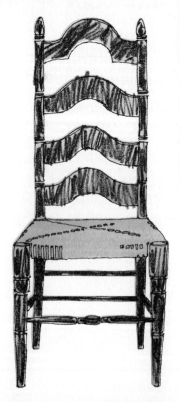

PART 7

ACCOUNTING FOR NOTES, ACCRUED REVENUE, AND ACCRUED EXPENSES

MOST BUSINESSES DEAL WITH NOTES AND INTEREST ON NOTES. When businesses need additional money to operate, they may issue notes payable. To grant an extension of time on credit sales, many businesses accept notes receivable from customers. Good accounting procedures maintain accurate records of notes outstanding and interest paid and received.

ADJUSTING ENTRIES FOR ACCRUED REVENUES AND ACCRUED EXPENSES ARE IMPORTANT. Accrued revenue is a revenue that has been earned but not yet received. Accrued expense is an expense that has been incurred but not yet paid. End-of-fiscal-period adjusting entries for accrued revenues and accrued expenses are essential if all revenues earned and expenditures incurred are to be included in the financial statements.

In Part 7 of this textbook, we shall learn how a business, *Pioneer Antiques*, accounts for notes receivable, notes payable, accrued revenues, and accrued expenses.

PIONEER ANTIQUES
CHART OF ACCOUNTS

Balance Sheet Accounts

(1) ASSETS	Account Number
11 Current Assets	
Cash	111
Petty Cash	112
Notes Receivable	113
Interest Receivable	114
Accounts Receivable	115
Allowance for Uncollectible Accounts	115.1
Merchandise Inventory	116
Supplies	117
Prepaid Insurance	118
12 Plant Assets	
Store Equipment	121
Accumulated Depreciation— Store Equipment	121.1
Office Equipment	122
Accumulated Depreciation— Office Equipment	122.1

(2) LIABILITIES	
21 Current Liabilities	
Notes Payable	211
Interest Payable	212
Salaries Payable	213
Accounts Payable	214
Employees Income Tax Payable	215
FICA Tax Payable	216
Federal Unemployment Tax Payable	217
State Unemployment Tax Payable	218
Sales Tax Payable	219

(3) CAPITAL	
L. R. Hays, Capital	311
L. R. Hays, Drawing	312
Income Summary	313

Income Statement Accounts

(4) OPERATING REVENUE	Account Number
Sales	411
Sales Returns and Allowances	411.1

(5) COST OF MERCHANDISE	
Purchases	511
Purchases Returns and Allowances	511.1
Purchases Discount	511.2

(6) OPERATING EXPENSES	
Bad Debts Expense	611
Delivery Expense	612
Depreciation Expense — Office Equipment	613
Depreciation Expense — Store Equipment	614
Insurance Expense	615
Miscellaneous Expense	616
Payroll Taxes Expense	617
Rent Expense	618
Salary Expense	619
Supplies Expense	620

(7) OTHER REVENUE	
Gain on Plant Assets	711
Interest Income	712

(8) OTHER EXPENSES	
Loss on Plant Assets	811
Interest Expense	812

The chart of accounts for Pioneer Antiques is illustrated above for ready reference in your study of Chapters 30 and 31 in Part 7 of this book.

Notes and Interest

30

A written and signed promise to pay a sum of money on demand or on a definite date is called a promissory note. A promissory note is frequently referred to simply as a note.

Promissory notes are used by individuals and businesses to borrow money or to obtain an extension of time on an account. Sometimes a business requests a note from a charge customer when the buyer wants credit beyond the usual time given for sales on account. Notes have an advantage over oral promises and open accounts. If the business wants its money before the note is due, the note, like a check, can be endorsed and transferred to a bank. The bank then gives the business cash for the note. Notes can also be useful in a court of law as evidence of a debt.

One form of a promissory note is illustrated at the right.

A promissory note

The terms defined below are used in analyzing this note.

Terms	Definitions	The Illustration
1 Date	The day the note is issued.	March 25, 1977
2 Time	The days or months from the date of issue until the note is to be paid.	Sixty days
3 Payee	The one to whom a note is payable.	Wentz Company
4 Principal	The amount the borrower promises to pay — the face of the note.	$800.00
5 Interest rate	The percentage of the principal that is paid for the use of the money.	8%
6 Maturity date	The date the note is due.	May 24, 1977
7 Maker	The one who signs the note and thus promises to make payment.	L. R. Hays
8 Number	Number assigned by the maker to identify the specific note.	3

579

INTEREST ON NOTES

A sum of money paid for the use of the principal of a note for a period of time is called interest. Most promissory notes require the payment of interest. Promissory notes that require interest payments are called interest-bearing notes. Promissory notes that do not contain a provision for the payment of interest are called non-interest-bearing notes.

The interest rate is stated as a percentage of the principal. Interest at 8% means that 8 cents will be paid for the use of each dollar borrowed for a full year. The interest on $100.00 for a full year at 8% is $8.00.

The principal of a note plus the interest on the note is called the maturity value. A one-year note for $100.00 with an 8 percent interest rate will have a maturity value of $108.00 ($100.00 principal plus $8.00 interest).

> Sometimes partial payments are made on a note each month. This is particularly true when an individual buys a car and signs a note for the amount owed. The monthly payment includes part of the money owed and part of the interest to be paid.

Computing interest

To compute interest for one year, the principal is multiplied by the interest rate. The interest on a 6% interest-bearing note for $600.00 for 1 year is:

Principal	×	Interest Rate	=	Interest for 1 Year
$600.00	×	.06	=	$36.00

To compute interest for a period of less than one year, the principal is multiplied by the interest rate and by the fraction of the year. The interest on an 8% interest-bearing note for $600.00 for 4 months is:

$$\text{Principal} \times \text{Interest Rate} \times \text{Fraction of Year} = \text{Interest for Fraction of Year}$$

$$\$600.00 \times .08 \times \frac{4}{12} = \frac{\$192.00}{12} = \$16.00$$

The time of a note is often stated as a number of days, such as 30 days, 60 days, or 90 days. For convenience in computing interest, 360 days is commonly used as the number of days in a year. The interest on an 8% interest-bearing note for $800.00 for 90 days is:

$$\text{Principal} \times \text{Interest Rate} \times \text{Fraction of Year} = \text{Interest for Fraction of Year}$$

$$\$800.00 \times .08 \times \frac{90}{360} = \frac{\$5,760.00}{360} = \$16.00$$

Determining the maturity date

The time between the date a note is issued and the date the note is due may be expressed in either years, months, or days. When the time of a note is stated in months, the maturity date is found by counting the number of months from the date of issuance. For example, a two-month note dated March 18 would be due on May 18.

When the time of a note is expressed in days, the maturity date is determined by counting the exact number of days. To determine this date, find the number of days remaining in the month the note was written. Then add the days in the following months until the total equals the required number of days. For example, a 60-day note dated March 18 is due on May 17. The maturity date is found as follows:

March 18 to 31.....................................	13 days (31 − 18 = 13)
April 1 to 30..	30 days
May 1 to 17..	17 days (maturity date)
Total...	60 days

NOTES PAYABLE

Promissory notes that a business gives creditors are called notes payable. Notes payable are classified as current liabilities of a business.

Issuing a note payable to borrow money from a bank

On April 1, 1977, Pioneer Antiques arranges to borrow money from its bank. A note payable is issued to the bank as evidence of indebtedness. The bank credits the checking account of Pioneer Antiques for the principal amount of the note.

April 1, 1977. Issued a 6-month, 8% note to the First National Bank, $500.00. Note Payable No. 6.

Analyzing the issuance of a note payable. A copy of the note is the source document used by Pioneer Antiques for recording the transaction. In this transaction the balance of the asset account Cash is increased and the balance of the liability account Notes Payable is also increased. Therefore, Cash is debited for $500.00 and Notes Payable is credited for $500.00. No entry is made for the interest until a later date when the payment of interest is made.

Cash	111
500.00	

Notes Payable	211
	500.00

Recording the issuance of a note and the receipt of cash. This transaction is recorded in the cash receipts journal as shown on page 582.

| | | | | | | GENERAL | | SALES | SALES TAX | ACCOUNTS | CASH | |
| DATE | ACCOUNT TITLE | Doc. No. | Post. Ref. | DEBIT | CREDIT | CREDIT | PAYABLE CREDIT | RECEIVABLE CREDIT | DEBIT | |

CASH RECEIPTS JOURNAL   PAGE *24*

| | | 1 | 2 | 3 | 4 | 5 | 6 | |

6	*Notes Payable*	NP6		500 00					500 00	6
7										7
8										8
9										9

Entry to record cash received
for a note payable

The letters *NP* in the Doc. No. column stand for *Note Payable*.

Paying principal and interest on a note payable at maturity

When cash is paid for interest, the amount paid is debited to an expense account titled Interest Expense.

October 1, 1977. Paid the First National Bank in full for Note Payable No. 6 (principal, $500.00; interest, $20.00), $520.00. Check No. 399.

Notes Payable	211
500.00	

Interest Expense	812
20.00	

Cash	111
	520.00

Analyzing the payment of principal and interest. The check stub is the source document for recording the transaction. In this transaction the balance of the liability account Notes Payable is decreased; the balance of the expense account Interest Expense is increased; and the balance of the asset account Cash is decreased. Therefore, Notes Payable is debited for $500.00; Interest Expense is debited for $20.00; and Cash is credited for $520.00.

Recording the payment of principal and interest. This transaction is recorded in the cash payments journal as shown below.

CASH PAYMENTS JOURNAL   PAGE *33*

| | | | | | GENERAL | | ACCOUNTS PAYABLE | PURCHASES DISCOUNT | CASH | |
| DATE | ACCOUNT TITLE | Check No. | Post. Ref. | DEBIT | CREDIT | DEBIT | CREDIT | CREDIT | |

| | | | | 1 | 2 | 3 | 4 | 5 | |

3	{ *Notes Payable*	399		500 00				520 00	3
4	{ *Interest Expense*			20 00					4
5									5
6									6
7									7

Entry to record paying principal and
interest on a note payable at maturity

Issuing a note payable for an extension of time

If a business is unable to pay for a purchase on account when payment is due, the business may ask for an extension of time. Sometimes, when a request for more time is made, the business offers to issue an interest-bearing note payable. The note does not pay the amount owed to the creditor, but the form of the liability is changed from an account payable to a note payable.

> April 24, 1977. Issued a 60-day, 8% note to the Antique Furniture Company for an extension of time on this account payable, $840.00. Note Payable No. 7.

Analyzing the issuance of a note payable. A copy of the note is the source document for recording the transaction. In this transaction the balance of the liability account Accounts Payable is decreased and the balance of the liability account Notes Payable is increased. The balance of the creditor's account, Antique Furniture Company, in the accounts payable ledger, is also decreased. Therefore, Accounts Payable is debited for $840.00; Notes Payable is credited for $840.00; and the creditor's account, Antique Furniture Company, is debited for $840.00.

GENERAL LEDGER

Accounts Payable	214
840.00	

Notes Payable	211
	840.00

ACCOUNTS PAYABLE LEDGER

Antique Furniture Company	
840.00	

Whenever the accounts payable account in the general ledger is decreased, the proper creditor's account in the accounts payable ledger must also be decreased the same amount.

Recording the issuance of a note payable. This transaction is recorded in the four-column general journal as shown below.

	GENERAL JOURNAL			PAGE 22
ACCOUNTS PAYABLE DEBIT	GENERAL DEBIT	DATE	ACCOUNT TITLE	POST. REF.	GENERAL CREDIT	ACCOUNTS RECEIV. CREDIT

1	2		3	4
840 00		24 Antique Furniture Company		
			Notes Payable	840 00	
			Note Payable No. 7.		

Entry to record the issuance of a note payable
for an extension of time on an account payable

When this entry is posted, the account payable account with Antique Furniture Company will be closed and replaced by the note payable.

Paying a note payable. Note Payable No. 7 is due on June 23. On that date, Pioneer Antiques issues a check for $851.20 to Antique Furniture Company in payment of the principal, $840.00, and interest, $11.20. This check is recorded in the cash payments journal in the same way as the payment of Note Payable No. 6 is recorded. Notes Payable is debited for $840.00; Interest Expense is debited for $11.20; and Cash is credited for $851.20.

Bank discount

Some banks require the borrower to pay all the interest in advance at the time that a note is signed. Interest collected in advance by a bank on a note is called bank discount. The amount received for a note after the bank has deducted the bank discount is called proceeds. A note on which interest is paid in advance is called a discounted note.

May 25, 1977. Discounted at 10% at the First National Bank our 6-month, non-interest-bearing note, $2,000.00. Note Payable No. 8. The bank credited our checking account for the proceeds, $1,900.00.

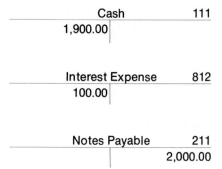

Analyzing the issuance of a discounted note payable. A copy of the note is the source document for recording the transaction. In this transaction, the balances of the asset account Cash and the expense account Interest Expense are increased. The balance of the liability account is also increased. Therefore, Cash is debited for $1,900.00; Interest Expense is debited for $100.00; and Notes Payable is credited for $2,000.00. The amount of interest is computed as:

Maturity Value	×	Interest Rate	×	Time	= Interest
$2,000.00	×	10%	×	$\frac{6}{12}$ Year	= $100.00

The proceeds are computed as:

Maturity Value	− Interest	= Proceeds
$2,000.00	− $100.00	= $1,900.00

Recording the issuance of a discounted note and the receipt of cash. This transaction is recorded in the cash receipts journal as shown at the top of the next page.

		CASH RECEIPTS JOURNAL					PAGE 27	
			1	2	3	4	5	6
DATE	ACCOUNT TITLE	Doc. No.	Post. Ref.	GENERAL		SALES CREDIT	SALES TAX PAYABLE CREDIT	ACCOUNTS RECEIVABLE CREDIT	CASH DEBIT
				DEBIT	CREDIT				
6	{25 Notes Payable	NP8			200000				190000	6
7	{ Interest Expense			10000						7

Entry to record cash received
for a discounted note payable

Recording the payment of a discounted note payable. When Note Payable No. 8 is paid on November 25, Check No. 452 is issued to the First National Bank in payment of the principal. No payment of interest is necessary at this time because the bank collected the interest in advance. This transaction is recorded in the cash payments journal as shown below.

		CASH PAYMENTS JOURNAL					PAGE 35	
			1	2	3	4	5	
DATE	ACCOUNT TITLE	Check No.	Post. Ref.	GENERAL		ACCOUNTS PAYABLE DEBIT	PURCHASES DISCOUNT CREDIT	CASH CREDIT
				DEBIT	CREDIT			
8	25 Notes Payable	452		200000				200000	8

Entry to record the payment of
a discounted note payable

NOTES RECEIVABLE

Promissory notes that a business accepts from customers are called notes receivable. Notes receivable are classified as current assets of a business.

Accepting a note receivable from a customer

A charge customer who is unable to pay an account on the due date may request additional time. A note may be accepted from the charge customer as a means of granting an extension of time for payment of the account. The note receivable does not pay the amount the customer owes, but the form of the asset is changed from an account receivable to a note receivable.

> May 12, 1977. Received a 3-month, 8% note from J. G. Haworth for an extension of time on this account receivable, $200.00. Note Receivable No. 23.

Analyzing the acceptance of a note receivable. The original copy of a note receivable is the source document for recording the transaction. In this transaction the balance of the asset account Notes Receivable is

GENERAL LEDGER

Notes Receivable	113
200.00	

Accounts Receivable	115
	200.00

*ACCOUNTS RECEIVABLE
LEDGER*

J. G. Haworth	
	200.00

increased and the balance of the asset account Accounts Receivable is decreased. The balance of the customer's account, J. G. Haworth, in the accounts receivable ledger is also decreased. Therefore, Notes Receivable is debited for $200.00; Accounts Receivable is credited for $200.00; and the customer's account, J. G. Haworth, is credited for $200.00.

Whenever the accounts receivable account in the general ledger is decreased, the proper customer's account in the accounts receivable ledger must also be decreased the same amount.

Recording the acceptance of a note receivable. This transaction is recorded in the four-column general journal as shown below.

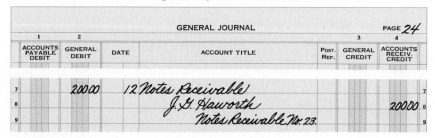

Entry to record a note received for an extension of time on an account

When this entry is posted, the account receivable account with J. G. Haworth will be closed and will be replaced by the note receivable.

Collecting principal and interest on a note receivable at maturity

The amount of interest received is credited to a revenue account titled Interest Income.

August 12, 1977. Received cash from J. G. Haworth in settlement of Note Receivable No. 23 (principal, $200.00; interest, $4.00), $204.00. Receipt No. 788.

Cash	111
204.00	

Notes Receivable	113
	200.00

Interest Income	712
	4.00

Analyzing the receipt of principal and interest. The receipt for the cash received from J. G. Haworth is the source document for recording the transaction. In this transaction the balance of the asset account Cash is increased; the balance of the asset account Notes Receivable is decreased; and the balance of the revenue account Interest Income is increased. Therefore, Cash is debited for $204.00; Notes Receivable is credited for $200.00; and Interest Income is credited for $4.00.

Recording the receipt of principal and interest. This transaction is recorded in the cash receipts journal as shown at the top of page 587.

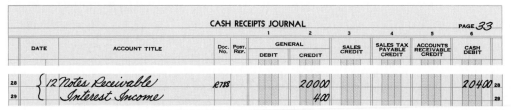

Entry to record collection of principal and interest on a note receivable at maturity

After the entry is recorded, Note Receivable No. 23 is marked *Paid* by the accountant and is returned to J. G. Haworth, the maker.

Dishonored note receivable

A note that is not paid when due is called a dishonored note.

The balance of the notes receivable account should show only the amount of those notes that probably will be collected. The amount of a dishonored note receivable should therefore be removed from the notes receivable account. The amount is still owed by the customer. Therefore, the amount owed should be debited to the accounts receivable account in the general ledger and to the customer's account in the accounts receivable ledger. The customer's account will then show the total amount owed by the customer, including the amount of the dishonored note. This information may be important if the customer requests credit in the future.

November 17, 1977. A. C. Debold dishonored Note Receivable No. 36, a non-interest-bearing note for $300.00 due today. Memorandum No. 301.

Analyzing a dishonored note receivable. The memorandum is the source document for analyzing and recording the transaction. In this transaction the balance of the asset account Accounts Receivable in the general ledger and the balance of the customer's account in the accounts receivable ledger are increased. The balance of the asset account Notes Receivable is decreased. Therefore, Accounts Receivable and A. C. Debold are each debited for $300.00; Notes Receivable is credited for $300.00.

GENERAL LEDGER

Accounts Receivable	115
300.00	

Notes Receivable	113
	300.00

ACCOUNTS RECEIVABLE LEDGER

A. C. Debold
300.00

Recording a dishonored note receivable. This transaction is recorded in the four-column general journal as shown on page 588.

If Mr. Hays, the payee, later decides that collection cannot be obtained from Mr. Debold, the balance of the account will be written off as a bad debt. At that time Allowance for Uncollectible Accounts will be debited, and Accounts Receivable and A. C. Debold's account will be credited.

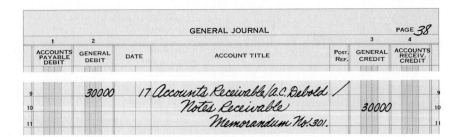

Entry to record a
dishonored note
receivable

REPORTING NOTES AND INTEREST ON
FINANCIAL STATEMENTS

The chart of accounts of Pioneer Antiques on page 578 shows where notes and interest appear on the financial statements.

Notes receivable and notes payable on the balance sheet

The asset account Notes Receivable is classified as a current asset and is reported on the balance sheet in the Current Assets section. The balance of the notes receivable account represents the total principal of the notes receivable on hand on the date of the balance sheet.

The liability account Notes Payable is classified as a current liability and is reported on the balance sheet in the Current Liabilities section. The balance of the notes payable account represents the total principal of the notes payable outstanding on the date of the balance sheet.

Interest income and interest expense on the income statement

Interest income does not result from the normal operation of a merchandising business. The revenue account Interest Income is therefore classified as other revenue and is reported on the income statement in the Other Revenue section. The balance of the Interest Income account represents the total amount of interest income for the fiscal period.

Interest expense is not an operating expense of a merchandising business. The expense account Interest Expense is therefore classified as other expense and is reported on the income statement in the Other Expenses section. The balance of the interest expense account represents the total amount of interest expense for the fiscal period.

**Using
Business
Terms**

✦ What is the meaning of each of the following?

- promissory note
- date of a note
- time of a note
- payee of a note

- principal of a note
- interest rate of a note
- maturity date of a note
- maker of a note

- number of a note
- interest
- interest-bearing notes
- non-interest-bearing notes

- maturity value
- notes payable
- bank discount
- proceeds
- discounted note
- notes receivable
- dishonored note

1. What are the two common uses of promissory notes?
2. What advantages, if any, does a note have over an open account?
3. What is the difference between the payee and the maker of a note?
4. What does "interest at 6%" mean?
5. What is the basic formula for computing interest for less than a year?
6. When the time of a note is expressed in days, how is the maturity date of the note determined?
7. What accounts are debited and credited when a business borrows from a bank on an interest-bearing note?
8. What accounts are debited and credited when a business issues an interest-bearing note payable to a creditor as an extension of time on its account payable?
9. What accounts are debited and credited when a business pays the principal on a note payable at maturity?
10. What accounts are debited and credited when a non-interest-bearing note payable is discounted at the bank?
11. What accounts are debited and credited when a discounted note payable is paid at maturity?
12. What accounts are debited and credited when a note is accepted from a customer as an extension of time on the customer's account?
13. What accounts are debited and credited when a business receives the principal and the interest on a note receivable at maturity?
14. What accounts are debited and credited when a customer dishonors a non-interest-bearing note receivable?
15. How are the accounts Notes Receivable and Notes Payable listed on the balance sheet?
16. How are the accounts Interest Income and Interest Expense listed on the income statement?

CASE 1 George Abbott, a druggist, maintains a cash balance in his bank account sufficient to pay all his business bills when they become due. Alice Schmidt, another druggist, finds it necessary to borrow money from her bank at frequent intervals in order to pay her business bills on time. Both druggists have an equal volume of sales. How will these practices affect the net income for each business? Why?

CASE 2 Alex Wilkinson purchased $2,500.00 worth of merchandise on account from Wiley Furniture on March 1. Wiley's terms of sale require payment on accounts within 30 days. However, Mr. Wilkinson purchased the merchandise with the understanding that he could issue an 8 percent note payable with payment due June 1.

As Mr. Wilkinson's accountant, when do you recommend he issue the note payable to Wiley Furniture? Why?

DRILL 30-D 1 Computing maturity dates and interest on notes receivable

The Vaught Music Company has issued five notes payable. These notes are shown at the top of page 590.

Instructions: For each of the notes compute (a) the maturity date and (b) the interest. Use the appropriate formulas on pages 580 and 581.

No. of Note	Date of Note	Time	Interest Rate	Principal
126	March 1	1 year	8%	$ 400.00
127	March 1	90 days	8½%	600.00
128	March 12	6 months	9%	900.00
129	April 23	75 days	9¼%	1,000.00
130	August 4	1 month	10%	200.00

DRILL 30-D 2 **Computing bank discounts and proceeds on notes payable**

During the current year Chevalley Contractors discounts five non-interest-bearing notes receivable at its bank. Each note is discounted on the date of the note.

No. of Note	Date of Note	Time	Interest Rate	Principal
281	January 1	30 days	7½%	$ 100.00
282	March 4	60 days	8%	600.00
283	April 15	2 months	8½%	2,000.00
284	May 28	3 months	9%	640.00
285	November 5	36 days	6%	400.00

Instructions: For each of the above notes compute (a) the amount of the discount and (b) the proceeds. Use the appropriate formulas on page 584.

PROBLEM 30-1 **Recording notes, interest, and bank discount**

The transactions given below were selected from those completed by Larry Walsh, a piano dealer, during April, May, and June of the current year.

Instructions: □ **1.** Record the following transactions, using a cash receipts journal (page 10), a cash payments journal (page 6), and a general journal (page 4) like those illustrated in this chapter. Source documents are abbreviated as: check, Ck; memorandum, M; note payable, NP; note receivable, NR; receipt, R.

Apr. 2. Received a 60-day, non-interest-bearing note from Jim Rapp for an extension of time on this account receivable, $200.00. NR42.
    5. Issued a 60-day, 8% note to Mobley Music Company for an extension of time on this account payable, $3,000.00. NP30.
    7. Discounted at 9% at the Boulder Bank our 60-day, non-interest-bearing note, $5,000.00. NP31. The bank credited our checking account for the proceeds, $4,925.00.
    9. Received a 30-day, 8% note from Gladys Hull for an extension of time on this account receivable, $675.00. NR43.
    16. Issued a 30-day, 8% note to Interstate Instruments for an extension of time on this account payable, $4,200.00. NP32.
    27. Issued a 2-month, 7½% note to the City Bank, $2,000.00. NP33. The bank credited our checking account for the principal.

May 9. Received a check from Gladys Hull in settlement of NR43 (principal, $675.00; interest, $4.50), $679.50. R112.

14. Received a 30-day, 8% note from Joe Salas for an extension of time on this account receivable, $600.00. NR44.

16. Paid Interstate Instruments for NP32 (principal, $4,200.00; interest, $28.00), $4,228.00. Ck208.

June 1. Jim Rapp dishonored NR42 due today, $200.00. Charged the amount of the note to his account. M135.

4. Paid Mobley Music Company for NP30 (principal, $3,000.00; interest, $40.00), $3,040.00. Ck246.

6. Paid the Boulder Bank for NP31, $5,000.00. Ck253.

13. Received a check from Joe Salas in settlement of NR44 (principal, $600.00; interest, $4.00), $604.00. R251.

20. Received a 30-day, non-interest-bearing note from Cora Guzman for an extension of time on this account receivable, $300.00. NR45.

27. Paid the City Bank for NP33 (principal, $2,000.00; interest, $25.00), $2,025.00. Ck275.

Instructions: □ **2.** Foot and prove the journals.

MASTERY
PROBLEM 30-M Recording notes, interest, and bank discount

Optional Problems

The transactions given below were completed by Lee Zink, a plumbing contractor, during May of the current year.

Instructions: □ **1.** Record the following transactions, using a cash receipts journal (page 20) and a cash payments journal (page 12) similar to those illustrated in this chapter. Source documents are abbreviated as: check, Ck; note payable, NP; note receivable, NR; receipt, R.

May 3. Paid Kooper Supply for NP21 (60-day, 8% note due today; principal, $800.00). Ck72.

7. Discounted at 9% at the Guaranty Bank our 30-day, non-interest-bearing note, $1,000.00. NP25. The Guaranty Bank credited our checking account for the proceeds.

8. Received a check from Jean Mingo in settlement of NR48 (20-day, 10% note due today; principal, $360.00). R38.

10. Paid the Peoples National Bank for NP16 (90-day, 9% note due today; principal, $1,500.00). Ck78.

16. Issued a 30-day, 8% note to Peoples National Bank, $1,800.00. NP26. The bank credited our checking account for the principal.

17. Received a check from A. C. Forsman in settlement of NR31 (6-month, 8% note due today; principal, $1,000.00). R41.

18. Paid Ellison Plumbing Supplies for NP22 (60-day, 9% note due today; principal, $850.00). Ck86.

24. Discounted at 9% at the Guaranty Bank, our 20-day, non-interest-bearing note, $800.00. NP27. The Guaranty Bank credited our checking account for the proceeds.

May 25. Received a check from Delbert Brock in settlement of NR49 (30-day, 8% note due today; principal, $672.50). R43.

28. Paid Aaron Plumbing Company for NP18 (90-day, 8% note due today; principal, $900.00). Ck95.

Instructions: ◻ **2.** Foot and prove the journals.

BONUS PROBLEM 30-B Recording notes, interest, and bank discount

The transactions given below were completed by D. R. Etzel, a paint distributor, during the current year.

Instructions: ◻ **1.** Record the following transactions, using a cash receipts journal (page 50), a cash payments journal (page 36), and a general journal (page 22) similar to those illustrated in this chapter. Source documents are abbreviated as: check, Ck; memorandum, M; note payable, NP; note receivable, NR; receipt, R.

Jan. 3. Received a 90-day, 8% note dated December 29 from Alvin Jaeger for an extension of time on account, $500.00. NR42.

6. Received a 30-day, 9% note dated January 5 from Clara Pollard for an extension of time on account, $200.00. NR43.

24. Issued a 30-day, 8% note to Starlite Products for an extension of time on account, $900.00. NP1.

Feb. 4. Received a check from Clara Pollard in settlement of NR43. R36.

23. Paid Starlite Products for NP1. Ck85.

Mar. 5. Issued a 90-day, 7% note to John Dunn & Co., for an extension of time on account, $3,000.00. NP2.

11. Purchased office equipment from Parkway Interiors, $1,500.00. Paid cash, $500.00, and issued a 60-day, 8% note for the balance, $1,000.00. Ck110; NP3.

Record the complete transaction in the cash payments journal in one combined entry.

29. Received notice from the bank that Alvin Jaeger dishonored NR42. Charged principal and interest to his account. M52.

May 3. Discounted at 9% at Sterling Bank our 30-day, non-interest-bearing note, $1,200.00. NP4. The bank credited our checking account for the proceeds.

10. Paid Parkway Interiors for NP3. Ck128.

June 2. Paid Sterling Bank for NP4. Ck171.

3. Paid John Dunn & Co. for NP2. Ck178.

Oct. 15. Received a check from Alvin Jaeger for half of the $510.00 balance charged to his account on March 29. R259. Wrote off the remainder of this account receivable as uncollectible. M104.

Record the check in the cash receipts journal. Record the write-off of the customer's account in the general journal.

Instructions: ◻ **2.** Foot and prove the journals.

Accrued Revenue and Accrued Expenses

31

Most journal entries that record revenue are made when the revenue is received. However, some revenue may be earned before it is actually received. For example, interest is earned for each day an interest-bearing note receivable is held. The interest is not received, however, until the maturity date of the note.

Most entries recording expenses are also made when the expense is paid. Some expenses though are incurred before they are actually paid. For example, salary expense is incurred for each day that an employee works. The payment for salary expense is not made, however, until the regular payday.

To record the revenue that has been earned but not yet received, an adjusting entry is made at the end of the fiscal period. Because of this adjustment, the revenue is reported for the fiscal period in which it is actually earned. An adjusting entry also is made at the end of a fiscal period to record the amount of an expense that has been incurred but not yet paid. As a result of this adjustment, the expense is reported for the fiscal period in which the expense is actually incurred.

ACCRUED REVENUE

Revenue that is earned in one fiscal period but collected in a later fiscal period is called accrued revenue. Accrued revenue is a receivable that is classified as an asset. At the end of a fiscal period, each type of accrued revenue is recorded by an adjusting entry. The income statement will then show all the revenue for the period even though some has not been received. The balance sheet will show all the assets, including the accrued revenue receivable.

593

Adjusting entry for accrued interest income

At the end of each fiscal period, the accountant for Pioneer Antiques examines the notes receivable on hand. The accountant determines the amount of interest income earned but not collected. Interest earned on notes receivable but not yet collected is called accrued interest income. On December 31, 1978, there is only one note receivable on hand. This is Note Receivable No. 41, a 60-day, 9% note for $1,000.00 from Larry Pruett, dated December 1, 1978. The accounting records should show all the interest income for the fiscal period. Therefore, an adjusting entry must be made to record the amount of interest earned to date on this note.

Analyzing the adjusting entry for accrued interest income. The interest on $1,000.00 at 9% for 30 days (December 1 to 31) is $7.50. The adjustment for accrued interest income is analyzed in the T accounts at the left.

Interest Receivable	114
7.50	

Interest Income	712
	7.50

Interest receivable is an asset. The asset account Interest Receivable is debited for $7.50 to show the increase in the balance of this account. The balance of the interest receivable account is the amount of interest income that has accrued at the end of the fiscal period. However, this revenue is not received until the next fiscal period.

Interest on notes receivable is a revenue of the business. The revenue account Interest Income is credited for $7.50 to show the increase in the balance of this account. The balance of the interest income account is the amount of interest income earned during the fiscal period.

Adjustment for accrued interest income on the work sheet. The adjusting entry for accrued interest income is planned on the work sheet along with the other adjusting entries. The adjustment is shown in the Adjustment columns on Lines 4 and 42 of the partial work sheet below.

			1	2	3	4	5	6	7	8	
	ACCOUNT TITLE	ACCT. NO.	TRIAL BALANCE DEBIT	CREDIT	ADJUSTMENTS DEBIT	CREDIT	INCOME STATEMENT DEBIT	CREDIT	BALANCE SHEET DEBIT	CREDIT	
4	Interest Receivable	114			(A.) 7 50				7 50		4
42	Interest Income	712		78 50		(A.) 7 50		86 00			42

Accrued interest income on the work sheet

On Line 4, Interest Receivable is debited for $7.50 in the Adjustments Debit column. This amount is extended to the Balance Sheet Debit column because it is an asset.

On Line 42, Interest Income is credited for $7.50 in the Adjustments Credit column. This amount, $7.50, is added to the amount in the Trial Balance Credit column, $78.50. The new balance, $86.00, is extended to the Income Statement Credit column because it is a revenue account.

Recording and posting the adjustment for accrued interest income.
The data needed to journalize the adjustment for accrued interest income
are obtained from the Adjustments columns of the work sheet. The adjusting entry in the general journal is shown below.

ACCOUNTS PAYABLE DEBIT	GENERAL DEBIT	DATE	ACCOUNT TITLE	POST. REF.	GENERAL CREDIT	ACCOUNTS RECEIV. CREDIT	
			GENERAL JOURNAL			PAGE 42	
			Adjusting Entries				10
	750	Dec. 31	Interest Receivable				11
			Interest Income		750		12

Adjusting entry for accrued interest income

After the adjusting entry is posted, the interest receivable account and
the interest income account appear as shown below.

Accounts after posting the adjusting entry for accrued interest income

ACCOUNT Interest Receivable   **ACCOUNT NO.** 114

DATE	ITEM	POST. REF.	DEBIT	CREDIT	BALANCE DEBIT	BALANCE CREDIT
1978 Dec. 31		J42	750		750	

ACCOUNT Interest Income   **ACCOUNT NO.** 712

DATE	ITEM	POST. REF.	DEBIT	CREDIT	BALANCE DEBIT	BALANCE CREDIT
Dec. 1		CR48		500		7850
31		J42		750		8600

The interest receivable account has a debit balance of $7.50. This is the
accrued interest income earned but not collected at the end of the fiscal
period. The interest income account has a credit balance of $86.00. This
is the total interest income for the fiscal period.

Reporting accrued interest income on the financial statements

The asset account Interest Receivable is listed on the balance sheet in
the Current Assets section. On Pioneer Antiques' balance sheet for December 31, 1978, Interest Receivable is listed as shown below.

Assets		
Current Assets:		
Cash		673400
Petty Cash		18000
Notes Receivable		100000
→ Interest Receivable		750
Accounts Receivable	553800	
Less Allow. for Uncoll. Accts.	63700	490100

Interest Receivable on the balance sheet

The account Interest Income is listed on the income statement in the Other Revenue section. When the income statement is prepared for the year ended December 31, 1978, Interest Income is listed as shown on the partial income statement below.

Other Revenue:		
Gain on Plant Assets	14470	
Interest Income	8600	
Total Other Revenue		23070

Interest Income on the income statement

Closing entry for the interest income account

One closing entry is made for the accounts listed in the Income Statement Credit column of the work sheet. Interest Income is included in the accounts whose balances are closed into the income summary account. The closing entry in the general journal on December 31, 1978, is shown below.

ACCOUNTS PAYABLE DEBIT	GENERAL DEBIT	DATE	ACCOUNT TITLE	POST. REF.	GENERAL CREDIT	ACCOUNTS RECEIV. CREDIT
			Closing Entries			
	8561600	1978 Dec. 31	Sales			
	129100		Purchases Returns & Allow.			
	297600		Purchases Discount			
	14470		Gain on Plant Assets			
	8600		Interest Income			
			Income Summary		9011370	

GENERAL JOURNAL — PAGE 43

Closing entry for the interest income account

After this closing entry is posted, the interest income account is closed.

Need for readjusting the interest receivable and interest income accounts

When cash is received for Note Receivable No. 41 on January 30, 1979, the cash will include the principal, $1,000.00, plus the interest, $15.00. The accountant for Pioneer Antiques records the receipt of cash by debiting Cash for the amount received, $1,015.00; crediting Notes Receivable for the principal of the note, $1,000.00; and crediting Interest Income for the amount of interest received, $15.00. But $7.50 of this interest has already been credited to Interest Income as accrued revenue at the end of the 1978 fiscal period, and only $7.50 applies to the 1979 fiscal period.

Accrued interest income recorded in a previous fiscal period should not be credited to the interest income account a second time when it is actually received in the following fiscal period. To avoid this double credit, the interest receivable account and the interest income account are readjusted at the beginning of a new fiscal period. A journal entry made at the beginning of a new fiscal period to readjust an adjusting entry made in the preceding fiscal period is called a reversing entry.

After the reversing entry has been recorded and posted, all interest income transactions throughout the new fiscal period are handled in the same way. That is, the full amount of interest is credited to Interest Income. Using reversing entries makes it unnecessary to analyze each receipt of interest to determine how much, if any, was earned during the previous fiscal period.

Reversing entry for accrued interest income

A reversing entry is exactly the opposite of the original adjusting entry. The adjusting entry for accrued interest income made by Pioneer Antiques on December 31, 1978, debited Interest Receivable for $7.50 and credited Interest Income for $7.50. The reversing entry made on January 1, 1979, reverses this adjusting entry.

Analyzing the reversing entry for accrued interest income. The reversing entry for accrued interest income is analyzed in the T accounts at the right. Interest Income is debited for $7.50 and Interest Receivable is credited for $7.50. This reversing entry closes the interest receivable account and transfers the original debit balance to the debit side of the interest income account. The debit to Interest Income is a temporary minus balance that represents uncollected interest income earned and recorded during the previous fiscal period.

Interest Income			712
Closing	86.00	Balance	78.50
		Adjusting	7.50
	86.00		86.00
Reversing	7.50		

Interest Receivable			114
Adjusting	7.50	Reversing	7.50

During the new fiscal period, receipts of interest income are credited to the interest income account. The portion of each receipt of interest that applies to the previous fiscal period will automatically be deducted because of the debit balance.

Recording and posting the reversing entry for accrued interest income. The reversing entry is made in the general journal as of January 1, 1979, under the centered heading *Reversing Entries* as shown below.

	1	2		GENERAL JOURNAL		3	4	PAGE 44
	ACCOUNTS PAYABLE DEBIT	GENERAL DEBIT	DATE	ACCOUNT TITLE	POST. REF.	GENERAL CREDIT	ACCOUNTS RECEIV. CREDIT	
1			1979	*Reversing Entries*				1
2		7 50	Jan. 1	*Interest Income*				2
3				*Interest Receivable*		7 50		3

Reversing entry for accrued interest income

After the reversing entry is posted, the interest receivable account and the interest income account appear as shown on page 598.

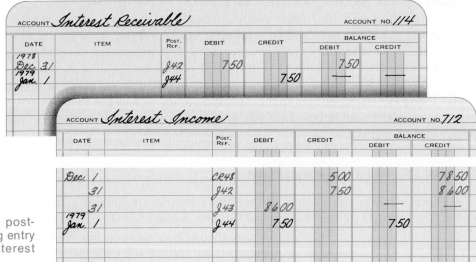

Accounts after posting the reversing entry for accrued interest income

The interest receivable account above has a zero balance at the beginning of the new 1979 fiscal period. The interest receivable account will not be used again until it is needed for an adjusting entry at the end of the 1979 fiscal period. The interest receivable account is needed for only one day each period to prepare complete financial reports.

The interest income account above has a debit balance of $7.50 on January 1, 1979. This balance on the first day of the new fiscal year is the result of posting the reversing entry for accrued interest income. During 1979 the interest income account will be credited each time cash is received for interest income. At the end of the 1979 fiscal period, the credit balance will show the amount of interest income that belongs to the 1979 fiscal period. At the end of the 1979 fiscal period there will be new accrued interest income, earned in 1979 but not collected in 1979. The accrued interest income on December 31, 1979, will be recorded in the same manner as the accrued interest income on December 31, 1978.

ACCRUED EXPENSES

Expenses incurred in one fiscal period but not paid until a later fiscal period are called accrued expenses. An example of an accrued expense is interest expense incurred during one fiscal period but not paid until the next fiscal period. Another example is salaries earned by employees in one fiscal period but not paid until the next fiscal period. At the end of a fiscal period, each type of accrued expense is recorded by an adjusting entry. The income statement will then show all the expenses for the period even though some expenses have not been paid. The balance sheet will show all the liabilities, including the amounts owed for accrued expenses.

Adjusting entry for accrued interest expense

At the end of each fiscal period, the accountant for Pioneer Antiques examines the notes payable on hand to determine the amount of interest expense incurred but not paid. Interest incurred on notes payable but not yet paid is called accrued interest expense. On December 31, 1978, there is only one note payable on hand. This is Note Payable No. 11, a 90-day, 8% note for $3,000.00 issued to the M. K. Danz Company on November 1, 1978. An adjusting entry is made to record the amount of interest expense incurred to date on this note.

Analyzing the adjusting entry for accrued interest expense. The interest on $3,000.00 at 8% for 60 days (November 1 to December 31) is $40.00. The adjustment for accrued interest expense is analyzed in the T accounts at the right.

Interest on notes payable is an expense of the business. The expense account Interest Expense is debited for $40.00 to show the increase in the balance of this account. The balance of the interest expense account is the total amount of interest expense incurred during the fiscal period.

Interest Expense	812
40.00	

Interest Payable	212
	40.00

Interest payable is a liability. The liability account Interest Payable is credited for $40.00 to show the increase in the balance of this account. The balance of the interest payable account is the amount of interest expense that has accrued at the end of the fiscal period but that is not paid until the next fiscal period.

Adjustment for accrued interest expense on the work sheet. The adjusting entry for accrued interest expense is planned on the work sheet along with the other adjusting entries. The adjustment is shown in the Adjustments columns on Lines 15 and 44 of the partial work sheet below.

On Line 44, Interest Expense is debited for $40.00 in the Adjustments Debit column. This amount, $40.00, is added to the amount in the Trial Balance Debit column, $190.00. The new balance, $230.00, is extended to the Income Statement Debit column because it is an expense.

On Line 15, Interest Payable is credited for $40.00 in the Adjustments Credit column. This amount is extended to the Balance Sheet Credit column because it is a liability.

	ACCOUNT TITLE	ACCT NO.	TRIAL BALANCE DEBIT	TRIAL BALANCE CREDIT	ADJUSTMENTS DEBIT	ADJUSTMENTS CREDIT	INCOME STATEMENT DEBIT	INCOME STATEMENT CREDIT	BALANCE SHEET DEBIT	BALANCE SHEET CREDIT	
15	Interest Payable	212				(u) 40.00				40.00	15
44	Interest Expense	812	190.00		(u) 40.00		230.00				44

Accrued interest expense on the work sheet

Recording and posting the adjustment for accrued interest expense. The data needed to journalize the adjustment for accrued interest expense are obtained from the Adjustments columns of the work sheet. The adjusting entry in the general journal is shown below.

Adjusting entry for accrued interest expense

			GENERAL JOURNAL		PAGE 42	
1	2			3	4	
ACCOUNTS PAYABLE DEBIT	GENERAL DEBIT	DATE	ACCOUNT TITLE	POST. REF.	GENERAL CREDIT	ACCOUNTS RECEIV. CREDIT
17	4000	31	Interest Expense			17
18			Interest Payable		4000	18

After the adjusting entry is posted, the interest payable account and the interest expense account appear as shown below.

Accounts after posting the adjusting entry for accrued interest expense

ACCOUNT Interest Payable — ACCOUNT NO. 212

DATE	ITEM	POST. REF.	DEBIT	CREDIT	BALANCE DEBIT	BALANCE CREDIT
1978 Dec. 31		J42		4000		4000

ACCOUNT Interest Expense — ACCOUNT NO. 812

DATE	ITEM	POST. REF.	DEBIT	CREDIT	BALANCE DEBIT	BALANCE CREDIT
Dec. 15		CP37	2000		19000	
31		J42	4000		23000	

The interest payable account has a credit balance of $40.00, which is the accrued interest expense incurred in the current fiscal period but to be paid in the next fiscal period. Interest Expense has a debit balance of $230.00, which is the total interest expense for the fiscal period.

Reporting accrued interest expense on the financial statements

The liability account Interest Payable is listed on the balance sheet in the Current Liabilities section. Interest Payable is listed on Pioneer Antiques' balance sheet for December 31, 1978, as shown below.

Interest Payable on the balance sheet

Liabilities		
Current Liabilities:		
Notes Payable	300000	
→ Interest Payable	4000	
Salaries Payable	12000	
Accounts Payable	374200	

The expense account Interest Expense is listed on the income statement in the Other Expenses section. On the income statement for the year ended December 31, 1978, Interest Expense is listed as shown on the partial income statement below.

Other Expenses:		
Loss on Plant Assets	21000	
→ Interest Expense	23000	
Total Other Expenses		44000

Interest Expense on the income statement

Closing entry for the interest expense account

One closing entry is made for the accounts listed in the Income Statement Debit column of the work sheet. Interest Expense is included in the accounts whose balances are closed into the income summary account. The closing entry in the general journal of Pioneer Antiques on December 31, 1978, is shown below.

	ACCOUNTS PAYABLE DEBIT	GENERAL DEBIT	DATE	ACCOUNT TITLE	POST. REF.	GENERAL CREDIT	ACCOUNTS RECEIV. CREDIT	
8		7610200	31	Income Summary				8
9				Sales Returns + Allow.		210710		9
10				Purchases		2271600		10
11				Bad Debt Expense		42840		11
12				Delivery Expense		187300		12
13				Depr. Expense-Office Equip.		224600		13
14				Depr. Expense-Store Equip.		411550		14
15				Insurance Expense		18000		15
16				Miscellaneous Expense		64715		16
17				Payroll Taxes Expense		296840		17
18				Rent Expense		60000		18
19				Salary Expense		3710800		19
20				Supplies Expense		67225		20
21				Loss on Plant Assets		21000		21
22				→ Interest Expense		23000		22
23								23

GENERAL JOURNAL   PAGE 43

Closing entry including the interest expense account

After this closing entry is posted, the interest expense account is closed.

Need for readjusting the interest payable and interest expense accounts

When Pioneer Antiques pays its Note Payable No. 11 on January 30, 1979, it will pay the principal, $3,000.00, plus the interest, $60.00. The payment will be recorded by debiting Notes Payable for the principal of the note, $3,000.00; debiting Interest Expense for the amount of interest paid, $60.00; and crediting Cash for the total amount paid, $3,060.00. But $40.00 of the interest paid has been debited to Interest Expense as accrued expense at the end of the 1978 fiscal period, and only $20.00 applies to the 1979 fiscal period.

Accrued interest expense recorded in a previous fiscal period should not be debited to the interest expense account a second time when it is actually paid in the following fiscal period. To avoid this double debit, the interest payable account and the interest expense account are readjusted at the beginning of a new fiscal period by a reversing entry. After the reversing entry has been recorded, every interest expense transaction during the new fiscal period is a debit to Interest Expense.

Reversing entry for accrued interest expense

The adjusting entry for accrued interest expense made by Pioneer Antiques on December 31, 1978, debited Interest Expense for $40.00 and credited Interest Payable for $40.00. The reversing entry made on January 1, 1979, reverses this adjusting entry.

Interest Payable			212
Reversing	40.00	Adjusting	40.00

Interest Expense			812
Balance	190.00	Closing	230.00
Adjusting	40.00		
	230.00		230.00
		Reversing	40.00

Analyzing the reversing entry for accrued interest expense. The reversing entry for accrued interest expense is analyzed in the T accounts at the left.

Interest Payable is debited for $40.00 and Interest Expense is credited for $40.00. This reversing entry closes the interest payable account and transfers its original credit balance to the credit side of the interest expense account. The credit to Interest Expense is a temporary minus balance that represents unpaid interest expense incurred and recorded during the previous fiscal period.

During the new fiscal period, payments of interest expense are debited to the interest expense account. The portion of each interest payment that applies to the previous fiscal period will automatically be deducted because of the credit balance.

Recording and posting the reversing entry for accrued interest expense. The reversing entry is made in the general journal as of January 1, 1979, as shown below.

Reversing entry for accrued interest expense

After the reversing entry is posted, the interest payable account and the interest expense account appear as shown below.

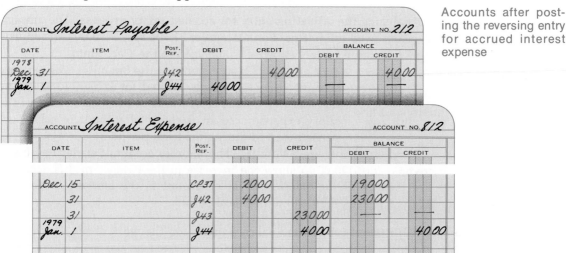

Accounts after posting the reversing entry for accrued interest expense

The interest payable account shown above has a zero balance at the beginning of the new 1979 fiscal period. Like the interest receivable account, the interest payable account will not receive any entries until the end of the 1979 fiscal period. Also, like the interest receivable account, the interest payable account is needed for only one day each period, just long enough to prepare complete financial reports.

The interest expense account shown above has a credit balance of $40.00 on January 1, 1979. This balance on the first day of the new fiscal year is the result of posting the reversing entry for accrued interest expense. During 1979 the interest expense account will be debited each time cash is paid for interest expense. At the end of the 1979 fiscal period, the debit balance will show the amount of interest expense that belongs to the 1979 fiscal period. Then, at the end of the 1979 fiscal period there will be new accrued interest expense, incurred in 1979 but not paid in 1979. The new accrued interest expense on December 31, 1979, will be handled in the same manner as the accrued interest expense on December 31, 1978.

Adjusting entry for accrued salary expense

Pioneer Antiques pays its employees weekly on Friday. At the end of the fiscal period on Sunday, December 31, 1978, one day's salary amounting to $120.00 is owed to employees for work performed on Saturday, December 30. This salary expense will not be paid until the next regular payday on Friday, January 5, 1979. The $120.00 owed is a salary expense of the 1978 fiscal period. The accounting records must show all the salary expense for the 1978 fiscal period. An adjusting entry is made to record the amount of salary owed at the end of December but to be paid in

January of the next year. Salary owed but not yet paid is called accrued salary expense.

Analyzing the adjusting entry for accrued salary expense. The amount of salary owed but not paid on December 31, 1978, is $120.00. The adjustment for accrued salary expense is analyzed in the T accounts.

Salary Expense	619
120.00	

Salaries Payable	213
	120.00

Salary owed is an expense of the business. The expense account Salary Expense is debited for $120.00 to show the increase in the balance of this account. The balance of the salary expense account is the total amount of salary expense incurred during the fiscal period.

Salaries payable are a liability. The liability account Salaries Payable is credited for $120.00 to show the increase in the balance of this account. The balance of the salaries payable account is the amount of accrued salary expense at the end of the fiscal period.

Adjustment for accrued salary expense on the work sheet. The adjusting entry for accrued salary expense is planned on the work sheet along with the other adjusting entries. The adjustment is shown below.

		1 TRIAL BALANCE DEBIT	2 CREDIT	3 ADJUSTMENTS DEBIT	4 CREDIT	5 INCOME STATEMENT DEBIT	6 CREDIT	7 BALANCE SHEET DEBIT	8 CREDIT	
ACCOUNT TITLE	ACCT. NO.									
16 Salaries Payable	213				(4)12000				12000	16
39 Salary Expense	619	3698800		(4)12000		3710800				39

Accrued salary expense on the work sheet

On Line 39, Salary Expense is debited for $120.00 in the Adjustments Debit column. This amount, $120.00, is added to the amount in the Trial Balance Debit column, $36,988.00. The new balance, $37,108.00 is extended to the Income Statement Debit column because it is an expense.

On Line 16, Salaries Payable is credited for $120.00 in the Adjustments Credit column. This amount is extended to the Balance Sheet Credit column because it is a liability.

Recording and posting the adjustment for accrued salary expense. The data needed to journalize the adjustment for accrued salary expense are obtained from the Adjustments columns of the work sheet. The adjusting entry in the general journal is shown below.

		GENERAL JOURNAL			PAGE 42	
1 ACCOUNTS PAYABLE DEBIT	2 GENERAL DEBIT	DATE	ACCOUNT TITLE	POST. REF.	3 GENERAL CREDIT	4 ACCOUNTS RECEIV. CREDIT
19	12000	31 Salary Expense				19
20		Salaries Payable		12000		20

Adjusting entry for accrued salary expense

After the adjusting entry is posted, the salaries payable account and the salary expense account appear as shown below.

Accounts after posting the adjusting entry for accrued salary expense

The salaries payable account has a credit balance of $120.00. This is the accrued salary expense incurred in the current fiscal period but to be paid in the next fiscal period. The salary expense account has a debit balance of $37,108.00, which is the total salary expense for the fiscal period.

Reporting accrued salary expense on the financial statements

The liability account Salaries Payable is listed on the balance sheet in the Current Liabilities section. The balance of the salaries payable account of Pioneer Antiques on December 31, 1978, is shown on the partial balance sheet on page 600.

The expense account Salary Expense is listed on the income statement in the Operating Expenses section. The balance of the salary expense account of Pioneer Antiques for the year ended December 31, 1978, is shown below on the partial income statement.

Salary Expense on the income statement

Closing entry for the salary expense account

Salary Expense is included in the closing entry made for the accounts listed in the Income Statement Debit column of the work sheet. The closing entry in the general journal of Pioneer Antiques on December 31, 1978, for the salary expense account is shown in the entry on page 601. After this closing entry is posted, the salary expense account is closed.

Need for readjusting the salaries payable and salary expense accounts

When the entry is made for Pioneer Antiques' next weekly payroll on January 5, 1979, the entire amount of salaries for the week, $720.00, is debited to Salary Expense. This entry is the same as that for each weekly payroll in 1978. But $120.00 of these salaries has already been debited to Salary Expense as accrued expense at the end of the 1978 fiscal period. Therefore, only $600.00 applies to the 1979 fiscal period.

Accrued salary expense recorded in the previous fiscal period should not be debited to the salary expense account a second time when it is actually paid in the following fiscal period. To avoid this double debit, the salaries payable account and the salary expense account are readjusted at the beginning of the new fiscal period by a reversing entry.

Reversing entry for accrued salary expense

The adjusting entry for accrued salary expense made by Pioneer Antiques on December 31, 1978, debited Salary Expense for $120.00 and credited Salaries Payable for $120.00. The reversing entry made on January 1, 1979, reverses this adjusting entry.

Analyzing the reversing entry for accrued salary expense. The reversing entry for accrued salary expense is analyzed in the T accounts at the left. Salaries Payable is debited for $120.00 and Salary Expense is credited for $120.00. This reversing entry closes the salaries payable account and transfers its original credit balance to the credit side of the salary expense account. The credit to Salary Expense is a temporary minus balance that represents unpaid salary expense incurred and recorded during the previous fiscal period.

Salaries Payable		213
Reversing 120.00	Adjusting	120.00

Salary Expense		619
Balance 36,988.00	Closing	37,108.00
Adjusting 120.00		
37,108.00		37,108.00
	Reversing	120.00

Recording and posting the reversing entry for accrued salary expense. The reversing entry is made in the general journal as of January 1, 1979, as shown at the top of page 607.

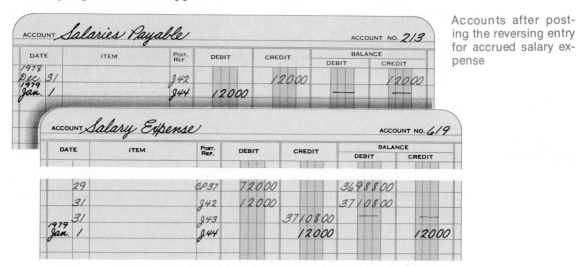

Reversing entry for accrued salary expense

After the reversing entry is posted, the salaries payable account and the salary expense account appear as shown below.

Accounts after posting the reversing entry for accrued salary expense

The salaries payable account shown above has a zero balance at the beginning of the new 1979 fiscal period. Like the interest payable account, the salaries payable account will not receive any entries until the end of the 1979 fiscal period.

The salary expense account shown above is credited at the beginning of the new 1979 fiscal period for the amount of salary expense that belongs to the 1978 fiscal period. This amount will be paid in 1979. During 1979 the salary expense account will be debited each time the weekly payroll is paid.

✦ What is the meaning of each of the following?

Using Business Terms

- accrued revenue
- accrued interest income
- reversing entry
- accrued expenses
- accrued interest expense
- accrued salary expense

Questions for Individual Study

1. When are most journal entries made that record revenue?
2. Why should revenue that has been earned but not received be recorded before financial statements are prepared at the end of a fiscal period?
3. What accounts are debited and credited in the general journal on page 595

to record the adjusting entry for accrued interest income?

4. Under what heading on the balance sheet is the balance of the interest receivable account listed?

5. Why are the interest receivable and interest income accounts readjusted at the beginning of a new fiscal period?

6. What accounts are debited and credited in the general journal on page 597 to record the reversing entry for accrued interest income?

7. Why should expenses that have been incurred but not paid be recorded before financial statements are prepared at the end of a fiscal period?

8. What accounts are debited and credited in the general journal on page 600 to record the adjusting entry for accrued interest expense?

9. Under what heading on the income statement is the balance of the interest expense account listed?

10. Why are the interest payable and interest expense accounts readjusted at the beginning of a new fiscal period?

11. What accounts are debited and credited in the general journal on page 602 to record the reversing entry for accrued interest expense?

12. Why are the salaries payable and salary expense accounts readjusted at the beginning of a new fiscal period?

Cases for Management Decision

CASE 1 At the end of the fiscal period, the accountant for Armstrong Hardware failed to record accrued interest income amounting to $300.00 on notes receivable outstanding. What effect does this omission have on (a) the income statement and (b) the balance sheet?

CASE 2 At the end of the fiscal period, the accountant for Jack's TV Service failed to record accrued interest expense amounting to $100.00 on notes payable outstanding. The accountant also failed to record accrued salary expense amounting to $200.00. What effect do these omissions have on (a) the income statement and (b) the balance sheet?

Drill for Mastering Principles

DRILL 31-D 1 Recording adjusting and reversing entries for accrued revenue and accrued expenses

Instructions: □ 1. Prepare a form similar to the one shown below. Enter each number and item on the form.

No.	Item	Account Titles Affected By			
		Adjusting Entry		Reversing Entry	
		Account Debited	Account Credited	Account Debited	Account Credited
1	Accrued interest income				
2	Accrued interest expense				
3	Accrued salary expense				

Instructions: □ 2. For each of the items of accrued revenue and accrued expense listed above, indicate the titles of the accounts to be debited and credited in making (a) the adjusting entry on December 31 of the current year and (b) the reversing entry on January 1 of the following year.

PROBLEM 31-1   Adjusting, closing, and reversing entries for accrued revenue and accrued expenses

Selected accounts from the ledger of J. F. Barnett and the balances on December 31 of the current fiscal year before adjusting entries are shown below.

Account Title	Acct. No.	Balance	Account Title	Acct. No.	Balance
Interest Receivable	114	——	Salary Expense	619	$8,918.00
Interest Payable	212	——	Interest Income	712	296.80
Salaries Payable	213	——	Interest Expense	812	122.50
Income Summary	313	——			

On December 31, accrued interest income on notes receivable outstanding is $27.30; accrued salaries are $169.40; and accrued interest expense on notes payable outstanding is $61.00.

Instructions: □ **1.** Open the general ledger accounts and record the balances.

□ **2.** Record on page 14 of the columnar general journal as of December 31 the adjusting entries for the accrued revenue and the accrued expenses.

□ **3.** Post the adjusting entries to the general ledger accounts.

□ **4.** Record in the four-column general journal the entries to close (a) the interest income account and (b) the salary expense and interest expense accounts.

□ **5.** Post the closing entries to the general ledger accounts.

□ **6.** Record the reversing entries on January 1 of the new year.

□ **7.** Post the reversing entries to the general ledger accounts.

PROBLEM 31-2   Work at the end of the fiscal period

The account numbers, titles, and general ledger balances of Allton's Greenhouse on December 31 of the current year are given below and on the next page.

Account Title	Acct. No.	Balance	Account Title	Acct. No.	Balance
Cash	111	$ 7,243.54	Office Equipment	122	$2,400.00
Petty Cash	112	90.00	Accumulated Depreciation—		
Notes Receivable	113	600.00	Office Equipment	122.1	300.00
Interest Receivable	114	——	Notes Payable	211	2,400.00
Accounts Receivable	115	5,538.50	Interest Payable	212	——
Allowance for Uncollectible			Salaries Payable	213	——
Accounts	115.1	201.78	Accounts Payable	214	1,480.50
Merchandise Inventory	116	12,778.58	Employees Income Tax Pay.	215	229.70
Supplies	117	972.66	FICA Tax Payable	216	112.54
Prepaid Insurance	118	763.20	Federal Unemployment Tax		
Store Equipment	121	4,965.00	Payable	217	56.82
Accumulated Depreciation—			State Unemployment Tax Pay.	218	48.60
Store Equipment	121.1	736.20	Sales Tax Payable	219	164.45

Account Title	Acct. No.	Balance	Account Title	Acct. No.	Balance
Eloise Allton, Capital	311	$17,948.40	Depreciation Expense —		
Eloise Allton, Drawing	312	4,320.00	Store Equipment	615	——
Income Summary	313	——	Insurance Expense	616	——
Sales	411	87,789.46	Miscellaneous Expense	617	$ 695.50
Sales Returns and Allowances	411.1	679.68	Payroll Taxes Expense	618	470.64
Purchases	511	50,278.45	Rent Expense	619	8,640.00
Purchases Returns and Allow.	511.1	487.20	Salary Expense	620	7,104.00
Purchases Discount	511.2	962.75	Supplies Expense	621	——
Advertising Expense	611	2,250.00	Utilities Expense	622	903.92
Bad Debts Expense	612	——	Gain on Plant Assets	711	36.00
Delivery Expense	613	2,052.72	Interest Income	712	18.00
Depreciation Expense —			Loss on Plant Assets	811	19.44
Office Equipment	614	——	Interest Expense	812	206.57

Adjustment data at the end of the fiscal period on December 31:

Accrued interest income, $9.60.

Additional allowance for uncollectible accounts, ½% of the total charge sales of $43,596.00.

Merchandise inventory, December 31, $10,360.50.

Supplies inventory, $304.94.

Value of insurance policies, $163.00.

Annual amount of estimated depreciation of store equipment, $467.50.

Annual amount of estimated depreciation of office equipment, $228.60.

Accrued interest expense, $24.00.

Accrued salary expense, $178.20.

Instructions: □ **1.** Prepare an eight-column work sheet for the annual fiscal period ended December 31 of the current year.

□ **2.** Prepare an income statement, a capital statement, and a balance sheet.

□ **3.** Record the adjusting and closing entries in a general journal, pages 15 and 16.

□ **4.** Record in the general journal the reversing entries for the accruals as of January 1 of the next year.

Optional Problems　**MASTERY PROBLEM 31-M** Adjusting, closing, and reversing entries for accrued revenue and accrued expenses

Selected accounts from the ledger of E. H. Toomey and the balances on December 31 of the current fiscal year before adjusting entries are shown below.

Account Title	Acct. No.	Balance	Account Title	Acct. No.	Balance
Interest Receivable	114	——	Insurance Expense	615	——
Prepaid Insurance	118	$ 540.00	Salary Expense	619	$18,952.50
Interest Payable	212	——	Interest Income	712	72.00
Salaries Payable	213	——	Interest Expense	812	165.00
Income Summary	313	——			

Adjustment data at the end of the fiscal period on December 31:

Accrued interest income on notes receivable outstanding, $33.75.

The $540.00 in the prepaid insurance account was the premium paid on July 1 covering a three-year period.

Accrued salaries payable, $372.00.

Accrued interest expense on notes payable outstanding, $60.00.

Instructions: □ **1.** Open the general ledger accounts and record the balances.

□ **2.** Record on page 8 of a four-column general journal as of December 31 the adjusting entries for the accrued revenue, the prepaid expense, and the accrued expenses. Post to the general ledger accounts.

□ **3.** Record the entries to close the revenue account and the expense accounts. Post the closing entries to the general ledger accounts.

□ **4.** Record the reversing entries for the accruals as of January 1 of the next year. Post the reversing entries to the general ledger accounts.

BONUS Adjusting, closing, and reversing entries for
PROBLEM 31-B accrued revenue and accrued expenses

Selected accounts from the ledger of Sharon LeBaron and the balances on December 31 of the current fiscal year before adjusting entries are shown below.

Account Title	Acct. No.	Balance	Account Title	Acct. No.	Balance
Interest Receivable	114	——	Salary Expense	618	$36,468.00
Rent Receivable	115	——	Interest Income	711	225.00
Interest Payable	212	——	Rent Revenue	712	1,500.00
Salaries Payable	214	——	Interest Expense	811	90.00
Income Summary	313	——			

Adjustment data at the end of the fiscal period on December 31:

Accrued interest income has been earned on a 60-day, 9% note for $6,000.00 dated November 21.

Accrued interest expense has been incurred on a 120-day, 8% note for $4,000.00 dated December 16.

Accrued rent receivable, $300.00.

Accrued salaries payable, $280.00.

Instructions: □ **1.** Open the general ledger accounts and record the balances.

□ **2.** Record on page 23 of a four-column general journal as of December 31 the adjusting entries for the accrued revenue and the accrued expenses. Post to the general ledger accounts.

□ **3.** Record the entries to close the revenue accounts and the expense accounts. Post the closing entries to the general ledger accounts.

□ **4.** Record the reversing entries on January 1 of the new year. Post the reversing entries to the general ledger accounts.

Carson & Bennett

PENRITE CORPORATION

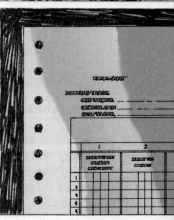

PARTNERSHIPS AND CORPORATIONS

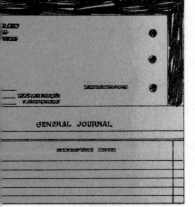

DIFFERENT FORMS OF BUSINESSES EXIST. Businesses are usually organized as (a) a sole proprietorship, (b) a partnership, or (c) a corporation. All the businesses described previously in this textbook have been sole proprietorships. The differences in accounting records for a partnership and a corporation are described in Part 8. Accounting procedures for the three kinds of businesses are much the same. The major difference is in the procedures used to account for the capital of the business.

ACCOUNTING FOR CAPITAL IS DIFFERENT FOR EACH FORM OF BUSINESS. The accounting procedures of a partnership, *Carson and Bennett*, are described in Chapter 32. The accounting procedures for a corporation, *Penrite Corporation*, are described in Chapter 33. The procedures described in these two chapters are for the recording of capital for each kind of business.

CARSON & BENNETT
CHART OF ACCOUNTS

(3) CAPITAL	Account Number
Otis Bennett, Capital	311
Otis Bennett, Drawing	312
Alton Carson, Capital	313
Alton Carson, Drawing	314
Income Summary	315

Capital accounts of a partnership

PENRITE CORPORATION
CHART OF ACCOUNTS

(3) CAPITAL	Account Number
Capital Stock	311
Retained Earnings	312
Income Summary	313

Capital accounts of a corporation

The capital section of the chart of accounts for the partnership (described in Chapter 32) and the capital section of the chart of accounts for the corporation (described in Chapter 33) are illustrated above for ready reference as you study Part 8 of this textbook.

Partnerships

32

Rainbow Car Wash, described in Part 1, is owned by an individual. Gift World, described in Part 2, is also owned by an individual. A business owned entirely by one person is called a sole proprietorship.

Two or more persons may become joint owners of a single business by combining their assets. Sometimes a business needs more capital than one owner can provide. Sometimes the nature of the business may require various kinds of management skills not possessed by a single individual. The form of business organization in which two or more persons combine their assets and abilities and agree to share in the profits or losses is called a partnership.

Partnerships are common in small retail stores, in personal service businesses, and in wholesale businesses. Partnerships also are often used for professional businesses such as medical clinics, law offices, and accounting firms. Each member of a partnership is called a partner.

FORMING A PARTNERSHIP

A partnership may be formed when the sole proprietor of an existing business agrees with one or more other persons to combine assets and skills. Partners may also start an entirely new business that has not existed before.

Articles of partnership

When two or more persons agree to form a business, a partnership comes into existence. A partnership agreement is a legal contract and may be oral or written. A written contract is more desirable than an oral one in avoiding future misunderstandings. The written agreement by which a partnership is formed is called the articles of partnership.

The articles of partnership usually include: (1) names of the partners, (2) name, location, and kind of business to be conducted, (3) length of time for which the partnership is to exist, (4) investment to be made by each partner, (5) duties and rights of each partner, (6) amount of salary to be paid each partner and the amount of withdrawals permitted each partner, (7) manner in which each partner shares profits, losses, and responsibilities, and (8) provisions for terminating the partnership.

The articles of partnership for the wholesale automotive supply business, Carson & Bennett, are shown below.

ARTICLES OF PARTNERSHIP

THIS CONTRACT, made and entered into on the fifth day of December, 1977, by and between Alton Carson and Otis Bennett, both of Billings, Montana.

WITNESSETH: That the said parties have this day formed a partnership for the purpose of engaging in and conducting a wholesale automotive supply business in the city of Billings under the following stipulations, which are a part of this contract:

FIRST: The said partnership is to continue for a term of ten years from January 1, 1978.

SECOND: The business is to be conducted under the firm name of Carson & Bennett at 159 West Gilbert Street, Billings, Montana 59101.

THIRD: The investments are as follows: Otis Bennett, cash, $30,000.00; Alton Carson, cash, $30,000.00. These invested assets are partnership property in which the equity of each partner is the same.

FOURTH: Each partner is to devote his entire time and attention to the business and to engage in no other business enterprise without the written consent of the other partner.

FIFTH: During the operation of this partnership, neither partner is to become surety or bondsman for anyone without the written consent of the other partner.

SIXTH: Each partner is to receive an annual salary as follows: Otis Bennett, $7,200.00; Alton Carson, $6,000.00. One twelfth of the annual salary is payable in cash on the last business day of each month. At the end of each annual fiscal period, the net income or the net loss shown by the income statement, after the salaries of the two partners have been allowed, is to be shared as follows: Otis Bennett, 60 percent; Alton Carson, 40 percent.

SEVENTH: Neither partner is to withdraw assets in excess of his salary, any part of the assets invested, or assets in anticipation of net income to be earned, without the written consent of the other partner.

EIGHTH: In case of the death or the legal disability of either partner, the other partner is to continue the operations of the business until the close of the annual fiscal period on the following December 31. At that time, the continuing partner is to be given an option to buy the interest of the deceased or incapacitated partner at not more than 10 percent above the value of the deceased or incapacitated partner's proprietary interest as shown by the balance of his capital account after the books are closed on December 31. It is agreed that this purchase price is to be paid one half in cash and the balance in four equal installments payable quarterly.

NINTH: At the conclusion of this contract, unless it is mutually agreed to continue the operation of the business under a new contract, the assets of the partnership, after the liabilities are paid, are to be divided in proportion to the net credit to each partner's capital account on that date.

IN WITNESS WHEREOF, the parties aforesaid have hereunto set their hands and affixed their seals on the day and year above written.

Alton Carson (Seal)

Otis Bennett (Seal)

Articles of partnership

Forming the Carson & Bennett partnership

Alton Carson and Otis Bennett agree to form a partnership to operate a wholesale automotive supply business. They sign the articles of partnership, page 616, in December, 1977, and agree to start business on January 1, 1978. Mr. Bennett has had experience in a wholesale automotive supply business. Mr. Carson has no experience in this kind of business, although he has worked in various other kinds of businesses.

Both Mr. Carson and Mr. Bennett agree to invest $30,000.00 each in the new business. In return, each partner is to receive (1) an annual salary and (2) a percentage of the remaining profits or losses. (See the sixth item in the articles of partnership, page 616.)

Partnership accounts in the general ledger

Two or more persons share in the ownership of a partnership. Therefore, the capital accounts in the general ledger must show each partner's share in the total owners' equity. A separate capital account and a separate drawing account for each partner are kept in the capital section of the general ledger.

The accounting work for a partnership is similar to that for a sole proprietorship. The major difference is in recording the division of ownership among the partners' capital accounts. The capital section of the partnership chart of accounts for Carson & Bennett is on page 614.

OPENING ENTRIES FOR A PARTNERSHIP

The opening entries for a partnership are similar to those for sole proprietorships. Ordinarily a separate entry is made to record the investment of each partner.

Opening entries for a partnership when only cash is invested

The articles of partnership, page 616, were signed by Alton Carson and Otis Bennett when they formed the partnership. According to the articles of partnership, each partner is to invest $30,000.00 in cash. To record the investment of each partner, the following entries are made in the cash receipts journal of the new partnership.

Opening entries for a partnership when only cash is invested

DATE	ACCOUNT TITLE	Doc. No.	Post. Ref.	GENERAL DEBIT	GENERAL CREDIT	SALES CREDIT	ACCOUNTS RECEIVABLE CREDIT	SALES DISCOUNT DEBIT	CASH DEBIT
1978 Jan. 1	Alton Carson, Capital	R1			30000 00				30000 00
1	Otis Bennett, Capital	R2			30000 00				30000 00

CASH RECEIPTS JOURNAL   PAGE 1

Opening entries to convert a sole proprietorship into a partnership

Sometimes a sole proprietorship is converted into a partnership by a merger with another business or by the investment of cash or other assets by other persons.

In some cases when a sole proprietorship is converted into a partnership, a new set of books may be opened. For example, Tom Moore operates a home decorating business. On March 1, 1978, he forms a partnership with Martha Hilsdale. Mr. Moore invests the assets of his business, and the partnership assumes the liabilities of his business. He has a net investment of $15,000.00. Miss Hilsdale invests $10,000.00 in cash. The new partnership, Hilsdale & Moore, opens a new set of books. A separate opening entry is made in the general journal for the investment of each partner so that all information about the initial investment is recorded in one place. The illustration below shows the two opening entries for the Hilsdale & Moore partnership.

Opening entries when a sole proprietorship is converted into a partnership

The cash investments of the partners are not recorded in the cash receipts journal, because the amount of cash is posted directly from the general journal. The total amount of cash is recorded as a memorandum entry on the first line of the cash receipts journal for future use in proving cash. The cash receipts journal of Hilsdale & Moore with the memorandum entry is shown below.

Beginning cash balance of a partnership recorded in a cash receipts journal as a memorandum entry

In some cases when a sole proprietorship is converted into a partner-ship, the partners may agree to continue using the books of the original business. When this is done, only the investment of the incoming partner is recorded as an opening entry.

RECORDING PARTNERS' SALARIES

Mr. Bennett, of the Carson & Bennett partnership, has operated a wholesale automotive supply business for several years. He has business experience that he is contributing to the partnership in addition to the assets he invests. Mr. Carson has had less business experience than Mr. Bennett and no experience in the automotive supply business. Because of the difference in experience of each partner, the partners agree to base salaries on past experience. Mr. Bennett is to receive an annual salary of $7,200.00. Mr. Carson is to receive an annual salary of $6,000.00. The salaries are payable monthly.

The federal income tax form filed by a partnership provides a space for reporting the payment of partners' salaries as an expense of the business. The partnership, therefore, debits the monthly salaries to an expense ac-count titled *Partners Salaries*. At the end of a fiscal period this expense account, together with the other expense accounts, is closed into Income Summary.

Partners are not considered to be employees of a partnership. Some accountants prefer to record partners' salaries as withdrawals. This is done by debiting the partners' drawing accounts for the amount of the salaries instead of debiting the expense account Partners Salaries.

Salary payments to partners are not subject to withholding for income taxes or FICA taxes. For tax purposes, each partner is treated as a self-employed person. Each partner's share of the net income from the busi-ness is subject to income tax and social security self-employment tax. The amount of income received from the partnership is reported on each partner's personal income tax return.

FINANCIAL STATEMENTS OF A PARTNERSHIP

The financial statements of a partnership are similar to those of a sole proprietorship. The major differences are: (1) the distribution of net in-come or net losses is reported separately for each partner; and (2) the equity of each partner is recorded in separate capital accounts and is reported separately on the financial statements.

> At the end of each year Carson & Bennett employs a certified public accounting firm to audit its books and prepare financial statements. This CPA firm uses automated equipment and supplies the partnership with computer printouts as shown on the next four pages.

Income statement of a partnership

The income statement of the Carson & Bennett partnership is similar to that of a sole proprietorship. The account Partners Salaries is listed with the other operating expenses. The income statement prepared for Carson & Bennett on December 31, 1978, is shown below.

```
                          CARSON & BENNETT
                          INCOME STATEMENT
                   FOR YEAR ENDED DECEMBER 31, 1978


OPERATING REVENUE
    SALES.................................              $97,015.10
    LESS    SALES RETURNS & ALLOWANCES       $    711.09
            SALES DISCOUNT............            456.38   1,167.47
    NET SALES..........................                   $95,847.63

COST OF MERCHANDISE SOLD
    MERCHANDISE INVENTORY, JAN 1, 1978      $19,950.00
    PURCHASES.......................  $68,875.07
    LESS    PURCHASES RETURNS & ALLOW.$  838.44
            PURCHASES DISCOUNT........ 1,097.36  1,935.80
    NET PURCHASES....................             66,939.27
    TOTAL COST OF MDSE AVAIL FOR SALE.            $86,889.27
    LESS MDSE INVENTORY, DEC 31, 1978.            26,278.34
    COST OF MERCHANDISE SOLD..........                    60,610.93

GROSS PROFIT ON SALES.................                    $35,236.70

OPERATING EXPENSES
    BAD DEBTS EXPENSE.................     $    173.96
    DELIVERY EXPENSE..................        1,667.57
    DEPRECIATION EXPENSE..............          955.50
    INSURANCE EXPENSE.................          242.00
    MISCELLANEOUS EXPENSE.............          824.04
    PARTNERS SALARIES.................       13,200.00
    PAYROLL TAXES EXPENSE.............          688.61
    PROPERTY TAXES...................           602.90
    SALARY EXPENSE...................         7,420.41
    SUPPLIES EXPENSE..................          359.37
    TOTAL OPERATING EXPENSES..........                    26,134.36

INCOME FROM OPERATIONS................                    $ 9,102.34

OTHER REVENUE
    INTEREST INCOME...................     $     74.66

OTHER EXPENSE
    INTEREST EXPENSE..................          445.64

NET DEDUCTION.........................                       370.98

NET INCOME............................                    $8,731.36
```

Computer printout of an income statement for a partnership

Distribution of net income or net loss of a partnership

The net income or net loss of a partnership may be distributed in any way agreed upon by the partners. The method is usually stated in the articles of partnership. Some of the ways that partners agree to share the net income or net loss are: (1) equally; (2) according to an agreed-upon ratio; (3) according to the ratio of their investments; (4) by allowing interest on each partner's investment; and (5) by a combination of two or more of these methods. Sometimes the articles of partnership do not include an agreement for distributing the net income or net loss. If no agreement is included, the distribution is assumed by law to be made equally to all partners.

The articles of partnership, page 616, show in the sixth item that the net income or net loss is to be distributed as: Otis Bennett, 60%; Alton Carson, 40%.

The distribution of net income or net loss of a partnership is usually shown in a separate statement. A financial statement that shows in detail the distribution of the net income or net loss to each partner is called a distribution of net income statement.

The distribution of net income statement prepared for Carson & Bennett on December 31, 1978, is shown below.

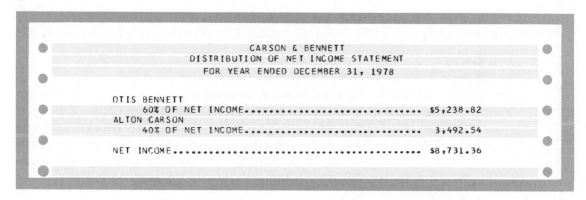

```
                    CARSON & BENNETT
            DISTRIBUTION OF NET INCOME STATEMENT
               FOR YEAR ENDED DECEMBER 31, 1978


   OTIS BENNETT
      60% OF NET INCOME................................. $5,238.82
   ALTON CARSON
      40% OF NET INCOME.................................  3,492.54

   NET INCOME......................................... $8,731.36
```

Computer printout of a distribution of net income statement of a partnership

Some businesses prefer to show the distribution of net income or net loss as part of the partnership income statement. When this is done, the information is placed at the bottom of the income statement below the double ruled lines. The heading *Distribution of Net Income* is written below the double ruled lines. The information following this heading is similar to that shown in the distribution of net income statement above.

Ruled lines are not shown in the illustration above because they normally are not included on computer printouts.

Capital statement of a partnership

Detailed data about changes in the capital of each partner during the fiscal period are shown in a partnership capital statement. The capital statement of Carson & Bennett prepared on December 31, 1978, is shown below.

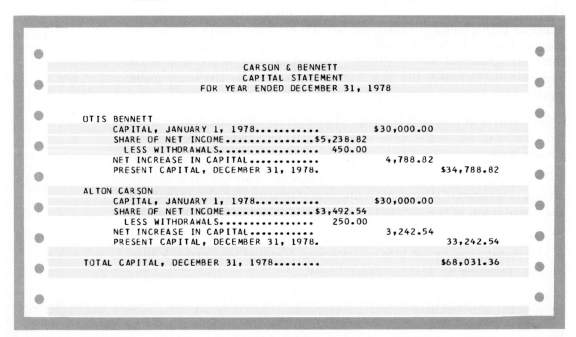

```
                            CARSON & BENNETT
                            CAPITAL STATEMENT
                     FOR YEAR ENDED DECEMBER 31, 1978


     OTIS BENNETT
        CAPITAL, JANUARY 1, 1978...........        $30,000.00
        SHARE OF NET INCOME...............$5,238.82
          LESS WITHDRAWALS.................  450.00
        NET INCREASE IN CAPITAL............          4,788.82
        PRESENT CAPITAL, DECEMBER 31, 1978.                     $34,788.82

     ALTON CARSON
        CAPITAL, JANUARY 1, 1978...........        $30,000.00
        SHARE OF NET INCOME...............$3,492.54
          LESS WITHDRAWALS.................  250.00
        NET INCREASE IN CAPITAL............          3,242.54
        PRESENT CAPITAL, DECEMBER 31, 1978.                     33,242.54

     TOTAL CAPITAL, DECEMBER 31, 1978........                   $68,031.36
```

Computer printout of a
partnership capital statement

Salaries of these partners are recorded as expenses of the partnership. The salaries are not shown on the capital statement of Carson & Bennett. The capital statement does show, however, that Otis Bennett withdrew $450.00 and Alton Carson withdrew $250.00. These withdrawals of cash or merchandise are in addition to the salaries that are paid to the partners. For this reason, the withdrawals are recorded in the partners' drawing accounts.

The total amount that each partner received from the partnership in 1978 is:

Partner	Salary	plus	Share of Net Income	equals	Total Income Received
Otis Bennett	$7,200.00	+	$5,238.82	=	$12,438.82
Alton Carson	$6,000.00	+	$3,492.54	=	$ 9,492.54

The total amount received is the amount each partner reports on his personal income tax return for the year. Mr. Bennett must report $12,438.82 and Mr. Carson must report $9,492.54.

Balance sheet of a partnership

The balance sheet for a partnership is similar to one for a sole proprietorship. The balance sheet for Carson & Bennett is shown below.

The difference between this balance sheet and one for a sole proprietorship is in the capital section. The present capital of each partner is shown separately.

Computer printout of a balance sheet for a partnership

```
                            CARSON & BENNETT
                             BALANCE SHEET
                          DECEMBER 31, 1978


                 ASSETS

CURRENT ASSETS
        CASH .......................................          $11,851.93
        PETTY CASH..................................              150.00
        NOTES RECEIVABLE............................            2,472.00
        ACCOUNTS RECEIVABLE....................$ 8,409.94
           LESS ALLOWANCE FOR UNCOLLECTIBLE ACCTS..      173.95 8,235.99
        MERCHANDISE INVENTORY......................           26,278.34
        SUPPLIES...................................            1,543.89
        PREPAID INSURANCE..........................              652.68

        TOTAL CURRENT ASSETS.......................                        $51,184.83

PLANT ASSETS
        EQUIPMENT..............................$ 5,720.00
           LESS ACCUMULATED DEPRECIATION--EQUIPMENT.     475.00  $ 5,245.00
        BUILDING...............................$ 9,000.00
           LESS ACCUMULATED DEPRECIATION--BUILDING..     180.00    8,820.00
        LAND...................................                    6,000.00

        TOTAL PLANT ASSETS.........................                         20,065.00

TOTAL ASSETS...................................                            $71,249.83

                 LIABILITIES

CURRENT LIABILITIES
        NOTES PAYABLE..............................           $ 1,520.00
        INTEREST PAYABLE...........................               34.20
        ACCOUNTS PAYABLE...........................            1,490.56
        SALARIES PAYABLE...........................               92.76
        EMPLOYEES INCOME TAX PAYABLE...............               43.29
        FICA TAX PAYABLE...........................               18.55
        FEDERAL UNEMPLOYMENT TAX PAYABLE...........               10.76
        STATE UNEMPLOYMENT TAX PAYABLE.............                8.35

        TOTAL CURRENT LIABILITIES..................                        $ 3,218.47

                 CAPITAL

OTIS BENNETT, CAPITAL..........................           $34,788.82
ALTON CARSON, CAPITAL..........................            33,242.54

TOTAL CAPITAL.................................                             68,031.36

TOTAL LIABILITIES AND CAPITAL.................                            $71,249.83
```

ADJUSTING AND CLOSING ENTRIES FOR A PARTNERSHIP

The adjusting entries for a business are similar whether the business is a sole proprietorship or a partnership. In either form of business, the Adjustments columns of the work sheet contain the data used for the adjusting entries.

The entries to close the general ledger accounts are similar for a sole proprietorship and a partnership with one exception. The income summary account is closed into the partners' capital accounts according to the way the net income is distributed. The data for most of the closing entries are taken from the work sheet. The data for recording the closing of the income summary account are taken from the distribution of net income statement.

The entries to close the income summary account and to close the partners' drawing accounts for Carson & Bennett are shown below.

				GENERAL JOURNAL			PAGE 14	
	1	2					3	4
	ACCOUNTS PAYABLE DEBIT	GENERAL DEBIT	DATE	ACCOUNT TITLE	POST. REF.	GENERAL CREDIT	ACCOUNTS RECEIV. CREDIT	
1				*Closing Entries*				1
20		873136	31	*Income Summary*				20
21				*Otis Bennett, Capital*		523882		21
22				*Alton Carson, Capital*		349254		22
23		45000	31	*Otis Bennett, Capital*				23
24				*Otis Bennett, Drawing*		45000		24
25		25000	31	*Alton Carson, Capital*				25
26				*Alton Carson, Drawing*		25000		26

Portion of the closing entries for a partnership

The first entry closes the income summary account and records the distribution of the net income to the capital accounts. This distribution of net income is the same as shown on the distribution of net income statement, page 621. The second and third entries close the partners' drawing accounts into their respective capital accounts.

✦ What is the meaning of each of the following?

- sole proprietorship
- partnership
- partner
- articles of partnership
- distribution of net income statement

1. What are two reasons why people may form a partnership?
2. When does a partnership actually come into existence?
3. Why is it best to have a partnership agreement in writing?
4. How is the capital section of a partnership general ledger different from that of a sole proprietorship?
5. How does the accounting work for a partnership compare with that for a sole proprietorship?

6. How does the opening entry for a sole proprietorship differ from the opening entries for a partnership?

7. Why are salaries for partners charged to a different account than that used for employees' salaries?

8. In what way does an income statement for a partnership differ from that of a sole proprietorship?

9. If the articles of partnership do not include an agreement on how profits and losses are to be distributed, how will the distribution be made?

10. For the two partners in the partnership Carson & Bennett, described in this chapter, what two items make up the total amount of income each partner receives from the business?

11. In what way does a balance sheet for a partnership differ from that of a sole proprietorship?

12. How do the closing entries for a partnership differ from those for a sole proprietorship?

CASE 1 Merle McCall owns a small store selling unfinished furniture. Some of his customers ask him where they can find someone to finish the furniture for them. Mr. McCall has a friend who does furniture refinishing and upholstery work. There is room in the building where Mr. McCall has his store to also have a workroom for furniture refinishing. What are some of the possible advantages and disadvantages to Mr. McCall in asking his friend to enter a partnership with him?

Cases for Management Decision

CASE 2 Jerome Masey owns a men's clothing store. He has been earning an average of 10% on his investment in the business. However, business has not increased much in the past 10 years. His younger brother, who has never been in business for himself, offers to invest an amount equal to Mr. Masey's current investment, work as a partner in the store, and share equally in the profits or losses. Mr. Masey's wife suggests that he sell the business, invest the proceeds from the sale in government bonds, and find another job working for someone else. Which plan might be best for Mr. Masey? (1) Continue as things are now, (2) enter into a partnership with his brother, (3) sell the business and seek another job. Why?

DRILL 32-D 1   Figuring the distribution of net income or net loss in a partnership

Drill for Mastering Principles

Instructions: □ **1.** Assume that each of the businesses shown at the right earned a net income of $20,000.00. What is the amount of net income to be distributed to each partner in each business? □ **2.** Assume that each of the businesses shown at the right had a net loss of $16,000.00. What is the amount of net loss to be distributed to each partner in each business?

Business	Partner	Capital Investment in the Business	Agreement on Sharing of Income or Loss
1	A B	$75,000.00 25,000.00	70% of income or loss 30% of income or loss
2	C D	$30,000.00 50,000.00	According to the ratio of their investment to total investment
3	E F	$20,000.00 30,000.00	No written agreement
4	G H I	$20,000.00 30,000.00 50,000.00	According to the ratio of their investment to total investment

PROBLEM 32-1 ○ Opening entries for cash investments
in a partnership

On May 1 of the current year, John Harris and Betty Edwards open a hobby shop.
Each partner invests $16,000.00 cash in the new partnership.

Instructions: Record the opening entries for the new partnership on page 1 of a
cash receipts journal like the one on page 617.

PROBLEM 32-2 ○ Opening entries for investments of cash and
other assets in a partnership

On April 1 of the current year, Jane Adams and Freda Leming form a partnership
to expand a retail store operated by Ms. Adams. The partnership is to be called
Adams and Leming. The partnership agrees to accept the assets and assume the
liabilities of Ms. Adams' present business. Ms. Leming is to invest cash equal to
Ms. Adams' investment. The balance sheet of Ms. Adams' present business is:

Jane Adams
Balance Sheet
March 31, 19—

Assets			Liabilities		
Cash...........................	3 806	96	Notes Payable.........................	850	00
Notes Receivable..................	634	48	Accounts Payable	2 554	71
Accounts Receivable	2 419	60	Total Liabilities.......................	3 404	71
Merchandise Inventory...........	8 985	32			
Supplies.............................	441	35	**Capital**		
Equipment	2 713	00	Jane Adams, Capital...............	15 596	00
Total Assets.........................	19 000	71	Total Liabilities and Capital	19 000	71

Instructions: □ **1.** Record the opening entry for each partner on page 1 of a general journal like the one on page 618. Receipt No. 1.

□ **2.** Record the cash balance on April 1 as a memorandum entry on page 1 of a
cash receipts journal like the one on page 618.

PROBLEM 32-3 ○ Distribution of the net income
of a partnership

Anthony Francisco and Daniel O'Leary are partners in a retail business. The following data were taken from the records on December 31 of the current year.

Partner	Capital Invested January 1	Balance of Drawing Account	Distribution of Net Income
Francisco	$40,000.00	$300.00	60%
O'Leary	$25,000.00	$100.00	40%

Instructions: □ **1.** Assume that on December 31 the partnership had a net income of
$14,000.00 as shown on the income statement.
Prepare a distribution of net income statement
for the year ended December 31 for the partnership of Francisco and O'Leary.

□ **2.** Prepare a capital statement.

☐ **3.** Assume that on December 31 all the data are the same as that on page 626 except that the partnership had a net loss of $900.00. Prepare a distribution of net income statement for the year ended December 31.

PROBLEM 32-4 Work at the end of a fiscal period for a partnership

The following trial balance was prepared on December 31 of the current year for the partnership of Gaylord and Newson.

Gaylord and Newson
Trial Balance
December 31, 19—

Account Title	Acct. No.	Trial Balance Debit	Trial Balance Credit
Cash	111	5 698 00	
Petty Cash	112	100 00	
Accounts Receivable	113	7 859 00	
Allowance for Uncollectible Accounts	113.1		409 00
Merchandise Inventory	114	26 269 00	
Supplies	115	381 00	
Prepaid Insurance	116	343 00	
Equipment	121	3 382 00	
Accumulated Depreciation — Equipment	121.1		845 00
Notes Payable	211		1 430 00
Interest Payable	212		—
Accounts Payable	213		2 358 00
Salaries Payable	214		—
Employees Income Tax Payable	215		49 00
FICA Tax Payable	216		19 80
Federal Unemployment Tax Payable	217		1 65
State Unemployment Tax Payable	218		8 91
Charles Gaylord, Capital	311		15 000 00
Charles Gaylord, Drawing	312	500 00	
Donald Newson, Capital	313		10 000 00
Donald Newson, Drawing	314	160 00	
Income Summary	315	—	—
Sales	411		93 071 64
Sales Returns and Allowances	411.1	566 00	
Purchases	511	57 012 00	
Purchases Returns and Allowances	511.1		264 00
Purchases Discount	511.2		625 00
Bad Debts Expense	611	—	
Delivery Expense	612	1 974 00	
Depreciation Expense — Equipment	613	—	
Insurance Expense	614	—	
Miscellaneous Expense	615	900 00	
Partners Salaries	616	12 000 00	
Payroll Taxes Expense	617	364 00	
Rent Expense	618	2 600 00	
Salary Expense	619	3 960 00	
Supplies Expense	620	—	
Interest Income	711		12 00
Interest Expense	811	26 00	
		124 094 00	124 094 00

Instructions: □ **1.** Prepare an eight-column work sheet for the partnership for the year ended December 31. The additional data needed to complete the work sheet are:

The balance of Allowance for Uncollectible Accounts should be equal to 5.5% of the balance of the accounts receivable account.
Ending merchandise inventory, $29,132.00.
Ending supplies inventory, $63.00.
Ending value of insurance policies, $85.00.
Annual amount of depreciation on equipment, $169.00.
Accrued interest expense, $7.00.
Accrued salary expense, $84.00.

Instructions: □ **2.** Prepare an income statement.

□ **3.** Prepare a distribution of net income statement. The net income is to be distributed equally to all partners.

□ **4.** Prepare a capital statement.

□ **5.** Prepare a balance sheet.

□ **6.** Record the adjusting entries on page 31 of a general journal.

□ **7.** Record the closing entries on page 32 of a general journal.

**MASTERY
PROBLEM 32-M** Opening entries for a partnership

On May 1 of the current year, Martin Ross and Morris Cohen combined their separate retail groceries into one business, a partnership. The partnership took over the assets and liabilities of each of the sole proprietorships as shown in the following balance sheets.

In addition to investing the assets and liabilities of his business, Mr. Cohen is to invest sufficient additional cash to make his total investment the same as that for Mr. Ross.

Martin Ross
Balance Sheet
April 30, 19—

Assets			Liabilities		
Cash	2 813 98		Notes Payable	1 320 00	
Notes Receivable	242 00		Accounts Payable	2 498 00	
Accounts Receivable	4 008 00		Total Liabilities	3 818 00	
Merchandise Inventory	9 467 67				
Supplies	186 35		**Capital**		
Equipment	3 850 00		Martin Ross, Capital	16 750 00	
Total Assets	20 568 00		Total Liabilities and Capital	20 568 00	

Morris Cohen
Balance Sheet
April 30, 19—

Assets				Liabilities			
Cash.............................	1	464	87	Accounts Payable		3 284	48
Accounts Receivable	3	968	07				
Merchandise Inventory...........	7	385	96				
Supplies...........................		122	30				
Prepaid Insurance..................		45	28	**Capital**			
Equipment	2	268	00	Morris Cohen, Capital............	11	970	00
Total Assets.......................	15	254	48	Total Liabilities and Capital	15	254	48

Instructions: ◻ **1.** Record a separate opening entry for the assets and liabilities contributed by each partner. (Remember to add sufficiently to the cash for Mr. Cohen to make his investment equal that of Mr. Ross.) Use page 1 of a general journal.

◻ **2.** Record the cash balance on May 1 as a memorandum entry on page 1 of a cash receipts journal like the one on page 618.

**BONUS
PROBLEM 32-B** Distribution of net income of a
partnership

A partnership called "Lights and Things" has three partners with investments on January 1 as follows: Mary Bloom, $30,000.00; Catherine Johnson, $35,000.00; Tina Worthington, $25,000.00.

The partnership agreement reads as follows: (1) Whether there is net income or net loss, each partner is to receive an amount equal to 3% of her investment. (2) The remainder of the net income or the resulting net loss is to be distributed equally to the three partners.

As of December 31 of the current year, the drawing accounts for each partner had the following debit balances: Ms. Bloom, $150.00; Ms. Johnson, $170.00; Ms. Worthington, $75.00.

Instructions: ◻ **1.** Assume the net income for the year ended December 31 of the current year is $15,000.00. Prepare a distribution of net income statement and a capital statement for the partnership.

◻ **2.** Assume that the net loss was $7,500.00. Prepare a distribution of net income statement and a capital statement for the partnership.

33

Corporations

A business may need more capital than can be provided by a sole proprietor or by two or more partners. Under these circumstances a third form of business organization may be used. A business that has a legal right to act as one person and that may be owned by many persons is called a corporation. In this form of business, many persons can invest capital and become part owners.

Most large businesses are organized as corporations by state authority. Some corporations, such as national banks, are authorized by the federal government.

CORPORATE FORM OF BUSINESS ORGANIZATION

Corporations exist under laws that vary from state to state. Most states require that three or more persons provide the initial assets of a new corporation. The persons who are responsible for the initial organization of a corporation and who provide the initial assets for a corporation are called incorporators.

Forming a corporation

Persons forming a corporation must apply to the proper state or federal government agency. When approved by a state or federal agency, the corporation comes into existence and is considered to be a "created person." As a "person" a corporation has the right to own property and the responsibility to use that property in a legal way. The corporation can make contracts and otherwise act as a real person. If laws are broken, the corporation can be sued, fined, or put out of business.

The corporation is considered to exist as a "person" separate from its owners. For example, a truck that is owned by a corporation is an asset of the corporation. The truck is not owned by the persons who own the corporation. Also, liabilities of the corporation cannot become liabilities of owners of the corporation.

Articles of incorporation. The written application to the proper state or federal agency requesting permission to form a corporation is called the articles of incorporation. The articles of incorporation are sometimes known as the certificate of incorporation. The specific information that must be included in the articles of incorporation varies from state to state. However, the major features of the articles of incorporation are those shown in the illustration below.

ARTICLES OF INCORPORATION

of

PENRITE CORPORATION

FIRST: The name of the corporation is Penrite Corporation.

SECOND: The principal office of said corporation is located at 210-214 Beckett Avenue, in the City of Wilmington, County of New Castle, Delaware 19805.

THIRD: The nature of the business, or objects or purposes to be transacted, promoted, or carried on, is to engage in the business of selling motorcycles and all business incidental to such sale.

FOURTH: The total number of shares of stock that the corporation shall have authority to issue is Two Thousand (2,000) and the par value of each of such shares is One Hundred Dollars ($100.00), amounting in the aggregate to Two Hundred Thousand Dollars ($200,000.00).

FIFTH: The amount of capital with which the corporation will begin business is One Hundred Thousand Dollars ($100,000.00).

SIXTH: The names and places of residence of the incorporators are as follows:

Joseph C. Dale........1336 Vine Place, Dover, Delaware 19901
Martha B. Morrison....2547 Trimble Avenue, Wilmington, Delaware 19808
Theodore S. Sahl......139 Beechcrest Road, Newport, Delaware 19804
Patricia S. Vinson....2614 Park Avenue, Wilmington, Delaware 19802

SEVENTH: The corporation is to have perpetual existence.

WE, THE UNDERSIGNED, being each of the incorporators hereinbefore named for the purpose of forming a corporation to do business both within and without the State of Delaware, under Chapter 65 of the Revised Code of Delaware, and the acts amendatory thereof and supplemental thereto, do make this certificate, hereby declaring and certifying that the facts herein stated are true and accordingly have hereunto set our hands and seals this fifth day of June, 1978.

In the presence of:

Bryant Ellison

Alice Carlson

Joseph C. Dale (SEAL)
Martha B. Morrison (SEAL)
Theodore S. Sahl (SEAL)
Patricia S. Vinson (SEAL)

State of Delaware   ) ss.:
County of New Castle)

BE IT REMEMBERED, that on this fifth day of June, A.D. 1978, personally came before me, Mary D. Manning, a Notary Public for the State of Delaware, all of the parties to the foregoing certificate of incorporation, known to me personally to be such, and severally acknowledged the said certificate to be the act and deed of the signers respectively and that the facts therein stated are truly set forth.

GIVEN under my hand and seal of office the day and year aforesaid.

Mary D. Manning
Notary Public

Articles of incorporation

Obtaining a charter. When the articles of incorporation are approved, the state agency furnishes a certified copy of the articles to the incorporators. The certified copy of the articles of incorporation is called a charter.

In June, 1978, four persons decide to organize Penrite Corporation to sell motorcycles and related accessories and services. These four persons prepare the articles of incorporation shown on page 631. The articles of incorporation are filed with the Secretary of State in the state in which the corporation is formed.

Ownership of a corporation

The ownership of a corporation is divided into units called shares. The owner of one or more shares of a corporation is called a stockholder. A stockholder is sometimes known as a shareholder or a shareowner.

Capital stock. The total shares of ownership in a corporation are called the capital stock. Each investor in a corporation buys shares of capital stock. The evidence of the number of shares owned by each stockholder is a certificate called a stock certificate. The stock certificate issued to Joseph C. Dale for his shares in Penrite Corporation is shown below.

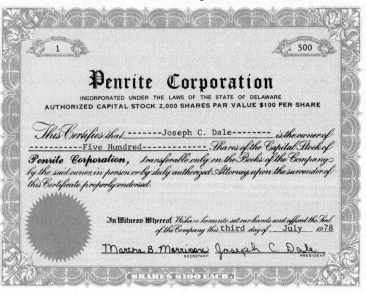

Stock certificate

The fourth paragraph of the charter, page 631, shows that Penrite Corporation is authorized to issue $200,000.00 in capital stock. The total amount of stock that a corporation may issue is called the authorized capital stock. The fourth paragraph of the charter also shows that the total authorized stock is divided into 2,000 shares. Each share has an authorized value of $100.00. A share of stock that has an authorized value stated on the stock certificate is called par-value stock.

A share of stock that has no authorized value stated on the stock certificate is called no-par-value stock. A charter will indicate the number of authorized shares of no-par-value stock that a corporation can issue.

A corporation may issue two kinds of stock. Stock issued by a corporation giving a stockholder preference in earnings or other rights is called preferred stock. Stock issued by a corporation that does not give the stockholder any special preferences is called common stock. The preferences are printed on the preferred stock certificates. Sharing income is the most commonly given preference for preferred stock. For example, investors holding preferred stock are usually entitled to a share of the income before any is paid to the common stockholders.

The Penrite Corporation is authorized to issue only one kind of stock. When a corporation has only one kind of stock, it must issue common stock. The Penrite Corporation is authorized to issue 2,000 shares of common stock with a par value of $100.00 each. The total authorized capital stock, therefore, is $200,000.00 of common stock.

Capital stock issued. Before applying for incorporation, the incorporators must give written promises to buy stock. In this way, the state can be sure that the corporation will begin operations with sufficient capital.

When Penrite Corporation files its application for incorporation, the incorporators promise to buy 1,000 shares of stock. The amount each incorporator promises to buy is:

Joseph C. Dale:	500 shares, to be paid for with assets of his existing business,	$ 50,000.00
Martha B. Morrison:	200 shares, to be paid for in cash,	20,000.00
Theodore S. Sahl:	200 shares, to be paid for in cash,	20,000.00
Patricia S. Vinson:	100 shares, to be paid for in cash,	10,000.00
Total	1,000 shares	$100,000.00

Management of a corporation

A corporation usually has many stockholders. A large number of stockholders would find difficulty in managing the day-to-day activities of the business. Therefore, at an annual meeting the stockholders elect a group of persons to manage the business. Each stockholder owning common stock is usually entitled to one vote for each share owned. Normally, the ownership of preferred stock does not include the right to vote. The preferred stockholder is usually assured a share of the net income before any is paid to owners of common stock. Therefore, the owner of preferred stock does not need a vote to protect the investment.

The group of persons elected by the stockholders to manage a corporation is called the board of directors. The board of directors makes and controls general policies for the corporation. The board of directors also elects the officers of the corporation. The officers carry out the day-to-day operations. The officers are responsible to and report to the board of directors. The board of directors, in turn, reports to the stockholders.

Advantages of the corporate form of business

A corporation has several advantages over a sole proprietorship or a partnership:

1. The amount of capital of a corporation is limited only by (a) its ability to sell authorized shares of stock and by (b) its ability to borrow. The amount of capital of a sole proprietorship or a partnership is limited by (a) the owners' wealth and by (b) the owners' ability to secure personal loans. Corporations can usually raise capital more easily than sole proprietorships or partnerships.
2. A stockholder is not personally liable for the debts of a corporation. The creditors can claim only the assets of the corporation. The most that a stockholder can lose is the amount personally invested in the corporation. A sole proprietor or a partner may lose the investment and any personal assets needed to pay creditors of the business.
3. The length of life of a corporation does not depend upon the natural life of the owners. A corporation charter may specify a specific number of years or perpetual life. A sole proprietorship or a partnership dissolves immediately upon death of one or all owners.

JOURNAL ENTRIES FOR THE CAPITAL OF A CORPORATION

The daily transactions of a corporation are journalized in the same way as they are for a sole proprietorship or a partnership. A corporation, however, records entries related to capital accounts differently than other forms of businesses.

Capital accounts of a corporation

The capital accounts in the capital section of the general ledger for the Penrite Corporation are:

Account Title	Account Number
Capital Stock	311
Retained Earnings	312
Income Summary	313

All investments through the sale of stock to stockholders are recorded in the capital stock account. The account balance represents the total value of the stock issued. The capital stock of Penrite Corporation is recorded at the par value stated in the charter and on the stock certificates.

The net income earned and retained by a corporation is recorded in the retained earnings account.

Opening entries for a corporation

The opening entry for a sole proprietorship consists of debits to assets, credits to liabilities, and a credit to the owner's capital account. The opening entries for a partnership are the same except that a credit is made to each partner's capital account. The opening entries for a corporation are also the same except that the capital account credited is titled Capital Stock.

Payment for stock by incorporators. On July 3, 1978, the four incorporators of Penrite Corporation pay for the 1,000 shares of capital stock they promised to buy. Mr. Dale transfers the assets and liabilities of his business to the new corporation in payment of his 500 shares. Ms. Morrison, Mr. Sahl, and Ms. Vinson pay a total of $50,000.00 in cash for their shares. A stock certificate is issued to each incorporator to show the number of shares of capital stock owned.

Opening entries for Penrite Corporation. The opening entries to record the receipt of cash and other assets from the incorporators are recorded in Penrite Corporation's general journal. One entry is made for Mr. Dale's investment of assets and liabilities. A second entry is made for the total cash investment of the other three incorporators.

ACCOUNTS PAYABLE DEBIT	GENERAL DEBIT	DATE	ACCOUNT TITLE	POST. REF.	GENERAL CREDIT	ACCOUNTS RECEIV. CREDIT	
	1258450	1978 July 3	Cash				1
	400000		Notes Receivable				2
	717600		Accounts Receivable				3
	3086800		Merchandise Inventory				4
	44150		Supplies				5
	25000		Prepaid Insurance				6
			Notes Payable		300000		7
			Accounts Payable		232000		8
			Capital Stock		5000000		9
			Balance sheet of				10
			Dale Sales Company,				11
			July 1, 1978.				12
	5000000	3	Cash				13
			Capital Stock		5000000		14
			Receipts No. 1-3.				15

Opening entries for a corporation when cash and other assets are received from the incorporators

Individual accounts for each stockholder are not kept in the general ledger of Penrite Corporation. The total par value of the capital stock issued is shown in one account, Capital Stock.

A memorandum entry is made in the cash receipts journal to show the balance of cash on hand.

							GENERAL							
													PAGE	
							1	2	3	4	5	6		
	DATE	ACCOUNT TITLE	Doc. No.	Post. Ref.	DEBIT	CREDIT		SALES CREDIT	ACCOUNTS RECEIVABLE CREDIT	SALES DISCOUNT DEBIT	CASH DEBIT			
1	1978 July 3	Balance on hand, $62,584.50		✓										1
2														2

Beginning cash balance of a corporation recorded
in a cash receipts journal as a memorandum entry

The cash balance includes the $12,584.50 received from Mr. Dale as well as the $50,000.00 received from the other three incorporators.

Issuing capital stock after incorporation

One way a corporation raises additional capital is by selling part or all of the unsold shares of authorized capital stock. The Penrite Corporation sold 1,000 shares of capital stock to the four incorporators at the time the corporation was formed. The corporation still has 1,000 shares of unsold authorized capital stock.

On November 6,1978, the corporation sells 100 shares of capital stock to Mr. Ron Sargant. The stock is sold at the par value of $100.00 a share. The entry to record this sale of capital stock is recorded in the cash receipts journal.

						GENERAL								
												PAGE 8		
						1	2	3	4	5	6			
	DATE	ACCOUNT TITLE	Doc. No.	Post. Ref.	DEBIT	CREDIT	SALES CREDIT	ACCOUNTS RECEIVABLE CREDIT	SALES DISCOUNT DEBIT	CASH DEBIT				
10	Nov. 6	Capital Stock	R281			1000000				1000000				10
11														11

Entry to record the sale of capital stock for cash

Cash is debited and Capital Stock is credited for the total par value of the stock sold to Mr. Sargant, $10,000.00. A stock certificate for 100 shares is also issued to Mr. Sargant.

FINANCIAL STATEMENTS OF A CORPORATION

The financial statements of a corporation are prepared from data on a work sheet. The same basic procedures are used by a corporation in preparing financial statements as are used by other forms of businesses. The board of directors of a corporation uses data on the financial statements in making managerial decisions. In addition, stockholders use the statements to determine the condition and progress of the business. Persons with money to invest may also analyze the financial statements to determine if the corporation appears to be a good investment possibility.

Work sheet of a corporation

A portion of the work sheet prepared for Penrite Corporation on December 31, 1978, is shown below.

Penrite Corporation
Work Sheet
For Six Months Ended December 31, 1978

ACCOUNT TITLE	ACCT. NO.	TRIAL BALANCE DEBIT	CREDIT	ADJUSTMENTS DEBIT	CREDIT	INCOME STATEMENT DEBIT	CREDIT	BALANCE SHEET DEBIT	CREDIT
1 Cash	111	6994758						6994758	
2 Petty Cash	112	20000						20000	
3 Accounts Receivable	113	640200						640200	
17 Federal Income Tax Pay.	218				(A)156715				156715
18 Capital Stock	311		11000000						11000000
19 Retained Earnings	312								
20 Income Summary	313			(b)3086800	(c)3475900	3086800	3475900		
21 Sales	511		4060856				4060856		
26 Interest Expense	811	30000		(g)5000		35000			
27 Federal Income Tax	812	170000		(h)156715		326715			
28		2875926	2875926	7395664	7395664	16689110	17669256	15294750	14314604
29 Net Income After Tax						980146			980146
30						17669256	17669256	15294750	15294750

Partial work sheet of a corporation

The two accounts related to capital are Capital Stock and Retained Earnings. In the Trial Balance Credit column the capital stock account shows a credit balance of $110,000.00. This is the amount of capital stock issued. This is the first work sheet of Penrite Corporation. Therefore, there is no balance shown for the retained earnings account in the Trial Balance Credit column.

In succeeding years, the amount in the Trial Balance Credit column for Retained Earnings will be the amount of the net income from previous years not yet distributed to stockholders. The distribution of net income to stockholders is described later in this chapter.

A corporation, as a "person," must pay federal and state income taxes. The estimated federal income tax must be declared and paid quarterly. Therefore, the debit balance for Federal Income Tax, Line 27, of the work sheet, page 637, represents the amount of federal income tax paid prior to December 31, 1978. The adjustment for federal income tax represents the additional tax that Penrite Corporation estimates it still owes at the end of the fiscal year, 1978. This amount still owed will be paid in January, 1979.

The adjustments on the work sheet for Penrite Corporation are similar to those for any other form of business. One additional adjustment for federal income tax owed is necessary for the corporation. This adjustment is not made for sole proprietorships or partnerships because income taxes are not paid by such businesses but are paid by the owners.

Figuring the federal income tax owed. The federal income tax paid by a corporation is not considered an operating expense of the business. Therefore, the account Federal Income Tax is listed in the Other Expenses section of the general ledger. To figure the amount of federal income tax from the data on the work sheet, the Penrite Corporation accountant does the following:

1. Completes all the usual adjustments on the work sheet and extends all amounts needed to the Income Statement columns.

2. Foots the Income Statement columns and finds the difference between the two footings. (This footing is shown below Line 26 of the illustration, page 637.) The amount of the difference between the footings is the net income before deducting the federal income tax.

Footing of Income Statement Credit column.................. $176,692.56
Less footing of Income Statement Debit column 163,623.95
Equals net income before federal income tax.................. $ 13,068.61

The amount of net income before federal income tax is deducted, $13,068.61, is not shown on the work sheet.

3. Figures the amount of federal income tax due on the "net income before federal income tax." (The Penrite Corporation accountant uses tax rate tables supplied by the Internal Revenue Service.) For Penrite Corporation, the amount of federal income tax for the first six months of operations ending December 31, 1978, is $3,267.15. Some of this tax, $1,700.00, has already been paid and recorded. The additional amount for which an adjustment must be made is figured as follows:

Total amount of federal income tax on net income.............. $3,267.15
Less amount already recorded in federal income tax account 1,700.00
Equals additional amount of tax to be recorded $1,567.15

Adjustment for federal income tax. The adjustment needed for federal income tax is shown in the T accounts at the right.

The amount of additional income tax owed by Penrite Corporation, $1,567.15, is debited to Federal Income Tax. The new balance of this account, $3,267.15, is the total amount the corporation must pay on its net income for the six months ending December 31, 1978.

Federal Income Tax		812
Bal.	1,700.00	
Adj.	1,567.15	

The amount, $1,567.15, is also credited to Federal Income Tax Payable. This amount is to be paid to the federal government in January, 1979.

Federal Income Tax Payable 218		
	Adj.	1,567.15

The adjustment for federal income tax owed is shown on the work sheet, page 637, as adjustment (h). Although the federal government does not consider the income tax to be an expense of the corporation, Penrite Corporation shows the tax as an expense when reporting to stockholders.

After the adjustment for federal income tax has been made on the work sheet, the work sheet is completed in the usual manner. The net income is labeled as *Net Income After Tax*. This is shown on the work sheet, page 637, on Line 29.

Income statement of a corporation

The income statement of a corporation is similar to the income statement for other forms of businesses. The exception is the listing of net income before and after federal income tax is considered. This is shown on the partial income statement below for Penrite Corporation.

```
                    PENRITE CORPORATION
                     INCOME STATEMENT
              FOR SIX MONTHS ENDED DECEMBER 31, 1978


       OPERATING REVENUE
          SALES.............................  $140,608.56
          LESS SALES RETURNS AND ALLOWANCES     1,325.60
          NET SALES .......................                139,282.96


             TOTAL OPERATING EXPENSES.........               24,298.93
       INCOME FROM OPERATIONS................              $ 13,418.61
       OTHER EXPENSE
          INTEREST EXPENSE..................                   350.00
       NET INCOME BEFORE FEDERAL INCOME TAX..             $ 13,068.61
       LESS FEDERAL INCOME TAX..............                 3,267.15
       NET INCOME AFTER FEDERAL INCOME TAX..             $  9,801.46
```

Computer printout of a partial income statement for a corporation

The income statement above shows that the corporation had a net income of $13,068.61, before it considered federal income tax. The federal income tax is $3,267.15 (part of this has already been paid, but all of it is an expense for this fiscal period). The net income remaining after the total federal income tax is paid is $9,801.46 ($13,068.61 − $3,267.15).

Balance sheet of a corporation

The only difference between a balance sheet of a corporation and that of a sole proprietorship or a partnership is in the capital section. The capital section shown below of the Penrite Corporation balance sheet is labeled *Stockholders' Equity*. Some corporations use the same label as sole proprietorships and partnerships: *Capital*. Either label is acceptable.

```
                    STOCKHOLDERS' EQUITY
CAPITAL STOCK  ........................... $110,000.00
RETAINED EARNINGS.........................    9,801.46
TOTAL STOCKHOLDERS' EQUITY................            119,801.46
TOTAL LIABILITIES AND STOCKHOLDERS' EQUITY           $152,947.50
```

Computer printout of the stockholders' equity
section of a corporation balance sheet

The amount earned by a corporation and not yet distributed to stockholders is called retained earnings. Other terms used are earned surplus, earnings retained in the business, retained revenue, retained income, and accumulated earnings. If costs and expenses exceed revenue, there is a net loss. The amount of net loss is called a deficit.

On the balance sheet above, the amount of net income for Penrite Corporation not yet distributed to stockholders is $9,801.46. This amount is listed on the line with the account title Retained Earnings. The amount of capital stock, $110,000.00, plus the amount of retained earnings, $9,801.46, equals the total stockholders' equity of Penrite Corporation, $119,801.46.

Adjusting and closing entries of a corporation

The adjusting entries are based on data in the Adjustments columns of the work sheet. With the exception of the adjustment for federal income tax, adjustments for corporations are similar to those for sole proprietorships and partnerships.

The closing entries are also similar to those for a sole proprietorship or partnership. However, there are no separate capital and drawing accounts for owners of a corporation. The amount of net income (which is also the balance of the income summary account) is closed into the retained earnings account. This closing entry for Penrite Corporation is shown on page 641.

			GENERAL JOURNAL			PAGE /4
1	2				3	4
ACCOUNTS PAYABLE DEBIT	GENERAL DEBIT	DATE	ACCOUNT TITLE	POST. REF.	GENERAL CREDIT	ACCOUNTS RECEIV. CREDIT
21	980146	31	*Income Summary*			21
22			*Retained Earnings*		980146	22
23						23

Entry to close the income summary account
into the retained earnings account

Post-closing trial balance

After the adjusting and closing entries have been posted, the accountant for Penrite Corporation prepares a post-closing trial balance. This procedure is the same as for other forms of businesses.

Reversing entries for a corporation

On the first day of a new fiscal period, a corporation makes reversing entries in the same manner as other forms of business. The Penrite Corporation has two reversing entries to make: (1) for the amount of interest payable recorded as an adjustment, and (2) for the amount of federal income tax payable recorded as an adjustment.

The reversing entries are shown below.

			GENERAL JOURNAL			PAGE /
1	2				3	4
ACCOUNTS PAYABLE DEBIT	GENERAL DEBIT	DATE	ACCOUNT TITLE	POST. REF.	GENERAL CREDIT	ACCOUNTS RECEIV. CREDIT
1			*Reversing Entries*			1
2	5000	1979 Jan. 1	*Interest Payable*			2
3			*Interest Expense*		5000	3
4	156715	1	*Federal Income Tax Pay.*			4
5			*Federal Income Tax*		156715	5

Reversing entries for
Penrite Corporation

After these reversing entries are posted, the work at the end of the fiscal period is complete. The books of Penrite Corporation are ready for the new fiscal period.

DISTRIBUTING INCOME TO STOCKHOLDERS

The net income earned by a corporation belongs to the stockholders. Some of this income may be retained by the business to provide for expansion and increased needs of the business. Some of the income can be given to the stockholders as a return on their investments. None of the income can be distributed to stockholders except by formal action of the board of directors. The amount of corporate earnings distributed to stockholders is called a dividend.

Declaring a dividend

The action of the board of directors to distribute a definite amount of corporate earnings to stockholders on a specific date is called declaring a dividend. The amount of the dividend is usually stated as a certain amount per share.

On January 3, 1979, the board of directors of Penrite Corporation declares a dividend of $1.00 a share on 1,100 shares of outstanding stock. The dividend is to be paid on January 31, 1979. This action of the board of directors transfers $1,100.00 from Retained Earnings to a liability account, Dividends Payable. Dividends Payable is a liability account showing the total amount of dividends owed to stockholders.

The entry in the general journal to record the dividend declared on January 3 is shown below.

Entry to record the declaration of a dividend

ACCOUNTS PAYABLE DEBIT	GENERAL DEBIT	DATE	ACCOUNT TITLE	POST. REF.	GENERAL CREDIT	ACCOUNTS RECEIV. CREDIT	
	1 1 0 0 00	3	Retained Earnings				9
			Dividends Payable		1 1 0 0 00		10
			January 3 minutes				11
			of Board of Directors.				12

GENERAL JOURNAL — PAGE 1

Paying a dividend

On January 31, 1979, Penrite Corporation mails a check to each stockholder for the amount of dividend owed. An entry is made in the cash payments journal to record the *total* payment of the dividend. Dividends Payable is debited for $1,100.00, and Cash is credited for $1,100.00.

CASH PAYMENTS JOURNAL — PAGE 2

DATE	ACCOUNT TITLE	CHECK No.	POST. REF.	GENERAL DEBIT	GENERAL CREDIT	ACCOUNTS PAYABLE DEBIT	PURCHASES DISCOUNT CREDIT	CASH CREDIT	
31	Dividends Payable	521- 526		1 1 0 0 00				1 1 0 0 00	29

Entry to record the payment of a dividend

Thus, two entries are required to record dividends: (1) at the time a dividend is declared, debiting Retained Earnings and crediting Dividends.

Payable; and (2) at the time a dividend is paid, debiting Dividends Payable and crediting Cash.

COOPERATIVE FORM OF BUSINESS

A business owned by its customers is called a cooperative. One of the chief differences between a cooperative and a corporation is the voting rights of owners. In a cooperative, each member has only one vote regardless of the number of shares owned. In a corporation, each stockholder has one vote for each share of common stock owned. Therefore, a few stockholders of a corporation may have the majority of votes at the annual stockholders' meeting. For example, if Mr. Dale (with 500 shares) and Ms. Morrison (with 200 shares) vote together, they will have a majority vote at stockholders' meetings. In fact, if Mr. Dale buys 51 more shares of stock from one of the other stockholders, he *alone* will have a majority of the issued shares of stock.

The net income of a cooperative is distributed to its members in two ways: (1) according to the amount of purchases made by each member during the fiscal year; and (2) according to the amount of investment each member has. The percentage of net income distributed to each member by a cooperative according to the amount of the member's annual purchases is called a participation dividend. The percentage of net income distributed to each member of a cooperative according to the amount of the member's investment is called a dividend on capital stock. A cooperative may use one or both methods of distributing net income.

The methods of recording business transactions for a cooperative are the same as for a corporation. The financial statements are identical.

Using Business Terms

✦ What is the meaning of each of the following?

- corporation
- incorporators
- articles of incorporation
- charter
- shares
- stockholder
- capital stock
- stock certificate

- authorized capital stock
- par-value stock
- no-par-value stock
- preferred stock
- common stock
- board of directors
- retained earnings

- deficit
- dividend
- declaring a dividend
- cooperative
- participation dividend
- dividend on capital stock

Questions for Individual Study

1. Who authorizes the formation of a corporation?
2. What is the relationship between a corporation and its stockholders?
3. When does a corporation come into existence?

4. What rights do holders of preferred stock usually have that holders of common stock do not have?
5. What rights do holders of common stock have that holders of preferred stock usually do not have?

6. What are three advantages of the corporate form of business?

7. What are the three capital accounts used by the Penrite Corporation?

8. What accounts are debited and credited if an incorporator invests cash and equipment in a corporation?

9. What accounts are debited and credited if an incorporator buys stock in a corporation for cash only?

10. How do adjusting entries for a corporation compare to those for a sole proprietorship?

11. How does the income statement of a corporation compare to that of a sole proprietorship?

12. How does the balance sheet of a corporation compare to that of a sole proprietorship?

13. What entry is made to close the income summary account and record the net income for a corporation?

14. What accounts are debited and credited when a dividend is declared?

15. What accounts are debited and credited when a dividend is paid?

16. How do the voting rights of owners of a corporation differ from voting rights of owners of a cooperative?

17. In what two ways, described in this chapter, might a stockholder control a corporation?

Cases for Management Decision

CASE 1 You have $15,000.00 to invest. You can buy stock in the Dorton Corporation, which has paid a dividend each year equal to 10% of the value of its capital stock. You can also become a partner in the firm of Melcross and Peake. The partnership has two partners at the present time. Each year the partners have earned an amount equal to 10% of their investment in the partnership. What factors would you consider before deciding to invest in either the corporation or the partnership?

CASE 2 A major stockholder criticizes the board of directors for not declaring larger dividends. During the past five years the net income annually has been equal to 15% of the investment in capital stock. The amount of dividend declared each year has been only 6% of the investment. As a stockholder in the same corporation, would you support a proposal to increase the size of the annual dividend? Why?

Problems for Applying Concepts

PROBLEM 33-1 Opening entry for a corporation

On January 3 of the current year a charter is obtained by McGrady Sales Corporation. The new corporation is authorized to issue 1,000 shares of common stock with a par value of $100.00, for a total authorized capital of $100,000.00.

The new corporation has agreed to take over the hardware business owned by John McGrady and to issue stock to him for his equity. In addition, Susan McLean is to invest $20,000.00 and Don Bell is to invest $10,000.00 in cash.

On January 3 the corporation takes over the assets and liabilities of Mr. McGrady's business as shown on the balance sheet on page 645. The corporation issues 400 shares of stock to Mr. McGrady.

On January 3, the corporation also receives cash from Ms. McLean, $20,000.00, and issues 200 shares of stock to her. Cash is received on the same date from Mr. Bell, $10,000.00, and 100 shares of stock are issued to him.

Instructions: □ **1.** Record the opening entries on page 1 of a general journal. Receipt No. 1.

□ **2.** Record the memorandum entry for the cash invested on page 1 of a cash receipts journal.

McGrady Hardware Company Balance Sheet January 3, 19—				
Assets		**Liabilities**		
Cash............................	3 454 60	Notes Payable................	2 704 00	
Accounts Receivable	6 524 85	Accounts Payable	4 383 85	
Merchandise Inventory....	19 598 15	Total Liabilities	7 087 85	
Supplies........................	910 25			
Equipment	16 600 00	**Capital**		
		John McGrady, Capital	40 000 00	
Total Assets	47 087 85	Total Liabilities & Capital	47 087 85	

PROBLEM 33-2 ● Declaring and paying a dividend

During the current year, the Bayside Corporation completed the following entries related to declaring and paying a dividend:

June 30. Transferred the credit balance of the income summary account, $24,950.00, to the retained earnings account by a closing entry.

July 1. Declared a dividend of $3.00 per share on 4,000 shares of common stock.

Aug. 1. Paid the dividend declared on July 1. Checks No. 148–165.

Instructions: Record each of the entries above on page 12 of a general journal and page 65 of a cash payments journal.

PROBLEM 33-3 ● End-of-year work for a corporation

The account balances in the general ledger of the Franklin Corporation for the fiscal year ended December 31 of the current year are shown on page 646.

Instructions: ◻ 1. Prepare an eight-column work sheet for Franklin Corporation. Additional data needed are:

Allowance for uncollectible accounts, 10% of balance of Accounts Receivable.
Merchandise inventory, December 31, $36,702.50.
Supplies inventory, December 31, $328.74.
Value of insurance policies, December 31, $850.00.
Annual estimated depreciation of equipment, $300.00.
Accrued interest expense on December 31, $225.00.
Federal income tax to bring the total federal income tax expense for the year up to an amount equal to 22% of the net income before federal income tax.

Instructions: ◻ 2. Prepare an income statement for Franklin Corporation. Use the partial income statement on page 639 as a model.

◻ 3. Prepare a balance sheet for Franklin Corporation. Use the partial balance sheet on page 640 as a model. To obtain the balance of the retained earnings account for the balance sheet, add the net income after federal income tax to the balance of the retained earnings account shown on the work sheet.

☐ **4.** Record the adjusting entries on page 29 of a general journal.

☐ **5.** Record the closing entries on page 30 of a general journal.

☐ **6.** Record the reversing entries for accrued interest expense and federal income tax as of January 1 of the next year. Record the reversing entries on page 30 of a general journal.

Account Title	Acct. No.	Account Balances Debit	Account Balances Credit
Cash	111	$ 18,320.96	——
Accounts Receivable	112	7,041.25	——
Allowance for Uncollectible Accounts	112.1	——	$ 624.16
Merchandise Inventory	113	40,725.78	——
Supplies	114	1,564.09	——
Prepaid Insurance	115	1,070.00	——
Equipment	116	8,800.00	——
Accumulated Depreciation — Equipment	116.1	——	660.00
Notes Payable	211	——	5,000.00
Interest Payable	212	——	——
Accounts Payable	213	——	1,132.75
Employees Income Tax Payable	214	——	302.15
FICA Tax Payable	215	——	62.28
Federal Unemployment Tax Payable	216	——	5.18
State Unemployment Tax Payable	217	——	28.03
Federal Income Tax Payable	218	——	——
Capital Stock	311	——	50,000.00
Retained Earnings	312	——	5,692.46
Income Summary	313	——	——
Sales	411	——	174,955.22
Sales Returns and Allowances	411.1	540.13	——
Purchases	511	141,646.00	——
Purchases Returns and Allowances	511.1	——	487.00
Purchases Discount	511.2	——	948.50
Advertising Expense	611	1,750.00	——
Bad Debts Expense	612	——	——
Delivery Expense	613	1,600.00	——
Depreciation Expense — Equipment	614	——	——
Insurance Expense	615	——	——
Miscellaneous Expense	616	173.00	——
Payroll Taxes Expense	617	1,146.32	——
Rent Expense	618	2,160.00	——
Salary Expense	619	12,460.00	——
Supplies Expense	620	——	——
Interest Expense	811	75.20	——
Federal Income Tax	812	825.00	——

CORPORATION

A Business Simulation

Environmental
Residential Apparatus

JOURNALS
& PAYROLL
REGISTERS

EMPLOYEES
EARNINGS
RECORDS

CHECKBOOK

ACCOUNTS
RECEIVABLE LEDGER
ACCOUNTS
PAYABLE LEDGER

The *ENVIROTROL* business simulation provides a review of the accounting principles discussed and illustrated in this textbook. It covers the transactions completed by a corporation that conducts a combination wholesale and retail business dealing in precision residential instruments such as humidifiers, dehumidifiers, electronic air cleaners, and climate control devices. The flowcharts on the next two pages show the accounting cycle of *ENVIROTROL*.

(The narrative is provided in the set available from the publisher.)

647

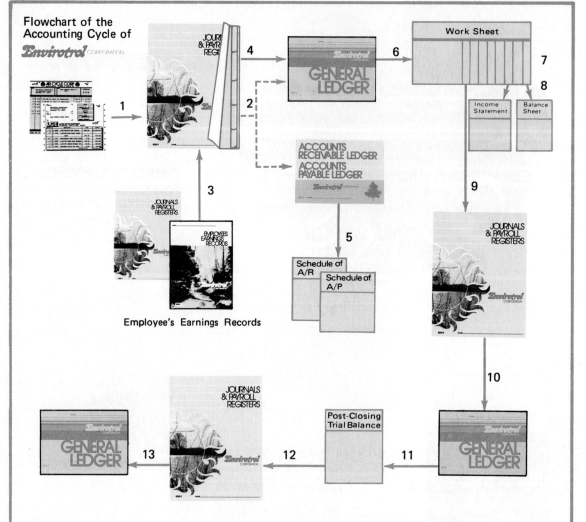

Flowchart of the Accounting Cycle of *Envirotrol* CORPORATION

Employee's Earnings Records

1 Journalize from the source documents to the appropriate special journals.
2 Post items to be posted individually to the accounts receivable ledger, accounts payable ledger, and general ledger.
3 Prepare the payroll and journalize the entries. Update the employee's earnings records.
4 Post the column totals to the general ledger.
5 Prepare schedules of accounts receivable and of accounts payable from the subsidiary ledgers.
6 Prepare the trial balance on the work sheet.
7 Enter the adjustments and complete the work sheet.
8 Prepare the financial statements.
9 Journalize the adjusting and closing entries from the work sheet.
10 Post the adjusting and closing entries to the general ledger.
11 Prepare a post-closing trial balance.
12 Journalize the reversing entries.
13 Post the reversing entries to the general ledger.

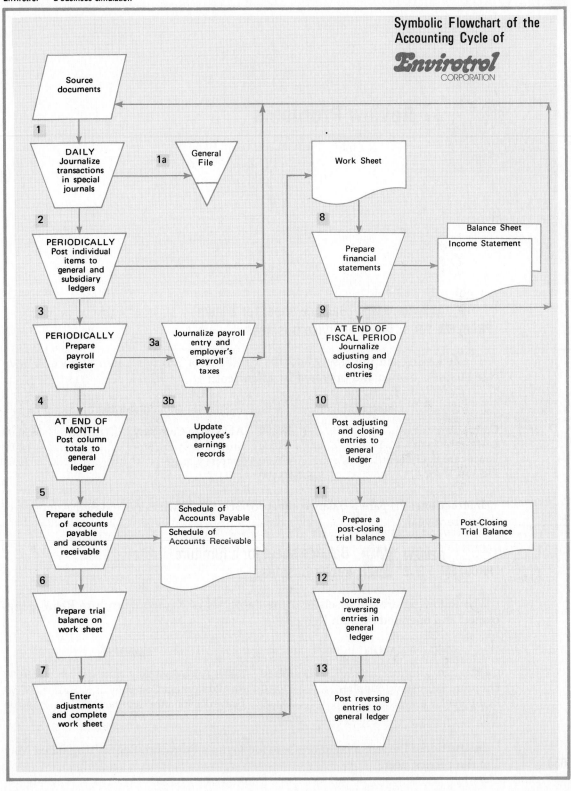

Symbolic Flowchart of the
Accounting Cycle of

Envirotrol
CORPORATION

1 Source documents

1 DAILY Journalize transactions in special journals

1a General File

2 PERIODICALLY Post individual items to general and subsidiary ledgers

3 PERIODICALLY Prepare payroll register

3a Journalize payroll entry and employer's payroll taxes

3b Update employee's earnings records

4 AT END OF MONTH Post column totals to general ledger

5 Prepare schedule of accounts payable and accounts receivable

Schedule of Accounts Payable
Schedule of Accounts Receivable

6 Prepare trial balance on work sheet

7 Enter adjustments and complete work sheet

8 Prepare financial statements

Work Sheet

Balance Sheet
Income Statement

9 AT END OF FISCAL PERIOD Journalize adjusting and closing entries

10 Post adjusting and closing entries to general ledger

11 Prepare a post-closing trial balance

Post-Closing Trial Balance

12 Journalize reversing entries in general ledger

13 Post reversing entries to general ledger

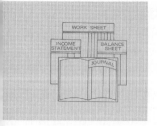

Review Problems

REVIEW PROBLEM 1-R 1 Balance sheet for a lawn service business

The following are the assets and the liabilities of Scotty's Lawn Service, a lawn care business owned and operated by Ellen Scott:

Assets		Liabilities	
Cash	$ 185.00	Auto Loan Company	$630.00
Lawn-care Tools	80.00	Burt's Hardware Store	60.00
Lawn-care Equipment	475.00	Empire Garage	40.00
Pick-up Truck	1,900.00		

Instructions: Prepare a balance sheet for Scotty's Lawn Service dated August 1 of the current year.

REVIEW PROBLEM 1-R 2 Balance sheet for a furniture repair business

The following are the assets and the liabilities of Kemp's Furniture Refinishing, owned and operated by Beth Kemp:

Assets		Liabilities	
Cash	$ 650.30	Keller Paint Company	$180.90
Furniture Refinishing Supplies	510.10	Rex Equipment Company	280.90
Equipment	840.40	Universal Finance Company	860.00
Truck	2,400.00		

Instructions: Prepare a balance sheet for Kemp's Furniture Refinishing dated May 1 of the current year.

REVIEW PROBLEM 2-R 1		Balance sheet and opening entry for a motorcycle repair service

Charles Tanner owns and operates Chuck's Cycle Shop where he repairs motorcycles. The following are the assets and liabilities of his business:

Assets		Liabilities	
Cash	$ 840.00	Cycle Tire Company	$ 185.00
Supplies and Parts	1,210.50	J & R Parts Company	110.00
Repair Equipment	3,880.50	Miller Equipment Company	1,215.00
Office Equipment	860.00		

Instructions: □ **1.** Prepare a balance sheet for Chuck's Cycle Shop dated October 1 of the current year.

□ **2.** Record the opening entry on page 1 in a general journal.

REVIEW PROBLEM 3-R 1		Recording and posting the opening entry for an attorney

The balance sheet of Margaret Warner, attorney, on May 1 of the current year is as follows:

Margaret Warner, Attorney
Balance Sheet
May 1, 19—

Assets			Liabilities		
Cash	917	00	Legal Book Company		47 00
Office Supplies	73	50	Modern Furniture Company		540 00
Law Library	510	00	Total Liabilities		587 00
Office Furniture	1 112	00			
Office Equipment	685	50	Capital		
			Margaret Warner, Capital		2 711 00
Total Assets	3 298	00	Total Liabilities and Capital		3 298 00

Instructions: □ **1.** Record the opening entry on page 1 of a general journal. Use May 1 of the current year as the date.

□ **2.** Open accounts in a ledger for all the account titles listed on the balance sheet. Allow one fourth of a page in your ledger for each account. Number the accounts as follows: asset accounts, 11 to 15; liability accounts, 21 and 22; and the attorney's capital account, 31.

□ **3.** Post the opening entry.

REVIEW PROBLEM 4-R 1		Analyzing transactions into their debit and credit parts

Mr. John Foley operates Foley's Tax Service. On July 1, his ledger contains the balance sheet accounts with balances as shown on page 652.

Cash		Elmex Business Machines	
Balance 1,700.00			Balance 430.00

Office Supplies		L & M Office Supplies	
Balance 80.00			Balance 79.00

Office Furniture		Wesley Office Furniture	
Balance 262.00			Balance 350.00

Office Machines		John Foley, Capital	
Balance 372.00			Balance 1,555.00

Instructions: □ **1.** On a sheet of paper, copy the T accounts as shown above with their balances. Allow seven lines for the cash account and three lines for each of the other accounts.

Cash	
Balance 1,700.00	
(1) 48.00	

Office Furniture	
Balance 262.00	(1) 48.00

□ **2.** Analyze each of the following transactions into its debit and credit parts. Write the debit amount and the transaction number on the proper side of the account. Write the credit amount and the transaction number on the proper side of the account.

The analysis of the first transaction and its effect on the accounts is shown at the left.

1. Received cash from sale of old office furniture, $48.00.
2. Paid cash to Wesley Office Furniture in payment of amount owed, $350.00.
3. Paid cash for new electric typewriter, $450.00.
4. Paid cash for office supplies, $19.00.
5. Received cash from sale of old office desk, $45.00.
6. Paid cash for new office desk, $300.00.
7. Paid cash to Elmex Business Machines in part payment of amount owed, $250.00.
8. Received cash from sale of old office chair, $15.00.
9. Paid cash for new office chair, $90.00.
10. Received cash from John Foley, the owner, as an additional investment in the business, $750.00.
11. Paid cash to L & M Office Supplies in payment of amount owed, $79.00.

REVIEW PROBLEM 5-R 1 ● Analyzing transactions into their debit and credit parts

Doris Krupa operates the Dolphin Swim Club and pays a monthly rent for the use of the pool and buildings. Her revenue is obtained from two sources: (1) annual membership dues, and (2) daily swim fees paid by nonmembers.

On March 1 her ledger accounts contain the following balances: Cash, $850.00; Office Furniture and Equipment, $1,110.00; Pool Equipment, $600.00; Nolan Equipment Company (creditor), $450.00; and Doris Krupa, Capital, $2,110.00.

Instructions: □ **1.** On a sheet of paper prepare a T account for each of the accounts above and record the account balance. Also prepare a T account for each of the following accounts: Membership Dues, Swim Fees, Electricity Expense, Pool Maintenance Expense, Rent Expense, and Water Expense. There are no account balances on March 1 in the two revenue accounts and the four expense accounts. Allow twelve lines for the cash account and allow three lines for each of the other accounts.

□ **2.** Analyze each of the following transactions into its debit and credit parts. Write the debit amount and the transaction number on the proper side of the account. Write the credit amount and the transaction number on the proper side of the account.

1. Paid cash for water bill, $57.00.
2. Paid cash for March rent, $250.00.
3. Received cash from membership dues, $575.00.
4. Paid cash for chlorine tablets, $35.00. (Pool Maintenance Expense)
5. Received cash from swim fees, $30.00.
6. Paid cash for pool treatment solution, $20.00. (Pool Maintenance Expense)
7. Paid cash to Nolan Equipment Co. in part payment on account, $100.00.
8. Received cash from membership dues, $345.00.
9. Received cash for sale of used pump and filter, $260.00.
10. Paid cash for new circulating pump and filter, $1,100.00.
11. Paid cash for electric bill, $28.00.
12. Received cash from swim fees, $40.00.
13. Received cash from Ms. Krupa as additional investment in the business, $500.00.
14. Paid cash for a new diving board, $85.00.
15. Received cash from membership dues, $950.00.
16. Received cash from sale of old office desk, $8.00.
17. Paid cash for new office desk, $220.00.
18. Paid cash for reclining pool chairs, $55.00.
19. Paid cash to Nolan Equipment Co. in part payment on account, $150.00.

REVIEW
PROBLEM 6-R 1   Journalizing cash transactions of a hunting lodge

After being closed during spring and summer, Moose Lodge reopened for the hunting season on October 15 of the current year.

Instructions: □ **1.** Prepare a cash journal similar to the one on page 77 by writing the proper headings at the top of each column. Note that the revenue account is called Room Sales. Number the page 8.

□ **2.** Record the beginning cash balance as of October 15 of the current year as a memorandum entry. The cash balance at the start of this new hunting season was $390.00.

□ **3.** Journalize the following transactions of Moose Lodge. Use the account titles shown in the chart of accounts below.

Moose Lodge Chart of Accounts			
(1) Assets	Account Number	**(4) Revenue**	Account Number
Cash.............................	11	Room Sales.............................	41
Housekeeping Supplies...............	12		
Furniture and Fixtures................	13	**(5) Expenses**	
Office Equipment	14		
		Advertising Expense...................	51
(2) Liabilities		Laundry Expense......................	52
		Miscellaneous Expense...............	53
Avery Plumbing Company...........	21	Rent Expense	54
Motel Furniture Company............	22	Utilities Expense	55
(3) Capital			
Karl Kleeb, Capital.....................	31		

Instructions: □ **4.** All cash payments were made by check. Number all checks beginning with Ck1. Receipt numbers are given for all revenue transactions.

Oct. 15. Paid cash to person for opening and cleaning the lodge, $40.00. (Miscellaneous Expense)
  15. Paid cash for rent of lodge for remainder of October, $80.00.
  16. Received cash from sale of old furniture, $20.50. Receipt No. 1.
  17. Received cash from room sales, $70.00. Receipts No. 2–8.
  19. Paid cash to Avery Plumbing Company in payment of amount owed, $28.00.
  20. Received cash from room sales, $70.00. Receipts No. 9–15.
  20. Paid cash for laundry, $21.00.
  21. Received cash from sale of old calculator, $15.50. Receipt No. 16.
  22. Received cash from room sales, $130.00. Receipts No. 17–29.
  23. Paid cash for installing road signs advertising the lodge, $55.00.
  26. Received cash from room sales, $110.00. Receipts No. 30–40.
  27. Paid cash for telephone bill, $7.50.
  28. Paid cash for laundry, $12.00.
  29. Paid cash for electric bill, $14.50.
  30. Received cash from room sales, $140.00. Receipts No. 41–54.
  30. Paid cash for advertisement in magazine, $18.00.

Instructions: □ **5.** Foot each of the amount columns of your cash journal. Use small pencil figures.

□ **6.** Prove the equality of debits and credits in your cash journal.

□ **7.** Prove cash. The last check stub shows a bank balance at the end of the month of $670.00. All cash received has been deposited.

□ **8.** Write the column totals on the Totals line of your cash journal. Write the word *Totals* in the Account Title column.

□ **9.** Rule the cash journal.

<table>
<tr><td align="right">**REVIEW**
PROBLEM 7-R 1</td><td></td><td>Journalizing and posting the transactions
of an attorney</td></tr>
</table>

You will need to prepare the ledger of Richard J. McCarron, a lawyer, before you can do the work in this problem.

Instructions: □ **1.** Open the twelve accounts in the ledger that will be needed for this problem. Place six accounts on each page of your ledger. A chart of accounts showing account titles and numbers is given below.

Richard J. McCarron, Attorney Chart of Accounts			
(1) Assets	Account Number	**(4) Revenue**	Account Number
Cash..	11	Fees Revenue............................	41
Automobile	12		
Office Furniture.........................	13	**(5) Expenses**	
Professional Library...................	14		
		Automobile Expense....................	51
(2) Liabilities		Miscellaneous Expense...............	52
		Rent Expense............................	53
Cummings Garage......................	21	Salary Expense...........................	54
Hoffman Company	22		
(3) Capital			
Richard J. McCarron, Capital........	31		

Instructions: □ **2.** Copy the following account balances on the appropriate sides of the proper accounts in the ledger. Use October 1 of the current year as the date. Whenever a balance is copied in a ledger account, write the word *Balance* in the Item column and place a check mark in the Post. Ref. column.

Cash $14,313.00; Automobile, $3,800.00; Office Furniture, $1,450.00; Professional Library, $645.00; Cummings Garage, $1,139.00; Hoffman Company, $184.50; Richard J. McCarron, Capital, $9,035.50; Fees Revenue, $16,400.00; Automobile Expense, $540.00; Miscellaneous Expense, $125.00; Rent Expense, $2,250.00; Salary Expense, $3,636.00.

□ **3.** Record the cash balance as a memorandum entry. Use page 10 of a cash journal like the one in Bonus Problem 6-B on page 85.

□ **4.** Journalize the transactions for October given below. The revenue column should be headed *Fees Revenue Credit*. Number all checks beginning with Ck216. Number all receipts beginning with R60.

Oct. 1. Paid cash for October rent, $350.00.
2. Received cash for legal services, $50.00.
3. Paid cash for office furniture, $145.00.
4. Received cash for sale of old office chair, $10.00.
9. Received cash for legal services, $85.00.
10. Paid cash to Hoffman Company on account, $184.50.
15. Paid cash for salary expense, $200.00.
15. Paid cash for automobile expense, $5.00.
17. Paid cash for taking a client to dinner, $9.50.
18. Paid cash for repairs to automobile, $21.50.
24. Received cash for legal services, $300.00.
25. Paid cash to Cummings Garage on account, $250.00.
26. Received cash for sale of old office furniture, $20.00.
26. Received cash for legal services, $125.00.
29. Received cash for legal services, $80.00.
30. Paid cash for telephone bill, $16.00.
31. Paid cash for electric bill, $8.00.
31. Paid cash for salary expense, $200.00.

Instructions: □ **5.** Post the individual amounts in the General Debit and General Credit columns to the accounts in the ledger.

□ **6.** Foot each amount column with small pencil figures.

□ **7.** Prove the equality of debits and credits in your cash journal.

□ **8.** Prove cash. The last check stub shows a bank balance at the end of the month of $13,593.50. All cash receipts have been deposited.

□ **9.** Total and rule the cash journal.

□ **10.** Post the totals of the three special columns. Place a check mark under the General Debit and General Credit columns to indicate that these totals are not to be posted.

REVIEW PROBLEM 8-R 1 Trial balance for a tree service

Bonus Problem 5-B on page 64 shows the accounts of Dan's Tree Service after twelve transactions were recorded in the accounts. Assume that these transactions were completed during March of the current year.

Instructions: □ **1.** Prove cash. The bank balance according to the checkbook on March 31 of the current year is $485.00. All cash receipts have been deposited.

□ **2.** Prepare a trial balance dated March 31 of the current year.

REVIEW
PROBLEM 8-R 2   ● Trial balance for a surgeon

The footings in the ledger accounts of Charlene C. Eaton, on October 31 of the current year are as follows:

Acct. No.	Account Title	Debit	Credit
11	Cash	$1,701.90	$ 401.60
12	Equipment	3,950.00	
13	Office Furniture	1,455.00	
21	Athens Equipment Company	250.00	675.90
22	Colby Medical Supply Company	75.90	75.90
31	Charlene C. Eaton, Capital		5,656.85
41	Fees Revenue		1,504.00
51	Miscellaneous Expense	66.45	
52	Rent Expense	440.00	
53	Salary Expense	375.00	

Instructions: □ **1.** Prove cash. The bank balance according to the checkbook on October 31 of the current year is $1,300.30. All cash receipts have been deposited.

□ **2.** Prepare a trial balance dated October 31 of the current year.

REVIEW
PROBLEM 9-R 1   ● Work sheet for an insurance agency

On July 31 of the current year, the end of a fiscal period of one month, the account balances in the ledger of the United Insurance Agency are:

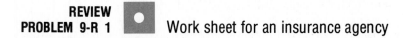

Cash 11	Brown & Company 21	Premiums Revenue 41	Entertainment Exp. 53
1,430.00	376.50	1,300.00	72.00

Automobile 12	Glen Motors 22	Advertising Expense 51	Miscellaneous Exp. 54
4,500.00	1,400.00	93.50	115.00

Office Furniture 13	Parker Products 23	Automobile Expense 52	Rent Expense 55
720.00	740.50	125.00	225.00

Office Machines 14	Karen Malone, Cap. 31
660.50	4,124.00

Instructions: Prepare a six-column work sheet for the United Insurance Agency for the period ended July 31 of the current year. Write the proper heading at the top of each column of the work sheet. Use the account titles, account numbers, and account balances shown above. Use as your model the work sheet illustrated on page 125.

REVIEW
PROBLEM 10-R 1
REVIEW
PROBLEM 10-R 1   Financial reports for a cinema

The work sheet for Plaza Cinema for the month of March of the current year is given below.

Plaza Cinema
Work Sheet
For Month Ended March 31, 19—

Account Title	Acct. No.	Trial Balance Debit	Trial Balance Credit	Income Statement Debit	Income Statement Credit	Balance Sheet Debit	Balance Sheet Credit
Cash	11	2 680 20				2 680 20	
Air Conditioning Equip.	12	3 800 00				3 800 00	
Projection Equipment	13	9 100 00				9 100 00	
Sound Equipment	14	938 50				938 50	
Allied Studios	21		107 30				107 30
Bader Films	22		33 10				33 10
Cline Films, Inc.	23		83 00				83 00
Gibson Sound Service	24		50 00				50 00
United Supplies, Inc.	25		48 20				48 20
Elsa Calvo, Capital	31		15 041 00				15 041 00
Admissions Revenue	41		2 938 60		2 938 60		
Advertising Expense	51	164 00		164 00			
Electricity Expense	52	136 20		136 20			
Film Rental Expense	53	1 015 00		1 015 00			
Maintenance Expense	54	83 00		83 00			
Projection Expense	55	42 30		42 30			
Rent Expense	56	300 00		300 00			
Water Expense	57	42 00		42 00			
		18 301 20	18 301 20	1 782 50	2 938 60	16 518 70	15 362 60
Net Income				1 156 10			1 156 10
				2 938 60	2 938 60	16 518 70	16 518 70

Instructions: □ **1.** Prepare an income statement.

□ **2.** Prepare a balance sheet.

The work sheet illustrated for Review Problem 10-R 1 will be used in Review Problem 11-R 1.

REVIEW
PROBLEM 11-R 1   Closing entries for a cinema

A work sheet for Plaza Cinema is given in Review Problem 10-R 1.

Instructions: Record the closing entries for Plaza Cinema on page 8 of a two-column general journal.

REVIEW
PROBLEM 12-R 1   Journalizing transactions in a combination journal

Barbara Miller, a retail hardware dealer, completed the following transactions during November of the current year. The November 1 cash balance was $1,920.00.

Instructions: ▢ **1.** Prepare page 8 of a combination journal by writing the headings at the top of each column. Use the headings shown on pages 188 and 189.

▢ **2.** Record the cash balance with a memorandum entry.

▢ **3.** Record the following transactions. Source documents are abbreviated as: check, Ck; memorandum, M; purchase invoice, P; receipt, R; sales invoice, S; cash register tape, T.

Nov. 1. Paid November rent, $360.00. Ck101.
2. Purchased merchandise for cash, $240.00. Ck102.
3. Sold merchandise on account to Olin Herzel, $100.00. S51.
5. Cash sales of merchandise for the week, $840.00. T5.
6. Bought supplies on account from Marie Diaz, $40.00. M10.
6. Purchased merchandise on account from Harry Delson, $125.00. P25.
7. Received on account from Judy Callie, $220.00. R54.
8. Paid on account to Marie Diaz, $130.00. Ck103.
9. Purchased merchandise on account from Bedford Company, $110.00. P26.
12. Cash sales of merchandise for the week, $900.00. T12.
14. Sold merchandise on account to Alice Toth, $230.00. S52.
14. Purchased merchandise for cash, $190.00. Ck104.
14. Received on account from Olin Herzel, $120.00. R55.
15. Paid salaries, $240.00. Ck105.
16. Purchased merchandise on account from Curtis and Son, $150.00. P27.
16. Paid on account to Harry Delson, $230.00. Ck106.
18. Paid telephone bill, $24.00. Ck107. (Miscellaneous Expense)
19. Cash sales of merchandise for the week, $980.00. T19.
21. Purchased merchandise for cash, $100.00. Ck108.
21. Sold merchandise on account to Judy Callie, $250.00. S53.
21. Issued check to owner for a cash withdrawal, $125.00. Ck109.
22. Discovered that supplies bought in October had been posted in error as a debit to Prepaid Insurance instead of Supplies, $30.00. M11.
22. Received on account from Liz Vernon, $80.00. R56.
26. Cash sales of merchandise for the week, $890.00. T26.
28. Paid on account to Bedford Company, $110.00. Ck110.
29. Purchased merchandise on account from Harry Delson, $155.00. P28.
29. Paid delivery expense, $37.00. Ck111. (Delivery Expense)
29. Paid on account to Curtis and Son, $80.00. Ck112.
30. Paid salaries, $240.00. Ck113.
30. Sold merchandise on account to Liz Vernon, $85.00. S54.
30. Cash sales of merchandise for the week, $625.00. T30.

Instructions: ▢ **4.** Pencil foot the columns of the combination journal and prove the equality of debits and credits.

▢ **5.** Prove cash. The balance on hand shown on the check stub for Check No. 114 is $4,469.00.

▢ **6.** Total and rule the combination journal. Use the illustrations on pages 190 and 191 as a guide in ruling.

REVIEW PROBLEM 13-R 1 Recording in a combination journal; posting to a general ledger, an accounts receivable ledger, and an accounts payable ledger

Instructions: □ **1.** Open the following customers' accounts in the accounts receivable ledger. Record the balances as of October 1 of the current year.

Customer	Address	Account Balance
Eva Lucero	1116 Putnam Street, Manchester, NH 03103	——
Janis Nash	2432 Valley Street, Manchester, NH 03102	——
Tempco Company	5120 N. River Road, Manchester, NH 03106	$300.00
Alma Wade	2243 Kelly Street, Manchester, NH 03104	400.00

□ **2.** Open the following creditors' accounts in the accounts payable ledger. Record the balances as of October 1 of the current year.

Creditor	Address	Account Balance
John Gulick, Inc.	8340 Cambridge Street, Boston, MA 02154	$360.00
Phillips Company	12860 Lincoln Avenue, Boston, MA 02126	——
Yeager's	2130 Hanover Street, Manchester, NH 03106	——

□ **3.** Open the following accounts in the general ledger of Link's Store. Record the balances as of October 1 of the current year.

Account Title	Acct. No.	Account Balances Debit	Credit
Cash	11	$2,560.00	——
Accounts Receivable	12	700.00	——
Merchandise Inventory	13	3,840.00	——
Supplies	14	250.00	——
Prepaid Insurance	15	150.00	——
Accounts Payable	21	——	$ 360.00
Orin Link, Capital	31	——	7,140.00
Orin Link, Drawing	32	——	——
Income Summary	33	——	——
Sales	41	——	——
Purchases	51	——	——
Delivery Expense	61	——	——
Insurance Expense	62	——	——
Miscellaneous Expense	63	——	——
Rent Expense	64	——	——
Salary Expense	65	——	——
Supplies Expense	66	——	——

Instructions: □ **4.** Record the following transactions on page 12 of a combination journal similar to the one shown on pages 208 and 209. The beginning cash balance is $2,560.00. Source documents are abbreviated as: check, Ck; memorandum, M; purchase invoice, P; receipt, R; sales invoice, S; cash register tape, T.

Transactions

Oct. 1. Paid rent expense, $220.00. Ck43.
   3. Purchased merchandise on account from Phillips Company, $700.00. P81.
   3. Paid on account to John Gulick, Inc., $360.00. Ck44.
   3. Purchased merchandise for cash, $270.00. Ck45.
   4. Received on account from Alma Wade, $400.00. R26.
   6. Sold merchandise on account to Tempco Company, $450.00. S32.
   8. Cash sales for the week, $900.00. T8.
  10. Purchased merchandise on account from Yeager's, $830.00. P82.
  12. Sold merchandise on account to Eva Lucero, $600.00. S33.
  15. Paid salaries, $500.00. Ck46.
  15. Cash sales for the week, $1,060.00. T15.
  17. Sold merchandise on account to Janis Nash, $630.00. S34.
  18. Purchased merchandise for cash, $1,100.00. Ck47.
  19. Paid miscellaneous expense, $60.00. Ck48.
  20. Received on account from Eva Lucero, $600.00. R27.
  22. Cash sales for the week, $1,150.00. T22.
  22. Issued check to Orin Link, owner, for cash withdrawal, $250.00. Ck49.
  24. Paid on account to Yeager's, $830.00. Ck50.
  25. Purchased merchandise on account from Phillips Company, $900.00. P83.
  26. Purchased merchandise on account from John Gulick, Inc., $500.00. P84.
  27. Sold merchandise on account to Alma Wade, $380.00. S35.
  28. Discovered that $75.00 debited to Supplies in September should have been debited to Prepaid Insurance. M10.
  28. Received on account from Janis Nash, $630.00. R28.
  29. Cash sales for the week, $925.00. T29.
  29. Paid delivery expenses, $90.00. Ck51.
  31. Paid salaries, $500.00. Ck52.
  31. Bought supplies for cash, $150.00. Ck53.
  31. Cash sales for balance of month, $275.00. T31.

Instructions: ▫ **5.** Pencil foot the columns of the combination journal and prove the equality of debits and credits.

▫ **6.** Prove cash. The balance shown on Check Stub No. 53 is $4,170.00.

▫ **7.** Total and rule the combination journal.

▫ **8.** Post from the combination journal the individual items recorded in the following columns: General Ledger Debit and Credit; Accounts Receivable Debit and Credit; and Accounts Payable Debit and Credit.

▫ **9.** Post the totals of the special columns of the combination journal.

▫ **10.** Prepare a schedule of accounts receivable and a schedule of accounts payable. Prove the accuracy of the subsidiary ledgers by comparing the schedule totals with the balances of the controlling accounts in the general ledger.

▫ **11.** Prepare a trial balance in the Trial Balance columns of a work sheet.

REVIEW PROBLEM 14-R 1 Writing checks and recording deposits in a checkbook

Miss Ann Shelby, owner of The Camera Shop, asked you (as her accountant) to write the checks listed below. As accountant, sign the checks.

Oct. 29. Paid November rent to Frantz Associates, $300.00. Ck183.
Nov. 1. Deposited in checking account at the bank, $492.73.
     1. Paid on account to Bell Camera Supplies, $287.70. Ck184.
     2. Deposited in checking account at the bank, $173.42.
     2. Bought supplies for cash from Blair Supplies, $48.30. Ck185.

Instructions: □ **1.** Write the balance of cash brought forward from Check Stub No. 182, $1,523.48, on the unused check stub for Check No. 183.

□ **2.** Write check stub and check for October 29.

□ **3.** Record deposit made on November 1 on unused Check Stub No. 184.

□ **4.** Write check stub and check for November 1.

□ **5.** Record deposit made on November 2 on unused Check Stub No. 185.

□ **6.** Write check stub and check for November 2.

REVIEW PROBLEM 14-R 2 Reconciling a bank statement for a business

On February 3 of the current year, G. L. Burch, owner of Burch Leather Goods, received the bank statement for the period ending January 31. A comparison of the bank statement with the checkbook of the business revealed the following:

The checkbook balance on Check Stub No. 516 at the close of business on February 3 was $3,647.75.

The bank service charge was $4.20.

The outstanding checks were: No. 508, $35.75; No. 514, $172.16; and No. 515, $12.43.

A deposit of $450.00 had been made on February 1, which did not appear on the bank statement.

The balance shown on the bank statement was $3,413.89.

Instructions: □ **1.** Prepare the reconciliation of the bank statement for Burch Leather Goods in the form as shown on page 230.

□ **2.** Record the bank service charge on page 23 of the combination journal. M37.

REVIEW PROBLEM 15-R 1 Work sheet for a merchandising business

On April 30 of the current year, the account balances, representing a one-month fiscal period, and the list of inventories are as shown on page 663.

Account Title	No.	Balance	Account Title	No.	Balance
Cash..........................	11	$ 3,014.90	Sales...........................	41	$19,821.60
Accounts Receivable	12	8,821.00	Purchases....................	51	18,181.30
Merchandise Inventory..	13	24,900.00	Delivery Expense..........	61	420.20
Supplies......................	14	552.20	Insurance Expense........	62	——
Prepaid Insurance.........	15	288.00	Miscellaneous Expense..	63	108.70
Accounts Payable	21	7,452.00	Rent Expense	64	480.00
Rosa Moreno, Capital....	31	31,509.50	Salary Expense	65	1,416.80
Rosa Moreno, Drawing..	32	600.00	Supplies Expense..........	66	——
Income Summary..........	33	——			

Inventories, April 30:	Merchandise inventory...	$26,524.00
	Supplies inventory...	438.20
	Value of insurance policies.......................................	192.00

Instructions: Prepare an eight-column work sheet for Moreno's Camera Shop. Use as your guide the eight-column work sheet shown on page 258.

REVIEW
PROBLEM 16-R 1 Financial reports for a merchandising business (net income; no additional investment)

A work sheet for Koehn's Toyland for the month ended April 30 of the current year is given below.

Koehn's Toyland
Work Sheet
For Month Ended April 30, 19—

		1	2	3	4	5	6	7	8
Account Title	Acct. No.	Trial Balance		Adjustments		Income Statement		Balance	
		Debit	Credit	Debit	Credit	Debit	Credit	Debit	Credit
Cash..........................	11	2 360 20						2 360 20	
Accounts Receivable	12	1 040 85						1 040 85	
Merchandise Inventory.	13	5 996 00		(b) 4 256 00	(a) 5 996 00			4 256 00	
Supplies.....................	14	434 90			(c) 110 00			324 90	
Prepaid Insurance........	15	120 00			(d) 20 00			100 00	
Accounts Payable	21		910 65						910 65
V. C. Koehn, Capital....	31		6 856 50						6 856 50
V. C. Koehn, Drawing..	32	400 00						400 00	
Income Summary.........	33			(a) 5 996 00	(b) 4 256 00	5 996 00	4 256 00		
Sales..........................	41		5 271 35				5 271 35		
Purchases...................	51	1 763 45				1 763 45			
Delivery Expense.........	61	210 30				210 30			
Insurance Expense.......	62			(d) 20 00		20 00			
Miscellaneous Expense.	63	62 80				62 80			
Rent Expense	64	300 00				300 00			
Salary Expense	65	350 00				350 00			
Supplies Expense.........	66			(c) 110 00		110 00			
		13 038 50	13 038 50	10 382 00	10 382 00	8 812 55	9 527 35	8 481 95	7 767 15
Net Income.................						714 80			714 80
						9 527 35	9 527 35	8 481 95	8 481 95

Instructions: □ **1.** Prepare an income statement similar to the one shown on page 269.

□ **2.** Prepare a capital statement similar to the one shown on page 272. Ms. Koehn did not invest any additional capital in the business during the year.

□ **3.** Prepare a balance sheet in report form similar to the one shown on page 275.

REVIEW PROBLEM 16-R 2

Work sheet and financial statements for a merchandising business (net income; additional investment)

The account balances and the inventories on June 30 of the current year, the end of a quarterly fiscal period, for the Fujita Men's Shop are shown below.

Account Title	No.	Balance	Account Title	No.	Balance
Cash	11	$ 3,567.60	Sales	41	$21,489.90
Accounts Receivable	12	4,973.62	Purchases	51	15,180.70
Merchandise Inventory	13	12,774.13	Delivery Expense	61	311.82
Supplies	14	254.95	Insurance Expense	62	——
Prepaid Insurance	15	268.90	Miscellaneous Expense	63	383.70
Accounts Payable	21	6,299.00	Rent Expense	64	1,080.00
Yoshiro Fujita, Capital	31	14,026.52	Salary Expense	65	2,100.00
Yoshiro Fujita, Drawing	32	920.00	Supplies Expense	66	——
Income Summary	33	——			

Inventories, June 30:	Merchandise inventory	$13,095.00
	Supplies inventory	126.98
	Value of insurance policies	150.00

Instructions: □ **1.** Prepare an eight-column work sheet similar to the one shown on page 261A.

□ **2.** Prepare an income statement similar to the one shown on page 269.

□ **3.** Prepare a capital statement similar to the one shown on page 274. Mr. Fujita made an additional capital investment of $1,200.00 on June 5 of the current year.

□ **4.** Prepare a balance sheet similar to the one shown on page 275.

REVIEW PROBLEM 17-R 1   Work at the end of a fiscal period

On September 30 of the current year, the end of a monthly fiscal period, the account balances in the ledger of Brookside Hardware and the list of inventories are as shown on page 665.

Instructions: □ **1.** Prepare an eight-column work sheet.

□ **2.** Prepare an income statement.

□ **3.** Prepare a capital statement.

□ **4.** Prepare a balance sheet.

□ **5.** Record the adjusting entries and the closing entries on page 12 of a combination journal.

Account Title	No.	Balance	Account Title	No.	Balance
Cash............................	11	$ 5,076.90	Sales..............................	41	$13,778.27
Accounts Receivable	12	2,876.50	Purchases........................	51	8,523.08
Merchandise Inventory......	13	16,044.60	Delivery Expense..............	61	738.38
Supplies.........................	14	849.42	Insurance Expense............	62	——
Prepaid Insurance.............	15	730.00	Miscellaneous Expense......	63	516.58
Accounts Payable	21	2,588.30	Rent Expense...................	64	570.00
Rita Mercer, Capital..........	31	20,728.89	Salary Expense	65	650.00
Rita Mercer, Drawing........	32	520.00	Supplies Expense.............	66	——
Income Summary..............	33	——			

Inventories, September 30:	Merchandise inventory......................................	$17,289.30
	Supplies inventory...	481.05
	Value of insurance policies................................	670.00

REVIEW PROBLEM 18-R 1 Chart of accounts setup form for a general ledger

The general ledger chart of accounts for Murphy Hardware Store, Client No. 684, is given below.

Account Number	(10000) ASSETS	Account Number	(40000) REVENUE
11000	Cash	41000	Sales
12000	Accounts Receivable		**(50000) COST OF MERCHANDISE**
13000	Merchandise Inventory		
14000	Store Supplies	51000	Purchases
15000	Prepaid Insurance		**(60000) EXPENSES**
16000	Store Fixtures		
		61000	Advertising Expense
	(20000) LIABILITIES	62000	Delivery Expense
		63000	Insurance Expense
21000	Accounts Payable	64000	Miscellaneous Expense
		65000	Rent Expense
	(30000) CAPITAL	66000	Salary Expense
		67000	Store Supplies Expense
31000	Jack Murphy, Capital		
32000	Jack Murphy, Drawing		
33000	Income Summary		

Instructions: Prepare a chart of accounts setup form for the *balance sheet* accounts of the general ledger chart of accounts illustrated above.

REVIEW PROBLEM 18-R 2 Chart of accounts setup form for a general ledger

Instructions: Prepare a chart of accounts setup form for the *income statement* accounts of the general ledger chart of accounts illustrated in Problem 18-R 1 above.

Recording the opening entry using a
journal entry transmittal

The balance sheet of the Murphy Hardware Store for November 30, 1977, is shown below. The store has few accounts in the accounts receivable and accounts payable subsidiary ledgers. Therefore, only the controlling accounts, accounts receivable and accounts payable, are included in the automated accounting system.

Murphy Hardware Store Balance Sheet November 30, 1977			
Assets			
Cash..	3 200 00		
Accounts Receivable	340 00		
Merchandise Inventory...	38 750 00		
Store Supplies...	580 00		
Prepaid Insurance..	360 00		
Store Fixtures...	6 120 00		
Total Assets		49 350 00	
Liabilities			
Accounts Payable		680 00	
Capital			
Jack Murphy, Capital		48 670 00	
Total Liabilities and Capital		49 350 00	

Instructions: Record the opening entry for the Murphy Hardware Store, Client No. 684, on a journal entry transmittal. Use December 1, 1977, as the date of the opening entry. Use the account numbers from the chart of accounts of Murphy Hardware Store illustrated in Review Problem 18-R 1, page 665.

Journalizing transactions using a
journal entry transmittal

Jack Murphy completed the following transactions on December 1, 1977. Mr. Murphy arranges all transactions by groups before recording the entries on the journal entry transmittal.

December 1, 1977. Summary of cash payments for the day:

Paid cash for December rent, $375.00. Ck561.
Paid cash for advertising expense, $42.00. Ck562.
Paid cash for delivery expense, $74.00. Ck563.
Paid cash for electricity, $48.00. Ck564.
Paid cash for salaries, $860.00. Ck565.
Paid cash for store supplies, $223.00. Ck566.
Paid cash for prepaid insurance, $135.00. Ck567.
Paid cash for purchase of merchandise, $483.00. Ck568.

Instructions: ◻ **1.** Record the transactions listed on page 666 on a journal entry transmittal. Use the account numbers from the chart of accounts of Murphy Hardware Store, Client No. 684, illustrated in Review Problem 18-R 1, page 665.

◻ **2.** Compute and record the control totals.

REVIEW PROBLEM 20-R 2

Recording the adjusting entries using a journal entry transmittal

On November 30 of the current year, the end of a fiscal period, the beginning and ending inventories and the value of the prepaid insurance of the Murphy Hardware Store, Client No. 684, appear as shown below.

	Beginning Balance	Ending Balance
Merchandise Inventory	$38,750.00	$36,500.00
Store Supplies	580.00	490.00
Prepaid Insurance	360.00	328.00

Instructions: ◻ **1.** On a journal entry transmittal form, enter the adjusting entries needed to bring the inventory and insurance accounts up to date.

◻ **2.** Compute and enter the control totals on the journal entry transmittal form.

REVIEW PROBLEM 21-R 1

Determination of earnings

The following table gives the hours worked and the hourly rate for ten employees. Each employee is paid his or her regular hourly rate for a maximum of 8 hours for Monday through Friday. If an employee works more than 8 hours on any of these five days, the worker receives time and a half for overtime. Each employee also receives time and a half for Saturday.

Name	Hours Worked						Hourly Rate
	M	Tu	W	Th	F	S	
Keith Allen	8	8	8	9	8	4	$2.60
Karen Bell	10	8	8	8	10	2	2.30
Gloria Denton	9	10	8	8	8		2.80
Susan Gomez	8	8	8	8	8	3	2.30
Sylvia Knapp	8	8	8	4	8	2	2.40
Robert Lenon	10	10	8	8	8	3	2.80
Barbara Simons	8	8	8	8	10		2.60
Doris Tresh	8	8	8	8	8	4	2.30
Warren Wells	8	8	9	8	8	3	2.70
Norman Zuker	8	10	8	10	8		2.50

Instructions: Determine the total earnings for the week for each employee and the total earnings for all employees.

REVIEW
PROBLEM 22-R 1   Recording payroll transactions

Teresa Balboa, owner of a garden supplies store, completed the following payroll transactions during May, June, and July of the current year.

May 31. Paid monthly payroll, $1,635.90, covering salary expense of $1,960.00 less a deduction of $206.50 for employees' income tax and a deduction of $117.60 for FICA tax. Ck133.

    31. Recorded employer's payroll taxes as follows: FICA tax, 6%; federal unemployment tax, .58%; state unemployment tax, 2.7%. M12.

June 9. Deposited with the bank the amount of the liabilities for the month of May for employees' income tax payable, $206.50, and for FICA tax payable, $235.20; total deposit, $441.70. Ck153.

    30. Paid monthly payroll, $1,591.05, covering salary expense of $1,920.00 less a deduction of $213.75 for employees' income tax and a deduction of $115.20 for FICA tax. Ck213.

    30. Recorded employer's payroll taxes at the same rates as in May. M15.

July 14. Deposited with the bank the amount of the liabilities for the month of June for employees' income tax payable, $213.75, and for FICA tax payable, $230.40; total deposit, $444.15. Ck255.

    31. Paid liability for state unemployment tax for the quarter ended June 30, $163.20. Ck273.

Instructions: Record the payroll transactions on page 31 of a combination journal.

REVIEW   Journalizing and posting transactions
PROBLEM 23-R 1   affecting purchases and cash payments

Instructions: □ **1.** Open the following creditors' accounts in the accounts payable ledger of Castleton Company. Record the balances as of July 1 of the current year.

Creditor	Terms of Sale	Account Balances
Boyer Supply Company, Wilmington, DE 19808	n/30	$103.20
Gadbury Company, Baltimore, MD 20206	n/30	——
Mickleson & Son, Troy, NY 12180	1/10, n/30	——
Shane Company, Charleston, WV 25309	n/30	225.00
Vance Company, Fanwood, NJ 07023	1/10, n/30	480.00
Edith Yancy & Company, Dover, DE 19901	1/10, n/30	——

Instructions: □ **2.** Open the accounts shown on page 669 in the general ledger of Castleton Company. Record the balances as of July 1 of the current year. (Only those general ledger accounts needed in this problem are included.)

□ **3.** Record the transactions beginning on page 669 affecting purchases and cash payments. Use page 7 of a purchases journal (similar to the one shown on page 428), page 5 of a general journal (similar to the one shown on page 441), and page 9 of a cash payments journal (similar to the one shown on page 433). Use July of the current year for all transactions. Source documents are abbreviated as: check, Ck; memorandum, M; purchase invoice, P; debit memorandum, DM.

Account Title	Acct. No.	Account Balance	Account Title	Acct. No.	Account Balance
Cash	11	$5,800.00	Purchases	51	——
Supplies	14	259.56	Purchases Ret. and Allow.	51.1	——
Accounts Payable	21	808.20	Purchases Discount	51.2	——
Emp. Income Tax Payable	22	96.36	Delivery Expense	61	——
FICA Tax Payable	23	100.80	Miscellaneous Expense	63	——
Federal Unemp. Tax Payable	24	29.22	Payroll Taxes Expense	64	——
State Unemp. Tax Payable	25	68.04	Rent Expense	65	——
James Dudley, Drawing	32	——	Salary Expense	66	——

Transactions

July 1. Paid July rent, $500.00. Ck170.
3. Purchased merchandise on account from Gadbury Company, $300.00. P82.
3. Returned merchandise to Shane Company, $14.00. DM27.
5. Purchased merchandise on account from Mickleson & Son, $90.00. P83.
6. Paid on account to Shane Company, $211.00, covering P78 for $225.00 less DM27 for $14.00; no discount. Ck171.

   Posting. Post the items that are to be posted individually. Post from the journals in this order: Purchases journal, general journal, and cash payments journal.

8. Paid on account to Vance Company, $475.20, covering P64 for $480.00 less a 1% discount of $4.80. Ck172.
10. Purchased merchandise for cash, $132.00. Ck173.
11. Issued a check to James Dudley, the owner, for a cash withdrawal for personal use, $100.00. Ck174.
12. Deposited the amount of liabilities for employees' income tax payable, $96.36, and for FICA tax payable, $100.80; total deposit, $197.16. Ck175.
12. Paid liability for state unemployment tax payable, $68.04. Ck176.
13. Paid on account to Mickleson & Son, $89.10, covering P83 for $90.00 less a 1% discount of $0.90. Ck177.
13. Bought supplies on account from Boyer Supply Company, $72.00. M56.

   Posting. Post the items that are to be posted individually.

15. Purchased merchandise on account from Edith Yancy & Company, $228.00. P84.
17. Purchased merchandise on account from Mickleson & Son, $120.00. P85.
19. Paid miscellaneous expense, $12.00. Ck178.
20. Returned merchandise to Gadbury Company, $36.00. DM28.

   Posting. Post the items that are to be posted individually.

22. Purchased merchandise on account from Edith Yancy & Company, $240.00. P86.
24. Paid on account to Gadbury Company, $264.00, covering P82 for $300.00 less DM28 for $36.00; no discount. Ck179.
24. Paid delivery expense, $18.00. Ck180.

July 25. Paid on account to Edith Yancy & Company, $225.72, covering P84 for $228.00 less a 1% discount of $2.28. Ck181.

25. Paid miscellaneous expense, $18.00. Ck182.

27. Paid on account to Boyer Supply Company, $72.00; no discount. Ck183.

27. Returned merchandise to Edith Yancy & Company, $10.00. DM29.

Posting. Post the items that are to be posted individually.

29. Purchased merchandise on account from Shane Company, $176.00. P87.

30. James Dudley, the owner, withdrew merchandise for personal use, $80.00. M57.

31. Paid monthly payroll, $693.24, covering salary expense of $840.00 less deductions for employees' income tax, $96.36, and for FICA tax, $50.40. Ck184.

31. Recorded employer's payroll taxes as follows: FICA tax, $50.40; federal unemployment tax, $4.87; state unemployment tax, $22.68; total payroll taxes expense, $77.95. M58.

Posting. Post the items that are to be posted individually.

Instructions: □ **4.** Total and rule the purchases journal. Post the total.

□ **5.** Foot, prove, total, and rule the general journal. Post the totals of the special columns.

□ **6.** Foot, prove, total, and rule the cash payments journal. Post the totals of the special columns.

□ **7.** Prepare a schedule of accounts payable similar to the one shown on page 215. Compare the schedule total with the balance of the accounts payable account in the general ledger. The total and the balance should be the same.

REVIEW Journalizing and posting transactions
PROBLEM 24-R 1 affecting sales and cash receipts

Instructions: □ **1.** Open the following charge customers' accounts in the accounts receivable ledger of Townsend Supplies. Record the balances as of May 1 of the current year. Terms of the sale for all charge customers are 1/10, n/30.

Charge Customers	Account Balance
Dora Ashley, 2318 Harvey Road, Ann Arbor, MI 48104	$120.00
Columbia House, 1417 Vine Street, Ann Arbor, MI 48104	430.80
C. J. Duane, 4703 Butler Way, Ann Arbor, MI 48104	——
Miller's Electric, 246 A Street, Ann Arbor, MI 48102	271.20
Ruth Parkison, 2785 Abbey Lane, Ann Arbor, MI 48104	——
S. D. Pole, 429 J Street, Ann Arbor, MI 48102	80.40
John C. Thiel, 2468 Orr Street, Ann Arbor, MI 48104	222.00

Instructions: □ **2.** Open the following accounts in the general ledger of Townsend Supplies. Record the balances as of May 1 of the current year. (Only those general ledger accounts needed in this problem are included in the list.)

Account Title	No.	Balance
Cash	11	$ 4,500.00
Accounts Receivable	12	1,124.40
Irma Townsend, Capital	31	36,000.00
Sales	41	——
Sales Returns and Allowances	41.1	——
Sales Discount	41.2	——

Instructions: ☐ **3.** The following transactions affecting sales and cash receipts were completed by Townsend Supplies during May of the current year. Record these transactions in a sales journal, a general journal, and a cash receipts journal like those illustrated in this chapter. Use page number 10 in each journal. Source documents are abbreviated as: memorandum, M; receipt, R; sales invoice, S; cash register tape, T; credit memorandum, CM.

May 1. Recorded the cash balance on May 1 as a memorandum entry in the cash receipts journal, $4,500.00.

2. Sold merchandise on account to C. J. Duane, $138.00. S41.

2. Received on account from Miller's Electric, $268.49, covering S38 for $271.20 less a 1% discount of $2.71. R230.

3. Received cash from the owner, Irma Townsend, as an additional investment in the business, $1,200.00. R231.

3. Received on account from Columbia House, $426.49, covering S36 for $430.80 less a 1% discount of $4.31. R232.

3. Sold merchandise on account to Dora Ashley, $139.80. S42.

4. Received on account from Dora Ashley, $120.00, covering S35 for $120.00; no discount. R233.

5. Discovered that a sale on account to Ruth Parkison on April 30 (S40) was incorrectly charged to the account of S. D. Pole, $80.40. M72.

7. Cash sales for the week, $1,111.68. T7.

Posting. Post the items that are to be posted individually.

9. Sold merchandise on account to Columbia House, $177.60. S43.

9. Received on account from Ruth Parkison, $79.60, covering S40 for $80.40 less a 1% discount of $0.80. R234.

10. Granted credit to Dora Ashley for merchandise returned by her, $19.80. CM12.

12. Received on account from C. J. Duane, $136.62, covering S41 for $138.00 less a 1% discount of $1.38. R235.

14. Cash sales for the week, $1,126.08. T14.

Posting. Post the items that are to be posted individually.

16. Sold merchandise on account to S. D. Pole, $264.00. S44.

17. Sold merchandise on account to Miller's Electric, $180.00. S45.

18. Received on account from Columbia House, $175.82, covering S43 for $177.60 less a 1% discount of $1.78. R236.

19. Granted credit to S. D. Pole as an allowance on damaged merchandise, $30.00. CM13.

May 21. Cash sales for the week, $920.40. T21.

> *Posting.* Post the items that are to be posted individually.

23. Sold merchandise on account to John C. Thiel, $102.00. S46.
25. Received on account from Miller's Electric, $178.20, covering S45 for $180.00 less a 1% discount of $1.80. R237.
26. Granted credit to John C. Thiel for merchandise returned by him, $24.00. CM14.
28. Cash sales for the week, $1,096.50. T28.

> *Posting.* Post the items that are to be posted individually.

31. Sold merchandise on account to C. J. Duane, $156.00. S47.
31. Received on account from John C. Thiel, $222.00, covering S39 for $222.00; no discount. R238.
31. Cash sales for the week, $256.80. T31.

> *Posting.* Post the items that are to be posted individually.

Instructions: □ **4.** Total and rule the sales journal. Post the total. Compare your work with the sales journal shown on page 451.

□ **5.** Foot, prove, total, and rule the general journal. Post the totals of the special columns. Compare your work with the general journal shown on page 441.

□ **6.** Foot the cash receipts journal and prove the equality of debits and credits.

□ **7.** Prove cash. The total of the Cash Credit column of the cash payments journal for Townsend Supplies is $7,911.84. The cash balance on hand on May 31 is $3,906.84.

□ **8.** Total and rule the cash receipts journal. Post the totals of the special columns. Compare your work with the cash receipts journal shown on page 455.

□ **9.** Prepare a schedule of accounts receivable. Compare the schedule total with the balance of the accounts receivable account in the general ledger. The total and the balance should be the same.

REVIEW PROBLEM 25-R 1 Recording selected transactions summarized on a cash proof and balances slip

On May 28 of the current year, the cashier for the Penrod Company prepared the cash proof and balances slip shown on page 673 and gave it to the accountant. Along with the cash proof and balances slip, the cashier gave the accountant a copy of Sales Slip No. 472 for a sales return on account to D. K. Carlson, $5.04.

Instructions: □ **1.** Using the steps outlined on pages 483–485, Chapter 25, check the amounts on the cash proof and balances slip.

□ **2.** On page 13 of a cash receipts-sales journal similar to the one on page 486, make the entry to record the data from the cash proof and balances slip for May 28.

☐ **3.** Check the equality of the debits and credits in the journal entry made for Instruction 2.

☐ **4.** On page 6 of a four-column general journal similar to the one on page 488, make the entry to record the sales return on account for D. K. Carlson.

Items	Accounts	Register Proof and Balances	
CASH PROOF AND BALANCES SLIP			
		CHANGE FROM CASH DRAWER	
1 Change to be Accounted for			77 00
2 Less Paid Out		MAY 28 -- 563	$00025.80PO
3 Balance of Change			51 20
		CASH PROOF	
4 Cash Sales		MAY 28 -- 564	$01092.83CA
5 Received on Account		MAY 28 -- 565	$00236.61RC
6 Total Received		MAY 28 -- 566	$01329.44TL
7 Cash in drawer by actual count	Debit Cash		1327 79 [7]
8 Cash Short	Debit Cash Short and Over		1 65 [1]
9 Cash Over	Credit Cash Short and Over		—— [2]
		SALES PROOF	
10 Department 1		MAY 28 -- 567	$00672.38-1
11 Department 2		MAY 28 -- 568	$00092.81-2
12 Department 3		MAY 28 -- 569	$00409.75-3
13 Department 4		MAY 28 -- 570	$00057.42-4
14 Total Sales	Credit Sales	MAY 28 -- 571	$01232.36TL [3]
15 Cash Sales		MAY 28 -- 572	$01092.83CA
16 Charge Sales	Debit Accounts Receivable	MAY 28 -- 573	$00139.53CH [4]
17 Total Sales		MAY 28 -- 574	$01232.36TL
		RECEIVED ON ACCOUNT	
18 Total Accounts Receivable	Credit Accounts Receivable	MAY 28 -- 575	$00239.01PB [5]
19 Less Sales Discounts	Debit Sales Discount	MAY 28 -- 576	$00002.40SD [6]
20 Received on Account		MAY 28 -- 577	$00236.61RC

Date _May 28, 19--_   Cashier's Signature _Kathy Botkins_

REVIEW PROBLEM 25-R 2   Establishing, proving, and replenishing the petty cash fund

Carmen Lopez owns and operates Carmen's Novelties. On October 3 of the current year, Ms. Lopez issued and cashed Check No. 261 for $150.00 to establish a petty cash fund. During the month of October, the cashier made payments from the petty cash fund and on October 31 submitted the report shown on page 674.

REQUEST TO REPLENISH PETTY CASH FUND	
PAYMENTS	
Account	Amount
Supplies	18.04
Sales Returns and Allowances	15.51
Delivery Expense	13.20
Miscellaneous Expense	3.58
Total needed to replenish	50.33

Date _Oct. 31_ 19 _--_   *Peggy Large*
                 Cashier

Check No. issued _____ Date _____ 19 _____

Accountant _____

Instructions: □ **1.** Record on page 14 of a cash payments journal like the one on page 493 the issuance of Check No. 261 on October 3 to establish the petty cash fund.

□ **2.** Prove the petty cash fund. At the end of the month, the amount of money actually remaining in the petty cash fund is $99.67.

□ **3.** Record the issuance of Check No. 275 on October 31 in the cash payments journal to replenish the petty cash fund.

REVIEW PROBLEM 26-R 1   Recording transactions in special journals

Instructions: □ **1.** Record the following selected transactions completed by Mullen Furniture Store during March of the current year. Use page 18 of a sales journal, page 26 of a general journal, page 14 of a cash receipts journal, and page 20 of a cash payments journal. Source documents are abbreviated as: check, Ck; memorandum, M; receipt, R; sales invoice, S; cash register tape, T; credit memorandum, CM.

Mar.   1. Record the cash balance on March 1 as a memorandum entry in the cash receipts journal, $2,646.99.

       1. Sold merchandise on account to Lloyd Cain, $47.30, plus sales tax of $1.89. S37.

       2. Received on account from Joan Halley, $93.50. R61.

       4. Sold merchandise on account to Ana Ferrer, $132.00, plus sales tax of $5.28. S38.

       5. Cash sales for March 1 to 5, $825.60, plus sales tax of $33.02. T5.

       8. Received on account from Harriet Kane, $165.00. R62.

       9. Discovered that S33 to David Miller on February 24 was incorrectly posted to the account of David Mueller, $28.60. M3.

     12. Cash sales for March 6 to 12, $924.00, plus sales tax of $36.96. T12.

     15. Paid sales tax collected during February to the State Tax Commission, $356.14. Ck316.

     15. Sold merchandise on account to Harriet Kane, $192.50, plus sales tax of $7.70. S39.

     16. Received cash for office supplies sold to accommodate a fellow merchant, $13.64. R63.

        Sales tax is not collected in this state on an accommodation sale.

     18. Received on account from Ana Ferrer, $110.00. R64.

     19. Cash sales for March 13 to 19, $803.40, plus sales tax of $32.14. T19.

Mar. 22. Granted credit to Lloyd Cain for merchandise returned by him on S37, $16.50, plus sales tax of $0.66. CM38.

24. Sold merchandise on account to Ruth Myers, $247.50, plus sales tax of $9.90. S40.

26. Received on account from Lloyd Cain, $32.03 for S37, $49.19, less CM38, $17.16. R65.

26. Cash sales for March 20 to 26, $1,078.00, plus sales tax of $43.12. T26.

29. Received on account from Berta Sanchez, $28.60. R66.

31. Sold merchandise on account to Joan Halley, $385.00, plus sales tax of $15.40. S41.

31. Cash sales for March 27 to 31, $313.50, plus sales tax of $12.54. T31.

Instructions: □ **2.** Foot, prove, total, and rule the journals.

REVIEW Recording transactions with bad
PROBLEM 27-R 1 debts expense

Lewis Industries has accounts in its general ledger for Allowance for Uncollectible Accounts and Bad Debts Expense. At the beginning of the current year, the credit balance of the allowance for uncollectible accounts was $255.80.

Selected transactions affecting bad debts are given below.

Instructions: □ **1.** Record the following selected transactions on page 15 of a general journal like the one on page 526.

Feb. 26. Wrote off past-due account of Daniel Katz as uncollectible, $46.35. M27.

Mar. 31. *End of first quarterly fiscal period.* Make adjusting entry for estimated bad debts expense. Increase allowance for uncollectible accounts by 1% of the total charge sales for the first quarter fiscal period, $13,029.50.

May 10. Wrote off past-due account of Miriam Green as uncollectible, $89.10. M62.

June 30. *End of second quarterly fiscal period.* Make adjusting entry for estimated bad debts expense. Increase allowance for uncollectible accounts by 1% of the total charge sales for the second quarterly fiscal period, $11,320.52.

Aug. 22. Wrote off past-due account of Diana Welker as uncollectible, $127.51. M107.

Sept. 30. *End of third quarterly fiscal period.* Make adjusting entry for estimated bad debts expense. Increase allowance for uncollectible accounts by 1% of the total charge sales for the third quarterly fiscal period, $12,422.57.

Nov. 30. Wrote off past-due accounts of these three customers as uncollectible: Orval Long, $31.90; Carol Ross, $165.11; Evald Tone, $85.47. M123. (Make one combined entry, debiting Allowance for Uncollectible Accounts for the total.)

Dec. 31. *End of fourth quarterly fiscal period.* Make adjusting entry for estimated bad debts expense. Increase allowance for uncollectible accounts by 1% of the total charge sales for the fourth quarterly fiscal period, $12,817.47.

Instructions: □ **2.** Foot, prove, total, and rule the general journal.

REVIEW PROBLEM 28-R 1 Figuring and journalizing depreciation expense; finding book value of plant assets

Marsha Riley bought the following items of equipment during the first three years she was in business:

Plant Asset	Date Bought	Original Cost	Estimated Salvage Value	Estimated Life
1	January 3, 1975	$3,600.00	$400.00	10 years
2	June 30, 1976	375.00	none	5 years
3	July 1, 1976	9,000.00	800.00	10 years
4	September 3, 1976	90.00	none	4 years
5	April 1, 1977	4,950.00	550.00	8 years
6	December 2, 1977	108.00	none	4 years

Instructions: ☐ **1.** Record on page 7 of a general journal the adjusting entry for the total depreciation expense (a) at the end of December 31, 1975; (b) at the end of December 31, 1976; and (c) at the end of December 31, 1977. Figure depreciation to the nearest number of months.

☐ **2.** Find the book value as of December 31, 1977, for each item of equipment.

REVIEW PROBLEM 29-R 1 Buying and disposing of equipment

Nilda Marino owns and manages a retail shoe store. She has these office equipment accounts in her general ledger: Office Equipment, 121; Accumulated Depreciation — Office Equipment, 121.1; Depreciation Expense — Office Equipment, 613.

Instructions: Record the following selected transactions completed by Ms. Marino through December of the current year. Use a cash receipts journal (page 16), a cash payments journal (page 21), and a general journal (page 27) like those shown in Chapter 29. Source documents are abbreviated as: check, Ck; memorandum, M; receipt, R.

Jan. 2. Bought a new typewriter, $510.00. Ck110.

Mar. 31. Recorded estimated depreciation for office equipment for the quarter ended March 31, $221.50.

Apr. 1. Discarded *two* office chairs with a book value of $15.00 *each* and an original cost of $70.00 *each*. M25.

June 30. Recorded estimated depreciation of office equipment for the quarter ended June 30, $218.50.

July 1. Sold for $18.00 cash, a used office desk with a book value of $12.00 and an original cost of $95.00. R129.

Aug. 15. Bought new filing cabinets, $250.00. Ck260.

Sept. 30. Recorded estimated depreciation of office equipment for the quarter ended September 30, $301.00.

Oct. 1. Bought a new typewriter for $280.00 cash plus trade-in of a used typewriter that had a book value of $50.00 and an original cost of $200.00. Ck304.

Nov. 1. Sold for $50.00 cash a used adding machine with an original cost of $250.00 and a book value of $70.00 *after* depreciation for it was recorded on September 30. Amount of depreciation each quarter on the used machine is $30.00.
(a) Record the depreciation for October. M88.
(b) Record the sale of the used adding machine. R416.

Dec. 31. Record estimated depreciation of office equipment for quarter ended December 31, $304.00.

| | REVIEW PROBLEM 30-R 1 | | Recording notes, interest, and bank discount |

The transactions given below were completed by Ruth Cotton, a bank employee, during part of the current fiscal year.

Instructions: □ 1. Record the following transactions, using a cash receipts journal (page 30), a cash payments journal (page 25), and a general journal (page 10) similar to those illustrated in Chapter 30. Source documents are abbreviated as: check, Ck; memorandum, M; note payable, NP; note receivable, NR; receipt, R.

Mar. 3. Issued a 30-day, 8% note to Lyman Publishing Co. for an extension of time on account, $1,200.00. NP1.

10. Received a 60-day, 9% note from Leo Vasquez for an extension of time on account, $800.00. NR22.

16. Discounted at 8% at the Central State Bank our 45-day, non-interest-bearing note, $2,000.00. NP2. The bank credited our checking account for the proceeds.

22. Received a 90-day, 8% note from Harry Armer for an extension of time on his account, $600.00. NR23.

Apr. 2. Paid Lyman Publishing Co. for NP1 (principal, $1,200.00; interest, $8.00), $1,208.00. Ck91.

20. Issued a 90-day, 8% note to the Central State Bank, $750.00. The bank credited our checking account for the principal. NP3.

30. Paid the Central State Bank for NP2, $2,000.00. Ck193.

May 9. Received a check from Leo Vasquez in settlement of NR22 (principal, $800.00; interest, $12.00), $812.00. R69.

10. Issued a 30-day, 7% note to Northwest Supplies for an extension of time on account, $900.00. NP4.

June 9. Paid Northwest Supplies for NP4 (principal, $900.00; interest, $5.25), $905.25. Ck295.

20. Harry Armer dishonored NR23 due today. Charged the amount of the note and the interest to his account (principal, $600.00; interest, $12.00), $612.00. M132.

July 19. Paid the Central State Bank for NP3 (principal, $750.00; interest, $15.00), $765.00. Ck348.

Instructions: □ 2. Foot and prove the journals.

REVIEW
PROBLEM 31-R 1 ● Adjusting, closing, and reversing entries
for accrued revenue and accrued expenses

The following selected accounts from the general ledger of Frances Fillro contain the balances shown below on December 31 of the current fiscal year before adjusting entries are made:

Account Title	No.	Balance	Account Title	No.	Balance
Interest Receivable	114	——	Salary Expense	619	$9,894.00
Interest Payable	212	——	Interest Income	712	$ 195.60
Salaries Payable	213	——	Interest Expense	812	——
Income Summary	313	——			

On December 31, accrued interest income on notes receivable outstanding is $29.40; accrued salaries are $223.70; and accrued interest expense on notes payable outstanding is $40.45.

Instructions: □ **1.** Open the general ledger accounts and record the balances.

□ **2.** Record on page 17 of a general journal the adjusting entries for the accrued revenue and the accrued expenses as of December 31.

□ **3.** Post the adjusting entries to the general ledger accounts.

□ **4.** Record in the general journal the entries to close (a) the interest income account and (b) the salary expense and interest expense accounts.

□ **5.** Post the closing entries to the general ledger accounts.

□ **6.** Record the reversing entries on January 1 of the new year.

□ **7.** Post the reversing entries to the general ledger accounts.

REVIEW
PROBLEM 32-R 1 ● Opening entries for a partnership

On April 1 of the current year, Walter Monroe and Karen Bush formed a partnership for the purpose of continuing and expanding a retail store operated by Mr. Monroe. The partnership is to be called the M & B Market. The partnership agrees to accept the assets of Mr. Monroe's present business and to assume his liabilities. Ms. Bush is to invest cash equal to Mr. Monroe's investment. The balance sheet of Mr. Monroe's present business is:

	Walter Monroe					
	Balance Sheet					
	March 31, 19—					

Assets			Liabilities		
Cash	4 644 68		Notes Payable	4 536 00	
Notes Receivable	479 75		Accounts Payable	1 410 52	
Accounts Receivable	1 697 31		Total Liabilities	5 946 52	
Merchandise Inventory	7 910 93				
Supplies	249 32		Capital		
Equipment	3 514 00		Walter Monroe, Capital	12 549 47	
Total Assets	18 495 99		Total Liabilities and Capital	18 495 99	

Instructions: ◻ **1.** Record the opening entry for each partner on page 1 of a general journal. Receipt No. 1 was issued to Ms. Bush.

◻ **2.** Record the cash balance on April 1 as a memorandum entry on page 1 of a cash receipts journal.

REVIEW PROBLEM 32-R 2 Distribution of net income in a partnership

Carla Rock and Lester Robin are partners in a business known as "Rock-Robin." As of January 1 of the current year, Ms. Rock's investment is $45,000.00 and Mr. Robin's is $20,000.00. Net income or net loss is to be distributed as: 70% to Ms. Rock and 30% to Mr. Robin. Neither partner has made any withdrawals.

Instructions: ◻ **1.** Assume that the net income for the year is $18,000.00. Prepare a distribution of net income statement and a capital statement for the business.

◻ **2.** Assume that the business had a net loss of $1,900.00 for the year. Prepare a distribution of net income statement and a capital statement for the business.

REVIEW PROBLEM 33-R 1 Opening entry for a corporation

The partnership of Downs and Kelly applied for a charter to form a corporation. On March 1 of the current year a charter was received for a corporation to be known as Downs & Kelly, Inc. The corporation is authorized 1,000 shares of capital stock with a par value of $60.00 per share, total capital, $60,000.00.

The corporation takes over the printing business of Jerry Downs and Roy Kelly and issues them 150 and 250 shares of stock respectively. In addition, D. Southerland invests $6,000.00 for 100 shares of stock, and Ann Delaney invests $3,000.00 for 50 shares. The balance sheet for the partnership of Downs & Kelly is shown below.

Downs & Kelly
Balance Sheet
February 28, 19—

Assets			Liabilities		
Cash......................................	5	194 03	Notes Payable		875 00
Notes Receivable..................		900 00	Accounts Payable	2	196 46
Accounts Receivable	3	169 31	Total Liabilities	3	071 46
Merchandise Inventory..........	6	009 12			
Supplies..............................		816 40	Capital		
Equipment	10	982 60	Jerry Downs, Capital.............	9	000 00
			Roy Kelly, Capital................	15	000 00
Total Assets	27	071 46	Total Liabilities and Capital ...	27	071 46

Instructions: ◻ **1.** As of March 1 of the current year, record on page 1 of a general journal the opening entries to record the investments of Downs & Kelly, of Mr. Southerland, and of Ann Delaney. Receipts Nos. 1 and 2 were issued.

◻ **2.** Record a memorandum entry for the cash invested on page 1 of a cash receipts journal.

REVIEW PROBLEM 33-R 2 Work at the end of a fiscal period for a corporation

The general ledger account balances for Northport Corporation on December 31 of the current year are:

Account Title	No.	Balance	Account Title	No.	Balance
Cash	111	$ 18,016.80	Retained Earnings	312	$ 3,997.62
Petty Cash	112	300.00	Income Summary	313	——
Accounts Receivable	113	9,329.23	Sales	411	113,050.12
Allow. for Uncoll. Accts.	113.1	281.60	Sales Returns and Allow.	411.1	521.30
Merchandise Inventory	114	32,299.49	Sales Discount	411.2	1,194.10
Supplies	115	2,383.75	Purchases	511	81,961.64
Prepaid Insurance	116	1,403.80	Purch. Ret. and Allow.	511.1	561.57
Equipment	117	4,800.00	Purchases Discount	511.2	2,321.65
Accum. Depr. — Equip.	117.1	570.00	Bad Debts Expense	611	——
Notes Payable	211	2,000.00	Delivery Expense	612	2,625.20
Interest Payable	212	——	Depr. Expense — Equip.	613	——
Salaries Payable	213	——	Insurance Expense	614	——
Accounts Payable	214	5,348.49	Miscellaneous Expense	615	3,729.10
Employees Inc. Tax Pay.	215	285.45	Payroll Taxes Expense	616	1,338.60
FICA Tax Payable	216	145.44	Rent Expense	617	3,500.00
Fed. Unemploy. Tax Pay.	217	6.06	Salary Expense	618	14,550.00
State Unemploy. Tax Pay.	218	32.72	Supplies Expense	619	——
Federal Income Tax Pay.	219	——	Interest Expense	811	16.30
Capital Stock	311	50,000.00	Federal Income Tax	812	631.41

Instructions: ☐ **1.** Prepare an eight-column work sheet for the fiscal year ended on December 31 of the current year. Additional data needed are:

Allowance for uncollectible accounts, 1% of balance of accounts receivable.
Merchandise inventory, December 31, $33,916.33.
Supplies inventory, December 31, $956.11.
Value of insurance policies, December 31, $494.90.
Annual estimated depreciation of equipment, $240.00.
Accrued interest expense, $8.30.
Accrued salary expense, $271.00.
Federal income tax to bring the total federal income tax expense for the year up to an amount equal to 22% of the net income before federal income tax.

☐ **2.** Prepare an income statement.

☐ **3.** Prepare a balance sheet.

☐ **4.** Record the adjusting entries on page 21 of a general journal.

☐ **5.** Record the closing entries on page 22 of a general journal.

☐ **6.** Record the reversing entries for accrued interest expense and accrued salary expense and for federal income tax payable as of January 1 of the next year. Record the reversing entries on page 22 of a general journal.

Index

681